A Companion to
Samuel Beckett

Blackwell Companions to Literature and Culture

This series offers comprehensive, newly written surveys of key periods and movements and certain major authors, in English literary culture and history. Extensive volumes provide new perspectives and positions on contexts and on canonical and post-canonical texts, orientating the beginning student in new fields of study and providing the experienced undergraduate and new graduate with current and new directions, as pioneered and developed by leading scholars in the field.

Published Recently

A COMPANION TO

SAMUEL BECKETT

EDITED BY

S. E. GONTARSKI

WILEY-BLACKWELL

A John Wiley & Sons, Ltd., Publication

This edition first published 2010

© 2010 Blackwell Publishing Ltd except for editorial material and organization © 2010 S.E. Gontarski

Blackwell Publishing was acquired by John Wiley & Sons in February 2007. Blackwell's publishing program has been merged with Wiley's global Scientific, Technical, and Medical business to form Wiley-Blackwell.

Registered Office
John Wiley & Sons Ltd, The Atrium, Southern Gate, Chichester, West Sussex, PO19 8SQ, United Kingdom

Editorial Offices
350 Main Street, Malden, MA 02148-5020, USA
9600 Garsington Road, Oxford, OX4 2DQ, UK
The Atrium, Southern Gate, Chichester, West Sussex, PO19 8SQ, UK

For details of our global editorial offices, for customer services, and for information about how to apply for permission to reuse the copyright material in this book please see our website at www.wiley.com/wiley-blackwell.

The right of S. E. Gontarski to be identified as the author of the editorial material in this work has been asserted in accordance with the Copyright, Designs and Patents Act 1988.

Wiley also publishes its books in a variety of electronic formats. Some content that appears in print may not be available in electronic books.

Designations used by companies to distinguish their products are often claimed as trademarks. All brand names and product names used in this book are trade names, service marks, trademarks or registered trademarks of their respective owners. The publisher is not associated with any product or vendor mentioned in this book. This publication is designed to provide accurate and authoritative information in regard to the subject matter covered. It is sold on the understanding that the publisher is not engaged in rendering professional services. If professional advice or other expert assistance is required, the services of a competent professional should be sought.

Library of Congress Cataloging-in-Publication Data

A companion to Samuel Beckett / edited by S. E. Gontarski.
          p. cm. – (Blackwell companions to literature and culture)
     Includes bibliographical references and index.
     ISBN 978-1-4051-5869-5 (hardcover : alk. paper)
     1. Beckett, Samuel, 1906-1989–Criticism and interpretation–Handbooks, manuals, etc.
I. Gontarski, S. E.   II. Title.   III. Series.
     PR6003.E282Z62114 2009
     848'.91409–dc22

                                                    2008047949

A catalogue record for this book is available from the British Library.

Set in 11 on 13 pt Garamond 3 by Toppan Best-set Premedia Limited
Printed and bound in Singapore by Fabulous Printers Pte Ltd

1   2010

Contents

Notes on Contributors

H. Porter Abbott is Research Professor Emeritus at the University of California, Santa Barbara. In addition to numerous essays on Beckett's work, his authored publications include *The Fiction of Samuel Beckett: Form and Effect* (1973), *Diary Fiction: Writing as Action* (1984), *Beckett Writing Beckett: The Author in the Autograph* (1996), and *The Cambridge Introduction to Narrative* (2nd edn., 2008). He is the editor of *On the Origin of Fictions: Interdisciplinary Perspectives* (2001).

Chris Ackerley is Professor and former Head of Department of English at the University of Otago, New Zealand. His speciality is annotation. Recent publications include *Demented Particulars: The Annotated* Murphy (rev. edn. 2006); *Obscure Locks, Simple Keys: The Annotated* Watt (2006); and, with S. E. Gontarski, *Companion to Samuel Beckett* (2004 and 2006). He has edited *Watt* for Faber (2009) and is currently working on a study of Beckett and Science.

David Bradby is Emeritus Professor of Drama and Theatre Studies at Royal Holloway, University of London. He is the author of *Modern French Drama 1940–1990* (1991); *The Theatre of Michel Vinaver* (1993); *Beckett: Waiting for Godot* (2001); and, with Annie Sparks, *Mise en Scène: French Theatre Now* (1997). His edited works include *The Paris Jigsaw: Internationalism and the City's Stages* (2002), with Maria M. Delgado, and two volumes of *New French Plays* (1989 and 1998). He has translated and edited two books by Jacques Lecoq: *The Moving Body* (2000) and *Theatre of Movement and Gesture* (2006) as well as plays by Michel Vinaver and Bernard-Marie Koltès (for Methuen). In 1997 he was awarded the title "Chevalier des Arts et Lettres" for services to French theater. He edits the CUP series Cambridge Studies in Modern Theatre and is joint editor with Maria M. Delgado of *Contemporary Theatre Review*.

Enoch Brater is the Kenneth T. Rowe Collegiate Professor of Dramatic Literature at the University of Michigan. His major studies on Beckett include *The Drama in the Text: Beckett's Late Fiction, Beyond Minimalism: Beckett's Late Style in the Theater, Why Beckett, The Essential Samuel Beckett*, and *Beckett at 80/Beckett in Context*. He is widely published in the field of modern and contemporary theater, most notably on Arthur Miller, and his work has been translated into Italian, French, Japanese, Spanish, Portuguese, and Polish.

Mary Bryden is Professor of French at the University of Reading, a former Co-Director of its Beckett International Foundation, and recent past president of the Samuel Beckett Society. She has published widely on Beckett and Deleuze. Her books include *Women in Samuel Beckett's Prose and Drama: Her Own Other* (1993), *Samuel Beckett and the Idea of God* (1998), and, as editor *Samuel Beckett and Music* (1998) and *Deleuze and Religion*. Most recently she has published *Gilles Deleuze: Travels in Literature* (2007).

S. E. Gontarski (Editor) is Robert O. Lawton Distinguished Professor of English at Florida State University where he is Director of Graduate Studies and where he edited the *Journal of Beckett Studies* (1992–2008). His most recent books are, with C. J. Ackerley, *The Grove Companion to Samuel Beckett: A Reader's Guide to His Works, Life, and Thought* (2004) and *The Faber Companion to Samuel Beckett: A Reader's Guide to His Works, Life, and Thought* (2006), and, with Anthony Uhlmann (eds.), *Beckett after Beckett* (2006).

Lois Gordon is University Distinguished Professor of English at Fairleigh Dickinson University, the author of books on Donald Barthelme (1981) and Robert Coover (1983) and of the first book in the United States on Harold Pinter, *Stratagems to Uncover Nakedness* (1969). She has subsequently edited *Harold Pinter: A Casebook* and *Pinter at 70* (2001). Her recent work has included *American Chronicle: Year by Year through the Twentieth Century* (1999), *The World of Samuel Beckett, 1906–1946* (1996) (translated into Chinese), and *Reading Godot* (2002). *Nancy Cunard: Heiress, Muse, and Political Idealist* (2007), which was reviewed on the front page of the *New York Times Book Review*, has been translated into Spanish and Chinese and been optioned for a film.

Graley Herren is Associate Professor of English at Xavier University in Cincinnati. He is the author of *Samuel Beckett's Plays on Film and Television* (2007) as well as numerous articles on Beckett and other modern dramatists. He was formerly Associate Editor of the *Journal of Beckett Studies* and currently edits *The Beckett Circle*.

William Hutchings is Professor of English at the University of Alabama at Birmingham and the author of *Samuel Beckett's* Waiting for Godot: *A Reference Guide* (2005). His other publications include two books on playwright David Storey and numerous articles on twentieth-century English and Irish fiction and drama.

James Knowlson is Emeritus Professor of French at the University of Reading. A friend of Samuel Beckett for almost 20 years, he wrote his authorized biography, *Damned to Fame: The Life of Samuel Beckett* which won the George Freedley Memorial Award in the USA in 1996 and the Southern Arts Non-Fiction Prize in the UK. Earlier, he had published a book on seventeenth- and eighteenth-century thinking about language, and written or edited ten other books on Beckett, including *Frescoes* *of the Skull* (with John Pilling) as well as numerous essays on modern European drama published in *Beckett in Dublin*, *Modern French Drama*, *Around the Absurd*, etc. He is general editor of the four-volume series of *The Theatrical Notebooks of Samuel Beckett* and also edited the *Krapp's Last Tape* volume and co-edited *Waiting for Godot* for that series. He published *Images of Beckett* (2003) with the British theater photographer, John Haynes. His latest book, with Elizabeth Knowlson, is *Beckett Remembering – Remembering Beckett* (2006).

Sean Lawlor completed his PhD at the University of Reading on quotation and allusion in Samuel Beckett's early poems. He has published essays on Beckett's poetry in *Samuel Beckett Today/Aujourd'hui* 18, *Fulcrum 6, An Annual of Poetry and Translation: 2008*, and *Beckett and Death*, ed. Matthew Feldman. He is co-editor, with John Pilling, of a critical edition of Beckett's *Poems and Translations*, currently in preparation.

Patrick A. McCarthy is Professor of English at the University of Miami (Coral Gables, Florida) and the author or editor of ten books, among them *Critical Essays on Samuel Beckett* (1986). His recent publications include a monograph essay, *Joyce, Family, "Finnegans Wake"* (2005); "Modernism's Swansong: Malcolm Lowry's *Under the Volcano*" in *A Companion to the British and Irish Novel 1945–2000*, ed. Brian Shaffer (Blackwell, 2005); and "Making Herself Tidal: Chapter I.8" in *How Joyce Wrote* Finnegans Wake: *A Chapter-by-Chapter Genetic Guide*, ed. Luca Crispi and Sam Slote (2007).

Xerxes Mehta is Professor Emeritus of Theatre at the University of Maryland, Baltimore County. A director known for his work on Beckett's short plays, he has toured productions to Beckett festivals in Strasbourg (1996) and Berlin (2000). His articles on Beckett's theater have appeared in the *Journal of Beckett Studies*, *Samuel Beckett Today/Aujourd'hui*, *The Beckett Circle/Le Cercle de Beckett*, and Lois Oppenheim's anthology *Directing Beckett* (1994). He has spoken on Beckett and organized panels and performances at international Beckett events, and is a former president of the Samuel Beckett Society.

Sinéad Mooney is a graduate of University College Cork and the University of Oxford and is currently a lecturer in the Department of English, National University of Ireland, Galway. She is the author of *Samuel Beckett* (2006), editor, with Kathryn Laing and Maureen O'Connor, of *Edna O'Brien: New Critical Perspectives* (2006) and has written a number of essays on Beckett and twentieth-century Irish women's writing. She is currently working on a study of Beckett's translation and self-translation, on a research fellowship from the Irish Research Council for the Humanities and Social Sciences.

Susan Mooney is Associate Professor of Comparative Literature at the University of South Florida and is author of *The Artistic Censoring of Sexuality: Fantasy and Judgment in the Twentieth-Century Novel* (2008). She is writing a monograph on masculinity and ethics in the modern novel.

Mark Nixon is Lecturer in English at the University of Reading, where he is also the Co-Director of the Beckett International Foundation. He has published more than twenty essays on Beckett's work, and has recently edited, with Matthew Feldman, *The International Reception of Samuel Beckett* (Continuum, 2009). He is an editor of *Samuel Beckett Today/Aujourd'hui*, reviews editor of the *Journal of Beckett Studies*, and the Co-Director of the Beckett Digital Manuscript Project. He is currently working on *Samuel Beckett's Library* with Dirk Van Hulle and is editing a book on *Beckett and Publishing* (British Library, 2010). He is also preparing, for Faber and Faber, an edition of Beckett's *Shorter Fiction 1950–1976*, and also for Faber, a critical edition of the unpublished short story "Echo's Bones."

David Pattie is Professor of Drama and Theatre Studies at the University of Chester. He is the author of *The Complete Critical Guide to Samuel Beckett* (2001) and has published widely on contemporary British theater, Beckett, and popular performance.

Marjorie Perloff is Sadie Dernham Patek Professor Emerita of Humanities at Stanford University and currently Scholar-in-Residence at the University of Southern California. She is the author of many books on twentieth- and twenty-first-century poetry and poetics, including *The Poetics of Indeterminacy: Rimbaud to Cage* (1981), *The Futurist Moment* (1986), *Wittgenstein's Ladder: Poetic Language and the Ordinary* (1996), and her cultural memoir *The Vienna Paradox* (1994). She has published many essays on Beckett's work.

John Pilling is Emeritus Professor of English and European Literature at the University of Reading, where he was Director of the Beckett International Foundation and from where he edited the *Journal of Beckett Studies* (o.s.), on whose advisory board he still serves. He is also on the advisory board of *Samuel Beckett Today/Aujourd'hui*. His books include: *A Samuel Beckett Chronology* (2006), *A Companion to* Dream of Fair to middling Women (2004), *Beckett before Godot* (1997), *Samuel Beckett* (1976), and, with James Knowlson, *Frescoes of the Skull: The Later Prose and Drama of Samuel Beckett* (1979). He is currently working on *Beckett in the 1930s*, on a gathering of his numerous uncollected essays in journals, and, with Sean Lawlor, on a critical edition of Beckett's *Poems and Translations* for Faber and Faber.

Jean-Michel Rabaté is Vartan Gregorian Professor in the Humanities at the University of Pennsylvania. He is one of the founders and executive directors of Slought Foundation. He is a member of the American Academy of Arts and Sciences and has authored or edited more than 30 books on modernism, psychoanalysis, contemporary art, philosophy and writers such as Beckett, Pound and Joyce. Recent books include *Given: 1) Art, 2) Crime* (2006), *Hélène Cixous – On Cities*, coeditor with Aaron Levy (2006), *Lacan Literario* (2007), *1913: The Cradle of Modernism* (2007) and *The Ethic of the Lie* (2008).

Antonia Rodríguez-Gago is Profesora Titular of English Literature at the University Autónoma of Madrid (Spain), where she teaches English Renaissance and Jacobean

Drama and Contemporary Anglo-American Theater. She has published extensively on contemporary theater, especially on Beckett, Pinter, Caryl Churchill, Sarah Kane, and Suzan-Lori Parks. Her book *Happy Days: Los días felices* was published in Madrid by Cátedra in 1986 (5th edn. 2006). *Rockaby, Ohio Impromptu* and *Catastrophe* were premiered in Spain, in 1985, in her authorized translations. Her most recent essays have appeared in *Drawing on Beckett: Portraits, Performances and Cultural Contexts*, ed. Linda Ben-Zvi (2007) and in *Beckett at 100*, ed. Angela Moorjani and Linda Ben-Zvi (2008).

Barney Rosset was the influential publisher of Grove Press and the *Evergreen Review*. He acquired the former with a list of three imprints in 1951 and created and edited the latter in 1957, and with both he embarked on a tumultuous career of publishing and political engagement that continues to inspire today's defenders of free expression. He was the first American publisher of acclaimed authors Samuel Beckett, Jorge Luis Borges, Jean Genet, Eugene Ionesco, Henry Miller, Alain Robbe-Grillet, Marguerite Duras, William Burroughs, Harold Pinter, Che Guevara, Tom Stoppard, Malcolm X, Frantz Fanon, Kenzaburo Oe, Tom Stoppard, and Malcolm X, among others, and he battled the US government in the highest courts to overrule the obscenity ban on groundbreaking works of fiction such as *Lady Chatterley's Lover*, *Tropic of Cancer* and *Naked Lunch*. In 2001 he received the National Book Critics Circle (NBCC) Lifetime Achievement Award.

Paul Shields is Assistant Professor of English at Assumption College in Worcester, MA, where he teaches courses in dramatic literature, critical theory, and composition. Recent essays on Beckett have appeared in *Samuel Beckett Today/Aujourd'hui* (2002), *Samuel Beckett's Endgame, Dialogues I*, ed. Mark S. Byron (2007), and *Transnational Beckett* (2008). A former associate editor of the *Journal of Beckett Studies*, he received his PhD in English from Florida State University in Tallahassee.

Brett Stevens is Associate Professor of Mathematics and Statistics at Carleton University, Ottawa where he specializes in Combinatorics and Combinatorial Optimization, but he is also active in Mathematical Biology. His main combinatorial work is in graph theory, specifically design and coding theory, and Gray code realizations. He is interested in industrial optimization, scheduling, and software testing problems, and, of course, Samuel Beckett. His research in biology is focused on the problem of the evolution of amphimixis and also demography.

Anthony Uhlmann is Associate Professor in the School of Humanities and Languages at the University of Western Sydney, Australia. He is the author of *Samuel Beckett and the Philosophical Image* (2006) and *Beckett and Poststructuralism* (1999, paperback 2008). He is the editor, with S. E. Gontarski, of *Beckett after Beckett* (2006) and, with Han van Ruler and Martin Wilson, of *Arnold Geulincx's Ethics with Samuel Beckett's Notes* (2006).

Dirk Van Hulle teaches English literature at the University of Antwerp. He recently edited a volume on Beckett's later prose for Faber and Faber. His research and publications focus on the writing methods of twentieth-century authors and include the monographs *Textual Awareness* (2004) and *Manuscript Genetics, Joyce's Know-How, Beckett's Nohow* (2008). He is Co-Director of the Beckett Digital Manuscript Project and is currently working with Mark Nixon on Beckett's Library.

Shane Weller is Reader in Comparative Literature and Co-Director of the Centre for Modern European Literature at the University of Kent at Canterbury. His publications include *A Taste for the Negative: Beckett and Nihilism* (2005), *Beckett, Literature, and the Ethics of Alterity* (2006), and *Literature, Philosophy, Nihilism: the Uncanniest of Guests* (2008). He is also editor of the Faber edition of Beckett's *Molloy* (2009).

Acknowledgments

Chapter 1: Excerpts from Samuel Beckett's letters to Jocelyn Herbert 22 April 1966; Thomas MacGreevy 17 July 1961, 3 March 1962, 11 August 1955, 27 November 1957, 4 June 1956; Etha MacCarthy 10 January 1959; A. J. Leventhal 22 April 1959; Pamela Mitchell 27 December 1954. © The Estate of Samuel Beckett. Reproduced by permission of the Estate of Samuel Beckett c/o Rosica Colin Limited, London.

Chapter 2: From Gontarski, S. (2001). *The Grove Press Reader, 1951–2001*. New York: Grove Press. Excerpts from Samuel Beckett's letters to Barney Rosset 16 April 1966, August 1954, 6 April 1957; Harry Joe Brown 26 March 1961; Richard Barr 25 September 1963. © The Estate of Samuel Beckett. Reproduced by permission of the Estate of Samuel Beckett c/o Rosica Colin Limited, London.

Chapter 5: Excerpts from Samuel Beckett's letters to Thomas MacGreevy early August 1931, 9 January 1935, 10 January 1935. © The Estate of Samuel Beckett. Reproduced by permission of the Estate of Samuel Beckett c/o Rosica Colin Limited, London. Extracts from *The Letters of Samuel Beckett, Volume 1* edited by Martha Dow Fehsenfeld, Lois More Overback, George Craig and Dan Gunn © The Estate of Samuel Beckett 2009, published by Cambridge University Press.

Chapter 8: From Badiou, A. (2003). "Tireless Desire." In *On Beckett*, ed. and trans. Alberto Toscano and Nina Power. Manchester: Clinamen Press. From Adorno, Theodor W. [1970] (1997). *Aesthetic Theory*, ed. Gretel Adorno and Rolf Tiemann, trans. Robert Hullot-Kentor. Minneapolis: University of Minnesota Press.

Chapter 15: From Beckett, Samuel (2006). *The Grove Centenary Edition*, Vol. 4: *Poems, Short Fiction, Criticism*, ed. Paul Auster. New York: Grove Press.

Chapter 16: Extracts from Belmont, Georges (2001). *Souvenirs d'outre-monde*. Paris: Calmann-Lévy © Editions Calmann-Lévy, 2001. Transcriptions of poems 'Text'/Text 1 and 'C'n'est au Pelican'/Text 2 from *Dream to Fair to Middling Women*, 1992; quotation from holograph *At last I find*; excerpt from introduction to 'Serena I', 13 September 1932; excerpt from 'Philosophy Notes', Samuel Beckett; excerpts from certain letters to Thomas MacGreevy,1 March1931, 11 March 1932, 3 November 1931 © The Estate of Samuel Beckett. Reproduced by permission of the Estate of Samuel Beckett c/o Rosica Colin Limited, London.

Chapter 17: From Beckett, Samuel (1995). *The Collected Short Prose 1928–1989*, ed. S. E. Gontarski. New York: Grove Press.

Chapter 18: From *Malone Dies: Postmodernist Masculinity* by Samuel Beckett. London: Faber and Faber Ltd. Reprinted by permission. From *Malone Dies* from *Three Novels* by Samuel Beckett, New York: Grove/Atlantic. Copyright © 1955, 1956, 1958 by Samuel Beckett. Used by permission of Grove/Atlantic, Inc.

Chapter 22: Alvin Klein's review in the *New York Times* 1990: 15. Murray Bramwell's review in the *Advertiser* 1991. Gerry Colgan in the *Irish Times* 1995: 15. Paul Taylor in the *Independent* 1996: 19. Robert Hanks in the *Independent* 1996: 9. Antonio Ballesteros González in *The Beckett Circle* 1997: 6. Helen Astbury in *The Beckett Circle* 1999: 3. Fintan O'Toole in the *Irish Times* 2001: 60. Annie Joly in *The Beckett Circle* 2001: 7. Diane Luscher-Moreta in *The Beckett Circle* 2002: 6. Laura Cerrato in *The Beckett Circle* 2004. Alexandra Poulain in *The Beckett Circle* 2006: 1.

Chapter 23: quotations from Asmus, Walter (1975). "Beckett directs *Godot*." *Theatre Quarterly* 5(19): 19–26., reprinted with permission from Cambridge University Press.

Introduction

S. E. Gontarski

The innumerable performances, conferences, and festivals that marked the centenary of Samuel Beckett's birth offered unprecedented opportunities for reviewing his achievement, his impact on the contemporary world, on the arts, and more broadly on the popular culture of the second half of the twentieth and the early years of the twenty-first centuries. The extent of such celebrations was, in the words of Marjorie Perloff, "a wonder to behold," and she outlined their scope in her presidential address to the Modern Language Association in December of 2006:

> From Buenos Aires to Tokyo, from Rio de Janeiro to Sofia, from South Africa (where Beckett did not permit his plays to be performed until Apartheid was ended) to New Zealand, from Florida State University in Tallahassee to the University of Reading, from the Barbican Theatre in London to the Pompidou Center in Paris, from Hamburg and Kassel and Zurich to Aix-en-Provence and Lille, from St. Petersburg to Madrid to Tel Aviv, and of course most notably in Dublin, 2006 has been Beckett's Year. Most of the festivals have included not only performances of the plays, but lectures, symposia, readings, art exhibitions, and manuscript displays. *PARIS BECKETT 2006*, for example, co-sponsored by the French government and New York University's Center for French Civilization and Culture, has featured productions of Beckett's entire dramatic oeuvre, mounted in theatres large and small all over Paris, lectures by such major figures as the novelists-theorists Philippe Sollers and Helène Cixous, the playwrights Fernando Arrabal and Israel Horovitz, and the philosopher Alain Badiou ... Who, indeed, more global an artist than Beckett? (Perloff 2007: 652)

Yet the amount of attention, even adulation, this "global artist" received, not only in the run up to and the centenary year itself but in its aftermath as well, has raised profound questions about the future of Beckett and his art. For some, such popular acceptance of so experimental an artist suggests the blunting of his avant-garde edge, the taming, domestication, and even gentrification of Beckett's work as he is accepted and celebrated by the broad middle class as a "classic" artist, studied in schools, required reading on set exams, alluded to in television sitcoms, and even the subject of TV quiz shows, broadly enough known to enter the popular as well as the literary culture, his iconic face a saleable commodity, immediately recognizable and so suitable for Apple computer adverts. A recent quick search of Google Images™ turned up over one quarter million possibilities for Samuel Beckett; a YouTube™ search turned up over 100,000 possibilities, and Facebook™ has a Beckett Wall. Such absorption into the fabric of global commerce raises questions of whether or not some essential ingredients of Beckett's art are lost in this mass, commercial, electronic appeal. And if something has been lost amid steadily increasing popularity, does one lament the loss or try to retrieve it? The former, however, is nostalgic, while the latter little more than a reactionary gesture. That is, does or can the avant-garde edge of Beckett's work, associated primarily with the deprivations of postwar Europe, play in a contemporary global economy as anything other than kitsch? In other words, what exactly does play in the after-Beckett?

Many of the centenary symposia and performances, moreover, were financially supported not only by universities, humanitarian foundations, and cultural arms of governments, but by banks, airlines, beverage companies, and other corporate entities. One might well ask what interest such agencies have in an esoteric Hiberno-Gallic poet. Since the premiere performance of *En attendant Godot* in January of 1953, Beckett's work has, of course, steadily accumulated what some materialist critics would call commercial capital, and the corporate embrace and commodification of the avant-garde in general has by 2006 been long established. But the modernist avant-garde as a popular culture, as indeed *the* decorative art of our time, and thus the avant-garde at the moment of its greatest appeal, simultaneously suggests its degradation, if not the instant of its annihilation, the inherent cultural critique smothered in mass embrace. Roland Barthes had already anticipated such rehabilitation of modernism's edge in the 1960s: "the bourgeoisie will recuperate [the avant-garde] altogether, ultimately putting on splendid evenings of Beckett and Audiberti (and tomorrow Ionesco, already acclaimed by humanist criticism)" (1972: 67–70 at 69). The festivities commemorating the year of Beckett may have been just such recuperation, such a series of "splendid evenings," Beckett's post-humanism smothered in humanist embrace.

Admittedly, the sort of reassessment that I am suggesting here is not driven by the tick of the clock or the flip of a calendar page. The year 2006 was significant, surely, but such reviewing, such resituating of Beckett, a Beckett not only for his time but for ours as well, that is, a rethinking of the space between Beckett past and Beckett future, between the aesthetic and the commercial, has been under way for some years in anticipation of the anniversary, but the centenary year provided an acceleration of that process. Considerable impetus for what might be termed a rehistoricizing of Beckett and his work was generated a decade earlier by James Knowlson's 1996 authorized biography, *Damned to Fame: The Life of Samuel Beckett*, which was based on and brought to light a wealth of primary documents previously unknown to the public: notebooks, diaries, abandoned manuscripts, and the like, all of which have expanded our understanding of Beckett's intellectual milieu as well as the canon itself and consequently has extended the voice of the author. Thus the 1996 biography alone spurred a reviewing of Beckett, as it offered detailed examination of his education, *L'Éducation sentimentale*, perhaps: analyses of what he was reading, formally and informally, when he was reading it, and how thoroughly he assimilated and reconstituted that reading. Such context has allowed us to situate him afresh as both the product and a reshaper of a particular age. Most immediately the Knowlson biography has provided the impetus for books like John Pilling's edition of *Beckett's Dream Notebook* (1999) and his subsequent thorough annotations to that enigmatic first novel in *A Companion to* Dream of Fair to middling Women (2003). C. J. Ackerley's diptych *"Demented Particulars": The Annotated* Murphy (1998) and *Complex Locks, Simple Keys: Annotations to* Watt (2005) belongs to the same category of historicizing or contextualizing. The corollary to Pilling's 1999 publication and annotation of the *Dream Notebook* is the publication in English translation of Arnold Geulincx's *Ethics* (2006) along with Beckett's detailed reading notes on that work. This remarkable achievement is translated by Martin Wilson from what Beckett (or the narrator of *Murphy*) called "the beautiful Belgo-Latin of Arnold Geulincx," the volume as a whole edited by Han van Ruler, Anthony Uhlmann, and Martin Wilson. The scholars leading this repositioning, Knowlson, Pilling, Ackerley, and Uhlmann, are all represented in this current volume with substantial new work.

The *Ethics* of Geulincx thus joins William Inge's *Christian Mysticism* (1899); Archibald B. D. Alexander's *A Short History of Philosophy* (1922); Wilhelm Windelband's *A History of Philosophy* (1893, 2nd edn. 1901); John Burnet's *Greek Philosophy, Part I: Thales to Plato*; R. H. Wilenski's *An Introduction to Dutch Art* (1929); Robert Burton's *The Anatomy of Melancholy* (1621); and Mario Praz's *The Romantic Agony* (1933) (among others) as seminal, foundational reading for any serious grounding in Beckett studies. Beckett's reading among these critics and philosophers is detailed as well in a special issue of the journal *Samuel Beckett Today/ Aujourd'hui: An Annual Bilingual Review*, "Notes Diverse Holo: Catalogues of Beckett's Reading Notes and other Manuscripts at Trinity College Dublin, with Supporting Essays," edited by Matthijs Engelberts and Everett Frost, with Jane Maxwell (2006) (see especially pp. 67–93, 141–55). On Beckett's reading of Wilenski, and particularly its influence on his theater, see also John Haynes and James Knowlson's *Images of Beckett* (2003) where, in three essays accompanying the stunning theatrical images of John Haynes, Knowlson outlines Beckett's debts to particular visual artists and notes that in 1935, he "revealed a special interest in the history and development of 'spotlight painting' … He had just been reading R. H. Wilenski." The essays gathered here in *a Companion to Samuel Beckett* continue such engagement with literature and culture, authors reviewing Beckett in terms of the post-biographical critical spirit, capitalizing on the energy and wealth of high-level discourse that the centenary-year celebrations generated, and emphasizing what we might call, perhaps, the new pragmatics or a return to the archives to parallel the burst of theoretical work done on Beckett during the decades of the 1970s and 1980s.

Reviewings

Such a collection, moreover, allows us to return to a central tenet of Samuel Beckett's creative spirit, a creative life marked by a series of reinventions, or better by a pattern of serial reinvention. Born into a middle-class, suburban, Anglo-Irish family with an interest in "sports of all sorts," his family's expectation for their eldest was that he step into and finally assume control of their construction business. Such expectation is detailed in what might be considered a supplement or coda to the 1996 biography, James and Elizabeth Knowlson (eds.), *Remembering Beckett/Beckett Remembering: Uncollected Interviews with Samuel Beckett and Memories of Those Who Knew Him* (2006) (see particularly pp. 3–21, "The Young Samuel Beckett"), as well as Lois Gordon's *The World of Samuel Beckett, 1906–1946* (1998). Instead, a young Sam remade himself into something other at university, developing into a bookish, semi-bohemian linguist with a passion for reading continental literature in the language of composition, casting himself at first in the image of his university mentor, Thomas Rudmose-Brown. In Paris in 1928, however, in order to pursue an academic career he reinvented that donnish demeanor under the influence of the Paris avant-garde and remade himself in the image of his subsequent mentor, fellow Dubliner James Joyce. The brash, Parisian Beckett cultivated the look and literary style of Joyce, indulging in youthful bohemian excesses, but writing an insightful if anti-academic treatise on French modernist, Marcel Proust, which volume was deemed sufficient for his alma mater, Trinity College, Dublin, to grant him an MA degree. As he began his formal academic career, he saw himself less as a don than a man of letters, a professional author, say, writing a handful of acerbic, almost angry reviews, a scattering of nearly impenetrable poems, and a pointedly anti-academic novel, *Dream of Fair to middling Women*, which traces the rejection of academia for bohemia, in the process savaging his early scholarly mentor who appears in the thin guise of the Polar Bear. Almost out-Joycing his new literary mentor in virtuosity and obscurantism, he touted himself in the contributor's section of Samuel Putnam's poetry anthology, *The European Caravan: New Voices* (1931), as the new Joyce, even hinting that the protégé might exceed the mentor. As he said of himself, apparently unblushingly, he "•as adapted the Joyce method to his poetry with original results." (So much for our image of a shy, diffident, modest Beckett.) Moreover, something of T. S. Eliot's donnish poem, *The Waste Land*, lingers amid the tortured syntax and vocabulary of Beckett's own footnoted early poem on Descartes and that whore, time, *Whoroscope*.

After World War II, however, and after a third masterful novel, *Watt*, that featured a rationalist, epistemological, narratological collapse, he recast himself not only as the other to Joyce but as anti-mastery itself in a trilogy of French novels whose principal subject, as he suggested to interviewer Israel Shenker, was precisely that rationalist collapse:

> the difference is that Joyce was a superb manipulator of material ... The kind of work
> I do is one in which I am not master of my material. The more Joyce knew the more

he could ... I'm working with impotence, ignorance ... My little exploration is that whole zone of being that has always been set aside by artists as something unusable – as something by definition incompatible with art. (Shenker 1956: 146–9)

This confession and all-out embrace of artistic impotence not only defined Beckett's difference to Joyce but became thematically and stylistically the anti-didactic stance that would dominate much of his subsequent work, a position that manifests itself succinctly as early as his summary dismissal of Balzac and his *Comédie humaine* in the novel *Dream of Fair to middling Women*: "*He is absolute master of his material*" (1932: 119; my emphasis). In fact Beckett's most profound anti-Victorianism emerges from the embrace of a literature that refuses to teach, hence its conspicuous abandonment of conclusion, ending, or resolution of any sort, and his rejection of what he referred to as "clarity" in a review called "Denis Devlin" published in 1938 in *transition* 27: "The time is perhaps not altogether too green for the vile suggestion that art has nothing to do with clarity, does not dabble in the clear, and does not make clear, any more than the light of day (or night) makes [clear] the subsolar, -lunar and -stellar excrement" (Beckett 1983). On his way to becoming the apostle of impotence, he dismissed "the loutishness of learning" in a poem called "Gnome," a quatrain he wrote to mark his resignation from Trinity College, and hence his abandonment of an academic career (published in 1934 in *Dublin Magazine* 9[3]: 8 and signed "Sam Beckett"). Subsequent Beckettian protagonists came to acknowledge and accept the defeat of ocular and auditory proofs, the world of the narrators inevitably, irremediably, ill seen, ill heard, hence, of necessity, ill (re)presented, and so immune from clarity, Beckett's enterprise a *Comédie post-humaine*. An increasingly confident Beckett would also separate himself from the likes of other modernist masters, T. S. Eliot, Ezra Pound, and even, for a time, William Butler Yeats, whom he castigated in 1934 in an essay entitled "Recent Irish Poetry," although writing under the pseudonym "Andrew Belis" (*The Bookman* 86 [515]: 235–44; see also Beckett 1983: 70–6.). At least privately, in a letter to his confidant Thomas MacGreevy, he noted that T. Eliot spelled backwards was toilet (this perhaps a riposte to MacGreevy's own scholarly effort, a monograph on T. S. Eliot in the same series in which Beckett published his *Proust*). In the process of remaking himself, over and again, Beckett was simultaneously overturning and reconstituting, perhaps unavoidably, every literary genre he turned his attention to.

In the midst of reinventing narrative, Beckett simultaneously began the process of dismantling and reassembling theater, writing the admittedly juvenile, anti-boulevard farce *Eleutheria* between *Molloy* and *Malone meurt*, and the more mature *En attendant Godot* between *Malone meurt* and *L'Innommable*. Enthusiastic about *Eleutheria*, and eager for its performance and publication, he later repudiated it, refusing to have it published, at least in his lifetime, and prohibiting any staging, apparently in perpetuity, but the play did, almost literally, sweep the stage clear of both boulevard hijinks and naturalist gravitas, the debris of rationalist, meliorist, and utilitarian philosophies tossed into the laps of the bourgeois audience, and so the much abused, often ham-fisted *Eleutheria* paved the way for the barren stage of what would become in English *Waiting for Godot* and subsequently for what are generally referred to as Beckett's "late plays."

British critic Harold Hobson captured something of the revolutionary scope of *Godot* as he noted that it

> knocked the shackles of plot from off the English [one might add Irish here as well] drama. It destroyed the notion that the dramatist is God, knowing everything about his characters and master of a complete philosophy answerable to all of our problems. It showed that Archer's dictum that a good play imitates the audible and visible surface of life is not necessarily true. It revealed that the drama approximates or can approximate the condition of music, touching chords deeper than can be reached by reason and saying things beyond the grasp of logic. It renewed the English theater in a single night. (Hobson 1967: 25–8 at 25)

Joyce may have celebrated "Ibsen's New Drama," but for Beckett "The Quintessence of Ibsenism" suffered from rampant didacticism that would infect followers like Shaw and the bulk of postwar British dramatists (Pinter excepted). Against such Ibsenism heralded by his fellow Irishmen, Beckett wrote to his American director in 1972, "All I know is in the text. 'She' [the protagonist of *Not I*] is purely a stage entity, part of a stage image and purveyor of stage text. The rest is Ibsen" (October 16, 1972). Hobson was doubtless ventriloquizing Beckett in his assessment, insisting that Beckett's art will *teach* us nothing (in both senses of that term).

Radical as it was, *Godot* was not, of course, the end point of Beckett's generic play, but only a point in a series. The composition and performance history of *Play*, for example, a decade later in 1963, not only moved the post-humanist project further but triggered an increase in Beckett's direct involvement in theater since it demanded a level of technical sophistication and precision unknown in his earlier work. It was the intricacies of staging *Play* that finally forced a reluctant, private Beckett into public space, as he began to assume full and public responsibility for the direction of his work; that is, directing allowed him to reinvent himself yet again, as a director whose relationship to his stage works would become as intrinsic as that of Bertolt Brecht to his. With *Play*, which met enormous resistance from producers in England and the United States because of the near unintelligibility of its delivery speed, Beckett moved further from what was recognizable theater; the work eschewed development of plot and character, mainstays of traditional theater, and shifted the theatrical ground from corporeality to incorporeality, from wholes to what we might call pieces of (and for) theater, spectacles we now loosely call Beckett's "late plays." After 1963, what is more, Beckett's became increasingly a theater of ghosts, his work itself the ghost or afterimage of commercial theater, his stagings, moreover, the ghost of his scripts, themselves, perhaps, ghosts of his prose. By force of will, Beckett remade himself into a man of the theater as he began directing most of his new work but also reworking, rethinking, and so revising or reinventing his previous oeuvre, even those works firmly established within the theatrical repertory.

Beckett's transformation from playwright to theatrical artist was one of the paramount developments of late modernist theater, and yet it is slighted, even denigrated, in the theoretical, critical, and historical discourse that privileges print over performance, the apparent stability of page over the vicissitudes of stage, the materiality of script over the ghosts of (and in) performance. Such neglect of Beckett's work on the boards distorts the arc of his creative evolution, however, and undervalues his emergence as an artist committed to the performance of his drama as its full, even if evanescent, realization. He would finally embrace theater not just as a medium where a preconceived work was given accurate expression, but as *the* means through which the work of art was continually created and recreated. As he wrote to his American publisher, Grove Press, of his new play *Happy Days*, on May 18, 1961, "I should prefer the text not to appear in any form before production and not in book form until I have seen some rehearsals in London. It can't be definitive without actual work in the theatre." On November 24,1964 Beckett reiterated the principle to Rosset: "I realize I can't establish definitive text of *Play* without a certain number of rehearsals. These should begin with [French director Jean-Marie] Serreau next month. Alan's [Schneider's] text will certainly need correction. Not the lines but the stage directions. London rehearsals begin on March 9th." From *Godot* onward, rehearsals would protract the creative process; performance would thus become an extension of composition. At times Beckett's complete vision would be realized only well after the original publication when as a director he turned a fresh eye on his text. Directing himself would allow him to implement and refine a personal creative vision, for, as his original director, Roger Blin, has noted,

> he had ideas about the play [in this case *Fin de partie*] that made it a little difficult to act. At first, he looked on his play as a kind of musical score. When a word occurred or was repeated, when Hamm called Clov, Clov should always come in the same way every time, like a musical phrase coming from the same instrument with the same volume. (Blin 1986: 233)

As Beckett evolved from being first a playwright, then an advisor on productions of his work, then a director taking full charge of its staging, the boards grew to be an extension of his writing desk, a platform for self-collaboration through which he reinvented his own theatrical output in more decidedly performative terms.

The Performative

The years of transformation from author to theater and television director were the early 1960s. Recently returned from New York, where he oversaw the filming of his *Film*, Beckett joined preparations (with Mariu Karmitz and Jean Ravel) for a film version of Jean-Marie Serreau's June 1964 staging of *Comédie* (*Play*). He rushed off to London to oversee taping of *Eh, Joe*, with Jack MacGowran and Siân Phillips, nominally directed by Alan Gibson but thoroughly visualized and overseen by Beckett (BBC 2 broadcast July 4, 1966). He oversaw two performances on vinyl for Claddagh Records, *MacGowran Speaking Beckett* and *MacGowran Reading Beckett's Poetry*. He then rushed back to Paris to oversee Jean-Marie Serreau's series of one-acts at the Odéon, Théâtre de France, including a reprise of *Comédie*, *Va et vient*, and his own staging of Robert Pinget's *Hypothèse* with actor Pierre Chabert, originally presented at the Musée d'Art Moderne (October 18, 1965). These opened on March 14, 1966. The first of his works for which he received full and public directorial billing, however, was the 1966 Stuttgart telecast of *He Joe* (broadcast by SDR to commemorate his sixtieth birthday on April 13, 1966). By 1966, Beckett the theatrical director had come out of the closet.

In 1967, after almost a full year of non-stop theater, he accepted his most public posture, an invitation from the Schiller-Theater to direct a play. He chose *Endspiel* [*Endgame*], the "favorite of my plays" he noted in his *Berlin Diary*. The monumental decision would begin the transformation of nearly all of his works for theater over the next two decades, as he prepared a complex *Regiebuk*, a thorough director's notebook, for each of his productions. Such notebooks would characterize his meticulous approach to directing and become a public record of a private vision as the series, transcribed, translated, and annotated, was published (with Beckett's full cooperation, participation, and financial assistance) as *The Theatrical Notebooks of Samuel Beckett* (1992–9). The *Notebooks* themselves have presented pressing issues for scholars and theater practitioners as they wrestle with their implication, particularly for performance: what long-term relationship exists between Beckett's own meticulously directed works of the last two decades of his creative life and future performances? That is, with what authority are we to view Beckett's stagings? Are his productions now the standard from which no deviation will be tolerated? This certainly is, roughly, the position of the Beckett Estate, which sanctions productions of his work. One result is that more than a few major directors have refused to work with Beckett's material (American directors Herbert Blau and Lee Breuer among them), and, worse, others have been prohibited from engaging it (including until recently Debra Warner and JoAnne Akailitus). If the future of Beckett production requires the fulfillment of legal contracts whose end is to ensure what for some might be called "authentic" productions, suspect as appeals to authenticity always are, for others such constraint ensures only Xerox copies of previous productions, or, to change the metaphor, Beckett's theater works become pinned butterflies under glass, audiences entering not theaters but the Beckett Museum. The inevitable question that wants direct confrontation is whether Beckett's drama is thereby becoming theatrically irrelevant to the twenty-first century in any meaningful terms. Put another way, will the centenary year of celebrations of Samuel Beckett's work, including innumerable productions, be its headstone as well?

The compilation of *A Companion to Samuel Beckett* will not, of course, necessarily resolve such questions, but the discourse here continues to engage the issues and is of a piece with contemporary attempts to look at the continued integrity of Beckett's art after his death and into the twenty-first century and so contributes to the reassertion of its vitality in the face of commodity culture. The collection is, finally, less a full reappraisal (although it is at least that), and so potentially retrospective, than a continued exploration of the potential of Beckett's oeuvre in a new century, among new cultures, amid changing economies, and on a global, transnational stage.

REFERENCES

Ackerley, C. J. (1998). *"Demented Particulars": The Annotated* Murphy. Tallahassee, FL: Journal of Beckett Studies Books.

Ackerley, C. J. (2005). *Complex Locks, Simple Keys: Annotations to* Watt. Tallahassee, FL: Journal of Beckett Studies Books.

Barthes, Roland (1972). "Whose Theater? Whose Avant-Garde?" Critical Essays, translated by Richard Howard. Evanston: Northwestern University Press.

Beckett, Samuel (1934). "Gnome." *Dublin Magazine* 9 (3): 8.

Beckett, Samuel (1983). "Recent Irish Poetry." "Denis Devlin." In *Disjecta: Miscellaneous Writings and a Dramatic Fragment by Samuel Beckett*, ed. Ruby Cohn. New York: Grove Press.

Beckett, Samuel (1999). *Beckett's Dream Notebook*, ed. and annotated with an introductory essay by John Pilling. Reading: Beckett International Foundation.

Blin, Roger (1986). "Blin on Beckett." In S. E. Gontarski (ed.), *On Beckett: Essays and Criticism*. New York: Grove Press, Inc.

Frost, Everett and Matthijs Engelberts with Jane Maxwell, eds. (2006). "Notes Diverse Holo: Catalogues of Beckett's Reading Notes and other Manuscripts at Trinity College Dublin, with Supporting Essays." *Samuel Beckett Today/Aujourd'hui*. 16.

Gordon, Lois (1998). *The World of Samuel Beckett, 1906–1946*. New Haven: Yale University Press.

Harmon, Maurice (ed.) (1998). *No Author Better Served: The Correspondence of Samuel Beckett and Alan Schneider*. Cambridge, MA: Harvard University Press.

Haynes, John and James Knowlson (2003). *Images of Beckett*. Cambridge: Cambridge University Press.

Hobson, Harold. (1967). "The First Night of 'Waiting for Godot.'" In J. Calder (ed.), *Beckett at Sixty: A Festschrift*. London: Calder and Boyars.

Knowlson, James (1996). *Damned to Fame: The Life of Samuel Beckett*. New York: Simon & Schuster.

Knowlson, James and Elizabeth Knowlson (eds.) (2006). *Remembering Beckett/Beckett Remembering: A Centenary Celebration*. New York and London: Arcade Publishing and Bloomsbury.

Perloff, Marjorie (2007). "Presidential Address 2006: It Must Change." *PMLA* 122 (3): 652–62.

Pilling, John (2003). *A Companion to* Dream of Fair to middling Women. Tallahassee, FL: Journal of Beckett Studies Books.

Putnam, Samuel (1931). *The European Caravan: New Voices*. New York: Brewer, Warren & Putnam.

Shenker, Israel (1956). "Moody Man of Letters," *New York Times* (May 5); rpt. in 1979 in L. Graver and R. Federman (eds.), *Samuel Beckett: The Critical Heritage*.

Uhlmann, Anthony, Han van Ruler, and Martin Wilson (2006). *Arnold Geulincx's Ethics with Samuel Beckett's Notes*. Leiden: Brill, 2006.

Part I
A Life in Letters

1
A Writer's Homes –
A Writer's Life

James Knowlson

38 Boulevard Saint-Jacques

Samuel Beckett and Suzanne Deschevaux-Dumesnil lived together in a small apartment at 6 rue des Favorites (a road which leads off the long, straight rue de Vaugirard and is close to the Métro station of Vaugirard) from 1938 until 1960. Increasingly, however, particularly in the 1950s, they found their living quarters not only cramped and uncomfortable but also totally unsuited to their differing lifestyles. Beckett frequently stayed out late at night drinking with his friends and wanted, therefore, to lie in bed late into the morning, while Suzanne followed a much more ordered, more conventional, even, some people thought, a more austere existence. As a result, when the great success of *Waiting for Godot* offered them the financial resources to move house, they decided in 1959 to buy two adjoining units in a new apartment block which was being built at 38 boulevard Saint-Jacques. "We simply must have our rooms where we can shut ourselves up, not possible at present," Beckett wrote to a friend in 1959 (SB, letter to Mary Manning, December 22, 1959).

Over the past few years, he had come to relish the isolation and privacy offered to him by the small country house that he had had built in Ussy-sur-Marne in 1953. This made him want to have a study-cum-library of his own in Paris in which he could concentrate undisturbed on his writing. The units that he and Suzanne chose had two separate entrances, for their plan was to have an apartment and a small studio which were interconnected yet which offered them both a greater degree of freedom and independence. In my biography of Beckett, I described the living arrangements of the new apartments as follows:

Suzanne had her own bedroom overlooking the tree-lined boulevard and, to the right, the Métro station of Place Saint-Jacques. A sitting room that they shared with a small piano also faced onto the Boulevard. There was only one kitchen. Through the kitchen was a small bedroom where Beckett slept in a somewhat monk-like cell that was lined with low grey cupboards. Beyond that, facing the tiny, forbidding, barred windows of the cells in the Santé prison, was his study and bathroom. With this arrangement it was possible for Beckett to come and go and for guests to call on him without disturbing Suzanne ... Unless either of them was eating out, they took their meals together at a simple formica table by the left-hand window in the sitting-room. (Knowlson 1996: 472–3).

These arrangements enabled them to live *parts* of their lives independently without one of them disturbing the other, if he or she did not wish to be disturbed. "We leave [the rue des] Favorites and the abominable rue de Vaugirard without a pang – after 23 years there," Beckett concluded in a letter to a friend (SB, letter to Thomas MacGreevy, September 22, 1960).

The apartments, which were reached by a small, narrow elevator, lay on the seventh floor. Beckett's study, situated at the rear of the building, was consequently well isolated from the noise of the traffic on the busy boulevard Saint-Jacques. It looked out onto quiet little town gardens and offered more distant views of the Val de Grâce, the Panthéon, and the cathedral of Notre Dame, as well as the less appealing sight of the nearby prison. One of the key features of Beckett's life there was that he was close enough to walk to all his old haunts in the Quartier Latin. Also, with the proximity of the Métro stations of Saint-Jacques or, only a short walk up the boulevard, the much busier hub of Denfert-Rochereau, he and Suzanne could easily meet up with their different sets of friends.

An even more important feature of his new apartment for Beckett, however, was the quietness of his rooms there. An average day in Paris would begin with him tackling his large correspondence, answering himself most of the letters that he received from family, publishers, agents, and friends in many countries. Most days he then used to wander up the boulevard to a local tabac to buy his daily newspaper (*Combat* and later *Libération*) and his cigarettes (or, later, cigarillos). His meetings with visitors often took place at the nearby Closerie des Lilas restaurant or the Îles Marquises on the rue de la Gaîté or, again later, mainly for coffee, at the PLM Hôtel Saint-Jacques, just down the road from his building. But he also had a number of regular ports of call, which he integrated into his long walks around the left-bank, its parks, and its gardens: his Irish friend, "Con" Leventhal's apartment on the boulevard Montparnasse (the rent of which he was paying); Barbara Bray's apartment in the rue Séguier; and the studio of painters, Avigdor and Anne Arikha, in the Square du Port-Royal. As often as he could, he tried to find the time to write, sitting at his desk in a meticulously organized study.

The study was lined with shelves of books along two of its walls. On the longer back wall, above the shelves, were a number of small cupboards, also full of books or papers. Behind him, as he sat at his dark green desk, was a row of shelves holding a few mementoes: on one shelf there was a sandstone mask of a face with its tongue sticking out (sent to him by the poet, Nick Rawson) and a small, square, brass-framed clock; on another there was a small sculpted figure with its head bent down between its knees like Dante's Belacqua; below that again was a very large watch, standing upright on a stand. To his left, underneath his row of dictionaries and reference books and above his black telephone with its red on–off button, were fixed two sloping containers which held paper, envelopes, and cards. Attached to the shelf to his left was a black, metallic, angle-poise lamp which illuminated the working area of the desk. Facing him on the opposite wall as he wrote, above a small settee, hung a large painting by his Dutch painter friend, Bram van Velde, "Composition 37." A small armchair, in which he often used to read, stood in a corner by the window. Outside, on a narrow balcony protected by a double metal rail, stood a sculpture sent to him as a gift by the Russian sculptor, Vadim Sidur (1924–86). It was from this window that, with a small pair of binoculars, Beckett used to scan the tiny, barred windows of the cells in the Santé prison, often feeling emotion for those who were imprisoned inside.

Although, as we shall see later, his country house at Ussy-sur-Marne was the place he much preferred for longer stretches of intensive creative writing, he did manage to create enough tranquility in his Paris apartment to write a number of entire manuscripts and many versions or parts of manuscripts there. His concentration was such that it was as if he were struggling (yet failing, of course) to recreate in the bustling city the life of a medieval monastic clerk working intently on his manuscript illuminations or, as he once described his situation to me, quoting the Parnassian poet José Marie de Heredia's poem, as if he were the sculptor, Benvenuto Cellini, working on the Ponte Vecchio in Florence, carving his miniatures on the pommel of a dagger, not even noticing the thronging crowd.

Of Beckett's late plays, both *Not I* (in 1972) and *Catastrophe* (in 1982), for example, seem to have been written entirely in Paris. On the other hand, *That Time* was written (in 1974) in both Ussy and Paris, the manuscript being transported several times on the train or in his little Citroen Deux Chevaux from one place to the other. *A Piece of Monologue* was begun in Paris but was completed in Ussy in October 1977. Of the prose works, while *Still* (in 1972) and *Worstward Ho* (in 1981) were both written in Paris, *Le Dépeupleur* (*The Lost Ones*) and the English translations of the *Foirades* (*Fizzles*) were again composed in both venues, *Le Dépeupleur* mainly in 1965 and 1966 and the translations intermittently between 1972 and 1975. (For more details on the places and dates of composition, see Admussen [1979] and Bryden, Garforth and Mills [1998].)

Increasingly, however, after his move into the new apartment, and with his fame growing rapidly in the 1960s, Beckett was inundated at times with appointments. His daily diaries allow us to focus on several different periods in his life over the two decades of the 1960s and 1970s, selecting either an animated or a quiet time and looking at the kind of people he was meeting and the nature of their meetings (in as much as this can now be ascertained) and seeing how, in spite of the demands that were made on his time, he still contrived to fit his writing into such a busy schedule.

The opening weeks of April 1966 are selected first for their hectic quality and also because it was the month in which his sixtieth birthday occurred, a significant enough

"awful occasion," as Krapp put it (*Krapp's Last Tape*, 1959: 11). He returned on April
1 from the studios of Süddeutscher Rundfunk in Stuttgart, where he had been directing Deryk Mendel and Nancy Illig in the first German version of his television play,
He Joe. After his return, he escorted the recently bereaved Jocelyn Herbert around
Paris for a few days, playing billiards with her and, following a matinée performance
of a "medley" of Ionesco, Beckett, and Pinget plays, taking her out to dinner on April
9 with the actress Madeleine Renaud, her husband Jean-Louis Barrault, and Beckett's
regular stage designer, Matias.

   But his meetings with Jocelyn were only a handful of many that he arranged in
what turned out to be a frantic few weeks. Some of his appointments were with close
friends; others were to do with his work or were with people whom he scarcely knew.
He spent the evening of his actual birthday, for instance (April 13) with good friends,
meeting (separately) both Madeleine Renaud and Mary Hutchinson, a 77-year-old
supporter of the arts, former member of the Bloomsbury group, and a huge admirer
of Beckett's work. The following night the French novelist, Robert Pinget, came
round to the apartment for dinner with him and Suzanne. On April 17 he had drinks
(and perhaps a meal) with the English dancer/actor Deryk Mendel, who had also just
come back from playing Joe in the German television production of *He Joe*. Beckett
also dined with his good friends the painter Avigdor Arikha (on April 11) and "Con"
Leventhal (on April 22). On Sunday, April 24, he met Georges Belmont (formerly
Pelorson) in the boulevard Saint-Jacques apartment at lunchtime and, most interestingly for Beckett scholars, two days later, sent him an inscribed copy of his first long
1930 poem *Whoroscope,* but one in which the text had been heavily corrected, indeed
virtually rewritten, probably around 1933. The new version (which still exists among
Belmont's papers) has not yet, as I write, been printed, even though it represents an
improvement on the original.

   Of the visitors he knew less well, one was the 28-year-old Italian film director,
Carlo di Carlo, with whom Beckett met on April 7 to discuss the film that di Carlo
was making of his mime *Act Without Words I*. His Danish translator, Christian
Ludvigsen, was also staying at the Hôtel des Deux Continents for a week and Beckett
managed to fit in an evening meeting with him on April 25, as well as supplying
him with a photocopy of his unpublished play *Eleutheria*. The Quartier Latin seemed
to be teeming with his American visitors: on April 7 he met the American playwright,
Edward Albee (who was in Europe for an extended trip and was currently writing his
play *A Delicate Balance*), for lunch at Albee's hotel, the Plaza Athénée; later in the
month, the theater scholar Ruby Cohn checked into the modest little Hôtel des
Balcons in the rue Casimir Delavigne for a four-day stay, and he dined with her on
April 23, while Al Capone's biographer, John Kobler, whom Beckett knew, was
staying for a few days, with his wife Evelyn, at the more upmarket Hôtel Cayré,
after being admitted as an emergency patient, suffering from a kidney-stone, at the
American Hospital in Paris (SB, letter to Jocelyn Herbert, April 12, 1966).

   Other lunches or dinners combined friendship and business. Beckett dined, for
instance, with his French publisher, Jérôme Lindon, on April 6 to discuss the

imminent publication of his short prose text *Assez*. On April 18, at the Closerie des Lilas, he met the young French film director Michel Mitrani, whom he had recently helped to make a film of his play *Comédie*. What might at first glance appear to be a series of social occasions with Madeleine Renaud over a period of two weeks were, in fact, for the rehearsals and the recording of his French translation of *Eh Joe* (*Dis Joe*) at the television studios of ORTF in the rue Cognacq Jay. Beckett later described Renaud's recording of the Voice to Jocelyn Herbert as "good." Both Renaud and her husband Jean-Louis Barrault, who acted the silent role of Joe in the television play, were already exhausted from rehearsing Roger Blin's production of Jean Genet's *Les Paravents*, which Beckett saw and found "not my bucket of scald"(SB, letter to Jocelyn Herbert, April 22, 1966). After attending rehearsals, Beckett also concluded that he was "tired" of *Eh Joe* and of his second television experience in two months (ibid.).

Meanwhile, Beckett had a wide variety of other things that he had to remember to fit in. He signed copies of his newly published prose text *Assez*, for example, at Les Editions de Minuit's *service de presse* on April 12 with his new "Rapido" fountain pen, an architect's drawing pen and a gift from Jocelyn Herbert, to whom he soon sent a signed copy (SB, letter to Jocelyn Herbert, May 6, 1966); he ordered tickets for *Les Paravents* for John Kobler and for Barbara Bray; he posted two shirts as a birthday present to his cousin, Sheila's husband, Donald Page; he sent a copy of the Bordas edition of *Murphy* to John Calder, as well as posting Calder's edition of *How It Is* to an English scholar, John Fletcher. He also fretted because he was only able to send Jocelyn Herbert 40,000 old francs – his share of the box-office for the Odéon Théâtre de France show – towards the award set up in the name of the founder of the English Stage Company, Jocelyn's late partner, George Devine (SB, letter to Jocelyn Herbert, April 22, 1966).

Dozens of such commitments were crammed into a period of less than a month. Even though the pressure was not exceptional, it was bad enough for Beckett to feel the need to leave Paris at the end of the month for his house in the country, where he remained for most of May. He tried hard to rest there but also took up his work again on the abandoned manuscript of *Le Dépeupleur* which he resumed on April 29 just before leaving Paris, then continued while he was in Ussy and later in June in the Hôtel Moderno in Courmayeur (see Bryden, Garforth, and Mills 1998: 151–2).

There were, of course, quieter phases when Beckett found time to write in Paris as well as in Ussy. The period between March and the beginning of April 1972, when we know that he was composing that astounding short monologue *Not I*, is one example. Returning from a holiday in Morocco on March 13, he began to write the actual text of the play on March 20. With the image of the djellaba-clad waiting figure seen in the street in El Jadida still in his head, an image which proved to be the inspiration for the figure of the Auditor in *Not I*, it looks as if he deliberately made very few appointments for the first few days of his return so that he would be freer to write.

The manuscript shows that, starting on Monday, March 20, he completed the holograph manuscript of the monologue, also in Paris, on Saturday, April 1. It does not follow, of course, that he was working on the draft all of that time. He does appear, however, to have restricted himself throughout a period of two weeks to only a few daytime meetings: a quick lunch with the French playwright Raymond Cousse at the Café Cluny (March 21); an afternoon with his friend, the English dramatist Harold Pinter, meeting him at Pinter's hotel (March 24); another with the writer Jean Demélier, whom Beckett befriended, indeed often funded (March 27); a third, for coffee, with his favorite stage designer, Matias Henrioud (March 25). But there were, in addition, quite a number of evening dinner appointments: with Mira Averech, the Israeli woman journalist with whom he had had a brief fling at the Akademie der Künste in Berlin in 1967 (March 22); with Ludovic Janvier, the French translator of *Watt* (March 24); with Danielle Collobert, an attractive but intensely depressed young French writer (March 27); and with his old friends Josette Hayden (March 26), Avigdor Arikha (March 30), and Con Leventhal (March 31). It is a busy enough schedule for anyone, let alone someone trying to finish a demanding play.

My own experiences of meeting Beckett in the 1970s suggest that, provided he had the rest of the day to concentrate on his writing or translating and to keep up with his extensive correspondence, he was fairly happy to relax over an evening meal, forgetting the intensely absorbing world that he had been creating during the day. Nonetheless, there were always obligations in Paris: people to see; books to sign; letters to write; phone calls to make. As a result, he used to take himself off as often and for as long as he could manage to his country retreat in Ussy.

The Silence of Ussy

It would be difficult to overestimate the importance of Beckett's "little house" in Ussy-sur-Marne to his creative life as a writer (SB, letter to Tom MacGreevy, July 17, 1961). Many of his novels and plays and a fair number of the *Mirlitonnades* were written at his large oak desk in the dull, unimposing house which he had had built on a hillside outside this village on the Marne in 1953. The short French prose texts such as *Bing* and parts of *Le Dépeupleur*, as we have seen, as well as the extraordinary long novel, *Comment c'est*, were all composed there. (As the five manuscript notebooks held in the Humanities Research Center in Texas reveal, *Comment c'est* could not, it would seem, have been written anywhere else.) Similarly, the English texts of *All that Fall* and *Eh Joe*, as well as their French translations, had Ussy as their place of genesis or "discovery." Most of the slow, patient, meticulous work of self translation of the major novels originally written in French took place in the silence of Ussy. It was there that these translations evolved into true works of recreation.

Sometimes Beckett's stays in the country lasted only a few days and were snatched almost furtively out of what we have seen was so often a frantically busy life in Paris. More often they were planned sufficiently well ahead to allow him to carve out substantial slabs of time – expressed as entirely white pages in his day-to-day appointment diaries – when he worked in the silence, seeing virtually no one.

Above all, his isolated country house meant peace, tranquility, and what he described as "invisibility" (SB to Thomas MacGreevy, March 3, 1962). It offered him the solitude that he badly needed in order to write. "I could live here contentedly now I think, all the year round. I seem to recuperate something in the silence and solitude," he wrote to his Irish friend Tom MacGreevy two years after the house had been completed (SB, letter to Tom MacGreevy, August 11, 1955). He even sought refuge there in the depths of winter. In January 1959, for instance, he wrote to the dying Ethna MacCarthy, "My silly old body is here alone with the snow and the crows and the exercise-book that opens like a door and lets me far down into the now friendly dark" (SB, letter to Ethna MacCarthy, January 10, 1959). Almost inevitably, after Suzanne stopped accompanying him to Ussy in the early sixties, he found it lonely and isolated at times. But he never thought of it as threatening, or, to use his own word, as "sinister" (SB, letter to Tom MacGreevy, November 27, 1957).

Beckett is, after all, the great poet of silence, a silence which allowed him to listen to that internal voice murmuring away relentlessly in his head or which emphasized so dramatically the tiny little sounds that so often pass unperceived. A fly buzzing around his worktable, for instance, was to make a companionable appearance later in his prose text *Company* as if it were an imaginary invention: "Let there be a fly. For him to brush away. A live fly mistaking him for dead" (*Company* in *Nohow On*, 1996: 20). The song of the nightingales or (less harmoniously) the hooting of the owls in the neighboring copse kept him company – or so at least he felt – at night when, as happened so often, he could not sleep. The sound of the leaves rustling in the wind, to which Beckett was always keenly sensitive, figures in his late writing: "She murmurs, Listen to the leaves. Eyes in each other's eyes you listen to the leaves. In their trembling shade" (ibid.: 35).

But Ussy was not only a privileged place for creative work. The recuperation he sought there found its expression in several different ways. He loved, for example, to work physically in his "grounds," which he did not like to call a garden. In the spring and summer he cut the grass (for which he had selected a cross between lawn seed and pampas grass), first with a little hand mower, then, later, with a three-wheeled scythe-mower driven by a two-stroke petrol engine, aiming to finish the large area of field in under three hours; he dug holes in the ground, heavy with stones and with marl-like putty, in order to plant a number of trees (a red chestnut, a cedar, two negundos, two apple trees, two limes, and a prunus); he repaired the barbed wire fence that separated his property from the little wood, filling in the gaps caused by the wild boar (SB, letter to Barney Rosset, May 17, 1959). Generally, to use his own word, he "pottered" about. "Pottering inertia" (SB to Thomas MacGreevy, June 4, 1956) helped to restore his mental and physical equilibrium which was threatened by too many rendezvous, too many late nights, and far too many whiskeys consumed in Paris. I remember dining with him at the Îles Marquises, his favorite seafood restaurant in the rue de la Gaîté, when he told me that he loved the calm, steady routine of raking up the leaves in the autumn, adding "I don't know why this gives me so much pleasure." In the summer, he used to sit out regularly in the sun, sometimes naked (SB, letter to Jocelyn Herbert, May 16, 1966) knowing that he was safe from the prying eyes of any passers-by because of the tall concrete wall that surrounded his property. He owned a bicycle as well as the little Deux Chevaux car and he used both, the first to take urgent letters to a postbox in the tiny hamlet of Molien and for exercise, the second to drive to the station at the larger town of La Ferté-sous-Jouarre to catch the train into Paris or simply to do his shopping in the grocer's shop or to buy his paper from the little tabac in the square. It was a hard slog to cycle as far as La Ferté, although he sometimes drove himself to do it, panting up the hills and arriving back home exhausted. Above all, Beckett adored walking, sometimes covering as many as 10, even, very occasionally, 20 kilometers a day on the quiet roads and footpaths around Molien and Meaux.

"How I adore solitude," he wrote in his private journal after a long walk in the Tiergarten in Berlin in 1936 (SB, German Diaries, notebook 3, December 31, 1936). Yet he was no hermit. This is one of the myths that has so often been perpetuated about Beckett. In fact, spending an evening with him could often be inspirational, as well as hugely entertaining. It was just that meeting so many people in Paris took a huge toll on him. Taking an active part in rehearsals of his plays, then later directing them himself, was also emotionally draining. The solitude of Ussy represented a counterbalance, a source of vital renewal of energy and, above all, of creative force.

He was rarely bored in the country. He listened regularly to concerts of classical music on his Telefunken radio and, after 1967, bought a Schimmel piano, taking it "out on Haydn and Schubert. My nose so close to the score that the keyboard feels behind my back. Get it by heart in the end and lean back" (SB, letter to Alan Schneider, April 24, 1967). At weekends, he listened on the radio to sound commentaries on rugby matches, above all to games between France and Ireland. He read and reread the great texts of Dante, Racine, Shakespeare, Goethe, Hölderlin, as well as – in the fond hope of getting to sleep – hundreds of crime novels in the French "série noire" that Henri Hayden regularly lent him. Some days he used to drive over to Reuil where the Haydens had a country house to play chess with Henri or to share a dinner prepared by Josette. More often though he would cook his own simple rice dishes or "asparagus and spuds" (SB, letter to A. J. Leventhal, April 22, 1959) and drink a few glasses of white wine. In the evening he would replay alone some of the chess games that he found in a collection of Mikhail Tal's "best games" or Alexander Alekhine's *My Best Games of Chess 1924–1937* or Reuben Fine's *Chess Marches On* (see SB, letter to Morris Sinclair, February 26, 1962). Other chess books by Alekhine, Capablanca, Spassky, and Fischer stood in a neat row on the shelves over his work desk. All of them were very well thumbed.

When the Haydens were staying in Reuil, he had a measure of companionship, but only when he specifically sought it out, whereas, in Paris, with his growing celebrity as a writer, his social life could, as the snapshots above have shown, become overwhelming, at times even nightmarish, as he raced around fulfilling what he perceived as obligations to family, friends, publishers, and directors as well as (since he was unwilling to have any secretarial help in his Paris apartment or at Ussy) struggling to keep abreast of his vast correspondence.

His relations with the village of Ussy itself became very acrimonious following a dispute with the commune about a strip of land that bordered Beckett's property. In spite of certain promises made to him by the mayor in 1952 when he bought his plot, and in spite of his own efforts to purchase the land after the death of the mayor, it was sold early in 1955 to someone else. Beckett was furious about what he saw as a personal betrayal and remained very bitter and stubbornly unforgiving for the rest of his life. After this reversal, he hardly ever went into the village itself, preferring to do all his shopping in La Ferté sous Jouarre. Yet he stayed deeply attached to the landscapes of the Monts-Moyens and always relished the peace and the isolation of the region. He never lost his affection either for some of its individual residents: above all, for the wife of the farmer down the road, Nicole Greub, who looked after his cottage for him when he was in Paris (as her mother-in-law had done before her) and to whom he left the house at Ussy after his death. He also had a friendly relationship with the garage owner, Stanislas Labeda, who took good care of his Deux Chevaux, and a local artisan, Aristide Barberis, who did odd jobs for him from time to time.

As well as being a place of refuge, Ussy represented occasionally a direct source of inspiration for Beckett's work. Although he wrote the short prose text "Still" ("Immobile") in English in his apartment on the boulevard Saint-Jacques in Paris it evokes some striking features of his French country cottage. The "small upright wicker chair with arm-rests" ("Still" in *The Complete Short Prose 1929–1989*, 1995: 240) in fact stood exactly like this in his sitting-room-cum-study in Ussy; "the valley window" looked out onto what Beckett sometimes referred to as "my Marne valley," which his painter friend Henri Hayden had painted so memorably; the windows had been placed strategically to offer different outlooks so that Beckett too, like the protagonist of his text, could in reality "turn head now and see it the sun low down in the south-west sinking"(ibid.).

There is another sense, however, in which his stays in the country impinged much more deeply on his late work. He spent many hours, we have seen, walking in the country. After just such a lengthy walk he made clear to Pamela Mitchell in a letter written in December 1954, only a few months after the death of his brother, "the real walk is elsewhere, on a screen inside, old walks in a lost country, with my father and my brother, but mostly with my father, long ago" (SB, letter to Pamela Mitchell, December 27, 1954). As a boy and a youth, he used to accompany his father at weekends up into the mountains (to Two Rock, Three Rock, and Tibradden) leaving his native village of Foxrock, County Dublin by the Ballyogan Road, "That dear old backroad" (*Company* in *Nohow On*, 1996: 16). So what he saw or heard on the walks in the Marne valley some 50 years later, or even the walks themselves, became intricately fused with memories of that distant past. Such memories are contained in Beckett's prose in images of striking immanence, as this passage from *Worstward Ho* beautifully illustrates:

> Bit by bit an old man and child. Hand in hand with equal plod they go. In the dim void bit by bit an old man and child. Any other would do as ill.

Hand in hand with equal plod they go. In the free hands – no. Free empty hands. Backs turned both bowed with equal plod they go. The child hand raised to reach the holding hand. Hold the old holding hand. Hold and be held. Plod on and never recede. Slowly with never a pause plod on and never recede. Backs turned. Both bowed. Joined by held holding hands. Plod on as one. One shade. Another shade. (*Worstward Ho* in *Nohow On*, 1996: 93).

Emotion for his family and his past has, one feels, been filtered in the course of those long, solitary walks around Ussy and Molien so that it can be depersonalized and crystallized to reach an evocation of human togetherness and tenderness which manages somehow to transcend death.

Beckett's stays in Ussy allowed him to focus with the minimum of interruption on the exploration of his own inner world. Images swam up freely from his unconscious; past and present memories merged; landscapes evolved which did not directly imitate life but assumed their own shapes and patterns. Tears welled up in Beckett's eyes as, during the last few months of his life when he was too frail and too infirm to travel there himself, I described my visits to his country house. Shortly after the death of Suzanne, he even asked me to go with Edith Fournier to the local cemetery in Ussy to see if there was a patch of shade under a tree where he might be buried when he died. Since we reported that there was not, he opted to be buried with Suzanne in the graveyard of Montparnasse.

The debt to Ussy that he himself acknowledged is much greater than most critics and readers of his work have ever recognized. It was not only a refuge and a lifeline. It provided him with ideal conditions for his creativity. Small wonder that he never sold the house.

References and Further Reading

Beckett's letters to Jocelyn Herbert are in the archives of the Beckett International Foundation at The University of Reading, those to Thomas MacGreevy are at Trinity College Dublin, those to Alan Schneider are at Boston College, those to Barney Rosset are at The University of New York at Syracuse, and those to Mary Manning, A. J. Leventhal, and Ethna MacCarthy are at the Humanities Research Center in Austin, Texas. His letters to Morris Sinclair and the appointment diaries are still in private hands. Beckett's German Diaries are in the archives of the Copies of Beckett International Foundation at The University of Reading.

Admussen, Richard (1979). *The Samuel Beckett Manuscripts: A Study*. Boston: G. K. Hall.

Beckett, Samuel (1959). *Krapp's Last Tape and Embers*. London: Faber and Faber.

Beckett, Samuel (1995). *The Complete Short Prose 1929–1989*. New York: Grove Press.

Beckett, Samuel (1996). *Nohow On*. New York: Grove Press.

Bryden, Mary, Julian Garforth, and Peter Mills (1998). *Beckett at Reading: Catalogue of the Samuel Beckett Manuscripts at the University of Reading*. Reading: Whiteknights Press and the Beckett International Foundation.

Gussow, Mel (1999). *Edward Albee: A Singular Life*. London: Oberon Books.

Knowlson, James (1996). *Damned to Fame: The Life of Samuel Beckett*. London and New York: Bloomsbury Publishing and Simon and Schuster, reissued by Grove Atlantic 2004.

2
Within a Budding Grove: Publishing Beckett in America

S. E. Gontarski

Gratitude is a poor word for the beautiful set of 13 and the affection it brings me from you all and the way it says how good things always were between us and always will be. (SB to BR and all at Grove, April 16, 1966)[1]

On June 18, 1953, Barnet Lee Rosset, Jr, the 31-year-old proprietor and sole editor of the budding Grove Press, took on a new author, Samuel Beckett, a little known Irish émigré living in Paris and writing (then) primarily in French: "It is about time that I write a letter to you – now that agents, publishers, friends, etc., have all acted as go-betweens. A copy of our catalogue has already been mailed to you, so you will be able to see what kind of publisher you have been latched onto. I hope that you won't be too disappointed." That initial letter began one of the most extraordinary relationships in publishing that lasted until Beckett's death on December 22, 1989. Its origins were modest: a little known writer (unknown in the USA) publishing arcane, experimental poems, plays, and novels with little prospect of commercial success championed by a neophyte American publishing house struggling to find its niche. Samuel Beckett went on, of course, to become one of the most influential writers of the twentieth century, his reputation solidified internationally by the award of the *Prix International de Littérature* in 1961, which he shared with Jorge Luis Borges, which in turn led to the Nobel Prize for Literature in 1969. Rosset, in turn, would guide what began as a small reprint house that he bought in 1951 for $3,000 into the most aggressive, innovative, audacious, politically active, and so sometimes reckless, publishing concern in the United States for over three decades. Through the turbulence, the successes and failures of the press, Beckett remained a featured, signature author.

In these early years Grove Press was a decidedly amateurish concern. Rosset was operating it from his 57 W. 9th Street flat in New York's Greenwich Village, filling orders himself, delivering parcels of books to the local post office in a shopping trolley. As business increased Rosset took on an assistant editor, Don Allen, whom he had met at a night class, "Editorial Practices and Principles of Book Publishing," offered at Columbia University by legendary Random House editor Saxe Commins (1892–1958). Allen went on to develop the influential Grove Press house magazine, *Evergreen Review*, and he was Grove's first translator of Eugene Ionesco (*Four Plays: The Bald Soprano, The Lesson, Jack or The Submission, The Chairs*, 1958) and edited two influential anthologies for Grove: *The New American Poetry: 1945–1960* (1960), and, with Robert Creely, *New American Story* (1965).

On March 30, 1953 *Newsweek* magazine described the budding enterprise thus:

> the Grove Press is housed on the ground floor of a Greenwich Village dwelling, with the shipping room in what used to be the dining room [... The office] overlooks one of those fine old Greenwich Village back yards of struggling trees, spare grass, spite-wall fences, clotheslines, and expanses of brick wall. Since the staff of the Grove Press consists only of a publicity man [John Gruen], a charming young German girl newly arrived in the United States [Hannelore (Loly) Eckert whom Rosset would marry on August 21, 1953], and a part time assistant who plays in bit parts in Broadway shows [Howard Turner], the overhead is not high.

What the *Newsweek* profile intimated was that the Grove staff lacked publishing experience. If Beckett had earlier thought of the group of editors publishing *Merlin* magazine in Paris as the Merlin juveniles, he now seemed to be dealing with the Grove Press juveniles. Debutantes that they were, however, Rosset and company were fully engaged in professional development.

The Rosset–Beckett match seemed, at the outset, unlikely, if not odd: a classically educated Irishman with a Master's degree in modern languages from the venerable Trinity College, Dublin transplanted to France, and a scrappy Chicagoan from a middle-class banking family who had failed to complete degree requirements at three major American universities transplanted to New York; a shy, bookish, taciturn artist with impeccable European (if not nineteenth-century) manners, on the one hand, and a brash, volatile, street-smart American more comfortable in the jazz clubs of Chicago than in any library or university. They were a generation apart in age as well; Samuel Barclay Beckett was born in Foxrock, County Dublin on April 13, 1906, Barnet Lee Rosset, Jr in Chicago on May 28, 1922. But over a 35-year period, a professional, personal, even spiritual bond developed between the upstart American publisher bent on challenging traditional restrictions on American publishing and the upstart Irish writer bent on challenging the literary traditions not only of his homeland but of Western Europe as a whole. The two actually had a great deal in common. Rosset had Irish roots on his mother's side, Mary E. Tansey (b. 1899), who married the son of Russian Jewish immigrants, Barnet Lee Rosset (b. 1899); as Rosset describes them: "My father was a Jewish Republican, my mother an Irish Democrat." Rosset and Beckett were, finally, children of privilege, sons of the upper middle class, raised in posh suburbs (Rosset on Chicago's Lakeshore Drive, Beckett in Foxrock) and products of private education. Both had a strong interest in sports: Rosset for (American) football and track; Beckett for cricket and golf. They shared an interest in tennis as well, Rosset having private courts built at each of his successive summer residences (in East

Hampton, NY). Sports "of all sorts" were part of their meetings in Paris, as Rosset remembers:

> We had found a common ground in games. I tried my hand at Beckett's favorite pastimes, chess and billiards, but found them too maddeningly demanding of precision for me to cope with. Beckett, on the other hand, enjoyed playing my more slapdash table tennis. As a spectator sport we settled on tennis, which we both had once played, and we attended matches at Roland Garros stadium outside Paris. Once we saw a match between the great American player Pancho Gonzales and the Australian champion, Lew Hoad, at a time when professionals could not compete against amateurs. The umpire was a Basque and an admirer of Beckett. He waved enthusiastically at Sam as he mounted his tall chair courtside. The stadium was jammed. A couple of sets later, before a booing crowd, he was ejected at Gonzales' request after making a number of calls against him. He paused to chat for a moment with Sam in the midst of his forced exit.

Both sought refuge in physical labor at their country homes, although Beckett's Ussy home was monastic compared with those that Rosset owned in East Hampton. Each was nearly obsessed with planting trees to surround his retreat. Each had a passion for music, though their musical tastes differed. Beckett was a proficient pianist who, throughout his life, could be moved to tears by Schubert. He had a piano in his Paris flat and another in his country house in Ussy-sur-Marne, the latter a Schimmel on which he played sonatas by Haydn, Beethoven, and Mozart, or accompanied himself in Schubert Lieder. Rosset, on the other hand, was committed to the jazz he grew up with and listened to in South Chicago nightclubs:

> I went into this very, very favorite bar of mine called Tin Pan Alley in Chicago that had Baby Dodds playing the drums and Laura Rucker, a blind woman, playing the piano ... A strange, narrow long bar with these two people huddled in one corner. You had to fall over them to get past them, the blind pianist and the old drummer. But they were wonderful.

The first issue of *Evergreen Review* would, then, juxtapose the life story of Baby Dodds with Beckett's poetry, and nearly all subsequent issues contained essays on or reviews of jazz and much Beckett.

They also shared a strong distaste for authority, and both developed a taste for revolutionary literature and avant-garde visual art. Central to Rosset's sensibility was his reading (as an undergraduate at Swarthmore College in 1940) of fellow countryman Henry Miller's banned novel *Tropic of Cancer* and his anti-American diatribe *The Air-Conditioned Nightmare*. Central to Beckett's sensibility was his reading of fellow countryman James Joyce's banned novel *Ulysses* and his *Work in Progress*, published as *Finnegans Wake*. Both had strong, early attachments to women who would eventually marry their best friends and subsequently die young from cancer. In Rosset's life the woman was fellow student at the Parker School in Chicago, Nancy Ashenhurst, who married his best friend cinematographer Haskell Wexler. In Beckett's case it was fellow Trinity College student Ethna McCarthy who married A. J. "Con" Leventhal in 1956 and who died in May of 1959. She is immortalized as the "feminine incarnate" in Beckett's poem "Alba," the character based on her in *Dream of Fair to middling Women*, as well. But Rosset finds the relationship with another failed love and her early death even more poignant and persistent, that between Beckett and his first cousin, Peggy Sinclair, who appears as the Smeraldina in his early work:

> In 1958 Sam wrote a major piece in English. It was *Krapp's Last Tape*. The texture is almost wildly emotional. The chess playing atmosphere in *Endgame* is less evident; the fabric provides a sort of a sudden oasis of piercingly romantic fulfillment followed by desperate loss. The prose becomes suffused with sensuality and then with tears. Krapp, now an old man, plays and replays tapes from his younger days, trying to find some meaning or hope in his life. One passage is excruciatingly passionate. His/their love has now been destroyed beyond retrieval ...
>
> Led to it by Beckett, I searched the German nineteenth-century novelist Theodor Fontane's *Effi Briest* for clues to this passage. Finally Beckett told me that, for him, it referred to a summer with his cousin Peggy in 1929 at a small resort on the Baltic Sea, at a time when Peggy was engrossed in the book about a young girl's calamitous life that ended with her death from tuberculosis. Although Beckett was only 23 at the time, his feeling for her, and the memory of their being together, survived her engagement to another man and her death in 1933, ironically also of tuberculosis.
>
> The story struck an incredibly strong chord in me. I had also suffered the loss of a young love, my Nancy, who went to high school with me in Chicago. During World War II, she married my best friend, and not much later died of cancer. I still grieve for Nancy and have dreams about her.

Unlikely as it seemed at first, their relationship would grow to be mutually influential. Beckett would become one of Grove's most respected and, finally, profitable authors, a mainstay of Grove Press through its financial successes and near bankruptcies. Rosset in turn would have a significant impact on Beckett's career as he made good the promise of his initial letter, "Believe me, we will do what we can to make your work known in this country." Grove would market the avant-garde writer aggressively, almost obsessively, in the United States.

Rosset's relationship with Beckett was to grow well beyond that of author and publisher as from 1957, after the first production of *Waiting for Godot*, until Beckett's death in December of 1989, he took on the added responsibility of acting as American theatrical agent, and in addition became the producer of a number of American stagings of Beckett's plays. Rosset had been intimately involved in American productions from the first, championing Beckett's appearance not in the more commercial Broadway theaters, but in the smaller, more intimate, off-Broadway theaters of Greenwich Village. Beckett first broached the matter of Rosset's becoming his sole American theatrical agent in a letter of April 6, 1957 as preparations for an American production of *Endgame* were taking final shape. Rather than a formal contract between the two, Beckett offered a letter in which he expressed his general confidence in Rosset even though the decision might "bring down, from Covent Garden [i.e., Curtis

Brown] and I suppose from [*Godot* producer Michael] Myerberg, thunderbolts upon my head, but the bloodiness and bowedness of that perishing appendix can hardly be augmented ... Let me know if you would be disposed to take it on." Beckett had already raised the issue with his American director, Alan Schneider, two days earlier, on April 4 – "I shall probably take control of U. S. A. performance rights away from Curtis Brown and give it to Rosset," a decision he conformed in his subsequent letter to Schneider of April 30 (Harmon 1998: 13–14). In a letter of March 26, 1961 to the producer of *Krapp's Last Tape*, Harry Joe Brown, Beckett outlined what became his standard position about productions in the United States: "all decisions with regard to productions rest with Grove Press and will be approved by me," the statement essentially repeated to producer/director Richard Barr on September 25, 1963: "There can be no question of my ever accepting arrangements for any of my plays in the USA that are not approved both by Barney Rosset and Alan Schneider." And as late as February 1, 1986, Beckett reaffirmed his commitment to and confidence in Rosset thus: "This is to confirm that I have appointed you as my exclusive theatrical agent for North America. This agreement shall remain in effect until such time as either one of us decides to terminate it." Soon after Beckett's death, however, a rift developed between Rosset and Beckett's estate, and the agreement was summarily terminated.

Between the 1957 Cherry Lane Theater *Endgame* and Beckett's death in 1989, Rosset would help make Beckett an off-Broadway fixture, most performances taking place in Rosset's beloved Greenwich Village. The Village, at that time, was an American echo of left-bank Paris, and Rosset's sensibility, like Beckett's, favored its inhabitants, particularly the dispossessed and the culturally marginal. For Rosset, then, Beckett and Greenwich Village were a perfect match, and he drummed that message to Beckett so frequently that he risked "being thought of as the village crank by you and Albery because I have conducted this monotonous diatribe about off-Broadway" (January 27, 1956).

So, politically and culturally, Rosset and Beckett had much in common, and through their thirty-six year relationship, Rosset would exert considerable influence on Beckett's professional career. As his initial letter shows, he had a vision for Beckett: "*En attendant Godot* [*Waiting for Godot*] should burst upon us as an entity in my opinion." Rosset would urge, prod, and coax a reluctant Beckett to translate his novels:

> The first order of the day would appear to be the translation [of *Molloy*] ... If you would accept my first choice as translator the whole thing would be easily settled. That choice of course being you. That already apparently is a satisfactory condition insofar as the play [*Godot*, which Beckett was then in the midst of translating] is concerned. The agent here tells me that you have agreed to our proposal, and he is drawing up a simple letter contract now which we will mail to you tomorrow.

Furthermore, Rosset would go on in the mid-1950s to encourage Beckett to return to writing in his native tongue, and Beckett would respond shortly thereafter with a radio play for the BBC, *All That Fall*, and the one-act masterpiece, *Krapp's Last Tape*. On February 5,1954 he wrote the following to Beckett: "I have been wondering if you would not get almost the freshness of turning to doing something in English which you must have gotten when you first seriously took to writing in French. A withdrawal from a withdrawal – English." Thenceforth, Beckett would write in both languages, translating his works himself from one language into the other. And Rosset was quick to see, perhaps the first, that translation for Beckett was *a part of*, not apart from, the process of creativity. Beckett could see no future to his writing in August of 1954 as he tended his dying brother Frank, and he wrote to Rosset from Ireland on the 21st of the month, "You know, Barney, I think my writing days are over. *L'Innommable* finished me or expressed my finishedness." On September 12 Rosset responded, his own father having recently and unexpectedly died, "Samuel, don't you think that the translation work in itself is still a form of writing for you? If you go on, as you have said you will, with your own translation of the last two books [*Malone meurt* and *L'Innommable*], don't you think it possible that somewhere within them you will find a lead to another deposit?" Beckett did and produced the 13 short pieces *Textes pour rien* (*Texts for Nothing*) and, by 1961, another stunning post-*Unnamable* novel, *Comment c'est* (*How It Is*).

Furthermore, in 1963 Rosset's passion for expanding his publishing house into other media culminated in Grove's commissioning a film script from Beckett. The result was the film (Beckett's one and only true venture into that medium and the only one of a planned series that Grove Press was developing that was made) entitled *Film*. The shooting occurred in New York during the summer of 1964, Beckett himself in attendance. He arrived in New York at what was then Idlewild (now Kennedy) Airport on July 10, 1964, spending the weekend at Rosset's East Hampton summer home, planning the shooting, playing some tennis, and then returning to Rosset's West Houston Street flat where he resided throughout the filming, departing for Paris on August 6. Beckett seemed awkward, even uncomfortable, during his New York stay, relaxing only at "The Emerald Isle," a Greenwich Village pub. Shortly thereafter, on his sixtieth birthday, Grove Press presented its featured author with a set of 13 specially bound copies of his books. Beckett was overwhelmed by the gesture: "Gratitude is a poor word for the beautiful set of 13 and the affection it brings me from you all and the way it says how good things always were between us and always will be" (April 16, 1966). At the end of his career and only two years before his death, Beckett dedicated the three stories of his late masterpiece *Stirrings Still* to Rosset.

Beckett in turn would steel Rosset for what would soon become Grove's crusade against censorship. In a letter of June 25, 1953 Beckett suggested not only his own uncompromising position toward his art but set the tone for Rosset's battles against censorship for the next two decades:

> With regard to my work in general, I hope you realize what you are letting yourself in for. I do not mean the heart of the matter, which is unlikely to disturb anybody, but certain obscenities of form which may not have struck you in French as they will in English, and which frankly (it is better that you should know this before we get going) I am not at all disposed to mitigate. I do not of course realize what is possible in America

from this point of view and what is not. Certainly as far as I know such passages, faithfully translated, would not be tolerated in England.

Rosset too was unsure what was possible in America. Cautioned by Beckett, and on advice of his legal staff, Rosset's initial parry with American authorities was tentative, circumspect. *Molloy* was published exclusively in hard cover at first, its distribution restricted to New York bookshops that had requested it: "Copies of *Molloy* are in all the New York City bookstores that wanted them," he wrote Beckett on September 24, 1955, "but distribution across the rest of the country has not yet gone out. The post office is now examining the book and I am sure their decision will be very amusing if not pleasing." In this instance the United States Post Office raised no objection to the book, and Rosset proceeded with a paperback publication the following year concurrent with the release of *Malone Dies*, which was published exclusively in paperback. (Although actually published in 1956, the paperback *Molloy* retained the 1955 publication date as if it were published simultaneously with the hard cover.) Rosset would subsequently persevere not only with the "obscenities of form" in Beckett but push on to publish and distribute through the mail, in defiance of Post Office interdictions, two famously banned novels: the unexpurgated *Lady Chatterley's Lover* in 1959, a book even Sylvia Beach of Shakespeare and Company, publisher of James Joyce's *Ulysses*, rejected in 1928 as unsavory, and Henry Miller's *Tropic of Cancer* in 1961 (although the legal battles over Miller's work persisted until 1964). These were books that shaped and fueled that social and political upheaval loosely called "the sixties." Battles against censorship became a crusade for Rosset and his Grove Press. In an interview with Italian publisher Giangiacomo Feltrinelli conducted in 1959 for the New York City educational radio station WNET, Rosset articulated what might be considered the ideology of his press: "Mr. Feltrinelli, I would like to interject here that I feel that personally there hasn't been a word written or uttered that shouldn't be published, singly or in multiples. I think that is stating my position" (Gontarski 2001: 8).

From its modest beginning with the publication of *Molloy*, Rosset's battle against censorship became virtually a battle against American legal authority in general. These turbulent years coincided with Richard Seaver's tenure at Grove (1959–71), and his summary of the period is couched in near military terminology:

> In 1961, one year after the *Lady Chatterley* litigation ended, we published Henry Miller's *magnum opus*. Ironically, because Lawrence had knocked out both the Post Office and Customs, and won a federal victory, there was no federal case this time. Instead, every local police chief and district attorney felt free to seize and sue, as indeed they did. At one point, Grove was defending some sixty cases around the country, and its paltry reserves were strained to the breaking point as lawyers were hired en masse to defend those attacked. Key staff members, from Barney on down, spent more time in court testifying than they did in the office.
>
> Frankly, I don't remember how we managed to survive the *Tropic of Cancer* litigations, but somehow we did and, bruised and battered but still standing, we went on to test a

few more waters: William Burroughs' *Naked Lunch* … available in France from Maurice
Girodias's Olympia Press but not in the author's native land; Jean Genet, whose dramatic works Grove had been publishing but whose novels, *The Thief's Journal* and *Our
Lady of the Flowers*, had generally been deemed too hot to handle even in France and had
been published there by a small but audacious publisher, Arbelète. Finally, in 1949 and
'51 respectively, the most prestigious French publisher, Gallimard, screwed its courage
to the sticking post and brought out both Genet novels. Armed with that house's near-
inviolable imprimatur, the Gallic censors, less ardent than the Anglo-Saxon, remained
in their corner. But we at Grove had no such illusions about their counterparts here if
and when we released those daring works in the States. In the wings close behind Burroughs were two younger Americans, John Rechy and Hubert Selby Jr., not to mention,
again from that country who produce so much of this censorable material, a mysterious
woman, Pauline Réage, whose *Story of O.* had since the mid-1950s been the talk and
rage of Paris; and, finally, the naughty granddaddy of them all: the infamous, garrulous
blasphemer and rebel *extraordinaire*, Donatien-Alphonse-François, a.k.a. the Marquis de
Sade …

    … In the next two to two and a half years we unleashed upon the world (with *Naked
Lunch* now safely behind us) no fewer than half a dozen works which, under normal
circumstances, we would have published over a five- or six-year period. In quick suc-
cession, and not necessarily in that order, came Frank Harris' monumental *My Life
and Loves* (with a final chapter by – pseudonymously – my old *Merlin* colleague and
Grove author Alex Trocchi), John Rechy's *City of Night,* Jean Genet's *Our Lady of the
Flowers* (the original Olympia Press translation being, to use a kindly term, wooden,
I was dispatched to Paris for a month to rework it, line by line, with the translator
Bernard Frechtman, a job of delicate diplomacy, since Frechtman "owned" the English
language rights and did not take kindly to criticism), followed a year later by his *The
Thief's Journal*, Selby's *Last Exit to Brooklyn,* and Pauline Réage's *Story of O.* (Gontarski
2001: 92)

This, then, would be the house to represent Samuel Beckett in the United States and
champion his professional development. And Beckett was in general sympathy with
what might be called the Grove spirit. As early as February 1938 he was approached
by Jack Kahane of Obelsik Press, father of Maurice Girodias who would begin to
publish Beckett through his Olympia Press, to translate *Les 120 Jours de Sodome*, which
Beckett thought, "one of the capital works of the 18th century" (Knowlson 1996: 269).
After considering how such a publication might damage his fledgling literary career,
however, he demurred. But he retained an interest in and a respect for many of the
books that Rosset was publishing at Grove. He was delighted to receive the Grove
edition of the long suppressed Frank Harris work *My Life and Loves*, which he acknowledged in his letter of November 24, 1963, and on November 26 he asked Judith
Schmidt to airmail a copy to Jack McGowran in London.
    During those years of aggressive publishing and battles against censorship, Beckett
did seem to take a back seat to a larger political agenda at Grove, but the politically
aggressive press began to unravel in the 1970s. Grove faced a dual assault from the
emerging women's movement, as employee Robin Morgan led a takeover of the Grove
offices, and as unlikely labor unions tried to organize the Grove employees. These

tandem events managed to accomplish what the force of American government could not: restrain, indeed muzzle Grove Press. Richard Seaver left shortly thereafter in 1971, as did Judith Schmidt. For the next decade and a half Grove was in a constant state of near collapse and bankruptcy. By March 1, 1985, Rosset would have to sell Grove Press in an effort to revitalize the flagging company. Rosset's thinking was that the new owners would provide "the infusion of capital" that he had been searching for for over a decade and that this would inject new life into the press, but it came at the price of the press itself.

Rosset tried several publishing ventures in the aftermath of Grove Press, but he could no longer generate substantial financial backing, and so they remained marginal. Beckett tried to supply him with additional material on occasion, promising at first to translate *Eleutheria* for him. Finding the juvenile work impossible to translate, he offered Rosset three new short texts, which he dedicated to his American publisher, and which Rosset (along with John Calder) published as *Stirrings Still*. But such short pieces had little impact on Rosset's ability to start, generate, and sustain a new publishing venture. By 1986, therefore, Barnet Lee Rosset, Jr was no longer a force in American publishing, but he still represented Beckett's theatrical interests in the United States. His publication, not long after Beckett's death, of *Eleutheria* brought that to an end, too, however. Although publishing Beckett's first full-length play in the face of the Estate's interdictions was the immediate cause of the rift, the letters detail a pattern of tensions from the earliest days over rights and royalties between American and French publishers, the latter of which became the Executor of Beckett's estate. Aside from the slight volume of stories, *Stirrings Still* (published through North Star Books), and the American rights to *Eleutheria* (published through Foxrock Books), Rosset's professional, and hence economic, connection was fully severed by 1995.

NOTE

1 The unpublished letters quoted in this chapter are available in the Rare Book Collection, The Wilson Library, The University of North Carolina at Chapel Hill, and in Rosset's personal archive.

REFERENCES AND FURTHER READING

Gontarski, S. E. (ed.) (2001). *The Grove Press Reader, 1951–2001*. New York: Grove Press.

Harmon, Maurice (ed.) (1998). *No Author Better Served: The Correspondence of Samuel Beckett and Alan Schneider*. Cambridge, MA: Harvard University Press.

Jordan, Ken (1998). "Barney Rosset: The Art of Publishing II" [an interview]. *The Paris Review* 145: 171–215.

Knowlson, James (1996). *Damned to Fame: The Life of Samuel Beckett*. London: Bloomsbury.

Newsweek (1953). "Advance-Garde Advance." March 30: 94–6.

Seaver, Richard (ed.) (1977). *"I Can't Go On, I'll Go On": A Selection from Samuel Beckett's Work*. New York: Grove Press.

3
Samuel Beckett and *Waiting for Godot*

Lois Gordon

The brief period during which Samuel Beckett began his major writing, usually referred to as the "siege in the room," occurred following World War II, after Beckett spent five years in the French Resistance fighting the Nazis. And it was during this "siege" that he wrote *Waiting for Godot*. Beckett could not have written this great play if he had not lived these astonishingly heroic years, in the midst of an otherwise unexceptional, if interesting, life. This remains of particular interest to me, because during most of his lifetime Beckett was incorrectly viewed as a solitary and eccentric man, a recluse who rarely left his apartment and who remained in bed much of the day contemplating abstract philosophy. In a similarly incorrect way, even after he received the Nobel Prize in 1969, *Waiting for Godot* was often read as a gloomy philosophical statement – as a negative vision of life – a play demonstrating the boredom and misery of life. In fact, and to the contrary, the play, like Beckett's life, is fully involved in the variety of elements that characterize most people's lives, especially the concrete issues of every day – what to eat, when to go to sleep, how to spend the day – just as it addresses the more abstract issues provoked by war, human suffering, and the mysteries of life. In other words, it is a play about the everyday problems of human survival and the meaning of life both in its pleasures and hardships, its humor and brutality. It is about how in life we shuttle between joy and sorrow. As Beckett expresses it in one of his most memorable lines, "The tears of the world are a constant quantity. For each one who begins to weep somewhere else another stops. The same is true of the laugh."

Beckett's life is central to understanding *Godot*, although many details are familiar by now. Beckett was born in Foxrock, Ireland, a wealthy Dublin suburb. His parents, and their parents as well, were part of the late nineteenth-century Protestant upper middle class. Although Irish by birth, they were English by style, temperament, and political orientation. They believed typically that progress through science, industry, and religion – certainly not through art – would better the lot of humankind, and that wealth and status were signs of divine grace. To most children of their class, there was little to do but follow in their elders' footsteps. Obviously, Beckett did not.

It was, as Beckett frequently remarked, a happy childhood, although he often added that he was always aware of the unhappiness around him. The family lived eight miles from Dublin in a village with unpaved roads, one general store, and any number of cows, sheep, hens, lambs, and dogs. Foxrock was within walking or biking distance of the Dublin mountains and a beautiful seaside and harbor. The Beckett three-story Tudor house, called Cooldrinagh, was handsome enough to be photographed for a prestigious architecture journal. It had stables, large lawns and gardens, wood-paneled rooms, house maids, a gardener, and numerous pets, including dogs, donkeys, and hens. The house was usually filled with the smells of fresh jam and lemon cakes that Mrs Beckett baked in her kitchen.

Beckett's father, not interested in university education, was a partner in the family's construction firm in Dublin. He had met Beckett's mother, Mary, when she was a nurse. Now a lady of leisure "May's" life goal was to be a good wife and mother. She instructed her two sons in proper manners and congenial hobbies, like piano playing, drawing, and singing, and she was also stern and religious. Beckett once said that he was raised "almost a Quaker," adding the caveat that he soon lost faith after leaving Trinity. Beckett's college days at Trinity would follow the failed 1916 Irish Uprising against England and World War I.

Beckett's father, Bill, shared his keen interest in sports with his boys and took them hiking regularly, and fished, bicycled, and played golf with them. He tried his best to understand his children. But he was strict and, in the style of the times, demanding of a kind of physical perfection and fearlessness. He would, for example, take the young boys to a granite promontory at an area called "Forty Foot" and force them to jump into the water. One of Beckett's friends said about this that early on, Sam acquired "a physical toughness" that would "stand him in good stead throughout his life" (Reid 1969: 68). To be sure, Beckett frequently described the enormous love both he and his brother, Frank, felt toward their father.

Beckett's parents may have had an enormous interest in their children's upbringing, but, like their neighbors, they had little interest in Irish culture or the popular Irish life around them. Their only contact with the Catholic world was with their servants, so that if "one preferred to think of oneself as English here in Foxrock, Ireland, there was really no reason not to." That they were isolated from the real world, in a sense, sheds light on Beckett's remark about his awareness of the unhappiness around him. First of all, beggars and tramps frequently roamed the countryside or sat with outstretched hands on the Dublin bridges. In addition, the Foxrock children who played together were very much aware of but confused by the retarded and mentally ill who were kept at home. Families would "hide" them. "I remember a family who hired a 'keeper,'" remarked one young friend, "for a man who played the same tune on his piano all day long. This [word] 'keeper' [also] puzzled us children, as it was used for the men who looked after lions and tigers in the zoo, but there were quite a few around" (Duckworth 1980: 61–2). Dublin also had two as-they-were-called "lunatic asylums," as well as several hospitals; tuberculosis was prevalent. After a military hospital opened near Beckett's home, the young boy saw patients every day in various stages of mental and physical disability.

Of greater importance in understanding Beckett's remark about the "unhappiness around him" – and one of the most memorable events of his life – was the evening his father took him to see Dublin in flames during the Easter Uprising. This was just one of several events Beckett witnessed involving Catholic Ireland's heroic but doomed effort to gain independence from Protestant England. Although he was only 10 in 1916, this was a period of national and global transformation that he would never forget. Continual bloodshed would anticipate years of dreams and disappointment, along with an increasingly brutal animosity between the English and Irish. And the Great War, which began in 1914, would end any lingering Victorian dreams of limitless power and expansion, and would end the prewar sentiment "How sweet it is to die for my country." Throughout his childhood, adolescence, and early manhood Beckett knew about the conflicts over the Irish being drafted into the British military at the same time that they were fighting for their independence from the British.

Beckett had been attending school in Dublin, and not only were many sections of the city devastated by bombs and other artillery but posters and flags decorated it with reminders of the terrible events of the time. The words of the great Irish patriot James Connolly were on banners everywhere, proclaiming, "We Serve Neither King Nor Kaiser But Ireland." To Connolly: "Irishmen are ready to die in order to win for Ireland those natural rights which the British government has been asking them to die to win for Belgium."

The result of the ill-planned and ill-executed Irish rebellion of Easter 1916 was massive looting and killing. And to many, certainly to Beckett's family, the executions and martial law that followed were not inappropriate. The great rebel heroes Connolly, Padraic Pearse, and Thomas MacDonough, and their followers, foresaw their roles as sacrificial figures and believed that only through violence and sacrifice could sufficient solidarity mount to ensure their victory. Connolly always qualified the sacred nature of their mission: "Men still know how to die for the holiest of all causes," for the "brotherhood of men"; "Without shedding of Blood there is no Redemption." Pearse's rhetoric was similarly irresistible: "Life springs from death and from the graves of patriots ... spring living nations." Indeed, the notion of suffering redeemed through camaraderie – and, if possible, altruistic action – would resound in *Waiting for Godot*, as each figure repeats in his own way "To every man his little cross," aware that salvation alone arises from hearing those "cries for help" addressed to "all mankind" when "all mankind is us." And Beckett's extraordinary activities during World War II suggest a similar sense of responsibility.

The Great War – World War I – with its unprecedented casualties caused unspeakable human grief. But in Ireland, long after the armistice, terrible losses persisted. The Great War may have ended for most of the world, but in Ireland violence continued through the fight for independence and the Irish Civil War, with ambushes, shooting, curfews, murders in the street, and every kind of horror. And it was in 1923 that Beckett enrolled at Trinity. Hence, his remark that he "was raised almost a Quaker," but "soon lost faith ... after leaving Trinity."

Beckett graduated from Trinity with many honors and went on to become the college's exchange lecturer with the École Normale Superiéur in Paris, but before that term, he taught French in Northern Ireland, in Belfast. It was, as he put it, a "grim" nine-month experience, "a terrible place ... full of bigotry." Belfast was suffering a terrible depression and Beckett, always sympathetic to the ill-treated, realized that "to be Protestant was to be privileged [and] to require that Catholics be visibly deprived; and to deprive Catholics was to build the social order on domination." (MacDonald 1986: 8)

During virtually half of his life, Beckett thus bore witness to human degradation, suffering, and humiliation: the Irish Uprising, World War I, the 1920s depression, and discrimination in Belfast; then the major economic depression that hit England in the 1930s when he moved there; and, finally, during World War II, when he lived in France, the Nazi occupation of Paris and Vichy puppet government in southern France. The world might have seemed to Beckett an unrelenting campaign of slaughter rising out of religious and ethnic prejudice. But Beckett also observed bravery and sacrifice. He came into his own with a profound sense that evil cannot go unattended and that the defense of the good, whether in dramatic or modest action, gives dignity and meaning to life.

Beckett's ideas about individual will and choice, and matters of good and evil, were, in part, the outgrowth of a lifelong interest in literature, philosophy, and debate. He had a number of gifted friends and artists, none more talented than James Joyce whom he met shortly after he went to teach in Paris in 1927. They developed an extraordinary friendship and were like father and son to one another. Although Beckett had to leave Paris to fulfill other obligations he returned in the late 1930s and actively continued his relationship with Joyce. The French press had been reporting Hitler's aberrant aims and activities, and this, along with Beckett's firsthand experience with the Nazi regime during 1936–7, when for six months he traveled to Germany, was crucial in his swift decision after Hitler moved his troops into Paris to resist the German evil actively rather than accept it passively. Perhaps he thought, as Vladimir says in *Godot*, "Let us not waste our time in idle discourse! ... Let us do something, while we have the chance!" As Alec Reid reported, after the Germans occupied Paris, the war suddenly became something "personal and with meaning" to Beckett. Like Joyce, he had many Jewish friends and he was incensed "by the constant public humiliations ... and the almost daily shootings by the Germans of innocent people taken as hostages." Beckett said, "almost apologetically, 'I couldn't stand with my arms folded'"(Reid 1968: 13–14).

Beckett was one of the earliest in 1940 to join the Resistance, when he learned of the organizations printing anti-Nazi propaganda and carrying out sabotage activities. Although he was always reluctant to discuss his war activities they are documented in the historical records of World War II. His Paris group, Gloria, was indirectly funded by Churchill's organization, the Special Operation Executive (SOE), which oversaw all underground activities in the occupied nations. Étoile was another of Beckett's groups. His assignments included collecting information (sometimes in code) regarding German troop movements, which he deciphered and typed or micro-filmed before it was smuggled out to London. In August 1942, after one of Gloria's members was tortured into a confession, the others faced imminent exposure. At 11:00 a.m., on August 15, Suzanne and Samuel Beckett received a telegram urging them to leave Paris immediately. By 3:00 p.m. they were gone, traveling mostly on foot and at night, toward Roussillon, a village in the so-far unoccupied zone in the south. Beckett in flight was known as a "key man" for whom Nazi bullets were marked.

By the time he arrived in Roussillon, the Germans had invaded the entire area, and anyone suspected of any kind of underground activity faced grave danger. Once there Beckett joined the maquis, and his clandestine activities included the delivery of ammunition for the destruction of railroad yards involved in transporting German supplies and setting up contacts between Resistance workers. Beckett dismissed his World War II activities as "boy-scout stuff," but following the war he was decorated by Charles de Gaulle with the Croix de Guerre, and his medal with its silver star indicated "specific acts of bravery." Beckett also received the Medaille de la Résistance. To both these honors, he responded with typical reserve and humility.

At this point one may ask how Beckett's life relates to the play. How is *Godot* about war or even about how most people live? It portrays two characters on a road that both goes nowhere and that comes from nowhere and how, on this road, they talk to each other, laugh, sing, cry, argue, and entertain some rather odd visitors, two other men, who act like master and slave to each other. Here Beckett is dealing with basics – with how the preponderance of our lives is devoted to the rituals of survival and how only occasionally are we asked to perform heroic or even altruistic acts. Beckett had an unusually heroic period in his life and he witnessed the terrible events I have mentioned, but the majority of his life was spent, like the lives of most people, facing the satisfactions and dilemmas of youth and adulthood, in a rather unremark-able way.

Why, one may also ask, are the main props on stage, beside the road and men, a tree and a rock? Here, too, Beckett is dealing with basics: the men, animal; the tree, vegetable; and the rock, mineral. And what of the two major characters? Do these costumed bums represent us? Of course, they're not really bums: they're perhaps shabby characters, and if not shabby, maybe just disheveled. They also wear bowler hats – of the sort that traditionally elegant men wear with their vests and three-button suits or whatever is stylish. Furthermore, on Beckett's figures, at least in the produc-tions that have respected Beckett's detailed instructions in his notebooks, their clothes don't fit. On the thin man, Vladimir, the pants and jacket are too short and tight (appropriate for a man who refrains from expressing his feelings); on Estragon, the heavier man, the clothing is too large (appropriate for his sensual, uninhibited partner). Often, one is dressed in striped pants, of the sort people in jail – or concentration camps – wear (or, symbolically, people captive to a universe over which they have no control), and the striped pants of one match the striped jacket of the other. The other half of each man's outfit is in a solid fabric, so that in dress the two visually comple-ment each other, like two halves of a whole. (In the second act the patterning is often reversed.) And there they are, in stripes or not, two people who actually keep each other going as friends do, telling jokes, comforting one another, arguing, dancing, doing whatever human beings do to pass the day, to pass a lifetime. Every once in a while, however, they reveal what is really on their minds: what are they doing with their lives? and why are they doing it? In fact, they are typical of most people in that their minds and hearts cry out for validation: "Why am I living the life I live? What is the payoff?" They, like we, need assurance that life has meaning and that actions have purpose. Can it be that there is no heaven, no purpose, no God-ordained pattern?

Specifically, Beckett's people are waiting on this road because they believe that clarity will come when Godot arrives. Thus, they wait for Godot – and it is hardly a coincidence that the word "Godot" contains the word God – who, as one suspects – will not appear. "Messengers" do, a different one each of the two "days" we see on stage, saying that a Mr Godot will arrive "tomorrow." But for most of the play, the characters wait; and if we look ahead to the climax, we find Beckett's figures acting heroically. They don't have a world war in which to participate, but they do help the suffering – the needy and the fallen – and that's quite enough to make them heroes. Following this, however, they return to waiting.

The very act of waiting – the busy-ness of waiting – becomes Beckett's image, his vision, of the games and routines people construct in order to pass the hours and years. That is, people assume a number of roles in the various areas of their lives – at work, home, school, social activities, and perhaps in a secret life. Vladimir and Estragon's relationship is similarly geared toward survival – to distract them from the boredom, depression, and paralysis that most people fall into without a structured life. In their case, the goal is a calm, egalitarian relationship. They have rejected a more self-indulgent interaction that permits the outlet of anger and frustration. Their visitors, the master named Pozzo and his slave named Lucky, pursue these less admirable roles – of the dictatorial sadist and submissive masochist. However, as offensive as that seems, as Pozzo admits, one needs a companion in this life, for "the road seems long when one journeys all alone." Although we don't enjoy watching Pozzo lead Lucky on a rope as if he were an animal to be ordered about, they are a couple, a perfect couple. What, after all, is a sadist without a masochist? Is one worse than the other: the masochist who says, "Hit me?" or the sadist who says, "No"? Each has a life, so to speak. Lucky is "lucky." He has a Godot, a purpose, to carry the bags, to be beaten, and to be directed here or there, even if it is at the end of a rope.

But Vladimir and Estragon assume a more humane, egalitarian relationship in which, with one assuming the more rational, philosophical role (Vladimir) and the other, the forgetful, emotional one (Estragon), they can aspire to some stability and sense of equality. In this way, they can pursue a relatively peaceful and predictable coexistence, unless, of course, something out of the ordinary disrupts their equanimity – such as the intrusion of strangers like Lucky and Pozzo. Should this occur – as it does – their roles might fragment, and the less savory aspects of themselves surface and break the equilibrium of their relationship. Thus, they await Godot, unsure of who or what "he" is and entirely unsure of the outcome of their awaited meeting. "Waiting" is the human condition, in which one constructs games or a lifestyle that makes the unknowable tolerable. They can, as they say, always hang themselves tomorrow.

Beckett's moving and significant climax occurs in Act 2, which, as his early critics and some directors today fail to realize, is not a repetition of Act 1. The climax of the second act is not as dramatic as a world war, but one in which the characters choose to act in a distinctly heroic way as they face an event that arouses the same impulse as the one that moved Beckett to fight – the impulse to help the suffering, the less fortunate, the victimized – here, of helping their visitors, the dictator and his slave when they return in a helpless state, both crawling on the ground, one mute; the other, blind. And this is what the play is about: survival and, when possible, heroic actions large or small on a road that Beckett might say is life, which ultimately comes from and goes nowhere.

Beckett is famous for mastering a theater without traditional elements like plot – the counterpart, for example, of modern music, with its dissonance, rather than traditional harmonies, melody, and rhythm; in modern painting, a splotch here and there, with nothing "photographically" realistic. *Godot* is distinctly constructed without traditional plot, characterization, or a dramatic climax that leads to final resolution. This is just a play about waiting, both before and after heroic activity. But is this not what our life is like, lacking a beginning, middle, and final resolution? More traditional writers incorporated a climax and subsequent denouement in their work, and they created soliloquies of great personal insight, storms, and breathtaking sunsets to convey these epiphanies. But, in truth, most of us live from day to day, and life is mostly "middle." We gain insights without fanfare – regarding how we will change careers, alter relationships, or make other vital decisions – when we are enacting the most banal of tasks, such as washing dishes or removing our shoes. And in Beckett's play, "nothing much," in traditional terms, happens. However, it's that word "nothing" that is significant.

Nothing usually means the absence of something, a void, a vacancy. However, in Shakespeare, after King Lear's most beloved daughter answers her father's demand for an expression of the nature/degree of her love for him, she says "Nothing," and, enraged, he replies, "Nothing will come of nothing." Something, however – a tragedy – comes of her saying "nothing." At the same time, Lear learns that everything that enriches and is meaningful in life may come from possessing nothing. What, then, does the word "nothing" mean?

Beckett's first words in *Godot* are "Nothing to be done," and Beckett means just that – there's nothing to be done – about fate or knowledge of the ultimate purpose of life. But although there may be nothing we can do about larger issues, about altering our fate or understanding it, there is – and I am using double negatives now – there is not nothing we can do in the meantime. We can live – and wait (and do whatever we can to pass the time).

Beckett uses the word "nothing" in a manner not unlike his contemporaries, the two French philosophers enormously popular during and after World War II – Jean-Paul Sartre, who called himself an existentialist, and Albert Camus, who preferred to describe the world as "absurd." Whatever their differences, each believed that despite both the oblivion in which life ends and the absence of a priori commandments regarding how to live, one is still obliged to lead a meaningful life. ("Man exists, turns up, appears on the scene, and only afterwards, defines himself … At first he is nothing … He himself will have made what he will be.") Conscious acts alone (as one "exists") define the quality of one's life (one's "essence"). Hence Sartre's famous proclamation: "existence precedes essence" (Sartre 1956: 19–25).

Sartre creates his own golden rule: "At every moment I'm obliged to perform exemplary actions"; at the same time he insists that "man is condemned to be free," that is, to live without divine imperatives. Although, as Sartre realizes, man becomes "intensely mystified" by having moral freedom without reward, he is still obliged to carry out good actions: "There is not a single one of our acts which does not at the same time create an image of man as we think he ought to be." (Sartre 1956: 439, 626) In various poetic evocations, *Waiting for Godot* repeats the conviction that if salvation exists, it arises from acting upon the "cries for help" addressed to "all mankind" when "all mankind is us."

If the terror of *No Exit* lies in its characters' inability to perform good acts in the absence of metaphysical verification, Beckett's figures are exemplary in carrying out Sartre's demand. *No Exit*'s figures are imprisoned by their repeatedly selfish, exploitative, "inauthentic" actions – condemned by their bad choices and indifference to the value of engaging in the principled "human freedom that precedes metaphysical oblivion." Beckett's couples are among literature's most authentic characters, and they are admirable in their good faith. Also unlike Sartre's characters who never contemplate the human condition, Beckett's couples are obsessed with it, and they do all they can do to distract themselves from continuously posing metaphysical questions that they can never answer. Beckett's figures construct the best way of surviving in a universe they will never comprehend.

As such, they are noble in the very fact of their survival. They contend with the most apparent alternative that existential (or absurd) anguish allows – suicide (which in their ridiculous attempts they reject) – and instead pursue a lifestyle whose goal is to bury their profound dread in the deepest recesses of their minds. In their activities of tender caretaking, warm camaraderie, and the joyous performance of their silly games, they are like Sisyphus in Camus's heroic interpretation, as he rolls his rock to the top of his mountain, certain that it will fall but defiant in again rolling it upward as he distracts himself by enjoying its texture and the blue of the sky. In their best moments, Vladimir and Estragon are, as Camus says of Sisyphus, "happy." They are alive; they are artists, conscious that their every act is an invention or a creation – their only evidence of being alive.

Beckett always insisted that he was not a philosopher, but Camus's remarks in "The Myth of Sisyphus" seem applicable to the artistic vision of *Godot*:

I can negate everything of that part of me that lives on vague nostalgias, except this ... need for clarity and cohesion ... I don't know whether this world has a meaning that transcends it. But I know that I do not know that meaning ... [I have just] these two certainties – my appetite for the absolute and for unity and the impossibility of reducing this world to a rational and reasonable principle.

He then adds a statement that is surely applicable to Beckett's alternately forlorn and high spirited people: "The absurd man ... feels innocent. To tell the truth, that is all he feels – his irreparable innocence." (Camus 1955: 38–9)

As each figure in *Godot* demonstrates a measure of primal innocence – and Beckett uses these allusions in the play – he assumes a kinship with Adam, Cain, Abel, and what some view as a suffering, unredeemed Christ, abandoned in his plea "My God, My God, why hast Thou forsaken me?" Beckett's vision implies an initial assumption of a humanity more sinned against than sinning. In Vladimir's terms, we are a "species" condemned not to hell but to death, gratuitously fallen through the mere act of birth, and we possess only the illusion of salvation. The reality of undeserved suffering and death is our only birthright. Underlying our every effort to seek salvation or direction is the haunting lament, "My God, My God, why hast Thou forsaken me?" However, Beckett entreats his fellow humans to defy the ultimate decree, the wasting and pining of body, mind and spirit, through the profound art of survival. During their good moments Vladimir and Estragon explain:

> ESTRAGON: ... I wasn't doing anything.
> VLADIMIR: Perhaps you weren't. But it's the way of doing it
>   that counts, the way of doing it,
>   if you want to go on living.
> ESTRAGON: I wasn't doing anything.
> VLADIMIR: You must be happy too, deep down ...
>   .   .   .   .   .
> ESTRAGON: Would you say so?
>   .   .   .   .
> VLADIMIR: Say, I am happy.
> ESTRAGON: I am happy.
> VLADIMIR: So am I.
> ESTRAGON: So am I.
>   .   .   .   .
>   We are happy. [*Silence.*] What do we do now, now
>   that we are happy ?
> VLADIMIR: Wait for Godot.

This kind of vaudeville routine fills the play – many very funny, some sad because they convey each man's unspoken anxiety. In moments of discouragement, there are numerous acts of tender caretaking ("Like a carrot?" one man asks his hungry partner) and joy.

Thus, as Vladimir and Estragon pursue a humane partnership where one assumes the more rational and philosophical role (Vladimir) and the other, the more emotional and sensual one (Estragon), they hope to pursue a relatively peaceful and predictable coexistence that distracts them from despair over the human condition. For example, Estragon intentionally avoids answering Vladimir's provocative "Do you remember the Gospels?" adding that one of the thieves was saved; one damned. In this reference to the gospels, he is speaking of the crucifixion of Christ, when, in the Gospel of Luke, Jesus promised redemption to one of the condemned men crucified alongside him. But pursuing this discussion for the two of them is dangerous, and Estragon, the less logical one, knows this; he is smart on an intuitive level. He knows that discussing the gospels and two thieves might, and later does, provoke a discussion of their own redemption, a subject they must avoid. After all, if they have not made contact with God/Godot, how can there be salvation? And even if there is, which one of them, like the thief, will be pardoned? Estragon therefore answers Vladimir's question about the gospels in a private, seemingly non-responsive way, connecting the gospels to a concrete visual image totally unrelated to the question of salvation. He talks about the Bible's geographical origins as a child might draw them: "I remember the maps of the Holy Land. Coloured they were. Very pretty. The Dead Sea was pale blue ..."

The very beginning of the play clearly establishes their role assignments and how the two complement each other. First, Beckett places them in opposing postures on the stage. Estragon, the heavier man, sits "huddled" (Beckett's term) on his rock downstage left. He faces the audience with his head down and his hands cupped before him. He has been struggling to remove his boot and his foot hurts. Vladimir, the thinner and taller man, stands diagonally across from Estragon, up stage right, with his back to the audience, his face lifted to the sky, and his hands at his side. The tableau is interrupted by Estragon's "listening" and Vladimir's "watching." Estragon makes three loud, staccato sounds (Beckett instructs: a "grunt" or "pant"), as he tries to remove his boot. Vladimir, who walks to Estragon, awkwardly and stiffly (at times, in a stylized, even comical, knock-kneed and pigeon-toed fashion), also seems to be in pain. Visually, their potential as suffering and comic ("tragicomic") characters is already suggested.

Exhausted and in pain after his futile attempts to pull off the boot, Estragon says, "Nothing to be done." Since his assigned role calls for concrete, not abstract, thinking, he is responding solely to his boot, which he can't remove. Yet, as we soon learn, he suffers spiritually as much as Vladimir. But in talking about his boot and foot he is able to conceal, at least verbally, his inner pain. Their game is thus begun, with the subject of suffering avoided. Vladimir, as the man of reason equally committed to minimizing their common condition, intentionally ignores both his own and Estragon's pain. He responds in an impersonal and abstract manner. As if he were deep in thought, he avoids Estragon's need for help with seemingly casual, *general* remarks, which seem directed more to the audience than to Estragon: "I'm beginning to come round to that opinion. All my life I've tried to put it from me, saying, Vladimir, be reasonable, you haven't yet tried everything."

Although the subject of pain never surfaces, Vladimir understands, and shares, what Estragon is saying, but he responds to it as if he were a philosopher ("I'm beginning to come round to that opinion … Boots must be taken off every day"). This leaves him in the mental state of "brooding," parallel to Estragon's physical "exhaustion," after wrestling with his boots. Facing Estragon for the first time, his concluding remark sets Estragon back on track: "So there you are again." It's as if Vladimir were relocating his partner back on the game board. In the first few minutes of the play five sequences of this sort demonstrate how, with one or the other man taking the lead, they allow their mutual pain to remain unspoken. If, on occasion, their roles reverse and they do connect with one another, that communication is short-lived, as one or the other steers the conversation back to one of their scripts. After Estragon's "feeble" "Help me!" Beckett writes, for example,

VLADIMIR: It hurts?
ESTRAGON [*angrily*]: Hurts? He wants to know if it hurts!

Immediately following Vladimir's response "No one ever suffers but you. I don't count …" Beckett gives the identical words, and the tone in which they are uttered, to his partner:

ESTRAGON: It hurts?
VLADIMIR [*angrily*]: Hurts! He wants to know if it hurts!

One of them always "pick[s] up the ball" and proceeds to change the subject, to tell a joke, or to simply cry out "STOP IT!" or "DON'T TELL ME."

And so it is that they busy themselves each day. That they share the most profound life goal – of determining a purpose for living – is clear in the very name of their quest: Godot. This may refer to a diminutive God from the external world who would provide a sense of direction (the "Mr Godot" they await), but their nicknames provide another explanation. Estragon, the more emotional, forgetful, non-rational figure, who is troubled with his boots and who limps through a great deal of the play, "stinks from his feet" and is called Gogo. Vladimir, the often-frustrated philosopher, is called Didi, a word derived from the French *dire* (to speak, to philosophize), and he stinks, we are told, from his mouth. With "Godot" almost a contraction of their nicknames, Beckett would seem to be suggesting that their salvation, however precarious, lies in themselves, in their interaction and games that distract and reassure, rather than in pure thought or action.

When their games aren't working, they say "Let's go", but this is always followed by the stage direction "*They do not move.*" After all, where would they go? Wherever they are, they need games, bits, and routines. Therefore, a simple boot routine is rationalized as meaningful, and they pass a boot or a hat back and forth:

VLADIMIR: It'd pass the time. [*Estragon hesitates.*] I assure
    you, it'd be an occupation.

ESTRAGON: A relaxation.
VLADIMIR: A recreation.
ESTRAGON: A relaxation.

.   .   .   .   .   .

We don't manage too badly, eh Didi, between the two of us?

.   .   .   .   .   .

We always find something, eh Didi, to give us the
impression we exist.

Their goal is "To try to converse calmly" according to their well performed script:

ESTRAGON: So long as one knows.
VLADIMIR: One can bide one's time.
ESTRAGON: One knows what to expect.
VLADIMIR: No further need to worry.
ESTRAGON: Simply wait.
VLADIMIR: We're used to it.

Virtually everything they do, however, is ultimately worthless, because it is performed in the face of mortality and cosmic indifference. This harsh truth is given its most extensive expression in Lucky's monologue. Once a philosopher, Lucky speaks with the presumption that there is – that there exists ("Given the existence ... quaquaquaqua") – a mysterious, erratic deity, "who ... loves us dearly with some exception for reasons unknown." In the second section of his speech, he describes humanity as wasting and pining in spite of every conceivable human achievement. In the last section he speaks of how only the stony remnants of each interrupted life remain within the benign indifference of the universe: "abode of stones ... alas alas abandoned unfinished ... the stones ... so calm ..."

Almost every activity in *Godot* echoes Lucky's remarks about human achievement and ultimate decay. Even the seemingly "successful" character, the wealthy master Pozzo, who believed he could control his life, concretely demonstrates the blindness of his ways when, in the midst of his grandiosity and ruthless control of Lucky, he becomes blind. Aware, like Lucky, that the end result of all human endeavor is excrement – in Lucky's words, "waste," "defecation," "caca" ("acacacacademy," the end product of study) – he becomes, like all of Beckett's figures, another spiritually and emotionally burdened innocent, a modern-day "Atlas," bearing the world's delusional hopes on his shoulders. Beckett clearly wanted Pozzo to be portrayed as a needy character and "not be played as a superior figure (as he usually is)." He explained that Pozzo "plays the lord – magnanimous, frightening – only because he is unsure of himself" (McMillan and Fehsenfeld 1988: 141), "abandoned unfinished."

Pozzo, humanized by his blindness, speaks of the way life passes, like day into night, in an instant. But if the one-time poet Lucky has taught Pozzo this, Pozzo's blindness and remarks teach or propel Vladimir toward a similar insight. It is like a chain reaction, for many of Vladimir's subsequent words are identical to Pozzo's, regarding the brevity of life and how birth and death ultimately seem to occur within seconds of one another.

> POZZO: They give birth astride of a grave, the light gleams an instant,
> then it's night once more.
> VLADIMIR: Astride of a grave and a difficult birth. Down in the hole,
> lingeringly, the grave-digger puts on the forceps.

Before and after these speeches Pozzo and Lucky function as agents releasing Vladimir and Estragon's frustration and hostility, muted during their games of camaraderie. That is, after observing that Pozzo and Lucky are seriously debilitated, Vladimir and Estragon become aggressive toward them. They verbally insult and physically abuse them. But they also change radically as they help them.

Beckett's vision may evoke our terror in this portrayal of human nature, but it arouses our pity as well, as Beckett goes on to render humanity's reaching beyond defensive or repressed anger or stoical survival to the performance of gratuitous acts of kindness. This last element, acts of altruism as actions of free will or free choice, grants Beckett's figures their heroic, if not tragic, status. Stoicism, kindness, and altruism may be unredemptive in terms of assuring one a place in heaven – in terms of a responsive cosmic agency – but to Beckett, they offer moments of personal regeneration.

And this is the heart of the play. Vladimir elaborates on matters of human kindness, altruism, and waiting, but in his comments he is like a pendulum, moving back and forth between hope and despair. In a very *positive* spirit he says that he and Estragon must uplift the fallen Pozzo and Lucky: "Let us do something, while we have the chance! It is not every day that we are needed. Not indeed that we personally are needed ...But at this place, at this moment of time, all mankind is us, whether we like it or not. Let us make the most of it, before it is too late!"

He and Estragon may be part of the "foul brood" of creation, rather than "saints," but this declaration makes Vladimir feel "blessed." When he asks "What are we doing here, *that* is the question ['to be or not to be']," he can confidently say, "We happen to know the answer. Yes, in this immense confusion one thing alone is clear. We are waiting for Godot to come – " affirming that "We have kept our appointment."

But the assurance that one can understand anything about one's life is short-lived, and Vladimir's mood swings to *despair*. A philosopher married to logic, he questions if life is a dream and if he can really verify his existence, including the experience of having kept the "appointment" he has just affirmed. Perhaps Estragon, with no memory, has a better hold on life. Then, briefly identifying with his "dozing" friend, Vladimir asks if he too has been "sleeping while the others suffered." Elaborating on his distrust of logic and memory – and on what he had taken to be the reality of his life – he says, "To-morrow, when I wake, or think I do, what shall I say of to-day? That with Estragon my friend, at this place ... I waited for Godot? ... But in all of that what truth will there be?" It seems to him that Estragon will "know nothing," and as such, may be the wiser one in understanding that reality is entirely irrational, an intellectual void, a nightmare, or just a dream.

Incapable of accepting this (or any) conclusion, Vladimir continues to shift from one position to another, first repeating that, even if it is forgotten the next day, the most meaningful human activity is that of caring for others: "[Estragon will] tell me about the blows he received and I'll give him a carrot." This alone alters the balance of tears and laughter that marks the human experience. Then, choosing the richly ambiguous word "nothing," he speculates that another figure – a person, Godot, or God – looks upon and judges him, as he does Estragon: "At me too someone is looking, of me too someone is saying, He is sleeping, he knows nothing, let him sleep on." A momentary "I can't go on" gives way to his final "What have I said?" and his subsequent actions – at least until the end of this "day" – affirm not only the virtue of waiting but also how waiting, with prescribed games and rituals ("habits"), is an anesthetic to the pain of being: "We have time to grow old. The air is full of our cries. [*He listens.*] But habit is a great deadener." Habit, as he said earlier, will save them from madness.

And so the game resumes with Vladimir's "brooding" – Beckett's description of him at the beginning of the play. Vladimir and Estragon are ready to greet Godot's messenger who will again say that Godot is not coming but will arrive tomorrow. Their concluding "Let's go."/"*They do not move*" recapitulates their return to their defining if inconclusive waiting as men filled with hope for tomorrow and a sense of what they will do even if they have an inkling of the pointlessness of it all. We leave Beckett's couple inspired by the nobility of their perseverance as they endure on this mysterious road we all travel.

After the war, Beckett hoped to return to Paris where Suzanne awaited him, but restrictions had been placed on resident aliens due to shortages in France. He was, after all, an Irish citizen. Beckett then volunteered to help build a hospital planned by both the Irish and French Red Cross in the south of France, where he performed the most menial and boring of tasks. After the business of fighting the war, his vocation would be in the service of rebuilding and healing. He would become an active participant in the restoration of one of most famous postwar ruins of the world, the once-exquisitely-beautiful village of St Lô, now a grotesque and broken world of ashes.

Beckett arrived at the beginning of the project. They would build 100 makeshift wooden huts as hospital facilities and plant flowers and trees. The patients, survivors of the bombings and concentration camps, suffered from tuberculosis and the other diseases prevalent during the war. Beckett worked alongside both local laborers and the 1,000 German POWs on loan from the French government. They all wore the same uniform. First, they sorted 250 tons of supplies. Then they built the huts. Beckett's behavior, as described by the workers and physicians who worked with him, attests to those attributes that became associated with him for the rest of his life: generosity, kindness, a sense of responsibility, and modesty.

After he returned to Paris – the time of his great creative "siege" and before writing *Godot* – he wrote a radio speech, "The Capital of the Ruins" (McMillan 1986: 71). The speech is an exceptional discovery for anyone interested in Beckett, because he is atypically explicit in his personal and philosophical reflections. In this beautiful and moving statement, Beckett celebrates two things: (1) the comfort to be drawn from the human capacity to surmount circumstances of the utmost gravity, such as the bombings of war, and (2) speaking for himself as a worker, as well as for the patients, the sustenance to be afforded and gained in moments of friendship, of giving.

He sets forth several articles of faith which would resound in *Waiting for Godot*. The first is his awareness of the human capacity to surmount circumstance: "What was important was ... the occasional glimpse obtained, by us in them and, who knows, by them in us ... of that smile at the human condition [that cannot] be extinguished by bombs ... the smile deriding [or surmounting the state] of having and not having." Beckett's second point would seem to be that while the material universe is passing, and meaning and even acts are fleeting, the spirit of mundane generosity is not. Beckett extols the human impulse to give of oneself to the suffering. This then is a steadfast thread in the human fabric, an aspect of life that is eternal. Implicit here is his faith, as he again writes in *Waiting for Godot*, that regardless of circumstance, humanity will, as Vladimir says, "represent worthily the foul brood to which a cruel fate consigned us."

In perhaps his most optimistic statement, Beckett declares that the act of giving uplifts the giver as well as the recipient: "Those who were in Saint-Lô will come home realising that they got at least as good as they gave." This, I believe he is saying, is our salvation as we await Godot. It is life's redeeming virtue. The individual's fate may be provisional, and the course of history may be conditional, but the "smile" and wish to heal is not. Its source is in the human spirit, and from this come healers of a moment – those who build hospitals, those who dance and amuse one another with tales. The hospitals, like the dancers and the tales, will fade, just as the names of the ordinary patriots and ordinary hero-victims of war, will be forgotten – but the spirit that moves them will not.

At the end of the speech, repeating what was perhaps for him the crucial wisdom that directed his future work, Beckett adds, "I may perhaps venture to mention another [possibility], more remote but perhaps of greater import ... the possibility that [we in Saint-Lô] ... got indeed what [we] could hardly give, a vision and sense of a time-honoured conception of humanity in ruins": we saw the human condition, I believe he is saying, as much as one can – bound to this mysterious, uniquely fascinating, sometimes-cruel, sometimes-kind world. That is, we gained an opportunity to understand to some extent – in Beckett's words, we received perhaps even "an inkling of the terms in which our condition is to be thought again." The willingness to give of oneself to the suffering is not only an abiding part of human nature. It is also *the very means through which* one can gain an "inkling" of the mystery of the human condition, the closest we can come to meeting Godot. Beckett now braced himself for the great creative task facing him. His remarkable play followed shortly.

REFERENCES AND FURTHER READING

Camus, Albert [1942] (1955). *The Myth of Sisyphus and Other Essays*, trans. Justin O'Brien. New York: Vintage.

Cronin, Anthony (1997). *Samuel Beckett: The Last Modernist*. London: HarperCollins.

Duckworth, Colin (1980). "Beckett's Early Background: A New Zealand Biographical Appendix." *New Zealand Journal of French Studies* 1: 59–67.

Foot, M. R. D. (1973). *SOE in France*. London: Paul Elek.

Foot, M. R. D. (1984). *An Outline History of the Special Operations Executive, 1940–1946*. London: BBC.

Gordon, Lois (1996). *The World of Samuel Beckett, 1906–1946*. New Haven: Yale University Press.

Gordon, Lois (2002). *Reading Godot*. New Haven: Yale University Press.

Graver, Lawrence (1989). *Waiting for Godot*. Cambridge: Cambridge University Press.

Kalb, Jonathan (1989). *Beckett in Performance*. Cambridge: Cambridge University Press.

Knowlson, James (ed.) (1994). *The Theatrical Notebooks of Samuel Beckett*, Vol. 1. New York: Grove.

MacDonald, Michael (1986). *Children of Wrath*. Cambridge: Polity Press.

McMillan, Dougald (1986). *As No Other Dare Fail*. New York: Riverrun Press.

McMillan, Dougald, and Martha Fehsenfeld. (1988). *Beckett in the Theatre*. London: John Calder.

Oppenheim, Lois (1994). *Directing Beckett*. Ann Arbor: University of Michigan Press.

Reid, Alec (1968). *All I Can Manage, More than I Could: An Approach to the Plays of Samuel Beckett*. Dublin: Dolmen Press.

Reid, Alec (1969). "The Reluctant Prizeman." *Arts* 29: 64–8.

Ryan, Desmond (1919). *The Man Called Pearse*. Dublin: Maunsel.

Ryan, Desmond (1924). *James Connolly: His Life, Work and Writings*. Dublin: Talbot Press.

Sartre, Jean-Paul [1943] (1956). *Being and Nothingness: An Essay on Phenomenolological Ontology*, trans. Hazel E. Barnes. New York: Philosophical Library.

Toscan, Richard (1986). "MacGowran on Beckett" [interview]. In S. E. Gontarski (ed.), *On Beckett: Essays and Criticism*. New York: Grove Press.

Wylie, Laurence (1974). *Village in the Vaucluse*. Cambridge, MA: Harvard University Press.

4
Beginning to End: Publishing and Producing Beckett

Barney Rosset

Sylvia Beach wrote to me in New York in 1953, asking for an appointment. She was the legendary proprietor of Shakespeare and Company, the great English-language bookstore in Paris, and had been the close friend and publisher of James Joyce. She knew most of the writers in Paris, but she came to me in New York to talk about Samuel Beckett, whom she had known for many years.

For me, her name was magical. In 1948 when I was living in France with Joan Mitchell, who in 1951 would become my first wife, Joan received a letter from her mother telling us to look up Sylvia Beach. Joan's mother used her maiden name, Marian Strobel, as a poet and later when she was the dynamo behind the scenes of Harriet Monroe's *Poetry* magazine. In a way you could think of *Poetry* magazine as Chicago's equivalent of Sylvia Beach's Shakespeare and Company, its offices and pages places where serious writers gathered. Chicagoans were first introduced to T. S. Elliot and Ezra Pound in the pages of *Poetry*, and through it we found not only poignant echoes of Walt Whitman but also the work of Chicago's Carl Sandberg, then Hart Crane, and that strange Jazz Age poet, novelist, and, finally, panhandler Maxwell Bodenheim, who ended up being murdered along with his wife on Greenwich Village's MacDougal Street in February of 1954 a few yards from where I got to know Allen Ginsberg, Jack Kerouac, and Gregory Corso. *Poetry* set a standard for me, for *Grove Press*, and for our own journal, *Evergreen Review*, which we began in 1957. However, Joan and I seemed to lack the courage and self-confidence in those days to approach so legendary a figure as Sylvia Beach. It would have been as unthinkable for us to ring her doorbell as it would have been to knock on, say, Picasso's door.

Beckett was Sylvia Beach's very specific reason for contacting me in 1953. She spoke of him in the warmest terms as a writer of growing importance. I agreed and asked Wallace Fowlie, my professor and friend at The New School where I took my degree, to read *Godot* and give me his opinion. He confirmed what Sylvia Beach had said, as well as confirming my own response, saying that Beckett would come to be known as one of the greatest writers of the twentieth century, and we quickly signed a contract to publish *En attendant Godot* (*Waiting for Godot*), the work that would change the course of modern theater, and the three French novels, *Molloy*, *Malone meurt*, and *L'Innommable*.

That summer, while on honeymoon with my then-wife Hannelore (Loly) Eckert in Europe, I first met Beckett in Paris. We met at the bar of the Pont Royal Hotel on rue Montalembert, next to France's largest literary publisher, Gallimard. Beckett came in, tall, taciturn, and wearing a trench coat. He was on his way to another appointment, he announced, and had time only for a single quick drink. "He arrived late," Loly remembered, "looked most uncomfortable, and never said a word except that he had to leave soon. I was pained by his shyness, which matched Barney's. In desperation, I told him how much I had enjoyed reading *Godot*. At that, we clicked, and he became warm and fun." The appointment forgotten, the three of us went to dinner and to various bars, ending up at Sam's old hangout, La Coupole on boulevard Montparnasse at three in the morning, with Beckett ordering champagne.

As his publisher I was faced with the immediate problem of who was going to translate *Godot* into English. Beckett had never been truly satisfied with any of his earlier English translators. I tried to persuade him to do the translation himself, and I finally succeeded, at least for the play. I think he always wanted to go back to writing in English, which he did, mostly, from then on, especially now that he had an American publisher. By the following winter we had galley proofs of the translation. I wrote my new author in January of 1954 from our bunkerlike East Hampton (NY) Quonset hut house,

> You will probably have the proofs of *Godot* before you get this letter. I hope that you do not find them too bad – both as to design and as to errors. Loly and I are spending our first nights in our new home at East Hampton and the galleys arrived after we left New York, so we have not yet seen them. It would help a great deal if you would correct them just as soon as you conveniently can and ship them off to us airmail – we are already behind schedule for our planned publication date and I do want to see the book out this spring so that we may capitalize on the *New World Writing* piece [the 5th Mentor Selection (1954) published the opening pages of *Molloy* (316–23), which Beckett himself had translated].

Our correspondence was formal at first, but warmed quickly, and I even tried to lure Sam to our house in East Hampton: "It's so nice where we are – snowed-in, quiet, and sootless, that I think you might like it." Sometimes Beckett typed his letters, at my rather brash request, and sometimes his letters were written in his almost indecipherable script. In a world where writers switch publishers at the first shake of a martini pitcher, our transatlantic communications seemed tranquil and based on mutual trust from the first.

Suzanne Deschevaux-Dumesnil, who finally became Sam's wife in 1961, had been his strongest supporter for many years. She was his manager and practical organizer, tending to his every need, protecting him from the world, and vigorously promoting his career, but not to his new American publisher. Handsome, and austere, she was even more reclusive than he, and never, as far as I know, learned English, walling herself off from his friends, particularly his English-speaking friends. I remembered her making an attempt to study English at Berlitz when we first met, but it seemed to go against her grain, and I never actually heard her speak anything but French. During the German occupation of Paris Sam and Suzanne, who were part of the Resistance and were in danger of arrest by the Gestapo, escaped Paris to the south of France and hid out on an isolated farm near Roussillon, in the Vaucluse, to which Beckett specifically refers in *Godot* as well as mentioning one of the local farmers, Bonnelly, by name, at least in the French text. There in the Vaucluse the emptiness and monotony of the days stretched for what must have seemed like an eternity to Beckett.

Beckett and Suzanne were mostly alone together in the Vaucluse for three years. The heart of *Godot* must be inextricably intertwined with the feeling of their being bored with each other, their not knowing how to pass the time, their wondering what they were doing there and when the hell they were going to get out, coupled with their not wanting ever to see each other again, and yet not being able to leave one another. In one exchange between the protagonists Estragon has gone off and is beaten up. Upon his return this exchange occurs:

VLADIMIR: You again! … Come here till I embrace you … Where did you spend the night?
ESTRAGON: Don't touch me! Don't question me! Don't speak to me! Stay with me!
VLADIMIR: Did I ever leave you?
ESTRAGON: You let me go.

While Beckett clearly indicates an all-male cast for *Godot*, and refused two top American actresses, Estelle Parsons and Shelley Winters, permission to perform it in 1969, writing Ms Parsons that "theater sex is not interchangeable," I believe he'd taken that very real situation, he and Suzanne on a farm, waiting, and converted it into an eternal predicament, a universal myth. The latent sexuality became much clearer in the 1988 Lincoln Center production of *Godot* in New York with Robin Williams as Estragon and Steve Martin as Vladimir. They pushed forward the male/female sides of their characters.

Beckett's life with Suzanne seemed to have had the despairing yet persevering, separate yet joined quality evident in many of his other plays as well. In *Endgame* the couple's exchange goes like this:

HAMM: Why do you stay with me?
CLOV: Why do you keep me?
HAMM: There's no one else.
CLOV: There's nowhere else.

Beckett was, of course, extremely precise about his stage directions, including the look and size of the sets, and I believe that the configuration of his and Suzanne's two

Paris apartments reflected their deepening impasse as graphically as did his instructions for the settings of his plays.

Their first apartment, at 6, rue des Favorites, was in a fairly lively neighborhood. It was a tiny duplex, two small rooms one above the other, the lower one sparsely furnished with just enough chairs for a few people to sit down, and a couple of paintings. It had a claustrophobic feeling, but at least it was accessible to friendly restaurants and bars once you got outside. I never saw the upstairs bedroom, but cannot imagine it to have been particularly sybaritic. When Sam and Suzanne fled Paris to escape from the Nazis their apartment was locked up and left that way; after the war they were able to reoccupy it without anything having been changed.

One night when they still lived there, Sam and I spent an evening together. I was driving and I remember that the dawn was just coming up as we got to rue Fremicourt. Then, all the street lights went out. An electricity strike had just started. In Paris you get into your house by pushing a button on the outside to get your door open. Without the *minuterie electronique* functioning you could get in or even warn somebody inside that you are outside.

So Sam and I drove to my hotel, Le Pont Royal. The front door was open but the elevator was not working. We trudged up seven floors to my isolated room at the top, briefly looked at the sun rising over Paris and climbed into a nice big double bed. Now I could say that I had been to bed with Samuel Beckett.

Sam and Suzanne moved into an even more appropriate setting in 1961, right across from the Santé prison, and the Becketts' flat had a view down into the exercise yard. Sam had a deep identification with prisoners, and this flat was near the outskirts of Paris where the Métro emerges from underground to run down the middle of boulevard St Jacques (he lived at No. 38). It was a grim, impersonal neighborhood as bleak as any Beckett setting. It's hard to find a place like that in Paris, a *banlieue* where there are hardly any bars or restaurants or little shops, or people in the streets, but he found one, next door to a garage near a cold new housing project, the Le Petit Café and the Bar Américan in the Hôtel Pullman St Jacques, where he usually met friends and associates.

Beckett's building had seven floors, a cramped entryway, and the usual tiny French elevator. On his landing, small in itself, were two doors leading to two apartments, separate but connected. To reach Sam's side, you turned right; to the left you would find Suzanne's side. There were two rooms in Sam's part, a small study with a lot of books and papers very neatly arranged, and a bedroom with a skinny cot and an ordinary bureau. Then there was a narrow little kitchen placed horizontally in the rear. It was rather like a corridor that connected the two apartments from the back. So the living spaces were connected but you could close them off, with doors placed at each end of the kitchen. Her friends could come and go to her place, and his friends could visit his place, but they didn't have to see one another if they didn't feel like it. It was a unique, chilly arrangement, and I never saw Suzanne again after the move. Later, I understand, she became ill, and increasingly difficult and withdrawn and perhaps saw no one. Sam and she were in Tunisia, the land of her birth, when his winning the Nobel Prize was announced.

Beckett had at least one close woman friend I know of during this time with Suzanne. She was an English woman, Barbara Bray, a translator who had worked for the BBC in London. Previously married with two children, Barbara was nearly 30 years younger than Sam. She was very attractive, slim, dark-haired, as I remember, and pretty in an English way. She was extremely intelligent and quite similar to Beckett: laid back and concerned with accuracy in translation. Barbara was very close to him and may well have been one of the strongest attachments in his life during the period I knew him. I remember several instances when he and I had been out drinking late, but not so late for us – only about 3 a.m. I'd offer to walk him home, but he said something like "No, I'm going to stop by and see Barbara." During this period Beckett continued to live with Suzanne. When he finally married her in Folkestone, England, in 1961, he was 54, she 61.

Barbara's close friendship with Sam continued. I remember one evening in particular, in 1965, when Harold Pinter was in Paris for the opening of the French production of his plays *The Collection* and *The Lover*. Barbara, Harold, Sam, a girlfriend of mine, and I were at a bar right off the boulevard du Montparnasse where Beckett liked to go. It was called the Falstaff and featured beer. To me, except for the name, it was as French as any place else.

I remember that we occupied a narrow table which butted up against a wall, and that Barbara and Harold were seated opposite each other, then Sam and my girlfriend next to each other, and me at the end. I began to notice that Barbara and Harold were discussing Sam, sort of as if he were a sacred object they were having an academic chat about, not involving him in the conversation at all. I could see that he was getting increasingly irritated, and finally Sam took his stein and banged it on the table hard enough to spill some beer in a rare show of anger. Then he got up and walked across the room in that ungainly gait he had before his cataract operation, which gave people the impression that he was drunk when he was just having difficulty seeing. I watched him slowly climb the narrow stairs to the men's room and disappear. A hush fell over our table. Then he reappeared and seemed to be making his way back to us when he stopped about 20 feet away and sat down at another table with two people whom I slowly realized were total strangers to him. He stared at us for a few minutes, then rejoined us without comment or excuse. I always suspected that he was if not jealous then sensitive of Harold and Barbara's relationship.

His friendship with Barbara Bray, I think, may well have been the inspiration for a short, extremely bitter 1963 work called *Play* in which a husband, wife, and mistress, encased up to their necks in urns, are trapped in an eternal triangle, condemned endlessly to repeat the details of the husband and mistress's affair under the glare of a harsh, inquisitorial spotlight.

Shortly after completing *Play*, which Alan Schneider directed at the Cherry Lane Theatre in Greenwich Village, Beckett made his only trip to the United States. It was in the summer of 1964 and he came for the shooting in New York of his motion picture, *Film*, which I had commissioned him to write.

In 1962 I had started a new unit outside of Grove Press itself called Evergreen Theatre. Very ambitiously, I made a list of writers – with the help of my associates – whom we asked to write scripts for us to produce. Those writers were, first and foremost, Samuel Beckett, and then Harold Pinter, Eugene Ionesco, Marguerite Duras, and Alain Robbe-Grillet. They all said yes to our request and wrote their scripts; Duras and Robbe-Grillet both wrote full length scenarios for us. We envisaged that the Beckett, Ionesco, and Pinter scripts would constitute three segments of a trilogy.

Another Grove author, Jean Genet, was asked. Fred Jordan and I went to London to ask him, but he said no. (Strangely, years later we became the US distributor of the one film he wrote and directed himself – a wonderful, short, silent, black and white film, entitled *Un chant d'amour*.)

I tried for two other scripts by writers who were not Grove Press authors, Ingeborg Bachman and Günter Grass. I trailed Bachman to Zurich (I think), Switzerland to get her no – and I then went on to Berlin to see Günter Grass who lived in what I recall as being a sort of bombed out area in a precarious, small building. You reached its second floor, if he wanted you to, via a ladder which he extended down to you in lieu of a staircase. He was charming and friendly, but the outcome was the same as with Bachman.

Out of the five scripts we did get we were only able to produce Samuel Beckett's *Film*. Fortuitously the head of a TV production company, an Irish American and a true student of Beckett's work, came along and financed the production of *Film*. Needless to say, as with Evergreen, he was not reimbursed, and at some early point he totally dropped out of sight. A bit amazing, but there it is. None of us can remember his name, but he was a guardian angel on this project.

So, I set out to create a production team to turn Sam's script into a motion picture. The most important member of that team was Sam himself. He wrote, guided, and kept the ship afloat. Alan Schneider had had no previous cinematic experience when I commissioned him to direct the film, but he had done a great deal of successful stage directing, including plays of Pinter, Albee, and especially Beckett. The other top two people on the team were Sidney Meyers and Boris Kaufmann. Meyers was an acclaimed filmmaker. In 1960 he had been awarded the Flaherty Documentary Award for *Savage Eye* (which he shared with Joseph Strick and Ben Maddow). Meyers was nominated for both the Venice Film Festival Golden Lion Award in 1949 and for an Academy Award for *The Quiet One* in 1950. He was also a consummate musician, a self-effacing, literate, and intelligent man. He got along beautifully with Sam. And, not incidentally, he had helped me in a very important and selfless way at the end of the production work on my first film, *Strange Victory*.

Boris Kaufman completed our crew. He was the brother of the famous Soviet directors Dziga Vertov and Mikhail Kaufman and had won the Academy Award in 1954 for *On the Waterfront*. But important to me was the fact that he was the cinematographer on Jean Vigot's great films, *Atalante* (1934), *Zero de conduite* (1933), and *A propos de Nice* (1930). These were among my favorite films of all time, and the filmmaker whom I had felt most akin to was Jean Vigo. Amos Vogel in his book *Film As A Subversive Art* said of Zero deconduite,

> In this anarchist masterpiece – a poetic, surreal portrayal of revolt in a boys' school – Vigo also summarizes the suffocating atmosphere of French petty bourgeoisie life, seen, as the rest of the film, through a child's eyes: the *pater familias* who never emerges from his papers, the kitsch décor, the girl, her underwear showing: though the hero is blind-folded, we know he sees it all.

Judith Schmidt, my invaluable assistant, had retyped the script after conferences we held and audiotaped in East Hampton, where we had brought Beckett to stay the night he arrived at the little East Hampton airport from Paris. It was a very dramatic landing – the airport had thrown on some searchlights, all reminiscent of *Casablanca*. After the weekend, we went back to New York City to shoot *Film*.

Alan Schneider had suggested Buster Keaton for the lead role in *Film*, and Sam liked the idea. So, Alan flew out to Hollywood to attempt to sign Buster for the project. He found the great silent star living in extremely modest circumstances. On arrival, Alan had to wait in a separate room while Keaton finished an imaginary poker game with, among others, the legendary but long dead Hollywood moguls Louis B. Mayer and Irving Thalberg. Keaton took the job offered. He would die a year and a half after completing the shooting of film.

Sometime after *Film* was finished and being shown, Kenneth Brownlow, a Keaton/Chaplin scholar, interviewed Beckett about working with Keaton. "Buster Keaton was inaccessible," he said.

> He had a poker mind as well as a poker face. I doubt if he ever read the text – I don't think he approved of it or liked it. But he agreed to do it and he was very competent. He was not our first choice. It was Schneider's idea to use Keaton, who was available … He had great endurance, he was very tough, and, yes, reliable. And when you saw that face at the end – oh [he smiled]. At last.

When Brownlow asked Beckett if he had ever told Keaton what the film was about, Sam said,

> I never did, no. I had very little to do with him. He sat in his dressing room, playing cards – patience or something – until he was needed. The only time he came alive was when he described what happened when they were making films in the old days. That was very enjoyable. I remember him saying that they started with a beginning and an end and improvised the rest as they went along. Of course, he tried to suggest gags of his own … His movement was excellent – covering up the mirror, putting out the animals – all that was very well done. To cover the mirror, he took his big coat off and he asked me what he was wearing underneath. I hadn't thought of that. I said, "the same coat." He liked that. The only gag he approved of was the scene where he tries to

get rid of the animals – he put out the cat and the dog comes back, and he puts out the dog and the cat comes back – that was really the only scene he enjoyed doing.

Brownlow asked Sam what the film meant, what it was about and he replied,

It's about a man trying to escape from perception of all kinds – from all perceivers, even divine perceivers. There is a picture which he pulls down. But he can't escape from self perception. It is an idea from Bishop Berkeley, the Irish philosopher and idealist, "To be is to be perceived," – "*Esse est percipi*." The man who desires to cease to be must cease to be perceived. If being is being perceived, to cease being is to cease to be perceived.

Beckett went on to say that distinguishing between the modes of being perceived was a major technical roadblock:

There was one big problem we couldn't solve – the two perceptions – the extraneous perception and his own acute perception. The eye that follows, that sees him, and his own hazy, reluctant perception of various objects. Boris Kaufman devised a way of distinguishing between them. The extraneous perception was all right, but we didn't solve his own. He tried to use a filter – his view being hazy and ill defined. This worked at a certain distance but for close-ups it was no good. Otherwise, it was a good job.

Besides the problem of capturing the two perceptions, another technical problem arose when we attempted to use "deep focus" in the film. Originally *Film* was meant to run nearly 30 minutes. Eight of those minutes were to have been used in one very long shot, based on a "deep focus" technique developed by Sam Goldwyn and his great cameraman Greg Toland, in which a number of actors would make their only appearance. A little later it was used to stunning effect by Orson Welles, again with Toland as cameraman, in *Citizen Kane*. Even when panning their camera, "deep focus" allowed objects from as close as a few feet to as far as several hundred feet to be seen simultaneously with equal clarity. Toland's work was so important to Welles that he gave his cameraman equal billing to his own. Sad to say, our "deep focus" work in *Film* was unsuccessful. Despite the abundant expertise of our group, the extremely difficult shot was ruined by a stroboscopic effect that caused the images to jump around. Beckett ultimately removed the scene from the script.

In his autobiography, *Entrances*, Alan Schneider says,

Sidney proceeded to do a very quick, very rough cut for Sam to look at before taking off for Paris. And that first cut turned out to be not far off from what we finally used. The editing was painstaking – and painful, Sidney always gently trying to break the mold we had set in the shooting, and Sam and I in our different ways always gently holding him to it. There was no question of sparring over who had the legal first cut or final cut or whatever. We talked, argued, tried various ways, from Moviola to screen and back again, to make it come out as much the film that Sam had first envisioned as we could.

In New York, Sam and Alan Schneider stayed with me and my wife Cristina in our Greenwich Village house on Houston Street while shooting the film. When it was over, all Beckett wanted to do was get back to France as soon as possible. We booked an early morning flight, set our alarm, and I promised to wake Sam at 7:30 a.m. in time to get to the airport. At 9:00 a.m. Cristina and I woke up, horrified to find that we had overslept, and we were appalled to stumble over Sam sitting outside our bedroom door, wearing his overcoat even though it was July. He had his packed bag on the floor next to him and he was sound asleep. It never occurred to him to knock on our door. I made another airline reservation for 5:00 p.m., and the three of us spent the day at the New York World's Fair in Flushing Meadows wandering among the exhibits. Cristina and I somehow managed to lose our homesick writer along the way. After a frantic search we found him on a bench, sound asleep again. We revived him enough for him to buy two knitted Greek purses – one for Cristina and one for Suzanne – whereupon we escorted Sam to an air-conditioned bar at what was then Idlewild Airport for drinks until departure time. "This is somehow not the right country for me," Sam said at the bar. "The people are too strange." Then he said, "God Bless," and got on the plane, never to return.

Once Sam was back in Paris, things went on as before. In the beginning he favored a restaurant called the Closerie des Lilas on the boulevard du Montparnasse, where Hemingway liked to go, and where names of famous writers were embossed on the tables. There was also the grandiose La Coupole, a small bar called Rosebud, and the allegedly English pub, the Falstaff, around the corner from La Coupole. But especially congenial was a seafood brasserie in a tough, nightlife neighborhood nearby called Ile des Marquises, where the patron revered Beckett and had a photograph of him on the wall along with huge glossies of Marcel Cerdan (the great Algerian heavyweight champion killed in a transatlantic crash), Sugar Ray Robinson (the great American fighter), and other assorted personalities.

One New Year's Eve in Paris in the early seventies, Matthew Josephson, the famed Hollywood agent, called to say he was representing Steve McQueen, who desperately wanted to make a film of *Waiting for Godot*. Money was no object; Beckett could have complete control and any other actors he chose; Laurence Olivier, Peter O'Toole, and Marlon Brando, who was then about to do *Apocalypse Now*, were mentioned. After I ascertained that the agent was very much for real, and that the top price for a film property seemed to be $500,000, then a princely sum, I wrote stipulating that amount. Josephson replied that the offer was $350,000 and it was absolutely firm. The matter was dropped until I saw Sam again on St Patrick's Day for dinner at the Ile des Marquises. Anxious to secure some money for him, I told him of the offer for the proposed film, playing up Steve McQueen and, for some reason, Brando. Beckett asked what this McQueen looked like and I, grasping at straws, summoned up an image of James Garner. "He's a tall, husky, good-looking guy," I winged it. And Marlon Brando? "Even bigger, a huge, heavy-set fellow." Sam thought for a while and then said, "No. It will never work. My characters are shadows."

Near the end, Beckett refused to go to his old haunts, and it all narrowed down to an ersatz bistro called Le Petit Café in The Pullman St Jacques, a monstrosity of a new hotel near his apartment. It had a garish, Vegas-like marquee, and I thought of its lobby as resembling a souped-up railway station at rush hour with busloads of German and Japanese tourists swarming up and down its long escalators. All it needed was a bank of slot machines. Visiting athletes were a specialty, and I remember the Scottish rugby team, brawny men in tartans and kilts, all drunk as lords, horsing around in the lobby to the astonishment of a tour group of early-teenage Japanese girls. I also recall a boxing ring being set up in the lobby, and a loudspeaker announcing: "Will the Australian trampoline team please report to the fourth floor." Beckett stayed oblivious to all this, totally out of place and impassive in the midst of all this international action.

I, after intricate maneuvering, once brought Beckett and photographer Richard Avedon together at Le Petit Café in one of the most awkward and enigmatic encounters of my life. The celebrated photographer said his technique of using a white sheet as a backdrop was philosophically derived from Beckett. He also had said to me that he'd shot everybody he wanted to with the exception of Greta Garbo and Beckett himself. I made arrangements for Avedon and Beckett to meet, and stressed to Avedon that there was no guarantee Beckett would actually agree to pose and that it would not be an easy task to convince him.

Avedon came from Tokyo and I from New York with my fourth wife Lisa, my daughter Tansey, and my 10-year-old son Beckett. Sam was his usual self, silent but listening. Lisa and my kids did the same, while Avedon, who seemed nervous, talked non-stop for about an hour until finally he said: "Okay, let's take the pictures." He asked Sam and my son Beckett to go with him, and the three of them crossed the street and disappeared into a passageway through the Métro overpass for about half an hour. When they returned, nobody described what had happened, but I assumed the pictures had been taken.

I heard nothing further for a couple of months until one day I received two superb, very moving photos of my son with Sam, beautifully mounted and framed and signed by Avedon. About a month later Sam himself, who had never before shown the slightest interest in such matters, asked what had happened to the photographs. I wrote Avedon, and received what I thought was a very peculiar response to the effect that he had taken very few pictures of Samuel Beckett alone that day because the writer had seemed "unhappy," but that, because I had gone to so much trouble, he had taken a few shots of the two Becketts together.

My son said that after crossing under the Métro overpass they'd come to a wall where a white sheet had been tacked up and an assistant waited for them in a car. There was a large camera fastened to a tripod. He described Avedon setting up the shot, then focusing his camera with a black cloth over his head, then stepping out and squeezing the bulb a few times for the two Becketts and then for Sam alone. The missing Beckett photos supposedly appeared in the French magazine *Egoiste*, but I have never seen them, but a portrait of Sam alone was in Avedon's retrospective at the Metropolitan Museum in New York in 2005.

A later, thornier encounter at Le Petit Café involved Beckett and Peter Getty, son of the famously wealthy Ann Getty who, with Lord Weidenfeld, had bought Grove from me in 1985. After promising to keep me as CEO, they ousted me without ceremony the following year. Smart and young, Peter Getty, who often borrowed his subway fare from Grove employees to get uptown to his Fifth Avenue apartment, had learned I was meeting Beckett in Paris, and asked to be introduced. I agreed, and Getty flew over, checked into a suite at the Ritz, and taxied out to Beckett's unlikely hangout, Le Petit Café, with a book he wanted autographed.

It was a short, tense meeting, the only time Sam was not friendly to someone I introduced him to. After autographing the book, he glared at Peter and asked: "How could you do this to Barney, and what do you plan to do about it?" Peter was very embarrassed, and mumbled something about consulting with his mother. Later, I heard that Beckett had told another suppliant from Grove, "you will get no more blood out of this stone," and he never allowed them to publish anything new of his again. To me and a group of others assembled in his honor at La Coupole for his birthday in 1986 he said, "There is only one thing an author can do for his publisher and that is write something for him."

And write something he did. *Stirrings Still*, dedicated to me, is the meditations of an old man contemplating death. It brought back to me an ether dream I had had as a little boy. I had an out-of-body experience, seeing myself as an object rocketing into space, zooming through a black void until I was transformed into a "knob of blackness." I knew I was experiencing the terror of my own death. Still, now, unable to sleep in a totally darkened room, I am hounded by that dream. When he wrote *Stirrings Still*, I don't know how much Sam was actually thinking of me, but I think I know why he wrote it. He was facing his own dream of death, which was fast approaching, and which, possibly, he finally made bearable by acceptance of that approaching darkness. "Such and much more such the hubbub in his mind so-called till nothing left from deep within but only ever fainter oh to end. No matter how no matter where. Time and grief and self so-called. Oh all to end."

Beckett's health was clearly failing, although I couldn't admit this to myself. We now met exclusively at Le Petit Café, which had become Beckett's "club," and a place where he was totally ignored by outsiders. Later I took to actually staying at the Pullman St Jacques in order to be near him, and sometimes I ate meals alone in the fast-food café off the hotel's lobby. At breakfast they gave you a set of plastic-coated photographs, not unlike a deck of cards. One card had an egg on it, another card two eggs, another card a strip of bacon, and so on. To order, you went to the cashier and handed her the cards you'd selected. In a funny way, it was like Beckett's late theater. They'd done away with the menu entirely, eliminating the need for words or translations of words; you could choose a meal in total silence. In the same vein, Beckett had made increasing use of the stage directions "pause" and "silence" in his work, and had pared down his vocabulary to fewer and fewer words.

At some point, Sam began having dizzy spells and falling in his apartment; apparently not enough blood was circulating to his brain. After brief stays in several hospitals he moved to a nursing home only a few blocks from where he lived. The desire to go on had lessened even more. He was unsteady on his feet and thinner, and therefore seemed taller and more and more like a rendering by his friend Giacometti who had given him a drawing of a thin, striding man. Sam gave it to Cristina and me as a wedding present, and we later used it on the cover of a reprint of Sam's novel *Molloy*. Now he was just a ghost of even that drawing.

The nursing home was on a side street, and looked like the other small buildings on the block, with only a discreet plaque announcing its institutional function. You entered a sparsely furnished sitting room in which a number of old women, some with walkers, watched a couple of ancient TV sets. Then you went through a little dining room out into a tiny courtyard with a walkway and some grass. There were a few rooms looking out onto it. Beckett was in the first room, a cubicle with space enough only for a bed, a table and two wooden chairs, with a small bath off it.

I visited Sam there a number of times and found it cell-like and depressing. His British publisher John Calder and I tried to devise ways to move him to more comfortable quarters, but it wasn't easy to do Beckett a favor. He seemed to resist attempts to make his life more pleasant, in his perverse fashion managing to get a phone on which he could not make overseas calls, declining to have a TV set, stereo equipment (although he loved music), a bookcase, or even a typewriter. He wrote things down in a little notebook in his small, intricate handwriting, kept his engagement records meticulously, and he always seemed to have a bottle of Irish whiskey handy.

With Beckett it was a mistake to suppose that problems readily leant themselves to solutions, or that one thing necessarily led to another. Sam had started to go for walks, and sort of boasted to me – if you could ever say that about him – that he walked farther than where his own apartment was. He had told me he needed some papers from his apartment, so I asked why he didn't go home and pick them up. I offered to go with him. Beckett threw up his hands. First roadblock: there was too much traffic on his boulevard; it made him dizzy. Well, let's go in a car, I said, pressing on. Beckett replied that he didn't have a car. Not to worry, I said, I'll get the car and we'll drive there. I was greeted with stony silence, and that was the end of that.

Perhaps a major factor was that Suzanne was still back at the apartment, and he was ambivalent about seeing her. It was such an archetypical Beckett situation. It was *Endgame* again. Now they were Nagg and Nell in their garbage cans, unable to reach each other. They were both ill, separated by only five blocks, and yet they couldn't see each other. He needed papers from his apartment, and yet he couldn't go there – all the entrances and exits were blocked.

The last time I visited I brought along an American TV set I had kept in Paris just for possible use with Sam, and a videotape of *Godot* performed by the inmates of San Quentin prison. I had previously carted all this heavy equipment, the set, a transformer, and a VCR in a huge shopping bag through customs to the Pullman St

Jacques, where Beckett used to actually come to my room. Now I lugged it all to the nursing home.

Sam was visibly moved by the tape; the inmates understood his play. I thought, now I've got something going that he can enjoy in this arid place: we can have a correspondence utilizing videotapes. But as I left, I casually asked him if he would store the set for future viewings. "Oh no, no, no," Sam answered, "I have no use for it." As I struggled out with my shopping bag, Beckett said: "Oh Barney, that's too heavy for you. You shouldn't carry that." Then he walked over, lifted it, turned to me, and said, "No, it's all right. You can." Again: You can't go on, you'll go on.

It was clear that the prospect of the introduction of ease or entertainment into his life distracted him from the larger endgame he was in the midst of playing. A few months later he was *Not I*, as in the title of one of his plays. There was, at last, an *Act without Words*. He was buried next to Suzanne not in the famous Père Lachaise cemetery but in the Cimetière du Montparnasse, less famous but in Sam's beloved 14th arrondissement.

REFERENCES

Brownlow, Kevin (1979). *Hollywood: The Pioneers.* New York: Harper Collins.

Schneider, Alan (1986). *Entrances.* New York: Viking Press.

Vogel, Amos (1974). *Film As A Subversive Art.* New York: Random House; rpt. London: Thames and Hudson 2005.

Part II
Charting Territories

5

A Critique of Aesthetic Judgment: Beckett's "Dissonance of Ends and Means"

John Pilling

The phrase "Dissonanz von Mitteln und Gebrauch" (more literally rendered by the late Martin Esslin as a "dissonance between the means and their use") occurs in the so-called German Letter of 1937 (July 9, 1937) to Beckett's Munich friend Axel Kaun (Beckett 1983: 53, 173), and I use it, with a slightly adapted English phrasing, to review the tensions in Beckett's aesthetic thinking after finishing *Dream of Fair to middling Women* in 1932, in his struggling towards *Murphy* in 1935–6, and in his moving on from there in the years before the outbreak of war in 1939. Questions of method, of "the means and their use" or, more loosely, "ends and means" were for Beckett intimately bound up with issues of genre. In the early 1930s the subject of poetry exercised Beckett's thinking more than any other. It was the area in which he most wanted to succeed, very conscious of what Dante, Racine, and Rimbaud (among others) had achieved, and it was the area in which he most despaired of success. Beckett thought of prose fiction, in its "modern" manifestation (as distinct from the realism of the nineteenth century, a subject he had addressed in his lectures to undergraduates at Trinity College Dublin) as aspiring to the condition of poetry by way of the prose-poem, as it had developed in France over the previous 50 years. In approaching matters this way Beckett was not obliged to confront the fact that none of the great modern prose writers (Proust, Joyce, Gide) had actually shown very much of an aptitude for poetry proper. The idea held good, anyway, for the kinds of novels and novelists he had come to admire, and it served also to distinguish them from the fiction which filled and fueled the literary monthlies and quarterlies, often kept going by short stories, which Beckett saw as the victory of "commodity" over "art."

By mid-1932 Beckett had discovered that "ars longa" – the novel – was something of a mixed blessing. It required time and effort, sufficient raw material for development, and a modicum of "architectonics" (1992: 168). While poetry could not wholly dispense with these requirements, its narrower focus – once epic and/or narrative poetry had been discounted – meant that "combustion of the spirit" (letter to Thomas MacGreevy, October 18, 1932) could conceivably promote, and in due course produce, expressive intensity. At this point in time, drama, for Beckett (in spite of his profound affection for Racine) was not even an also-ran. He could choose, it seems, to go to the theater (*The Wild Duck*; letter to Thomas MacGreevy, November 11, 1932) or not go (*Peer Gynt*; letter to Thomas MacGreevy, October 18, 1932) without feeling that the choice necessarily had anything to do with his own creative imperatives. Besides, he found too many new plays "vulgarly conceived and vulgarly written" (of Lady Gregory, folklorist and dramatist, champion of Irish culture; letter to Thomas MacGreevy, January 5, 1930). Poetry remained to some extent, like the novel, a matter of volume, or rather of *a* volume, since only with a sufficient number of poems could he approach publishers (this was also true of short stories, as is reflected in a letter to Thomas MacGreevy, May 13, 1933). If "ars longa" was a problem in the sphere of prose fiction, "ars brevis" had necessarily to be more than just a handful of poems. If what had become commodified could (perhaps) be circumvented, what could be quantified could not.

A curious instance of how poetry and the short story could come close to one another is Beckett thinking of the "poem-scum" which might make "a Swift poem" (letter to Thomas MacGreevy, January 5, 1933), and coming up instead with the story "Fingal." (Something similar had occurred in the late summer of 1930 when, in an undated letter, Beckett had told MacGreevy that he was going to write a Proust poem, at a time when he had still not written a word of his *Proust* essay.) But stories, given the amount of work actually expended on them (as distinct from what was expended on poems), he found less labor-intensive, because they were "only" stories. Eleven stories were in due course reduced (by the rejection of "Echo's Bones") to ten. But "POEMS by Samuel Beckett," as they were first planned to be during the writing of *More Pricks*, amounted to only 27 items (Leventhal papers; HRHRC), and in eventually becoming *Echo's Bones and Other Precipitates* in 1935 they were reduced to 13. Also reduced, because publishers had shown so little interest, was the print-run; a limited edition of 327 copies was brought out by George Reavey's Europa Press, with Beckett meeting some of the costs. (Chatto and Windus, by contrast, had printed 1,500 sheets of *More Pricks Than Kicks*, even though only 500 copies were ever bound up.) In "working over the poems, in the expectation of proofs [of *Echo's Bones and Other Precipitates*] which have not come" (letter to Thomas MacGreevy, September 8, 1935), Beckett must have hoped that inspiration might provide him with a few poems more, if not for inclusion in *Echo's Bones* then for a later collection. But neither inspiration nor perspiration made very much difference: "I had no application for a poem," Beckett told MacGreevy a little over a fortnight later (on September 23, 1935), by which time any lingering inclination to turn poems into short stories was long beside the point.

Of Beckett's subsequent "application" for poems I shall have more to say presently, but I want now to go back a little, to just after the completion of *More Pricks* in the late autumn of 1933, which was probably when Beckett began two separate but related projects, neither of which proceeded much beyond the "notesnatching" (letter to Thomas MacGreevy, probably early August 1931) stage. These have both survived in the Trinity College Dublin papers (hereafter TCD) (MS 10971/2, as itemized in SBTA 17) under the headings "Trueborn Jackeen" and "Cow." Both deal, somewhat unexpectedly, in the aftermath of the Dublin depicted in *More Pricks*, with specifically "Irish" material, and in a way point forward to the distinctively Irish material in *Murphy*, even if *Murphy* is best seen as very much a "novel of London." One of the details from the "Cow" notes was used by Beckett in the story "Echo's Bones," but "Cow" occupies only a page or two and does not seem to have been continued with, or worked on, for very long. Nor, in the event, did "Trueborn Jackeen" amount to very much either, although it was clearly a more serious enterprise. In February 1934 Beckett told Nuala Costello, "I am thinking that I might well employ these long, sober (Kia-Ora and the wildest scenes of virtue) evenings in writing a *True-born Jackeen* on the model of Defoe's *True-Born Englishman* [a poem, a 'Satyr', in two parts, with an introduction and conclusion, first published in 1700], though of course infinitely more amusing and competent. He [their mutual friend Percy Ussher] shall have it then hot from the vinegar" (letter in private hands). The vinegar did not marinate the *True-born Jackeen* very successfully. In May 1934 Beckett wrote to A. J. Leventhal to say, "*True-born Jackeen* is too great an undertaking" (Harry Ransom Humanities Research Center, hereafter HRHRC). Whether the undertaking ever amounted to much more than a dozen or so pages of notes (taken from the *Encyclopaedia Britannica*) we shall presumably never know; it seems unlikely. But for Beckett to have considered it at all is an index of the way his thoughts kept reverting to Ireland now that he seemed to be stuck in England. "I saw," he told Nuala, "*Man of Aran* [Robert Flaherty's famous film of 1934] and felt I am afraid irretrievably glued to the seat. Very smart no doubt as far as it goes, sea, rocks, air and granite gobs very fine, but a sensationalisation of Aran wouldn't you say, as [erasure] Synge's embroidery [*The Aran Islands*] is a sentimentalisation" (letter of May 10, 1934). (It is not difficult to imagine what Beckett would have made of Tim Robinson's two volumes *Pilgrimage* (1989) and *Labyrinth* [*Stones of Aran*] (1995), if he had lived to see them.)

The *True-born Jackeen* notes are part of a prevalent tendency of Beckett's, at and about this time, to concern himself with history, and historical materials, and with life-histories of a kind. We know that between 1932 and 1935 Beckett read the historian J. R. Green (undated letter of early 1933), Albert Sorel (letter to Thomas MacGreevy, February 14, 1935), G. P. Gooch (Knowlson 1994: 216 and 746n. 114), J. G. Lockhart's *Life of Napoleon* ("Dream" notebook), Jean-Jacques Rousseau (*Confessions*), Alfieri (*Memoirs*), and even Shakespeare's history plays (much inferior, he thought [letter to Thomas MacGreevy, January 1, 1935], to George Eliot's *The Mill on the Floss*). It was a self-imposed "programme" of *Bildung* or education, given extra perspective by reading Spanish classics (late 1932), English literature (see my essay in SBTA 17), and by readings in the European Bildungsroman: Thomas Mann's *Buddenbrooks* and, later, in Germany, Gottfried Keller's *Der grüne Heinrich* and Adalbert Stifter's *Nachsommer*. Later, in 1936, Beckett derived a good deal of pleasure from reading Machiavelli's *Florentine History* (*Storie fiorentine*), alongside a collection of Early Lives of Dante, and a number of historical plays by Goethe and Schiller, all of which are mentioned in letters to MacGreevy. But it seems safe to say that none of these bulk large in our received idea of Beckett as a whole, and all of them are perhaps best seen as relatively momentary enthusiasms which, allied with his new interest in Dutch painting of the seventeenth century as aroused by the magnificent London collections, were to go towards the making of *Murphy*, a book about the Irish, but for the most part out of Ireland. But all of these authors, to a greater or lesser degree, nevertheless suggest that Beckett was at this point in time more interested in tracing "life-lines," or the lines of lives, than he was ever to be again.

TCD MS 10971/2 is the slender surviving relic of a mind alert to the need to know from what it needs to distance itself. No doubt the very fact that neither project came to fruition was further proof, if further proof was necessary, of Ireland's incapacity to furnish Beckett with the requisite motives for creativity. The evidence from *Disjecta* complicates the picture only in the sense that the "Irish issue" is never wholly separated from the "life-line" issue. Of the twelve items collected in *Disjecta* under the heading "Words About Writers" ("Other Writers," part 2A) one ("MacGreevy on Yeats") was only published in 1945, even though much of its argument can be found adumbrated in a letter to MacGreevy of January 31, 1938, not long after Beckett had set up, this time for good, in Paris. Of the eleven other pieces six are on Irish subjects: MacGreevy's poems, O'Casey's plays, the two essays (unpublished at the time) on Censorship and on "Recent Irish Poetry" (the initials of which condemn its poets to a kind of death), on Jack Yeats's novel *The Amaranthers*, and "Denis Devlin." But the first four of these effectively reflect Beckett's temporary role as "Irish correspondent" in the weeklies and monthlies of literary London, even when a close personal friendship is also the stimulus. Five other pieces (Mörike, Feuillerat on Proust, Rilke, Ezra Pound, and "Papini on Dante") reorientate our correspondent in the direction of international departures. The review of Jack Yeats's novel merits closer analysis (for my purposes) than anything else on the Irish side of the equation; on the other side the same could be said of Beckett's assessment of Feuillerat on Proust. There is no "life-line" in the Feuillerat review (as there inevitably is in the Mörike), but something similar to one is present in Beckett addressing, reassessing, and effectively rewriting the genesis of Proust's great novel, as painstakingly reconstructed by the academic Feuillerat. The Jack Yeats review continues this tendency by openly removing the discussion into some "out of time and space" situation, as if Beckett were determined to deny the relevance of any back-projection. There is, however, in both these reviews, a tension between what is actually there (in the books supposedly under review) and what is not there but might be. In the Feuillerat we find "the search, stated in the full complexity of all its clues and blind alleys" set over against the "*compte rendu* after the event, of a round trip" (Beckett 1983: 65). In the Jack Yeats review we find "[a]n imaginative adventure" set over against "reportage," with the latter also notionally tainted by consorting with "allegory," "symbol," and "satire" (ibid.: 89–90), and doubtless other horrors too terrible to be named. What, we might want to ask ourselves – with Beckett on the way towards *Murphy*, and also aiming beyond it, as with hindsight we know him to have been – can this tell us about the novel as we have it? At least two questions can be asked: (1) is *Murphy* the "search" or something of a "round trip"? and (2) is the novel "an imaginative adventure" (in Beckett's sense of what that might be), or unavoidably mired in "reportage"? It seems to me likely that any critical (in the neutral sense of the word) treatment of the novel, while happy to admit that both poles have their parts to play along an imaginary axis, is in practice likely to emphasize one of them at the expense of the other. And it is in this spirit that I wish to think the unthinkable. Could *Murphy*, wonderfully lively and engaging novel that it so often is, actually (in Beckett's sense of the fitness of things) be gravitating towards the two negative poles? Even if, generically speaking, *Murphy* only nods occasionally in the direction of "allegory," "symbol," and "satire," there is certainly "reportage" aplenty, and more than in any other Beckett fiction. But we may also find in *Murphy* more than a whiff of the *"compte rendu,"* the account rendered, since the book's relative fidelity to a line-of-life and -of-death cannot reasonably be expected to avoid it altogether. There was no doubt much more involved in Beckett's idea of a *"compte rendu"* than conventional thinking would look for, or expect to find, in a novel. But perhaps the real issue is whether or not *Murphy* can get far enough away from this familiar way of carrying on for the specter of a "round trip" to be exorcised successfully.

Murphy "solved" the "Irish issue" by situating most of its action in London, by which ruse it could (almost unobserved) administer another blow to Irish prestige. The novel's characters may be in "exile" but they are also in "asylum," except for Murphy, who has to find his asylum at the literal level. (Another black mark against him!) Beckett told MacGreevy on July 7, 1936 that he found all the characters "hateful," even Celia. The remark could be plausibly read as suggesting that Beckett was really hating the part of him (the very phrase is applied to the lead character early on) that had, for a number of reasons, left Ireland for England (like his characters), and that had now found he could not live comfortably there either. (Celia's nostalgia for Ireland is, significantly enough, for its light and its air.) If nowadays Anglo-American readers find the characters "charming," this is surely because they are so obviously "Irish," whether in Ireland, or out of it. They are stage Irish, participating in situations and dialogues artificially staged to serve purposes other than characterization: a tart with a heart, a few pub philosophers, some willing slaveys, all of them figures who, however central they may be to the novel (at least in terms of the time and space they occupy), are on the fringes of society. The further we get from Murphy himself the more stereotypical the action becomes, kept alive as it is by the ruses and resourcefulness of the ever-watchful omniscient narrator. Ironically enough, after a time even Murphy's actions come to seem mechanical; the mechanistic basis of the story (even if Beckett had not forgotten what he had told his students at Trinity College about Bergson's attitude to mechanical intelligence as over against instinct) colors all, the observer infects the observed (cf. *Proust*) with his own limitations.

With the "Irish issue" only partially solved, the "life-line issue" could not be as successfully negotiated as Beckett would doubtless have liked. His Trinity College lectures pursue the idea that the author needs to be stated at the same time as his material, but the balance in *Murphy* has shifted back from the material towards the "author," a lesser Fielding (whom Beckett had first read in 1932, and read again in 1934). But the real author behind the implied author, in accepting the convention that a narrative must move purposively towards some predetermined end – Beckett told MacGreevy after it was all over (in the letter of July 1936 published in *Disjecta*) that he had known how it would end from the outset – was working against the grain of his real convictions. There was a "dissonance of means and ends"; this, surely, is why Beckett found the finished book "not very honest" (letter to Thomas MacGreevy, May 23, 1936). The very things that had made a completed book possible were the problem. Perhaps history (or History) was in some ways to blame, as in Mr Deasy's tentative, and manifestly inadequate, suggestion to Stephen Dedalus in Chapter 2 of *Ulysses*, but this time in the more restricted sense that Beckett had been reading too many books with a relatively clear and progressive "life-line." The narrative shifts in the novel *Murphy* mock this convention openly, but they are so prominently sign-posted that they can hardly be said to dislodge it. They become the line that we follow, because we know them to be a part of what will emerge. Perhaps psychoanalysis was also to blame. In encouraging free association (since the patient notes, in the very nature of the case, are never likely to surface, we can only suppose this to be the expert and sensitive approach of Wilfred Bion, his psychoanalyst for the two years following his father's death), analysis nevertheless assessed material as if it were part of an overarching "plot."

What "hobble[d]" *Murphy* (Jupiter; 1963: 155) was the "only possible" solution to making it a publishable entity. Design – not a Beckettian thing at all – had been mocked as "architectonics" in *Dream* (Beckett 1992: 186), and over the shorter run of *More Pricks* had not been required. But *Murphy* presents characters (or "puppets," itself quite a give-away) in interaction, and in relationship, in every sense of the word. Family and families matter, the fictionally historical past matters, the foreordained future matters. Should the notebooks in which *Murphy* was written ever make their way to a public archive we can confidently expect to find in them plans and plot schemes keeping Beckett's frequently flagging hopes alive, relatively little deviation from a proposed purpose or putative development (I have suggested elsewhere, in *Beckett Before Godot*, 1997, that the novel must have been written in much the same order in which we read it, a conviction which over the course of time has only strengthened), and almost certainly a good deal of the stock-taking (number of words written, and the like) currently only available for scrutiny in the letters to MacGreevy.

What the letters to MacGreevy further show is that Beckett set to with a will, completing most of what would be the first six or seven chapters, more than half the whole, within some eight weeks of starting. At that point a fairly well-oiled mechanism, and an increasingly substantial work, ran into severe difficulties, agonies of will-lessness. It seems reasonable to suppose that, after months of very committed writing, there was a slight falling-off coming up to Christmas 1935 (on return to Dublin!). Certainly in the New Year Beckett struggled terribly, and even once he had recovered at least something of his early impulse (in spite of Dublin, as it were) never again enjoying the productivity of late August to early December 1935, except when, towards the end, predictably enough perhaps, some fluency returned. In the "fallow" periods we have to imagine a "driven" man driving nowhere, or not quite sure what he was driving *at* (as distinct from *towards*). If the discovery of Geulincx helped, or appeared likely to help, even as Murphy became "break down" (letter to Thomas MacGreevy, January 10, 1936), it is not very clear how he did so, given that the philosopher's presence in the novel is spotty, and effectively concentrated in just one or two places, even if some aspects that are not explicitly influenced by him can be shown to resemble aspects of his thinking. It is as if Beckett knew deep down that Geulincx could not be the really effective ghost in this machine, not least because Geulincx's whole ethic precluded him from playing any such dominant, even if latent, role. Geulincx helped Beckett explain himself to himself, but could supply relatively little narrative impulse, because as a philosopher he had, quite legitimately, no "story" to tell. A potentially presiding genius (of a kind) had been found too late to be of any assistance, and could not supply the required assistance in any case. This the novelist Malraux, as distinct from the "occasionalist" philosopher Geulincx, might have supplied. But Malraux, it seems, who had interested Beckett earlier in the 1930s (the novels *Les Conquérants* and *La Vie royale* are mentioned in a letter to Thomas MacGreevy, January 25, 1931), and whose more recent *La Condition humaine* supplied the epigraph to "section" nine, interested him much less than Geulincx in 1936. *Murphy* was indeed "broken down," but not "between" Geulincx and Malraux (as Beckett's correspondence with MacGreevy phrases it) except in the very separatist sense: neither Geulincx nor Malraux really had a word to say to one another. In the event succor came from neither, and if and when it came it was more by miracle than design (so, closer to Geulincx than to Malraux, again), and by Beckett facing up to another three months of work, another three notebooks, and to *his own* sense of "need." In early 1936 there were not *two* needs, as there would be in 1938 with "Les Deux besoins" (*Disjecta*), but only one: to get an initially lively but increasingly torpid enterprise actually done with. None of the "helps" had helped, so it was back to square one (as the chess game seems both to imply and actually dramatize), and back to number one. Murphy, potentially a hero of a kind, had to be swallowed up by the "puppets." It was only by way of them that, as in the very last words of the novel, they could "ALL" go "OUT," as if wished away. At the end the principal *raison d'être* of the whole enterprise thus far had to be absent (though still actually present in body) to enable the ceremonies to come to an end. There is, surely, a curiously ceremonial tone operative over the closing scenes of the novel, as of dissonances resolved. But it would perhaps be more accurate to say that dissonances have been silenced, and left to float in the beautiful last paragraphs, describing a scene imagined at the *beginning* of writing.

Peter Murphy's conviction (in his *Cambridge Companion to Beckett* essay) that Spinoza and Kant have their place in the thinking behind *Murphy* has to make its way against the fact that, in the book as we have it, Spinoza is nothing more than the epigraph to "section six" and something of a one-off afterthought (literally so, when Beckett,

prompted by his friend Brian Coffey, tried, and failed, to dig into Spinoza, but only
after *Murphy* had been sent out to publishers), and that there is nothing directly from
Kant at all. Beckett had, however, alluded to Kant *en passant* as early as "Le Concen-
trisme" (November 1930), and he obviously knew something about Kant from reading
Schopenhauer, Windelband, and others (Jules de Gaulthier [*Dream* and *Whoroscope*
notebooks] certainly, and perhaps Mauthner, although I date "Beckett's Mauthner"
to mid-1938). It is certainly reasonable to think, as I shall try to show, that Beckett
thought through his various dissonances with some Kantian categories to hand. Even
in the absence of anything unambiguously Kantian in the *Murphy* we have, we know
that in January 1938, after *Murphy*, Beckett received an 11-volume *Works* of Kant
from Munich, one volume of which was Ernst Cassirer's study of the life and thoughts
of the philosopher. Material from this edition figures in the *Whoroscope* notebook mixed
in with material from Mauthner, and among that material one brief, but telling, entry
offers

> (Kant): Zweckmässigkeit ohne Zweck
> (?): Zweck ohne Zweckmässigkeit

The first of these items – usually translated as "purposiveness without purpose" is a
famous definition from Kant's *Critique of Aesthetic Judgment*, part one (it is discussed
in the English translation of Cassirer [1981: 312–13, 325–6]). Kant argues, as S.
Körner explains ([1955] 1966: 185), that there are similarities to be observed between
an organism and a beautiful object, both of which exhibit a complex independence
of their constituent parts, but that only the organism, and not the beautiful object,
is referred to a specific purpose. On encountering this definition Beckett characteristically felt moved to invert it, to mean something like "a drive with no endpoint in
mind." In Kantian terms, in reversing this notion, he was undertaking a revolt of
"means" against "ends." Kant's ethical position (ibid.: 146ff.) was that in treating
man as a means, we ignore the fact that, as a rational being, he is an "end in himself"
and as such "stands outside all causal chains and consequently outside every hierarchy
of means and ends." This is a long way, and in more than just time, from Geulincx's
Ethics, and Beckett certainly did not share Kant's idea of man as "a rational being."
Indeed, his own position is not unfairly summed up in a letter to Mary Manning
Howe of August 30, 1937 (HRHRC): "There is an end to the temptation of light …
There is an end to making up one's mind." In Beckett's position there is an "end,"
in one sense, but no "end" (in the sense of "purpose") because there is no "purposiveness," and no "means" available to service it anyway. This was Beckett's way of
"organizing" a revolt of means against ends, without denying that there would have
to be some kind of conclusion.

   It was perhaps only by acting within a temporary Kantian frame – assuming, as I
do, that Beckett was familiar with the bare bones of the arguments I summarize above,
even without his own copy of Kant to refer to at the moment of composition – that

he could employ sufficient "means" to get *Murphy* finished with. But this could only occur at the cost – as in the Kaun letter – of exploiting a "dissonance" between a useful strategy and the use (*Gebrauch*) to which it might be put. And it brought Beckett no satisfaction, as the letter to Mary Manning Howe indicates: "I write the odd poem when it is there and that is the only thing worth doing." This skates over the evidence of the German Diaries, where Beckett's ability to find a poem "there" fluctuated markedly. After visiting Ohlsdorf cemetery in October 1936 Beckett "thought a poem would be there," but it was not. A month later he was determined to "write a poem about Paternoster, Heraclitus etc." (and underlined it in his diary), but nothing came of this either. In February 1937 he wrote "two lines and a half" (German Diaries, February 2, 1937; see my essay, in German, on Beckett's "German fever" in *Der unbekannte Beckett*, Suhrkamp, 2005: 112–23), and eight days later a piece of doggerel in French also ground to a halt (German Diary February 15, 1937; also in a letter to George Reavey of the same date). Early in March Beckett jotted down, and then revised, eight lines of poetry or proto-poetry beginning "I wish I were an old man." In August 1937, by then back in Dublin, Beckett wrote "Ooftish" (under the title "Whiting"). Not until early 1938 did he achieve any fluency, however, and by then it was in Paris and writing in French. But even an improved rate of frequency could not wholly silence the old worry over the question of quantity: "When I have enough," Beckett told MacGreevy (June 15, 1938), "I thought of taking them to Eluard." The obvious concern, which for *Echo's Bones and Other Precipitates* had been a kind of virtue, was that there might be too few.

Later again, Beckett admitted (letter to Thomas MacGreevy, April 18, 1939): "I do not know what [the poems in French] are worth. The few people I have shown them to liked them, but they are friends." He had raised this very question of "worth" in the "German Letter of 1937," where he told Axel Kaun that personally he could not avoid the self-confessedly "naive alternative" of doing what was "worthwhile" rather than what was "not worthwhile" (Esslin translation). The only "use" (*Gebrauch*) Beckett would countenance was to work towards what was "worthwhile." It was not much to set against what had obviously been years of much huffing and puffing, not unproductive at the mere level of words written down, but profoundly frustrating given what Beckett had hoped to achieve. The inherently unstable dynamic of "Dissonance" was the only way Beckett had of keeping the competing claims of ends and means at bay, and it became, if by no means a "definition," at least a way of expressing his own critique of aesthetic judgment.

REFERENCES

Beckett, Samuel (1935). *Echo's Bones and Other Precipitates*. Paris: Europa Press.

Beckett, Samuel (1963). *Murphy*. London: John Calder.

Beckett, Samuel (1965). *Proust and Three Dialogues with Georges Duthuit*. London: John Calder.

Beckett, Samuel (1974). *More Pricks Than Kicks*. London: John Calder.

Beckett, Samuel (1983). *Disjecta: Miscellaneous Writings and a Dramatic Fragment*, ed. Ruby Cohn, London: John Calder.

Beckett, Samuel (1992). *Dream of Fair to middling Women*, ed. Eoin O'Brien and Edith Fournier, Dublin: Black Cat Press in association with Faber and Faber.

Beckett, Samuel. *German Diaries; "Dream" Notebook; "Whoroscope" Notebook*, Beckett International Foundation, University of Reading.

Beckett, Samuel. "Echo's Bones" (unpublished short story of 1933), Dartmouth College, New Hampshire.

Beckett, Samuel. Letters to Thomas MacGreevy, Department of Books and Manuscripts, Trinity College Dublin.

Beckett, Samuel. Letters to Nuala Costello (in private hands).

Beckett, Samuel. Letters to Mary Manning Howe, A. J. Leventhal, George Reavey, Harry Ransom Humanities Research Center, University of Texas, Austin.

Cassirer, Ernst (1981). *Kant's Life and Thought*, trans. James Haden, New Haven and London: Yale University Press.

Knowlson, James (1994). *Damned to Fame: The Life of Samuel Beckett*. London: Bloomsbury.

Körner, S. [1955] (1966). *Kant*. Harmondsworth: Penguin.

Murphy, P. J. (1994). "Beckett and the Philosophers." In John Pilling (ed.), *The Cambridge Companion to Beckett*. Cambridge: Cambridge University Press.

Pilling, John (ed.) (1994). "Beckett's English Fiction." In *The Cambridge Companion to Beckett*. Cambridge University Press.

Pilling, John (1997). *Beckett Before Godot*. Cambridge: Cambridge University Press.

Pilling, John (ed.) (1999). *Beckett's "Dream" Notebook*, Reading: Beckett International Foundation.

Pilling, John (2005). "Dates and Difficulties in Beckett's 'Whoroscope' Notebook." In Dirk Van Hulle (ed.), *Beckett the European*. Tallahassee: Journal of Beckett Studies Books, 2005.

Pilling, John (2005). "Beckett und 'the German Fever'": Krisis und Identität in den 1930ern." In Therese Fischer-Seidel and Marion Fries-Dieckmann (eds.), *Der unbekannte Beckett: Samuel Beckett und die deutsche Kultur*. Frankfurt: Suhrkamp.

Pilling, John (2006). "Beckett and Mauthner Revisited." In S. E. Gontarski and Anthony Uhlmann (eds.), *Beckett after Beckett*. Gainesville: University Press of Florida.

Pilling, John (2006). "'For Interpolation': Beckett and English Literature." In Matthijs Engelberts, Everett Frost, and Jane Maxwell (eds.), *Notes {D}iverse{s} {H}olo (Samuel Beckett Today/ Aujourd'hui 16)*. Amsterdam: Rodopi.

Windelband, W. (1907). *A History of Philosophy*, 2nd edn., trans. James H. Tufts, New York: The Macmillan Company.

6

The Legacy of Samuel Beckett:
An Anatomy

H. Porter Abbott

A legacy is a bequest. It is something handed down, usually money or items of property, and though the meaning of the word "legacy" has been enlarged, both literally
and figuratively, the ground is firmest when you are considering the inheritance of
some thing. Legacies are big in the law, and the law is most comfortable dealing with
things. So I am starting this essay on Beckett's legacy with a definition deployed not
as a guide but a foil. The object is not to make the term work by some extensive
conceit, but to see if we can sort out some of the differences when the bequest is not
some *thing* fixed or quantifiable but something that exists by replication and reception.
There is copyright law that applies to some small extent, but I am interested in where
it does not apply. The bequest under consideration here, moreover, has, most of it,
been given to everyone to do with as they wish. And finally, in this particular case,
what has been given has powers that distinguish it from most other legacies of the
kind. I will call these three facets of Beckett's legacy the repeatable, the recombinant,
and the revelatory – not the best labels, but the best I can come up with. The distinctions between them are what I hope to make clear.

Repeatable Beckett

This facet of the legacy includes an actual bequest, as specified in a will and administered by two executors, Beckett's nephew, Edward Beckett, and the late Jérome
Lindon, his publisher in France of 45 years. The executors have taken considerable
heat from many who felt they were being awfully strict in the way they carried out
their charge. But one of them has already passed on, and the other will in time follow
him, and eventually even the copyrights will expire. In the meantime, these two men
have tried to be good soldiers, by their lights, seeking to preserve what one might
call, imperfectly, Absolute Beckett: the most exact replication of Beckett's intentions
regarding the publication and performance of his oeuvre. In this work they have been

assisted by the diligent research of scholars like Jim Knowlson, S. E. Gontarski, John Pilling, and Ruby Cohn, and the sensitivity to Beckett's intentions of directors like Walter Asmus, Robert Scanlan, and the late Alan Schneider, and, most importantly, by the late Beckett himself, who was, more than most authors, on the alert for productions that violated his intentions, even to the point of legal intervention.

One problem with this interpretation of Beckett's legacy is that his intentions changed. Why privilege the latest last wishes of an aging man whose views and valuations of his work evolved over the course of his many years? There was not, nor has there ever been, an Absolute Beckett, on paper, on the stage, or in himself. And how could there be, especially in the case of an author so much of whose work is about the absolute absence of the absolute? "The mistake they make, of course, is to speak of him as if he really existed, in a specific place, whereas the whole thing is no more than a project for the moment" (Beckett 1965: 371). In the worlds Beckett created, "everything oozes" (Beckett 1954: 39). So the problem here is much more than a question of changing intentions. You do not have to be much of a poststructuralist to understand that Beckett's efforts, like all referential efforts, are to some degree a matter of missing the mark, particularly in the case of a writer who in his own opinion achieved at best an "unlessenable least best worse" (Beckett 1996: 106). Any work of any complexity is perforce simply the latest version of a potentially infinite process of revision. Not only were Beckett's works no exception to this important insight, but they actually performed it as Beckett translated his work from language to language, and from medium to medium, and from production to production.

So, when we talk about Beckett we are really talking about a moving target. And by "Beckett" I mean here not only the man but the things he wrote. They, too, are objects in constant motion even after the death of their creator. If his "final" drafts were "things" fixed enough to satisfy both his publishers and the law, this did not stop them from changing, and not just through the inevitable differences in production but also as they took their varying shapes in the minds that bring them to life. In other words, to repeat is not to duplicate.[1] And to confuse repetition with duplication is to abandon the legacy altogether, since duplication is a form of displacement rather than preservation. It displaces the living author with an icon, inviting worship as it confers sainthood, which is a way of sending an artist (this one, at least) to Hell, a place where Lucifer, according to Dante, is frozen stiff for eternity.

Such deep Deleuzean, indeed Beckettian, insights have given fuel to those who would open the floodgates to "tampering with" Beckett's works, putting "marbles in Gogo's boots during intermission" (Delrogh 1990: 103). For do we not, when we try to close these floodgates, constrain the vitality of what Beckett left us? Well, no, not if they are closed in the right way, since it is only within these constraints that the distinct vitality of these radiant objects flourishes. These constraints are also what go by the name of Beckett. Call them the traces of his signature; they are what make Beckett repeatable. It is why we don't tamper with the texts of his novels. And to the extent that one does tamper with any of his works, to that extent one engages in, among other things, false marketing. The name Beckett resonates in many ways (I will get to some of these in the next section), but it would not resonate at all did it not point to the fact that work of inimitable art appeared on this earth by the agency of the bearer of this name. This work bore his particular impress, that "absolute predicament of particular human identity" that he shared with the rest of us and that preoccupied him to the end of his life (Beckett 1983: 91). So it makes good sense to keep working to preserve this facet of the legacy, including its constraints as well as its infinite indeterminacies. In this way we pass on the experience of the beauty, wit, energy, and radiance, the intense feeling, both nuanced and deep, and the sheer intelligence of these works in as close proximity as we can achieve to their emergence.

Recombinant Beckett

Recombinant Beckett is the opposite of Repeatable Beckett. It involves Beckett's inevitable and necessary dismemberment and redistribution in a process of productive thievery. This is Beckett consumed without constraints, the infinitely flexible instrument of the culture (now globally and electronically extended) that tears him apart. In quantitative terms, this will be, in fact already is, Beckett's most abundant, most diverse, and most haphazard legacy, since it trades on his availability to any and all users. Right from the start, it shows up in theatrical production, which is where the authorial product as repeatable legacy is most vulnerable because it is necessarily mediated for consumers by sensibilities other than the author's own. Despite Beckett's best efforts (though occasionally with his consent), the threads of his original conceptions began pulling apart even during his lifetime, with an all-women *Godot* in Holland, an *Endgame* in a subway in Boston, a *Godot* in Strasbourg featuring a fog-filled hanger with a street scene, including a bar and a barman, and a *Godot* in Haifa staged as a construction site, with Didi and Gogo speaking Arabic and Pozzo and Lucky speaking Hebrew. Famously, and to Beckett's enduring outrage, the tiny play *Breath*, which he contributed in good faith to Kenneth Tynan's *Oh! Calcutta*, was staged in its first appearance with live naked bodies for props. With Beckett's passing, despite the continuing best efforts of his executors, the threads continue to unravel. Krapp has been played as a clown, *Not I* has been produced any number of times with the whole woman in view, and all of the radio plays have been staged. Most famous, or infamous, of these unravelments is Susan Sontag's 1993 one-act *Godot* in Sarajevo, staged with a female Pozzo, an adult "boy," and three sets of tramps played by two men, two women, and a woman and a man, all of them on stage throughout the play.[2] Of all these creative divergences from Beckett's intentions, only one actually registered its divergence in its title, which would have been the ethical (if not necessarily the legal) way to go, honoring as it does the immense importance of Repeatable Beckett.[3]

But ethical or unethical, legal or illegal, radiant or ridiculous, these adaptations of Beckett's plays are parts of a legacy that goes way beyond them, indeed way beyond all of them gathered together from here to the end of time. They are a small fraction of a "memetic" explosion of all Beckett-related things large and small. Richard

Dawkins proposed the word "meme" in 1976 for any of the tens of thousands of units of cultural meaning crowded in each of our minds. Memes come in almost any form – a word, an idea, an image, a musical phrase, a gesture – and once expressed, they replicate, mutate, combine, and recombine like genes (Dawkins 1976).[4] They do so, only much faster than the generation-by-generation slog of biological evolution. Replicated, they swarm in our media and our conversation, mutating and recombining with other memes either by accident or by design, and often in every succeeding moment of expression. This is a reproductive process that can be as lawless and randomized as natural selection, but also, like natural selection, it requires some principle of attraction for reproduction to get off the ground in the first place. In this regard, the Bible and the works of Shakespeare are perhaps Beckett's most salient precursors. With their great wealth of attractive material, they have not just survived but multiplied in a lush and enduringly useful afterlife. A legacy of this sort is an honor that a culture bestows in varying degrees. Many are those whose cultural DNA, greatly productive in their time, has all but gone extinct (Colley Cibber, Nahum Tate, James Macpherson, Coventry Patmore, Mrs Humphrey Ward). There are some who have predicted a similar fate for the works of Beckett, but, 18 years after his death, Beckett is not dead yet. In fact, few have been and, I am predicting, will be so frequently stitched and restitched into the fabric of our global culture.

At the micro level, this legacy pops up as *Worstward, Ho!* the punk rock CD by Shinobu and as "Krapp's Last Bottle" by the Wine Detective. It is an advertisement for a retirement plan featuring Nag and Nell in their ash cans and a cartoon about two tramps waiting at a bus stop for the Godot bus. It is the hawk-like image of Beckett himself circulating on posters and tee-shirts and coffee cups. It is the Godot Company, the Brasserie Godot, Godot the interactive adventure, Godot the robot at the University of Edinburgh School of Informatics, Godot the online art gallery, Godot Technology, Godot the Go-playing applet, and the comic book hero Buck Godot, Zap-Gun for Hire. There are thousands of such Beckettian memes replicating and evolving even as I type this.

Memeticists like also to talk about "meme complexes" or "memeplexes." These are the larger agglutinations of memes that tend to replicate together. The cartoon referenced above is a modest example involving the tramps, the waiting, and Godot, all drawn from the still larger memeplex of the play itself. The radicalized versions of Beckett's plays that I referred to above are examples of evolving memeplexes. The memeplex of *Not I* mutates into an installation featuring ruby lips on six monitors set in a circle.[5] Beckett's revolutionary style (another kind of coalescence of memes) recombines with other styles in the plays of Harold Pinter and the novels of Raymond Federman. Tom Stoppard rips off two minor characters from *Hamlet* and recreates them under the influence of "the way in which Beckett expresses himself."[6] This goes on and on. Beckett himself reappears and evolves as a character in the plays of other playwrights.[7] And, finally, all the facets of his special way of seeing, saying, and thinking have been raided from the 1950s on by analytic professionals – philosophers, linguists, semioticians, psychologists, cultural historians. Perhaps one reason for

Beckett's usefulness in this regard is the great many ways in which Beckett achieved limit-cases in the domains of human relations, language, genre, the representation of consciousness, and other areas of knowledge. His legacy is, in Heidegger's sense, *zuhanden*, "ready-to-hand." It can be used with admiring affirmation (Adorno) or hostile disapproval (Lukacs), pulled out of context (Foucault), or erected as scaffolding for one's own thinking (Badiou).

Such appropriations have been and will continue to be more or less egregious in their reductions and distortions (for they always distort and reduce). It is possible to rise above them, to see them as parts of the whole process I have outlined in this section and to contemplate with a detached and steely gaze how "something is taking its course" (Beckett 1958: 32). But I like to think that all this hubbub of recombination is, on balance, a healthy feature of any society that has a robust and living art, and is busy arguing with itself on issues large and small. Viewed as such, the works of Beckett, along with what we think we know of Beckett himself, have become, and promise to continue to be, a powerful collection of instruments for art, thought, feeling, judgment, pleasure, and, yes, pain as well.

Revelatory Beckett

The third legacy returns us to Repeatable Beckett, but with a difference. Where Repeatable Beckett is Beckett re-rendered within that range of particularity that makes Beckett Beckett, Revelatory Beckett reveals or regenerates kinds of understanding that are rarely if ever available elsewhere. As I discussed above, the ways are many in which disciplines appropriate Beckett and other authors. As a repository of poetic and narrative exemplar, any literature enables a productivity of this sort that is at least potentially infinite. Look long enough and you can find anything in a literary text that you want; this is what the recombinant legacy of Beckett allows. But what Beckett provides, in addition to this abundance of cultural availability, is the fresh acquisition, and reacquisition, of kinds of knowledge. This is not the "how true" effect – "what oft was thought but ne'er so well expressed" – but something more like the rich science that Wordsworth argued was what poetry delivered when it was at its best: "the primary laws of our nature ... not standing upon external testimony, but carried alive into the heart by passion."[8] Yet even Wordsworth's phrasing can be read as a reformulation of what people have always known about literature: that we lose ourselves in it in a process of immersion, getting inside the narrative, feeling and thinking with the characters in a process variously called projection, identification, empathetic understanding. This is the acclaimed distinction of literature: representations that come alive in ways that the representations of analytical discourse do not. But then, we are able to know what characters are feeling because we know those feelings. And this is one of the things that allows literature to work so well as a compendium of demonstration texts for organized discourses of knowledge that thrive beyond its borders. It is intellectually exploitable – which is also a problem.

Commenting on the field of cognitive literary studies, Tony Jackson once asked whether there is a way for literature to "talk back" to science – that is, to lift it from the status of handmaiden to the knowledge industry. The same could be asked of literature's relations with philosophy, linguistics, or any of the other disciplines I referred to above. Jackson's larger concern was that, in the transaction between scientific theory and literary investigation, "the originating theory cannot, even in principle, be recursively affected by the investigation." He is right about this, insofar as literature does not give us in return the organized, analytical language that is the discursive lifeblood of the sciences (Jackson 2000: 319; 2002: 177).[9]

But there are instances when literature, in its individually particular way, actually can be said to "talk back" to science, reversing the common appropriative flow in which outside knowledge, pre-existing the text, pulls out what it needs from inside the text. Such talking back is one of the special things that Beckett's art is good at. It does so by immersing us experientially not in what we already knew but in what we either did not already know or had forgotten that we knew. One can talk around such knowledge, but the knowledge itself is not analytically convertible to other discourses without serious distortion. It is "news that stays news," to appropriate Pound's epigram. You can label it with wise old saws (I will produce one later), but you cannot get at it without reimmersion. Such a view of what art can give us restores interpretation as a delicate art of service, pointing the way, without displacing.[10]

"The stories of Mahood are ended. He has realized they could not be about me, he has abandoned, it is I who win, who tried so hard to lose, in order to please him, and be left in peace" (Beckett 1965: 348). The problems of reading this short, representative passage from *The Unnamable* are latent in its third word, the modest preposition "of." On the face of it, the stories of Mahood are the stories the narrating voice told *of* the creature he invented and named Basil, and then renamed Mahood. Yet they are stories *of* Mahood in the sense that they are also stories told by Mahood, a reminder that is cued by the first words of the next sentence: "He has realized ..." And were this to be the end of it, the reader's problem would be no more than a problem familiar to students of autobiography (which can actually be quite a bit of a problem, if you are required to think about it). Mahood has been both subject and narrator of these pathetic stories: "the teller and the told" (312). He has been, but, then again, he has not, for the ostensible subject, as the next words declare, is *me*: "He has realized they could not be about me ..." This triple weight on the preposition "of," together with the inter-identification of *he, me, I, him,* and *Mahood*, have in fact accompanied the reader for the preceding 37 pages, ever since the retroactive christening of Mahood: "It was he told me stories about me, lived in my stead, issued forth from me, came back to me, entered back into me, heaped stories on my head. I don't know how it was done" (311). Here again, one can point out that autobiographies, fictional and non-fictional, have occasionally been narrated in the third person. But rarely has the disturbance caused by this tripling of self reference been foregrounded for long and never, I would venture, with the kind of sentence-by-sentence grammatical vertigo that Beckett sustains.

And it gets worse:

> Having won, shall I be left in peace? It doesn't look like it, I seem to be going on
> talking. In any case all these suppositions are probably erroneous. I shall no doubt be
> launched again, girt with better arms, against the fortress of mortality. What is more
> important is that I should know what is going on now, in order to announce it, as my
> function requires. It must not be forgotten, sometimes I forget, that all is a question of
> voices. I say what I am told to say, in the hope that some day they will weary of talking
> at me. The trouble is I say it wrong, having no ear, no head, no memory. Now I seem
> to hear them say it is Worm's voice beginning, I pass on the news, for what it is worth.
> (Beckett 1965: 348)

By the end of this (arbitrarily severed) passage, two more personal pronouns have
entered the referential mix for the same subject/object, *they/them* and an implicit *you*
("in order to announce it," "I pass on the news, for what it is worth"). In grammatical
terms, this is a crisis of "person deixis," that is, of the necessary dependence of personal
pronouns on context to determine their reference. Personal deictics like *he, him, me,
I, they, you* have no referential value until it is delivered by their interaction with other
elements in any communication. Perhaps Otto Jespersen's term "shifters" works better
to express the fluid condition of these open lexical templates.[11] Once they are established, we rely on them in turn to let us know who is talking and who is being talked
about. But if I am right in my reading of this passage, its abundance of shifters all
have the same referent. Or more accurately, they do and they do not. And to make
our reading experience even more dizzying, the voice has included two proper names,
Worm and Mahood, that appear to share the same referential ambiguity. If these
names are not exactly pronominalized, they are similarly maintained as referential
templates without content except as temporarily deployed.

From this perspective, it is worth looking at another curiosity of narrative grammar,
which is in a way the obverse of what Beckett has created here and almost everywhere
in these hundred pages. I'm referring to what Ann Banfield first identified as an
"empty deictic center" (Banfield 1987). In this instance, deictics, largely of time
and place, strongly suggest a narrating "subjective center" within the storyworld
but with insufficient personal pronominal clues to know whose voice it is – as, for
example, in Katharine Mansfield's "At the Bay": "and there was the splashing of
big drops on large leaves, and something else – what was it? – a faint stirring and
shaking, the snapping of a twig and then such silence that it seemed someone was
listening" (Mansfield 2006: 250).[12] The empty deictic center is a subjective center
without a subject. But – and here is the point I want to emphasize – it is a condition
most readers of modernist texts by authors like Woolf, Mann, Joyce, and Mansfield
have learned to "naturalize" and thus accept without much strain or bother as one
scenic representation follows the next. In stark contrast, Beckett has crammed the
subjective center with a superabundance of personal deictics, a conflict of grammatical
schemata which cannot be naturalized and thus never loses its power to disturb
the reader.

The main caution, then, for this facet of Beckett's legacy is to resist settling into such fall-back interpretive conclusions as "foregrounding the operations of language" or "the limits of representation" or "the inadequacy of subject reference" or "the incompatibility of self and narrative," whatever truth value they may have. In the interpreting business, there has of course always been the risk of taking refuge in the language of analytical assessment. But here the risk is especially acute, because these very "failures" of language and narrative, and all the narratorial whinging and cursing that goes on about them, are tools that work very much in Beckett's favor. They allow him to generate direct experience of news from the interior, our own interior, enabled by his uncompromising focus on the enduring and exotic aporia of selfhood.

The revelatory knowledge that Beckett specialized in concerned, most often, conditions of unknowing that we spend much of our lives bracketing or pasting over. It is, moreover, produced not in the form of representation but actual contact. Put simply, he gives us experiential knowledge of our ignorance. He has devised textual mechanisms through which we experience individually specific consciousness as a moving point of self presence in a constancy of self absence. It is neither one nor the other but both at once and thus, arguably, impossible to realize without our constantly flipping deictic references from sentence to sentence and even phrase to phrase. Still, he gets us as close, perhaps, as most of us are likely to get to the condition of non-understanding that evolutionary necessity and its agent, grammar, for good practical reasons have kept from our daily awareness. After all, burdened as we are with consciousness as no other animal before us, it helps enormously to believe that we are unitary beings with a sense of self well within the grasp of language. It confers a competitive advantage.

So, if I am right that what I have tried to triangulate here is real knowledge that comes to us from within our transaction with the text, is it useful knowledge? Or is it perhaps, even, debilitating knowledge? I would answer that it is, now more than ever, not only useful but urgent. We live, after all, in a world in which the threat of cultural relativization increasingly provokes a backlash of cultural absolutism.[13] With it comes an increasingly strenuous and volatile absolutism on issues of identity. In such a world, the awareness Beckett offers is at the least chastening. It reminds us that we at present cannot, and probably will never, crack the aporia of selfhood. To produce the old saw promised above, Beckett reminds us that what wisdom we have is incomplete without the awareness of our ignorance. This is a point that Socrates made long ago. But Socrates made the case logically, confounding in argument all the so-called wise men of Athens. Beckett goes about the task much differently. He requires of his readers (if they are really reading him and not some other text overlaying the text) that they "let go" just as the author did before them. The first lesson, then, is how to read. As he continually maneuvers readers and audiences into spaces where they must give up preconceptions, Beckett forces them to experience not just liberation but the recognition of how tenaciously they ordinarily experience art by processes of appropriation. Here, what I mean by "appropriation" is more restricted than what I meant when I spoke above of the Recombinant Beckett. This kind of appropriation operates under the guise of interpretation, but in fact makes Beckett into what he is not. This is probably a reflexive move, prompted by the way we are wired. In recent neurological work on hemispheric specialization, Michael Gazzaniga and his colleagues have shown how the left hemisphere of the brain "persists in forming hypotheses about the sequence of events even in the face of evidence that no pattern exists." Neurologically, in other words, we are always alert "to find order in chaos" (Gazzaniga, Ivry, and Mangun 2002: 436). In readings of Beckett, I am inclined to see such misappropriations as acts of control, motivated often by under-standable, if unacknowledged, anxiety. But whatever terms are imported to explain why the mind is tempted to swerve while reading Beckett, to the extent that it stays with the text, the knowledge is *in* the experience of the text in such a way that we cannot even get near to it from the outside.

There is an art to immersing oneself in this set of contradictions, but only in achieving it does one approach the unnamable of language and cognition. It is to experience "the rapture of vertigo, the letting go, the fall, the gulf, the relapse to darkness, to nothingness, to earnestness, to home" (Beckett 1965: 195). There is deep knowledge in not knowing what is going on, but it is rarely attained. Our nature is set against it, since it means letting go even of one's best attempt to say what is going on here. In this regard, talking about Beckett is like explaining a joke. The logic is the same, for the joke works only if you let go of the explanation. The reason for this is that the knowledge of explanation paradoxically cancels the knowledge freighted in the unexplained. To appropriate the words of Molloy, knowledge enters in only when one is "beyond knowing anything" (Beckett 1965: 86).

NOTES

1 Steven Connor's *Samuel Beckett: Repetition, Theory, and Text* was the first and is still the most lucid application of this distinction to Beckett's works.

2 For a discussion of this production, see Oppenheim (1995).

3 *Ils allaient obscures sous la nuit solitaire: d'après* En attendant Godot *de Samuel Beckett*, directed by André Engel for the National Theatre of Strasbourg, 1980. For more on this fascinating adaptation, see Anne C. Murch (1984).

4 Later, in *A Devil's Chaplain* (2003), Dawkins distinguished between highly mutable cultural memes and "self-correcting" rule-bound memes (the same as what I refer to as "duplications" above). The trouble I have with his proposed binary is that it does not take into account the important distinction I wish to

make in this essay between repeatable (not self-correcting) meme complexes and recombinant ones.

5 Directed by Neil Jordan, the installation invited the viewer to experience the delivery of the text on six separate 13-minute takes with cameras set at six different angles. The film was produced by Blue Angel Films, and the production opened at the Irish Museum of Modern Art in February 2007. For a rich and buoyantly affirmative survey of the permutations of Beckett's theater, see Gontarski (2006).

6 Stoppard's own words to Giles Gordon (Hayman 1977: 8).

7 A few examples: Sean Dixon's *Sam's Last Dance* (1997), Justin Fleming's *Burnt Piano* (1999), and Michael Hastings's *Calico* (2004).

For an informative critical discussion of these plays, see Zeifman (2006).

8   Alexander Pope, *An Essay on Criticism*, pt. 2, l. 98; William Wordsworth (1963: 239, 251).

9   For an implicit response in Beckett criticism that not only runs parallel to my own, but goes further in attributing something like the scientific method to Beckett, see Elizabeth Drew's unpublished dissertation "Samuel Beckett's Late Prose and the Limits of Consciousness" (Trinity College Dublin). Drew analyses Beckett's late works as "experimental in the sense that they break new ground by attempting a literature that probes the stream of consciousness" and in fact "are themselves experiments; they perform controlled enquiry into the nature of cognition" (103).

10 "To serve art," of course, is an old cliché for the craft of interpretation, but it can also be a kind of cooptation for the ends of worship rather than experience. It is as much a displacing move as the appropriation for the uses of theory that I referred to above, only "in the old high way" (to misappropriate Yeats), freezing the art into an icon. This is by now old news: that putting art on a pedestal quarantines its influence.

11 The term, "shifters," was given prominence by Roman Jakobson, particularly in his essay "Shifters, Verbal Categories, and the Russian Verb." In his lucid and impeccably organized *Lectures on Deixis*, Charles J. Fillmore (1997) distinguishes five categories of deixis: person deixis, place deixis, time deixis, discourse deixis, and social deixis.

12 For a critique that identifies the missing subject with the reader, see Fludernik (1996: 192–201).

13 Strong arguments for this connection can be found in Robertson (1992), Waters (2001), and Campbell (2005).

References

Banfield, Ann (1987). "Describing the Unobserved: Events Grouped around an Empty Centre." In N. Fabb, D. Attridge, A. Durant, and C. MacCabe (eds.), *The Linguistics of Writing: Arguments between Language and Literature*. New York: Methuen.

Beckett, Samuel (1954). *Waiting for Godot*. New York: Grove.

Beckett, Samuel (1958). *Endgame*. New York: Grove.

Beckett, Samuel (1965). *Three Novels: Molloy, Malone Dies, The Unnamable*. New York: Grove.

Beckett, Samuel (1983). "'Intercessions,' by Dennis Devlin." In *Disjecta*, ed. Ruby Cohn. London: Calder & Boyers.

Beckett, Samuel (1996). *Nohow On*. New York: Grove.

Campbell, George van Pelt (2005). *Everything You Know Seems Wrong: Globalization and the Revitalizing of Tradition*. Lanham, MD: University Press of America.

Connor, Stephen (1988). *Samuel Beckett: Repetition, Theory, and Text*. Oxford: Blackwell, 1988.

Dawkins, Richard (1976). *The Selfish Gene*. New York: Oxford University Press.

Dawkins, Richard (2003). *A Devil's Chaplain*. London: Houghton-Mifflin.

Delrogh, Dennis (1990). "Still Waiting: Chaikin Directs Beckett's *Godot*." *Village Voice* (April 24): 103.

Fillmore, Charles J. (1997). *Lectures on Deixis*. Stanford, CA: CSLI Publications.

Fludernik, Monica (1996). *Towards a "Natural" Narratology*. London: Routledge.

Gazzaniga, Michael S., Richard B. Ivry and George R. Mangun (2002). *Cognitive Neuroscience: The Biology of the Mind*, 2nd edn. New York: Norton.

Gontarski, S. E. (2006). "Reinventing Beckett." *Modern Drama* 49 (4 [winter]): 427–50.

Hayman, Ronald (ed.) (1977). *Tom Stoppard*. The Contemporary Playwrights Series. London: Heinemann.

Jackson, Tony (2000). "Questioning Interdisciplinarity: Cognitive Science, Evolutionary Psychology, and Literary Criticism." *Poetics Today* 21: 319–47.

Jackson, Tony (2002). "Issues and Problems in the Blending of Cognitive Science, Evolutionary Psychology, and Literary Study." *Poetics Today* 23: 161–79.

Jakobson, Roman (1971). "Shifters, Verbal Categories, and the Russian Verb." *Selected Writings*, Vol. 2. The Hague: Mouton.

Jespersen, Otto (1949). *Language: Its Nature, Development, and Origin*. New York: Macmillan.

Mansfield, Katherine (2006). "At the Bay." In Vincent O'Sullivan (ed.), *Katherine Mansfield's Selected Stories*. New York: Norton.

Murch, Ann C. (1984). "Quoting from Beckett: Trends in Contemporary French Theatre." *Journal of Beckett Studies* 9: 113–29.

Oppenheim, Lois (1995). "Playing with Beckett's Plays: On Sontag in Sarajevo and Other Directo-rial Infidelities." *Journal of Beckett Studies* 4.2: 35–46.

Robertson, Roland (1992). *Globalization: Social Theory and Global Culture*. London: Sage.

Waters, Malcolm (2001). *Globalization*, 2nd edn. London: Routledge.

Wordsworth, William (1963). "Preface 1800 Version." In R. L. Brett and A. R. Jones (eds.), *Lyrical Ballads*. London: Methuen.

Zeifman, Hersh (2006). "Staging Sam: Beckett as Dramatic Character." *Hunter On-Line Theatre Review*. http://www.hotreview.org/articles/stagingsam.htm.

7

Beckett and Philosophy

Anthony Uhlmann

While many critics take it for granted that Beckett is a philosophical writer – indeed, among the most philosophical of writers – this idea is not universally acknowledged, with objections largely being based on comments Beckett made separately to Tom Driver and Gabrielle d'Aubarède in 1961, which have been taken to disavow any interest in philosophy.[1] It is necessary, then, to establish the basic point of the importance of philosophy to Beckett's works at the outset, and I will briefly outline this case before turning to some of the ways in which this interest in philosophy informs readings of his works and elements within these works themselves.

Beckett never formally studied philosophy: his degree from Trinity College Dublin was in Modern Languages and he then went on to begin an abortive MA thesis on "Unanimism" (a French school of poetry which already had a strong philosophical focus concerned with "collective consciousness" derived in part from an understanding of some of Henri Bergson's writings) focusing in particular on the work of Pierre-Jean Jouve.[2] Deirdre Bair notes that Beckett saw the absence of any formal study of philosophy as a gap in his education (1990: 96); he began to address this, and possibly even became aware of it, from 1929, after arriving in Paris in late 1928 to work as a *lecteur* in English at the École normale supérieure, when James Joyce asked him to write an essay for a collection dedicated to his "Work in Progress." This essay, "Dante ... Bruno.Vico..Joyce" draws upon philosophers who interested Joyce and Beckett recounted its genesis to Knowlson:

> It was at [Joyce's] suggestion that I wrote "Dante ... Bruno.Vico..Joyce" because of my Italian. And I spent a lot of time reading Bruno and Vico in the magnificent library, the Bibliothèque of the École Normale. We must have had some talk about the "Eternal Return", that sort of thing. He liked the essay. But his only comment on it was that there wasn't enough about Bruno; he found Bruno rather neglected. They were new figures to me at the time. I hadn't read them. I'd worked on Dante, of course. I knew very little of them. I knew more or less what they were about. I remember reading a

biography of one of them. (Knowlson 1996: 100; for an extended account of this interview see *Beckett Remembering*, Knowlson and Knowlson 2007: 44–5)

At the École normale supérieure Beckett also met a French philosophy student, Jean
Beaufret, who discussed philosophy with him and brought him books from the library
(Knowlson 1996: 96–7).[3] From this time on Beckett undertook private study, closely
reading background materials ranging over the history of philosophy; the best attempt
to date this process, which seemed to begin with a somewhat *ad hoc* reading before
developing into a more systematic study of the history of philosophy, is Everett Frost's
fine overview to Beckett's notes (see the introductions to each of the manuscripts,
written by Frost in Engelberts, Frost, and Maxwell 2006). While some important
materials, such as a notebook related to his reading about Descartes which L. E.
Harvey (1970) mentions, have been lost, much survives and has only recently been
made available to scholars. In the course of this chapter I will discuss these notes,
which were taken over a period of several years, probably beginning around 1932 (see
Frost in Engelberts, Frost, and Maxwell 2006: 68–73), and recent work dedicated to
them, but suffice it to say for the moment that they indicate Beckett's commitment
to developing a solid knowledge of the history of Western philosophy, a knowledge
which other evidence indicates was augmented by the close reading of particular
philosophers.

Beckett's correspondence, especially that written to Thomas MacGreevy (Beckett
TCD MS 10402), also indicates his interest in philosophy, with specific mention being
made of Schopenhauer, (letters 3, 4, 8, 1930), Diderot (letter 33, 1932) Leibniz, (letter
57, 1933), Geulincx, (letters 85, 91, 1936), G. E. Moore, (letter 85, 1936), Berkeley
(letter 85, 1936), Spinoza (letters 103, 105, 108, 1936), the complete works of Kant
(letter, 150, 1938), Bergson (letter 155, 1938), Malebranche (letter 175, 1948).
Indeed, some of the enthusiasm with which he had consulted these works, as well as
an indication of the coming to an end of a hiatus in this study forced by World War
II is conveyed in the last reference listed here. Beckett asks MacGreevy in 1948 if he
had read Malebranche, before continuing that he had been too restless and nervous to
read anything for a long time, but that he now feels the old desire for study returning. There is a paragraph dedicated to his use of the pre-Socratics in a letter to Alan
Schneider concerning *Endgame* in 1957 (Beckett and Schneider 1998: 23). No doubt
other references will be drawn to light when the complete correspondence appears.

A good knowledge of Bergson, and his influence on French literature, is also evident
in notes taken by Rachel Burrows to lectures Beckett delivered in 1931 on Racine
and Gide at Trinity College Dublin (Burrows 1931) and in a letter to MacGreevy of
February 1931, which indicates that his short dramatic piece, *Le Kid*, a burlesque of
Corneille's *Le Cid*, draws upon Bergson (Knowlson 1996: 124).[4] The outlines of an
understanding of Bergson's theories of habit are also noticeable in Beckett's short
monograph of 1931, *Proust*.[5] Proust effectively inverts Bergson's theory of memory,
yet both discuss the role of habit in similar ways (though with different value judgments), and Beckett was well aware of the links that had been made between Bergson

and Proust as well as the different understandings of time each developed. Burrow's notes to his lectures which show a thorough knowledge of the then contemporary French intellectual context (which was the subject both of his aborted thesis and this course of lectures) within which Bergson played a major part demonstrate this: "*Julien Benda* tried to clarify Bergsonian conception of intelligence & intuition – says that B's intuition *is* highest intelligence – *l'intelligence passionelle* ... *Proust* detached from Bergson's conception of time but interested in this opposition – instinct & conscious intelligence. Bergson insists on absolute time: Proust denied it. In Proust it's a function of too many things – local but not absolute reality" (Burrows 1931: 5).

A good deal more information than this is supplied by Knowlson, who tells us in his biography that Beckett read Plato, the Gnostics, and Aristotle on Thales at the British Museum in 1932 (1996: 161), and in addition to those mentioned above (which he at times expands upon) he underlines Beckett's interest in Parmenides, Pythagoras, Democritus, Heraclitus, G. E. Lessing (whose house Beckett visited and whose complete works he had shipped back to Ireland [ibid.: 242]), and Schiller, as well as documenting his acquaintance with the work of contemporaries such as Sartre, Camus, Heidegger, and Adorno.

The list is impressive in its scope yet it also hints at some principles of interest. That is, Beckett seemed particularly drawn to Ancient Greek philosophy, to seventeenth-century rationalism (Descartes, Spinoza, Geulincx, Leibniz, Malebranche), to Idealism (Berkeley, Schopenhauer), and to elements of the German philosophical tradition (Kant, Schiller, Lessing). While it would no doubt be difficult to develop a reading drawing together all those elements of his aesthetic practice which find points of resonance in the various philosophical works which interested him, one might at least suggest that certain themes or problems drew Beckett to certain philosophers. The pre-Socratics, Democritus, and others within the tradition of Ancient Greek philosophy (such as Plato, Aristotle, and the Stoics) outline fundamental problems which have haunted Western philosophy ever since: the problem of the relationship between existence and non-existence, being in the world and non-being, the ideal realm and the real realm (sets of problematics to which philosophy has returned again and again). The seventeenth-century rationalists, for their part, drew particular attention to the problem of the nature of the self and its relationship to knowledge, the difficulty of accounting for the means of interaction between the mind and body, the self and the world, and the problem of human freedom in the face of what appears, from a rationalist perspective, a predetermined, mechanical universe (with each offering somewhat different responses to these problems). Following on in some ways from this tradition, and foreshadowing later developments in phenomenology and psychology, the idealists focus on the problem of human subjectivity: what it means to *experience* the world.

All of this is sufficient to allow the affirmation that Beckett had a clear interest in philosophy; following this the interrelated questions of how he made use of philosophy and how critics might make use of philosophy in considering his works impose themselves.

As I have mentioned, Beckett began to make use of philosophy with his first published work, "Dante ... Bruno.Vico..Joyce." In this essay Beckett sets out a number of principles with regard to the relationship between philosophy and literature, principles to which, for the most part, he seems to have more or less consistently held. His first sentence offers the caution that "The danger is in the neatness of identifications" [between the work of the philosopher and the work of the poet] (Beckett 1983: 19). Later in the essay he develops a distinction between poetry and philosophy, which, while somewhat rudimentary, nevertheless might also be thought to hold through much of what he was to affirm about literature and philosophy much later. He states, "Poetry is essentially the antithesis of Metaphysics. Metaphysics purge the mind of the senses and cultivate the disembodiment of the spiritual; Poetry is all passion and feeling and animates the inanimate; Metaphysics are most perfect when most concerned with universals; Poetry, when most concerned with particulars. Poets are the sense, philosophers the intelligence of humanity" (ibid: 24). Rather than dismissing philosophy, his comments to d'Aubarède in 1961 (Beckett 1979: 217) might be read in light of this distinction, something which affirms both that Beckett sees himself as a poet rather than a philosopher, but equally recognizes that he *is* concerned with the same kinds of problems which interest philosophers: problems of being (and non-being), problems of knowing (and not knowing) problems of meaning (and failing to mean). That is, the poet and the philosopher might be thought to encounter the same problems but to approach them from opposite ends, the poet concerned with the particular experience or *feeling* of the problem, the philosopher with the problem in general and abstract terms:

> "I wouldn't have had any reason to write my novels if I could have expressed their subject in philosophic terms."
> "What was your reason then?"
> "I haven't the slightest idea. I'm no intellectual. All I am is feeling. *Molloy* and the others came to me the day I became aware of my own folly. Only then did I begin to write the things I feel." (Beckett 1979)

Beckett's writings are not disciplinary philosophy, then, but in finding themselves concerned with problems which are also encountered by philosophy they draw our attention to the very problem of the nature of the possible relation between philosophy and literature, between the world of feeling and the world of abstract understanding. Indeed, this is a problem that has many sides in Beckett. The evidence cited above indicates Beckett's clear and ongoing interest in certain philosophical ideas, and this brings to light a number of questions. How might critics make use of philosophy in reading his works so as to shed light upon those works? How does Beckett make use of philosophy? That is, how can philosophy be thought to be integrated within his works, and what strategies does he use to effect this integration? Are Beckett's works themselves "philosophical" in the sense that they are provocative to philosophers and readers of philosophy? And might they genuinely be thought to have any effect on the discipline of philosophy?

Critics have offered two main responses to the question of how Beckett might be read in relation to philosophy. Although these approaches are quite often intermixed within works of criticism they can be divided for the sake of clarity. One response has been to consider the references that Beckett clearly makes to philosophers, both in his works and in other primary sources such as his published comments and critical writings, his correspondence, his manuscripts and notebooks, and to draw these into relation with his works. Another response has been to identify themes or problems in the works and draw these into relation with cognate themes in the work of philosophers.

Critics have developed readings related to allusions in Beckett from the beginning, with Hugh Kenner establishing a trend that closely associated Beckett's works with ideas drawn from René Descartes, the subject of Beckett's first published poem *Whoroscope*. Kenner found Cartesian elements throughout Beckett's works and such themes were further traced by many others (such as Fletcher 1964, 1967, Federman 1970, Harvey 1970). One of the key features of Matthew Feldman's *Beckett's Books* (2006) is a sustained attack on Cartesian readings of Beckett, but it is likely that Feldman's position will itself be challenged. While he forcefully establishes that the links to Descartes are overstated and distort Beckett's works, he may himself go a little too far toward the opposite extreme of expunging Descartes from the scene altogether. In doing this he places some strain on his own empirical method (a challenge to the field and philosophical readings of Beckett in particular).[6] While he is no doubt right to force the field to reassess this old model, there is, nevertheless, a good deal of evidence that Beckett did have an enduring interest in seventeenth-century rationalism, a movement strongly marked by Descartes, including reactions to and divergences from him in Leibniz, Geulincx, and Malebranche, and references to these writers can be found, directly and indirectly, in many post-*Murphy* works such as the "Four Novellas," the "Trilogy," and *How It Is*, for example. Scholars wishing to investigate the nature of these links, therefore, I would argue, remain justified in doing so.

Many critics have sought to add depth to our readings either by identifying and drawing out the implications of allusions to many other philosophers and thinkers other than Descartes and using them to develop their own readings, or by identifying problems to which others have responded via philosophical readings: Ruby Cohn, James Knowlson, John Pilling, Enoch Brater, Linda Ben-Zvi, and Stan Gontarski, are among the better known of these critics, and most recently Chris Ackerley has added a body of impressive scholarship both by drawing upon recently available material and through the patient tracing of references he perceives in the works themselves.

Critics such as Steven J. Rosen, Paul Davies, and Judith Dearlove exemplify another tendency, which is to develop sustained readings drawing upon theoretical ideas outlined in Beckett's own highly sophisticated critical writings: Davies makes use of "the ideal real" from *Proust*, Dearlove the idea of "nonrelation" from the "Three Dialogues with Georges Duthuit" (Beckett 1987), while Rosen (1976) weaves together a fabric of allusions drawn from throughout Beckett's works in tracing what he calls "the pessimistic tradition" throughout the history of philosophy and developing readings of philosophers within this tradition to shed light on Beckett's works. Rosen's list, which includes the pre-Socratics, Socratics, Cynics, Stoics, Christian theologians, Montaigne, Schopenhauer, Nietzsche, Descartes, and Sartre is all the more impressive given that he did not have access to Beckett's notes to his reading of philosophy (which confirm his knowledge of these traditions and most of these philosophers).

As touched upon above, however, readings of this kind are currently undergoing renovation because of important materials that have only become available to scholars since 2002. These items, held at Trinity College Dublin, include significant notes that Beckett made while studying philosophy (and psychology) in the 1930s.

Key sources among these papers include his extended notes (267 pages recto and verso) to his reading of the history of philosophy. Everett Frost and Jane Maxwell offer invaluable descriptions of these notes in "Notes Diverse Holo," a special edition of *Samuel Beckett Today/Aujourd'hui* published in late 2006. These are drawn, according to Frost, largely from three sources: Archibald Alexander's *A Short History of Philosophy*, a set text in the Trinity College Dublin course on philosophy offering a rudimentary overview, which Beckett used to begin with but abandoned halfway through. Probably by tracing references from Alexander, Beckett moved to two more advanced sources: Wilhelm Windelband's exhaustive and magisterial two-volume work, *A History of Philosophy*, and a source which Windelband himself cited as among the best two available on that topic at that time (and the only one of these available in English), John Burnet's *Greek Philosophy, Part I, Thales to Plato*. Beckett read both of these texts in full (see Frost in Engelberts, Frost, and Maxwell 2006: 67–89). One might suggest that having completed this extended study, which involved cross-referencing these initial sources with various other sources, some of which are yet to be identified (see Frost in Engelberts, Frost, and Maxwell), Beckett had educated himself in the history of philosophy at least to the level of a competent university graduate. These notes would not only have served as a foundation upon which to build other knowledge (as from then on he would have had a sophisticated understanding of the main philosophical forms and debates which would have allowed him to place and contextualize any subsequent philosophical text he might choose to read), they also amount to a treasure trove of material related to Beckett's interest in philosophy, which in turn he might have made use of in his creative writing.

Chris Ackerley draws on Windelband in developing recent work (Ackerley 2004, 2006; Ackerley and Gontarski 2004), and Feldman (2006) draws upon these notes and sources in developing his readings of the manuscripts in the first study devoted to this topic. There is an enormous amount still to be said, however. For example, while, as Feldman contends, more than half the notes Beckett makes (146 pages recto and verso) refer to Ancient Greek Philosophy, only 66 of these pages (recto and verso) specifically refer to the pre-Socratics whom Feldman focuses upon in his reading of MS 10967. That is, while Feldman is right to point to the importance of the pre-Socratics, Beckett's interest in other Greek traditions as well as other periods (to which he dedicates 121 pages) are also very much worthy of critical interest (see Engelberts, Frost, and Maxwell).

In addition there are Beckett's notes to his reading of sources in psychology (Beckett TCD MS 10971/7 and TCD MS 10971/8), which cross over into philosophy: Karin Stephen, for example, whose work *The Wish to Fall Ill* Beckett takes notes to, was not only a cousin of Virginia Woolf, but also a strong advocate of the work of Henri Bergson (so that one might consider the extent to which her understanding of psychology is influenced by her reading of Bergson). So too Mauthner's theory of language, to which Beckett took extensive notes (Beckett TCD MSS 10971/5/1–4), includes an important dialogue with the history of philosophy and resonates with the work of many twentieth-century theorists who also draw upon language and consider its importance to what we can know. Equally important are Beckett's notes to his reading of Arnold Geulincx (Beckett TCD 10971/6). Geulincx's *Ethics* has now been translated in full for the first time in an edition that includes Beckett's notes to his reading of Geulincx, which is cross-referenced to Geulincx's work to highlight the kinds of selections Beckett made in developing his reading of Geulincx (see Geulincx 2006). These are meticulously made, and while they are only drawn from Treatise I and the Annotations to this,[7] it should be noted that this Treatise was considered a complete work by Geulincx and published as a separate book in both Latin and Dutch editions during his lifetime (see Land 1891; van Ruler 2004). It was only after Geulincx's death that the additional five Treatises were added by the former students who assembled them from posthumous notes. That is, while one can understand why Feldman makes the point that Beckett does not seem to complete his reading of the *Ethics* (Feldman 2006: 132–3), when seen in this context it is apparent that his notes cover the greater part of by far the most important Treatise, one which is sufficient in and of itself to an understanding of the key elements of Geulincx's ethical system.

In addition to this, the opening lines to *The Unnamable* are so strikingly close to a passage in Treatise VI of the *Ethics* (see Geulincx 1891–3: 141; Geulincx 2006: 152) that one must wonder whether Beckett had this passage in mind even though he did not take notes to it. That is, while the notes can prove that Beckett read and was in a position to make use of certain texts, they cannot prove that he did not also read other texts, a knowledge of which might be postulated through the kind of strong textual resonance apparent here.

Important work has begun in what will no doubt be an extended process of digestion of all these sources. The best overview of all the available material is offered by Engelberts, Frost, and Maxwell (2006); Ackerley has effectively drawn on many of these notes in developing his recent work. Matthew Feldman's book (2006) offers the first extended study of all of these sources and develops many interesting arguments. My own recent book (Uhlmann 2006), *Samuel Beckett and the Philosophical Image*, draws upon Beckett's notes to Geulincx and the new translation of his *Ethics* to develop a reading which considers, among other things, the manner in which Beckett borrows images from philosophers and reuses them in his texts. Yet all of this only begins what will no doubt be an ongoing process: one which will, more than probably, significantly change the ways in which we understand Beckett.

The best scholars adopting the second approach that I have outlined above have developed a variety of interesting responses to Beckett's works. An early trend in the field involved aligning Beckett's works with French existentialism. While these links are open to criticism there is no doubt that they have proved influential and that popular understanding of the nature of Beckett's works have been marked by Esslin's idea of the "Theatre of the Absurd" (Esslin 1968) (drawing upon ideas developed by Albert Camus and little valued by Beckett himself),[8] for example. A number of other critics, such as Lance Butler (1984), Edith Kern (1970) and L. A. C. Dobrez (1986), look to existentialism to understand Beckett, something that was felt to be justified by the proximity between this group and their exact contemporary Samuel Beckett. Clearly assertions made by Beckett himself are not necessarily the final word on these issues: that is, his works might exceed or miss his intentions at various times as he himself recognizes in the production of *Film* (see Beckett and Schneider 1998: 166), and therefore it is valid to examine his works in the light of ideas developed within the contexts he inhabited.

In each case, the final point by which works of this kind need to be judged, is through their demonstrated fidelity to Beckett's works themselves. In the case of critics proceeding through reference to manuscript sources, critical writings, and correspondence, readers must first develop an interpretation of the relationship between these sources and the creative process and then consider whether intentions, where these are expressed, remain consistent with the finished works. In the case of critics proceeding through an understanding of shared problems or apparent affinities between Beckett's works and ideas expressed by philosophers, readers need to consider whether the ideas outlined are actually drawn from Beckett's texts, or whether alien philosophical systems are being superimposed over ideas within these texts. In each case, the onus falls upon the critic to justify their claims, in the first instance through evidence found in the works themselves.

I would contend that while there are some interesting points of relation between Beckett and existentialism his own work had already begun to look beyond the problems that existentialism encounters towards others which would come to interest the next generation of French philosophers.[9] Yet, in both cases, readers are drawn to considering Beckett in relation to French philosophy because of the fact that they shared common contexts: the France of World War II and immediately after; the France defeated by the Nazis, marked by the French resistance and the "guerre franco-française"; the France of the postwar purge and the willed forgetting instituted by General de Gaulle; the France of the Algerian War. This was a history which, in the words of Michel Serres, left people with a "taste for disobedience" (Serres with Latour 1995: 20). Given that Beckett shared such an uncommon history with two generations of thinkers who also sought to come to grips with the problems which emerged from this period, it does indeed seem important to take an interest in the French intellectual contexts that Beckett inhabited and marked with his presence, even if he was not openly engaging with these thinkers. Indeed, similar arguments might be made for the links between Beckett and German philosophy. For example, even if Beckett felt Adorno had misinterpreted him (Knowlson 1996: 478–9), Adorno's reading remains of interest to us because it helps us to understand the kind of impact his work had within the world in which it emerged, and the manner in which it was heard by philosophy and by philosophers at that time, something which will in turn influence how it might be understood now.

Implicit in these kinds of philosophical readings is the understanding that Beckett's works themselves offer important ways of thinking, of understanding the world – that in some sense they offer us a kind of knowledge which might only come to light in the forms and through the processes Beckett creates. Yet this poetical thinking is so powerful that we cannot avoid attempting to draw it into a framework which might allow us to try, at least, to understand it: while this process is perilous it remains justified, because refusing to engage with the works on this level involves a severe limitation on their capacity to affect us.

Angela Moorjani (1982) was perhaps the first critic to bring Beckett's works into relation with the work of the post-Sartre generation of French philosophers, a generation of thinkers which amounted to one of the most extraordinary flowerings of philosophical creativity at one time and in one place to have occurred in the history of philosophy. Beckett was certainly aware of these thinkers, at least late in life (see Bernold 1992) and they were certainly very well aware of, and even influenced by, him. The process started by Moorjani was taken up in earnest by a number of critics, beginning with Steven Connor in 1988 and Leslie Hill, Carla Locatelli, and Thomas Trezise in 1990. Bruno Clément's book on Beckett in 1989 also opened the way to new French critical interpretations to add to the important French works offered by philosophers such as Deleuze and Badiou. The interest in linking Beckett to philosophy and contemporary French philosophy in particular has continued from that time on with works in English and French by a number of critics including Begam, Bryden, Casanova, Gibson, Grossman, Lane, Oppenheim, and Sheehan.

We are left, then, with the difficult questions of how philosophy might be integrated within Beckett's works, and whether Beckett's works themselves are philosophical. With regard to the first of these: most of the readings mentioned above offer suggestions as to how this interaction might come about, yet, to my mind, this remains an extremely difficult question to answer and the question remains open.

With regard to the second question, it is clear that Beckett's works have been and remain provocative to philosophers and readers of philosophy, and that they *have* had an effect on the discipline of philosophy. Bruno Clément has written an excellent essay (2006: 116–37) examining how French philosophers such as Blanchot, Bataille, Deleuze, and Badiou have made use of Beckett in their works. While Clément emphasizes how these philosophers offer somewhat selective readings, which draw upon those aspects of Beckett which most agree with their own systems, one might equally emphasize that there is evidence that Beckett has not only been "used" in this way but that, in addition, his works have affected his readers (and indeed Clément's subtle readings do take into account this idea that the readers have been changed by what they have read). In support of this one might cite the by now well-known statements made by Michel Foucault, who used ideas drawn from Beckett in the *Archaeology of Knowledge* (1989), *L'Ordre du discours* [*The Order of Discourse*] (1971), and "What is an Author?" (1977). Asked how he came to be the kind of philosopher he turned into

Foucault said, "I belong to that generation of people, who, when they were students, were enclosed within an horizon marked by Marxism, Phenomenology, Existentialism, etc. ... I was like all the other students of philosophy at that time, and for me, the rupture came with Beckett: *Waiting for Godot*, a breath-taking spectacle" (Foucault 1985: 105).

Others have felt a close affinity to Beckett, without writing on him, such as Derrida who, asked why he had never written on Beckett, stated, "This is an author to whom I feel very close, or to whom I would like to feel myself very close" (Derrida 1992: 60).

This, too, is a question that is still to be fully explored as it relates to the effect of Beckett's works. The works *are* philosophical in that they have had and continue to have profound effects on philosophical discourse: both engaging with and influencing philosophers, and influencing and changing how Western culture in general has come to think about particular problems. Yet questions concerning how we might understand this process are only beginning to come into focus. How do these works make us think? How have they changed our understanding of what it means to think and to be in the world?

NOTES

1 For an example of a critic who claims Beckett has little interest in philosophy see Cronin's comments (1996: 231). I have argued in detail against taking Beckett's comments to d'Aubarède as a simple disavowal elsewhere (see Uhlmann 2006: ch. 4).

2 See Knowlson (1996: 75–6), Knowlson and Knowlson (2007: 32–3 and 39), and Ackerley and Gontarski (2004) on Jouve, Unanimisme.

3 Beaufret was to go on to have a very distinguished career as a philosopher in France, being most closely associated with the reception of Martin Heidegger after World War II, a reception complicated by Heidegger's association with the Nazi Party. Beaufret not only brought Heidegger into immediate contact with postwar French philosophy by urging him to write his "Letter on Humanism," which critiques Sartre and existentialism, but also brought students to meet Heidegger in Germany, and introduced Heidegger to the work of Jacques Derrida. Although Beckett's friendship with Beaufret petered out after Beckett left Paris in the early 1930s his comments to Knowlson show he was well aware of Beaufret's later career (see 1996: 97). Everett

Frost has also noted that Beaufret also wrote two books related to Greek philosophy (Engelberts, Frost, and Maxwell 2006: 71).

4 Burrows further indicates that Beckett made references to Nietzsche in his lectures.

5 I discuss these relations in *Beckett and Poststructuralism* (Uhlmann 1999: ch. 2).

For example, Feldman tends to dismiss a now lost notebook containing Beckett's notes to his reading of and about Descartes as unimportant (see 2006: 46, 157 n. 22) and further suggests that Beckett probably only read a digest version of Descartes because this was the only collection of Descartes's works in Beckett's library after his death. Both claims are difficult to sustain with reference to available evidence: a source which is known to have existed but is now lost cannot simply be assumed to be of a lesser importance than extant sources. Equally, Feldman has no logical grounds from which to assert that Beckett only read the work on Descartes which survives in his library: there are numerous witnesses who claim Beckett gave away many books, borrowed and returned others, and as we have seen he spent a good deal of time in libraries.

6   The notes begin at page 3 after the title page 1 and blank page 2 of Land's edition, and end at page 59, six pages from the end of Treatise I. As for the Annotations to Treatise I, Beckett's notes begin on the second page of the Annotations, page 154, and break off twenty pages from the end of all Annotations at page 257 (Geulincx, *Opera Philosophica*).

7   See the summary in Ackerley and Gontarski (2004: 2).

8   I develop an extended argument concerning Beckett's affinities with the post-Sartre generation of French philosophers in *Beckett and Poststructuralism* (Uhlmann 1999).

REFERENCES AND FURTHER READING

Ackerley, C. J. (2004). *Demented Particulars: The Annotated Murphy*. Tallahassee: Journal of Beckett Studies Books.

Ackerley, C. J. (2006). *Obscure Locks, Simple Keys: The Annotated Watt*. Tallahassee: Journal of Beckett Studies Books.

Ackerley, C. J., and S. E. Gontarski (2004). *The Grove Companion to Samuel Beckett*. New York: Grove.

Adorno, Theodor W. (1988). "Trying to Understand *Endgame*." In Harold Bloom (ed.), *Modern Critical Interpretations: Samuel Beckett's "Endgame."* New York: Chelsea House.

Alexander, Archibald (1908). *A Short History of Philosophy*. Glasgow: Maclehose.

Badiou, Alain (2004). *On Beckett*, trans. Andrew Gibson and Alberto Toscano. Manchester: Clinamen Press.

Bair, Deirdre (1990). *Samuel Beckett: A Biography*. London: Vintage.

Bataille, Georges (1951). "Le silence de Molloy." *Critique* 7: 387–96.

Beckett, Samuel, *TCD MS 10402, Letters to Thomas MacGreevy*, Manuscripts Department, Trinity College Library Dublin, Republic of Ireland.

Beckett, Samuel, *TCD MSS 10967, Philosophy notes*, Manuscripts Department, Trinity College Library Dublin, Republic of Ireland.

Beckett, Samuel, *TCD MSS 10971/5/1–4, Notes to Mauthner*, Manuscripts Department, Trinity College Library Dublin, Republic of Ireland.

Beckett, Samuel, *TCD 10971/6, Notes to Geulincx*, Manuscripts Department, Trinity College Library Dublin, Republic of Ireland.

Beckett, Samuel, *TCD MS 10971/7 and TCD MS 10971/8, Psychology notes*, Manuscripts Department, Trinity College Library Dublin, Republic of Ireland.

Beckett, Samuel (1979). "Interview with Gabriel d'Aubarède," trans. C. Waters. In L. Graver and R. Federman (eds.), *Samuel Beckett, the Critical Heritage*, London: Routledge and Kegan Paul.

Beckett, Samuel (1983). *Disjecta: Miscellaneous Writings and Dramatic Fragment*, ed. Ruby Cohn. London: John Calder.

Beckett, Samuel (1987). *Proust and Three Dialogues with Georges Duthuit*. London: John Calder.

Beckett, Samuel (1999). *Beckett's Dream Notebook*, ed., annot., and introd. John Pilling. Reading: Beckett International Foundation.

Beckett, Samuel, and Alan Schneider (1998). *No Author Better Served: The Correspondence of Samuel Beckett and Alan Schneider*, ed. Maurice Harmon. Cambridge, MA: Harvard University Press.

Begam, Richard (1996). *Samuel Beckett and the End of Modernity*. Stanford: Stanford University Press.

Ben-Zvi, Linda (ed.) (2003). *Drawing on Beckett: Portraits, Performances, and Cultural Contexts*. Tel Aviv: Assaph Books.

Bernold, André (1992). *L'Amitié de Beckett: 1979–1989*. Paris: Hermann.

Blanchot, Maurice (1986). "Where Now? Who Now?" In S. E. Gontarski (ed.), *On Beckett, Essays and Criticism*. New York: Grove.

Brater, Enoch (1990). *Beyond Minimalism: Beckett's Late Style in the Theater*. Oxford: Oxford University Press.

Bryden, Mary (1993). *Women in Samuel Beckett's Prose and Drama: Her Own Other*. Lanham, MD: Barnes & Noble Books.

Bryden, Mary (2007). *Gilles Deleuze: Travels in Literature*. London: Palgrave.

Burnet, John (1914). *Greek Philosophy, Part I, Thales to Plato*. London: Macmillan.

Burrows, Rachel (1931). "*Notes to lectures by Samuel Beckett on Gide and Racine at Trinity College Dublin*," TCD MIC 60, Manuscripts Department, Trinity College Library Dublin, Republic of Ireland.

Butler, Lance St John (1984). *Samuel Beckett and the Meaning of Being*. St Martin's Press: New York.

Casanova, Pascale (1997). *Beckett l'abstracteur*. Paris: Seuil.

Clément, Bruno (1989). *L'Oeuvre sans qualités: Rhétorique de Samuel Beckett*. Paris: Seuil.

Clément, Bruno (2006). "What the Philosophers Do with Samuel Beckett," trans. Anthony Uhlmann. In S. E. Gontarski and Anthony Uhlmann (eds.), *Beckett after Beckett*. Gainesville, FL: University Press of Florida.

Cohn, Ruby (1973). *Back to Beckett*. Princeton: Princeton University Press.

Connor, Steven (1988). *Samuel Beckett: Repetition, Theory and Text*. Oxford: Basil Blackwell.

Cronin, Anthony (1996). *Samuel Beckett: The Last Modernist*. London: Harper Collins.

Davies, Paul (1993). *The Ideal Real: Beckett's Fiction and Imagination*. London and Toronto: Associated University Presses.

Dearlove, Judith E. (1982). *Accommodating the Chaos: Samuel Beckett's Nonrelational Art*. Durham: Duke University.

Deleuze, Gilles (1997). "The Exhausted," trans. Anthony Uhlmann. In Daniel W. Smith and Michael A. Greco (eds.), *Essays Critical and Clinical*. Minneapolis: University of Minnesota Press.

Deleuze, Gilles (1997). "The Greatest Irish Film." In *Essays Critical and Clinical*, trans. Daniel W. Smith and Michael A. Greco. Minneapolis: University of Minnesota Press.

Derrida, Jacques (1992). "'This Strange Institution Called Literature': An Interview with Jacques Derrida" [with Derek Attridge], trans. Geoffrey Bennington and Rachel Bowlby. In Derek Attridge (ed.), *Acts of Literature*. New York: Routledge.

Dobrez, L. A. C. (1986). *The Existential and Its Exits: Literary and Philosophical Perspectives on the Works of Beckett, Ionesco, Genet, and Pinter*. London: Athlone.

Driver, Tom F. (1961). "Beckett by the Madeleine." *Columbia University Forum* (Summer): 21–5.

Engelberts, Matthijs, Everett Frost, and Jane Maxwell (eds.) (2006). *Notes Diverse Holo: Catalogues of Beckett's Reading Notes and Other Manuscripts at Trinity College, Dublin, with Supporting Essays*, Samuel Beckett Today/Aujourd'hui 16. Amsterdam: Rodopi.

Esslin, Martin (1968). *The Theatre of the Absurd*. London: Penguin.

Federman, Raymond (1970). "Beckettian Paradox: Who Is Telling the Truth?" In Melvin J. Friedman (ed.), *Samuel Beckett Now*. Chicago: The University of Chicago Press.

Feldman, Matthew (2006). *Beckett's Books: A Cultural History of the Interwar Notes*. London: Continuum.

Fletcher, John (1964). *The Novels of Samuel Beckett*. London: Chatto and Windus.

Fletcher, John (1967). *Samuel Beckett's Art*. London: Chatto and Windus.

Foucault, Michel (1971). *L'Ordre du discours: Leçon inaugurale au Collège de France prononcée le 2 décembre 1970*. Paris: Gallimard. (Translations from this source are my own.)

Foucault, Michel (1977). "What is an Author?" In Donald F. Bouchard (ed.), *Language, Counter-Memory, Practice: Selected Essays and Interviews*, trans. Donald F. Bouchard and Sherry Simon. Ithaca: Cornell University Press.

Foucault, Michel (1985). "Archéologie d'une passion" [interview with Charles Ruas]. *Magazine littéraire* 221 (July–August): 100–5.

Foucault, Michel (1989). *The Archaeology of Knowledge*, trans. A. M. Sheridan Smith. London: Routledge.

Geulincx, Arnold (1891–3). *A. Geulincx Antverpiensis Opera philosophica*, Vol 3, ed. J. P. N. Land. The Hague: Martin Nijhoff.

Geulincx, Arnold (1999). *Metaphysics*, trans. Martin Wilson. Wisbech: Christoffel Press.

Geulincx, Arnold (2006). *Arnold Geulincx's Ethics: With Samuel Beckett's Notes*, ed. Han van Ruler, Anthony Uhlmann, and Martin Wilson, trans. Martin Wilson. Amsterdam: Brill.

Gibson, Andrew (2007). *Beckett and Badiou: The Pathos of Intermittency*. Oxford: Oxford University Press.

Gontarski, S. E. (1985). *The Intent of Undoing in Samuel Beckett's Dramatic Texts*. Bloomington: Indiana University Press.

Gontarski, S. E., and Anthony Uhlmann (eds.) (2006). *Beckett after Beckett*. Gainesville: University Press of Florida.

Grossman, Evelyne (2004). *Défiguration: Artaud – Beckett – Michaux*. Paris: Éditions de Minuit.

Harvey, Lawrence E. (1970). *Samuel Beckett Poet and Critic*. Princeton: Princeton University Press.

Hill, Leslie (1990). *Beckett's Fiction in Different Words*. Cambridge: Cambridge University Press.

Kenner, Hugh (1968). *Samuel Beckett: A Critical Study*. Berkeley: University of California Press.

Kern, Edith (1970). *Existential Thought and Fictional Technique: Kierkegaard, Sartre and Beckett*. New Haven: Yale University Press.

Knowlson, James (1996). *Damned to Fame: The Life of Samuel Beckett*. London: Bloomsbury.

Knowlson, James, and Elizabeth Knowlson (eds.) (2007). *Beckett Remembering, Remembering Beckett*. London: Arcade.

Knowlson, James, and John Pilling (1979). *Frescoes of the Skull: The Later Prose and Drama of Samuel Beckett*. London: John Calder.

Land, J. P. N. (1891). "Arnold Geulincx and His Works." *Mind: A Quarterly Review of Psychology and Philosophy* 16: 223–42.

Lane, Richard (ed.) (2002). *Beckett and Philosophy*. London: Palgrave.

Locatelli, Carla (1990). *Unwording the World: Samuel Beckett's Prose Works after the Nobel Prize*. Philadelphia: University of Pennsylvania Press.

Moorjani, Angela B. (1982). *Abysmal Games in the Novels of Samuel Beckett*. Chapel Hill: University of North Carolina Press.

Murphy, P. J. (1994). "Beckett and the Philosophers." In John Pilling (ed.), *The Cambridge Companion to Beckett*. Cambridge: Cambridge University Press.

Oppenheim, Lois (2000). *The Painted Word: Samuel Beckett's Dialogue with Art*. Ann Arbor: University of Michigan Press.

Pilling, John (1976). *Samuel Beckett*. London: Routledge and Kegan Paul.

Pilling, John (1997). *Beckett before Godot*. Cambridge: Cambridge University Press.

Rosen, Steven J. (1976). *Samuel Beckett and the Pessimistic Tradition*. New Brunswick, NJ: Rutgers University Press.

Serres, Michel with Bruno Latour (1995). *Conversations on Science, Culture, and Time*, trans. Roxanne Lapidus. Ann Arbor: University of Michigan Press.

Sheehan, Paul (2002). *Modernism, Narrative, and Humanism*. Cambridge: Cambridge University Press.

Trezise, Thomas (1990). *Into the Breach: Samuel Beckett and the Ends of Literature*. Princeton: Princeton University Press.

Watson, David (1991). *Paradox and Desire in Samuel Beckett's Fiction*. London: Macmillan.

Windelband, Wilhelm (1958). *A History of Philosophy*. 2 vols. New York: Harper.

Uhlmann, Anthony (1999). *Beckett and Poststructuralism*. Cambridge: Cambridge University Press.

Uhlmann, Anthony (2006). *Samuel Beckett and the Philosophical Image*. Cambridge: Cambridge University Press.

van Ruler, Han (2004). "Arnout Geulincx." In Wiep van Bunge, Henri Krop, Han van Ruler, and Paul Schuurman (eds.), *The Dictionary of Seventeenth and Eighteenth-Century Dutch Philosophers*. London: Thoemmes Continuum.

8
Philosophizing with Beckett: Adorno and Badiou

Jean-Michel Rabaté

Philosophy begins at the beginning, and thus, in order to deal with Beckett's loaded links with philosophers and philosophies, I will start with the first two letters of the alphabet. This will not even be an ABC of philosophy as revisited by Beckett, since I will stop before reaching letter C. Doing this, I'll quote the only letter I received from Samuel Beckett. In 1984, after I had edited the collection entitled *Beckett avant Beckett*, I mailed a copy to Beckett via the Editions de Minuit. Almost immediately, I received a polite thank-you note neatly handwritten on both sides of a medium-sized visiting card with his name printed on it. Beckett thanked me kindly for the volume and referred to it by its abbreviation, *B. A. B.* Such modesty was consistent with his reputation. Then, looking better, I saw a small "a" added after the second B. It dawned on me that Beckett had played on the abbreviation, calling the collection not just "B. A. B." but "*B. A. BA*," which, in French, commonly means a "primer" or a "beginner's guide." Did he imply that his first steps in literature were barely worth a collective effort, or was he slyly suggesting that our genealogical approach was in dire need of a method, like a Cartesian return to foundations? Without being sure about this, I sensed that he was insisting upon beginnings. A little earlier, he had punned on the fact that, in French, "how it is" sounds exactly like "to begin" (*Comment c'est*). Our collective effort, which attempted to survey his own literary beginnings (a sort of "*Comment c'était*"), was good provided it brought about an actual beginning (*Comment c'est? Commencez!*).

This foundational concern is shared by the two philosophers I will examine here. I will bring them into play not because their initials follow the alphabet but because they have meditated on Beckett in a consistent and systematic manner. Theodor W. Adorno and Alain Badiou do not just quote Beckett once in a while, they do not only devote one or two brilliant essays to some of his works, as, for instance, Gilles Deleuze and Stanley Cavell have done (Deleuze working mostly on *Film* and *Quad* [see 1997a: 23–6; 1997b: 152–74] while Cavell tackled *Endgame* [see 1969:115–62]). For them, indeed, Beckett entirely belongs to the history of philosophy. His writings represent a major theoretical problem that has to be addressed and responded to with new concepts. In order to do this they deploy all the resources of their dialectical skills. Needless to say, both are strong readers who are not above a slight misreading here and there. This is because they never forget that theoretical confrontations come first, and that a preliminary discussion of principles is inevitable since any encounter with Beckett should trigger an irresistible urge to philosophize differently. Adorno and Badiou may embody a more general tendency here. We have been made increasingly aware that Beckett's works, although they make sense by themselves, also require theoretical frameworks.

This is confirmed by the dramatic proliferation of theoretical approaches to Beckett. Far from being swamped or diluted, Beckett has profited by the theoretical deluge. In support of this, I will draw on my experience of having presented Becket's *Film* at Slought gallery in Philadelphia; the occasion was a debate with Branka Arsic in 2003. We first saw the film, discussed for an hour the main themes of her book *The Passive Eye* (Arsic 2003), then screened *Film* once more. All those who were in the audience felt a qualitative jump after the second screening. The debate on Deleuze's definition of time, on the paradoxes of vision and blindness, on Beckett's fascination for silent movies from the 1930s, on Berkeley's immaterialism and theological phenomenology, all this made sense concretely when confronted with a second viewing of *Film*. To be sure, ideally, the philosophical framework that helps us engage with Beckett's works should be double: it should take into account the philosophical allusions that pepper the texts (as with Berkeley's *esse est percipi* in *Film*), and evoke a more comprehensive discourse which does not shrink from basic definitions, never taking for granted terms like subjectivity, love, truth, knowledge, language, being, desire.

One might object that this theoretical detour risks encompassing the whole spectrum of metaphysical entities. Is it simply that one has replaced earlier discussions of the absurd and the pathos of the human condition with concepts culled from a more sophisticated library? In answer to this objection, what is distinctive with Badiou and Adorno is that they do not bow to the changes of fashion, precisely because they continually historicize Beckett, both in his works and in his reception. They insist on our urgent need to read Beckett, and see him as an author who marks a divide in the history of Western philosophy. Indeed, one could say that for Adorno Beckett occupies the role that Kafka or Schönberg played in his earlier essays. As for Badiou, Beckett takes his place next to his favorite French poets, Rimbaud and Mallarmé. On the whole, Adorno and Badiou presuppose that any respectable intellectual should be conversant with the most minute details of Beckett's *oeuvre*; his *oeuvre* helps readers find their bearings in matters of ethics, dialectics, politics, and why not, more intimate issues of love and beauty. Their efforts aim at producing a speculative accompaniment to purely literary readings and are therefore quite demanding.

Let us assume that Adorno and Badiou suffice, as a beginning, to provide our "B. A. BA to Beckett's philosophers." However, if one compares their interpretations of Beckett, one notes immediately an almost complete reversal in their starting point as their general evaluations evince a dramatic shift from the negative to the positive that will prove to be revealing. Spanning half a century of philosophical discussions of Beckett, their points of departure stand at antipodal ends while emphasizing the exemplarity of Beckett's work. Adorno, writing in the late 1950s and 1960s at the end of a long career,[1] begins with Beckett's negativity, a dialectical negativity that should not be confused with nihilism; Badiou, writing in the late 1980s and 1990s, quickly brushes aside any suggestion of nihilism or negativity in order to stress the purely affirmative character of Beckett's writings.[2] These two philosophical readings of Beckett imply in each case a set of original concepts brought to bear on the texts and called up by the texts themselves. They try to provide exhaustive readings dealing with the entire Beckettian canon grasped in its most general problematic. They manage not to be reductive; that is, Beckett's texts do not turn into mechanical exemplifications of their concepts or hermeneutic programs. In both cases, the philosophical starting point does not elide a certain specificity of art and literature, while working with abstract concepts and not just playing with the signifiers of the texts in a psychoanalytic or deconstructive mode. Adorno and Badiou never allow themselves to be impressed by the mystical autonomy of the text that one finds in Blanchot, for instance. Nevertheless, their interpretive procedures are buttressed on sustained exercises in close reading, Adorno with *Endgame* and later with *The Unnamable*, Badiou with *Sans* and *Worstward Ho*.

Can one pin down the change of tone and philosophical problematic to the fact that they belong to different generations? Badiou, born in 1937, 34 years after Adorno (1903–69), is more aware of the historicity of his reading, and if he never mentions having met Beckett in the flesh, he begins his book on Beckett with an autobiographical account of his first encounter with the works. When he evokes the strong impression left on him then he is aware that this is bound up with the Sartrian context of his youth. Interestingly, this point is also mentioned by Adorno, but in a more negative way; his first long essay on Beckett begins with: "Beckett's oeuvre has many things in common with Parisian existentialism" (1991: 241). But Adorno proceeds to excoriate existentialism. For his part, Badiou explains that he discovered Beckett as a young man, actually barely 20 in the mid-1950s, and also a devoted disciple of Sartre. It was at that time that Beckett left an indelible mark on Badiou, which can be explained in part by his youth.

This is the principal task of youth: to encounter the incalculable, and thereby to convince oneself, against the disillusioned, that the thesis "nothing is, nothing is valuable" is both false and oppressive.

But youth is also that fragment of existence when one easily imagines oneself to be quite singular, when really what one is thinking or doing is what will later be retained as the typical trait of a generation. Being young is a source of power, a time of decisive encounters, but these are strained by their all too easy capture by repetition and imitation. Thought only subtracts itself from the spirit of the age by means of a constant and delicate labor. It is easy to want to change the world – in youth this seems the least that one could do. It is more difficult to notice the fact that this very wish could end up as the material for the forms of perpetuation of this very world. This is why all youth,

as stirring as its promise may be, is always also the youth of a "young cretin". Bearing
this in mind, in later years, keeps us from nostalgia. (Badiou 2003: 37–8)

I have quoted the translation provided by Nina Power and Alberto Toscano in their
invaluable collection of Badiou's complete essays on Beckett. Nevertheless, this fine
translation glosses over Badiou's participation in what came before and after the student's unrest in 1968. A more literal rendering of the ending would be: "Thought
can only avoid being reduced to Zeitgeist by strenuous and delicate labor. It is easy
to want to change the world, as at this time this was *for us* the least one could do. It
is more difficult to realize that this very wish may be nothing but material used by
the forms of the same world's perpetuation." Badiou clearly alludes to his political
commitment, and to a whole generation, the generation that came of age in May
1968. Until recently, he would declare that he was a Maoist philosopher; this passage
contains a discreet admission that he had recanted somewhat, using here the Aristotelian opposition between "form" and "material." He implies that the students' unrest
was nothing but a way for France to catch up with the world at large, impelled by
the historical necessity to enter the homogeneous space of globalized culture. This is
relevant in the context of a discussion that brings in Adorno, as we'll catch a glimpse
of the older philosopher's dismay at being called a "reactionary mandarin" by the
Frankfurt students to whom he had taught critical thinking and negative dialectics.

Regardless of the background against which we situate Badiou's remarks, the
passage implies also that the term "young cretin" can apply to us as well: haven't we
all been young cretins once? Evidently, the term does not spare Samuel Beckett
himself, especially if we think of the young Beckett in the 1930s, a brilliant but
priggish amateur trapped between Dublin and Paris, possessed by the desire to write
without having found a theme, fated as it were to succeed by radically failing first.
Cretins were thought to be the consequence of intermarriages brought about by geographical isolation. At least this was the case, so the story goes, with the hapless
people called "*Crétins des Alpes*," the debilitated offspring of endogamic Alpine communities. They were charitably dubbed "Christians" – or *crétins* – by priests who
wanted to assert that they were no less human for all that. No less charitably, and
with a view to avoid theoretical isolation, I will connect French theory with German
"critical theory" and link schools that are rarely set in dialogue with one another.

Adorno's Negative Aesthetics[3]

Beckett and Adorno did meet a few times, the first occasion being in November 1958,
when Adorno went to Paris to give a series of lectures at the Sorbonne. He called up
Beckett and they had a long discussion on *Godot* and *Endgame* at the Coupole and later
in a Montparnasse restaurant. At this occasion, Adorno jotted down a few condensed
statements that gave, as it were, keys for his reading. Among these, he heard Beckett
making unspecified "reproaches" against Kafka, which tempered his earlier decision

to develop a systematic comparison between the two writers. One of the most revealing notes is this: "Beckett (after Godot). Not abstraction but subtraction" (Tiedemann
1994: 25; all my quotations from this work come from pages 18–77 and are my own
translations.) This is linked with what Adorno shrewdly perceives as Beckett's decision
to debunk existentialism, to reduce philosophy to a string of meaningless clichés. By
so doing, Beckett will radicalize the attempts at subjective foundation provided earlier
by phenomenology. He begins by opposing an "existentialist jargon" that gives a
mystified image of the human condition, since it essentializes it thanks to a "process
of abstraction that is not aware of itself." Fundamentally, Beckett opposes such an
abstract vision of man: "To this kind of unacknowledged process of abstraction,
Beckett poses the decisive antithesis: an avowed process of subtraction" (Adorno 1991:
246). Beckett's work is thus an anti-formalist machine, even if it is based upon a new
concept of form.

It is important to understand this reversal, as this is a point that Badiou will make
again later, but with a different slant. When Adorno sums up existentialism, he has
in mind less Sartre and the then fashionable discourse of existentialism than Heidegger,
whom he was to attack with savage wit and relentless virulence in *The Jargon of
Authenticity* written in 1963–4 (in condensed essay form in Adorno 2003: 162–81)
Beckett's "subtraction" would then oppose the "abstraction" of those who negate
concrete life and its historical determination in the name of a reified concept of existence. Beckett's process of subtraction works with a reduced subject, and this subject
then reduces the abstractions of existentialism to an utterly laughable absurdity. He
derides philosophical abstraction and all the remainders of late modernism by creating
an impasse, a dead end from which one can only be saved by a regressive laughter
that spares nothing.

For Adorno, it would be a mistake to refuse this process in the name of the plenitude of life, as Lukacs attempted to do.

> True to official optimism, Lukacs complains that in Beckett human beings are reduced
> to their animal qualities … Just as it is ridiculous to impute an abstract subjectivist
> ontology to Beckett and then put that ontology on some index of degenerate art, as
> Lukacs does, on the basis of its wordlessness and infantilism, so it would be ridiculous
> to put Beckett on the stand as a star political witness. (Adorno 1991: 247–8).

After he had completed his preparatory work, Adorno announced to his friends that
his essay about Beckett's *Endgame* should be understood as a refutation of Lukacs's
position. The famous Marxist critic was attacking an "absurdist" theater deemed to
be nothing but "petty-bourgeois nihilism." For Adorno, Beckett's supposed apolitical
stance was in fact highly political, and it exposed both the disingenuousness of Marxist
humanism and the sterility of Heidegger's ontological essentialism. In that context,
Adorno can be ferocious: "Adherents of totalitarianism like Lukacs, who wax indig-
nant about the decadence of this truly *terrible simplificateur*, are not ill-advised by the
interest of their bosses. What they hate in Beckett is what they betrayed" (ibid.: 243).

One can follow the transformation from an apolitical Beckett to a figure of resistance to totalitarianism of any kind, and of salutary cynicism facing the complacent illusions of the bourgeoisie about living well without a purpose.

In his jottings, Adorno duly noted that Beckett compared *Endgame* to a chess problem (an endgame): even if all is lost from the beginning, the game has to be played to the end all the same. He registered Beckett's passion for music and rhythm as well: "B. said that his plays were as much music as play, following a purely immanent logic of sequences, not of meaning" (Tiedemann 1994: 24). This must have echoed with Adorno's habit of dotting his copies of Beckett's works with marginal F (*forte*) or FFF (*fortissimo*). Here and there, he voices some incomprehension, and, quite symptomatically, this is about the issue of negativity: "Very enigmatic remark about a kind of positivity contained in pure negativity. In view of such absolute negativity, one could be said to *quasi* live"(ibid.). This last note sums up what is most baffling for Adorno, and this is a point that he will meditate on again and again, teasing out its consequences in various ways. It reappears in the notes that Adorno took in the summer of 1960 about *Endgame*. In all these, we see him pondering the Beckettian paradox of: "Life does not live."

Beckett and Adorno met again in Frankfurt in the spring of 1961 when the latter gave a lecture using the substance of "Trying to understand *Endgame*." This time, Beckett was to have mixed feelings about Adorno; Beckett, always a stickler for literary detail and historical precision, he found to his dismay that although he had explained to Adorno that the name "Hamm" contained no reference to Hamlet, Adorno went on imperturbably and developed his thesis on the links between *Hamlet* and *Endgame*.[4] One can still find this idea in "Trying to understand *Endgame*."[5] From then on, Adorno would embody for Beckett the stereotypical German professor whose watertight architecture of concepts is impervious to facts. This is probably what triggered Beckett's dismissive remark when questioned about *Endgame* in 1967: "*Endgame* will be just play. Nothing less. Don't worry about enigmas and solutions. For these, we have well-equipped universities, churches, cafés du commerce and so on."[6]

In January 1968, Beckett and Adorno met more cordially, for a last time, in Paris where Adorno had come to give a lecture at the Collège de France. He talked for two hours with Beckett. During that conversation, Beckett stated (in English) that his work amounted to a "desecration of silence" (Tiedemann 1994: 25), a phrase which found its way into the pages of *Aesthetic Theory*: "An artwork is, as Beckett wrote, a *desecration of silence*" (Adorno [1970] 1997: 134). Betraying an incipient minimalism, Beckett confided cryptically that everything that mattered in life depended not upon "man's maximum" but on "man's minimum." After the encounter, Adorno left Paris for Cologne, where he participated in a heated discussion of Beckett's works with Martin Esslin and a few others for a German radio network. In the discussion, entitled "It would be criminal to think optimistically," Adorno reiterated the principle of "negative dialectics." Beckett's negativity would be a "determined negation." The phrase is repeated several times at the end when the discussion becomes lost in a cacophonic medley of voices. Adorno never met Beckett again, but wrote to him in

February 1969 announcing his *Aesthetic Theory*'s imminent publication. He added ruefully that he had been shocked at being called a "reactionary" by his own students. In his answer, Beckett tried to reassure him on the issue of the politics of German students: "I have not yet been *conspiré* [an obvious misreading for *conspué*, meaning "booed" or "heckled"] so far as I know and that is not far, by the *Marcusejugend*. As you said to me once at the Iles Marquises [the Paris restaurant where they had dined together], all is *malentendu*. Was ever such rightness joined to such foolishness?" (Tiedemann 1994: 26).

Adorno died soon after, and *Aesthetic Theory* was published posthumously. Among his unfinished projects was a series of marginalia to the *Unnamable* – a novel that he had come to consider as Beckett's masterpiece – followed by the draft of an essay on it. The notes betray a distinctively German slant, pointing to parallels with Brecht, Benn, Kafka, Benjamin, Bloch, Wittgenstein, Hegel. Also Gertrude Stein, James Joyce, and Descartes are each mentioned once. The discussion would have been philosophical indeed, with a new motto: "The path of the novel: reduction of the reduced" ("Die Bahn des Romans: Reduktion des Reduzierten" [ibid.: 38]). The same idea will be pushed further by Badiou: for Adorno as for Badiou, Beckett's method is very close to a Husserlian phenomenological reduction, but it reduces what has already been reduced. Hence, Beckett's method goes back not only to Descartes but to Husserl and to the phenomenological element present in Proust. Indeed, Adorno identifies the speaking "I" of the *Unnamable* with the "I" that one hears at the beginning of Proust's novel: "The 'I' of the beginning and the 'I' of the beginning of *La Recherche*" (Tiedemann 1994: 61). Moreover, like Proust, Beckett strove for a point of confusion or indifferentiation between narrative and theory (ibid.). Unsurprisingly, Adorno still harps on the dialectics of negativity: "L'innommable is the negative subject-object" (ibid.: 67). "With Beckett, positive categories like hope become absolutely negative categories. Hope is hope for nothingness" (ibid.: 44). The last pages of the draft meditate on the specific nature of Beckett's nothing: "Is the nothing only nothing? This is the central issue in Beckett. Absolute rejection, because hope is only where there is nothing to keep. A plenitude of nothing. This is the explanation of his remaining in the zero-point" (ibid.: 73). At least, this emphasis on negativity should refute any imputation of "absurdist" allegiance in Beckett, who, by this time, has nothing more to do with Ionesco.

The draft takes up seven pages only but it is highly condensed and testifies to the seriousness with which Adorno dedicated himself to his task. The essay was to constitute the core of the fourth volume of his *Notes to Literature*. Adorno had also decided to dedicate his forthcoming *Aesthetic Theory* to Samuel Beckett – which highlights his importance to a book that was to crown its writer's critical *oeuvre*, and which can be taken as a point of departure since it condenses Adorno's views on Beckett. Here is a passage that revisits the *Endgame* analysis.

> Beckett's plays are absurd not because of the absence of any meaning, for they would
> be simply irrelevant, but because they put meaning on trial; they unfold its history. His

work is ruled as much by an obsession with positive nothingness as by the obsession with a meaninglessness that has developed historically and is thus in a sense merited, though this meritedness in no way allows any positive meaning to be reclaimed ... Artworks that divest themselves of any semblance of meaning do not thereby forfeit their similitude to language. They enunciate their meaninglessness with the same determinacy as traditional artworks enunciate their positive meaning. Today this is the capacity of art: Through the consistent negation of meaning it does justice to the postulates that once constituted the meaning of artworks. Works of the highest level of form that are meaningless or alien to meaning are therefore more than simply meaningless because they gain their content through the negation of meaning. (Adorno [1970] 1997: 153–4)

Here, Adorno rewrites his earlier essay on *Endgame* and generalizes its conclusions so as to encompass Beckett's main plays. An Aristotelian opposition underpins the analysis of Beckett's main plays. "The negativity of the subject as the true form of objectivity can only be presented in radically subjective form, not by recourse to a purported higher reality ... In all art that is still possible, social critique must be raised to the level of form, to the point that it wipes out all manifestly social content" (ibid.: 250). A similar dialectics of content and form coupled with a Hegelian return of the principle of negativity can be found in the "draft introduction":

In Beckett the negative metaphysical content affects the content along with the form ... A relation, not identity, operates between the negativity of the metaphysical content and the eclipsing of the aesthetic content. The metaphysical negation no longer permits an aesthetic form that would itself produce metaphysical affirmation; and yet this negation is nevertheless able to become aesthetic content and determine the form. (ibid.: 347–8)

The terms used for Beckett throughout remain the same: form determines content and then sublates negativity to another level. What is stressed, therefore, is the domination of parody (in the realm of ideas) and of slapstick comedy in the realm of the theater. An oxymoronic coupling of immobility with dynamism underpins the whole oeuvre. Beckett combines the stymied movements of his characters with a formal dynamism that conjures up an ever-receding horizon of disaster.

One of the consequences of Beckett's exemplary position is that he will have a political impact even when he does not explicitly engage with politics. For Adorno, it was symptomatic that the right-wing junta of colonels who had seized power in Greece banned Beckett's works: "Greece's new tyrants knew why they banned Beckett's plays in which there is not a single political word" (ibid.: 234). This is because Beckett always exemplifies the spirit of resistance in art, a spirit of obstinate ethical perseverance facing barbarism. Such perseverance does not have to shout its name or be explicit. The idea is developed at the end of *Negative Dialectics*:

Beckett has given us the only fitting reaction to the situation left by concentration camps – a situation he never calls by name, as if it were subject to an image ban. What is there, he says, is like a concentration camp. He spoke once of a lifelong death penalty, implying as only hope for the future that there will be nothing any more. This, too, he rejects. From the rift of inconsistency thus found it is the imagery of the Nothing as Something that emerges, and it will then stabilize his poetry. (Adorno 1970: 371–2; trans. 380–1)

The particular negativity deployed by Beckett is not a pure "nothing," since it manages to retain its historical and dialectical properties: "Such nihilism implies the contrary of an identification with nothingness"(ibid.). Beckett would thus, like Paul Celan but with different rhetorical strategies, provide the only possible answer to Adorno's self-imposed quandary: how to write "poetry" after Auschwitz? Let us note here that Adorno, like Badiou, tends to see Beckett's oeuvre as inscribed in the genre of poetry. To write poetry or *Dichtung* after Auschwitz entails a number of paradoxes. In the end, what Adorno finds to praise in Beckett's alleged "nihilism" is that it appears as the opposite of nihilism. Beckett is a "true nihilist" because he opposes the false positivities of a post-Auschwitz moment that saw the restoration of older values in which it is impossible to believe. Even if Badiou brushes off all "negative dialectics," he will find his starting point there as well.

Badiou's Affirmative Logics

Badiou starts from what he saw as a *doxa* in Beckett's reception in the late 1950s: he is "a writer of the absurd, of despair, of empty skies, of incommunicability and of eternal solitude" (Badiou 2003: 38). To reject what he sees as a prevalent negativist view, Badiou inscribes on the back of the cover of his Beckett book a strong disclaimer: "No, Beckett's oeuvre is not what was always said about it – that it was despair, absurdity of the world, anxiety, solitude, decrepitude." This resolute and defiant "No" to nihilism defines the tone of the book on Beckett entitled *Beckett: L'Increvable Désir* (Badiou 1995; I will quote from the English translation in Badiou 2003). This is a user-friendly guide which restates in less technical language the dense pages devoted to Beckett in "The writing of the generic" from 1989. Badiou had devoted a whole chapter to *Worstward Ho* in his *Handbook of Inaesthetics* from 1998 – a condensed book that comes as a rejoinder to Adorno's huge and sprawling *Aesthetic Theory*. As I suggested earlier, Badiou's position had been prefigured in the USA by the groundbreaking essay that Stanley Cavell devoted to *Endgame* in 1964. Cavell's main thesis is that Beckett's play has nothing to do with *Angst* but is to be thought of within the logic of everyday conversation: "The discovery of *Endgame*, both in topic and technique, is not the failure of meaning (if that means the lack of meaning) but its total, even totalitarian success – our inability *not* to mean what we are given to mean" (Cavell 1969: 117). Cavell approaches Beckett via Wittgenstein and Austin, while Badiou refers to Althusser, Lacan, Deleuze, Dedekind, Cantor, and a few others. Now, a book has been published on Badiou and Beckett: Andrew Gibson (2006) is straightforward in his sense that one must understand the whole of Badiou's philosophy to gauge his relevance in the Beckett canon. Gibson's book is honest and courageous, and never tries to hush certain doubts facing Badiou's treatment of Beckett's texts. Gibson even complements Badiou with a few philosophical references of his own, like Françoise Proust, Giorgio Agamben, Jacques Rancière, and Antonio Negri, whom he quotes when he finds Badiou wanting.[7] Fundamentally he follows the path of Badiou, which is conceptual and systematic, and attempts to either find in Beckett's texts or apply to Beckett's texts typical concepts developed by Badiou. The list includes "subtraction, restricted action, actual infinity, the event, subjectification, the logic of appearance, naming, fidelity, apagogic reason, the waiting subject, investigation, inexistents, patience, vigilance, objectivity; undecidables, indiscernibles, and unnameables, *événementialité* or the event of the event" (ibid.: 285). While I cannot help voicing some skepticism as to whether Beckett's work includes *all* these concepts, I will return later to one crucial concept, at least according to Gibson's reading, that of event or *événementialité*, and will focus only the terms directly deployed by Badiou when he tackles Beckett.

The temptation is great to take the book on Beckett as a shortcut leading to the heart of Badiou's philosophy while bypassing all the rather technical allusions to mathematical logic and recondite authors. His point of departure is parallel to that of Adorno since both pay attention to the context of Beckett's reception in the 1950s. Like Adorno in the essay on *Endgame*, Badiou notes affinities between Beckett's works and the theses of existentialism; like him, he refuses this tempting homology in order to go further. If Adorno equates Beckett with Kafka and Schönberg, Beckett belongs to the artists who throne in Badiou's pantheon, next to Mallarmé, not far from Rimbaud, Pessoa, and Celan. These writers all designate crucial theoretical issues better broached by artists than by philosophers. More than a poetological reading of the Irish writer, the philosophical reading provided here places Beckett in a long discursive tradition. Badiou sees Beckett as straddling two schools, phenomenology and classical rationalism: fundamentally wedged between Descartes and Husserl, his writing sets in motion a whole series of gestures calling up Heraclitus, Parmenides, Plato, and Kant. However, Badiou does not forget to pay close attention to the literality or to the exact signifiers of Beckett's texts, which he follows in all their varied and cunning rhetorical strategies.

We saw that there was little nostalgia in the autobiographical opening of the book: Badiou's first response facing Beckett was emblematic of a misreading. The dominant fashion in 1956 was to read Beckett as a nihilist, a pessimist, or an absurdist. Beckett was seen as a dark comedian whose metaphysical clowns wandered under an empty sky, ruminating on an absent god while expressing the despair inherent to man's estate. A little later, he would be portrayed as a modernist for whom language had become the central concern. He was then seen as haunted by the question of pure writing, endlessly restating the aporia of language's opacity and intransitivity. If one tried to compound these views, the Sartrean reading insisted on man as a "useless passion" but forgot the question of language in the name of ethics, commitment, and politics, whereas Blanchot and his followers saw the problematic of silence, negativity, and disappearance as dominant, until the writer's voice would dissolve in the neutral space of post-Hegelian negativity. Accordingly, Badiou's program in the late 1950s aimed at reconciling Sartre's negative ontology with Blanchot's mysticism of a purely self-referential language. Such an endeavor would have meant to "complete the Sartrean theory of freedom through a careful investigation into the opacities of the signifier" (Badiou 2003: 39).

Even today, this might look like a worthwhile pursuit, one could even recommend it as a dissertation topic. However, this now appears to Badiou as misguided, since such a reading program would risk missing or downplaying an essential part in Beckett's trajectory. It would not focus on the ethical imperative of "courage" – the courage to keep on desiring via personal fidelity to certain signifiers. Such an imperative implies a whole ethics of desire, which owes not a little to Lacan's seminar on the ethics of psychoanalysis, while leading toward an aesthetics of Beauty as suggested by Lacan's discussion of Antigone.[8] Thus, the desire for truth and the contemplation of beauty condense for Badiou the most vital impulse in Beckett's works.

Badiou remembers how he had memorized Beckett's most cynical, darkest textual nuggets, how he would quote these sentences while missing the exact import of their irony and their energy. Being too much in love with the prose of *The Unnamable*, he could not see that this was a dead end, for which Beckett paid by several years of silence. Just as Beckett needed some time to overcome the writer's block created by the trilogy, it took Badiou a few years to undo the cliché of Beckett the existentialist absurdist, the nihilist. He had also to refuse the opposite version offered soon after, that is Beckett viewed as a "thin Rabelais" (Badiou 2003: 40) only interested in postmodern derision, sending off literature in a grotesque slaughter of all values. Then he had to reassert the priorities as it were: "Neither existentialism nor a modern baroque. The lesson of Beckett is a lesson of measure, exactitude and courage" (ibid.). Thus it is, above all, an ethical Beckett that Badiou wants to sketch. Beckett would be a writer who teaches something that is fundamentally true about desire, language, being, and humanity. In spite of some obvious moralistic overtones, Badiou does not presuppose a humanistic reading of Beckett. His position owes more to Lacan's uncompromising ethics of unconscious desire. Beckett is thus one of the rare writers who know that it is essential never to yield to one's desire. Such a lesson rings truer when one faces collapse, fiasco, moral perversion, intellectual bankruptcy, and writerly impotence. Beckett's ethical affirmation gives the courage to keep on living and creating precisely because he heaps up quasi impossibilities and difficulties on this path.

Badiou insists squarely on a chronological divide in Beckett's career, which he reads less teleologically than as marked by gaps and dehiscence. Here, even Gibson, usually enthusiastic about Badiou's approach, expresses some reservations. Badiou sees *Texts for Nothing* as marking the termination or the exhaustion of Cartesian solipsism, and assumes that *How It Is* is the sign of a new opening to the Other. As Gibson writes, such a narrative of Beckett's career "reaching a crisis point from which it has to recover" (2006: 186) can be suspected of idealization. Badiou's reading of the *Unnamable* as pure torment and despair misses important elements of irony, parody, and aggression (ibid.: 187). The chronology seeing a break in 1960 followed by a new departure does not accommodate easily those texts on which Adorno insists, such as *Endgame*, begun in 1955, *All that Fall*, written in 1956, and *Krapp's Last Tape*. Badiou simplifies the issue, lumping together all the works leading to the first trilogy which culminates with *The Unnamable*, then assumes a moment of stuttering or quasi silence between *Texts for Nothing* (1950) and *How It Is* (1960). The new departure of *How It Is* would be marked by a new minimalism, followed by an unblocking, leading to daring experiments with the theater and new media like film and television. This would culminate with the second trilogy of *Nohow On*, which, in Badiou's reading, should condense the highest point of Beckett's language and thought.

What is refreshing here is that Badiou refuses to either treat Beckett's oeuvre as a single block, which is, as we have seen, Adorno's temptation, or as a linear progression leading toward formal minimalism so as to fulfill an earlier nihilistic philosophical project (Badiou 2003: 40). Badiou sees Beckett's oeuvre as punctuated by hesitations and caesuras while always underpinned by a set of original abstractions that push forward a phenomenological reduction. Beckett's is an inverse phenomenology to be sure, since it is not just the world and all the objects offered to consciousness that are "reduced," but the subjectivity itself when it is caught in the world. This procedure allows Beckett to offer affirmative statements through poetic variations on a few essential themes. Thus his works cannot be inscribed in any given genre: he blurs the distinction between novel and short story, theatrical play and performance. The progression in his problematic would be underpinned by original answers provided to Kant's three fundamental questions: "Where would I go if I could go?" "What would I be if I could be?" and "What would I say if I had a voice?" (ibid: 41). After the alleged 10-year hiatus, according to Badiou, Beckett added a fourth question concerning other people: "Who am I, if the other exists?" (ibid.).

These four questions are not meant to remain without an answer or aporetic, as most commentators have thought, on the contrary they end up finding an answer and a positive one at that: "In a manner that is almost aggressive, all of Beckett's genius of Beckett tends toward affirmation. He is no stranger to the maxim, which always carries with it a principle of relentlessness and advancement" (ibid.) Typically, Badiou refuses to take Beckett at his word when the latter stresses negative factors when he has to explain his compulsion to write. Shortly before his death, Beckett answered the questionnaire sent to him by *Libération* asking: "Why do you write?" He wired back the most condensed statement possible: "*Bon qu'à ça!*" ("Only good for that" or "That's all I'm good for" would be equivalents.) Following Beckett's own qualification in "Enough": "Stony ground but not entirely" (Beckett 1995: 187), a sentence that he admires and quotes several times, Badiou gently rebukes Beckett: "Not completely, Beckett, not completely! That's all, but not completely!" (ibid.: 42). As Bruno Clément has shown, Badiou adapts a trope that recurs in Beckett, the epanorthosis, or a qualifying modification that rhetorically transforms the meaning of a passage, often pushing it from surface negativity to a quasi positive.[9]

A section from *Ill Seen Ill Said* can be taken as a blueprint: "Was it ever over and done with questions? Dead the whole brood no sooner hatched. Long before. In the egg. Over and done with answering? With not being able. With not being able not to want to know. With not being able. No. Never. A dream. Question answered" (Beckett 1992: 80). Even the passage apparently concludes that there are no answers, it nevertheless answers, precisely by unleashing the verbal energy that heaps precisions, qualifications, rectifications, double negatives, and tangled contradictions. No, indeed, "it" will never end or reach an absolute period. Here is the site explored by Beckett's later prose, a paradoxical space that Badiou starts describing in terms of basic devices or "operations" (Badiou 2003: 44). Badiou concludes that the specific beauty of the work forces us to be responsible to truth and to beauty. Beckett forces us to be more responsible to the "letter of beauty" (ibid.).

How then is this letter written? Badiou shows that Beckett's operations reiterate a "methodical askesis" that goes back to Descartes and Husserl in its wish to "suspend" everything that is inessential – the only rigorous path to reach the real and the true. All the trappings of the clownish humor and the nihilistic elements of despair and anxiety are instrumental in that context. When Beckett reduces human subjects to paralyzed cripples, to mere ectoplasms stuck in a jar, when he wedges Winnie in a hole in *Happy Days* and imagines the narrator of *The Unnamable* as an egg-like sphere with a few apertures, this is a way of returning to a Cartesian and Husserlian *epoché* (ibid.), finally exposing what is truly "generic" in man. Beckett would initiate a systematic and serious investigation of "thinking humanity" (ibid.), and if he proceeds by way of destruction, it is in order to discover what resists, what remains indestructible at the bottom. Such a fundamental indestructibility yields the only stable foundation for ethics. Before, it will have questioned the role of the event, of its meaning and the links between infinity, truth, and the void.

Watt is, for Badiou, a sounding board in that it moves from a Cartesian universe still dominant in *Murphy* to a world in which the enclosure of being in itself does not rule out infinite calculations; it starkly opposes the infinity of serial proliferation to the unique occurrence of an incomprehensible event. This is crucial for Badiou's theory of the event. A chapter entitled "The Event and Its Name" lays down the foundations for what would be Beckett's goal, the investigation of the minimal conditions of freedom, an investigation needed if one wants to know the conditions of possibility of any event, even if this entails hollowing out dominant modes of rationality (ibid.: 55). *Watt* is a novel in which "the prose oscillates between grasping indifferent being and the torture of a reflection without effect" (ibid.: 56). The novel is saved from a "Kafkaian" dead end or a negative theology by foregrounding the emergence of "events" outside the law, events called "incidents" by Watt. They are almost negligible, and the first of these is, as we will recall, simply the arrival of piano tuners, the Galls, who exchange perfunctory remarks and go about their business. We never know why this "event" is chosen among others, yet it provides a conceptual riddle that has to be solved. This is how Beckett reflects on it:

> The incident of the Galls ... ceased so rapidly to have even the significance of two men, come to tune a piano, and tuning it, and exchanging a few words, as men will do, and going, that this seemed rather to belong to some story heard long before, and instant in the life of another, ill-told, ill-heard, and more than half-forgotten.
>
>   So Watt did not know what had happened. He did not care, to do him justice, what had happened. But he felt the need to think that such and such a thing had happened then, the need to be able to say, when the scene began to unroll its consequences, Yes, I remember, that is what happened then. (Beckett 1953 : 71)

This can be taken as a gloss on Badiou's ethics of the event. In order to be an "event," the "incident" or symptomatic "occurrence" has not only to be deployed outside the law but also to question the law. These events are "paradoxical supplements" (Badiou 2003: 56) generically defined, to quote *Watt*, by "great formal brilliance and indeterminate purport" (Beckett 1953: 71). Even when Badiou notices that *Watt* still hovers at the limit of the religious sphere, with a hero obsessed by the need to provide meaning when there is none (Badiou 2003: 57), the novel's main focus is the place of the law. By measuring themselves with an invisible law, Becket's texts reach a structural unnamability: they inevitably encounter a limit or foreclosure of their language.

Watt's foreclosure and disclosure of this law leads to the postulation of a sadistic ethics; it generalizes the "torture" generated by the constant struggle of thought against itself and applies it to other people. Here, a Cartesian *cogito* turned against itself clashes against the perversion of the Kantian law. Badiou often repeats the idea that Beckett's sadism stages the "torture of the cogito" (Badiou 2003: 49, 51, 52–6, 59, 72). Following the insights provided by Adorno and Horkheimer in *Dialectics of Enlightenment*, I have attempted to bring Badiou and Adorno closer by suggesting that *Watt* demonstrates links between Kant's morality, capitalism, technology (Watt was the name of the inventor of the steam engine) and Marquis de Sade's erotic machines (the orgy, a complex montage of bodies that will leave no one idle, sexually speaking) buttressed by a rhetoric of excess and pain (see Rabaté 2004: 71–83 and 2005: 87–108).

This principle of torture opens up to the question of the Other, a question that Beckett would discover later, according to Badiou's chronology. This issue can indeed found to lie at the core of *How It Is*, less a meditation on post-apocalyptic survival than a deployment of everyday-life paradoxes centering on love – defined by Badiou as making two with "ones." This is also Badiou's approach to *Worstward Ho*. He compares the last section of the second trilogy with Heraclitus' poetic maxims, with Plato's *Sophist* or with Mallarmé's *Un Coup de Dés*. The essay devoted to the second trilogy in the *Handbook of Inaesthetics* defines it as a "short philosophical treatise, as a treatment in shorthand of the question of being" (Badiou 2003: 80). Badiou's reading is both intensely abstract and philosophical, all the while managing to use almost only words, concepts, and phrases that are found in Beckett's text. As he generally does, Badiou breaks down *Worstward Ho* in a series of theoretical propositions (Badiou 2003: 81–96). I will sum these up, remaining as close as possible to Badiou's language.

1   "On" signals the "imperative of saying" which the first and only law of the text.

2   Pure being is equated with the "void" in a systematic exercise in disappearance.

3   We are all inscribed in being, as are the emblematic characters of this fiction: the one of a woman, the two of an old man and a child. The universe is a void infested by shades. "Dimness" is the condition of being. Whatever or whoever is inscribed in being is defined as that which can "worsen." Existence is a constant "worsening" brought about by language, since it is always possible to say "worse" or "iller" what has already been said badly. However, the worst that language is capable of can never let itself be captured by an absolute Nothing.

4   Thought is the recollection of (1) and (3), and is produced by a head or a skull in whose confines the old drama of the cogito is being replayed endlessly.

5   The exercises in worsening are of three types or three "shades": they can bear on the one, they can bear on the two, and finally they can bear on the head or brain or skull. In all these exercises in worsening that all testify to the sovereignty of language, addition is equal to subtraction.

6   Worsening is a labor that demands courage, the courage of truth. Since there can be no termination to the process of saying, such courage is founded upon a strong rapport between words and truth.

7   If the void is unworsenable as an absolute limit, nevertheless worsening aims at getting ever closer to the void. The void is crossed by an event that remains always unspeakable.

8   What has been gained by exercises in worsening is, first, a more rigorous definition of the two of love as the root of migration and change and then a sense of joy and beauty deriving from the link between words and truth. Beauty surges when we understand that the path of words goes counter to the demand of thought.

9   Finally, at the end, on the last page, we can go beyond the set-up (*dispositif*) linking being, existence, and thought. There, we witness something like the irruption of an event. It is similar to the "constellation" which appears on the page and in the sky at the end of Mallarmé's *Un Coup de Dés*. "Enough," in the penultimate paragraph, introduces a rupture with what precedes. The old woman has turned into a grave. However, the imperative of language remains and all must begin again. Thus Mallarmé, the French faun, meets Beckett the Irish insomniac.

Once more, the "lesson" is primarily ethical: Beckett exemplifies the courage of a truth to which he testifies in his writings (ibid.: 96). Such courage derives from words themselves, in so far as they keep a link with truth. "The courage of effort is always drawn out against its own destination. Let us call this the torsion of saying: the courage of the continuation of effort is drawn from words themselves, but from words taken against their genuine destination, which is to worsen" (ibid.: 97). This justifies Badiou's strategy, which is to quote the terms provided by Beckett and to rearticulate them in his logical categories. His commentary's length is the double of Beckett's prose poem; it includes it almost entirely, while incorporating it forcibly into his own philosophical system – a rare feat of close reading allied with a radical translation.

The key concept in Badiou, as we have seen, is that of an event, and it is perhaps a problematic idea when one wants to see its emergence in a text. The main idea here is that of a progressive opening of Beckett's text, until it can accept the idea of an event rendered all but impossible in *Watt*: "Little by little – and not without hesitations and regrets – the work of Beckett will open itself up to chance, to accidents, to sudden modifications of the given, and thereby to the idea of happiness. The last words of *Ill Seen Ill Said* are indeed 'Know Happiness'" (ibid.: 55). However, when Badiou comments on *Ill Seen Ill Said*'s moving finale ("First last moment. Grant only enough remain to devour all. Moment by glutton moment. Sky earth the whole kit and boodle. Not another crumb of carrion left. Lick chops and basta. No. One moment more. One last. Grace to breathe that void. Know happiness.") he takes "know happiness" at face value, as if it was a philosophical injunction. One could see it as similar to Murphy's end, a Nothing that is finally met by the character and engulfs all the rest. Isn't the reference to happiness partly ironical since it is coupled with death? Isn't Badiou missing out on the latent ironies and the sense of dark humor that pervade Beckett's text?

A similar authoritarian affirmativeness distinguishes his decision to see the emergence of the "event" on the last page of *Nohow On*. There is a recapitulation of the parameters of existence followed by a sort of explosion.

> But once the recapitulation is complete there brusquely occurs – in a moment introduced by "sudden" – a sort of distancing of this state to a limit position ... there emerges, in a suddenness that amounts to a grace without concept, an overall configuration in which one will be able to say "nohow on." Not an "on" ordained or prescribed to the shades, but simply "nohow on" – the "on" of saying reduced, or leastened, to the purity of its possible cessation. (ibid.: 109–10)

It is true that the penultimate paragraph seems to call up a sudden emergence of something: "Enough. Sudden enough. Sudden all far. No move and sudden all far. All least. Three pins. One pinhole. In dinmost din. Vasts apart. At bounds of boundless void. Whence no farther ..." (Beckett 1992: 128). Let us note that this is not the first time that Beckett uses "sudden" (see, for instance, "Next sudden gone the twain. Next sudden back" [ibid.: 107]). One could praise Badiou's subtle rhetoric and the way in which he uses an intertextual detour via Mallarmé to justify a forced reading, no doubt brought about by his own philosophical problematic, and leave it at that, were it not that the followers of Badiou have taken all too seriously the notion of an extra-textual event that would somehow percolate into the text and leave a "hole" for the emergence of truth.

This may be the case with Andrew Gibson, since he ends up identifying modernity with the event: "The event defines modernity" (2006: 257). As Badiou always insists on the paucity of events, Gibson lists just a few: the French Revolution, Kant, Wordsworth, and, I suppose, Beckett. Gibson at first accepts Badiou's reading of the last page of *Worstward Ho*, only to retreat a little when he suggests that the text could be, after all, just describing the "*événementialité* of the event." Elsewhere, Gibson hedges the thesis, as when he writes that "Beckett's commitments to aporetics is precisely a commitment to a writing that, in the absence of events, produces and sustains a consciousness of *événementialité*" (ibid.: 287). He tries to show that in *Fizzles* 3 Beckett "holds the event at several removes" (ibid.: 289). However, his conclusion still alludes to "the passage about the event in *Ill Seen Ill Said*" (ibid.: 288)

A reader not familiar with Badiou might ask: what is the "event" of which we are we talking? Badiou would refuse the promise of Derrida's hospitality to the Other, or his concept of a time to come defined by a "messianicity without a Messiah" as too religious. The event entails for Badiou a type of fidelity and is often linked with either a political revolution or with a qualitative jump in science. Does it help to put it at a remove, as Gibson does when he talks of the *Unnamable*, for instance: "the arduous fidelity of the Unnamable … is to *événementialité*, the event of the event" (Gibson 2006: 197)? It is here that Adorno could help Badiou, even though it would run against the grain of Badiou's own *Ethics*, a book that staunchly refuses to talk of the Shoah as an absolute or an exception embodying radical evil. For Adorno, indeed, the event has taken place, and it is what he calls "Auschwitz." As we know, Beckett has been decidedly discreet on the topic. Nevertheless, one text at least comes as close as possible to a direct naming of this "event": *Lost Ones*. The ending of the French text of *Le Dépeupleur* is more explicit when it quotes Primo Levi's *Si ce fut un homme* in the last lines: "Voilà en gros le dernier état du cylindre et de ce petit peuple de chercheurs dont un premier si ce fut un homme dans un passé impensable baissa enfin une première fois la tête si cette notion est maintenue" (Beckett 1970: 55).

Surprisingly, Gibson never mentions Primo Levi in his discussion of *The Lost Ones*, whereas the allusion to Levi's *Se quest'un uomo* in *The Lost Ones* has been analyzed at some length by Antoinette Weber-Caflisch in *Chacun son dépeupleur* (1994). Weber-Caflisch glosses the astonishing calculation mistakes in the description of the surface of the cyclinder within which men and women move around. She shows that "*si c'est un homme*" used twice in the last section of the text quotes directly Primo Levi's book *Si c'est un homme (Se quest'un uomo)* (1990: 41–3). The questers, called here the "vanquished," do resemble those concentration camp inmates who had abandoned all hope and who, as Levi narrates, were dubbed "Muslims" by the others still endowed with the will to survive. If this can be called an "event," and if it has something to do with literature, as Adorno always states, it is an "event" that cannot be named directly but only evoked obliquely, silently, by the effects of torsion that it produces on language. Beckett's *Lost Ones* would then come close to Paul Celan's tortured German syntax. This is something that Adorno had seen when describing a paradoxical silence at work in *Endgame*. For him, the play had less to do with the cold war and the hysterical fears of atomic annihilation than with "Auschwitz." The event was such that it could not be named. "The violence of the unspeakable is mirrored in the fear of mentioning it. Beckett kept it nebulous. About what is incommensurable with experience as such one can only speak in euphemisms, the way one speaks in Germany of the murder of the Jews" (Adorno 1991: 245–6). Thus the restraint of a muted reproach impressed Adorno all the more. "Beckett too could claim what Benjamin praised in Baudelaire, the ability to say the most extreme things with the utmost discretion; the consoling platitude that things could always be worse becomes a condemnation" (ibid.: 266). Could the "event" whose conditions of possibility are limned in Beckett's later prose happen both in the future and in the past?

The answer to this question depends upon the kind of subjectivity that we imagine behind the condemnation. Badiou and Adorno meet when they see this subjectivity as the end product of a long "torture" associated with Western rationality. Moreover, Adorno seems to have anticipated Agamben when he talks of reducing subjects to mere existence or "bare life" in "Trying to Understand *Endgame*": "He extends the line taken by the liquidation of the subject to the point where it contracts into a 'here and now,' a 'whatchamacallit,' whose abstractness, the loss of all qualities, literally reduces ontological abstractness *ad absurdum*, the absurdity into which mere existence is transformed when it is absorbed into naked self-identity" (ibid.: 246). Or, again, in *Aesthetic Theory*, about Beckett's novels: "they present the reduction of life to basic human relationships, that minimum of existence that subsists *in extremis*" (Adorno [1970] 1997: 30). Finally, if one is to speak of an event, or of the mere possibility of events, it seems to me that Adorno makes better sense, at least in so far as Beckett's oeuvre is concerned.

Conclusion

Can one think the unthinkable and attempt to approach Beckett both via Badiou and Adorno together? I tried to point out points of convergence: the concept of reduction or subtraction, the anti-dialectical dialectics of a Nothing that reverts to a positive affirmation, the insight that Beckett bridges the gap between ontology and ethics. Taken from another angle, Adorno's critical legacy will be severely tested if we focus on the later Beckett. Adorno praised the heroism of modernist artists who rejected a bourgeois mass culture dominated by kitsch. Beckett follows after Schönberg and Kakfa who debunk the shallowness of late capitalism and its alienated and commodi-fied culture. This view has led to a misunderstanding about modernism that is preva-lent among German critics. The myth is that high modernism is by nature opposed to popular culture, hence is "elitist" and reactionary. Still adhering to Adorno's point of departure, the socio-critical attack on modernism blamed for its elitism became the hallmark of German-oriented critics like Peter Bürger and Andreas Huyssen. If their analyses are more relevant when dealing with German culture, the great divide that they see splitting high modernism from a feminized mass culture loses its edge as soon as we deal with Anglo-American-Irish modernism, as any reader of *Ulysses* and *The Waste Land* will know.

Yet we cannot bracket off the discussion between Adorno and Walter Benjamin on the topic of mass culture, film, and trash. Benjamin's task had been to redeem the trash of history (especially in the culture of Paris in the nineteenth century) via his own brand of "magical materialism." In this important dialogue, Beckett would appear closer to Benjamin than to Adorno. He stands out as a defiant bearer of negativity who debunks a world dominated by the ethical entropy of late capitalism, *and* he identifies his characters with the trash of a debased culture. He moves between the remnants of a tattered classical culture that he mercilessly parodies *and* he may well be the embodiment of a latter-day Platonist capable of giving us reasons to believe in the Good and the Beautiful, as Badiou claims. If *Aesthetic Theory* leaves us a portrait of Beckett as a paradoxical negativist it is because Beckett allowed Adorno a doubly posthumous reconciliation with Walter Benjamin – and Badiou could broker the reconciliation:

> The *"Il faut continuer,"* the conclusion of Beckett's *The Unnamable,* condenses this antinomy to its essence: that externally art appears impossible while immanently it must be pursued ... The political significance, however, which the thesis of the end of art had thirty years ago, as for instance indirectly in Benjamin's theory of reproduction, is gone; incidentally, despite his desperate advocacy of mechanical reproduction, in conversation Benjamin refused to reject contemporary painting: Its tradition, he argued, must be preserved for times less somber than our own ... But the function of art in the totally functional world is its functionlessness; it is pure superstition to believe that art could intervene directly or lead to an intervention. The instrumentalization of art sabotages its opposition to instrumentalization; only where art respects its own immanence does it convict practical reason of its lack of reason. (Adorno [1970] 1997: 320–1)

Here, Adorno identifies in Beckett's work a refusal of the idea of progress – a refusal duly allegorized by the lack of movement in his plays. Here is a passage that can be brought closer to Agamben:

> The gesture of walking in place at the end of *Godot,* which is the fundamental motif of his work, reacts ... to this situation. Without exception his response is violent. His work is the extrapolation of a negative καιρός. The fulfilled moment reverses into perpetual repetition that converges with desolation. His narratives, which he sardonically calls novels, no more offer objective descriptions of social reality than – as the widespread misunderstanding supposes – they present the reduction of life to basic human relationships, that minimum of existence that subsists *in extremis*. These novels do, however, touch on fundamental layers of experience *hic et nunc* which are brought together into paradoxical dynamic at a standstill. (ibid.: 30)

Adorno, for all his stress on dialectics and negativity, seems to agree here with Badiou. It is not a coincidence that this should occur at a moment when the expression of "dialectics at a standstill," an expression used repeatedly by Walter Benjamin to define his method in the *Arcades Project*, is echoed by Adorno in his evocation of Beckett's program. Moreover, Adorno, like Badiou, understands that the act of thinking is similar to music for Beckett, and that this does not entail a total adherence to Schopenhauerian mysticism. If the "music of thinking" stresses form more than content, it is a "brilliant" form capable of opening holes in knowledge. Such a deliberately twisted or halted development dynamizes the dialectics of its own images in order to criticize the foundation of our belief in humanity's progress. The text thinks its own form and makes it become almost radiant, furthering new concepts and chains of reasoning. In a similar vein, Badiou stresses that Beckett's texts always "think," even when they seem to play the bow and the fiddle of metaphysical *ritournelles* (to use Deleuze's and Guattari's term). As long as these texts assert the force of desire they allow us to understand that "words go counter to the demands of thought," while signaling the unremitting power of beauty through words.

NOTES

1   His most systematic confrontation with Beckett was to remain posthumous – it appeared in *Aesthetic Theory* (Adorno [1970] 1997).

2   His first lecture on Beckett, which contains all the theses on Beckett further elaborated in later works, was given in June 1989 as "Samuel Beckett: L'Ecriture du Générique et l'Amour" (see Badiou 1989).

3   This subtitle quotes the title of Marc Jimenez's excellent introduction to Adorno's aesthetics (Jimenez 1983). Beckett is often mentioned in this book which gives a good survey of the debates in the late seventies about the role of negativity in art and cultural politics. They would dominate in Paris at the time Badiou was elaborating his own "inaesthetics," and tried to start from a radically different point of view. Jimenez (ibid.: 250–1) quotes a book by P. V. Zima (1978) in which a discussion opposing Adorno and Lucien Goldmann about

the "positivity" or "negativity" of Beckett's *oeuvre* was a key moment.

4   See Siegfried Unseld's account, as reported by James Knowlson (1996: 428).

5   In a very muted manner, to be true (see Adorno 1991: 267).

6   This is my translation of: "*Endspiel* wird blosses Spiel sein. Nichts weniger. Von Rätseln und Lösungen also kein Gedanke. Es gibt für solches ernstes Zeug Universitäten, Kirchen, Cafés du Commerce usw" (Beckett 1983: 114).

7   "Agamben, Rancière, and Proust all shed an important light on a dimension of Beckett's work that Badiou conspicuously neglects." (Gibson 2006: 284).

8   I have discussed this in *Jacques Lacan: Psychoanalysis and the Subject of Literature* (Rabaté 2001: 69–84).

9   See Clément 1994 for an analysis of this recurrent trope.

REFERENCES

Adorno, Theodor W. (1970). *Negative Dialektik*. Frankfurt: Suhrkamp. [English translation *Negative Dialectics*, trans. E. B. Ashton, New York: Seabury 1973.]

Adorno, Theodor W. (1991). "Trying to Understand *Endgame*," *Notes to Literature*, Vol. 1, trans. Shierry Weber Nicholsen. New York: Columbia University Press.

Adorno, Theodor W. [1970] (1997). *Aesthetic Theory*, ed. Gretel Adorno and Rolf Tiemann, trans. Robert Hullot-Kentor. Minneapolis: University of Minnesota Press.

Adorno, Theodor W. (2003). *Can One Live after Auschwitz? A Philosophical Reader*, ed. Rolf Tiedemann. Stanford: Stanford University Press.

Arsic, Branka (2003). *The Passive Eye: Gaze and Subjectivity in Berkeley (via Beckett)*. Stanford: Stanford University Press.

Badiou, Alain (1989). *Samuel Beckett: L'Ecriture du Générique et l'Amour*. Paris: Editions du Perroquet.

Badiou, Alain (1995). *Beckett: L'Increvable désir*. Paris: Hachette.

Badiou, Alain (2003). "Tireless Desire." In *On Beckett*, ed. and trans. Alberto Toscano and Nina Power. Manchester: Clinamen Press.

Beckett, Samuel (1953). *Watt*. London: John Calder.

Beckett, Samuel (1970). *Le Dépeupleur*. Paris: Minuit.

Beckett, Samuel (1983). *Disjecta: Miscellaneous Writings and a Dramatic Fragment*. London: John Calder.

Beckett, Samuel (1992). "Ill Seen Ill Said." In *Nohow On*. New York: John Calder.

Beckett, Samuel (1995). *The Complete Short Prose 1929–1989*. Grove Press: New York.

Cavell, Stanley (1969). "Ending the Waiting Game: A Reading of Beckett's *Endgame*." In *Must We Mean What We Say?* New York: Charles Scribner's Sons.

Clément, Bruno (1994). *L'Oeuvre sans qualités: Rhétorique de Samuel Beckett*. Paris: Seuil.

Deleuze, Gilles (1997a). "The Greatest Irish Film," trans. Daniel W. Smith and Michael A. Greco. In Daniel W. Smith and Michael A. Greco (eds.), *Essays Critical and Clinical*. Minneapolis: University of Minnesota Press.

Deleuze, Gilles (1997b). "The Exhausted," trans. Anthony Uhlmann. In Daniel W. Smith and Michael A. Greco (eds.), *Essays Critical and Clinical*. Minneapolis: University of Minnesota Press.

Gibson, Andrew (2006). *Beckett and Badiou: The Pathos of Intermittency*. Oxford: Oxford University Press.

Jimenez, Marc (1983). *Vers une esthétique négative: Adorno et la Modernité*. Paris: Le Sycomore.

Knowlson, James (1996). *Damned to Fame: The Life of Samuel Beckett*. New York: Simon and Schuster.

Levi, Primo (1990). *Si c'est un homme*, trans. Martine Schruoffeneger. Paris: Julliard.

Rabaté, Jean-Michel (2001). *Jacques Lacan: Psychoanalysis and the Subject of Literature*. Houndmills: Palgrave.

Rabaté, Jean-Michel (2004). "*Watt*/Sade: Beckett et l'humain à l'envers." In Marie-Christine Lemardeley, Carle Bonnafous-Murat and André Topia (eds.), *L'Inhumain*. Paris: Presses Sorbonne Nouvelle.

Rabaté, Jean-Michel (2005). "Unbreakable B's: from Beckett and Badiou to the Bitter End of Affirmative Ethics." In Gabriel Riera (ed.), *Alain Badiou: Philosophy and Its Conditions*. Albany: SUNY Press.

Tiedemann, Rolf (1994). "'Gegen den Trug der Frage nach dem Sinn': Eine Dokumentation zu Adornos Beckett-Lektüre." *Frankfurter Adorno Blätter III*. Munich: Edition Text+Kritik.

Weber-Caflisch, Antoinette (1994). *Chacun son dépeupleur: Sur Samuel Beckett*. Paris: Éditions de Minuit.

Zima, P. V. (1978). *Pour une sociologie du texte littéraire*. Series 10/18. Paris: Union Générale d'Editions.

9
Beckett and Ethics

Shane Weller

Ethical Beckett

Within the ever-expanding field of Beckett studies there have been numerous attempts to treat the question of "Beckett and philosophy," "Beckett and psychology," and, more recently, "Beckett and politics." A conspicuous absentee from this list has been "Beckett and ethics." It would certainly be a mistake, however, to assume that commentators have simply neglected or avoided the question of the ethical in Beckett. Indeed, for all the changes in intellectual fashion, from existentialism to post-structuralism to the mathematical ontology of Alain Badiou, to name just three influential approaches to Beckett since the early 1950s, the ethicality or otherwise of his oeuvre has remained an abiding critical preoccupation.

For reasons that lie only partly in the nature of his works, attempts to address the ethical in Beckett have tended to begin with whether or not those works are "nihilist" in their orientation. Maurice Nadeau, one of the very first critics in France to write on Beckett, argues in his April 1951 review of *Molloy* (1951) that, for Beckett, the human being is thrown into "the world of the Nothing where some nothings which are men move about for nothing" (Graver and Federman 1979: 53). Less than a year later, in his March 1952 review of *Malone meurt* (1951), Nadeau proceeds to describe Beckett's novels as "nihilist." It should be noted, however, that the label "nihilist" is certainly not intended by Nadeau as a criticism of Beckett; indeed, Beckett's "nihilism" is, for Nadeau, an achievement, a veritable "conquest of Nothingness" (Graver and Federman 1979: 78). Since Nadeau's early reviews the debate on whether or not Beckett's works are nihilist has continued unabated, although it has to be said that almost all the major commentators have insisted that, far from being nihilist, Beckett's oeuvre is in fact anti-nihilist (on this influential critical tradition, see Weller 2005). Among the more recent advocates of this position is Alain Badiou, who claims that "Beckett will *never* be a nihilist" (Badiou 2003: 15).

"Nihilism" is, however, a highly problematical term with a long and complex history, and commentators on Beckett have certainly meant very different things by it. For some, nihilism is to be understood as the doctrine that nothingness is the ultimate reality; for others, it consists in a rejection of all possible determination of value, not least ethical value. In John Burnet's *Greek Philosophy* (1914), a work on which Beckett himself took copious notes in the early 1930s, these two basic forms of nihilism are labeled "cosmological nihilism" and "ethical nihilism," the former being associated with the pre-Socratic philosopher Gorgias of Leontini, and the latter with the pre-Socratics Kallikles and Thrasymachos (see Burnet 1914: 121–2).

Rather than entering into a consideration of whether or not Beckett's oeuvre is in fact the expression of "cosmological" and/or "ethical" nihilism as defined in Burnet, it might seem more appropriate to quote Beckett's own well-known remark on the subject of nihilism: "I simply cannot understand why some people call me a nihilist. There is no basis for that" (Beckett in Büttner 1984: 122). This statement has understandably often been deployed by commentators attempting to demonstrate not only that Beckett's oeuvre is not nihilist but that it is in fact anti-nihilist. As I hope to demonstrate in what follows, however, Beckett's relation to nihilism, both "cosmological" and "ethical," is considerably more complex than the statement recorded by Büttner suggests.

From at least as early as the 1950s, then, Beckett has been read not only in relation to the ethical, but as a writer whose work is essentially ethical in nature. Early French commentators such as Nadeau tend to take a broadly existentialist line, finding in Beckett an idiosyncratic form of existentialist ethics. To give just one example of this approach, Jean Pouillon argues, like Nadeau before him, that Beckett presents his readers with an "absurd" and "meaningless" reality, but, more explicitly than Nadeau, Pouillon makes clear the ethical dimension by claiming that *Molloy* "offers a morality, the most classical one, that of an absolute, almost scientific conscience." This "classical" morality would lie, according to Pouillon, in Molloy's being "a man who refuses to play," a figure who holds that "one should do no more than see, although without imagining that one then sees something" (Graver and Federman 1979: 66–7). Put slightly differently, Molloy is, for Pouillon, a kind of *résistant*, someone who refuses to collaborate with that absurd world into which he has been thrown. Such passive resistance is an ethical stance in that it would constitute the only kind of freedom remaining to the human being – or, more precisely, to what Beckett himself, in an unbroadcast radio script of 1946, terms "humanity in ruins" (Beckett 1995: 278).

In the course of the 1950s, Beckett continues to be considered within a broadly existentialist frame, with the emphasis falling as much on the ethical as it does on the ontological side of existentialism. Thus, for instance, in her March 1956 review of *Nouvelles et Textes pour rien* (1955), Geneviève Bonnefoi argues that while Beckett's "major obsessions" include decrepitude, death, and solitude, the "I" in his prose texts exhibits an "extreme exigency of truth." This exigency is located above all in the relentless attempts made by this "I" to grasp itself, despite its recognition of the impossibility of any such grasping. The exigency at work here, Bonnefoi concludes, constitutes "the honor of Samuel Beckett at a time when literature is all too often an inconsequential game" (Graver and Federman 1979: 144). In existentialist terms, Beckett's works would exhibit an exemplary authenticity: his protagonists would commit themselves knowingly to the impossible, enduring that aporia generated by both the need to grasp the essential self and the impossibility of so doing. And, indeed, such commitment would not be limited to Beckett's hapless protagonists; his art as a whole might be seen to commit itself to the impossible by seeking time after time to "eff" the "ineffable," as it is put in *Watt* (1953). While such an art may be "doomed to fail, doomed, doomed to fail" (Beckett 1976: 61), its ethicality would lie precisely in this failure. Beckett's statement in the last of the *Three Dialogues* (1949) that "to be an artist is to fail, as no other dare fail" (Beckett 1965: 125) may be read, then, as a statement concerning the ethics of art as such.

An existentialist ethics – closer to Camus than to Sartre – is not the only kind of ethics to have been identified by early commentators on Beckett. Another, no less influential, ethicalizing reading finds early expression in Alfred Simon's December 1963 review of *Oh les beaux jours* (1963). Simon proposes a Gnostic Beckett, in key respects closer to Kafka than to either Camus or Sartre. According to Simon, "The evil God weighs heavy upon Beckett's universe. It is the dead God. God has killed himself out of wickedness, out of hatred of man" (Graver and Federman 1979: 270). For Simon, then, the world of Beckett's works is the creation of an evil God, and is itself evil. It is essentially a world of endless, meaningless suffering, of torturers and victims, with each individual playing both roles. In such a universe, the only ethical action becomes a complete negation of being.

In fact, Simon's Gnostic Beckett is anticipated by Theodor Adorno, who benefited from conversations with Beckett prior to the writing of his now celebrated lecture on *Endgame*, delivered in Frankfurt am Main, in Beckett's presence, on February 27, 1961. Adorno opens the published version of this lecture with the claim that, while Beckett's oeuvre "has many things in common with Parisian existentialism," Beckett in fact "dismisses existentialist conformity, the notion that one ought to be what one is" (Adorno 1991: 241). In *Negative Dialectics* (1966), Adorno proceeds to substitute an essentially Gnostic Beckett for the existentialist Beckett:

> To Beckett, as to the Gnostics, the created world is radically evil, and its negation is the chance of another world that is not yet. As long as the world is as it is, all pictures of reconciliation, peace, and quiet resemble the picture of death. The slightest difference between nothingness and coming to rest would be the haven of hope, the no man's land between the border posts of being and nothingness. Rather than overcome that zone, consciousness would have to extricate from it what is not in the power of the alternative. The true nihilists are the ones who oppose nihilism with their more and more faded positivities, the ones who are thus conspiring with all extant malice, and eventually with the destructive principle itself. Thought honors itself by defending what is damned as nihilism. (Adorno 1973: 381)

Adorno certainly considers Beckett's oeuvre to have been "damned as nihilism" – even if, as we have seen, it was also celebrated as nihilism – and that oeuvre is undoubtedly honored by Adorno. Above all, Adorno champions Beckett's works for what he sees as their unrelenting resistance of positivism, their refusal to offer us anything but a negative image of "reconciliation" (*Versöhnung*), by which Adorno means that which "would release the nonidentical, would rid it of coercion, including spiritual coercion; it would open the road to the multiplicity of different things and strip dialectics of its power over them" (Adorno 1973: 6). For Adorno, the "destructive principle" that Beckett resists is quite simply the principle of identity. By refusing to give in to the lure of identity-thinking, by insisting in work after work on the non-coincidence of the subject with itself, and thus upon that subject's irreducible openness to alterity, Adorno's Beckett produces the only possible ethical art in the post-Holocaust age of total administration. As an art of impotence, Beckett's works would stage the failure of any integrative, totalizing program, the failure of any dream of mastery, even a mastery of the negative: for, according to Adorno, even the nothing fails to coincide with itself in Beckett, leaving open what Adorno describes as a "haven of hope" for the future.

Just as Adorno's ethical Beckett shares much with the existentialist Beckett, so his ethicalizing reading anticipates in a number of key respects the broadly deconstructive approach to Beckett that finds expression in the Anglo-American world, in, among others, Connor (1988), Hill (1990b), Trezise (1990), Begam (1996), and Critchley (1997). Although there are certainly some important distinctions to be made between these commentators' takes on Beckett, and although they do not all refer explicitly to the ethicality of Beckett's works, it is nonetheless the case that for each of them Beckett's oeuvre proves to be governed by an ethics of alterity or difference, which is to say by an irreducible openness not just to the other but to the other *in its value*. Hill formulates this position most succinctly when he claims that an attentive reading of Beckett will discover "the power of Beckett's commitment to an ethics of writing, his respect for the trace of otherness, the alterity and difference at the heart of assumed identity that, for Beckett, was what was at stake in literature" (Hill 1990a).

In an irony of literary-critical history that certainly warrants analysis, Adorno's argument on the ethicality of Beckett's oeuvre also anticipates the position taken by Alain Badiou, whose reading of Beckett is prefaced by a radical rejection not only of the existentialist approach to Beckett but also what might broadly be called the post-structuralist approach, which arguably first finds expression in Maurice Blanchot's celebrated 1953 essay on the trilogy (see Blanchot 2003). According to Badiou, in the critical analysis of Beckett there has long been an "alliance between nihilism and the imperative of language, between vital existentialism and the metaphysics of the word, between Sartre and Blanchot" (Badiou 2003: 39). Badiou declares himself to be "entirely opposed to the widely held view according to which Beckett moved towards a nihilistic destitution" (ibid.: 55).

Badiou's Beckett is ethical in two key respects. First, "all of Beckett's work" is tied together by the "question of love" or the *"existence of the Two"* (ibid.: 5). Within this unity, however, Badiou identifies a fundamental division: "Beckett's evolution goes from a programme of the One – obstinate trajectory or interminable soliloquy – to the pregnant theme of the Two, which opens out onto infinity" (ibid.: 17). For Badiou, it is above all in *Comment c'est* (1961) and the works that come after it – especially *Assez* (1965), a text "devoted to love" (Badiou 2003: 30) – that Beckett explores this "pregnant theme." Beckett's treatment of love is to be radically distinguished from the romantic treatment of it in that Beckett never makes a One of the Two: "Love [in Beckett] is never either fusion or effusion" (ibid.: 28). This passage from the One to the Two is the passage from "solipsism to the infinite multiplicity of the world" (ibid.: 31). Within the category of "love," Badiou includes the many "pseudocouple[s]" (to use the term deployed by Beckett in *The Unnamable*: see Beckett 1959: 299) that populate both his prose and his drama: these include Mercier and Camier, Vladimir and Estragon, Hamm and Clov, Winnie and Willie, and Listener and Reader, to name only a few. Badiou does not worry unduly over the possibility that these "pseudocouples" are often violently homo-fraternal in nature, or that they tend to be governed by the endlessly reversible principle of desire – that is, love and hate – which Beckett found stated in both Racine and Sade, and which, in a letter of December 29, 1957 to the director Alan Schneider, he expressed as "*nec tecum nec sine te*" (neither with you nor without you) (Beckett 1998: 24).

Secondly, Badiou finds in Beckett an "ethic of truth," the fundamental imperative of which is "Keep going!" (*Continuez*). Crucially, this keeping going is to be distinguished from a mere "perseverance of being" (Badiou 2001: 91). Indeed, according to Badiou, "all of Beckett's genius tends towards affirmation" (Badiou 2003: 41). In what is only an apparent paradox, this affirmation is achieved through a labor of negation – that is, an ascetic or subtractive operation, functioning in a manner akin to Cartesian doubt and accomplishing the writing of a "generic humanity," beyond all local (including sexual) differences, and determined by three basic functions: going, being, and saying.

From this necessarily brief survey of the critical reception of Beckett since the early 1950s, then, we can see that the question of the ethical has indeed remained absolutely central, with an existentialist ethics of authenticity being replaced by a poststructuralist ethics of alterity or difference, and this in turn being replaced by an ethics of truth. Such a concern with the ethical is arguably more than justified in Beckett's case, since, as we shall see in the next section, Beckett himself exhibits a preoccupation with the relation between art and ethics throughout his writing life. That said, we shall also see that the ethicalizing reading of Beckett carried out by all of the above commentators entails the avoidance of a complication in Beckett's own treatment of the ethical.

The Ethics of Negation and Affirmation

In his first book publication, the 1931 monograph on Proust, Beckett insists that there can be no relation at all between art and morality. In À *la recherche du temps perdu*, he argues, "Proust is completely detached from all moral considerations. There is no right and wrong in Proust nor in his world. (Except possibly in those pages dealing with the war, when for a space he ceases to be an artist and raises his voice with the plebs, mob, rabble, canaille)" (Beckett 1965: 66–7). Over 40 years later, in response to Charles Juliet's claim that the "artistic enterprise is inconceivable without rigorous ethical standards urgently upheld," Beckett observes: "What you say is correct. But moral values are not accessible and not open to definition. To define them, you would have to make value judgements, and you can't do that. That's why I have never agreed with the idea of the theatre of the absurd. Because that implies making value judgements" (Beckett in Juliet 1995: 148–9). In this later statement, Beckett appears to elide the important distinction between morality and ethics: while Juliet refers to "ethical standards," Beckett speaks only of "moral values." And, in fact, while he will continue to believe that art can have nothing to do with morality, Beckett certainly does not separate art and ethics in any simple fashion. Indeed, he concerns himself from very early on in his writing life with the relation between art and ethics, and with the possibility and the nature of an ethical art. Above all, it will, for Beckett, be a question of an ethics of negation and an ethics of affirmation.

That negation is almost everywhere in Beckett scarcely requires emphasis. Indeed, his entire oeuvre might be seen as one long labor of negation. To give just a few examples: the Belacqua of Beckett's first novel, *Dream of Fair to middling Women* (written in 1931–2), seeks to withdraw into the "wombtomb"; in his first published novel, *Murphy* (1938), Murphy idolizes Mr Endon for his having accomplished a seemingly complete withdrawal from the "outer reality"; many of the later novels, plays, and short prose explore the workings – or, more precisely, the unworkings – of what Freud terms the "death drive" (*Todestrieb*); *Ill Seen Ill Said* (1982) ends with a plea for "Grace to breathe that void. Know happiness" (Beckett 1982: 59); while *Stirrings Still* (1988) ends "Oh all to end" (Beckett 1995: 265). Negativity in Beckett also often takes the form of murderous violence, not least in *Molloy* (1951) and *Endgame* (1957). There can be no doubt that Sade, whose *Les 120 Journées de Sodome* Beckett read in early 1938 and by which he was very impressed, exerts an influence on Beckett's oeuvre, not least on *Comment c'est*. Surprising as it may seem, this does not necessarily mean that Beckett is engaged in a critique of violence as such. Indeed, even the least palatable forms of negation in Beckett may be said to fall within a general conception of an ethics of negation.

Beckett encountered the theory of just such an ethics of negation in Schopenhauer's *The World as Will and Representation*, which he first read in the summer of 1930. In a July 1930 letter to Thomas MacGreevy, Beckett declares that Schopenhauer warrants attention not for his "philosophy" but rather for his "intellectual justification of unhappiness – the greatest that has ever been attempted" (quoted in Knowlson 1996: 118). What Beckett found in Schopenhauer was a theory of life as an endless oscillation between suffering and boredom, neither of which has any value. For Schopenhauer, the Kantian "Thing-in-Itself" (or noumenon) becomes the will (*Wille*), constantly at war with itself in the phenomenal realm of representation (*Vorstellung*). The first step, according to Schopenhauer, is to recognize this situation; that is, to overcome the "the egotistical distinction" within the phenomenal realm between self and other by recognizing their identity. Torturer and victim are in fact one and the same. Having seen through the "veil of Maya" that deludes us into distinguishing subject and object, the individual comes to take "as much interest in the sufferings of other individuals as in his own" (Schopenhauer 1969: 378).

This recognition of life as pointless suffering and of the unity of the will is not enough, however. There is, Schopenhauer argues, another crucial step to be taken, namely the denial (*Verneinung*) of the will. According to Schopenhauer, it is not least the artist who can achieve such a denial, although art itself remains only an "occasional consolation" (*einstweilen ein Trost*) (Schopenhauer 1969: 267). A complete negation of the will can be achieved only by those saintly figures who withdraw altogether from the phenomenal realm, including the still sensuous realm of art. What remains for them is precisely "nothing."

For Schopenhauer, the denial of the will is ultimately an ethical obligation, since it is the only path towards the reduction of suffering and the achievement of true happiness. In *Proust*, which he wrote shortly after reading Schopenhauer, Beckett redefines original sin as "the sin of having been born," for which life becomes the "expiation" (Beckett 1965: 67). This he derives from Calderón's *Life is a Dream* by way of Schopenhauer. The ethical negation of the will finds its clearest expression in *Proust*, however, when Beckett refers to "the wisdom of all the sages, from Brahma to Leopardi, the wisdom that consists not in the satisfaction but in the ablation of desire" (ibid.: 18). It should also be borne in mind that it is in Schopenhauer that Beckett encounters that Gnosticism which Adorno detects in Beckett's own work: that is, the conception of being as radically evil, and the ethical response to this evil a negation of being as such, and thus the pursuit of the nothing. In short, then, Schopenhauer introduces Beckett to what might be termed a kind of ethical nihilism.

The ethics of negation that Beckett encounters in Schopenhauer is complemented by a similar ethics in a number of his other readings of the 1930s, above all Thomas à Kempis's *De Imitatione Christi* and Arnold Geulincx's *Ethica* (1675). As John Pilling has established, Beckett probably read Kempis's *De Imitatione Christi* in August–September 1931, and took notes on this text in his *"Dream" Notebook*. While undoubtedly impressed by Kempis's claim that "He who knows the secret of enduring will enjoy the greatest peace" (a phrase that is boxed in the *"Dream" Notebook* and quoted in an important letter of March 10, 1935 to Thomas MacGreevy; see Beckett 1999: 85), Beckett undertakes what C. J. Ackerley describes as a secularization of Kempis's Christian quietism, substituting "self" for "God" and "goodness," and theorizing in the letter to MacGreevy his own "abject self-referring quietism." In the same letter, he goes on to state that he "cannot see how 'goodness' is to be made a foundation or a beginning of anything" (quoted in Ackerley 2000: 85).

As Mark Nixon has observed, after his extended reflections on Thomas à Kempis in the above letter to MacGreevy, Beckett's "pursuit of the quietist question resurfaces in his admission to Arland Ussher in March 1936 that his interest in Geulincx is based on '*his* fourth cardinal virtue, Humility'" (Nixon 2006: 265, quoting from

Beckett's letter to Ussher of March 25, 1936). In Geulincx, a summary of whose philosophy he had already encountered in Wilhelm Windelband's (1893) *History of Philosophy* (which he read in 1932), and whose *Ethica* he read in early 1936, Beckett found a radicalization of Descartes's founding distinction between mind and body. Rejecting any possible communication between the two, Geulincx maintains that "I [as mind or soul] am a mere spectator of this machine [the body or world], whose workings I can neither adjust nor readjust; wherein I neither devise nor destroy anything: the whole thing is someone else's affair" (Geulincx 1999: 25). Given this radical separation, ethical behavior will take the form of humility (*humilitas*), giving up all claim to that over which one can have no power. According to Geulincx, humility involves: (1) the inspection of oneself (*inspectio sui*), and (2) contempt for oneself (*despectio sui*). The ethical imperative at which Geulincx arrives, and which Beckett cites approvingly in *Murphy*, is: "*Ubi nihil vales, ibi nihil velis*" (where you are worth nothing, there you should want nothing) (Beckett 1938: 178). In Beckett's novel, it is in the world of the body that one is worth nothing, and it is from that world and its needs that Murphy attempts to withdraw. As Ackerley observes, Kempis and Geulincx are "reconciled in their renunciation of the will and affirmation of humility" (Ackerley 2000: 87).

The importance of Geulincx to Beckett more generally is clear from the latter's remark in a letter of June 14, 1967 to Sighle Kennedy that were he (Beckett) to find himself in the "unenviable position" of having to study his own work, one of his two "points of departure" would be Geulincx's "Ubi nihil vales, ibi nihil velis." The other, he writes, would be the "Naught is more real ..." of Democritus of Abdera (see Beckett 1983a: 113). This identification of a second "point of departure" takes us beyond Schopenhauer's notion of the "nothing" as that which would remain after the complete denial of the will, and which is experienced as "positive peace" by Murphy shortly before his death. For, soon after his reading of Schopenhauer, Beckett encountered a much earlier philosophical conception of the nothing, namely the one proposed by the pre-Socratic atomist philosophers Leucippus and Democritus, and it is to the pre-Socratics that we must turn for another key element in Beckett's thinking of an ethics of negation. As Feldman (2006) has demonstrated, Beckett's knowledge of pre-Socratic philosophy derived principally from his reading in the early 1930s of three histories of philosophy: Archibald Alexander's *Short History of Philosophy*, from which Beckett takes the precise phrasing of the atomist paradox, "Naught is more real ..." (see Alexander 1922: 39); Wilhelm Windelband's *History of Philosophy* (1893); and John Burnet's *Greek Philosophy* (1914). It was in these works, too, that Beckett learned of two fundamental forms of nihilism. As mentioned above, these are what Burnet refers to as the "cosmological nihilism" of Gorgias of Leontini and the "ethical nihilism" of Kallikles and Thrasymachos.

Gorgias of Leontini (c.483–376 bc) was a Sicilian philosopher, perhaps best known as a teacher of rhetoric, author of the extant *Encomium of Helen*, and the first of Socrates' interlocutors in Plato's *Gorgias*. However, he was also reputed by a number of classical writers to have been the author of a lost treatise entitled *On Nature or the Non-Existent*

(*Peri phuseōs e tou me ontos*). Beckett's notes on the "three famous propositions" summing up the argument of *On Nature* follow closely the phrasing in Alexander: "1st, nothing exists; 2nd, even if anything did exist, it could not be known; 3rd, and even if it could be known, it would be incommunicable" (Alexander 1922: 51; cf. Beckett TCD MS 10967/48).

Gorgias is a "cosmological nihilist," then, because he believes that nothingness is the ultimate reality. While, unlike both Democritus and Heraclitus, Gorgias may not appear by name in Beckett's published works, he is nonetheless a crucial figure in Beckett's deployment of the nothing. As C. J. Ackerley has shown, Gorgias's tripartite paradigm arguably recurs in *Watt* (see Ackerley 2005). Furthermore, evidence that Beckett continued to reflect on Gorgias's cosmological nihilism decades after having read about him is to be found in a letter of April 21, 1958 from Beckett to his friend A. J. Leventhal in which Beckett repeats Gorgias's three propositions and refers to the third – "If anything is, and can be known, it cannot be expressed in speech" – as the "coup de grâce" (quoted in Feldman 2006: 76).

As for what Burnet describes as the "ethical nihilism" of Kallikles and Thrasymachos, this is "the doctrine that there is no natural distinction between right and wrong" (Burnet 1914: 120). Beckett duly notes that the nihilism of Thrasymachos is "complete ethical nihilism" because "according to him there is no Right at all, and what we call by that name is only 'the interest of the stronger' which he is able to force the weaker to accept as lawful and binding on themselves in virtue of his strength" (ibid.: 121; cf. Beckett TCD MS 1097/48.1). Now, if Gorgias's cosmological nihilism undoubtedly finds its place in Beckett's oeuvre, the same can also be said for the ethical nihilism of Kallikles and Thrasymachos, although Beckett will strip it of that proto-Nietzscheanism to which Burnet refers. Evidence for this lies in Beckett's repeated insistence to Charles Juliet that one simply cannot make "value judgements" (Beckett in Juliet 1995: 148). This is not to say, however, that Beckett's oeuvre is simply the expression of nihilism – be that nihilism cosmological or ethical in nature. Rather, both cosmological and ethical nihilism may be said to haunt that oeuvre.

Thus far we have considered the ethics of negation in Beckett principally by way of his readings in philosophy during the 1930s. We have now to consider the ethics of affirmation that has a no less important role to play in his works – and indeed in his life. From as early as his first novel, *Dream of Fair to middling Women*, Beckett presents his readers with figures who, for all their exhaustion, for all their desire to withdraw from a world of suffering, nonetheless find themselves compelled to "go on." At the end of *Dream*, this compulsion emanates from a literal figure of the law: a policeman. By the time of *The Unnamable*, it has been disembodied: "you must go on ... I'll go on" (Beckett 1959: 418). By the time of *Worstward Ho* (1983b), it has been completely displaced from any "I," to be relocated not in another but as a performative utterance tied to no identifiable subject: "On. Say on. Be said on. Somehow on. Till nohow on. Said nohow on" (Beckett 1983b: 7).

As the above quotation from *Worstward Ho* makes clear, affirmation is far from being restricted to the matter of Beckett's work. It is also apparent in its manner or form. Indeed, the following remark, recorded by Juliet in October 1973, suggests that Beckett eventually comes to endorse an affirmative ethics of aesthetic form: "Paradoxically, it's through form that the artist can find a kind of solution – by giving form to what has none [i.e. what Beckett elsewhere terms not being but the "mess"]. It is perhaps only at that level that there may be an underlying affirmation" (Beckett in Juliet 1995: 149). This statement stands in striking contrast not only to the view expressed by the narrator of *Dream*, whose dreams include an art that would be the "authentic extrinsecation" of an "incoherent reality" (Beckett 1992: 102), but also to Beckett's own view of *The Unnamable*, in which, he says, there is "complete disintegration" (Beckett in Graver and Federman 1979: 148). As numerous commentators have argued, Beckett's later works may indeed be seen as attempts to "get out of the attitude of disintegration," to "find a form that accommodates the mess" (Beckett in Graver and Federman 1979: 219). Such forms are apparent not least in *Comment c'est* (1961), *Play* (1963), and *Not I* (1973), in each of which the "chaos" or "mess" is framed by aesthetic form, often musical in nature.

Anethical Beckett

In Beckett, then, one finds both an ethics of negation and an ethics of affirmation. It is on the basis of one or other of these, and sometimes by trying to reconcile them, that commentators on Beckett have generally sought to argue that his art is in fact a privileged form of resistance to nihilism. For Adorno, it is the "slightest difference" within the negative that constitutes the ethicality of Beckett's work. For Badiou, it is an "affirmation" both of the "Two" and of the "on" (Badiou 2003: 41). Beckett's own notes on Ernest Jones's *Treatment of the Neuroses* (1920), which he read in the mid-1930s, suggest, however, that this imperative to "go on" might also be read in a very different way – as indicative, for instance, of obsessional neurosis (*Zwangsneurose*), or what one of Jones's own patients describes as a "feeling of mustness," a phrase duly noted by Beckett (see Beckett TCD MS 10971/8/23).

In an irony the implications of which are considerable, to insist upon ethicalizing this affirmative compulsion is in fact to negate its radical opacity. Furthermore, to place the emphasis ultimately upon the compulsion to "go on" is to negate – in the interests of the ethical – that other imperative: the imperative to end. That, in Beckett, this imperative to end may be no less compelling, and indeed no less ethical, than the imperative to go on is suggested not least by the final words of the postwar novella "The End" (1946), where Beckett juxtaposes "the courage to end" with "the strength to go on" (Beckett 1995: 99). Once one takes account of this double imperative, it becomes clear that Beckett's creatures – and indeed his conception of the artist/writer – constitute a strange purgatorial pseudocoupling of Dante and Belacqua, at once committed to remaining under the shadow of the rock and to climbing Mount Purgatory. This being racked by a double imperative makes of Beckett's pseudocouples creatures caught within the reversibility of the palindrome "no"/"on," which arguably finds its fullest expression in the "nohow on" that punctuates *Worstward Ho*.

To see Beckett's oeuvre as the expression of either an ethics of negation or an ethics of affirmation, to label it as quietist or stoic, is to avoid that very doubleness of the "pseudocouple" that inhabits the Beckettian no man's land. This "pseudocouple" is not ethical, but rather the conjunction of two, antithetical imperatives: to end and to go on, at once negation and affirmation. As I have sought to demonstrate elsewhere (see Weller 2006), this experience of competing imperatives produces neither the ethical nor the unethical, and not even the non-ethical, but rather what might be termed the *anethical*, in which the prefix "an" signals both a movement towards (as in the Latin *an-*) and a movement away from (as in the Greek *an-*) the poles of ethicality and unethicality.

This anethicality may also be seen as a form of failure, namely the failure of both negation and affirmation, the failure of both ethical and unethical comportment. As Beckett puts it to Juliet: "Negation is no more possible than affirmation. It is absurd to say that something is absurd. That's still a value judgement. It is impossible to protest, and equally impossible to assent" (Beckett in Juliet 1995: 165). In the January 18, 1937 entry in his German Diaries (1936–7), Beckett refers back to the recently completed *Murphy*, stating that Murphy's withdrawal from the "outer reality" is an expression of the "fundamental unheroic" (quoted in Ackerley 2000: 89). As Ackerley observes, this unheroism stands in direct contrast to what Beckett sees as the heroism of Joyce. In their *Companion to Beckett* (2004), Ackerley and Gontarski go on to claim that the "fundamental unheroic" is Beckett's formulation of a "more complex *ethics*" (Ackerley and Gontarski 2004: 474). To this judgment I would add only that this more complex ethics may perhaps be more accurately termed an "anethics," in which neither negation nor affirmation can be accomplished, and in which it is no longer possible to determine any action – or indeed any inaction – as either ethical or unethical.

REFERENCES AND FURTHER READING

Ackerley, C. J. (2000). "Samuel Beckett and Thomas à Kempis: The Roots of Quietism." *Samuel Beckett Today/Aujourd'hui* 9: 81–92.

Ackerley, C. J. (2005). *Obscure Locks, Simple Keys: The Annotated "Watt."* Tallahassee, FL: JOBS Books.

Ackerley, C. J., and S. E. Gontarski (2004). *The Grove Companion to Beckett.* New York: Grove.

Adorno, Theodor W. (1973). *Negative Dialectics*, trans. E. B. Ashton. London: Routledge & Kegan Paul.

Adorno, Theodor W. (1991). "Trying to Understand *Endgame*." In *Notes to Literature*, Vol. 1, trans. Shierry Weber Nicholsen. New York: Columbia University Press.

Alexander, Archibald B. D. (1922). *A Short History of Philosophy*, 3rd edn. Glasgow: J. Maclehose & Sons.

Badiou, Alain (2001). *Ethics: An Essay on the Understanding of Evil*, trans. Peter Hallward. London: Verso.

Badiou, Alain (2003). *On Beckett*, ed. Nina Power and Alberto Toscano. Manchester: Clinamen Press.

Beckett, Samuel (1938). *Murphy*. London: George Routledge & Sons.

Beckett, Samuel (1959). *Molloy, Malone Dies, The Unnamable*. London: John Calder.

Beckett, Samuel (1965). *Proust and Three Dialogues*. London: Calder & Boyars.

Beckett, Samuel (1976). *Watt*. London: John Calder.

Beckett, Samuel (1982). *Ill Seen Ill Said*. London: John Calder.

Beckett, Samuel (1983a). *Disjecta: Miscellaneous Writings and a Dramatic Fragment*, ed. Ruby Cohn. London: John Calder.

Beckett, Samuel (1983b). *Worstward Ho*. London: John Calder.

Beckett, Samuel (1992). *Dream of Fair to middling Women*, ed. Eoin O'Brien and Edith Fournier. Dublin: Black Cat.

Beckett, Samuel (1995). *The Complete Short Prose, 1929–1989*, ed. S. E. Gontarski. New York: Grove.

Beckett, Samuel (1998). *No Author Better Served: The Correspondence of Samuel Beckett and Alan Schneider*, ed. Maurice Harmon. Cambridge, MA: Harvard University Press.

Beckett, Samuel (1999). *"Dream" Notebook*, ed. John Pilling. Reading: Beckett International Foundation.

Begam, Richard (1996). *Samuel Beckett and the End of Modernity*. Stanford, MA: Stanford University Press.

Blanchot, Maurice (2003). "Where Now? Who Now?" In *The Book to Come*. Stanford: Stanford University Press.

Burnet, John (1914). *Greek Philosophy, Part I: Thales to Plato*. London: Macmillan.

Büttner, Gottfried (1984). *Samuel Beckett's Novel "Watt,"* trans. Joseph P. Dolan. Philadelphia: University of Pennsylvania Press.

Connor, Steven (1988). *Samuel Beckett: Repetition, Theory and Text*. Oxford: Basil Blackwell.

Critchley, Simon (1997). *Very Little ... Almost Nothing: Death, Philosophy, Literature*. London: Routledge.

Feldman, Matthew (2006). *Beckett's Books: A Cultural History of Samuel Beckett's "Interwar Notes."* New York: Continuum.

Geulincx, Arnold (1999). *Metaphysics*, trans. Martin Wilson. Wisbech: Christoffel Press.

Geulincx, Arnold (2006). *Ethics, with Samuel Beckett's Notes*, trans. Martin Wilson. ed. Han van Ruler, Anthony Uhlmann, and Martin Wilson. Leiden: Brill.

Graver, Lawrence, and Raymond Federman (1979). *Samuel Beckett: The Critical Heritage*. London: Routledge & Kegan Paul.

Hill, Leslie (1990a). Beckett Obituary. *Radical Philosophy* 55.

Hill, Leslie (1990b). *Samuel Beckett: In Different Words*. Cambridge: Cambridge University Press.

Juliet, Charles (1995). *Conversations with Samuel Beckett and Bram van Velde*, trans. Janey Tucker. Leiden: Academic Press.

Knowlson, James (1996). *Damned to Fame: The Life of Samuel Beckett*. London: Bloomsbury.

Nixon, Mark (2006). "'Scraps of German': Samuel Beckett Reading German Literature." In *"Notes Diverse Holo": Catalogues of Beckett's Reading Notes and Other Manuscripts at Trinity College Dublin, with Supporting Essays*. Amsterdam: Rodopi.

Schopenhauer, Arthur (1969). *The World as Will and Representation*, Vol. 1, trans. E. F. J. Payne. New York: Dover. Originally published 1818.

Trezise, Thomas (1990). *Into the Breach: Samuel Beckett and the Ends of Literature*. Princeton: Princeton University Press.

Weller, Shane (2005). *A Taste for the Negative: Beckett and Nihilism*. Oxford: Legenda.

Weller, Shane (2006). *Beckett, Literature, and the Ethics of Alterity*. Basingstoke: Macmillan.

Windelband, W. (1893). *A History of Philosophy*, trans. James H. Tufts. London: Macmillan.

10

Beckett and Germany in the 1930s: The Development of a Poetics

Mark Nixon

On September 29, 1936, Samuel Beckett embarked on a six-month trip to Germany, sailing to Hamburg from the port of Cobh on board the SS *Washington*. Even without the advantages of hindsight, Beckett's decision to travel through Nazi Germany at this time appears somewhat surprising. As he was undoubtedly aware, the political situation within Germany had changed radically since his last visit in 1932; in the intervening years the wider intentions of the Nazi regime had started to become apparent. By September 1936, Germany had reoccupied the demilitarized Rhineland (March 1936) and nearly established its complete hold on the political, social, and cultural life within its borders. Indeed, barely a week after his arrival in Germany, Beckett acknowledged in his diary that he was traveling through a country that might well be at war in the near future: "They 'must' fight soon (or burst)" (German Diaries [hereafter GD], October 6, 1936, quoted in Knowlson 1996: 261). This awareness may well have contributed to Beckett's decision to undertake the trip in the first place, in order to further his knowledge of German culture and language and to study the vast treasures of painting held in German galleries before the country became inaccessible to foreigners. Moreover, the writing of *Murphy*, which he completed towards the end of June 1936, had left him with no clear sense of what do to next; he undoubtedly hoped that the journey would yield new material for his writing. After all, by 1936, Germany and its culture had established itself as a large influence on Beckett. Indeed, the importance of German culture on the young writer's aesthetic development in the 1930s can hardly be overestimated. Even the most cursory glance through Beckett's early poetry, prose, critical essays, manuscript notebooks, and correspondence reveals the extent of his engagement with German literature, art, and philosophy.

It is also possible that Beckett wanted to return to a cultural space which had a personal significance to him, and which in the past had offered emotional intensity in the form of his relationship with his cousin Peggy Sinclair. In a letter to Thomas MacGreevy, written shortly after his arrival in Hamburg in October 1936, Beckett hinted at this: "It is nice to be away, but when I have seen the pictures + struggled with the language I don't think I'll be sorry to go. I begin to think that Germany's charm is perhaps after all mainly for me a matter of associations. I feel sad enough + often enough for that to be so" (Letter to MacGreevy [hereafter TM], October 9, 1936, quoted in Fries-Dieckmann 2005: 216). As the letter suggests, for Beckett, Germany was also a site of personal memory in the form of Peggy, connected with feelings of love, sexuality, and, ultimately, loss and sadness (especially following her death from tuberculosis in 1933). That Beckett's emotional attachment to Germany is linked to his interest in a particular strand of its culture is something this essay will sketch out in what follows, by focusing on the importance of Germany to Beckett's writing and his developing poetics in the 1930s and beyond.

The "German Comedy" – *Dream of Fair to middling Women*

Beckett's relationship with Peggy Sinclair, and the ultimately painful separation in late 1929, initiated a correlation, an "association," between Germany's cultural heritage and his own emotions. When viewed in this light, it is hardly surprising that when Beckett came to deal with his relationship with Peggy (and other women) in *Dream of Fair to middling Women* (written 1931–2 but unpublished in Beckett's lifetime), the book would be permeated with German words and phrases, as well as fragments of German literature. These instances chiefly occur in the sections describing the Smeraldina-Rima (modeled on Peggy) and Belacqua's time with her in Vienna. Beckett acknowledged the connection in a letter to MacGreevy by referring to his book as the "German Comedy" (TM, May 29, 1931). Yet the designation of the book as "comic," which it undeniably is in parts, obscures Beckett's rather less light-hearted intention in writing the novel: the "purging of a recent past and an even more recent present" (Pilling 1997: 62). As James Knowlson has shown, *Dream* is set within a framework which draws on Beckett's own experiences from 1928 to 1932 (Knowlson 1996: 83–5).

Ultimately, and despite the "fever to have done" with painful memories (Beckett 1992: 195), German or otherwise, the writing of *Dream* did not quite have the desired effect. In a letter written six months after the completion of the novel, his attachment to Germany was still very much alive. As he told MacGreevy in a letter of November 21, 1932, "I am reading German and learning a little that way. Always when its [*sic*] coming up to Xmas I get the German fever" (quoted in Nixon 2006a: 260), but he went on to add that "soon I will be tired of the Brothers Grimm's machinery" (quoted in Pilling 2005: 113). Even as the "Brothers Grimm's machinery" threatened to turn Beckett's memories of past Christmases at Kassel with Peggy Sinclair into a distant fairy tale, the involuntary state of "fever" continued to govern an intricate web of personal associations equating Germany with his emotional, or rather sexual, feelings. The "Homer dusks" and the "red steeples" of this letter relate explicitly to the poem "Dortmunder," written early in 1932, which tells of a visit to a brothel. In Beckett's annotated copy of the collection *Echo's Bones* held at the Harry Ransom Center in Austin, the poem is appended with the words "Kassel revisited," providing a link to the implied visit paid by Belacqua in *Dream* to a brothel during New Year's Eve 1929 (when Beckett and Peggy separated). A further visit to a Nuremberg brothel is equally signposted in *Dream* through a set of German references. The details of this passage, such as the allusions to the town's artistic legacy (the "Haus Albrecht Dürer" and the sculptor "Adam Kraft") and the torture chamber in the castle, derive from Beckett's own short stay in Nuremberg on his way to Kassel in Spring 1931. In *Dream*, details from the visit to the torture chamber (such as the smoking prohibition) are used to transmit the sexual content of the text. Thus the brothel becomes its own kind of torture chamber, as the admonition "no effing smoking do you hear me in the effing Folterzimmer [torture chamber]" and the later reference to "The Cast-Iron Virgin of Nürnberg" sign posted (Beckett 1992: 72, 182). The subtext of this passage is indicated by the diminutive dismissal of the "whorchen," a German–English hybrid similar to the later reference to the "Jungfräulein," a diminutive young virgin (ibid.: 72, 130). Moreover, in that she is a "little bony vulture of a whorchen" she is linked to Dürer ("dürr" is German for "skinny"), just as the sculptor's name "Adam Kraft" evokes a (now lost) power inherent in the edenically pure first man. Although the passage is on the whole rather impenetrable ("I *won't* tell you everything", ibid. 72), the fact that it is there at all attests to a specifically German complex established by Beckett in his endeavors to come to terms with his separation from Peggy.

Shades of separation, loss, and unhappiness are cast throughout the early writing, which acts like a codified map to events in Beckett's life: an intricate network of references encompassing his travels, opinions, relationships, his reading and artistic preoccupations. Within this network it is ultimately the German discourse that engenders Beckett's most private references. Prey to attacks of melancholy reflection and introspection, this discourse constructs an autobiographical and confessional tonality, which is subsequently often disguised and buried beneath either a layer of erudite references or humorous strategies of textual instability.

"Scraps of German"

The humor of *Dream* often manifests itself in Beckett's use of German phrases and words. By 1932, Beckett's command of the German language was already quite good, having obviously benefited, as we shall see, from his reading. Yet *Dream* indicates that on the written level he was relying on the German acquired during his time in Kassel, inserting the odd word or expression he would have picked up through conversations. Thus colloquial terminology such as *quatsch* (nonsense), *Sauladen* (mess), or *abknutschen* (smother with kisses, or to hug) jostle with proverbial wisdom: *Der Mensch* [sic] *ist ein Gewohnheitstier* (the human being is a creature of habit) (Beckett 1992: 19, 82, 14, 75). These terms contribute to the general irreverent tone of the book, compounded by Beckett's mocking attitude towards the German language and the pedantry it so often expresses. This is particularly evident in the fun Beckett has with compound nouns, a German speciality, when coming up with names such as *Arschlochweh* (pain-in-the-arse) or *Herr Sauerwein* (Mr Sourwine) (ibid.: 61, 106). The jewel in the compound crown is the Joycean expletive: "Himmisacrakrüzidirkenjesusmariaundjosefundblütigeskreuz!" (ibid. 239). It is in the section "The Smeraldina's Billet Doux" that the satirical treatment of all things German finds its apotheosis, culminating in the irreverent use of the German national anthem, the "Deutschlandlied": "I love you über alles in dieser Welt, mehr als alles auf Himmel, Erde und Hölle [I love you above all else in this world, more than everything in heaven, earth, and hell]" (ibid. 58).

However, Beckett's use of German in *Dream* obscures his admiration for the language. In his essay on Joyce's "Work in Progress," Beckett had praised the German language for its precision, commending the word "Zweifel" for giving a "sensuous suggestion of hesitancy, of the necessity for choice, of static irresolution," which the English "doubt" failed to do (Beckett 1983: 28). In *Dream*, Beckett inserted a small private joke in "The Smeraldina's Billet Doux," when Smerry asks "how could you ever doupt me?" Unlike French and Italian, German was not a language Beckett had studied at Trinity College Dublin, but his interest in the language and his desire to read German literature in the original led him to expand his knowledge of the language in the early 1930s. Two notebooks now held at the Beckett International Foundation Archive in Reading (UoR MS5002 and UoR MS5006) from early 1934 show Beckett improving his German vocabulary and writing skills. In an essay written in order to practice recently acquired words, the program of study is clearly set out: "Aber die Lektüre deutscher Bücher, scheint von allen möglichen Methoden die beste zu sein, um einen reichen Wortschatz zu erlangen" (But the reading of German books seems to be the best of all possible methods to acquire a rich vocabulary) (UoR MS5002: 6r, quoted in Nixon 2006a: 261). Over the course of the next two years, Beckett would engage extensively with German literature. Before 1934, however, his knowledge of German literature was somewhat vague, and the intertextual fragments that are used in *Dream* and other early work do not appear to have derived from any sustained reading of primary material. Indeed, Beckett's first encounter with German culture came in the form of philosophy and music, or more specifically, Schopenhauer and Schubert.

Beckett started reading Schopenhauer in 1930, and the philosopher furnished him with a system of thought remarkably similar to his own: an essentially pessimistic view of human existence wherein the path to any semblance of redemption led through the artistic creative act. Beckett's reading of what he termed Schopenhauer's "intellectual justification of unhappiness" in *Die Welt als Wille und Vorstellung* (*The World as Will and Idea*) had a lasting effect on both his work and his view of life (TM, undated [July 25? 1930], quoted in Knowlson 1996: 118). Beckett immediately purloined the Schopenhauerian combination of philosophy and emotional utterance, and its underlying pessimism, for his critical monograph *Proust*, written in late August and early September 1930. Beckett's discovery – in the words of *Dream* – of "the darkest passages in Schopenhauer" (Beckett 1992: 62) instigated a persistent exploration of a distinct strand in German culture, not only in literature and philosophy, but also in the fields of the visual arts and music. The frustrated striving of the individual in a meaningless universe, preoccupations with melancholy, solitude, and loss were themes Beckett found within this tradition, all enunciated with the dark and heavy, even tragic, quality of the German language. Beckett's awareness of the effect that the German language had on his emotional state is illustrated by a (as so often self-deprecatory) passage in *Dream*: "Scraps of German played in his mind in the silence that ensued; grand, old, plastic words" (Beckett 1992: 191). The implication of a brooding indulgence in the self and an immersion in German writing and language is evident in Beckett's confession to MacGreevy that he was "wallowing in ... German" (TM, November 11, 1932, quoted Nixon 2006a: 260).

An important part in this assemblage of personal and aesthetic associations was Schubert. Beckett's attraction to Schubert and the poems he set to music in his Lieder was also based upon the way he expressed a certain mood rather than an intellectual system. It is probable that the source of the German fragments incorporated in the early poems and prose is Schubert's Lieder, with which Beckett was familiar from an early date (Knowlson 1996: 98). Even in later work, Beckett's use of German poetry was often via their musical setting. It is thus significant that Goethe's appearance in *First Love* is by way of a song: "I did not know the song, I had never heard it before and shall never hear it again. It had something to do with lemon trees, or orange trees, I forget" (Beckett 1995: 37). The song that the prostitute Lulu (or Anna) sings for the narrator is Mignon's Song from Goethe's *Wilhelm Meister*, one of Schubert's most well-known settings. Schubert's Lieder remained important to Beckett throughout his life, and in the 1982 television piece *Nacht und Träume* he used Schubert's Lied of that same name, with the text slightly modified from Heinrich Josef von Collin's poem (Knowlson 1996: 681). The confluence of musical mood and textual message was something Beckett admired, and a line copied into the "Sottisier" notebook in 1981, together with its musical provenance, serves as an example to illustrate what he admired: "Nur wer die Sehnsucht kennt, weiss was ich leide ([Goethe's] W. M. [Wilhelm Meister] Mignon. Schubert. Wolf.)" (Only he who has experienced yearning knows how I suffer, UoR MS2901: 15r, quoted in Nixon 2007b: 115). If Schopenhauer was useful to Beckett for providing an "intellectual justification of unhappiness," Schubert and the poets he set to music expressed a melancholy disposition close to Beckett's own aesthetic temperament.

Essentially, Beckett was less interested in the romantic concept of *Sehnsucht* – the longing for love or immortality or spiritual transcendence – than in a particular, melancholy strand of German romanticism encapsulated by the German word "Schwermut" (variously translated as "sadness," "weariness," "melancholy," or "wistfulness"). On the whole, Beckett's cultural awareness throughout the 1930s (and indeed beyond) was shaped by his attraction to this tradition, the coordinates of which he traced from Schopenhauer, Schubert, Goethe (tellingly, as a poet, not as a playwright), Grillparzer,

Heine to Hölderlin and Georg Trakl. To be sure, Beckett did not only find this kind of sentiment in German literature, and other authors such as, among others, Leopardi (the "unhappy writer," as he is called in the *Watt* notebooks), Keats, Burton, Geulincx, and Thomas à Kempis also contributed to Beckett's development of an aesthetic of melancholy.

Reading German Literature

Beckett's most intense and focused study of German literature and language began in earnest in the early months of 1934 following another painful separation, the death of his father in June 1933 (see Nixon 2006a). During this period, Beckett's engagement with German literature proved to be a creative stimulus as well as a vital influence on his developing poetics. Beckett prepared himself for his course of study by reading and taking exhaustive handwritten notes from J. G. Robertson's *A History of German Literature* (first published in 1902). Beckett's notes meticulously record the life dates, salient biographical features, and major works (at times with bibliographic reference) of a large portion of authors mentioned in Robertson's book, paying particular attention to the Middle High German period (1050–1350) and the main romantic period around Goethe.

Beckett's reading of Robertson's book influenced his immediate creative and critical endeavors. In Spring 1934 he penned the poem "Da tagte es," which draws on the generic theme of the inevitability of loss in the coming of dawn as expressed in medieval *Tagelieder* by authors such as Heinrich von Morungen and Walther von der Vogelweide (the latter's poem "Nemt, frowe disen kranz" resurfaces repeatedly in Beckett's writing up until *Stirrings Still*). Furthermore, Beckett was also able to draw on his freshly gained knowledge of German literary history in the critical reviews he wrote during 1934, such as "Humanistic Quietism" (on MacGreevy's poetry) and "Recent Irish Poetry."

Robertson also guided Beckett's reading of Goethe, although he had previously already read (in entirety or parts) *Die Wahlverwandschaften*, *Wilhelm Meister*, and *Die Leiden des Jungen Werther*. He also admired Goethe's poetry (most probably in Schubert's Lieder), fragments of which are woven into Beckett's early work. In particular, Beckett was attracted to the poems "Prometheus," a typed copy of which survives in a manuscript notebook, and "Der Erlkönig," used in the unpublished short story "Echo's Bones" of November 1933. Once again, it is the more melancholy poems that left the greatest impression on Beckett, and that creatively inspired him. Thus Beckett's poem "The Vulture," probably written early 1935, draws on the images of instability and artistic creation outlined by Goethe's "Die Harzreise im Winter." And the poem "Wandrers Nachtlied II" furnished Beckett with a resigned mood that he also found in parts of Keats or Leopardi, and he cited it in a variety of texts from *Dream* to the so-called German Letter to Axel Kaun of 1937:

> Über allen Gipfeln
> Ist Ruh,
> In allen Wipfeln
> Spürest du
> Kaum einen Hauch;
> Die Vögelein schweigen im Walde.
> Warte nur, balde
> Ruhest du auch.
> [Now stillness covers
> All the hill-tops;
> In all the tree-tops
> Hardly a breath stirs.
> The birds in the forest
> Have finished their song.
> Wait: you too shall rest
> Before long.]
>   (Goethe 1992: 236; 1999: 35)

In these lines, the evocation of peace is at once metaphysical and solitary, the promise of rest, in sleep or death, quietly anticipated. When Beckett turned to his most intense study of Goethe in 1935, and concentrated on his drama, he was disappointed by the lack of such lines. Indeed, Beckett's judgment of *Torquato Tasso* and *Iphigenie in Taurus* in March 1936 was hardly flattering; he found "some good rhetoric" in the former but on the whole thought "anything more disgusting would be hard to devise" (TM, March 8, 1936, quoted in Nixon 2006a: 271). Nevertheless, he transcribed passages from *Torquato Tasso* into a notebook, together with extensive quotation from Goethe's *Dichtung und Wahrheit*, which he read in early 1935. Beckett's transcriptions from Goethe's autobiography run to over 40 pages and are only outdone by the German notes on *Faust* in sheer length. Indeed, taken together these notes reveal the extent of Beckett's engagement with Goethe in the 1930s: in all of Beckett's notebooks of the 1930s, no literary writer, German or otherwise, is accorded as much space.

The transcriptions show Beckett's by-now comfortable use of the German language as he faultlessly alters tenses when summarizing or altering quotes. By March 1935 he had read more than half of the 700-odd pages of *Dichtung und Wahrheit*, telling MacGreevy that he found parts of it absorbing, particularly those sections dealing with Goethe's early artistic development (TM, March 10, 1935).

"Why Must One Always Find Something to Say" – From Goethe to Hölderlin

Whereas previously Beckett had used Goethe as inspiration and as a textual source for his work, his reading of *Dichtung und Wahrheit* (and subsequently *Faust*) contributed to his developing poetics. Accordingly, and despite the large volume of notes taken from *Dichtung und Wahrheit*, very little of this reading was explicitly integrated into Beckett's writing. Thus, for example, Beckett was interested in Goethe's style of writing, and his use of irony, a topic he further noted when later (in the summer of 1938) reading Fritz Mauthner's discussion of Goethe in his *Beiträge zu einer Kritik der Sprache*.

Having finished *Murphy* at the end of June 1936, and with his plans to go away for a long period to Germany now finalized, Beckett began to read Goethe's masterpiece *Faust* at the beginning of August, telling MacGreevy that he had "been working at German and reading Faust"(TM, undated [August 19, 1936], quoted in Knowlson 1996: 748n.168). However, the extensive transcriptions, from Robert Petsch's introduction and the first two parts of *Faust*, in two notebooks (UoR MS5004 and MS5005), give an insight into both Beckett's opinion of Goethe and his own creative thinking at this time.

Beckett's reading of *Faust* allowed him to engage with the idea of onwardness, of going on, or not going on, in textual and personal terms. Beckett's main criticism of *Faust* was that "the <u>on and up</u> is so tiresome ... the determined optimism à la Beethoven" (TM, undated [August 19, 1936], quoted in Nixon 2006a: 272). As Dirk Van Hulle has argued (Van Hulle 2006), Beckett in this letter is commenting on Petsch's introduction to the book, which remarks on the fact that "Faust ... stetig <u>aufwärts</u> streben muss" (must always strive upward) (Goethe 35; Uor MS5004, 17r–18r). Beckett's dismissal of this Faustian *Vorwärtsstreben* is further explained in a German diary passage, written after he had read a German novel by Walter Bauer, *Die Notwendige Reise* ("The Necessary Journey"), in January 1937. In this diary entry he distances himself from the "heroic, the nosce te ipsum, that these Germans see as a journey": "<u>Das notwendige Bleiben</u> [the necessary staying-put] is more like it. That is also in the figure of Murphy in the chair, surrender to the thongs of self, a simple materialisation of self-bondage, acceptance of which is the fundamental unheroic" (GD, January 18, 1937, quoted in Nixon 2006a: 272).

Ultimately, however, Beckett's reading of Goethe's *Faust* had a profound influence on his creative writing, revealed in his move toward a brevity and directness of utterance. At the beginning of August 1936 he told MacGreevy that there was a "surprising amount of irrelevance" in *Faust*, partly because Goethe "couldn't bear to <u>shorten</u> anything" (TM, August 7, 1936, quoted in Van Hulle 2006: 286). Beckett experienced a growing impatience as he continued to read the book, and, having finished the first part, he was left with the "impression of something very fragmentary, often irrelevant + too concrete, that perhaps Part 2 will correct. Auerbach's Cellar, the Witches kitchen and Walpurgisnacht, for example, – little more than sites + atmospheres, swamping the corresponding mental conditions" (TM, August 19, 1936, quoted in Knowlson 1996: 748n.168). Halfway through Part 2, however, Beckett abandoned the book, telling MacGreevy that "the 'Klassische Walpurgisnacht' was too much for me." It appears that Beckett's evaluation of Goethe, already formulated several months previously during the reading of *Torquato Tasso*, as a "machine à mots" (TM, March 8, 1936) was now incontrovertible.

These comments have a direct bearing on Beckett's poem "Cascando," written at the same time (July 1936) as he was immersing himself in Goethe's work. "Cascando" is essentially an emotional utterance, unencumbered by the erudition that had previously characterized his writing. The poem's "stale words" – "love love love" – reflect Beckett's growing preoccupation with both the inadequacy of language as well as the need to strip away the inessential. Beckett initially sought to solve the problem of the "unalterable whey of words" by making his first foray into a foreign language, translating "Cascando" into German (Beckett 1977: 30). In this translation, made on August 18, 1936, the same day he finished reading the first part of Goethe's *Faust*, the spurned love of the English version is replaced by a focus on the word "words." This emphasis on language is also achieved by a more insistent use of repetition.

It would not be false to say that Beckett's thinking in the late 1930s revolved primarily around the nature of language. Indeed, it is telling that apart from a handful of poems, a few reviews, and the aborted attempts to write *The Journal of a Melancholic* (while in Germany) and *Human Wishes* (a play on Dr Johnson), Beckett produced very little until he began to compose *Watt* in 1941. Beckett's struggle to find an adequate way of expression was, more often than not, played out through an engagement with German literature and philosophy, and against his underlying belief that the creative enterprise should be born out of necessity rather than habit. Various pronouncements support this, such as Beckett's dismissal of Schiller's *Maria Stuart*, which he read while in Germany in 1937: "Why must one always find something to say" (GD, January 6, 1937, quoted in Nixon 2006b: 107).

Beckett's German diaries reveal the extent of his ruminations on the linguistic conundrum, as he comments on the "word's inadequacy" and states that "communication is impossible" (GD March 26, 1937 and GD March 31, 1937, quoted in Nixon 2006b: 113). Beckett's belief in the limitations and restrictions of language finds its clearest and most forceful expression in his well-known letter to Axel Kaun of July 1937, in which he adumbrates a "Literature of the Unword" (1983: 173). Discussions of this letter tend to ignore Beckett's actual reason for composing it, which was to turn down the offer of translating Ringelnatz's German poetry into English. He does so by stating that "als Dichter aber scheint [Ringelnatz] Goethes Meinung gewesen zu sein: *Lieber NICHTS zu schreiben, als nicht zu schreiben*" (But as a poet [Ringelnatz] seems to have shared Goethe's opinion: it is better to write NOTHING than not to write at all) (52; trans. 171). Beckett's reference here represents a summation of his engagement with Goethe's writing over the previous years. Moreover, it neatly encapsulates his differentiation between necessary, essential acts of writing and incidental utterances, and can be brought to bear upon the first line of his poem "Cascando," a poem undoubtedly affected by the reading of Goethe: "is it better abort than be barren" (Beckett 1977: 29). Indeed, toward the end of the 1930s, the question of whether to "abort" or be "barren," that is to say, not to start writing at all, loomed large in Beckett's mind. In a sense, he had maneuvered himself into a corner, which he could only resolve aesthetically rather than creatively.

As already intimated, three German writers played a large part in helping Beckett to find a way forward. In autumn 1937 he returned to reading Schopenhauer, and in the summer of 1938 he studied Fritz Mauthner's critique of language, from which he took copious notes (in his "Whoroscope" notebook and on separate sheets). Mauthner's emphasis on the "Grenzen der Sprache" ("limits of language") tended to affirm Beckett's own sense of the inadequacy of verbal signs to convey meaning.

But it was a poet who, arguably, gave a practical demonstration of how these boundaries and limitations could be integrated into the writing process. Beckett's reading of Friedrich Hölderlin in 1938 and 1939 had a profound impact on him. In Hölderlin, Beckett found a writer who fulfilled the aesthetic criteria he had been formulating over the previous two or three years. Hölderlin first appears in Beckett's notation of the first two-and-a-half lines of "Mnemosyne" (Third Version) in the "Dream" notebook. Strangely, Beckett omitted the second half of the third line in his notebook, but then proceeded to complete the missing half of the third line when he used it in *Dream* itself (Beckett 1992: 138).

Beckett's more intense engagement with Hölderlin, however, only came after he had acquired a copy of the poet's complete works. His personal copy, preserved at the Beckett International Foundation's archive in Reading, contains various annotations, and carries the inscription "24/12/37." In terms of his own developing poetics, Beckett could not have read Hölderlin at a more suitable time. In his review of the poems of Denis Devlin ("Intercessions"), he praises the poem "The Statue," stating that "the extraordinary evocation of the unsaid by the said has the distinction of a late poem by Hölderlin," and in brackets cites the line "Ihr Lieblichen Bilder im Tale" (Beckett 1983: 94; see Nixon 2005 for a discussion of the "unsaid" in Beckett). The reference here is to Hölderlin's poem "Der Spaziergang," which impressed Beckett to such a degree that it influenced the writing of his own poem "Dieppe" in 1938. Furthermore, as the Devlin review makes clear, Beckett was in particular attracted to the German poet's late work, or, as he told Charles Juliet in 1977, the "mad poems" (Juliet 1995: 167). These late poems, marked by fragmentation and, simultaneously, obscurity and visionary insight, were indeed written by Hölderlin at a time when he had lost his sanity. Beckett further referred to these poems in a letter to Arland Ussher, probably written in June 1939, as the "terrific fragments of the Spätzeit [late period]" (letter to Arland Ussher, undated [June 14, 1939], quoted in Weller 2008: 41). Indeed, it is precisely the fragmentariness of Hölderlin's late poetry that was of interest to Beckett. If Goethe, according to Beckett, was a poet who would carry on writing when he had nothing to say, Hölderlin chose to be silent. As Beckett told Patrick Bowles in 1955, Hölderlin "ended in something of this kind of failure. His only successes are the points where his poems go on, falter, stammer, and then admit failure, and are abandoned. At such points he was most successful" (Bowles 1994: 31). With respect to the time at which it was made, this comment has a bearing on the *Trilogy* ("you must go on, I can't go on, I'll go on" [Beckett 1959: 418]), but it also reveals much about the way in which Beckett's reading of Hölderlin in 1938–9 was to have a long-lasting effect on his own creative enterprise. Crucially, Beckett read Hölderlin at the precise moment when he himself was embracing "failure" as an artistic concept, one that admitted incoherence and unknowing. It is thus all the more fitting that when Beckett quoted the closing stanza of Hölderlin's "Hyperions Schicksalslied" at the end of *Watt* (1976: 239), he did so in an extremely fractured manner.

It is worth noting, in this context, that Beckett's increasing emphasis on incoherence was sharpened during his trip through Nazi Germany in 1936/37. The German diaries kept at the time reveal his criticism of the Nazis' totalitarian discourse (see Nixon 2007a). This was most obviously expressed in a diary entry which records a conversation with Axel Kaun about his attempts to buy a reference book on German history:

> I say I am not interested in a "unification" of the historical chaos any more than I am in the "clarification" of the individual chaos, + still less in the anthropomorphisation of the inhuman necessities that provoke the chaos. What I want is the straws, flotsam, etc., names, dates, births + deaths, because that is all I can know ... I say the background + the causes are an inhuman + incomprehensible machinery + venture to wonder what kind of appetite it is that can be appeased by the modern animism that consists in rationalising them. Rationalism is the last form of animism. Whereas the pure incoherence of times + men + places is at least amusing. Schicksal [Fate] = Zufall [Chance], for all human purposes. (GD4, January 15, 1937; quoted in Knowlson 1996: 228)

Beckett's distrust of the political and historical assertions he encountered in Nazi Germany are here combined with his general resistance to accepting any rationalizing system of thought. Moreover, the emphasis here on the "individual chaos" shows that, by 1937, Beckett had fully embraced the belief in an "incoherent reality" already postulated in *Dream* in 1932 (Beckett 1992: 102).

Beckett's engagement with irrationality, and with vain striving, intensified after his return from Germany. As noted, he turned again to Schopenhauer, having bought a complete edition of the philosopher's works while there. It reconfirmed his belief that the German philosopher had always been "one of the ones that mattered most," and his experience of reading him was, Beckett noted, "like suddenly a window opened on a fug" (TM, September 21, 1937, quoted in Knowlson 1996: 268).

Indeed, by late 1937, Beckett appeared to have achieved a dimension of recognition, and of acceptance, with regard to the question of irrationality and the way in which his writing was to proceed. In a letter to Mary Manning Howe, which only thinly veils the influence of Schopenhauer, he stated,

> I write the odd poem when it is there, + that is the only thing worth doing ... The real consciousness is the chaos, a grey commotion of mind, with no premises or conclusions or problems or solutions or cases or judgements. I lie for days on the floor, or in the woods, accompanied + unaccompanied, in a coenaesthetic of mind, a fullness of mental self-aesthesia that is entirely useless. The monad without the conflict, lightless + darkless. I used to pretend to work, I do so no longer. I used to dig about in the mental

sand for the lugworms of likes + dislikes, I do so no longer. The lugworms of understanding. (Letter to Mary Manning Howe, August 30, 1937, quoted in Knowlson 1996: 269)

This is a remarkable letter, considering that Beckett had, since his student days, been burrowing far and wide in order to acquire knowledge and understanding, and it is possible to say that it is an aesthetic formulation from which he proceeded to generate his postwar writing. As the poem "Gnome" jokingly states, the 1930s were indeed *Wanderjahre*, in which Beckett sought ways to find a poetics that did not rely on the "loutishness of learning" (Beckett 1977: 7).

Within the struggle to attain this creative position, Beckett's engagement with German literature, art, and culture played a decisive role. Despite stating categorically in a letter to MacGreevy of March 1931 that "I don't want to be a professor," Beckett's attitude and writing was marked by his academic background. Indeed, the reader's report on his essay *Proust* that same year remarked that its author's prose "reminds one of the proverbial Teutonic professor." But in the years that followed, Beckett followed the trajectory he himself highlighted in a play on (German) words in the "Whoroscope" notebook and then used in his review of Denis Devlin's poems in 1938 (Beckett 1983: 91): changing "Gelehrte" ("scholars") to "Geleerte" ("emptied out people").

References

Beckett, Samuel. Letters to Arland Percy Ussher. Harry Ransom Humanities Research, The University of Texas at Austin.

Beckett, Samuel. Letters to Mary Manning Howe. Harry Ransom Humanities Research, The University of Texas at Austin.

Beckett, Samuel. TCD MS10402. Letters to Thomas MacGreevy. Trinity College Library Dublin, Republic of Ireland.

Beckett, Samuel. TCD MS10971/1. Notes on German Literature. Trinity College Dublin, Republic of Ireland.

Beckett, Samuel. UoR MS2901. "Sottisier" notebook. Beckett International Foundation Archives, University of Reading.

Beckett, Samuel. UoR MS3000. "Whoroscope" Notebook. Beckett International Foundation Archives, University of Reading.

Beckett, Samuel. UoR MS5000. "Dream" Notebook. Beckett International Foundation Archives, University of Reading.

Beckett, Samuel. "German Diaries" (6 notebooks). Beckett International Foundation Archives, University of Reading.

Beckett, Samuel. UoR MS5002 and MS5006. German Vocabulary notebooks. Beckett International Foundation Archives, University of Reading.

Beckett, Samuel. UoR MS5004 and MS5005. *Faust* notebooks. Beckett International Foundation Archives, University of Reading.

Beckett, Samuel (1959). *The Trilogy: Molloy, Malone Dies, The Unnamable*. London: John Calder Publications.

Beckett, Samuel (1976). *Watt*. London: John Calder.

Beckett, Samuel (1977). *Complete Poems in English and French*. New York: Grove Press.

Beckett, Samuel (1983). *Disjecta: Miscellaneous Writings and a Dramatic Fragment*, ed. Ruby Cohn, London: John Calder.

Beckett, Samuel (1992). *Dream of Fair to middling Women*. Dublin: Black Cat Press.

Beckett, Samuel (1995). *The Complete Short Prose 1929–1989*, ed. S. E. Gontarski. New York: Grove Press.

Bowles, Patrick (1994). "How to Fail: Notes on Talks with Samuel Beckett." *PN Review*, 96 (20): 24–38.

Fischer-Seidel, Therese and Marion Fries-Dieckmann (eds.) (2005). *Der Unbekannte Beckett: Samuel Beckett und die deutsche Kultur*. Frankfurt am Main: Suhrkamp.

Fries-Dieckmann, Marion (2005). "Beckett lernt Deutsch: The Exercise Books." In Therese Fischer Seidel and Marion Fries-Dieckmann (eds.), *Der Unbekannte Beckett: Samuel Beckett und die deutsche Kultur* (pp. 208–23). Frankfurt am Main: Suhrkamp.

Fries-Dieckmann, Marion (2007). *Samuel Beckett und die deutsche Sprache: Eine Untersuchung der deutschen Übersetzungen des dramatischen Werks*. Trier: WVT.

Goethe, Johann Wolfgang von (1992). *Gedichte*. Frankfurt am Main and Leipzig: Insel Verlag.

Goethe, Johann Wolfgang von (1999). *Selected Poetry*, trans. David Luke. London: Libris.

Hölderlin, Friedrich n.d. *Sämtliche Werke*. Leipzig: Insel-Verlag (Beckett's personal copy, UoR).

Hulle, Dirk Van (2006). "Beckett's *Faust* Notes." *Samuel Beckett Today/Aujourd'hui* 16: 283–97.

Hunkeler, Thomas (2000). "Un cas d'hyperthermie littéraire: Samuel Beckett face à ses 'juveniles expériences allemande.'" *Samuel Beckett Today/Aujourd'hui* 10: 213–22.

Juliet, Charles (1995). *Conversations with Samuel Beckett and Bram van Velde*. Leiden: Academic Press Leiden.

Knowlson, James (1996). *Damned to Fame: The Life of Samuel Beckett*. London: Bloomsbury.

Nixon, Mark (2005). "Becketts 'German Diaries' der Deutschlandreise 1936/37: 'Eine Einführung zur Chronik' and 'Chronik der Deutschlandsreise Becketts 1936/37.'" In Therese Fischer Seidel and Marion Fries-Dieckmann (eds.), *Der Unbekannte Beckett: Samuel Beckett und die deutsche Kultur*. Frankfurt am Main: Suhrkamp.

Nixon, Mark (2006a). "'Scraps of German': Samuel Beckett Reading German Literature." *Samuel Beckett Today/Aujourd'hui* 16: 259–82.

Nixon, Mark (2006b). "'Writing': Die Bedeutung der Deutschlandreise 1936/37 für Becketts schriftstellerische Entwicklung." In Lutz Dittrich, Carola Veit, and Ernst Wichner (eds.), *Obergeschoss Still Closed – Samuel Beckett in Berlin*, Texte aus dem Literaturhaus Vol. 16. Berlin: Matthes & Seitz.

Nixon, Mark (2007a). "Gospel und Verbot: Beckett und Nazi Germany." In Michaela Giesing, Gaby Hartel, and Carola Veit (eds.), *Das Raubauge in der Stadt: Beckett liest Hamburg* Göttingen: Wallstein Verlag.

Nixon, Mark (2007b). "'The Remains of Trace': Intra- and Intertextual Transferences in Beckett's *Mirlitonnades* Manuscripts." In S. E. Gontarski, William J. Cloonan, Alec Hargreaves and Dustin Anderson (eds.), "*Transnational Beckett*," *Journal of Beckett Studies* 16.1–2 (Fall 2006/Spring 2007): 121–34.

Pilling, John (1997). *Beckett before Godot*. Cambridge: Cambridge University Press.

Pilling, John (2005). "Beckett und 'the German fever': Krise und Identität in den 1930ern." In Therese Fischer Seidel and Marion Fries-Dieckmann (eds.), *Der Unbekannte Beckett: Samuel Beckett und die deutsche Kultur*. Frankfurt am Main: Suhrkamp.

11

Samuel Beckett and Science

C. J. Ackerley

I am reminded of the famous exchange between Napoleon and the Marquis de Laplace, when the celebrated author of the *Méchanique célestiale* was reproached for his failure to have mentioned *le bon Dieu*:

LAPLACE: "Sire, I had no need of that hypothesis."
NAPOLEON: "But it is a fine hypothesis. It explains so many things." (*Discours de la sortie*, Jean du Chas)

Science, for Samuel Beckett, is inseparable from its shadow, religion. It is best understood in terms of the German *Wissenschaft*, emphasizing knowledge, but equally ways of knowing; a close synonym might be *epistemology*, despite Beckett's rejection of what he called in his 1934 quatrain, "Gnome," the "loutishness of learning" (Beckett 2006: 4.9).[1] Beckett's attitude toward epistemology was largely shaped by Wilhelm Windelband's *A History of Philosophy* (1901), from which, in the 1930s, he took copious notes.[2] In particular he was influenced by Windelband's insistence that philosophy entails "the scientific treatment of general questions relating to the universe and human life" (Windelband 1901: 1) and that its history describes a process that challenged theology as scientific insight supplied a theory of the world and human life where religion could no longer meet this need (ibid.: 4). The conflict of *mythology* (including religion) and *science* (including philosophy) and the emergence of the one ("intelligence which seeks knowledge methodically for its own sake") from the other ("mythical fancy") in terms of explanatory power (ibid.: 24) is Windelband's controlling thesis, and one that Beckett respected.

Yet Beckett is a major religious writer, however steeped in agnosticism or atheism. He makes intricate reference to Christian symbols and rituals, and his curiosity about the theological quags into which the pre-Socratics wandered, to be followed by the early Church fathers and the seventeenth-century rationalists, testifies to his obsession with the paradoxes of faith, even as it precludes affirmation of any systematic belief (see Ackerley and Gontarski 2004: 479–81). His acute religious sensibility coexisted with a fundamental skepticism and a pervasive sense of absurdity (*"quia impossibile est"* as much as *"quia absurdum est"*). *Waiting for Godot*, his best-known work, is finely balanced between an insistent allegory of Christian salvation and an antithetical atheistic universe in which the persistence of hope is the cruelest joke of all. *Watt* is predicated on the basic question ("What?") and an equivocal answer ("[K]not"). It offers a critique of the mystical experience (Arsene's mysterious moment in the sun); of the bond between master and servant; of witnessing (with the Berkeleyan twist that if God is not witnessed then how can he exist?); and of the rationalism (Cartesian or Christian) by which Watt moves from apprehension of the clear and distinct not unto knowledge of Mr Knott but to the asylum.

The narrator of *Watt* considers how best to talk to God: as though he were a man ("which to be sure he was, in a sense, for a time"), or a termite (Beckett 2006: 1.229–30)?[3] The rational process is suspect, foisting a meaning where no meaning appears and evolving from the "meticulous phantoms" that beset Watt "a hypothesis proper to dispense them" (Beckett 2006: 1.230). Such attempts, we are told, are neither wholly successful, nor unsuccessful; rather, the hypothesis soon loses its virtue and must be replaced by another, "which in its turn had to be replaced by another, which in due course ceased to be of the least assistance, and so on." Or, rather, not "on": that preposition (a mirror-inversion of "no") implies progress, duty, and exhortation in a world apparently without purpose. Compare *The Unnamable*: "it's not a question of hypotheses, it's a question of going on, it goes on, hypotheses are like everything else, they help you on" (Beckett 2006: 2.397). The sequence curiously anticipates Karl Popper and Thomas Kuhn on scientific method, but Watt's attempts to construct hypotheses that advance understanding, to "saddle" events with meaning, meet resistance, and the formulae through which they are mediated fail as though they had not been. Any attempt, therefore, to saddle Beckett with a scientific temperament, let alone a scientific methodology, runs into an impasse generated by Beckett's deep distrust of the rational process. His rejection of rationalism entails a rejection of scientific methodology, less the process of uncertainty and fallibility ("Try again. Fail again. Fail better") than the capacity of reason and its handmaiden hypothesis to shape a sufficient understanding of the natural world.

What this inquiry offers, then, is neither an acceptance nor a rejection of Beckett's "scientific" knowledge but rather a map, or graph, of his conceptual world. To which I add in haste, as in Chapter 6 of *Murphy* where a justification of "Murphy's mind" is attempted, that what follows does not concern that world as it really was ("that would be an extravagance and an impertinence"), but, perhaps, as it felt and pictured itself to be. I offer accordingly an analogue of how Beckett's consciousness might have structured the natural world, a synthesis arising (in the words of Belacqua in *Dream of Fair to middling Women*) from the "refractory constituents" of his various writings that bind, however reluctantly, into a "composure," the value of which can be ascertained only with respect to how well the "succession of terms" approximates "the cubic unknown" (Beckett 1992: 118–20, 124–5).[4] More simply, such a map may have some heuristic and explanatory value.

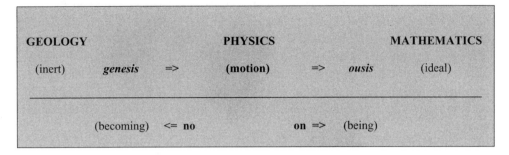

GEOLOGY			PHYSICS			MATHEMATICS
(inert)	*genesis*	=>	(motion)	=>	*ousis*	(ideal)
	(becoming)	<= no		on =>	(being)	

Figure 11.1 From *genesis* to *ousis*

A first essay is to graph the natural world along a horizontal axis from *geology* (representing the inert sciences) to *mathematics* (the universe of Ideas); and as reflecting the process (from *genesis* to *ousis*) of coming into being, as shown in Figure 11.1. James Knowlson (1996: 29) testifies to Beckett's early love of stones, which Beckett later rationalized as a fascination with the mineral, with things dying and decaying, with petrification; linking these to Freud's pre-birth nostalgia of return to the mineral state.[5] Diderot's "Le Rêve de d'Alembert" articulates the paradox of life generated from the plane of inert sediment, and returning to that state – his literal reading of Genesis 3:19: "for dust thou art, and unto dust shalt thou return" (one of the texts with which Beckett was obsessed). In his *Méthode* (Part 3), Descartes determined to find the ground of assurance, casting aside loose earth and sand to reach the rock and clay. Early drafts of *Watt* invoke "auto-speliology," the desire to go "deep down in those palaezoic profounds," to descend into the self. *How It Is* enacts the struggle of incipient form to emerge from existential formlessness, the mud an amorphous plane between the rock below and the light above. In "Rough for Radio II" Fox returns to the depths, "all stones all sides," with lichens, tunnels, and a voice that cries: "Let me out! Peter out in the stones!" Stones and bones inform Beckett's writings, from the early poetry of *Echo's Bones* to the Unnamable's sense of being trapped in his head like a fossil in a rock (Beckett 2006: 2.386) and the dark figure of Woburn in the radio play "Cascando," face in the stones, in the sand, in the mud, crashing his way to the sea, that littoral threshold of a consciousness ultimately denied its metamorphosis and so destined to return to the mineral from which it somehow arose.

At the other end of the horizontal axis is *mathematics*, the science that most closely approximates the Platonic ideal. In simple terms: the *idea* of a circle, or triangle, is a *universal* that encompasses all individual circles, or triangles, and thus has a perfection of form to which particular circles, or triangles, only approximate. Therein lies the problem that haunts Beckett: not only the ontological status of such universals but the relationship and finally the *gulf* between them and the particulars that they subsume. The obvious "bridge" is the rational faculty, but this proves suspect. A footnote to *Whoroscope* (1930) records that Descartes "proves God by exhaustion" (Beckett 2006: 4.7). This phrase is used of a circle with an inscribed polygon: the figure inscribed, be it a square or chiliagon, can be calculated exactly; and the more complex the polygon, the closer to the precise area of the circle. This is also true of the perfect sphere with an inscribed cube, dodecahedron, or icosahedron. However exhaustive, the method is approximate only; an infinitesimal gap between the perfect circle (or God) and *ratio* (reason) remains, for the gulf between the ideal and the real (the infinite and the finite, universal and particular, *esse in intellectu* and *esse in re*, God and man) cannot be crossed. The existence of *pi* indeed constitutes an offense against the deity.[6]

To understand the *essence* of his master, Watt lists his *accidents* in paradigms of increasing complexity. This parodies the third precept of the Cartesian method ("to order his thoughts beginning with the most simple and rising step by step to the knowledge of the most complex") (Baillett in Ackerley 2006: 43 [my translation]), for he fails to comprehend that the gulf between the rational and the transcendental cannot be overcome thus. Molloy, lost in the dark wood, but his head full of useful knowledge, recalls Descartes's advice that a traveler lost in a forest should proceed in a straight line; equally, though, he knows the fallacy of this, that one intending a straight line goes round in a circle. He instead describes a circle, hoping thereby to go in a straight line. This has limited success, in that he does not trace a circle, "and that at least was something" (Beckett 2006: 2.84), so he refines his method by altering course with every few jerks, permitting if not a circle at least a great polygon: "perfection is not of this world" (a motto suitable for this study). The day finally comes, by chance or exhaustion (the pun is implicit), when he reaches the *limit*, a tangent perhaps, the ditch adjacent to the forest.

Windelband (1901: 122) considers Plato's "unfortunate thought" of developing his ideas in accordance with Pythagorean number theory. The thought is unfortunate (he argues) because (1) it asserted mathematical forms not simply as universals but as ideas of a higher reality, thereby (2) insinuating an ethical principle (God as the One and an ideal transcendent being), and, further, (3) creating a disjunction between two ways of knowing, that of *perception* (the senses) and that of *reason* (the mind), the former but a shadow of the latter. Watt cannot relate a "pot" to the ideal Pot, for it evades, if only by a hairsbreadth, the nature of the true Pot. Godot, similarly, exists in the ideal realm and is inaccessible to sensory experience, but his existence cannot be discounted. The impasse consigns Vladimir and Estragon to an eternity (metaphorically speaking) of waiting.

According to Windelband (1901: 111), the two categories of corporeal being are *ousia*, ever the same with itself, and *genesis*, in process of change. The preoccupation of Greek thought, he contends (ibid.: 73), concerns the relationship between the unchanging order of things and the world of change. Greek ethics, he notes, began with a problem that paralleled the initial problem of physics: the essence of things that abide and survive all change. The Greek mind, seeking a permanent in the mutation of occurrence, found it in the great relations, such as the revolution of the stars, which *abide* (ibid.: 57). Like the stars, or Godot, Mr Knott *abides*; like Estragon and Vladimir, his servants *come and go*. Watt comes into the "establishment," works on the ground floor, moves to the first floor, then goes out as another comes in – but he never crosses the invisible threshold that might let him know Mr Knott; indeed, his failure to comprehend Arsene's "short statement" (a mystical intuition of *being* out of time) confirms his inability ever to do so.

The essential difference between *being* and *becoming* is *motion*.[7] Belacqua in "Ding-Dong" gives the Furies (his creditors) the slip by "setting himself in motion" (Beckett 2006: 4.99); his need to "move constantly" reflects a first law of physics, keep moving the only virtue, "gress" that is neither "pro" nor "re" (hence the tension between "**on**" and "**no**"). According to Arnold Geulincx, "Motus enim duas habet partes: *abesse* et *adesse*" ("Motion thus has two forms, *from being* and *to being*") (in Ackerley and Gontarski 2004: 385). Murphy's "When he came to, or rather from" (Beckett 2006: 1.65) is not a quibble but an Occasionalist conclusion, that he is coming *from* the realm of his mind *to* that of his body. Malone opines: "in order not to die you must come and go, come and go" (Beckett 2006: 2.225); but to die is the natural order of things, and the alternative to motion is death or homeostasis. The world of *Endgame* is "winding up" (or running down), with the death of all that is natural; and Winnie in *Happy Days* restates Aristotle's premise that "something must happen, in the world" (ibid.: 3.290) if she is to move again; but mobility is a curse (ibid.: 3.295–6) and earth a great extinguisher.

The diagrams in this chapter (Figs 11.1–5) center about *physics*, once defined by its scholastic opposition to *metaphysics*, but here describing the mechanics of motion. Physics mediates between the inert sciences (geology), in terms of the constitutive qualities of the natural world (Gk. *physis*) and the ideal sciences (mathematics), in terms of the laws by which the physical universe (its comings and goings) may be known. Both the ideal and material universes are intimated, but also the role of *motion* in terms of the classical Newtonian paradigm and the strange new world of quantum physics.[8] Figure 11.2 shows how these matters may be represented. (I note, parenthetically, that *biology* might form this fulcrum, but, in the first place, this is implicit in the *genesis* of life from the plane of the inert, and, in the second place, the biological sciences illustrate less efficiently the interaction of *nature* and *law*.)[9]

Beckett's early novels, *Murphy* and *Watt*, annihilate, if not the visible universe, then at least its rationalist foundations. Superficially, *Murphy*'s world is part of the Newtonian universe, where reason and harmony ("APMONIA") hold sway, where matter is governed by principles of *equilibrium*. In Wylie's words (Beckett 2006: 1.38), "The horse leech's daughter is a closed system. Her quantum of wantum cannot vary." This derives from Windelband (1901: 546), who argues that in nature substance is permanent, "its quantum can neither be increased nor diminished." The Newtonian universe is subject to entropy and the First Law of Thermodynamics (consider *Endgame*), but at the human level it is also subverted by the irrational Proustian ethos of *desire*. In the quantum state, classical laws that regulate the macrocosmic machinery do not apply; entities such as electrons exist in two states simultaneously, matter and/or energy; electromagnetic radiation behaves as waves and/or particles (*quanta*); Beckett considered this a better analogue of the mind.

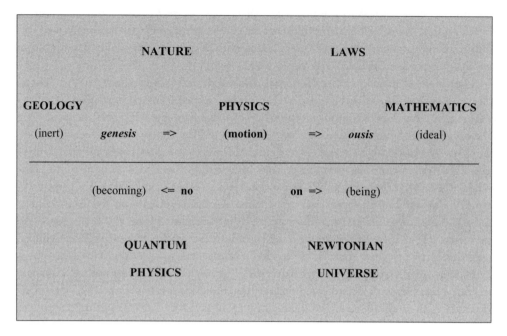

Figure 11.2   The physical world

The third zone of Murphy's mind, like Belacqua's "dark gulf," offers "a tumult of non-Newtonian motion." Here Murphy is a mote in the dark of absolute freedom, a point in the "ceaseless unconditioned generation and passing away of line," a missile without provenance (Beckett 2006: 1.70). This is the "matrix of surds," or womb of irrationality, a realm of mental being free from the contingencies of the contingent world. Molloy likewise feels, as identity fades, the "namelessness" of "waves and particles" (*Molloy*, Beckett 2006: 2.27), nameless things, thingless names. "A" and "C" act like particles in an undulating landscape, "which caused the road to be in waves" (Beckett 2006: 2.5); their meeting is the kind of random coincidence that binds other characters in the novel, whose encounters release destructive energies. Forces move about the fixed central figure of the Unnamable in an image of the planetary and atomic systems; the latter suggesting a splitting of the Cartesian atom of self to reveal curious particles within, of which no final understanding is reached. This drives the search for the most elusive matter of all, the location and nature of the *voice*.

Many of these concerns were anticipated by the pre-Socratics. By insisting that all flows, nothing abides, Heraclitus defined cosmic process as a continuous Becoming; whereas Parmenides accentuated the centrality of Being, the illusory nature of the senses, and The One. This drew an absolute distinction between the natural world of *genesis* and change, and that of mathematical forms and Being: "The Becoming of Heraclitus produces no Being, as the Being of Parmenides produces no Becoming" (Windelband 1901: 50). Crucially, this teleological principle informed a theory of knowledge, associated with Protagoras, whose celebrated dictum, that man is the measure of all things, affirmed the subjectivity of sense perception. Denying all knowledge of what *is*, Protagoras asserted the objects of sensory perception as a transient and relative reality, distinguishing in a remarkably pre-Kantian way between two kinds of knowledge, that of perception to a changing actuality (*phenomena*), and of thought to a reality (*noumena*) absolute and abiding (ibid.: 104–6).

The Platonic doctrine of knowledge and its allegiance to an immaterial reality, Windelband argues (ibid.: 116–18), is rooted explicitly in this rationalist theory of perception, man's allegiance to the higher (unchanging) order of things reflecting a principle of anthropomorphism that has shaped a sense of the natural world so intricately that Western history and philosophy has simply taken it for granted. For Windelband, the main divide in Greek thought was not that between Aristotelian materialism and Platonic ideas, for both assert the immortality of the soul, but rather between these schools and the atomists (Democritus, Epicurus, Lucretius); the triumph of Christianity led to the acceptance of the one and the eclipse of the other. Beckett's distrust of anthropomorphism is rooted in precisely this aspect of atomist thought, and he challenged it in three important ways (an argument I first made in Ackerley 2005: 1–20; see also Ackerley 2007):

1   His loyalty to a counter tradition (*atomism*), from Democritus through Epicurus and Lucretius, which took the form of pessimistic dissent and denied allegiance to a higher order, in particular, any possibility of the soul's survival after death, as explicit in the tradition of Graeco-Christian thought from Socrates, Plato, and Aristotle through Augustine, Neo-Platonism, and Christian rationalism to Descartes and beyond. Instead, Beckett affirmed an intrinsic irrationality, the absurdity of existence.

2   A growing suspicion of the unqualified relationship between the perceiving subject and that which is perceived; a distrust which questioned knowledge of the self as mediated by representation and affirmed the need to rupture the lines of communication between subject and object. This became a crucial concern in Beckett's later writings.

3   An aesthetic that rejected "the itch to animise," seeing nature as incommensurate with human expression, landscape as indifferent to mankind. Only with difficulty can the anthropomorphic mind disengage itself from its preconceptions (Knott is invariably "Mr Knott"); Beckett, however, rejected "the impulse towards anthropomorphism" by seeing nature as ultimately unintelligible and making the absence of rapport his working principle.

One consequence of what Windelband terms "a reciprocal interpenetration of cosmological and anthropological bodies of thought" (1901: 99) was the growth of theories of knowledge that attempted to ground metaphysics in principles of perception, and thus a tradition of scholasticism that for two thousand years reformulated the Platonic ideas and Aristotle's dicta by the precepts of Christian theology. The great question concerned the metaphysical significance of logical genera, of how uni-versals relate to reality (ibid.: 271; see also "scholasticism" in Ackerley and Gontarski [2004: 507–10]). *Realists* maintained the independent (Platonic) existence of genera and species; *nominalists* saw in universals only designations that apply commonly. Beckett's fascination with scholastic intricacies took many forms: the "Eucharistic sophistry" of *Whoroscope* that reconciles transubstantiation with the Cartesian physics of corporeal motion; Watt's "ancient error" of trying to understand the essential Knott by his accidents; Murphy's syllogistic explanation to Celia of the condition of their walking away (Beckett 2006: 1.12); or Mercier's "contribution to the controversy of the universals" (*Mercier and Camier*, Beckett 2006: 1.447, 458). Consider, too, the failure of Jackson's pink and gray parrot to complete the scholastic dictum: it could manage *Nihil in intellectu* ("There is nothing in the mind"), but the "celebrated restric-tion," *quod non prius fuerat in sensu* ("that was not first in the senses") was too much for it: "all you heard was a series of squawks" (*Malone Dies*, Beckett 2006: 2.211–12).

The epistemological principles may be reduced to two simple paradigms: (1) the Protagorean distinction between perception and knowing, in the familiar Kantian terms of *phenomena* and *noumena*; and (2) the dialectic of nominalism and realism, as shown in Figure 11.3. These principles require some explicitation. Broadly, *phenomena* and *nominalism* tend to the particular, and appear on the left (material) side of the figure, whereas *noumena* and *realism* tend to the universal, and appear on the right (ideal) side. I include the opposition of *macrocosm* and *microcosm*, as defined by Murphy (Beckett 2006: 1.107–8) in terms of the mind's attraction toward the Big World (Celia, ginger biscuits) against its pleasure in the little (*Ubi nihil vales, ibi nihil velis*). As *phenomena* and *noumena* tend to the macrocosm, they appear in the upper segments; as *nominalism* and *realism* tend to the microcosm, they appear in the lower. Specifically:

1 *Phenomena:* in *Murphy* (Beckett 2006: 1.11), Mr Willoughby Kelly urges Celia to be less "beastly circumstantial," with fewer "demented particulars." Underlying this admonition is Beckett's belief that the only things that can be known are the straws and the flotsam (scattered particulars) of human history, and that any attempt to rationalize them is a futile form of animism (Beckett German Diaries 4 in Ackerley 2004: 46–7 n. 13.2).[9] As Windelband notes (1901: 296), the *metaphysics of individual-ism* that accompany such a theory of knowledge assert that only particulars can be regarded as truly real (he invokes Roscellinus). This was a position that Beckett accepted, one that acknowledges the immediacy of demented particulars.

2 *Noumena:* the Kantian distinction between *phenomena* and *noumena* reflects that between our knowledge of objects as mediated by perception and the *Ding an sich*, the object that exists in the conceptual realm inaccessible to the senses. I have appro-priated "fluxions" from J-M. Rabaté, who uses this, Newton's term for the derivatives of a mathematical function, to suggest (in Berkeley's words) "the ghosts of departed quantities": invisible entities of plays like *Ghost Trio* or *Eh Joe*, but equally flickers of

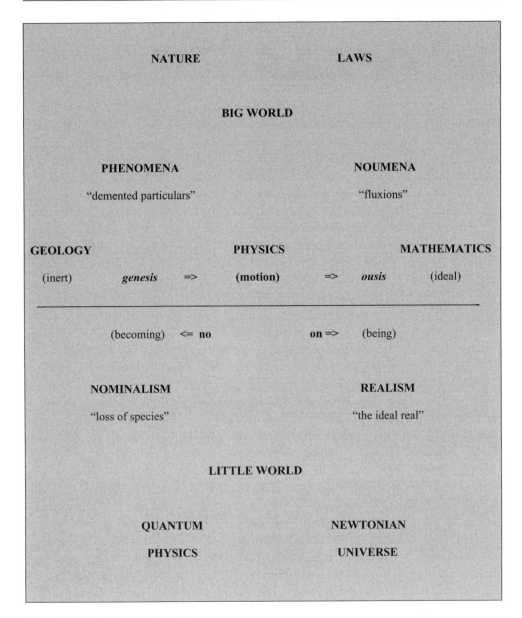

Figure 11.3   The phenomenal world

consciousness, memories, intertextual and auditory intimations, and fleeting intui-
tions of inevitable failures of vision amidst the deepening shades (see Rabaté 1996).
For all his particularity, Beckett did not deny the force of fluxions.

 3   *Nominalism:* in his "German Letter of 1937" to Axel Kaun, Beckett suggested
that he was seeking "the literature of the unword": a form of nominalist irony as "a

necessary stage" of tearing apart the veil of language, "to get at the things (or the Nothingness) behind it" (Beckett 1983: 173, 171). Nominalism reflects the scholastic opinion of universals as names only; but the irony thus defined is Beckett's critique of Fritz Mauthner's more radical nominalism, which would deny language the capacity to represent either universals or individuals (Ackerley and Gontarski 2004: 359). Beckett shares the sense of a blasted linguistic landscape in which signs are barely discernible, but his is a crucial qualification of Mauthner: a denial "bedeviled by the compulsion to express, so that even as expression is denuded an antic mask may be assumed" (Ackerley and Gontarski 2004: 360). The anonymous narrator of *How It Is* considers his individuality as a "loss of species" (Beckett 2006: 2.427): this may be construed in the biological sense (belonging to a larger unit, classified, not *unnamable*, not "a monster of the solitudes"), but also as defined by Windelband (1901: 127): "the ethical ideal of the Platonic philosophy lay not in the ability and happiness of the few, but in the ethical perfection of the species." Loss of species, like loss of language, is the loss of what makes one One with others; hence the unnamed narrator's tragic conclusion (a final Nominalist irony) that he is "sole elect."

4   *Realism:* Murphy, contemplating his lunch with reverence and satisfaction (Beckett 2006: 1.51), ponders the logical realism of Guillaume de Champeaux, to the effect that the universal is present in all its individuals (Windelband 1901: 294), so that by ingesting the biscuits he will also ingest their creator. To the Realist, the universal "*contains within itself the particular* (the species and ultimately the individual)"; universals are therefore not only substances (*res*, hence "realists"), but they are "*the more Real in proportion as they are the more universal*" (ibid.: 290). The question of the kind of reality that belongs to universals and their relation to individual things known to the senses is perhaps irresolvable (Murphy dimly recalls the eternal Kick "in its correlated modes of consciousness, the kick in *intellectu* and the kick *in re*" [Beckett 2006: 1.68]); but Realism was for Beckett an untenable doctrine, if only because it conflicted with demented particularity. Even so, traces remain in his thought, most clearly in his discussion of involuntary memory: the Proustian experience as "at once imaginative and empirical, at once an evocation and a direct perception, real without being merely actual, ideal without being merely abstract, the ideal real, the essential, the extratemporal" (Beckett 2006: 4.544). Even if this says more about Proust than himself (I would dispute this), or if "real" hovers uncertainly between the language of the academy and that of the market place, it nevertheless constitutes a lasting element of Beckett's aesthetic.

The two paradigms (*phenomena/noumena* and *nominalism/realism*) reflect modes of epistemology. A vertical axis suggests the further agency of the mind and continues the principle of dialectical opposition, first by contrasting *physics* with *metaphysics* (that which transcends *physis*, or nature); then by contrasting *physics* with *psychology* (see Fig. 11.4). As Hamm might say (Beckett 2006: 3.114), perhaps we are beginning to mean something. The paradigms added are Beckett's own: an ascent through three stages of perception (*petites perceptions, perception, apperception*) toward the *mystical*, as defined by Dean Inge in *Christian Mysticism*: "the immanence of the temporal in the eternal, and of the eternal in the temporal" (Ackerley and Gontarski 2004: 397), and an equal but opposite descent through three stages of consciousness (*light, half-light, dark*) that structure the minds of Belacqua and Murphy. The two paradigms reflect classical doctrines of the tripartite soul as well as more recent analogues (Freud, Jung) of the unconscious. The upper movement is from the self as center of being (whatever that means) toward the outer light; the lower is the antithetical movement from that self into its inner dark.

The upper axis reflects Beckett's fascination, albeit tempered by skepticism, with Leibniz's *Monadology* (Ackerley and Gontarski 2004: 314–15). For Leibniz, the monad is indestructible, and its essence is activity, or motion; each monad is an individual, distinct from all others (Windelband 1901: 423). The world is an infinite set of monads, mutually accommodated by a principle of pre-established harmony; and Leibniz asserts an ascent toward perfection from the lowest to the highest, culminating in the Supreme Monad. Murphy, hermetically sealed in his greatcoat, is a monad in motion, a *microcosm*, illustrating in human terms the laws of the physical universe as iterated in the *Monadology*. Tragically, his encounter with Mr Endon (Gk. meaning "within") reveals that his mind is not body-tight.

One of Leibniz's distinctions, reflecting the pre-Socratean paradoxes from which it arose, is that between *virtual* and *actual*, terms Beckett uses in his description of Murphy's mind, with respect to perception. *Petites perceptions* reflect what might be called "unconscious mental states" (Windelband 1901: 424); these are virtual, but in their totality (imperceptible drops of water breaking as a wave; innumerable grains of millet making up a heap) they may become actual; thus, they are both *ideal* and *real*. The term represents Leibniz's dissatisfaction with the clear and distinct; Descartes's mistake, he said, was to take no account of that which was not apperceived, "for it treats as non-existent those perceptions of which we are not consciously aware." (Ackerley and Gontarski 2004: 215).

For simplicity, I assume *perception* as a given, as intermediate between *petites perceptions*, or mental states below the threshold of awareness, and *apperception*, the mind's awareness of its own perceptual processes. Berkeley's *esse est percipi* ("to be is to be perceived"), another of Beckett's obsessional dicta, shapes his work ironically from *Murphy* (the encounter with Mr Endon) to *Film* (a vain attempt to escape the all-seeing Eye/I) and beyond (the mind creating the image in "La Falaise"). This is a vast realm of inquiry, but I prefer simply to restate the Protagorean (or Kantian) assertion that sensory perception yields phenomena radically different from things-in-themselves.

Apperception, for Leibniz and Kant, is the active process of the mind's reflecting upon itself, the consciousness of being conscious. Thus it defines the process whereby unconscious states of mind are rendered clear and distinct, *petites perceptions* translated into self-awareness. As Beckett was aware, this involves a paradox of infinite regression, in that the "I" that perceives itself must yet be aware of the *gulf* between that which perceives and that which is perceived; this requires a third faculty to unite them, and so on. This *regressus ad infinitum* Kant short-circuited, to use Murphy's term

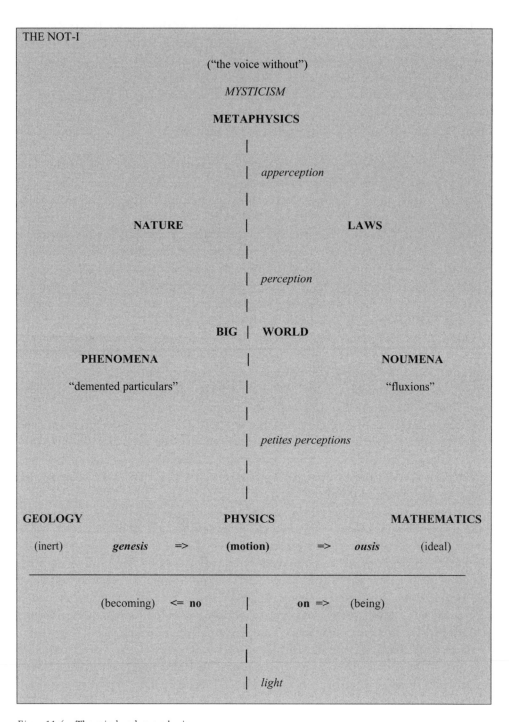

Figure 11.4   The mind and metaphysics

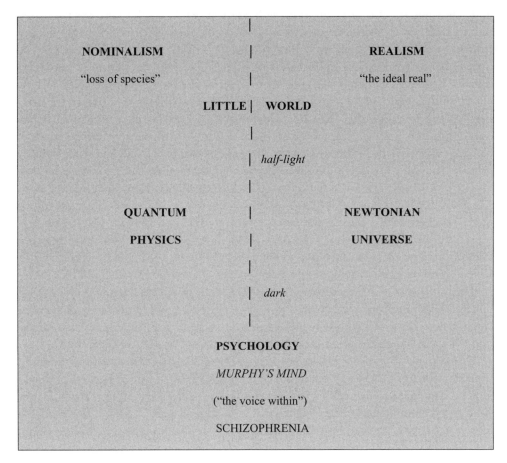

NOMINALISM | REALISM
"loss of species" | "the ideal real"

LITTLE | WORLD

| *half-light*

QUANTUM | NEWTONIAN
PHYSICS | UNIVERSE

| *dark*

PSYCHOLOGY

MURPHY'S MIND

("the voice within")

SCHIZOPHRENIA

Figure 11.4   Continued.

(Beckett 2006: 1.5), by the synthetic unity of consciousness; Beckett increasingly distrusted the synthetic unity of the perceiving subject, however, despite (or because of) what "O" in *Film* terms the "flight from extraneous perception breaking down in the inescapability of self-perception" (see Ackerley and Gontarski 2004: 17).

I deploy *metaphysical* in broad opposition to the Greek *physis*, "nature"; and iterate an earlier point: Beckett's simultaneous skepticism of yet attraction to the mystical. His skepticism is evident: in the discussion of mysticism in *Dream*, Belacqua finally calling himself a dud mystic, a John of the Crossroads (Beckett 1992: 186); in *Watt*'s attempts to eff the ineffable; in the eternal waiting for Godot that defers revelation; and in the conclusion of *How It Is*, that "life in the light" is "all balls." Yet the attraction persists, as in the incessant theological buzzing of the *Three Novels*, the Gnosticism of *Krapp's Last Tape*, and the spectral fluxions of "Ghost Trio" and other late works.

Above all (as it were) is the *voice*. A mystery concerns its location, without or within ("la voix ... ma voix") (Beckett 1952: 177),[10] and its authenticity, whether transcendental or delusional. From *Echo's Bones* to *What Where*, Beckett was fascinated and frustrated by this enigma; the attempt to hear and identify the voice is the ongoing concern of the great fiction, from *Watt* to *How It Is*. This is treated at length in the *Companion* (Ackerley and Gontarski 2004: 607–18) in perhaps the most important entry in that volume; here I wish merely to identify the problem of the voice and the knotty intransigence of its nature and location. One explanation (tending to the mystical) might be called the "Not-I": an external Other, as invoked by St Paul when considering the authority by which he spake (I Cor. 15:10): "not I, but the grace of God that was with me." This defines the voice as external to the self, and the allegiance owed to it as an imperative, presumably theological. In their different ways Molloy, Moran, and Malone acknowledge this voice, which each must learn to hear and follow. The Unnamable takes up the theme of "this voice that is not mine, but can only be mine" (Beckett 2006: 2.301), and the paradox of "this meaningless voice which prevents you from being nothing" (Beckett 2006: 1.364). But the distinction between the self that "utters" and the Not-I is not easily drawn (as in the play entitled *Not I*). Given *The Unnamable* as structured by the imagery of atomic physics, and its activity as the splitting of the Cartesian atom of self (the "I, of whom I know nothing"), an unhelpful resolution may be framed in terms of Bohr's Complementarity or Heisenberg's Uncertainty principles: in the quantum world of the mind the voice can be heard but not located, or vice versa; but not heard and located simultaneously.

This is unhelpful because the voice may yet be delusional. That issue is addressed in the lower part of the vertical axis, which graphs Murphy's mind as Beckett perceives it to be. The first account of this paradigm is in *Dream* (Beckett 1992: 120–5), where Belacqua is described as *trine*: "centripetal, centrifugal, and … not." The model is refined in *Murphy*, the mind pictured as a hermetic (monadic) sphere with three zones: the light, the half-light, and the dark. In the first, "forms with parallel" are perceived by the consciousness, and their reconfiguration (in Proustian terms) is voluntary. In the second, "forms without parallel" indicate that consciousness is relaxed, its activity involuntary. In the third or dark zone, the mind experiences total freedom; this is the atomist void, the Freudian unconscious, Schopenhauer's will-lessness, and/or the world of quanta and non-Newtonian motion, often imaged as the embryonic state of primal pleasure.[11] This structure is manifest in the *Three Novels* (the rational Moran regressing to the condition of Molloy, who enters the twilight world of Malone, who is reborn into the dark zone of the Unnamable), and in the circles of light and darkness of *Krapp's Last Tape*. Its relation to the paradigm above (*petites perceptions*, *perception*, *apperception*) is both complementary and ambivalent, but the contraries (in Bruno's terms) are curiously identified, so that the descent into the inner darkness emulates the ascent to the light.

On October 2, 1935 Beckett, with his analyst, Wilfred Bion, attended a lecture at the Tavistock Clinic at which Jung displayed a diagram "showing the different spheres of the mind and the dark centre of consciousness in the middle" (Ackerley 2004: 125 n. 111.3). Jung's diagram helped Beckett define the structure of Murphy's mind, the descent into the darkness of inner being, and the compatibility of his paradigm with recent trends in psychology. At this lecture Jung described how complexes may appear in visions and speak in voices, assuming identities of their own, and emancipating themselves from conscious control. In *Murphy*, Dr Killiecrankie has had "experience of the schizoid voice" (Beckett 2006: 1.111), and Watt's psychic disintegration is heralded by his experience of voices, from within or without he cannot tell. The Unnamable, too, experiences the sense of other voices imprisoned in his head, that oubliette. In *Embers*, the voices heard by Henry may be the product of his imagination or echoes of the past, but in *Eh Joe* the voice within (perhaps that of conscience, or God) becomes an assailant, emanating from "that penny farthing hell" he calls his mind. In *Company*, "a voice" comes from the dark, but its images are ill-heard, figments whose role seems to be that of aesthetic play, of "devising" company, so that the narrator is at the end as he was in the beginning, alone. *How It Is* introduces the paradox of the voice that was "once without" but now seems to be "in me." The narrator's understanding moves from "an ancient voice in me not mine" (ibid.: 2.411) to "only one voice here yes mine yes" (ibid.: 2.519), the intertextual echoing of the end of *Ulysses* mocking univocality even as it denies the alternative. The "resolution" to the problem of the transcendental or delusional voice, then, is weighted toward a nominalist irony; but this conclusion is fragile.

What remains is to complete the diagram by linking the cardinal points (Geology, Mathematics, Metaphysics, and Psychology) with a circle to indicate the conceptual relationship (whether dialectical opposition or pseudo-coupling) between recurrent epistemological concerns: *epiphany* and *God*; *consciousness* and *death*; *tomb* and *womb*; *rational* and *irrational*.[12] I have added a further axis, that of "memory," with time's arrow imagined as passing through the center of the graph but on a separate trajectory, another plane, so that it disrupts the two-dimensional (for the moment) diagram, complicating its synchronic stability by intimating a diachronic process of incessant change (Fig. 11.5).

The following relations now arise:

1   *Mathematics–Metaphysics (epiphany, God):* This arc (with its positive polarity) represents what Arsene in *Watt* (ibid.: 1.203) calls "existence off the ladder"; that is, those moments in and out of time that constitute the mystical experience, the Joycean epiphany, or the Proustian moment. This is Arsene's moment in the sun, when something in the time–space continuum seems to "slip." His experience, in the Proustian sense, is both *real* and *ideal*; it was not, Arsene insists, an illusion, but he is buggered if he can understand how it could have been anything else. Like Joyce and Proust, Beckett acknowledges the experiential reality of the mystical (similar moments are intimated throughout his work), but unlike them he withholds any transcendental validation of it. That skepticism is manifest later in *Watt* (ibid.: 1.279–80), in the Frog Song, where the series of different intervals is determined by a Fibonacci sequence (3, 5, and 8) that renders inevitable (after 120 beats) their merging in a chord; this is a perfect illustration of the mathematical *machinery* of the transcendental experience.

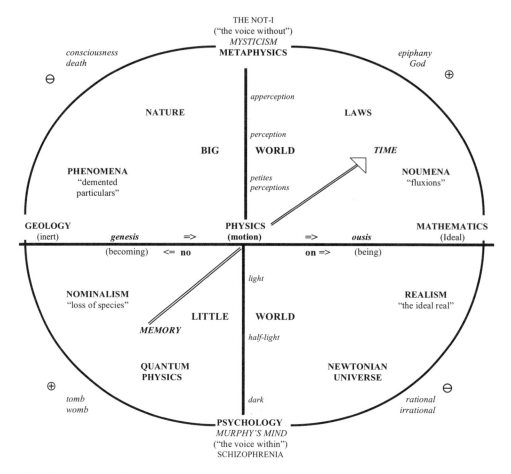

THE NOT-I
("the voice without")
MYSTICISM
METAPHYSICS

consciousness   *epiphany*
death   *God*

⊖   ⊕

apperception

NATURE   **LAWS**

perception

BIG   **WORLD**   *TIME*

PHENOMENA   *petites*   **NOUMENA**
"demented   *perceptions*   "fluxions"
particulars"

GEOLOGY   **PHYSICS**   **MATHEMATICS**
(inert)   *genesis*   =>   **(motion)**   =>   *ousis*   (Ideal)
                (becoming)   <= **no**   **on** =>   (being)

light

NOMINALISM   **REALISM**
"loss of species"   "the ideal real"

LITTLE   **WORLD**

MEMORY

half-light

QUANTUM   **NEWTONIAN**
PHYSICS   **UNIVERSE**

⊕   ⊖

tomb   *dark*   *rational*
womb   *irrational*

PSYCHOLOGY
MURPHY'S MIND
("the voice within")
SCHIZOPHRENIA

Figure 11.5 The monad

2 *Metaphysics–Geology (consciousness, death):* Beckett noted in "Proust" that the
world of our latent consciousness is "the only world that has reality and significance"
(ibid.: 4.513), and yet consciousness of being entails the knowledge (one of Beckett's
four certainties) that one day we will die. Consciousness somehow constitutes the self,
yet what Hesla calls "the reflecting-reflected dyad" (Ackerley and Gontarski 2004:
110) cannot reconcile that which reflects and that which is reflected. This arc (with
its negative polarity) traces the dialectic of awareness between the impulse to the light
and the return to the mineral. Beckett shared the atomist conviction of the dissolution
of the "soul" with that of the body; life is imaged as a process of slow crucifixion, and
he is deeply skeptical of the facile optimism that would seek consolation beyond the
grave. A wry jest informs every reference to nature (Malone when he is dead will be
"natural" at last), for death is the natural order of things. Yet it retains its mystery:
Molloy has always preferred slavery to death (that is, being put to death), "For death

is a condition I have never been able to conceive to my satisfaction" (Beckett 2006: 2.62). Yet there is a tonal shift at the end of Beckett's career, with plays like *Ghost Trio* and *Nacht und Träume* cautiously intimating something beyond.

3 *Geology–Psychology (tomb, womb):* This arc complements the previous one, but with a positive polarity: frequent images of the embryo testify to Beckett's desire to return to the womb, or, as Belacqua puts it in "Fingal," to be back "in the caul, on my back in the dark forever" (ibid.: 4.94). This is not polymorphous perversity for its own sake, although it reflects Otto Rank's sense of the "intrauterine primal pleasure" as interrupted by birth, so that life consists in uterine regression; this definition of the pre-oedipal relationship with the mother offering Beckett his most important psychoanalytic myth (Ackerley and Gontarski 2004: 170–1). More importantly, it offered Beckett a paradigm for the desire of the mind to go "wombtomb" (Beckett 1992: 121), that is, to enter its dark zone.

4 *Psychology–Mathematics (rational, irrational):* Whatever his sentiments about the loutishness of learning, Beckett could not ignore what he calls in *Murphy* (Beckett 2006: 1.115) the "rational prurit," the intellectual urge to scratch the spot that itches. This arc (with its negative polarity) represents his ongoing quarrel with the rationalist tradition wherein the right pursuit of reason is the highest activity of the immortal soul, leading finally to the love and understanding of God. Beckett's early fictions dispute with Descartes: *Dream* invokes the "incoherent continuum" of particulars neither clear nor distinct (Beckett 1992: 102ff); *Murphy* enacts the "Cartesian catastrophe" of failing to reconcile the dualism of body and mind; *Watt* is predicated on the *Méthode*, a rational path that, alas, leads to the asylum rather than to God; and the *Three Novels* interrogate the *cogito* as the frustrum of thought. Despite Windelband's contention that "rational science is mathematics" (1901: 389), the Pythagorean story Beckett retells in *Murphy* is that of Hippasos, drowned in a puddle (Beckett 2006: 1.38) for having betrayed the incommensurability of side and diagonal, the irrational at the center of being. Arsene's *risus purus*, the "dianoetic laugh" or Democritean guffaw that laughs at that which is unhappy (ibid.: 1.207), also mocks its source: Windelband's note on Aristotle concludes that "the dianoetic virtues are the highest"; that the highest perfection of thought is achieved by the rational nature of man in knowledge; and that man thereby "gains a participation in that *pure thought*, in which the essence of the deity consists" (1901: 154).

The axis of *memory* and *time* upsets the diagram's stability. As I have argued in *Demented Particulars* (Ackerley 2004: 118 n. 10.4), this Proustian fly in the ointment of microcosmos is a function of the monad's existence in time. Figure 11.5 maps the synchronic relations between its constituent parts, but it fails to acknowledge that identity thus constituted is ever changing, the past incessantly reformed by memory both fugitive and unreliable. It therefore must be re-imagined not just in terms of a complementary diachronic process, but as one of an infinity of successive synchronous states (a chess game with innumerable moves), each existing in a moment of time and with no certain relation to any other (a further intimation of the gulf between *being* and *becoming*). Beckett in "Proust" distrusts voluntary memory as a means of regaining the past, but he sees involuntary memory as an "accidental and fugitive salvation," a "mystic experience" (Beckett 2006: 4.124) that resolves the Proustian equation by recreating the experience as both *real* and *ideal*, thereby overcoming the hydra of time. This trust did not last, despite the epiphantic moments in such works as *Krapp's Last Tape* or *Words and Music*. In the late short prose, memory gives way to measurement, as something to be *counted on* when the mind fades.

Let me return to my Figure 11.5, without thus dissolving it in the teacup of Time. At this point some imaginative topology is required, beyond my geometric skills to depict, whereby the circle may be inflated into a sphere, with "PHYSICS" at its center, the nucleus of an atom of Being, in effect. This turns the two-dimensional graph into a three-dimensional *kosmos*, a self-contained world structured by intrinsic principles of harmony and dialectical contrast. The resulting *microcosm* might be called a *monad*, independent and self-contained; less irreverently, it resembles Newton's apple, or that of William Tell, with time's arrow passing through its center as an independent axis, thereby intimating a fourth dimension.

For those who cannot accept (as Beckett could not) Leibniz's doctrine of pre-established harmony that is his necessary validation of the activity of the monad, this structure has its problems, in terms of its accommodation to the natural or physical world. Let me recount one of Beckett's esoteric philosophical jests. Murphy's greatcoat is not quite vapor-tight, for when Celia gives it "a bit of a dinge" it fills out, "as a punctured ball will not retain an impression" (ibid.: 1.87). As Murphy retraces his steps, hissing, his strange figure excites the derision of some boys playing football in the road. Murphy on the jobpath embodies the monad in motion; a football is the commonest everyday embodiment of the Pythagorean dodecahedron, of all solids, Burnet claims (not entirely correctly, for the icosahedron with its 32 faces does so better), it "approaches most nearly to the sphere" (Ackerley 2004: 71 n. 47.9). A curious image suggests itself: the monad spiked by the exigencies of Job (allegiance to the Big World), and a hiss as the vital element of air escapes. What is attractive about this image is its incongruity; for, in the absence of Leibniz's God, if the monad is to retain any conceptual validity it must somehow accommodate the absurd.

The monadic structure offered in this essay has (I believe) an explanatory power that survives such mockery. For, at the center of this "large hollow sphere" (*Murphy*, Beckett 2006: 1.67) resides the abiding mystery of the conscious self and its relation to the world (that relation ever compromised by *desire* or *appetition*, which, as Neary bears witness, undermines rational behavior). As Stan Gontarski has remarked, the idea of character as a representation of self, a coherent and discrete entity, became for Beckett increasingly problematic.[13] Influenced by Freud and psychoanalysis, he found the Cartesian self (the "I" that Descartes finally could not doubt) not only unstable but finally unrepresentable, an incoherent continuum. New forms had to evolve to acknowledge the resistance of self to representation, to contain the chaos. In the 1960s, following the impasse of *How It Is*, Beckett turned from stories of motion toward vignettes of stillness and "closed space," and thence to the disembodied voices and voiceless bodies of the later short works. Jung had talked of the *integration* of self, but (as Molloy's Jungian quest testifies, by stripping away the psychoanalytical myths to reach the unaccommodated man) any representation of Beckett's monadic calculus of being (my "new form" to contain his chaos) must rather admit the *dis-integration* (or *differentiation*) of self.

There is no easy resolution to the enigma of the monadic self and its location in the world, but in an article entitled "What is Reality?" in the fiftieth anniversary issue of *New Scientist* Roger Penrose (2006: 32–9) responded to the Cartesian conundrum in a way, perhaps, that Beckett intuited but was unable to articulate, or, if this is too speculative, one that at least puts the concerns of this essay into an intriguing perspective. Initially, Penrose accepts that the universe consists of "actual things made of matter" but equally "the reality of our minds" (32) – hence, the familiar paradox of the world as existing independent of perception, yet its existence entirely dependent upon its being perceived by an individual consciousness. But Penrose finds this unsatisfactory, arguing that it is particularly difficult to see "how the extraordinary precision that we seem to observe in the workings of the natural world should find its basis in the musings of any individual" (34). He argues, in effect, that mathematical models of the physical world model reality with a precision far beyond that of our direct (or multi-personal) sense experiences (36); the agreement, he contends, is extraordinary, "revealing accord between physical behaviour at its deepest level and a beautiful, sophisticated mathematical scheme" (36).

The nub of Penrose's argument is that the mathematics is *there* in the behavior of physical things, and not merely imposed (perceived) by us; consequently, "the common-sense reality of chairs, tables and other material things would seem to dissolve away, to be replaced by a deeper reality inhabiting the world of mathematics" (38); the seemingly abstract world of Platonic forms accommodating with comfort physical reality. He therefore allows the Platonic mathematical world its own timeless and locationless existence, "while allowing it to be accessible to us through mental activity" (39). His viewpoint, he concludes, allows for three different kinds of reality: "the physical, the mental and the Platonic mathematical, with something (as yet) profoundly mysterious in the relations between the three" (39).

The importance of this reasoning for my study is that it breaks away from the usual Cartesian dualism to offer a different model: one that first tries to reconcile the plane of the inert (geology) with the realm of the ideal (mathematics); but one that senses, as Beckett seems to have done, the curious and fundamentally absurd relationship of the perceiving and disintegrating self to this continuum (whatever its ontological status), the absurdity arising from the fact that any real knowledge is limited to that of a few demented particulars, while reason gets stuck in the quags. That structure might therefore be used (or abused, some may hiss) to validate the monadic model I have been trying to advance. Penrose, let me hasten to add, does not imply let alone encourage any such nonsense; however, his integration of the physical with the mathematical, his avoidance of theology (like the Marquis de Laplace, he has no need for that hypothesis), and his setting of this continuum against what he calls "mental activity" permits the passage of the godforsaken monad as a suitably absurdist image of the self in motion, while largely evading the charge of "anthropomorphic insolence" (*Watt*, Beckett 2006: 1.334).

For Beckett, following Windelband, the central epistemological issue of the relation of the perceiving self to the world was framed in terms of the emergence of scientific (philosophical) inquiry from mythical fancy (religion), but this introduced into his conceptual framework three thousand years of religious impedimenta of the kind that Penrose in his more detached perspective can set aside. In the final analysis, perhaps, it is not the universe that is the absurdist structure (though one must "naturally" remain agnostic as to this), but rather the agency of the human mind that must accommodate itself to the only possible, the demented particulars of quotidian reality, in rare moments only being able to intuit the deeper laws that frame them, and so being left, like Arsene, with the fugitive memory of experiences that are not illusory, though we are buggered if we can understand how they could be anything else.

NOTES

1 References to Beckett's published work, unless otherwise indicated, are to this edition. The gnomic title and form (an echo of Goethe's "Xenien," an intricate pattern of participles, rhythms, and rhymes) subverts the sentiment without quite denying it; such irony characterizes Beckett's entire attitude to knowledge.

2 Beckett's notes from Windelband, some 266 folio pages, are now at Trinity College, Dublin (TCD MS 10967); for their description, see Frost, Engelberts, and Maxwell (2006: 13–199). See also Feldman (2006).

3 See Ackerley (2006: 96–7) for this critique of anthropology, negative theology, and scientific method. The "hypothesis" section was a late addition to the manuscript. Compare *Molloy* (Beckett 2006: 2.35): "What I liked in anthropology was its inexhaustible faculty of negation, its relentless definition of man, as though he were no better than God, in terms of what he is not."

4 Attempting to define the essential Belacqua while admitting that the attempt is doomed to failure: "He is in marmalade" (Beckett 1992: 125), this perhaps puns on "compote" ("composure" or "confiture").

5 My examples derive from the entry on Geology in Ackerley and Gontarski (2004: 219–21).

6 "B" notes in the *Three Dialogues* (Beckett 2006: 4.563) "a kind of Pythagorean terror, as though the irrationality of pi were an offence against the deity, not to mention his creature."

7 Examples from the entry on Motion in Ackerley and Gontarski (2004: 384–6).

8 See the entries on Equilibrium and Physics in Ackerley and Gontarski (2004: 181–2, 435–6).

9 At Durham University (December 2006), I was asked if my paradigm was compatible with Teilhard de Chardin's sense of the *lithosphere*, *biosphere*, and *noosphere*. My reply was, well, yes, but that paradigm does not reflect the absurdity of Beckett's world.

10 The euphony in French renders the distinction more poignant than it can be in English.

11 See Ackerley (2004: 125ff.) and the entry on "Murphy's Mind" in Ackerley and Gontarski (2004: 388–9) for further discussion of these points.

12 My thanks to Karen McLean for help with this diagram and for her interest in the theme.

13 I cite for convenience the entry on Character in Ackerley and Gontarski (2004: 91–3), but Gontarski (1985) explores this notion more fully.

References and Further Reading

Ackerley C. J. (2004). *Demented Particulars: The Annotated Murphy.* 2nd edn., rev. Tallahassee, FL: Journal of Beckett Studies Books.

Ackerley C. J. (2005). "Inorganic Form: Samuel Beckett's Nature." *AUMLA* 104 (November): 1–20.

Ackerley C. J. (2006). *Obscure Locks, Simple Keys: The Annotated Watt.* Tallahassee, FL: Journal of Beckett Studies Books.

Ackerley C. J. (2007). "Samuel Beckett and Anthropomorphic Insolence." In Dirk van Hulle and Philip Laubach-Kiani (eds.), *Beckett and Romanticism.* Amsterdam: Rodopi.

Ackerley C. J., and S. E. Gontarski (2004). *The Grove Companion to Samuel Beckett.* New York: Grove Press.

Baillett, Adrien (1691). *La Vie de Monsieur Des-Cartes*, Vol. 1. Paris: Daniel Hortemels.

Beckett, Samuel. TCD MS 10967. Notes from Windelband. Trinity College Dublin.

Beckett, Samuel (1952). *L'Innommable.* Paris: Minuit.

Beckett, Samuel (1983). "German Letter of 1937." In *Disjecta: Miscellaneous Writings and a Dramatic Fragment by Samuel Beckett*, ed. Ruby Cohn. London: John Calder.

Beckett, Samuel (1992). *Dream of Fair to middling Women*, ed. Eoin O'Brien and Edith Fournier. Dublin: Black Cat Press.

Beckett, Samuel (2006). *Samuel Beckett: The Grove Centenary Edition*, 4 vols, ed. Paul Auster. New York: Grove Press.

Burnet, John (1950). *Greek Philosophy: Thales to Plato*, rpt. London: Macmillan. Originally published 1914.

Feldman, Matthew (2006). *Beckett's Books: A Cultural History of Samuel Beckett's "Interwar Notes."* London: Continuum.

Frost, Everett and Matthijs Engelberts with Jane Maxwell (eds.) (2006). "Notes Diverse Holo." *Samuel Beckett Today/Aujourd'hui* 16: 13–199. Amsterdam: Rodopi.

Geulincx, Arnold (1891). *Metaphysica.* In *Opera Philosophica*, Vol. 2, ed. J. P. Land. Hague Comitum: Martinum Nijhoff.

Gontarski, S. E. (1985). *The Intent of Undoing in Samuel Beckett's Dramatic Texts.* Bloomington: Indiana University Press.

Hesla, David (1971). *The Shape of Chaos.* Minneapolis: University of Minnesota Press.

Inge, William Ralph (1912). *Christian Mysticism*, 2nd edn., rev. London: Methuen. Originally published 1899.

Knowlson, James (1996). *Damned to Fame: The Life of Samuel Beckett.* London: Bloomsbury.

Leibniz, Gottfried (1898). *The Monadology and Other Philosophical Writings*, trans. Robert Latta. London: Oxford University Press.

Penrose, Roger (2006). "What is Reality?" *New Scientist* 2578: 32–9.

Rabaté, J.-M. (1996). "Beckett's Ghosts and Fluxions." *Samuel Beckett Today/Aujourd'hui* 5: 23–40.

Rank, Otto (1929). *The Trauma of Birth.* London: Kegan Paul, Trench, Trubner & Co.

Windelband, Wilhelm (1901). *A History of Philosophy, with Special Reference to the Formation and Development of its Problems and Conceptions*, trans. James H. Tufts. 2nd edn., rev. London: Macmillan. Originally published 1893.

12

A Purgatorial Calculus: Beckett's Mathematics in "Quad"

Brett Stevens

Introduction

Mathematics appears frequently in Samuel Beckett's writing. Molloy, the protagonist in the novel *Molloy*, the first book of Beckett's famed French novels, plays mathematical games with himself. Malone, the protagonist of *Malone Dies*, the second book in the series, tells a story of a young boy, Saposcat, who enjoys the manipulation of numbers: "He made a practice, alone and in company, of mental arithmetic. And the figures then marshaling in his mind thronged it with colours and with forms" (Beckett 1965: 4). Beckett uses mathematics extensively to set the scene in some of his later works, including *Ping*, *Imagination Dead Imagine*, *The Lost Ones*, and *Quad*. Beckett even created *Lessness*, a short prose piece, stochastically (randomly) by placing sentences in a container and drawing them out to determine their order (Cohn 1973: 265–6). Moran, the second main character in *Molloy*, makes reference to Craige, a mathematician of the late seventeenth and early eighteenth centuries (Nash 1991: 2–3, 19–22, 54–5, 81–3). The literature already contains a few analyses of mathematics in Beckett's works. This essay is a mathematician's attempt to come to terms with Beckett's use of mathematics in a single piece, the late teleplay *Quad*.

Mathematicians rarely have the chance to see atypical uses of their familiar constructs and processes. We often think that the objects we study have no interest outside of our own domain or only see them applied in fields linked to industry, technology, and commerce. That these constructs are used in such humanistic, aesthetic, and expressive endeavors is a refreshing reminder of the flexibility and ubiquity of human ideas. However, the mathematics in *Quad* is not a unidirectional application of mathematics to literature but a cross-fertilization between mathematics and literature.

Overview: Mathematics and Beckett

A story told in a classroom lecture by Professor M. Worton of University College London provided me with my first glimpse into Beckett's use of mathematics. According to the story, and we should add that there is really no textual evidence to support this, Beckett had originally thought to write *Waiting for Godot* in three acts: the traditional structure of theater pieces. However, after browsing through a mathematics text at a bookseller's stall along the Seine he promptly cut the third act. The story claims that Beckett had read an explanation of induction, a mathematical proof technique. Mathematical induction demonstrates the truth of a statement for all positive integers (the whole numbers: {1, 2, 3, …}): if it can be established as true for 1 (the first positive integer), and it can also be shown that if the statement is true for the integer n, then it is also true for the integer $n + 1$. This proof is inherently a two-step process because it requires one to establish the truth for the first number and then show that the truth can always be extended to the next number. Reportedly, the textbook expressed this principle by claiming that the transition from zero to one in the integers is the analogue of creation and that the next step from one to two implies the rest of the journey to infinity. Thus, according to the story, Beckett reasoned that two acts would be enough to posit the eternal state of affairs experienced by Didi and Gogo. The first act establishes the mode of existence, and the second implies that it continues without end. Elizabeth Klaver notes that Beckett made a similar reduction of *Krapp's Last Tape*. The early version of the play focuses on tapes from two distinct periods. However, Beckett decided to only use one tape in the final version. The tape contains a recording of Krapp at age 39 about, as he discusses, the experience of listening to a tape he had made earlier in his life. Klaver notes that this has the effect of producing "indefinite allegorizations" and enables the "production of the library of all texts" (1990: 59); the play cycles to infinity.

The repeating cycles of time found in Beckett's plays are reinforced by geometric cycles on the stage. In *Beckett in Theatre*, Dougald McMillan and Martha Fehsenfeld discuss the choreographed cyclic stage movements of Gogo and Didi in a production of *Waiting for Godot* (1988: 99–106). In the play, Gogo or Didi trace out half a circle on stage in Act I and complete the circle on the stage at the corresponding time in Act II. This kind of reiterated theme between the visual and mathematical is also apparent in *Quad*.

Vivian Mercier was one of the first to discuss a mathematical bent in Beckett's works. He proposed the idea that the length and "content" of Beckett's early novels are negatively correlated (1959: 145). Many other scholars have followed in the wake of Mercier and sought to discover the mathematical imagery, equations, and structures in Beckett's works. In *Samuel Beckett: Repetition, Theory and Text*, Steven Connor postulates that mathematics provides a "consolation of order" in the novel *Watt* (1988: 173), but, as Ackerley and Gontarski discovered, this order becomes monstrous (2004: 351). When discussing this transition to the monstrous, Katz writes, "measuring in

Beckett seems hardly a way of ordering or controlling the world, a Cartesian 'method' of mastering it, but rather an activity that becomes its own *raison d'être*" (2003: 248); in short, the mathematics "leads to nothing" (ibid.: 252). Beckett frequently subverts the clarity and precision of mathematics in his texts by inserting errors into the calculations of his characters or narrators. For example, Molloy miscalculates his rate of farting, and the narrator's lengths, areas, and volumes in *The Lost Ones* are untrustworthy (Ackerley and Gontarski 2004: 353; Brater 1985: 97–103). We will see that *Quad* defies this model and moves beyond errors and pathological mathematical compulsions, using mathematics in a deeper self-extinguishing manner.

Despite Beckett's use of mathematics as a destabilizing force in the aforementioned works, he also uses the "precision of mathematics" to create structure, especially in his later plays (Chang 2003: 147). Phyllis Carey argues that Beckett's mathematics is a way of escaping from meaning (1988: 147). Cohn views Beckett's permutative play with the bowler hats in *Waiting for Godot* as a "transition to the resonances Beckett obtains from numbers, as few other playwrights do" (Cohn 1983: 5). Beckett was constantly looking for ways to escape the common use of words. This tendency was a result of his belief that a lack of text "transfer[ed] the problems of a linguistic text onto a different semiotic field" (Klaver 1990: 99). Mathematics offered a readily available means of doing this (Chang 2003: 153, 271, 276; Herren 1998: 124; Klaver 1990: 168, 189, 194; Sherzer 1987: 49–50). Steven Connor asserts that "mathematics can have the function of a 'metalanguage,' a language used to comment on another 'object' language. Employing mathematics as a metalanguage can place and subordinate the more slippery, perishable forms of verbal language" (1988: 173). Similarly, Chinhong Lim Chang suggests that Beckett moved from English to French (a "less familiar language") to give "himself more room for creative manipulation" (Chang 2003: 153, 208, 260, 271, 276). If one accepts this theory, then it follows that Beckett would have been attracted to mathematics for its potential to avoid the pitfalls inherent in all language.

Ackerley and Gontarski separate understanding Beckett's use of mathematics into four categories and discuss these in detail:

1   irrationality;
2   seriality;
3   the postwar texts;
4   memory and measurement in the later works (2004: 347).

Mathematics in *Quad*

Quad *itself*

In Samuel Beckett's *Quad*, four players in robes repeatedly traverse the square given in Figure 12.1 according to the paths given in Table 12.1. The players are set apart

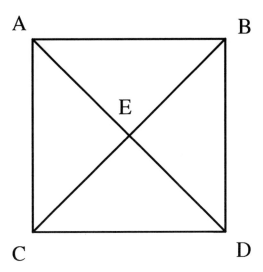

Figure 12.1 Square figure on which players move

Table 12.1 The paths for the four players

player 1	AC	CB	BA	AD	DB	BC	CD	DA
player 2	BA	AD	DB	BC	CD	DA	AC	CB
player 3	CD	DA	AC	CB	BA	AD	DB	BC
player 4	DB	BC	CD	DA	AC	CB	BA	AD

Table 12.2 The schedule of appearances on set by the players

1	13	134	1342	342	42
2	21	214	2143	143	43
3	32	321	3214	214	14
4	43	432	4321	321	21

from one another by the colors of their robes and the unique percussion sound that is played when they enter the set.

The play starts with player 1 traversing his or her path. When player 1 finishes the first cycle, player 3 enters the scene, and they traverse their courses together. They are then joined by player 4 who is in turn followed by player 2. Each player traverses the square once in his or her prescribed pattern of sides each time that he/she appears on set. After each complete traversal, either exactly one player leaves or exactly one player enters.

Whenever there are two or more players on set, their courses require them to cross the center at the same time. This is not possible, so Beckett designed the modified courses for the players shown in Figure 12.2. The arrow labels denote the directions

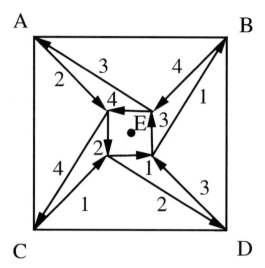

Figure 12.2   Revised square figure that enables players to avoid colliding with one another

the players take when they embark on the modified diagonal paths. The labels also indicate the first player to use each path. The play returns to its starting configuration when player 2 leaves player 1 alone on set. It begins to repeat as the piece ends.

After Beckett saw a version of *Quad* on a black and white studio monitor he wrote a sequel, *Quad II*. In this play, the robes have no color, the movement is slow, and the only sound is now the synchronized footsteps of the players. Beckett has explained that this play is set 100,000 years after *Quad I* (Brater 1985: 52–3). Unless I note otherwise, the term "*Quad*" will be used to refer to the action of both plays from this point forward.

Previous Investigations of the Mathematics in *Quad*

Many scholars have paid particular attention to the revised courses that the players take to avoid colliding with one another. However, Beckett suggests that the players' avoidance of the center also has deep meaning. He referred to *E* (the very center) as a "supposed danger zone" (Beckett 1984: 293) and told Martha Fehsenfeld that "gradually one realized they [the players] were avoiding the center [rather than each other]. There was something terrifying about it … it was danger" (Fehsenfeld 1982: 360).

Garner, Carey, and Okamuro suppose the center to be the self or "Being" and argue that *Quad* draws attention to the presence of the self's absence. However, scholars have been unable to come to a consensus about what this absence signifies. Okamuro connects this to Mandalas, Carl Jung, and the difficulty of reconciling the conscious and unconscious minds (1997: 127–8,132). Carey and Garner see the absence as a reference to humanity's struggle (and failure) to understand human existence and the self (Carey 1988: 145–9; Garner 1994: 29, 76, 135–6). Martin Esslin has postulated that the missed center represents the "impossibility of genuine contact" (1987: 72). Chinhong Lim Chang argues that the avoidance of the center is a way of establishing a tension and dynamism that make the plays much more powerful (2003: 234, 242–5). Klaver sees the center as a representation of the self and imagines that the players' avoidance of it signifies the void. She bases this claim on Derrida's rejection of "presence" as a center and his insistence that "difference" becomes the means of accessing "Being."

Beckett makes the players as alike as possible to subvert the audience's ability to identify them as individuals (Herren 1998: 127–9; Klaver 1990: 79–80, 83, 180). He uses the mathematical symmetries of the square to further break down differences between the players: each of their paths is a rotation of the others. In fact, if the set is viewed from a different corner, the players might be misidentified.

The dynamics and direction of the movement in *Quad* also possess great significance. The players always turn left or counter-clockwise. This is also the direction of movement of the damned in Dante's *Inferno*, which has caused many to see the play as "infernal" (Carey 1988: 147; Fehsenfeld 1982: 361; Gontarski 1983: 137). Antoni Libera has noticed that the players come to each side of the square (both inner and outer) in clockwise order, which is the direction of those eventually saved in Dante's *Purgatory* but continually turn counter-clockwise, which is the direction of the damned. John Freccero discusses similar associations of movement but has the association switched (1961: 168–81). He also introduces a sense in which the opposite directions are confounded with each other: "So the pilgrim's journey through hell, upward although a descent in humility, and to the right when it seems to the left, is a composite movement" (ibid.: 172). Libera sees a simultaneous duality in *Quad* in which the players move "away from and towards God" simultaneously (Connor 1988: 145). Such tensions in coinciding dualities permeate the criticism of *Quad* and also appear in discussions of a plethora of other binarily opposed features, such as internal and external reality (Herren 1998: 160), verbal and visual stimuli (Klaver 1990: 179), inside and outside, and freedom and constraint (Bryden 1995: 113–20; Connor 1988: 144–6). Thus, one should see *Quad* as more of a precariously balanced purgatory than a one-sided hell.

Connor combines the players' avoidance of the center and the movement with the notion of repetition and examines "oscillations" in *Quad*. He claims that the spatial oscillations between the center and periphery bring the simultaneity of opposing dualities and the avoidance of the center together and, thus, decenter, or destabilize, the balance of the many dichotomies (1988: 144–5).

Further Investigation into the Mathematics in *Quad*

Overall, however, the critical literature has not fully revealed the significance of mathematics in *Quad*. Connor feels that the silence of Beckett's mimes forces us to "supply the silent commentary" ourselves (1988: 165). Similarly, Phyllis Carey suggests that the viewer "is implicated in the process of *Quad*, creating with his/her perception the evanescent design the figures are tracing" (1988: 148). However, mathematics has a far more subtle and integral presence in the play, which can be discerned when the play is observed through a completely mathematical lens. Essentially, two primary kinds of mathematics are evoked by the play: geometry and combinations.

Beckett uses geometry as a means of plotting the literary structure of *Quad*. In order to create this structure, he uses the centers of mass of the various combinations of players on set and employs geometric figures (squares and cubes) to give a mathematical form to the trajectory of the play. When this mathematical structure is viewed on a Cartesian plane adopted for graphing literature, one can see that the play plots a course towards eventual zero.

In mathematics, the center of mass is a point in space that represents where the average of all the matter present exists. Mathematicians use it to simplify calculations. For example, the mass of the earth, sun, and moon is considered to be at their centers when calculations of gravity and orbits are performed. When dealing with a small finite number of objects, the centers of mass for systems are relatively easy to calculate. When there is a single player on set in *Quad*, the center of mass is in exactly the same place as the player. When there are two players on set, the center of mass is at a point halfway between them. Thus, if the pair is situated on opposite sides of the square, {1,4} or {2,3}, the center of mass is near the center of square *E*, not exactly at the center because the players are not exactly the same. Similarly, when there are four players, the symmetry of the square puts the center of mass near the center of the square.

The more interesting formations of players occur when three players are on set, and when two of them are adjacent to one another (as opposed to opposite). Tracing the midpoint between two adjacent players yields the center of mass following the dark gray path in Figure 12.3. The center of mass for the three players is located at the point of intersection of the three medians of the triangle that they form. The median is the line drawn from the corner of a triangle to the midpoint of the opposite side. For example, if the players 1, 3, and 4 are frozen at the points at which they start (A, C, and D respectively) then the medians and the center of mass form the pattern displayed in Figure 12.4. The center of mass of the three players traces the black path in Figure 12.3. The dark gray and black squares have side lengths equal to the side length of the original square divided by $\sqrt{2}$ and 3 respectively. The players movements set up the principal theme and their physical oscillations occur several times in each course. The oscillations of the centers of mass, on the other hand, are like harmonic overtones of the principal theme and occur once every series. This adds to and amplifies the total effect of the oscillations. As the number of players on set increases and decreases, the center of mass traces an identical path closer to and yet further from the center. Even if they cannot physically reach the center themselves, their movements are coordinated so as to bring their centers of mass close to the center

A   B

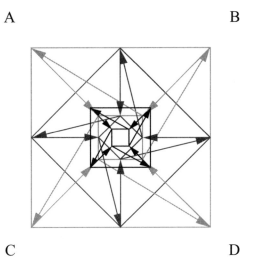

C   D

Figure 12.3   The paths of the center of mass of the players

A   B

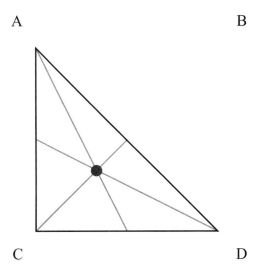

C   D

Figure 12.4   Using the medians of a triangle to calculate the center of mass of players at its vertices

of the square. The overlaid paths of the centers of mass also look like a spiral, which is a frequent shape of Beckett's literary structures.

The other two geometric aspects of the play are simpler in nature. The first is that the amended diagram in Figure 12.2 is a perspective drawing of a three-dimensional cube. The geometric combinations in *Quad* also form a four-dimensional cube. Secondly, and most notably, when *Quad I* and *Quad II* are compared to one another, we see what Connor, Herren, and Okamuro describe as an infinite process of increasing

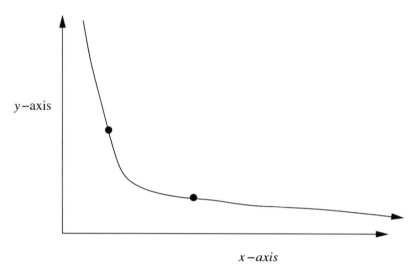

y−axis

x−axis

Figure 12.5   A curve asymptotic to the x-axis

entropy, tending towards eventual lack (Connor 1988: 94, 121–2; Herren 1998: 135–6; Okamuro 1997: 126, 128). In mathematics, such an infinite process of approach is called a *limit* or *asymptote*; a curve that is asymptotic to zero and is shown in Figure 12.5. If the *x*-axis represents time and the *y*-axis represents energy or movement, then the two points depict *Quad I* and *Quad II*. Part of the definition of an asymptotic trend is that it only converges to its limit at "infinity" (that is, never). Thus, this mathematical dilemma is another zero, or void (center), that is implied, approached, but never reached.

Combinatorics is the mathematics of finite sets, their combinations and permutations, and it can also be used to disclose information about *Quad*. The structure and order of the various combinations formed by the players reveal an avoidance of the center and another oscillation. Combinatorics will also reveal the existence of another cube formation. Most significantly, examining the schedule of the combinations of players reveals them to be a vehicle that Beckett used to reiterate powerful dichotomous purgatorial imagery, to play with representations of freedom, and to employ profound subversion of mathematics as a system of meaning.

There are $16 = 2^4$ possible combinations of the four players. Each combination has an alternative name that is a four-letter "word" in the "letters" 0 and 1. A 0 in the first position indicates that player 1 is not on the set, and a 1 in the first position indicates that player 1 is on the set. Similarly, the second, third, and fourth "letters" of the word will encode the status of players 2, 3, and 4 respectively. Table 12.3 lists the 16 combinations and their corresponding words; the $\varnothing$ denotes the combination of none of the players.

Any pair of the words can be added position by position in binary and the result is always another of the 16 words. The binary addition table is shown in Table 12.4 along with a sample addition.

Table 12.3 The 16 combinations of {1, 2, 3, 4} and their corresponding binary "words"

Ø	0000	{3, 4}	0011
{1}	1000	{1, 3, 4}	1011
{1, 2}	1100	{1, 2, 3, 4}	1111
{2}	0100	{2, 3, 4}	0111
{2, 3}	0110	{2, 4}	0101
{1, 2, 3}	1110	{1, 2, 4}	1101
{1, 3}	1010	{1, 4}	1001
{3}	0010	{4}	0001

Table 12.4 Binary addition

+	0	1		0101
0	0	1		+1100
1	1	0		1001

This addition has several properties that would have been useful to Beckett. Because $0 + 0 = 1 + 1 = 0$, the number of ones in the sum is precisely equal to the number of positions where the two words have different symbols (that is, where they disagree). Furthermore, the number of positions in which the two words disagree function as a kind of "distance" between them; this distance is known as the *Hamming distance*. The number of ones in any word is called its *weight*. When 0000 is added to anything, it remains unchanged, which means that 0000 is a *zero* in this system. Because this system of arithmetic uses many similarities to the coordinate geometry of x and y axes shown in Figure 12.5, 0000 is also called an *origin*. It is the center of such a system just as zero is the center of a number line. In mathematics, such an algebraic system is called a *group* or *vector space*, and the existence of a zero is one of the primary axioms of such a system.

Length n binary words correspond to subsets of a finite set with n elements and can uniquely label the corners of an n-dimensional cube. In Figure 12.6, two- and three-dimensional cubes are shown in two different perspectives. The edges are drawn between each adjacent pair of corners and their words have a distance of one; that is, they only disagree in one position.

The list of combinations in Table 12.3 is written in an order in which consecutive words have a distance of one and the last word has a distance of one from the first word. Such a list of binary words is called a cyclic Gray code (Wikipedia 2008a). When each word from a cyclic Gray code is located on the corner of the higher dimensional cube, the Gray code provides a repeatable (it ends precisely where it started) tour along the edges of the cube and visits each corner once. The thickened lines in the third cube in Figure 12.6 are an example of a Gray code. Since *Quad* ends

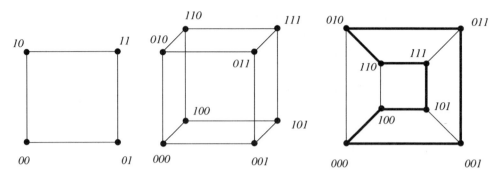

Figure 12.6   Cubes of dimension two and three

where it starts (with player 1 on set) the empty set $\emptyset$ never appears after the play begins to repeat.

We are now in a position to see the four different ways that Beckett invokes but avoids the center:

1   The players rush towards the center, which signifies it, but then swerve away suddenly, never reaching it. The three others are avoidances of origins, which have been identified as centers above;

2   Connor argues that the origin is "always missing from the repetition," and since *Quad* is a play with an indicated repetition, this center is missed. Connor also notes that the "origin and repetition are to be understood as moments in an unending process of mutual definition and redefinition" so that the missing origin is still signified by the repetition (1988: 5);

3   As *Quad* repeats, all combinations except the empty set appear, which means that the play describes a tour through the four-dimensional cube without ever reaching its center, the corner 0000. This zero is conspicuous because of the contrast between its absence and the importance of the axiom of zero in a group. This contrast causes 0000 to be strongly signified;

4   The sequence established in *Quad I* and *Quad II* gives a trajectory (depicted in Figure 12.5) that is asymptotic and tends to (and thus references) the x axis, which defines the center of the y axis of movement.

As I mentioned above, the meaning of Beckett's referencing and avoidance of the center is ambiguous. While the mathematics emphasizes the importance and difficulty of the center, it does not necessarily pick one meaning.

Just as there are multiple centers in *Quad*, there are also several oscillations. We have already seen an oscillation in the form of the players' movement towards the center and back out and an oscillation in the arrangement of the centers of mass from the periphery towards the center and back. Another oscillation can be seen when one considers how close each combination is to the origin, or zero (0000), in the Hamming distance, which in this case is equal to the combination's weight. The four series of combinations on set form a repeating movement around the edges and corners of the cube. The distance to zero oscillates between one and four and back to one in each series. This oscillation is in perfect synchrony but opposes the oscillation of the centers of mass. The center of mass is further out when fewer players are on set, but this is precisely the moment when the combination is closest to the center in Hamming distance. Similarly, the center of mass is closest to the center when all four players are on set, which is also the moment when they are the furthest out in Hamming distance. Not only are the oscillations between poles of opposing dichotomies, but these oscillations oppose each other too. How precariously balanced is *Quad* between all its dualities? Herren calls *Quad* "too pristine, too correct, too well ordered" (1998: 142). However, I argue that its balance and perfections are delicately resting at an unstable equilibrium that could collapse at any moment.

This four-dimensional cube is simply one of a number of squares and grids that appear in *Quad*. Carey and Klaver note that the paths traced by the players recreate the quadrangle of the television, which enables the play to reference its own medium (Carey 1988: 148; Klaver 1990: 191). Klaver argues that a "three-dimensional Klein bottle" and a "three-dimensional grid" are also present in *Quad* (ibid.: 189, 178). A Klein bottle is a three-dimensional cube that has its opposite sides glued together with a twist (this twisting and gluing must be done in the fourth dimension). The diagram in Figure 12.2 is a perspective drawing of the three-dimensional cube from Figure 12.6 with the additional diagonal lines generating a twist. For Klaver, these structures, their dimension, and their complexity come from the complex spirals of signifiers, especially the broken and self-referring ones (1990: 167–95). This design may also refer to Beckett's recurring crucifixion motif. Chang sees the grid and play with dimensionality as a common aesthetic principle between Mondrian and Beckett and concludes that both attempt to "incorporate the fourth dimension in the work" (2003: 192). She also views *Quad* as an instance of Beckett's gradual transition from three-dimensional drama to theater with a two-dimensional visual field (ibid.: 253). Thus, when Beckett flattens three dimensions to two in *Quad* as part of his reductionist process, he expands the signifiers into the fourth dimension by having the schedule of combinations describe a repeating walk on the four-dimensional cube.

The final mathematical examination of *Quad* focuses on the schedule of the players' entrances and the resulting order in which the combinations occur. At the end of each circuit, either exactly one player leaves the set or exactly one player enters the set. In regards to the words that correspond to the combinations, this means that precisely a single "letter" is changed at the end of every course. As a result, two consecutive words (combinations) have a distance of one. Since each of these transitions corresponds to an edge in the four-dimensional cube, the schedule of combinations in *Quad* represents a repeating walk on the four dimensional cube. As mentioned above, this cube visits every corner except the one labeled 0000. The empty set, $\varnothing$, is present at the start of the first series, but will not appear in any of the repetitions. Notably, the player leaving the set is always the one who has been on set the longest (perhaps this is because he or she is the most tired player). This is a first-in/first-out rule, which in mathematics is called a *queue*.

In order for the schedule to function, it must adhere to the follow properties:

- every combination must be given
- each change must consist of a single player coming on or off
- the process must repeat (end in the same state that it began)
- the first-in/first-out rule for the players' exits must be followed

The simplest schedule would achieve each combination only once without duplications. Beckett probably sought (but failed to find) this efficient schedule when creating the work; he draws attention to the fact that some combinations appear different numbers of times, even compared to other combinations of the same size (Beckett 1984: 291–2), which seems to indicate that the inefficiency of *Quad*'s schedule bothered him.

Before we decide if such a schedule is even possible, I offer a possible motivation behind each component of the existent schedule. Ackerley and Gontarski distinguish between Beckett's various uses of permutations and combinations. This distinction can be used as a tool for decoding Beckett's works. For example, in *Murphy*, the full enumeration of permutations has a transcendent imagery as he contemplates the possible combinations of eating five biscuits (Ackerley and Gontarski 2004: 57).

As *Quad* is a kind of purgatory, transcendence is at least one of the things signified by the achievement of all combinations, as it is in *Murphy*, and this transcendence can be identified with the principle of maximizing freedom. The limiting force in *Quad* is the extreme constraint that governs the attempts to produce all the combinations: all transitions involve exactly one player entering or exiting. With the addition of just one more constraint, the system would break down entirely. For example, if there was a first-in/first-out principle operating off-set and only the most refreshed player were permitted to enter at any given time, then it would not be possible to achieve all combinations. In fact, when n players is substituted for 4, such a constrained system would only allow for a tiny minority of combinations. On the other hand, relaxing any single constraint would make it trivial to find many (examples of these less restrained system are provided in Table 12.5). Thus, the properties demanded in the existent schedule represent the optimal level of constraint: more and the problem becomes categorically insoluble; less and it is too easy. Beckett has maximized the constraint.

The schedule implicit in the play both maximizes and minimizes freedom simultaneously. The demand that the schedule repeat falls into the pervasive theme of repetition in Beckett's work. Through this repetition, the schedule of combinations in *Quad* reiterates Libera's interpretation of the play's simultaneous movement towards and away from the divine. In fact, Libera and Connor go beyond the theistic and use the same idea of reference, that of moving "away from or towards freedom" (Connor 1988: 145). *Quad* perfectly superimposes the two primary aspects of its mathematics: geometry and combinatorics.

Table 12.5 Several examples of easily found schedules when any single constraint is relaxed

Not first-in/first-out	Not single player transitions	Not repeating
∅	∅	∅
1	12	1
12	2	12
2	23	2
23	3	23
123	34	3
13	342	34
3	42	4
34	421	41
134	4213	413
1234	213	13
234	13	132
24	134	1324
124	4	324
14	41	24
4	1	241

A schedule is termed a *Beckett-Gray code* if it meets the following requirements:

- all combinations are achieved exactly once
- each transition is the entrance or exit of a single player
- the exits follow a first-in/first-out rule

If this schedule repeats, it is *cyclic*. While it is known that cyclic Beckett-Gray codes exist for schedules containing one, two, five, six, seven, and eight players, they cannot be achieved with three or four players. In other words, the "ideal" schedule, the one with the most "trim," does not exist. The eight distinct Beckett-Gray codes for *n* = 5 are given in Table 12.6.

Beckett was clearly familiar with the mathematics of combinatorial orderings. His list of all the possible arrangements of the furniture in Mr Knott's room in *Watt* follows a strict additive pattern in a finite group ($\mathbb{Z}_4 \times \mathbb{Z}_5 \times \mathbb{Z}_4$) (Beckett 1959: 204–7). Furthermore, his list of the physical attributes of Mr Knott permutes the figure, stature, skin, and hair in a slightly modified Gray code ordering. The combinations of attributes themselves are generated in an order that shows a remarkable but twisted similarity to both Gray codes and alphabetical iterative generation methods. In fact, since consecutive combinations are the patterns that are the farthest away from one another in Hamming distance, his list forms a kind of "anti-Gray" code. I should also note that although the existence of Beckett-Gray codes for $n \geq 6$ requires the use of a computer, the existence for *n* = 1,2,5 and non-existence for *n* = 3,4 are within the scope of pencil and paper calculations. Although I am not aware of such calculations

Table 12.6 The eight distinct Beckett-Gray codes for n = 5

∅	∅	∅	∅	∅	∅	∅	∅
1	1	1	1	1	1	1	1
1 2	1 2	1 2	1 2	1 2	1 2	1 2	1 2
2	2	2	2	2	2	1 2 3	1 2 3
2 3	2 3	2 3	2 3	2 3	2 3	2 3	2 3
2 3 1	2 3 1	2 3 1	2 3 1	2 3 1	2 3 4	3	2 3 4
3 1	2 3 1 4	2 3 1 4	2 3 1 4	2 3 1 4	2 3 4 5	3 4	2 3 4 1
3 1 4	3 1 4	3 1 4	3 1 4	2 3 1 4 5	3 4 5	4	2 3 4 1 5
1 4	1 4	3 1 4 5	3 1 4 5	3 1 4 5	4 5	4 2	3 4 1 5
4	1 4 5	1 4 5	1 4 5	1 4 5	4 5 1	4 2 5	4 1 5
4 2	4 5	4 5	4 5	4 5	5 1	4 2 5 1	1 5
4 2 1	5	5	5	4 5 3	5 1 3	4 2 5 1 3	5
4 2 1 5	5 1	5 1	5 3	5 3	1 3	2 5 1 3	5 4
2 1 5	5 1 3	5 1 3	3	3	3	5 1 3	5 4 2
2 1 5 3	1 3	1 3	3 1	3 4	3 4	1 3	4 2
1 5 3	3	3	3 1 5	3 4 2	3 4 1	1 3 4	4 2 1
5 3	3 5	3 5	1 5	3 4 2 5	3 4 1 5	1 3 4 5	4 2 1 5
3	3 5 2	3 5 2	1 5 2	4 2 5	3 4 1 5 2	3 4 5	2 1 5
3 4	5 2	5 2	5 2	2 5	4 1 5 2	4 5	2 1 5 3
3 4 5	5 2 4	5 2 4	5 2 4	2 5 3	1 5 2	5	1 5 3
4 5	5 2 4 3	2 4	2 4	2 5 3 1	5 2	5 3	5 3
4 5 2	2 4 3	2 4 3	2 4 3	5 3 1	5 2 4	5 3 2	3
5 2	4 3	4 3	4 3	3 1	2 4	5 3 2 4	3 1
5 2 3	4 3 5	4 3 5	4 3 5	3 1 4	4	3 2 4	3 1 4
5 2 3 4	4 3 5 1	4 3 5 2	4 3 5 2	1 4	4 1	3 2 4 1	1 4
2 3 4	4 3 5 1 2	4 3 5 2 1	3 5 2	4	4 1 2	2 4 1	4
2 3 4 1	3 5 1 2	3 5 2 1	3 5 2 1	4 2	4 1 2 3	4 1	4 3
2 3 4 1 5	5 1 2	5 2 1	3 5 2 1 4	4 2 1	1 2 3	4 1 5	4 3 5
3 4 1 5	5 1 2 4	5 2 1 4	5 2 1 4	4 2 1 5	1 2 3 5	1 5	4 3 5 2
4 1 5	1 2 4	2 1 4	2 1 4	2 1 5	2 3 5	1 5 2	3 5 2
1 5	2 4	1 4	1 4	1 5	3 5	5 2	5 2
5	4	4	4	5	5	2	2

for *Quad*, Beckett does similar mathematics in his notebooks for *Watt* and for *J.M. Mime*, a never produced piece (Ackerley and Gontarski 2004: 352–3, 628–9, 631; Gontarski 1985: 201–8).

Many writers argue that Beckett's use of mathematics was part of an attempt to replace the "distrusted words" with alternative modes of expression (Herren 1998: 124, 139; Klaver 1990: 11, 66, 99, 194). They also cite his move from prose to theater as part of this process. But just as Beckett inserts errors into his work to subvert even the mathematical mode of meaning, he performs a deeper subversion in *Quad*. One of the strengths of mathematics lies in its precision of definitions and the unique and clear "ideal" objects that the definitions engender. At first, it seems like Beckett is attempting to use mathematics in *Quad* to express the inexpressible, to describe the presence of absence, as he does in previous works that use mathematics. However, as soon as the aspects of the mathematical object are clear, it becomes evident that no concrete mathematical solution exists to the problem.

Conclusion

The easiest ways of subverting mathematics would be to insert errors in calculations or pose problems that either are broadly insoluble in all their instances or widely known to have no solution. However, Beckett chooses to go beyond simply subverting mathematical calculations. Furthermore, he also chooses to avoid positing mathematical structures and constructions that do not exist. He has defined a novel structure that is sensible, exists in many instances (probably almost all instances), and yet he builds a play around one of the two known (probably the only two) instances that do not exist. Thus, *Quad* subverts the very power of mathematics and, in the process, exemplifies an even more powerful application of math: expressing the inexpressible, presenting the absent. The motif of structuring that which cannot be structured also appears in some of Beckett's other works. Klaver describes a similar construction of a semiotically insoluble structure in *Ohio Impromptu* (1990: 168). Federman discusses Beckett's notion of the "confrontation of *l'objet-obstacle* and *l'oiel-obstacle*" in painting. This is where the "object itself prevents us from seeing it clearly, and the eye itself is an obstacle to clear perception of the object" (Federman 2002: 169). The mathematical axioms of the object defined in *Quad* are its own obstacles to its own existence.

The Beckett-Gray code's payoff is its powerful literary analysis, but Beckett-Gray codes are also of significant interest within the mathematics and computer science community. Gray codes in general have many applications, and the fact that the Beckett-Gray code uses the first-in/first-out rule, or queue, means that a computer that uses it could run twice as efficiently as a computer that relies on other methods. When a player exits, it is not necessary to specify which player since only one of the players is "next" in the queue. These savings are limited to half because the identity of the player entering must still be specified (Cooke, Dewar, North, and Stevens: n.d.), but they are still substantial. Gray codes are often used for scheduling industrial processes efficiently, and the positions in the binary words often correspond to mechanical or electrical components. The first-in/first-out rule governing Beckett-Gray codes means that in a code with n positions (n players), no component can be turned on (be a "1") for more than $2n-2$ consecutive turns. As a result, Beckett-Gray codes offer an excellent solution for components that cannot be run continuously for indefinite periods of time (due to overheating, wear, lubrication, etc.). Beckett-Gray codes for $n = 5$ and 6 have been completely enumerated. Several examples for $n = 7$ and 8 are known, but a proof that they exist for all $n \geq 9$ is elusive and an open problem of active research in the mathematical community (ibid.).

References and Further Reading

Acheson, James and Kateryna Arthur (eds.) (1987). *Beckett's Later Fiction and Drama: Texts for Company*. Houndmills: Macmillan Press.

Ackerley, C. J. and S. E. Gontarski (2004). *The Grove Companion to Samuel Beckett*. New York: Grove Press.

Alvarez, A. (1973). *Samuel Beckett*. New York: The Viking Press.

Beckett, Samuel (1959). *Watt*. New York: Grove Weidenfeld.

Beckett, Samuel (1965). *Molloy, Malone Dies, The Unnamable*. New York: Grove Press.

Beckett, Samuel (1973). *Murphy*. London: Picador.

Beckett, Samuel (1983). *Disjecta: Miscellaneous Writings and a Dramatic Fragment*. London: John Calder.

Beckett, Samuel (1984). *Collected Shorter Plays of Samuel Beckett*. London: Faber and Faber.

Brater, Enoch (1983). "Mis-takes, Mathematical and Otherwise in *The Lost Ones*." *Modern Fiction Studies* 29 (1): 93–109.

Brater, Enoch (1985). "Toward a Poetics of Television Technology: Beckett's 'Nacht und Träum' and 'Quad.'" *Modern Drama* 28: 48–54.

Bryden, Mary (1995). "'Quad': Dancing Genders." In Catharina Wulf (ed.), *The Savage Eye/L'Oeil Fauve. Samuel Beckett Today/Aujourd'hui*, 4: 109–22. Amsterdam: Rodopi.

Carey, Phyllis (1988). "The 'Quad' Pieces: A Screen for the Unseeable." In Robin J. Davis and Lance St J. Butler (eds.), *Make Sense Who May: Essays on Samuel Beckett's Later Works*. Gerrards Cross: Colin Smythe.

Carey, Phyllis and Ed Jewinski (eds.) (1992). *Re: Joyce'n Beckett*. New York: Fordham University Press.

Chang, Chinhong Lim (2003). *"Unveil the Veiled: An Interdisciplinary Study of Aesthetic Ideas in the Works of Piet Mondrian and Samuel Beckett."* Diss. Ohio University.

Cohn, Ruby (1973). *Back to Beckett*. Princeton: Princeton University Press.

Cohn, Ruby (1983). "Beckett's Theater Resonance." In Morris Beja, S. E. Gontarski, and Pierre Astier (eds.), *Samuel Beckett: Humanistic Perspectives*. Ohio State University Press.

Connor, Steven (1988). *Samuel Beckett: Repetition, Theory and Text*. Oxford: Basil Blackwell.

Cooke, M., Dewar, M., North, C., and Stevens, B., n.d. "Beckett-Gray codes," submitted to *Journal of Combinatorial Mathematics and Combinatorial Computing*.

Esslin, Martin (ed.) (1965). *Samuel Beckett: A Collection of Critical Essays*. Englewood Cliff, NJ: Prentice-Hall.

Esslin, Martin (1987). "A Poetry of Moving Images." In Alan Warren Friedman, Charles Rossman, and Dina Sherzer (eds.), *Beckett Translating/Translating Beckett*. University Park and London: The Pennsylvania State University Press.

Federman, Raymond (2002). "The Imaginary Museum of Samuel Beckett." *Symploke* 10 (1–2): 153–72.

Fehsenfeld, Martha (1982). "Beckett's Late Works: An Appraisal." *Modern Drama* 25 (3): 355–62.

Freccero, John (1961). "Dante's Pilgrim in a Gyre." *PMLA* 76: 168–81.

Garner, Stanton B. Jr (1994). *Bodied Spaces: Phenomenology and Performance in Contemporary Drama*. Ithaca and London: Cornell University Press.

Gluck, Barbara Reich (1979). *Beckett and Joyce*. Lewisburg: Bucknell University Press.

Gontarski, S. E. (1983). "'Quad I & II': Beckett's Sinister Mime(s)." Review of "Quad I & II," by Samuel Beckett. *Journal of Beckett Studies* 9: 137–8.

Gontarski, S. E. (1985). *The Intent of Undoing in Samuel Beckett's Dramatic Texts*. Bloomington: Indiana University Press.

Herren, Graley (1998). *"The Ghost in the Machine: A Study of Samuel Beckett's Teleplays."* Diss. The Florida State University.

Homan, Sidney (1992). *Filming Beckett's Television Plays*. Lewisburg: Bucknell University Press.

Johnson, S. M. (1963). "Generation of Permutations by Adjacent Transpositions." *Mathematics of Computation* 17: 282–5.

Katz, Daniel. (2003). "Beckett's Measures: Principles of Pleasure in *Molloy* and 'First Love.'" *Modern Fiction Studies* 49 (2): 246–60.

Kenner, Hugh (1968). *Samuel Beckett: A Critical Study*. Berkeley: University of California Press.

Klaver, Elizabeth (1990). *"Postmodernism and Meta-textual Space in the Plays of Beckett, Ionesco, Albee and Mamet."* Diss. University of California, Riverside.

Knuth, Donald (2005). *Volume 4 of The Art of Computer Programming, Fascicle 2: Generating All Tuples and Permutations.* Reading, MA: Addison-Wesley.

Krance, Charles (1989). "Sam w Polsce / Sam in Poland." *The Journal of Beckett Studies* 11–12: 131–52.

Levy, Shimon (1995). "Spirit Made Light: Eyes and other I's in Beckett's TV Plays." In Catharina Wulf (ed.), *The Savage Eye/L'Oeil Fauve. Samuel Beckett Today/Aujourd'hui,* 4: 65–82. Amsterdam: Rodopi.

McMillan, Dougald and Martha Fehsenfeld (1988). *Beckett in Theatre.* London: John Calder.

Mercier, Vivian (1959). "The Mathematical Limit." *The Nation* (February 14): 144–5.

Nash, Richard (1991). *John Craige's Mathematical Principles of Christian Theology.* Carbondale: Southern Illinois University Press.

Okamuro, Minako (1997). "'Quad' and the Jungian Mandala." In Marius Buning, Matthijs Engelberts, and Sjef Houppermans (eds.), *Samuel Beckett, Crossroads and Borderlines. Samuel Beckett Today/Aujourd'hui.* Rodopi, 6: 125–33.

Pountney, Rosemary (1995). "Beckett and the Camera." In Catharina Wulf (ed.), *The Savage Eye/L'Oeil Fauve. Samuel Beckett Today/Aujourd'hui.* Amsterdam: Rodopi. 4: 41–52.

Saltz, David (1997). "Beckett's Cyborgs: Technology and the Beckettian Text." *Theatre Forum* 11: 38–48.

Sherzer, Dina (1987). "Words About Words: Beckett and Language." In Alan Warren Friedman, Charles Rossman, and Dina Sherzer (eds.), *Beckett Translating/Translating Beckett.* University Park and London: The Pennsylvania State University Press.

Trotter, H. F. (1962). "PERM (Algorithm 115)." *Communications of the ACM* 5: 434–5.

Wikipedia, The Free Encyclopedia (2008a). "Frank Gray (researcher)." <http://en.wikipedia.org/w/index.ph?title=Frank_Gray_(researcher)&oldid=209841629>. Accessed August 29, 2008.

Wikipedia, The Free Encyclopedia (2008b). "Squaring the Circle." <http://en.wikipedia.org/w/index.php?title=Squaring_the_circle&oldid=234391818>. Accessed August 29, 2008.

13
Beckett and Obsessional Ireland

David Pattie

The Irish Beckett

Ireland has a rather odd place in Beckett Studies. It is there and not there: Beckett scholars know that he never surrendered his Irish passport, and that, when asked if he was English, he replied *"au contraire"* – and yet, Beckett is still treated as someone whose Irishness has to be excavated laboriously, and whose relation to the development of Irish literature and culture in the twentieth century is tangential. The attempt has been made – by Christopher Ricks, Vivian Mercier, Eoin O'Brien, Mary Junker, Ronan MacDonald, and others; but, as a recent panel on Beckett and Ireland (held at one of the centenary conferences in 2006, in Florida) attested, for Beckett scholars the relation between Beckett and the land of his birth remains unclear. As Ronan MacDonald noted in 2002, this obscurity is itself further evidence of a long-established strand in the study of Beckett's work:

> In much criticism of his work the importance of history or politics, the contextual concerns of Beckett's cultural moment, are underplayed in the emphasis on absolute, transcendent articulations of the human plight or, more recently, in the emphasis on postmodern self-referentiality. History is seen simply as a pretext for those concerns. Like Murphy, anxious to retreat into the self-contained, authentic core of his own mind, Beckett's art is seen as loftily uninterested in the tawdry distractions of day to day life. And, or so the story goes, as history and politics are jettisoned in the interests of universal authenticity, geography and national locale are shed along with it – we are left with the characteristically rootless Beckettian landscape. (MacDonald 2002: 141)

And, along with it, comes the usual inference: the more rootless the Beckettian landscape, the more universal the territory his characters cover.

This is not a mistake made by those who write on Beckett from within Irish Studies. His characteristic preoccupations – the unreliability of language, the instability of meaning, and the obligation to express a sense of the distress of existence – can be, and have been, linked to the state of Ireland in the first half of the twentieth century. In particular the sense of loss and dislocation which runs through Beckett's novels, plays, and poetry gives his work, it has been argued, a peculiar relevance. This is the argument advanced, for example, in one of the key texts of contemporary Irish Studies, Declan Kiberd's *Inventing Ireland*:

> The voices that Beckett heard and committed to paper ... were unambiguously Irish. Occasionally, they bore faint Wildean echoes, as in the inversion of a famous quotation or proverb, but more often they were austere, pared back. The promise of Yeats and Joyce to take revivalist rhetoric and wring its neck was being brought to a strict conclusion. Yet Irish these voices steadfastly remained ... The Irish landscape of south county Dublin in particular was celebrated through famous passages of the trilogy in the concrete, chaste, descriptive style of the Celtic nature poets, without the burden of abstract metaphorical meaning, without any patriotic eroticising of this or that landscape as a synecdoche for the whole of Ireland. But, as with Celtic nature poetry, what was offered in such passages was an exile's celebration, which seemed once again to illustrate a bleak law; the imaginative possession of the Irish landscape seemed possible only to those who were removed from it. (Kiberd 1996: 535)

This is an insightful passage, and worth quoting in full: however, there is a paradox embedded in it. If Kiberd is right, then Ireland is at its most celebrated in Beckett's work when it is at its least apparent. Kiberd is correct to identify Dublin, and the landscape that surrounds it, as the archetypal Beckettian landscape; Eoin O'Brien's exhaustive *The Beckett Country* provides photographic proof of the recurrence of Irish locations in Beckett's work, from the earliest texts to the novels and plays of his maturity. After a certain point, though, something happens to these locations; either they are described but not named (W. J. McCormack notes that the city described in *Molloy* has two canals, just like Dublin, but correctly identifies this as a piece of relatively arcane knowledge for those who do not know the city (McCormack 1994: 399)), or they are named but not described (the sudden irruption of Croker's Acres into the monologue in *Not I*, for example). The fact that these images recur in Beckett's work is itself evidence of his continued imaginative dialogue with the landscape of his birth; but, from *Watt* onward, Beckett's fictional returns to Dublin are sharply distinct from those of James Joyce, for example. Where Joyce finds more and more levels of association (to the extent that, in *Finnegans Wake*, the city contains everything), Beckett drains the Dublin landscape of most of its culture and history.

Why does he do this? Is it simply that, as a Protestant in the new republic, Beckett was a deracinated representative of a deracinated culture? This argument is tempting, and there were certainly moments (the aftermath of Oliver Gogarty's libel trial, for example) when Beckett felt himself completely at odds with Irish life. However, Beckett himself seems not to have thought of Irish locations in his writing, either as exercises in "imaginative possession," or as a refracted image of the longing expressed by other Anglo-Irish writers, chief among them Elizabeth Bowen, for the old Ireland

of the Ascendancy. Interviewed by his official biographer, James Knowlson, he suggested another way of reading them:

> In the first interview with Beckett intended specifically for this book, I said that
> although I understood perfectly well what he meant when he spoke of a separation
> between his life and his work, I could not agree that such a separation was as absolute
> as he claimed. I then quoted some of the images of his childhood in Ireland that often
> appear in his work, even in his late prose texts; a man and a boy walking hand in hand
> over the mountains; a larch tree turning green every year a week before the others; the
> sounds of the stone cutters chipping away in the hills above his home. Dozens of such
> images could be cited, I maintained, which bridge his life and his work. At this point,
> Beckett nodded in agreement: "They're obsessional," he said, and went on to add several
> others. (Knowlson 1996: xxi)

In what follows, I will argue that Beckett's work, as it develops, burrows deeper and
deeper into Ireland: that the overt references to Irish life and culture in Beckett's early
work form a thoroughgoing rejection of the culture that surrounded him in his teens
and early twenties – and that the "obsessional" references to the Ireland of Beckett's
childhood (which begin with *Watt*, and which recur in his work until the end of his
life) are, in fact, an indication that, far from being engaged in the exile's celebration
of his homeland, Beckett's invocations of Ireland were based on the understanding
that a landscape that is obsessional, by its very nature, cannot be finally possessed. It
could be said that, as Beckett develops as a writer, his relation to his home country
changes from distanced, dismissive irony to immanence; the characters exist within
landscape – a landscape in which they are immersed but which is too close to them
to be named. In the rest of the chapter, I will discuss how that immanence – rooted
as it is in the obsessional nature of the images Beckett describes – evolved; and, as I
do so, I will argue that the relation between Beckett and Ireland is not simply that
between the exile and the homeland but rather between the individual artist and the
evolving territory his work attempts to define. In other words, Beckett's relation to
Ireland has none of the imaginative certainty of Joyce's; as he progresses, he is more
and more unsure of the Ireland his characters occupy; paradoxically, however, this
serves to make the relation between his work and Ireland more rather than less
immanent.

"His native city had got him again": Ireland in the Early Work

In *Murphy*, published in 1938, Neary, the title character's spiritual mentor, commits
cultural and political sacrilege in the Post Office:

> In Dublin a week later … Neary minus his whiskers was recognised by a former pupil
> called Wylie, in the General Post Office, contemplating from behind the statue of
> Cuchulain. Neary had bared his head, as though the holy ground meant something to

him. Suddenly, he flung aside his hat, sprang forward, seized the dying hero by the thighs and began to dash his head against his buttocks, such as they are. The Civic Guard on duty in the building, roused from a tender reverie by the sound of blows, took in the situation at his leisure, disentangled his baton and advanced with measured tread, thinking he had caught a vandal in the act. Happily Wylie, whose reactions as a street bookmaker's stand were as rapid as a zebra's, had already seized Neary round the waist, torn him back from the sacrifice and smuggled him halfway to the exit. (Beckett 1980a: 28)

The statue of Cuchulain had only recently been unveiled, by De Valera, on Easter Monday 1935; it is possible that Beckett, who was living in London at the time, saw it very soon after (he spent three weeks at home in Foxrock in April in 1935). The figure of Cuchulain was, of course, a very careful choice. The dying hero (as Beckett put it) not only stood in for Pearse, MacDonagh, Connolly, and the other rebels; it also made abundantly clear that the martyrs of 1916 were in a direct line of descent from the Ur-hero of Irish mythology. When Neary attacks Cuchulain, he is not simply expressing his disgust at the current state of Dublin municipal statuary: he is defaming the "holy ground" of the new republic.

This is not a single act of cultural sabotage: it is of a piece with the rest of Beckett's early writings, fictional and critical. In the essay "Recent Irish Poetry," published in *The Bookman* in 1934, Beckett takes his critical axe to the mythological underpinnings of the Revival, in a (characteristically) overblown passage:

> The device common to the poets of the Revival and after, in the use of which even beyond the jewels of language they are at one, is that of a flight from self awareness, and as such might perhaps be described as a convenience. At the centre there is no theme ... But the circumference is a iridescence of themes – Oisin, Cuchulain, Maeve, Tir-nanog, the Tain Bo Cuailgne, Yoga, the Crone of Beare – segment after segment of cut and dried loveliness. (Beckett 1983: 71)

And, as Sinead Mooney has recently argued (2005: 29–41), even those Irish poets who seem to escape Beckett's strictures (the rather more conventionally modernist McGreevey, Devlin, and Coffey) are at best the recipients of faint praise. Beckett, unlike other Protestant writers (Yeats and Synge being, of course, the most notable examples), did not find any cultural mileage in the mythic history of his country and its possible application to the Ireland of the early twentieth century. In rejecting it, he might be said to be reacting in a way that was, for a member of his religion and class, at least, understandable. Even though De Valera, in particular, had made overtures to the Protestants in the new republic, a lapsed Protestant like Beckett (who, nonetheless, by his own admission found the ingrained mental structures of Protestantism hard to shake off) might find himself out of sympathy with the religious tenor of the new state.

However, this is to assume that Beckett's reaction to the new country was solely determined by one aspect of his background: his Protestant upbringing. To argue this is to underestimate just how thoroughgoing is his rejection of all aspects of Irish culture; Beckett does conform, on the face of it, to the image of the Irish writer as migrant, but his exile is not simply from a new country that is in some way inimical to the Anglo-Irish. The rejection of Ireland in Beckett's early work comes close to a rejection *tout court*. The rituals of Protestant belief are satirized:

> *God bless dear Daddy*, he prayed vaguely that night for no particular reason before getting into bed, *Mummy Johnny Bibby* (quondam Nanny, now mother of thousands by a gardener) *and all that I love and make me a good boy for Jesus Christ sake Armen*.
> That was the catastasis their Mammy had taught them, first John, then Bel, when they were tiny. That was their prayer. What came after that was the Lord's Their prayer was a nice little box and the Lord's was a dull big box. You went down in a lift and your only stomach rose up into your craw. (Beckett 1992: 8–9)

So, too, the day to day life of Dublin:

> In this black city of ours that comes out seventh in occidental statistics, or did, such painful scenes are of daily occurrence. Men of the high standing of the Polar Bear [a caricature of Rudmose-Brown, one of Beckett's professors at Trinity], men of culture and distinction, occupying positions of responsibility in the City, permit themselves, condescend, to bandy invective with the meanest of day-labourers. Gone is patrician hauteur, gone, it almost seems, with the Garrison. The scurvy dog has taught the snarl to his scurvy master, the snarl, the fawn, the howl and the cocked leg: the general coprotechnics. And we are all dogs together in the dogocracy of unanimous scurrility. (ibid.: 159)

Not, as Beckett notes in the following paragraph, that the days of the Garrison had anything to commend them. The Dublin intellectual is mocked:

> "I don't wonder at Berkley," said Neary. "He had no alternative. A defence mechanism. Immaterialise or bust. The sleep of sheer terror. Compare the opossum."
> "The advantage of this view," said Wylie, "is, that while one may not look forward to things getting any better, at least one need not fear their getting any worse. They will always be the same as they always were."
> "Until the system is dismantled," said Neary.
> "Supposing that to be permitted," said Wylie. (Beckett 1980a: 36)

One might see this as an early exploration of the idea of stasis in Beckett's fictional world: however, in the novel, it renders a simple conversation about the whereabouts of Murphy needlessly (and comically) complex. Even the figure of the Irish migrant intellectual is guyed: in the second story of *More Pricks than Kicks*, "Fingal," Belacqua, and his lover, Winnie, take in the view from the hill of Feltrim near Dublin:

> "When it's a magic land" he sighed, "like Saone-et-Loire."
> "That means nothing to me," said Winnie.

"Oh yes" he said, "bons vins et Lamartine, a champaign land for the sad and serious, not a bloody little toy kindergarten like Wicklow."

You make great play of your short stay abroad, thought Winnie. (Beckett 1980b: 26)

It is not so much that Beckett's early work can be read as a thoroughgoing satire on Ireland; rather, Ireland is distanced from the narrator (and from the reader) through the liberal application of an all-embracing irony. However, the ironic treatment of the mores of contemporary Ireland is not balanced against any nostalgia for pre-republican days; there is, in Beckett, no mourning of the Ascendancy, no hankering back to the days when the Anglo-Irish section of Irish society could draw legitimacy from British rule. Partly, this was because of Beckett's own position: as his Irish biographer, Anthony Cronin, makes clear, Beckett's background ensured that his experience of the uprising, the civil war and the new republic was different to that of, for example, W. B. Yeats or Elizabeth Bowen. Beckett's family were mercantile Protestants: the family firm did not suffer any great upset during the 1910s or 1920s; Foxrock, where Beckett grew up, was overwhelmingly Protestant, but those who lived there did not suffer any great hardships either; during the civil war, Beckett was at school in the North. The version of Protestant Ireland that Beckett experienced was not evanescent; rather than fading into history it remained solid and unchanging – and that, indeed, was the problem. The version of Conservative Protestantism embraced by Beckett's family – and especially by Beckett's mother – was not necessarily that far out of step with Conservative Catholicism: it disavowed sexuality, censured excess, prized the overt display of Godliness, and allowed only the most token expressions of discontent. Rather than a country which had changed utterly, Ireland, to Beckett, seemed monumentally static, at all levels from the governmental to the domestic. Indeed, his biographies (and the excerpts from his letters published in Knowlson, in Cronin, and in others) strongly suggest that, after his first experiences of life in Europe, each return home simply revealed the same society, the same attitudes, and the same deadening routines. To the young Beckett, the static philistinism of Irish cultural life could be seen in the Government's decision to ban "unwholesome" literature; the article "Censorship in the Saorstat" grimly records statements such as,

"Give me the man broad-minded and fair who can look at the thing from a common sense point of view. If you want to come to a proper conclusion upon what is for the good of the people in a question of this kind, I would unhesitatingly *plump* for the common sense man" (Beckett 1983: 85, original emphasis)

It was also clearly visible in the unthinking adherence to social ritual that was very much a part of his family's world. Writing to Thomas McGreevey after his brother Bill's wedding, Beckett commented despairingly:

Watching the presents come along has been painful. The awful unconscious social cynicism that knows what the relationship comes down to in the end is gongs and tea-trolleys, that without them there is no "together". Till it seems almost a law of marriage that the human personal element should be smothered out of existence from the word go, reduced to a mere occasion for good housekeeping and house chat, the eggcup in the pie of domestic solidity. (Knowlson 1996: 266–7)

For the young Beckett, Ireland was frozen from the top down and from the bottom up: more than this, it was sick – Dublin especially was a "cultural backwater," as John Pilling described it (Pilling 2004: 5), which was rapidly turning foul. His first novel, *Dream of Fair to mddling Women*, contains images of infection which are related directly to the city; Belacqua, the central character, has returned home only to find "his native city had got him again, her miasmata already had all but laid him low, the yellow marsh fever that she keeps up her sleeve for her more distinguished sons had clapped its clammy honeymoon hands upon him, his moral temperature had gone sky-rocketing aloft, soon he would shudder and kindle in hourly ague" (Beckett 1992: 69). Dublin, and by extension Ireland, was diseased; to live there was to catch a plague which could only lead to creative death.

As a defensive strategy, one which would hold the young writer apart from the contamination that Ireland threatened, Beckett employed two tactics, both of them steeped in irony. Firstly, as Jose Fernandez Sanchez has pointed out, in the early work Dublin is simply named. Locations are not subject to the kind of detailed invocation that one might expect from an exile writing about his origins; whereas in Joyce the city is evoked in a series of directly sensual images, the early Beckett's Dublin is flat:

> As if eschewing closeness with the city and its inhabitants, the narrator maintains a detached perspective on the urban setting, without describing in detail routes, directions or the physiognomy of streets and houses. Names of places are simply used as points of reference for the action as in: "The Polar Bear came cataracting – too late; the tram had gathered way, now it is screaming past the Mansion House. He tore at the strap. 'Can't the bloody thing be stopped?' he cried. 'Next stop the Green' said the conductor." (Sanchez 2006: 9)

The early Beckettian protagonist moves through this flat landscape, but he is careful to keep himself distant from it: "Of the two [public] houses that appealed spontaneously to these exigencies, the one, situated in Merrion Row, was a home from home for Jarveys. As some folk from hens, so Belacqua shrank from Jarveys. Rough, gritty, almost verminous men. From Moore to Merrion Row, moreover, was a perilous way, beset at this hour with poets and peasants and politicians" (Beckett 1980b: 52). Note the "almost verminous": the city's inhabitants, like the city itself, are a risk – both physical (the gritty Jarveys, the peasants) and intellectual (the poets and politicians).

On the other hand (and as so often in the early fiction) Irish locations are so encrusted with association as to be almost invisible, as in this passage from *More Pricks than Kicks* in which a drunken Belacqua has noticed the neon Bovril sign that used to shine over College Green:

Bright and cheery above the storm of the Green, as though coached by the star of Bethlehem, the Bovril sign danced and danced through its seven phases.

The lemon of faith jaundiced, annunciating the series, was in a fungus of hopeless green reduced to shingles and abolished. Whereupon the light went out, in homage to the slain. A sly ooze of gales, carmine of solicitation, lifting the skirts of green that the prophecy might be fulfilled, shocking Gabriel into cherry, flooded the sign. But the long skirts came rattling down, darkness covered their shame, the cycle was at an end. Da capo.

Bovril to Salome, thought Belacqua, and Tommy Moore there with his head on his shoulders. Doubt, Despair and Scrounging, shall I hitch my bath-chair to the greatest of these? (ibid.: 53)

This is a good invocation of the sequential illumination of the sign, which was a prominent Dublin landmark. The network of allusions that weave themselves around the image, however, do not form themselves into a completed pattern – "the jaundiced lemon of faith," "the long skirts came rattling down," and so on. There is a suggestion in the passage that recent Irish history is being mocked ("hopeless green reduced to shingles and abolished," "in homage to the slain"), but the nature of the reference is too ambiguous to function as successful satire – if, indeed, that is what it is. A parallel between the star announcing Christ's birth and the sequence of the sign is suggested (but not illuminated), and the whole is tangled up in incidental allusion (the quick, passing reference to the sculpture of Thomas Moore, raised on the site of Dublin's largest public urinal – a reference impenetrable to those who do not know their Dublin statuary). As so often in Beckett's earliest work, accretion replaces illumination; the meaning of the sign, for Belacqua, for Ireland, for Christianity, and for us, is lost somewhere in the web of allusions that Beckett weaves around the image. What remains, though, is the sense that an icon of Beckett's home city is only of interest because it sparks the jaundiced Belacqua into reflection.

These ironic techniques – the separation of the author surrogate from Irish (and especially Dublin) life and the flattened or ornately allusive treatment of Irish locations – might seem to echo those employed by Joyce, and they do fulfill something of the same function. They do establish Beckett's early writing as undeniably the work of a migrant looking back on his home culture and attempting a summary of his relation to it. However, in Joyce, we never lose the sense that the central consciousness of the artist surrogate is, although unformed, a guide to the world that surrounds him (even though his view of the world might be partial and incomplete). Stephen's early attempts at personal and artistic expression might be treated with some amusement, but there is no doubt that Joyce intends him as a positive image of the migrant artist. There is no such certainty in Beckett; the migrant artists and intellectuals in the early fiction do not illuminate the Ireland of the time – in fact, quite the opposite. They manage only to obscure it. To go back to Kiberd; what is offered in the early fiction is the polar opposite of an "exile's celebration." Rather, it is an exile's dismissal: an ironic rejection of the Ireland of his early life.

"...*Quag up to the knees...*": Ireland in the Later Work

A road still carriageable climbs over the high moorland. It cuts across vast turfbogs, a thousand feet above sea-level, two thousand if you prefer. It leads to nothing any more. A few ruined forts, a few ruined dwellings. The sea is not far, just visible beyond the valleys dipping eastward, pale plinth as pale as the pale wall of sky...The city is not far either, from certain points its lights can be seen by night, its light rather, and by day its haze Even the piers of the harbour can be distinguished, on very clear days, of the two harbours, tiny arms in the glassy sea outflung, known flat, seen raised. And the islands and promontories, one has only to stop and turn at the right place, and of course by night the beacon lights, both flashing and revolving. (Beckett 1974: 97–8)

If there is an ur-landscape in Beckett's mature fiction, it is this one: a version of the bog and moor lands in the Dublin hills, with a view to the city below, the harbor, and the sea beyond. It is evoked in *Mercier and Camier* (in the passage quoted above), the trilogy, and the Nouvelles: features of the landscape – the mud and the stones in particular – recur throughout the later fiction and drama (*Godot*, the *Texts for Nothing*, *How It Is*, and *Ill Seen Ill Said*, for example). Even the pale sky features, in *Endgame*'s "Grey ... Light black, from pole to pole" (Beckett 1990: 107) and the "grey cloudless sky" of *For to end yet again* (Beckett 1999: 243). That the location is of profound significance to the narrator figures in the later work is undeniable. Molloy, approaching the ramparts of his home town (a town which sits between the mountains and the sea), comments, "For my native town was the only one I knew, having never set foot in any other" (Beckett 1959: 31); and the narrator of *The Expelled* calls his home town the "scene of my birth and of my first steps in the world, and then of all the others" (Beckett 1980c: 36). And yet the town, and the landscape that surrounds it, is never named. Not only that, but its features are both familiar and unfamiliar: the narrator of *The End*, expelled from the institution that has housed him at the beginning of his story, finds himself adrift in a town he does not recognize:

In the street I was lost. I had not set foot in this part of the city for a long time and it seemed greatly changed. Whole buildings had disappeared, the palings had changed position and on all sides I saw, in great letters, the names of tradesmen I had never seen before and would have been at a loss to pronounce. There were streets where I remembered none, some I did remember had vanished and others had completely changed their names. The general impression was the same as before. It is true I did not know the city very well. Perhaps it was quite a different one. (ibid.: 74)

It has been argued by Sean Kennedy, in a recent conference paper (2006), that this passage might reflect the changes in Irish society brought about in the wake of the constitutional changes enacted by De Valera's government. According to James Knowlson, it also reflects Beckett's estrangement from Dublin at the end of World War II. However, in the world that Beckett describes, even those elements that seem familiar are also uncanny. Trying to find a familiar part of the city, the narrator of

The End makes his way to the river. He is reassured to find, as he tells us, that the (unnamed) river still gives the impression of "flowing in the wrong direction" (Beckett 1980c: 75).

The profound change in Beckett's worldview, brought on by a number of factors – the breakdown after his father's death, and the therapy he received in London; the turn to French in the late 1930s; his experience of World War II and of the reconstruction after the war's end; and, finally, the moment of revelation described in *Krapp's Last Tape*, has been well documented (in Knowlson [1996] and elsewhere). Its constituent elements are also well known: a new-found willingness to embrace the possibility of failure, and to replace ironic omnipotence with a radical uncertainty. Beckett himself had noted, in his early monograph on *Proust*, that for the modern artist "[the] only fertile research is excavatory, immersive, a contraction of the spirit, a descent" (Beckett 1965: 65). However, it would be wrong to say that this was the path that the early Beckett pursued: as argued above, at least in relation to Ireland, he is more concerned with the attempt to stand apart from the world he describes, and with the maintenance of an ironic distance which serves to confirm the author's mastery over, and his rejection of, the world evoked in his fiction. However, after the change in his outlook in the late 1930s and 1940s, the work that Beckett undertook was genuinely excavatory in two ways. First, the work became more personal, not autobiographical but, in H. Porter Abbot's resonant phrase, autographical. As Abbott argues, it is possible to argue that Beckett's work comes to occupy "that rarely occupied subset … [which is] writing governed not by narrative form nor any species of tropological wholeness but by that unformed intensity of being in the present which at every point in the text seems to approach itself" (1996: 18). Secondly, it is excavatory in a more direct sense. In the early work, Beckett's central figures hold themselves apart from the physical world (Murphy retreating into his chair to escape the disasters of the external world and to lose himself in the "pure forms of commotion" [1980a: 66] is the paradigmatic example of this). In the later work, even if a character has apparently been removed from the real world, memories and images of that world continually recur; there is no escaping them, even for the figure on his back in the dark in *Company*.

The new status of the Beckett protagonist is neatly caught in the opening of the *Texts for Nothing*:

> Suddenly, no, at last, long last, I couldn't any more, I couldn't go on. Someone said, you can't stay here. I couldn't stay there and I couldn't go on. I'll describe the place, that's unimportant. The top, very flat, of a mountain, no, a hill, so wild, enough. Quag, up to the knees, faint sheep-tracks, troughs scooped deep by the rains. It was far down in one of these I was lying, out of the wind. Glorious prospect, but for the mist that blotted out everything, valleys, loughs, plain and sea. (Beckett 1999: 100)

The Beckett protagonist no longer distances himself from the landscape by papering it over with layers of allusion; now, the protagonist is immersed in landscape: Molloy leaning against his rock at the beginning of *Molloy*, Moran's journey from an ordered garden to the wilderness that Molloy inhabits, the mud of *How It Is*, the bare rocks of *Ill Seen Ill Said*. In these works, landscape is immanent; it is more clearly present to many of the protagonists in the later fiction and drama precisely because their physical existence is inextricably bound up with it. Winnie, sinking into the earth, is an instructive example; Beckett might, in rehearsal, claim that she is a creature of air, but what we see is a character for whom the earth is an extension of the body.

There are moments of such immanence in the early fiction, moments where figure and landscape come in to direct relation (Celia, in *Murphy*, lifting her face to the sky "simply to have that unction of soft, sunless light on her eyes which was all she remembered of Ireland" [1980a: 157] – a precursor of the grey, pale skies of the later fiction, of which more below). However, the transition from the landscapes in Beckett's early fiction to the landscapes of the later work takes place decisively in *Watt* – and the transition takes place in the landscape of Beckett's youth. *Watt* begins in the allusive, comic landscape of *More Pricks than Kicks*; the opening dialogues, although written more sparely, strike the same note of bizarrely polite emptiness as the dialogues in the early short stories. However, the location, although clearly identifiable as the Dublin suburbs, is never named as such. Here, the location is simply described, and when the novel shifts to Watt entirely, we find him on the platform, waiting to board a train on the Dublin Slow and Easy – the line which went past Beckett's childhood home – but immanent description has replaced flat or baroque reinterpretation. Mr Knott's house, Watt's final destination, is identifiably an amalgam of Cooldrinagh (the Beckett family home) and Glencairn, the nearby home of the millionaire Boss Croker (whose name recurs in Croker's Acres, cited memorably in *Not I*) – but again, the link is only apparent to those who have read the posthumous biographies, or O'Brien's *The Beckett Country* (1986). In *Watt*, the biographical resonance of the location is hidden, rather than overt; significantly, though, the figure who, in Beckett's work, most incarnates the process of immanence inhabits the space occupied, in Beckett's life, by those people most committed to stasis. Mr Knott cannot be understood through the application of strict descriptive terms; he will never settle to a single meaning. The name Knott not only suggests absence and nothingness; it also suggests constant transformation, not one fixed thing, but everything: "For one day Mr Knott would be tall, fat, pale and dark, and the next thin, small, flushed and fair, and the next sturdy, middle-sized, flushed thin and ginger, and the next tall, yellow, dark and sturdy, and the next fat, middle-sized, ginger and pale" (Beckett 1964: 209) – and so on, for the next two pages. The only way to understand Mr Knott is to abandon the process of understanding, and to immerse oneself in the immanence of the character; something that Watt, throughout the novel, signally fails to do. However, it is not simply that one character within the novel incarnates immanence: everything within Knott's house exists simultaneously in a fixed relation and also in immanent flux.

The irony is that Watt, the failed rationalist, already inhabits such a landscape. On his way to Mr Knott's house he tires, and has to sit on a path which is, as Beckett describes it, "hedged with thick neglected grass" (ibid.: 31) And then, in an attempt to escape the light of the moon, he "rolled himself into the ditch, and lay there, on his face, half buried in the wild long grass, the foxgloves, the hyssop, the pretty nettles, the high, pouting hemlock, and other ditch weeds and flowers" (ibid.: 32). At the novel's end, Watt has been ejected from Knott's house into an immanent Ireland; his relation to the physical landscape of the country is now that of an inescapable immersion:

> And often he struck against the trunks of trees, and in the tangles of underwood caught his foot, and fell to the ground, on his back, on his face, on his side, or into a great clump of brambles, or of briars, or of thistles, or of nettles. But ever he picked himself up and unmurmuring went on, toward his habitation, until I saw him no more, but only the aspens. (ibid.: 213)

This is a new landscape, contiguous with the protagonist, almost an extension of the self (note that, at the end of the quotation, the aspens stand as a silent, displaced echo of Watt, their presence inescapably bound up with his absence). The Beckett protagonist will move through a similar landscape for the rest of his writing life: the figure in *Stirrings Still*, Beckett's last prose text, imagines himself "[moving] on through the hoar grass resigned to not knowing where he was or how he got there or where he was going" (Beckett 1999: 263). Whether the location is urban or rural, it will have the same impact on the protagonist: it will be simultaneously proximate and unknowable; it will be an extension of the self, and at the same time an immanent physical presence, no longer held at a distance from the protagonist – and it will, time and time again, take its form and its structure from the landscapes of Dublin and its surrounding countryside.

In a recent essay, Paul Davies (2006) has pointed out the recurrence of particular climatic conditions in Beckett's work – rain, or grey skies, lightening, at least on the horizon, to admit a gleam of light before the sun is finally extinguished. Davies quite rightly notes that these conditions are familiar to anyone who has lived in Ireland; he also, interestingly, argues that the sun's last gleaming carries strongly metaphysical associations:

> This gives birth to Beckett's recessive yet recurrent philosophy of the sudden gleam. It leaps the boundary between the document of climate and the figurement of a state of mind ... The Irish rain, falling all day to leave the sun only moments to appear, offers Beckett one of his profoundest literary discoveries: in that sudden gleam is contained all eternity, and a magnificent reminder of the Heraclitean proverb that the one and only changeless attribute of the universe is its changeableness (2006: 70)

As above, so below; the Irish landscape, which in the later Beckett is a fixed chaos of entangled plants, mud, or, conversely, of a city either disturbingly crowded, forcing itself in on the protagonist (in *The Expelled*) or denuded of people save for the sudden appearance of a crowd that sweeps around the central character before disappearing again (*The Calmative*), suggests not so much eternity, as experience. It bears the traces of the character's passing; it is marked by the protagonist, and it marks the protagonist, in a way that the named locations of the early fictions never did. The central figure in *Company*, for example, conjures the memory of walking across a pasture; and the memory that is invoked is of the trace his feet have left on the land: "You look behind you as you could not then and see their trail" (Beckett 1980d: 52). A location meticulously named, only to be converted in the act of description into an interior landscape, is now a landscape which has to be lived through: it cannot be turned either into a theatrical flat or an overly abstracted meditation – it has to be encountered in the present, as a tangible force in the characters' lives.

We have, therefore, moved quite some distance from the exile's celebration that Kiberd identifies. We are in the territory described by Beckett as obsessional; an obsessional landscape is by implication indefinable (if a final definition could be achieved, obsession would be unnecessary). It cannot be held still: this landscape, and by implication the culture that is tied to the landscape, resists the process of reification that Beckett tried to impose upon it in his earlier work. It figures in Beckett's later writing as a physical presence; its precise relevance to the characters is never clear, perhaps because it is always at the point of construction: immanent presence has replaced distanced, ironic analysis. This does not mean, though, that Ireland has been transmuted in Beckett's later work into a representation of an interior landscape – it is too immediate, too close to the protagonists, for that. It is in this direction, toward the idea that Irish locations as immediate, physical, obsessional elements in the lives of Beckett's protagonists, that, I would argue, we have to look, if we want to understand the relation between Beckett's work and his cultural background. This is not the recreated Ireland of the exile (it cannot be named); neither is it another version of the relation between writer and landscape that the revisionist historian R. F. Foster (1993) identifies as a feature of Irish writing as a whole – again, because the relationship between the protagonist and the location is far too close. There are no final lessons to be drawn from this relation, no final summation of the relation of an Irish writer to his culture. But, also, I would argue that we are quite a distance from any notion of a "Beckett country"; the locations explored in the later fiction might be exactly contiguous with the protagonists, but, no matter how close the relation, the landscape of the later work is not a landscape of the mind. Rather, we have moved into a relation between self and world which has been described most appositely by the Scottish writer and critic Neal Ascherson; Scotland, like Ireland, has been caught up in the search for origins, but Ascherson argues that this is not the only way to read the Scottish landscape. Rather than searching for the authenticity of the stones, we should remember that "[instead] of authenticity, stones have biographies. Some of the biography is incised or chipped or rubbed into them. Some of it – the different uses, mythical or practical, to which they have been put by humans – can be read in a written document or inferred from other material evidence ... Much of it remains unreadable" (Ascherson 2003: 8).

Beckett's later work is, I would argue, an attempt to create a biography (or perhaps, to use Porter Abbott's phrase, an autography) of those Irish locations which figure obsessionally in his writing. Rather than the exile's celebration of a country which is fixed in the moment of writing, Beckett's work gives us the sense of an immanent, obsessional Ireland rendered with all the "unformed intensity of being in the present" that informs the rest of his art.

REFERENCES AND FURTHER READING

Abbot, H. Porter (1996). *The Author in the Autograph*. Ithaca: Cornell University Press.

Ascherson, Neal (2003). *Stone Voices*. London: Granta.

Beckett, Samuel (1959). *The Trilogy*. London: John Calder.

Beckett, Samuel (1964). *Watt*. London: John Calder.

Beckett, Samuel (1965). *Proust and Three Dialogues*. London: John Calder.

Beckett, Samuel (1974). *Mercier and Camier*. London: John Calder.

Beckett, Samuel (1980a). *Murphy*. London: John Calder.

Beckett, Samuel (1980b). *More Pricks than Kicks*. London: John Calder.

Beckett, Samuel (1980c). *The Expelled and Other Novellas*. London: Penguin.

Beckett, Samuel (1980d). *Company*. London: John Calder.

Beckett, Samuel (1983). *Disjecta*. London: John Calder.

Beckett, Samuel (1990). *Complete Dramatic Works*. London: Faber and Faber.

Beckett, Samuel (1992). *Dream of Fair to middling Women*. Dublin: Black Cat Press.

Beckett, Samuel (1999). *Complete Shorter Prose*. New York: Grove Press.

Cronin, Anthony (1996). *Samuel Beckett: The Last Modernist*. London: Harper Collins.

Davies, Paul (2006). "Strange Weather: Beckett from the Perspective of Eco-criticism." In S. E. Gontarski and A. Uhlmann (eds.), *Beckett after Beckett*. University of Florida Press.

Foster, Roy (1993). *Paddy and Mr Punch: Connections in Irish and English History*. London: Allen Lane, the Penguin Press.

Junker, Mary (1995). *Beckett: The Irish Dimension* Dublin: Wolfhound Press.

Kennedy, Sean (2006). "*Historicising Beckett: Aspects of the Four Novellas*," delivered at Beckett at 100: New Perspectives, Florida State University, February 9–11.

Kiberd, Declan (1996). *Inventing Ireland: The Literature of the Modern Nation*. London: Vantage.

Knowlson, James (1996). *Damned to Fame: The Life of Samuel Beckett*. London: Bloomsbury.

McCormack W. J. (1994). *From Burke to Beckett: Ascendancy, Tradition and Betrayal in Literary History*. Cork: Cork University Press.

MacDonald, Ronan (2002). *Tragedy and Irish Literature: Yeats, Synge, Beckett*. London: Palgrave.

Mooney, Sinead (2005). "Kicking Against the Thermolators." *Samuel Beckett Today/Aujourd,hui* 15: 29–41.

O'Brien, Eoin (1986). *The Beckett Country: Samuel Beckett's Ireland*. Dublin: Black Cat Press.

Pilling, John (2004). *A Companion to Dream of Fair to middling Women*. Tallahassee, FL: Journal of Beckett Studies Books.

Ricks, Christopher (1993). *Beckett's Dying Words*. Oxford: Oxford University Press.

Sanchez, Jose Maria. "'They took the dull coast road home': Images Of Ireland In Samuel Beckett's Dream Of Fair To Middling Women." In Maria Jose Carrera, Anunciacion Carrera, Enrique Camara, and Celsa Dapia (eds.), *The Irish Knot: Essays on Imaginary/Real Ireland*. Valladolid: University of Valladolid Press.

14
Beckett in French and English

Sinéad Mooney

When asked in 1956 by Niklaus Gessner why he had begun to write in French, Beckett replied, "Parce qu'en français c'est plus facile d'écrire sans style" (Gessner 1957: 32). To Herbert Blau he wrote that French "had the right weakening effect," and to Richard Coe that he feared English "because you couldn't help writing poetry in it" (Coe 1968: 14). Such statements have been read as cumulatively testifying to Beckett's postwar adoption of French as a language of original composition as part of a conscious aesthetics of self-impoverishment. On the other hand, if Beckett's switch to French is repeatedly linked to reduction, weakening, and self-impoverishment, other scattered comments made by him on the topic suggest that writing in French was as much an assertion of self as an abdication. Ruby Cohn quotes him as saying, perhaps flippantly, that he had switched to French "pour faire remarquer moi" (Cohn 1962: 95); the Israel Shenker interview reports him as saying he had switched to French because "it was more exciting for me – writing in French"; while his complaints on the "lack of brakes" he perceived to be inherent in English indicate a need to assert authorial control rather than to renounce it (Shenker 1956: 2.3).

In fact, Beckett's bilingual oeuvre – the existence of virtually all of his work in French and English versions which maintain a frequently problematic, not to say "pseudo-couplish," relation to one another – operates less upon a single moment of renunciation or ascesis than upon a career-long embrace of an activity traditionally considered ancillary and derivative, but which is, in Beckett's writing, hauled to center stage – that of self-translation. In Beckett's hands a procedure modulating between self-occlusion and self-aggrandizement, self-translation both doubles and abolishes the original by compromising its originality. It plays the shadowy figure of the translator off against the author – even when they are combined in the same person – and continues the repudiation of appeals to an essential recoverable "sense" made by Beckett's "original" work. Self-translation, thus, is not merely something performed upon the inert body of a completed text, but comes to constitute some of the most characteristic effects of an oeuvre traversed with alien voices, splittings, hauntings, and simulacra.

Traditionally, translation is considered an "impossible" art, or at best, one predicated upon an inevitable loss between original and translated version, and performed by largely invisible figures, characterized by "a willingness to play second fiddle, to meld into the identity of a primary creator" (Thiem 1995: 90). Conventionally, its highest aspiration is considered to be self-effacement, an unremarked communication or transfer of essential meaning. The author is viewed as primary and the translator as secondary, even when the two positions can, as in the case of Beckett, be occupied by the same person. It is clear that Beckett, whose early translations of the surrealists found more contemporary favor than his derivative "original" prewar work in English, initially began to translate his own work, beginning with his first published novel, *Murphy*, with the purely pragmatic motive of reaching two linguistic communities. Further, his correspondence of the 1950s and 1960s, larded with references to ongoing "arrears of self-translation," make it clear that he to some extent, at least in the casual space of letters to friends, shared the conventional conception of translation as essentially a practical, subsidiary task, as opposed to actual composition. To Thomas McGreevy he writes of the experience of working on the translation of *Molloy* with Patrick Bowles as "an indigestion of old work with all the adventure gone" (Beckett TCD10402/1–233), and, almost a decade later, to Alan Schneider of being "faced now with even more than the usual wilderness of self-translation – *Comment c'est* into English, *H.D.* [*Happy Days*] into French, *Play* into French, i.e. all real work blocked out for at least six months" (Harmon 1998: 131). Yet this account is crucially contradicted by the evidence of the second versions themselves, which testify to a complex poetics of self-translation which exploits the principle that, just as languages cannot simply be mapped onto one another, texts cannot simply be repeated without disrupting the regulatory function of the author, and flaunting the inherent failure of closure of the "original." The "wilderness of self-translation," in which author mingles with the more shadowy persona of the translator, is *about* the inherent lack of harmonization (linguistic dissonance and incommensurability, things getting "lost in translation," a paucity of orderly equivalents for what the translator is trying to convey from one language to another) that Beckett's work regards as axiomatic. The generation, via self-translation, of textual pseudo-couples undermines the myth of textual or authorial autonomy, dislocates the hierarchical binary of original/copy, and threatens an uncontrollable proliferation of meaning.

Beckett has, along with Nabokov, who also exchanged a mother tongue for a foreign language in mid-career, been held to be one of the very few writers to have flouted the dictum that active multilingualism inevitably hampers literary expression. However, unlike Nabokov, who spoke frequently of the "private tragedy" of his forced abandonment of his "infinitely rich and docile Russian ... for a second-rate brand of English" (Nabokov 1978: 15), Beckett, never willing to comment on his own creativity, refrained from elaborating on the reasons for his switch of languages. He remained even more reticent about his anomalous position as a writer who sedulously chose to write much of his mature work in an adopted language and then, with equal assiduousness, render it "back" into his mother tongue. This reticence, perhaps, has fostered a corresponding critical mutedness on the existence of virtually the entire Beckett canon in French and English, self-translated with varying degrees of fidelity by the author; the conventional invisibility of the translator has led in this instance to Beckett being regarded a special kind of authorized translator, to the extent that the translated status of much of his "original" work can be discounted because it is just as "valid" as the original.

Of course, Beckett, unlike Nabokov and Russian, did not in fact "abandon" his native English at all, or only briefly. In the midst of the fertile first flush of French composition he announced in a December 1946 letter to his friend and one-time agent, the Irish publisher–poet George Reavey, that he did not think he would write much in English in the future, but by the end of the "siege in the room," with a tally of four novels, four novellas, three plays, and thirteen short prose pieces, all in French, Beckett was already engaged in what he termed "the wastes and wilds of self-translation" as the *succès de scandale* of *Godot* saw him fielding requests for an English production. By 1956, the year he credited his turn to French to a desire for stylelessness, he was already far embarked on a career straddling two languages, with the publication of *Malone Dies* and the English *Godot*, and the beginnings of a return to English as a language of original composition, as witnessed by the publication of the prose fragment *From an Abandoned Work*, the writing of *All That Fall* for the BBC, and the theater fragment "The Gloaming." For the rest of his writing career, Beckett's work would involve this idiosyncratic combination of original composition in either French or English, alongside self-translation, sometimes performed close in time to the writing of the original, producing a "sibling text," or, alternatively, sometimes done years, even decades, after the writing of the original.

The casual reader could be forgiven for missing altogether the insidious fault-line of self-translation running through the core of Beckett's writing: his texts often bear only a token "traduit par l'auteur"/"translated by the author" when they are the second version. The Grove Press *Complete Short Prose 1929–1989* charts in bountiful detail the frequently bewildering mutations of short pieces, their journal publications or appearance in limited editions, but largely ignores, in its notes, the *translatedness* of the majority of the texts it contains. Yet the implications for critical consideration of his work are considerable: the blurring of boundaries by the existence of two imperfectly matched versions of most texts, among which the reader can find no clear sense of the definitive or authoritative, renders the idea of the individual work oddly porous. Self-translation effortlessly interrupts and complicates any attempt to outline a straightforward chronology of Beckett's work; the apparent binaries of French and English Beckett break down, and discontinuity runs riot through chronologies with which we think we are familiar. The anglophone Beckett reader is accustomed to thinking of, for instance, the *Texts for Nothing* as belonging to the famous, post-*L'Innommable* period of barrenness, but it is, of course, the case that most of the actual English words, with their haunting, halting cadences, were written some 15 years later in 1966, at roughly the same time *Watt* was even more belatedly making the opposite translatorial journey, and the complex of texts that would eventually result in *Le Dépeupleur/The Lost Ones* was well under way.

Common sense objects that the *Texts for Nothing* really "belong" to the textual moment of their original, whenever they were translated, but the double chronology nonetheless involves the reader in the double-bind of clinging to the both the words on the page before us as constituting the *real* text and simultaneously insisting that their moment in time is that of their original. Whichever way we might attempt to rationalize this quasi-Proustian textual flickering between widely divergent moments in time, we are forced into the realization that Beckett's writings are never fully present to themselves, but are radically distracted from their textual moment. Ultimately, the double inscription of each work in French and English denies the reader access to any unified or originary surface of interpretation, consciousness, or meaning.

Beckett's bilingualism and career-long recourse to self-translation is too often treated as straightforwardly anomalous, when, in fact, he came of age as a writer amid intense modernist investment in translation as a mode of literary production. Both the intensity and diversity of effort that mark the modernist concerns with, and practice of, translation suggest a conviction that the establishment of personal and cultural identity requires engaging with multiple others of foreign languages and traditions. The Francophone Eliot of "Dans le restaurant" and "Mélange Adultère de Tout" (*Poems 1920*) makes his presence strongly felt in *Echo's Bones*, and is likely to have prompted Beckett's first experiments in writing French poetry. While Eliot's venture into the brittle, ironic French of Laforgue was of brief duration, in contrast to Beckett's lifelong immersion in the impersonal French of no one in particular, both were seeking in French a quality absent from their own immediate literary surroundings. A somewhat older Eliot wrote in "Yeats" (1940) that the kind of writing he had needed to teach him the use of his own poetic voice "did not exist in English at all; it was only to be found in French" (Eliot 1957: 252), echoing a similar sentiment in Beckett's *Dream of Fair to middling Women*, which puts forward the notion that "perhaps only the French language can give you the thing you want" (Beckett 1992: 46). Beckett's "Ex Cathezra," "Dante ... Bruno.Vico..Joyce," and his 1937 letter to Axel Kaun – all manifestly influenced by the polyglot exhibitionism of Pound – also endorse Pound's influential assumptions that certain foreign texts have perceptions not available in English, and that these testify to a road not taken by English. The Pound of "Cavalcanti," who rages at "Victorian language" and the "crust of dead English, the sediment present in my own available vocabulary," shares with the Beckett of "Dante ... Bruno.Vico.. Joyce" (who complains of English "being abstracted to death") a dissatisfaction with the current state of English (Pound 1971: 399). Of course, even more than a perceptible influence from the *Cantos*, Beckett was marked by his involvement with that other unwieldy modernist undertaking in which the multiplicity of its constituent languages at once reflects an abiding thematic concern and plays a crucial role in the formal articulation of the text, *Work in Progress* – a section of which he co-translated, laboriously, into French, at Joyce's behest, in 1930.

In fact, far from rendering him anomalous, Beckett's early poetic experiments with French, and his interest in translation from and into French, are entirely characteristic of the work of the faction of anti-Revivalist Irish poetic modernism to which this phase of his career demonstrably belongs. Rather than focusing on "antiquarian"

translation from Irish myth and legend, as the poets of the Revival did, Thomas
MacGreevy, Denis Devlin, and Brian Coffey, along with Beckett – an otherwise dis-
parate group united by time spent in Paris and a self-alignment with European
experimentalism – embraced poetic translation from European languages. All, like
Beckett, contributors to *transition*, their pronounced openness to foreign texts and
influences makes of translation a radical rejection of national insularity, a textual following in the footsteps of Joyce which they would all also literally make, and a
(somewhat belated) declaration of belonging to a form of European modernism which
derives more from Pound, Eliot, and the surrealists, as well as Joyce, than from
W. B. Yeats.

     While between the late twenties and the late thirties Beckett translated Joyce's
"Anna Livia Plurabelle," Eluard, Breton, Char, Apollinaire, Rimbaud, and the mul-
tifarious contributions to Nancy Cunard's *Negro: An Anthology*, alongside writing
poetry in English and French, he was symptomatic of rather than exceptional among
his generation of Irish modernist poets. Denis Devlin translated, among others, St-
John Perse, Char, and Eluard; Brian Coffey made versions of Pablo Neruda, Eluard,
and later Mallarmé, while George Reavey translated from the French as well as
Russian, and ran an international translation bureau with close links to surrealist
outlets. Many of Thomas MacGreevy's poems do not exist in a single language; drafts
show a poem begun in Spanish being annotated and rewritten in French and reworked
in English, while others appear to be worked on simultaneously in both English and
French. The early career of Denis Devlin, whose *Intercessions* Beckett defended in 1938
from a dismissive review in the *Times Literary Supplement*, is marked by a lack of clear
distinction as to which language he should be writing in – later, his English is heavily
inflected by Irish and French, the two other languages and literatures in which he was
steeped. In all of these, as in Beckett's work, texts straddle other languages, and poetic
voice takes on hybrid or interstitial forms involving translating and moving back and
forth between different literary traditions and languages.

     Beckett's 1930s translations of the work of others, the Poundian serenas, albas and
enuegs of *Echo's Bones*, his exhibitionistically polyglot sub-*Wakean* prose and the
poems in French known as "Poèmes 1937–1939," give way, in the period immediately
after the war, to original prose composition in French. His co-translation of *Murphy*
into French with Alfred Péron, his "Anna Livia Plurabelle" collaborator, in 1938–40,
is also, bar a scattering of poems, the inaugural moment of self-translation. By the
time it was published in 1947, its co-translator and dedicatee was dead after intern-
ment in a concentration camp, and Beckett was engaged on *Molloy* and *Malone meurt*,
in which indistinct terrains are traversed by outsiders, exiles, refugees, who imbricate
the apartness of their author's Irish Protestantism with elements of the high modernist
conception of Jewishness as a type of cultural instability. These figures, in their
troping of a perplexed relationship between the subject and the grounds of its historical and cultural belonging, figure forth the process of translation.

     This lack of continuity between the self and its language, or lack of safe linguistic
ground underfoot, is pre-empted in Beckett's war-time novel *Watt*, a form of farewell

to English, whose manuscript contains marginalia in French, and which is characterized by the deformation of English away from its usual syntactical forms and by an
abundance of Gallicisms. Written, as he told Rubin Rabinovitz, "with a view to not
losing my reason," the novel shows signs of an incipient linguistic breakdown and a
growing disengagement from English, as well as the difficult, peripatetic circumstances of its composition. These two sets of circumstances dovetail in the text's
anxious preoccupation with language's desertion of the self for which it had previously
provided a "pillow of old words," and with coded language and encryption. Words
literally fail Watt, as events and objects become incapable of yielding "semantic
succour," consenting to be named, if at all, "with reluctance" (Beckett 1981: 79). The
novel moves between the poles of the intricately reversed, cryptic idiolect Watt speaks
in the asylum, and which the narrator, Sam, has to decipher or translate, and, on the
other hand, a nostalgia for "the old words, the old credentials" (ibid.: 81). From a
writer not given to Nabokovian communiqués on the pain of switching languages of
composition, what Leslie Hill has influentially dubbed *Watt*'s "loss of filiation" within
language is the only indication that Beckett struggled with what many bilingual
writers appear to experience as a lack of psychic sanction, a sense of illegitimacy, at
the abandonment both of the inhibiting mother-tongue and its allied deep-seated
restraints and strictures (Hill 1990: 23). No wonder that, as Erika Ostrovsky has
noted, Beckett's first French prose works, which follow *Watt*, are marked by the frequent use of words such as *jeter, abandoner, perdre* (Ostrovsky 1976).

Beckett's early French prose, with its ejections and rejections, shows traces of its
composition by what George Steiner terms a writer "linguistically unhoused ... not
thoroughly at home in the language of his production, but displaced or hesitant at
the frontier" (Steiner 1970: 120). The novellas, however, while they cast off many of
the trappings usually associated with the form, are characterized less by figures deliberately getting rid of things than by vagabonds, tramps, and solitaries who are themselves expelled, cast off or abandoned. Anticipating the trilogy in their half-familiar,
half-strange locations, which appear to be part Ireland, part continental Europe, the
four stories from 1946 constitute a series of symbolic births, banishments, or expul-
sions which seem congruent with beginning work in a new genre in a new language,
as the elderly waifs who inhabit them are inexplicably ejected from the security of
some form of shelter, in a manner suggestive of the birth trauma. That this rebirth
is also linguistic is evident from the manuscript of the first to be composed, "Suite"
(revised as "La Fin"), which shows that it was begun in English, and that the switch
to French took place after almost a month of writing, while the stories' insecure
lodging in French appears in references by the francophone narrator of "Premier
amour" to the foreign accent which has him mispronouncing his lover's name.

This sense of the subject balancing on a cusp is also a thematic and formal preoccupation in the trio of limpid bilingual poems "je suis ce cours de sable" ("my way
is in the sand flowing"), "que ferais-je dans ce monde sans visage sans questions"
("what would I do in this world faceless incurious") and "je voudrais que mon amour
meure" ('I would like my love to die') which were composed at about this time and

appeared in parallel text form in *Transition Forty-Eight*; among the few properly bilingual works by Beckett, their order of composition – whether initially in French or
English – is unknown. The poem, or pair of poems, leaves the speaker in his eerily
doubled, riven state, between the shingle and the dune, between a French and English
which refuse to gloss one another but insist on deferring meaning still further. "Three
poems"/"Trois poèmes" pull away from the linguistic and cultural center of each
language towards their own bilingual realm, opening the syntax and imagery of his
language to one another, and towards flexible, continuously reanimated meaning.
"Betweenness" in these poems is a hinge-state between linguistic worlds.

It is, however, with the trilogy and *Godot*, in both their languages, that Beckett
begins to fully inhabit an almost Bakhtinian space in which writing in a foreign
language – and the subsequent translation of that work back into the mother tongue
which is thus itself explicitly "marked" by translation – constitutes an important part
of the works' literary effects. The pair of trilogies, *Molloy*, *Malone meurt* (both written
in 1947 and published in 1951) and *L'Innommable* (written 1949–50, published 1953),
and *Molloy*, *Malone Dies*, and *The Unnamable* (published 1955, 1956, 1958) continue
more radically the novellas' exploitation of the state of linguistic and cultural betweenness, and an absconding from the condition of belonging. The trilogy seizes on the
previously unexplored no-man's-land between original and translation, French and
English (or Hiberno-English, itself a composite), presence and absence. One entirely
pragmatic reason for this is that the writing of the French trilogy becomes enmeshed
both with its own translation (work on the typescript of *L'Innommable* was still
ongoing alongside the translation of the *Mexican Anthology* when Beckett was asked
to translate sections of *Molloy* into English for Georges Duthuit's *transition* in 1950)
and the prodigious amount of jobbing translation work which underwrites it.

Despite the traditional account of the "siege in the room" as a period of solitary,
single-minded fertility in original creation – the discovery by Beckett of his own
"voice" in French – he was, throughout the poverty-stricken late 1940s and 1950s,
lending out his voice to anyone prepared to pay him. As well as translating for
UNESCO, Georges Duthuit's *The Fauvist Painters* and for the American journal *Art
News*, he contributed a translation, often more than one, to virtually every issue of
Georges Duthuit's revamped postwar *transition*, translating work by Duthuit himself,
Emmanuel Bove, Henri Michaux, Alfred Jarry, André du Bouchet, Suzanne Dumesnil,
poems by Eluard, Char, Jacques Prévert, Henri Pichette, Gabriela Mistral, and
Guillaume Apollinaire (Federman and Fletcher 1970: 97–9, Knowlson 1996: 369,
774–5). Beckett's translations – whether viewed as ventriloquism, ghosting for other
writers, or his placing of himself in "others' words," to elaborate on a trope that
dominates *L'Innommable/The Unnamable* in particular – manifest themselves in visible
"traces" of translation left in the trilogy texts.

It is not simply a matter of a tension between Irish names and Irish, or cod-Irish,
proper nouns and a French voice, though the jarring of an imperfect fit between language and name gives even the reader of the French "originals" of the trilogy novels
the sensation of always already reading a translation. The proximity, even the mutual

infection, of translation and composition, is evident in the trilogy's frequent deployment of foreignisms in both its languages, drawing attention to the narrator as translator – between languages, swerving between naturalizing and "foreignizing" translation styles. Early criticism of the trilogy often admired Beckett's skill in finding equivalent textual effects in his other language, but, in line with Beckett's frequent disobedience as a translator of others, his self-translations in fact resemble his prewar poetry translations in their frequent refusal of equivalence. From the novellas onward, texts that are already in their original forms mined with narrative and linguistic deviations, gaps, and incongruities develop in translation further unsettling linguistic markers or references to another linguistic universe, reneging still further on the realist contract.

If the French trilogy appears already to look back to a non-existent English original, sitting uneasily in French in its queasy combination of francophone, Irish-named figures and references to pence and Bastille Day, to Irish Republican politics and the *Times Literary Supplement*, to Condom being on the River Baise and imperial pints, then the subsequent English trilogy is equally ill-at-ease in English. Lacunae in the original narratives of the trilogy are sometimes sites of even greater pleasurable reader distress in the translation, aporias twice over, alerting the reader to the existence of not one but two translation worlds between which the implied translator continually moves for specific effects. The refusal of parity conservation is itself an important effect, as the translation wavers between a francophone world reported on by an implied English or Hiberno-English consciousness and an anglophone mirror-universe. Like the later plays, traversed by ghostly figures who never quite amount to the status of full characters, the trilogy novels are about the condition of never quite "being there," uncannily resisting the condition of full embodiment, enacted in a kind of writing that is never quite at home in either of its versions.

Deliberately inconsistent translation strategies, such as Beckett absorbed from his translation of others, thus contribute largely to the trilogy's radical oddness as a literary artifact. However, his self-translations are far from offering the consummation of a process of total evacuation of reference or representation, nor do they constitute works entirely free from dependence on or derivation from an extra-textual point of origin. Although shying away from any form of mimetic representation of postwar France or Ireland, translation also, inevitably, draws attention, albeit obliquely, to the question of linguistic, national, and authorial identity. This takes place precisely via the trilogy's perversely simultaneous inhabitation of positions that appear to be mutually exclusive according to the classificatory systems of nation, language, and canon. Translation cannot be considered an inviolate literary space, or an activity devoid of political content; it inevitably involves an agenda and negotiation with the ideological configurations and cultural discourses in which the translation is produced; it is more than a technical or supplementary practice, and an intervention which is inescapably value-bearing. Its inevitable choices – between words, registers, or which texts are translated – are rarely innocent. Beckett's self-translations need to be read in terms of their response to specifically Irish post-independence national anxieties, which center on fears of hybridity, which is seen as indicative of the perceived inauthenticity of the colonized culture and as evidence of the contamination of an original Irish essence which must be recuperated. If the aesthetic of nationalism subordinates all other aesthetic considerations to the demand for representative unity, a homogenized nation and an authenticating difference from the imperial culture, the trilogy represents cultural and linguistic hybridization, heterogeneity, and disintegration.

The adulterated, hybrid subject of the trilogy constitutes a rebuttal of the ideal subject of Irish cultural nationalism – what David Lloyd characterizes as the "individual's ideal continuity with the nation's spiritual origins"– in its romantic concern with the capacity of original "genius" to depict and embody the "spirit of the nation" (Lloyd 1993: 88). Simply put, the French trilogy, with its Irish names and landscapes, its references to the Republican graves of Glasnevin cemetery, and the hunger-striking Lord Mayor of Cork, all strikingly at odds with the French language in which they are narrated – is actively recalcitrant to the monologic demands of literary nationalism for a total identification with the nation. It circles, like Joyce's "Cyclops," thematically and stylistically around adulteration as the constitutive anxiety of nationalism. Translation – Douglas Hyde and his fellows in the Literary Revival having devoted themselves to de-anglicization and a recuperation of an "authentic" Irish identity through the translation of folklore – is crucial to this preoccupation with linguistic and cultural recovery. The trilogy, on the other hand, performs something akin to the adulteration of interpenetrating discourses of Joyce's *Ulysses* (though not the latter's fascination with adultery and adulteration in Irish history) by multiplying, in translation, its rampant internal heterogeneities. It offers a Bakhtinian multiplicity of contending, ill-integrated linguistic universes in direct contradistinction to a desired unified national identity as defined and represented in a national literature imbued with its "spirit." Where nationalism is devoted to the production of a single voice, cognate with the Irish subject and a collective national identity, continually identifying individual and nation to underwrite legitimate rights to "originality" hence legitimate independence, Beckett in the trilogy prevents any one voice being understood as internally coherent or stable. The autonomous national voice, and the possibility of its faithful reproduction, are undercut.

The Beckett reader is, thus, confronted with the six volumes of the trilogy, a curiously contrapuntal pair of triplets, in an initial French which seems always to gesture ahead to an English version which only came into being subsequent to its writing, and which appears in its turn to be looking over its shoulder to a lost fullness never in fact possessed by the "original." Both versions mourn a secondariness, or absence of plenitude – what Walter Benjamin terms "abjection" – which is the inevitable lot of the translated work, but which, in Beckett's self-translations, reaches back to abolish the notion of originality. Between the two texts translated by the author, there is no original, no possibility of origin. The self-translating writer is aware of not coinciding with himself; rather than confirming by repeating each other, at the level of the individual phrase and the entire work, the trilogy novels provide unsettling "company" for themselves, via the jarring of an imperfect fit. Writing everything twice, in French and English, means that every word, every phrase, is both more and less than itself; each is haunted by the ghost of its potential or actual translation.

Doubleness thus haunts the trilogy as a permanent component or circumstance of its vitality. It also offers a characteristic riposte to the demands of realist narrative for consistency, what Barthes has termed control by "the principle of non-contradiction." At every opportunity, he argues, it stresses "the *compatible* nature of circumstances, by attaching narrated events with a kind of logical 'paste.' Everything must 'hold together' as well as possible" (Barthes 1974: 156). However, the kinds of contradiction thrown up by the incommensurability of languages and Beckett's inconsistent translation strategies act as a major source of his writing's non-realist vitality. What Bakhtin says of Dostoevsky – that he constantly hears "two contending voices" in a single voice, that in his every expression there is a crack "and the readiness to go over immediately to a contrary expression" – is all the more true of Beckett, where contending voices and linguistic fissures occur across languages as well as across language (Bakhtin 1984: 30).

When Christopher Ricks writes in his *Beckett's Dying Words*, that "as so often in Beckett, his original French reads like a highly talented translation of a work of genius and not as the thing itself," he is celebrating what he believes, along with many other critics, to be the greater semantic richness of the English texts, regardless of whether they precede or follow the French (Ricks 1993: 4). Yet the distinctly "translated" feel of Beckett's subsequent version of a text, particularly in his post-trilogy work, constitutes an important set of textual and referential effects, which, ironically, celebrate as a literary gain the loss which is inevitably part of the translation process. It is hardly a surprise that Beckett, with his interest in an aesthetic of failure and impotence, should have seized on the potential for the loss of vitality in translation – the convention expressed in so Beckettian a way by Dryden's fear that "in pouring [a text] out of one language into another, there will remain nothing but a *caput mortuum*" (Dryden 1961: 241). His references to self-translation in letters continually emphasize loss and belatedness – *Endgame* is only one of the texts he claims "will inevitably be a poor substitute for the original," and, also, to Alan Schneider, five years later, he complains that "all the arrears of self-translation have me paralysed" (Harmon 1998: 14, 125). Beckett's distress at re-encountering, via the necessity to self-translate, work produced years or even decades earlier is evident: *Mercier et Camier*, written in French in 1946, translated into English in 1974, is "hateful old hat from the late Forties," while "Premier amour," written the same year as *Mercier et Camier* and translated in 1973, is "ancient prose painful to go back on" (Harmon 1998: 269, 300). This nexus of age, belatedness, and self-translation becomes a method of forwarding, haltingly, his later work's insistent deathward urge, manifested as an increasingly impoverished lexicon, a move towards shorter and sparer texts, and an increasing thematic preoccupation with the death of the imagination and the senescence of the body.

In its latter phase in particular – perhaps prompted by the unwelcome task of belatedly translating *Mercier et Camier* and "Premier amour" rather more than 20 years after their composition – Beckett's bilingual oeuvre seizes on this inevitable "loss" and negation in translation, producing deliberately bleached, lifeless, and archaic-seeming second versions in order to heighten the effect of pitting language against itself. Many critics have noted the tendency for the second versions of Beckett's texts to be somewhat "lessened" or contracted, as the second acts of plays such as *Godot* and *Play*, which are an entropic, reduced version of the first, or, as in *Endgame*, where the translated version is itself a cut-down "second act" of the original. Beckett's late self-translations allow for this "second act" (Connor 1988: 88–114). At times, as in the belatedly translated *Mercier and Camier*, the second versions are significantly cut, while in other texts, such as *The Lost Ones*, the translation acts as a space in which the entropic, dwindling, worsening suggestions implanted in the original *Le Dépeupleur* may be further played out, with textual spaces contracted, the cylinder-world smaller, and the language correspondingly diminished. *Mal vu mal dit* (1981), despite being translated shortly after it was written, becomes in English a considerably more archaic affair, the relatively contemporary original French transforming via a death-dealing translation into an elaborately obsolete Victorian English, larded with words such as "collatement," "dimmen," "washen," "viewless" (Mooney 2002). The translation has selected an entirely different diction to that of its original, and one which incarnates, even flaunts, the lexical obsolescence deprecated by writing on translation which, conventionally, fears the letter killing the spirit. That Beckett's later self-translation chooses to forgo fluency for consciously pallid or threadbare second versions suggests a development of his poetics of self-translation which constitutes a set of gestures towards the cessation of language, conveyed through language – the "literature of the unword" he first prescribed in his letter to Axel Kaun in 1937 (Beckett 1983a: 54).

In a particularly localized version of Beckett's earlier rhetoric of necessary artistic failure, his late self-translations sidestep the more conventionally effective pieces of writing they might have been, and choose instead a strategy of warpage, self-deadening, and senescence. In the context of the production of increasingly minimal pieces of work in prose and drama, this late poetics of self-translation is imbricated with the weakly insistent urge of Beckett's late, death-haunted writing to see beyond its own end, in the silence after the drying up of language which, always threatened and longed for, never quite happens. When one text has written itself into silence in its original language, the disliked but curiously necessary process of self-translation to which Beckett subjects his works starts up the silenced voice of the text again in the other language, indomitably, but a little more weakly, in a recursive trajectory. The title of *Stirrings Still* speaks of continued, if vestigial life, of motion and fluidity, or at worst the slow draining away of vitality – "stirrings" becoming "still" – while the French *Soubresauts* ("death pangs" or "convulsions") has become more comprehensively lethal. Self-translation here takes an ambivalent pleasure in killing off the work of the "other" language and the "other" self. "Vitality" being valued positively in the translation process and archaism devalued, Beckett chooses the latter as best suiting his work's infinitely slow deathward trend.

Even *Worstward Ho*, the 1983 text written in a form of pidgin English and notable for never having been translated into French by Beckett (though a version by Edith Fournier exists), constitutes within its single language a miniature parable of "worsening" translation. A 40-page study in comparative forms of the negative, the text continually tries to set up a kind of automatic translation device: each time the text says "say," the reader must instead understand the word as "missaid," or "be missaid," and a recurrent uneasiness emerges when the language does not go "from bad to worsen" as unerringly as it might (Beckett 1983b: 7). Here the self-translation machine is part of a characteristically Beckettian shrinking from further generation of text; sentences repeat one another in order to worsen one another, to "back unsay" one another, to unweave while weaving; "on" and "no" structure a corrosive dynamics of subtraction which is representative of the late self-translation in general. Each "say" has to be translated into sufficient inadequacy and weakness, properly "missaid."

The later self-translations, thus, form part of Beckett's extended meditation on eschatology in the texts of the 1970s and 1980s, as his translation from the Spanish puts it: "Not to the end that life may be preserved/But to inflict a more protracted death" (Beckett 1958: 84). Self-translation in the late texts continues and complicates the ongoing project of finding a syntax of sufficient weakness to meet the mania for qualification that Beckett's writing manifests from *Watt* onward, to be sufficiently *in*adequate to the needs of the ageing body, and to excoriate still further the notion of a literature unproblematically servicing a full, potent, and self-expressive extra-textual reality. The deliberately deadly late self-translations, incorporating archaism, a pallor of phrasing, and a willed tonelessness, make of the movement to another language a slow-motion vision of catastrophe as a continual grinding down to a continually deferred standstill.

Finally, Beckett's career-long commitment to self-translation between his two languages may be seen as powering his work's efforts to find a form which would "accommodate the mess," and act as a crucial weapon in its attempts to repudiate conventional forms of narrative "tidiness" or consistency, as well as received notions of origins, originality, and authorship. The radical incommensurability of languages and the semi-concealed pressure of another language on each set of texts in French and English are an important factor in his work's avoidance of the kind of "sweet reasonableness" he discerned in the work of Balzac and Austen, and its preference for the "principle of disintegration" – "perturbations and dislocations," "grave dissonances in compatibilities, clashing styles," "discords and dissension" (Beckett 1983a: 63–4). Self-translation, continually generating its mutually orbiting pseudo-couples, acts in Beckett's work as a fertile zone in which two languages make one another foreign, and dislocate the lexical accents of the voice, so that the native becomes unfamiliar and the foreign close to home. The nebulous *Zwischenwelt* of the translator feeds the indeterminacy of Beckett's writing, neither Ireland nor France, neither dead nor alive, neither speaking nor silent; it refuses strict distinctions between interior and exterior, self and other, home and abroad, and continually reinstates a processual account of both self and world, so that selves and writings are always in production, insistently formless and resistant to closure.

REFERENCES AND FURTHER READING

Bakhtin, M. (1984). *Problems of Dostoevsky's Poetics*, ed. Wayne C. Booth, trans. Caryl Emerson. Manchester: Manchester University Press.

Barthes, R. (1974). *S/Z: An Essay*, trans. Richard Miller. New York: Hill and Wang.

Beckett, Samuel. TCD MS 10402/1–233, Letter to Thomas McGreevy dated September 27, 1953, Samuel Beckett Papers, Trinity College Dublin.

Beckett, Samuel (1958). *Anthology of Mexican Poetry*, ed. Octavio Paz. Bloomington: Indiana University Press.

Beckett, Samuel (1981). *Watt*. London: John Calder.

Beckett, Samuel (1983a). *Disjecta: Miscellaneous Writings and a Dramatic Fragment by Samuel Beckett*, ed. Ruby Cohn. London: John Calder.

Beckett, Samuel (1983b). *Worstward Ho*. London: John Calder.

Beckett, Samuel (1992). *Dream of Fair to middling Women*, ed. Eoin O'Brien and Edith Fournier. Dublin: Black Cat Press.

Coe, R. (1968). *Beckett*. New York: Grove Press.

Cohn, Ruby (1962). *Samuel Beckett: The Comic Gamut*. New Jersey: Rutgers University Press.

Connor, S. (1988). *Samuel Beckett: Repetition, Theory and Text*. Oxford: Blackwell.

Dryden, J. (1961). *Essays of John Dryden*, Vol 1., ed. W. P. Ker. New York: Russel and Russel.

Eliot, T. S. (1957). *On Poetry and Poets*. London: Faber and Faber.

Federman, R. and J. Fletcher (1970). *Samuel Beckett: His Works and His Critics*. Berkeley, London: University of California Press.

Gessner, N. (1957). *Die Unzulänglichkeit der Sprache: eine Untersuchung über Formzufall und Beziehunglosigkeit bei Samuel Beckett*. Zurich: Junis Verlag.

Harmon, M. (ed.) (1998). *No Author Better Served: The Correspondence of Samuel Beckett and Alan Schneider*. Cambridge, MA: Harvard University Press.

Hill, L. (1990). *Beckett's Fiction: In Different Words*. Cambridge: Cambridge University Press.

Knowlson, J. (1996). *Damned to Fame: A Life of Samuel Beckett*. New York: Simon and Schuster.

Lloyd, D. (1993). *Anomalous States: Irish Writing and the Post-Colonial Moment*. Dublin: Lilliput.

Mooney, S. (2002). "'An Atropos All in Black' or, *Ill Seen* Worse Translated: Beckett, Self-translation and the Discourse of Death." *Samuel Beckett Today/Aujourd'hui* 12: 163–77.

Nabokov, V. (1978). *Strong Opinions*. London: Weidenfeld and Nicolson.

Ostrovsky, E. (1976). "*Le Silence de Babel*," *Cahiers de l'Herne Samuel Beckett*: Paris: L'Herne.

Pound, E. (1971). *Make It New*. Michigan: Scholarly Press.

Ricks, C. (1993). *Beckett's Dying Words*. Oxford: Oxford University Press.

Shenker, Israel (1956). "Moody Man of Letters: An Interview with Samuel Beckett." *New York Times* (May 5) section 2, p 3.

Shields, K. (2000). *Gained in Translation: Language, Poetry and Identity in Twentieth-Century Ireland*. Oxford and New York: P. Lang.

Steiner, G. (1970). "Extraterritorial." *Triquarterly* 17: 117–31.

Thiem, J. (1995). "The Translator as Hero in Postmodern Fiction." *Translation and Literature* 4: 88–96.

Part III
Acts of Fiction

15

Beckett the Poet

Marjorie Perloff

Beckett's lyric poetry presents the critic with a fascinating anomaly. When the *Collected Poems in English and French* first appeared in 1977, Richard Coe, reviewing the volume for the *Times Literary Supplement*, remarked:

> It is a singular fact that the writer who has exercised the most profound influence over the third quarter of our by-and-large unpoetic century should be a poet whose formal "poems" oscillate between the obscure, the imitative and the awkward, who at one point abandoned his own language for another precisely in order to avoid writing poetry, and who has finally fashioned a form of linguistic denudation – words used like a child's set of building-blocks – so utterly opposed to poetry in the Tennysonian sense that it suggests not so much stoicism as suicide. (Graver and Federman 1979: 354)

The key epithet here is Tennysonian. The language of Beckett's schooldays, if not his Irish childhood, was, after all, the language of canonical English literature, as taught to Anglo-Protestant boys at the Portora Royal School in the Northern Ireland of the early 1920s. Such a schoolboy would have been subjected to heavy doses of Shakespeare and Elizabethan poetry, of Milton, and, more immediately, of the great romantic and Victorian poets. The iambic pentameter quatrains of Tennyson's *In Memoriam* would thus be engraved in the young Beckett's mind. Indeed, as I shall suggest below, echoes of the "great" English poets from Shakespeare to Yeats haunt the later plays and fictions that were written in English.

But the early poems collected in Beckett's first volume of poetry, *Echo's Bones and Other Precipitates* (1934), published by George Reavey's Europa Press in Paris in a minuscule edition (327 copies), are not just straight "Englit" either. At Trinity College Dublin, Beckett did his honors work in French and Italian: Dante and Provençal poetry now entered the mix, and then, during his *École Normale* year (1926–7), the philosophical discourse of Descartes and Spinoza, as reflected in Beckett's first published poem, "Whoroscope" (1930). Finally – and most important for the early poetry – there was the example of James Joyce, whom Beckett first met in 1928 and quickly came to regard as his master. The language of *Echo's Bones* is indeed heavily Joycean: it was not till the watershed of World War II that Beckett was able to "write without style," as he put it to Niklaus Gessner – which meant, in his case, to write in French. Indeed, as he confessed to Richard Coe, he had – at least for the moment – to give up English because "you couldn't help writing poetry in it" (Coe 1969: 14).

This insight did not come easily. Throughout the thirties, Beckett's attitude toward his lyric poems and translations was ambivalent: on the one hand, he reworked many of them and tried his best to get them published (Knowlson 1996: 207–8); on the other, he knew there was something wrong: consider the following letter (October 18, 1932) to his poet friend Tom MacGreevy:

> my feeling is, more and more, that the greater part of my poetry, though it may be reasonably felicitous in its choice of terms, fails precisely because it is *facultatif* [optional] whereas the 3 or 4 I like, and that seem to have been drawn down against the really dirty weather of one of these fine days into the burrow of the "private life," *Alba* and the long *Enueg* and *Dortmunder* and even *Moly*, do not and never did give me that impression of being *construits* [constructed]. I cannot explain very well to myself what they have that distinguishes them from the others, but it is something arborescent or of the sky, not Wagner, not clouds on wheels, written above an abscess and not out of a cavity, a statement and not a description of heat in the spirit to compensate for pus in the spirit. (Knowlson 1996: 209)

Here Beckett recalls the words of his other Irish master, Yeats: "Our words must seem to be inevitable" (1964: 61). Poems that are *construits* and *facultatifs* are those that have no inevitability, no necessity; they are merely artful contrivances. To avoid such contrivance, the poet must eschew all Wagnerisms (presumably bombast, high artifice), and the "clouds on wheels" born of self-pity (lyric "written above an abscess") or mere despair (the "pus in the spirit" rather than its heat).

Consider the long "Enueg I" (1931), the second of 13 poems in *Echo's Bones* (2006b: 11–13) and, in Beckett's own estimate, one of the more successful poems in the volume. The *enueg* is a Provençal genre; its title, from the Latin *inodium*, means literally "vexation," and designates, as Lawrence Harvey explains, "a poem which treats the annoyances of life from mere trifles to serious insults, from improprieties at the table to serious misdemeanours." "The most striking feature of the *enueg* is the ... absence of continuity of thought; each line or group of lines is absolutely without relation to those which precede or follow. The only link is the poet's dislike which is applied indiscriminately." Harvey adds that, whereas most *enuegs* are witty and epigrammatic, Beckett's two poems by that title are, perhaps more properly understood as *planhs* (Provençal for complaints), expressing as they do personal suffering as well as vexation (Harvey 1970: 80–1).

Here and in many of his other early poems – "Alba," the two *sanies* and three *serenas* – Beckett thus adapts Provençal verse forms. But his are very different from, say, Ezra

Pound's troubadour adaptations. Let me list a few characteristics of "Enueg I" so as to understand how the young Beckett construed the poetic act.

1   Beckett's poem is a tissue of literary allusions. It appears, to begin with, in a book whose title alludes to Ovid's *Metamorphoses*: Echo, spurned by Narcissus, "frets and pines, becomes all gaunt and haggard, / Her body dries and shrivels till voice only / And bones remain, and she is voice only / For the bones are turned to stone" (see Harvey 1970: 68). The Ovidian frame contains references to Dante (the "secret things" of line 4 are the *segrete cose* of *Inferno* 3); T. S. Eliot ("the stillborn evening turning a filthy green" recalls both Prufrock's evening "spread out against the sky / Like a patient etherised upon a table" and the dank evening landscape of *The Waste Land*); the *Anatomy of Melancholy*, whose author Robert Burton wrote under the pseudonym Democritus Junior, here presented as a sad old man, "scuttling along between a crutch and a stick"; and the Isolde of the Tristan legend, recalled here indirectly in the place names – "Chapelizod" (literally "Isolde's Chapel") and "Isolde Stores" – of the Dublin suburbs, as drawn by Beckett from *Finnegans Wake* (Friedman 1976: 146–9).

2   Not only is "Enueg I" highly allusive; from its Latin opening, "*Exeo* in a spasm," to its reference to the Sumatran plant *Rafflesia* in line 48, the poem exhibits a fascination with obscure, exotic, and technical vocabulary: the poet is "tired of my darling's red *sputum*"; his skull feels "strangled in the cang of the wind" – a *cang* being a Chinese torture instrument, a kind of pillory – Democritus is described as "wearish," an obsolete term for "sickly" or "feeble"; the walker crosses "a travesty of champaign" (or open field); the "sweaty heroes" descend from the playing field to the pub for a pint of beer, here coyly referred to as "nepenthe" or "moly" – the narcotics of classical antiquity. Animal and plant life is everywhere diseased: the hens are "gray and verminous," the toadstool "great mushy" and "green-black, / oozing up after me," the sky an "ink of pestilence," and flowers perceived as "blotches of doomed yellow in the pit of the Liffey," where "a slush of vigilant gulls" animate "the grey spew of the sewer." Far from "direct treatment of the thing," the mode of "Enueg" is one of artifice, circumlocution, verbal excess, elaborate metaphor. Indeed, in its display of learning and dependence on modernist literary texts, Beckett's enueg thus resembles another first poem of the 1930s, Zukofsky's "Poem beginning 'The'."

3   At the same time – and here the Joycean influence comes in – the poem establishes a tone of documentary veracity. The depicted circular walk – from the Portobello Nursing Home (where the narrator evidently visits his dying sweetheart) near Dublin's Merrion Square across the Parnell Bridge out into the countryside and back again via the suburb of Fox & Geese and the village of Chapelizod, past the Isolde Stores and along the quays of the Liffey back into Dublin – can be traced on a map of Dublin and its environs; indeed Lawrence Harvey (1970: 126–34) has shown exactly where Beckett's walk took place and how accurately the landmarks, like the signpost "hoarding" above the "livid canal," are described.

4   The poem's sound structure is on a par with its overwrought exotic vocabulary. Alliteration and internal rhyme abound, as in "*trundle* along *rapidly* now on my *ruined* feet," "*manuring* the night *fungus* / *and* the *mind annulled*," "soaking up the *tatt*ered *sky like* an *ink* of *pestilence*," or "a *slu*sh of vigi*l*ant *gulls* in the grey *spew* of the *sewer*." At the same time – and this is odd given its debt to a highly wrought Provençal form, "Enueg I" is written in free verse with line and phrase usually coinciding in a less than tensile rhythmic pattern. Lines range from two syllables ("So on") to nineteen ("come hastening down for a pint of nepenthe or moly or half and half"), from one stress ("the wáter") to seven or eight in the long lines. Some passages are prosaic – for example, the conversation with the "child fidgeting at the gate" to the ball field (lines 36–42); others, like line 5, use metrical feet, in this case a string of anapests followed by a dactyl: "and tóil to the crést of the súrge of the steép périlous brídge." The overall impression is one of arbitrariness: what, the reader wonders, does lineation do for this lyric?

5   Finally – and this relates to the allusiveness I discussed above – Beckett's early lyric displays the marked influence of French modernist lyric. The structure of "Enueg I," to begin with, departs from the usual catalogue of disconnected items that characterizes the Provençal form, adopting instead the promenade structure of Apollinaire's "Zone." The walking poem is, of course, a familiar genre, extending in English from at least Wordsworth's "An Evening Walk" to Frank O'Hara's "I do this, I do that" poems like "A Step Away from Them." But "Zone," which Beckett translated at about the same time he wrote "Enueg I" (1977: 106–21, 147), has a direct bearing on Beckett's poem. Its solitary speaker too wanders through the modern city, crossing its bridges, and taking in its unpleasant screeching sounds; he too feels the despair of a lost love:

> *Maintenant tu marches dans Paris tout seul parmi la foule*
> *Des troupeaux d'autobus mugissants près de toi roulent*
> *L'angoise de l'amour te serre le gosier*
> *Comme si tu ne devais jamais plus être aimé* …

which Beckett translates as:

> Now you walk in Paris alone among the crowd
> Herds of bellowing buses hemming you about
> Anguish of love parching you within
> As though you were never to be loved again (1977: 112–13)

And the pub scene in "Enueg I" is matched by the image of the "bar crapuleux" ("crapulous café"), where the poet of "Zone" finds himself in the early morning hours. The death note of Apollinaire's conclusion – *Soleil cou coupé*, translated by Beckett as "Sun corseless head" – the sun as maimed body – resounds throughout "Enueg I."

If Apollinaire's poem is a structural model for Beckett's poem, its conclusion comes from Rimbaud's great prose poem "Barbare," whose vision of paradisal pleasure is rendered, as is typical of the *Illuminations*, in the paradoxical image of red meat bleeding on silky seas and arctic flowers:

> Le pavillon en viande saignante sur la soie des mers et des fleurs arctiques; (elles n'existent pas.)

which Beckett renders as:

> Ah the banner /
> the banner of meat bleeding
> on the silk of the seas and arctic flowers
> that do not exist.

In "Barbare" the strophe is repeated and the poem ends on the words "Le pavillon," which are abruptly broken off. The vision is closely integrated into the poem's framework, with its hot tears and arctic grottoes, its embers and waves and stars, so that although *elles n'existent pas*, the dream imagery is wholly real. In "Enueg I," by contrast, nothing earlier in the poem anticipates any sort of beauty or richness. Nothing happens to counter the poet's gloom and disgust, so that the note of joy and beauty introduced by the "Barbare" citation is somewhat hollow – a kind of afterthought.

To recapitulate: we might say that Beckett's early lyric poetry is a poetry of uneasy graft – "Enueg I" is Provençal *planh* with a modernist French twist in its deployment of the walker-in-the-city structure of Apollinaire's "Zone." The poem couples exotic, recondite, highly allusive diction with "realistic" documentation. Its sound structure oddly brings together a loose, prosaic free-verse line with marked secondary sound features like alliteration and internal rhyme. This is a poetry that represents what we might call *le côté Stephen Dedalus* of Sam Beckett. Like the young artist of the *Proteus* chapter of *Ulysses*, who strolls along the beach, brandishing his ashplant and assuming a bravado he sadly lacks, the Beckett of "Enueg I" is learned, sardonic, and clever – too clever perhaps to make his *enueg* (the analogue of Stephen's "villanelle") come to life. And indeed, the astonishing thing about Beckett's poetic development is that, by the late forties, he had come to something like Joyce's understanding that a Stephen Dedalus needed a Leopold Bloom for balance. In *Texts for Nothing* and the French–English pieces that followed, Beckett's early lyric structures were turned inside out. Fixed Provençal forms gave way to the prose paragraph, long Latinate words and foreign borrowings to a pared down monosyllabic diction, documentary place names to indeterminate reference, and clotted sound structure to what looks like a neat quasi-mathematical grid. The change coincides, at least in part, with Beckett's experience in the war and his shift to writing in French. When, late in life, English again becomes the language of choice, some of his earlier *Dedalisms* come in by the back door – but this time in a postmodern manner quite different from that of *Echo's Bones*.

The Trembling of the Veil

Beckett's own dissatisfaction with his early lyric mode (or, for that matter, with the Joycean comic mode of *Murphy*) is evident by the late thirties. When in 1937 his German friend Axel Kaun asked him to translate poems by a Joachim Ringelnatz, Beckett responded with a long letter, explaining why he felt this "Rhyme Coolie," as Beckett called the German poet dismissively, was not worth the trouble. Not only did Ringelnatz's "rhyming fury" disgust him, but his own English now seemed equally problematic:

> more and more my own language appears to me like a veil that must be torn apart in order to get at the things (or the Nothingness) behind it. Grammar and style. To me they seem to have become as irrelevant as a Victorian bathing suit or the imperturbability of a true gentleman. A mask. Let us hope the time will come ... when language is most efficiently used where it is being most efficiently misused ... To bore one hole after another in it, until what lurks behind it – be it something or nothing – begins to seep through: I cannot imagine a higher goal for a writer today. Or is literature alone to remain behind in the old lazy ways that have been so long ago abandoned by music and painting? ... Is there any reason why that terrible materiality of the word surface should not be capable of being dissolved, like for example the sound surface, torn by enormous pauses, of Beethoven's seventh Symphony? (Beckett 1984: 171–2)

This is one of the most telling statements we have of Beckett's later aesthetic, and in the paragraph that follows he makes clear that "with such programs [that is, programs for the renewal of poetic language], the latest work of Joyce has nothing whatever to do." Indeed, "the logographs of Gertrude Stein are nearer to what I have in mind" (ibid.: 172).

What Beckett now understood – and no doubt his study of German expressionist painting in 1936 had something to do with it – is that whereas modern painting or music had been revolutionized, had come to understand that the modernist ethos demanded new modes of representation, in poetry, "the old lazy ways" remained the order of the day. Poetic diction had become a "Victorian bathing suit": like Yeats, Beckett felt he had for too long made his "song a coat / Covered with embroideries / Out of old mythologies / From heel to throat," and, like Yeats, he could now declare, "Song, let them take it, / For there's more enterprise / In walking naked" (1916). Even Joyce's language, in this scheme of things, was "covered with embroideries." Accordingly, when, after the war, Beckett began to write in French, he produced such a lyric poem as the following:

> *je suis ce cours de sable qui glisse*
> *entre le galet et la dune*
> *la pluie d'été pleut sur ma vie*
> *sur moi ma vie qui me fuit me poursuit*
> *et finira le jour de son commencement*

> *cher instant je te vois*
> *dans ce rideau de brume qui recule*
> *où je n'aurai plus à fouler ces long seuils mouvants*
> *et vivrai le temps d'une porte*
> *qui s'ouvre et se referme*
>
> (1977: 56)

What is immediately striking to the reader accustomed to *Echo's Bones* is the absence of arcane citation, of foreign and obsolete words, and of all documentary reference. The opening line is enigmatic: does *Je suis* mean "I follow" or "I am"? Beckett's translation "My way is in the sand flowing" doesn't resolve this mystery. But then where and what is this sandy path between the shingle and the dune, and what house or shelter does the "shingle" belong to? Nowhere in the stanza are these questions answered: the summer rain *pleut sur ma vie* (an ironic allusion to Verlaine's *Il pleure dans mon coeur / comme il pleut sur la ville*) without seeming cause. Life both escapes and pursues the pursuer; it will end the day of its beginning. The language here is chaste, abstract, general, the main stylistic element being intensive repetition, whether of sound (*je suis ce cours de sable*; *suis / fuit / poursuit*; *pluie / pleut / poursuit*); word (for example, *vie*) or phrase (*sur ma vie / sur moi ma vie*). In the second stanza, the epiphany (*cher instant je te vois*) found in the mist that recedes, is that there will be no more elusive thresholds to cross; rather the poet will live *le temps d'une porte* – the brief time between the opening of a door and its closing.

In *je suis ce cours*, Beckett is still trying to find his way: conceptually, if not stylistically, the poem is, ironically, a more traditional lyric than "Enueg 1" – a short, personal meditation on life and death. The pathetic fallacy is in evidence, what with the summer rain raining on the poet's life and the receding mist that allows the poet to "see." Oddly, in his English version of the poem, Beckett roughs it up a bit, archaicizing its smooth flow:

> my way is in the sand flowing
> between the shingle and the dune
> the summer rain rains on my life
> on me my life harrying fleeing
> to its beginning to its end
>
> (1977: 57)

where "harrying fleeing / to its beginning to its end" disperses movement rather than completing the circle of the French *et finira le jour de son commencement*; the Verlaine echo also fades in the English rendition. In the second stanza, Beckett omits the first line completely, as if the idea of a *cher instant* were too embarrassing, and the time of a door oddly becomes "the space of a door." Whereas the French poem emphasizes the fleeting moment, the English version is more concerned with framing, with the daily limitations one must negotiate. In either case, *door, thresholds, shingle, dune, mist* and *rain* are unmodified nouns that lack all specificity. No "blotches" here "of doomed yellow in the pit of the Liffey"; the aim is to dissolve what Beckett called "the terrible materiality of the word surface."

Beckett wrote only a handful of lyrics in the vein of *je suis ce cours*. By the 1960s, in the wake of his great fictional and dramatic inventions, lineation, regarded by the young Beckett as the sine qua non of the lyric poem, began to give way to a poetic prose more flexible and supple than the *enuegs* and *sanies* (the word means morbid discharge) and *serenas* (evening songs) of the thirties. Beckett's short prose pieces, beginning with the *Texts for Nothing* of 1952–3, and including such important works as *Imagination Dead Imagine*, *Enough*, *Lessness*, and *Ping*, are not usually classified as poems, most obviously because they are not lineated, but also, no doubt, perhaps because they contain vestiges of the narrative of the *Trilogy* as well as echoes of the monologic plays like *Krapp's Last Tape* and *Not I*, or perhaps because most of Beckett's critics come to the short writings in question from his fiction or drama. These later texts have been called "residua" (Beckett's own term), "lyrics of fiction" (Ruby Cohn's), "monologues," or, perhaps most commonly, "pieces." In the new Grove centennial edition, they are included with the poems in Volume IV but classified as "Stories, Texts, Novellas." J. M. Coetzee, in his introduction to this volume, refers to *Ping* and *Lessness* as "quasi-musical compositions whose elements are phrases and sentences" (Beckett 2006b: xi).

But what is a quasi-musical composition whose elements are phrases and sentences but a form of poetry? It was Northrop Frye who first made the critical distinctions in this regard. "Verse," as he puts it, is by definition "some form of regular recurrence, whether meter, accent, vowel quality, rhyme, alliteration, parallelism, or any combination of these." "Prose," at the opposite pole, is "the arrangement of words … dominated by the syntactical relations of subject and predicate," in other words the sentence." Prose is "language on its best behavior, in its Sunday clothes, aware of an audience and with its relation to that audience prepared beforehand" (Frye 1963: 21). Yet there is another possibility, which Frye calls the *associative rhythm* and the French theorist Henri Meschonnic, the "third rhythm." In Frye's words:

> The naïve assumption that any poetry not in some recognizable recurrent pattern must really be prose clearly will not do, and we have to assume the existence of a third type of conventionalized utterance. This third type has a peculiar relation to ordinary speech, or at least to soliloquy and inner speech. We may call it an oracular or associational rhythm, the unit which is neither the prose sentence nor the metrical line, but a kind of thought-breath or phrase. Associational rhythm predominates in free verse and in certain types of literary prose. (1974: 886; cf. Perloff 1996: 135–54; Perloff 1998: 132–40)

Beckett, as we saw in the case of "Enueg I," was never really at home with verse, free or otherwise, perhaps because the notion of regular recurrence – and even most earlier free verse from Whitman to Pound exhibits the recurrence of rhythmic phrasing – went against his underlying sense of fracture, of dislocation and dissolution of the speaking subject. The "associative rhythm," the "thought-breath or phrase" became Beckett's métier, even as, like the concrete poets of the 1960s, he understood that in a technological age like ours – and, of course, materiality is even more intrinsic to the form of poetry since the advent of the computer screen – poetry has a strong visual component. Consider the short piece called "Still," first published in 1974 in a limited edition accompanied by original etchings by Beckett's friend Stanley William Hayter and then included in *Fizzles* (see Perloff 1981: 201–13). Interestingly, although its first appearance was as a "verbal" unit complemented by a visual analogue, the prose poem's own visual dynamic precludes the need for illustration. Here is the first part (approximately one third) of the single paragraph which is "Still":

> Bright at last close of a dark day the sun shines out at last and goes down. Sitting quite still at valley window normally turn head now and see it the sun low in the southwest sinking. Even get up certain moods and go stand by western window quite still watching it sink and then the afterglow. Always quite still some reason some time past this hour at open window facing south in small upright wicker chair with armrests. Eyes stare out unseeing till first movement some time past close though unseeing still while still light. Quite still again then all quite quiet apparently till eyes open again while still light though less. Normally turn head now ninety degrees to watch sun which if already gone then fading afterglow. Even get up certain moods and go stand by western window till quite dark and even some evenings some reason long after. Eyes then open again while still light and close again in what if not quite a single movement almost. Quite still again then at open window facing south over the valley in this wicker chair though actually close inspection not still at all but trembling all over. But casually in this failing light impression dead still even the hands clearly trembling and the breast faint rise and fall. Legs side by side broken right angles at the knees as in that old statue some old god twanged at sunrise and again at sunset. (Beckett 2006b: 415–17)

This minimalist text tracks a person of unspecified gender, sitting in a wicker chair by an open window, watching the sun go down. Overtly, this is all that happens, but the minute description of body movements produces unexpected tension, especially since the point of view is neither properly external nor internal. The voice that originally seems like that of an outside observer, watching the person in the chair from a distance, often knows only what the seated figure knows, for example, "Even get up certain moods and go stand by western window still quite dark." Then, too, as Enoch Brater and others have noted (see Brater 1977: 8; Kenton 1994: 171), that which is ostensibly "still" is, ironically, not still at all but always – and however slightly – moving. Sentence by sentence, things change. The passage has reference to body parts – in this case, eyes, skull, head, cheekbone, nape, breast, forearms, arms, elbow, hands, thumb, index, fingers, trunk, knees, and legs – but there is no indication as to how these body parts actually relate to one another or to the "torso" of the person in the "small upright wicker chair armrests" to whom they presumably belong. We only know that in the course of the narrative, the room becomes darker and the "right hand" is finally raised in a motion that seems to mimic the circle of the sun "till elbow meeting armrest brings this last movement to an end and all still once more." But even then all is not still. For when, at last, the "dark eyes [are] closed," they are closed "not enough and perhaps even more than ever necessary that no such thing," the sentence trailing off so that we do not know what such a thing might be. And the final sentence reads: "Leave it so all quite still or try listening to sounds all quite still head in hand listening for a sound."

From "still" to the "listening" (note the sound echo of *s-t-i-l* in *l-i-s-t*) for "sound": this is the trajectory of Beckett's poem, which exhibits precisely the tearing of the "veil" of "grammar and style" Beckett spoke of in his letter to Axel Kaun. The poem is largely made up of monosyllabic ordinary words: the first sentence has 17: "Bright at last close of a dark day the sun shines out at last and goes down." The same words are repeated again and again, making the appearance of a new longer word or phrase like "southwest" in the second sentence, "afterglow" in the third, and "upright wicker chair with armrests" in the fourth surprising deviations. The strangeness of the passage is enhanced by its syntax: Beckett's sentences are less coherent units than congeries of phrases, phrases discontinuous, repetitive, and heavily accented (see Perloff 1998: 132–40):

> Bríght at lást
> clóse of a dárk dáy
> the sún shines óut at last and góes dówn.
> Sítting quîte stíll at válley wíndow
> nórmally túrn héad nôw and sée ît
> the sún lów in the sóuthwêst sínking ...

The unit of rhythm here and throughout "Still" is the short phrase of irregular rhythm and primitive syntax Northrop Frye defined as the associative rhythm. This rhythm is entirely appropriate for a poem that, as I remarked above, has no identifiable voice and where repetition ("at last"), internal rhyme ("close"/"goes"), and eye rhyme ("window"/"now"/"low") are introduced only to give way to the verbal slippage whereby "quite" turns into "quiet," "end of rests" into "rest on ends," "quite still" into "till quite," and so on. All that is "still" is regularly "not still at all" but "trembling all over."

What makes these verbal tensions all the more remarkable is the overall *verbivoco-visual* (Joyce's term) form of Beckett's composition. In an earlier study of the brilliant collaboration between Beckett and Jasper Johns that resulted in their artist's book *Foirades/Fizzles*, I argued that the incantatory aural repetition of key motifs is matched by the visual design of the page itself, by the configuration, for example, made by the morphemic/lettristic potential of the title word in the opening page of "Still," where the reader's eye cannot help but note the visual constellations produced by the words **still, till, time, light, quite, quiet, while**, with a secondary tier of monosyllabic words (and individual syllables of disyllabic and trisyllabic words) that contain the letters **s, t, i** and **l** in various combinations (see Perloff 2002).

Indeed, it could be argued that in producing such texts-to-be-seen Beckett shows his affinities to the visual and sound poets who were his contemporaries. But there is one striking difference. Unlike, say, Eugen Gomringer's well-known "Wind" (Solt 1971: 93) –

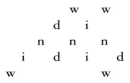

– "Still" creates a dense verbal fabric only to interrupt it with curiously dissonant notes. Just when we think the person in the chair by the window and her observer can only express themselves in broken, monosyllabic discourse, we get references to "ninety degrees," or "close inspection," or – more surprisingly, "Legs side by side broken right angles at the knees as in that old statue some old god twanged at sunrise and again at sunset." Is this a reference to the Buddha and hence related to the East–West imagery of the passage, or perhaps to one of the broken colossi of Memnon who, following the earthquake that broke them, produced a musical sound at sunrise as the stone was warmed by the sun? And through whose mind does the thought of the statue filter? "Still" raises many such questions, resolving none of them in its passage from still to sound, light to darkness, life to impending death.

Recovering the Roots

In the poetic pieces of Beckett's last decade (he died in 1989), the minimalism of "Still" gives way to a more personal and highly wrought "literary" mode. In *Worstward Ho*, written in English in 1983, and *Ill Seen Ill Said* (originally published in French as *Mal vu, mal dit* in 1981, but very different in English), the basic unit is not the grid-like paragraph of "Still" but a tightly packed strophe – a strophe closer to prose than to verse but not fully either (see Perloff 1985 *passim*).

Like "Still," *Ill Seen Ill Said* (Beckett 2006b: 451–70) features a solitary person, this time referred to unambiguously as "she," at a window, contemplating the night sky. But here the room in what seems to be an isolated cabin is part of a larger land-scape, which contains a pasture and a "zone of stones" that may or may not be a cemetery. The cabin houses a set of obsessive objects: a kitchen chair, a skylight, a buttonhook hanging from a nail on the cabin wall, an antique coffer, a trap door. In the course of Beckett's narrative, the woman is seen as in series of film stills, sitting in her chair and watching the moon rise outside her window (as in "Still"), or eating a bowl of slop, or opening the antique coffer and finding a "scrap of paper" on whose "yellowed face" appear "in barely legible ink two letters followed by a number. Tu. 17. Or Th." (462–3). These indoor scenes are punctuated by outdoor shots of the woman, occasionally followed by a lamb but mostly alone, making her way toward the zone of stones where she is confronted by the enigmatic "twelve," alternately advancing and receding, as she is drawn again and again to one particular stone (apparently her husband's tombstone although Beckett never specifies): "Blindfold she could find her way." In this Stonehenge-like setting, the nameless woman tries to make out the "trace" of a lost "face," but in the poem's penultimate strophe, we read, "Till no more trace. On earth's face. Instead of always the same place. Slaving away forever in the same place. At this and that trace" (470).

As these primitive rhyming units suggest, *Ill Seen Ill Said* is essentially a chant:

> From where she **lies** she sees Venus **rise. On.** From where she **lies** where the **skies** are clear she sees Venus **rise** followed by the **sun.** Then she rails at the source of all life. **On.** (451)

Here internal rhyme and refrain create a strophic pattern, with clusters of stresses coming together. In keeping with *chant*, the language has an almost Pre-Raphaelite cast in its word choice. Such phrases as, "She sits on erect and rigid in the deepening gloom," or "The buttonhook glimmers in the last rays" (456) recall the young Yeats, whose "shadowy horses" are "glimmering white" even as in "Innisfree," his "midnight's all a glimmer and noon a purple glow." And even the later Yeats of "A Prayer for my Daughter" gives us the locution:

> And for an hour I have walked and prayed
> Because of the great gloom that is in my mind –

These gloom notes are echoed, perhaps parodically, in such Beckett locutions as "In the dim light the skylights shed. An even dimmer light. As panes slowly dimmen. All in black she comes and goes" (456). And the voice that registers this dimness is also aware of "withered flowers" (454), "slow wavering way" (454), "Black night fallen" (466), "the westering sun" (466), "olden kisses" (466), "dim the light of day" (467), and "towards unbroken night" (467).

The archaisms and allusions of Beckett's earliest poetry – his *enuegs* and *sanies* – thus return, although now intricately jumbled. For example:

1   *Ever scanter even the rankest weed* (451–2)
    A predominantly trochaic pentameter line whose sound structure alludes parodically to Milton's "Lycidas" ("As killing as the canker to the rose"), even as its imagery also recalls *Hamlet* act 2, scene 1: "'tis an unweeded garden / That grows to seed. Thinks rank and gross in nature / Possess it merely." Again, in *Hamlet* act 3, scene 4: "And do not spread the compost on the weeds, / To make them ranker."
2   *Invisible nearby sea. Inaudible* (452)
    Joyce's *Ulysses*, opening of the "Proteus" chapter: "Ineluctable modality of the visible ... seaspawn and seawrack."

3 *Unshepherded they stray as they list* (452)
Burlesque of St Peter's speech in "Lycidas": "Of other care they little reck'ning make, / Than how to scramble at the shearers' feast ... And when they list, their lean and flashy songs / Grate on their Scannel Pipes of wretched straw."
4 *Averts the intent gaze. Incriminates the dearly won. Forbids divining her* (454)
These tightly woven three-stress lines recall Satan's first view of Eve in *Paradise Lost*, canto 4: "When Satin still in gaze, as first he stood ..."
5 *Things and imaginings* (456)
Yeats, "The Tower," part 3: "I have prepared my peace / With learned Italian things / And the proud stones of Greece, / Poet's imaginings ..."
6 *Stark the skeleton chair death-paler than life* (464)
John Keats, *La Belle Dame sans Merci*: "Pale warriors, death-pale were they all."
7 *Ghost of an ancient smile* (466)
Play on Ezra Pound's "host of an ancient people" ("The Return")

It would be tedious to list all the other literary echoes in Beckett's text – echoes, for example, from Gerard Manley Hopkins, Shelley, and Tennyson, not to mention the King James Bible (see Perloff 1990: 164–8). What is important is that, unlike the early "Whoroscope" and "Enueg I," which wear their learning rather ostentatiously, showing off the poet's cleverness, disgust, and morbidity, in *Ill Seen Ill Said* the combination of citation and colloquialism, elegant phrasing and contemporary argot creates a densely mannered discourse – one carefully distanced from the simulation of natural speech. For example,

> Suddenly enough and way for remembrance. Closed again to that end the vile jelly or opened again or left as it was however that was. Till all recalled. First finally by far hanging from their skirts two black greatcoats. Followed by the first hazy outlines of what possible a hutch when suddenly enough. Remembrance! When all worse there than when first ill seen. The pallet. The chair. The coffer. The trap. Alone the eye has changed. Alone can cause to change. In the meantime nothing wanting. Wrong. The button-hook. The nail. Wrong. There they are again. Still. Worse there than ever. Unchanged for the worse. Ope eye and at them to begin. But first the partition. It rid they too would be. It less they be as much. (468)

Here the "third rhythm" becomes a kind of shorthand in which the impersonal narrative voice distances the thoughts and feelings of the nameless woman by turning her responses into enigmatic elliptical statements, some serious, some parodic, that raid the poet's unconscious for emblems of the past. The "remembrance" mentioned in the first sentence recalls Proust's *Remembrance of Things Past*, one of the novels most important to Beckett. But why does "remembrance" come suddenly? The second sentence alludes to Edmund's terrible words to the blinded Gloucester in *Lear*: "Out vile jelly! Where is thy lustre now?" Whether the subject's eyes are open or closed doesn't change anything: everything is "left as it was however that was. Till all recalled." The two black greatcoats, the pallet, the chair, the coffer, the trap, the button-hook, the nail: these become leitmotifs, never disclosing their full meaning as they appear and reappear in shifting contexts. At the same time, Beckett invokes his own titles – "Enough," "Still," "For to End Yet Again," and even "Ill Seen ..." – as if to suggest that the memories are his own and that he can now revisit his earlier texts as well as the one before us. Such burlesque statements as "Unchanged for the worse," collide with the archaic imperative, "Ope eye and at them to begin." But to begin is to reverse word order: the final "It rid they too would be" means "They too would be rid [of] it," whereas the final sentence – "it less they be as much" – is missing most of its connectives and cannot be deciphered at all. It becomes what John Ashbery was to call, with reference to Gertrude Stein, "an open field of narrative possibilities" (1972: 41).

Ill Seen Ill Said is an elegy for missed opportunities, lost chances, erotic desire, remembered pain. The "voice from within us" and the woman's consciousness merge to dredge up incoherent images and memories but finally – and surprisingly for Beckett – "Grace to breathe that void. Know happiness" (Beckett 2006b: 470). The associative monologue, non-linear and non-coherent, weaves in and out of the present, unable any longer to separate the literary echo from the poet's own invented word pool. What matter who's speaking?

Not everyone admires the mannered poetic prose of Beckett's last decade; certainly it is less immediately artful than the spare permutations of "Lessness" or "Ping," "How It Is," or "Still." Still, to trace the possibilities of that word, the late texts usher in a different phase in which Beckett comes full circle from the "*facultatif*" lyrics of his youth through the French modernist phase of *Je suis ce cours* to the minimalist explosive poetic word blocks of his maturity, to the strophic lyric poems, densely layered, allusive, and elegiac, to – finally – lineation once more.

The return to lineation is, of course, partially prefigured in the poetic extracts cited above from *Ill Seen Ill Said* – extracts like "Ghosts of an ancient smile" with its Poundian echo. Then, too, the later plays introduce verse passages, as when the character Words in *Words and Music* chants,

> Age is when to a man
> Huddled o'er the ingle
> Shivering for the hag
> To put the pan in the bed
> And bring the toddy
> She comes in the ashes
> Who loved could not be won
> Or won not loved
> Or some other trouble
> Comes in the ashes
> Like that old light
> The face in the ashes
> That old starlight
> On the earth again.
> (Beckett 2006a: 337)

The inflections of these musical three-stress lines, with their heavy alliteration and assonance, are markedly Yeatsian, especially the Yeats of "The Tower," Part III, who commemorates "The death of friends, or death / Of every brílliant eye / That made a catch in the breath / Seem but the clouds of the sky" (Yeats 1989: 199). Again, the central question in Part II of "The Tower": "Does the imagination dwell the most / Upon a woman won or a woman lost?" (ibid.: 197) provides the source for Beckett's "She comes in the ashes / Who loved could not be won / Or won not loved."

This return – or rather this turn, since Beckett's early poetry was so much more florid, allusive, exotic, and metrically clotted than Yeats's – to the mode of "The Tower" is confirmed anecdotally by Anne Atik (the wife of the artist Avigdor Arikha, who was one of Beckett's close Paris friends) in her recent memoir of Beckett, *How It Was*. The recitation of canonical poems was evidently one of Beckett's favorite occupations; indeed Atik recalls that, on one of his visits, Beckett recited Mallarmé and Nerval, Rimbaud, and Apollinaire, as well as Shakespeare's sonnets and Shelley's "Ode to the West Wind" (Atik 2005: 24–5). But Beckett's favorite was Yeats: he recited from memory the *Crazy Jane* songs, "Under Ben Bulben," and especially "The Tower," whose "congruence of language with visual imagery" he praised (ibid.: 68). The last time Atik saw Beckett, in the nursing home where he was to die on December 22, 1989, he recited, she recalls, the conclusion of "The Tower" Part III, which begins "Now shall I make my soul," concluding with the "bird's sleepy cry / Among the deepening shades," followed by his own "Age is a when to a man / Huddled o'er the ingle," from *Words and Music* (Beckett 2006a: 337).

The question remains: why, if he was so keen on the "soul making" of Yeats's "Tower" – a rhetorical mode he had known intimately since his Dublin student days – did Beckett abandon formal lyric so completely in his own postwar writing? One reason, surely – and I mentioned this *vis-à-vis* "Enueg I" – is that Beckett had little taste for lineation, much less for metrics. He could, of course, readily construct a formal lyric and place it within the dissonant context provided by Morton Feldman's music, a context that, together with the verbal dislocations of *Words and Music* or *Cascando*, would give the lyric in question a parodic edge. But he needed that edge, for a dramatic formal verse stanza like Yeats's could not accord with the semantic disjunctions so central to his work.

What, then, do we make of what was evidently Beckett's last piece of writing, the lineated piece, "What is the Word" (1988), a translation of his earlier *Comment dire* (1982)? This poem (or, at least, it is considered a poem by Beckett's editors; see 2006b: 566) has 50 lines and a coda that repeats the title. It begins as follows:

> folly –
> folly for to –
> for to –
> what is the word –
> folly from this –
> all this –
> folly from all this –
> given –

> folly given all this –
> seeing –
> folly seeing all this –
> this –
> what is the word –
> this this –
> (2006b: 50–1)

The poem continues in this minimal way, permutating the same word set, with the gradually intercalated addition of the words "glimpse," "seem," "what," "where," "over," "afar," "away," "afaint," and culminating in the long line: "folly for to need to seem to glimpse afaint afar away over there what – " followed by "what – / what is the word – " and then a space, and the coda.

Here prosody has a predominantly visual function: we see each line separately, a broken phrase followed by a dash, that tries to correct or enlarge itself but never seems to find that missing word. The poem's diction is rigidly constricted, "afar" and "afaint" being the only words that go outside the circle of everyday discourse. And yet the language is not so ordinary after all: "what is the word," for starters, puns on the almost equivalent and very common phrase, "what in the world," so that we have to remind ourselves as we read along that "in" is "is" and "world" "word." And the referent for "this" becomes more rather than less obscure as the poem unfolds.

When heard, the lines of "What Is the Word" are not inherently different from the abrupt breath units of Beckett's later plays, for example, *Not I* or *Rockaby*. The "look" of the poem is thus ambivalent, and it is this ambivalence that characterizes Beckett's view of lyric throughout his career. Poetry, especially poetry as dense, dramatic, rhetorical, and rhythmically compelling as Yeats's later lyric was a touchstone, a source of pleasure, especially when recited to one's friends. But Beckett's own "folly for to need to seem to glimpse what where" demanded a less bravura, indeed a more interrogative mode. Construction, even when it was as dazzling as Yeats's or Mallarmé's, represented the *facultatif* that Beckett found so troubling. The doors of perception, so far as his own poetic texts were concerned, had to remain defiantly *open*, elusive, indeed self-contradictory. It must go on. It can't go on. It goes on.

REFERENCES AND FURTHER READING

Ashbery, John (1972). *Three Poems*. New York: Viking Press.

Atik, Anne (2005). *How It Was*. London: Shoemaker & Hoard.

Beckett, Samuel (1977). *Collected Poems in English & French*. New York: Grove Press.

Beckett, Samuel (1984). *Disjecta: Miscellaneous Writings and a Dramatic Fragment*, ed. Ruby Cohn. New York: Grove Press.

Beckett, Samuel (2006a). *The Grove Centenary Edition, Vol. 3: Dramatic Works*, ed. Paul Auster. New York: Grove Press.

Beckett, Samuel (2006b). *The Grove Centenary Edition, Vol. 4: Poems, Short Fiction, Criticism*, ed. Paul Auster. New York: Grove Press.

Brater, Enoch (1977). "Still/Beckett: The Essential and the Incidental." *Journal of Modern Literature* 6: 3–16.

Coe, Richard (1969). *Samuel Beckett*. New York: Grove Press.

Cohn, Ruby (1973). *Back to Beckett*. Princeton: Princeton University Press.

Friedman, Melvin J. (1976). "Introductory Notes to Beckett's Poetry." In Edouard Morot-Sir, Howard Harper, and Dougald McMillan (eds.), *Samuel Beckett: The Art of Rhetoric*. Chapel Hill: University of North Carolina Press.

Frye, Northrop (1963). *The Well-Tempered Critic*. Blooomington: Indiana University Press.

Frye, Northrop (1974). "Verse and Prose." In Alex Preminger, Terry V. F. Brogan, and Frank J. Warnke (eds.), *Princeton Encyclopedia of Poetry and Poetics*. Princeton: Princeton University Press.

Graver, Lawrence and Raymond Federman (eds.) (1979). *Samuel Beckett: The Critical Heritage*. London: Routledge and Kegan Paul.

Harvey, Lawrence E. (1970). *Samuel Beckett Poet & Critic*. Princeton: Princeton University Press.

Kenton, Andrew (1994). "From the Residua to 'Stirrings Still'." In John Pilling (ed.), *Cambridge Companion to Beckett*. Cambridge: Cambridge University Press.

Knowlson, James (1996). *Damned to Fame: The Life of Samuel Beckett*. New York: Grove Press.

Perloff, Marjorie (1981). "The Space of a Door: Beckett and the Poetry of Absence." In *The Poetics of Indeterminacy: Rimbaud to Cage*. Princeton: Princeton University Press.

Perloff, Marjorie (1985). "Between Verse and Prose: Beckett and the New Poetry." In *The Dance of the Intellect*. Cambridge: Cambridge University Press.

Perloff, Marjorie (1990). "Un voix pas la mienne: French/English Beckett and the French/English Reader." In *Poetic License: Essays on Modernist and Postmodernist Lyric*. Evanston: Northwestern University Press.

Perloff, Marjorie (1998). "Lucent and Inescapable Rhythms: Metrical Choice and Historical Formation." In *Poetry On & Off the Page*. Evanston: Northwestern University Press.

Perloff, Marjorie (2002). "Light Silence, Dark Speech: Reading Johns's Images, Seeing Beckett's Language in *Foirades/Fizzles*." *Fulcrum* 1: 83–105.

Solt, Mary Ellen (ed.) (1971). *Concrete Poetry: A World View*. Bloomington: Indiana University Press.

Yeats, W. B. (1964). *Letters on Poetry from W. B. Yeats to Dorothy Wellesley*. London: Oxford University Press.

Yeats, W. B. (1989). *The Collected Works: Vol. 1, The Poems*, ed. Richard J. Finneran. New York: Macmillan.

16
The "Dream" Poems:
Poems in Personae

Sean Lawlor

He was making up his piece, almost an occasional one (Dream of Fair to middling Women)

He was making up his piece, d'occasion perhaps in both senses ("A Wet Night," More Pricks Than Kicks)

Dream of Fair to middling Women ([Beckett 1992] hereafter *Dream*) is a treasury of verse, original and *d'occasion*, in the five major European languages. The Smeraldina, who competes with the Syra-Cusa to be the least literary character in the book, annexes to her *billet-doux* Goethe (Gretchen's song at the spinning wheel [59]) and Grillparzer ("Der Tag wird kommen und der stille Nacht" [60]). The Alba quotes James Clarence Mangan ("woe and pain, pain and woe," [172]), recites a dirty Spanish ditty ("No me jodas en el suelo" [209]), and alludes to "the Ronsard" ("Magie, ou Délivrance de l'amour" [175]). Belacqua applies Leopardi to himself ("Or posa per sempre … stanco mio cor. Assai palpitasti" [62]) and adapts Goethe's "Wandrers Nachteid II" to goad (or "gird") the Smeraldina (80). He draws on Tennyson to describe his mind, "brilliantly lit, canalised and purling," after a few drinks: "Clear and bright it should be ever, / Flowing like a crystal river, / Bright as light and clear as wind" (87). When the occasion demands, the omniscient narrator indulges himself in a verse. Having "got the substance of the Syra-Cusa" he applies an obscene quatrain from the *Roman de la rose* to her ("*Toutes êtes, serez ou fûtes, / De fait ou de volonté, putes …*" His "good friend" Chas will later recite the "iniquitous quatrain" at the close of the Frica's party (51 and 231).

As well as these second-hand pieces of verse, there are four original poems in *Dream*, which rise to their various occasions. All are ascribed to characters in the book, so that, given the author's relentlessly satirical attitude to his creatures, the seriousness with which we might entertain these poems is undermined. Liebert is credited with *"C'n'est au Pélican"* (21), "At last I find in my confused soul" (70–1) is Belacqua's, while "Calvary by Night" is "made up" by the "homespun poet" for the Frica's party

(213). The prose poem ("Text" in the *New Review*, April 1932), which is inserted as a relief from "bad dialogue" (83), voices the Smeraldina's yearnings whether it is her composition or not. All of these poems also have a life outside of *Dream*. "At last I find" exists in three versions, as a typescript with "Whoroscope" (Beckett HRHRC), as part of "Sedendo and Quiescendo" (1932), and in *Dream*. "Calvary by Night" was revised for inclusion in *More Pricks Than Kicks* (Beckett [1970] hereafter *MPTK*). However, neither it nor "At last I find" are included in the contents list for *POEMS* (Beckett Leventhal Papers). In this list, *"C'n'est au Pélican"* is revised as "Text 2" to form a trio of Texts with the prose poem ("Text"/"Text 1") and the long poem – "Text 3," which begins "Miserere oh colon" – also rather confusingly called "Text" on its publication in the *European Caravan*. This suggests that despite their ascription to his fictional creatures in *Dream*, these two "texts" maintained, in Beckett's view, sufficient integrity to be considered as free-standing pieces, whereas the revisions to "At last I find" and "Calvary" had effectively pushed them too far into pastiche to be salvageable. Ironically, when Beckett's "long list" of poems was pruned for publication neither of these *Dream* poems (Texts 1 and 2) was collected, and they have not been republished in collections of Beckett's poems to this day. Calder did, however, include in *Poems 1930–1989* "Calvary by Night" and "At last I find," retitled "Sonnet" (Beckett 2002: 194 and 198) that Beckett apparently rejected for *POEMS*.

John Pilling suggests that "At last I find" may be the poem that Beckett submitted to the *Irish Statesman* about March 1929 (2006: 19). If so, this would make it the earliest poem of Beckett's that we have. Similarities of wording in the mystical climax which it shares with the short story "Assumption" (1929) seem to support this argument: "he was released, achieved the blue flower, Vega, GOD" and "one with the birdless, cloudless, colourless skies, in infinite fulfillment" (Beckett 1995: 6, 7). However, since the holograph variant of the poem is found on the reverse of the last page of the *Whoroscope* manuscript it seems probable that both poems were written about the same time. While the legend of *Whoroscope*'s composition overnight on the evening of June 15, 1930 is dubious, it seems unlikely that it could have been written as early as spring 1929. Paradoxically, the discipline of the sonnet form may have offered Beckett some relief after the *vers libre* exactions of *Whoroscope*, which had to be reduced to fewer than 100 lines for the *Hours Press* competition. The Jacobean punning on death and engulfing that brings "Assumption" to its end fits well with the constraints of the sonnet and its association with the literary conceit. Whatever its merits, the *bona fides* of the poem are questioned by the way it is introduced in *Dream* as one of the "finest Night of May hiccupsobs that ever left a fox's paw sneering and rotting in a snaptrap." The reference is to de Musset's *Nuits de mai* and specifically to the "Allégorie du Pélican," with its mournful definition of what makes a fine poem: "Les plus désespérés sont les chants les plus beaux, / Et j'en sais d'immortels qui sont de purs sanglots" (The most beautiful songs are those that are most despairing and I know immortal verses made purely from sobs). The integrity of the poem is further undermined by the "sublimen of blatherskite" that follows hot on its tail.

> At last I find in my confusèd soul,
> Dark with the dark flames of the cypresses,
> The certitude that I cannot be whole,
> Consummate, finally achieved, unless,
>
>   I be consumed and fused in the white heat
> Of her sad finite essence, so that none
> Shall sever us who are at last complete,
> Eternally, irrevocably one,
>
>   One with the birdless, cloudless, colourless sky,
> One with the bright purity of the fire,
> Of which we are, and for which we must die,
> A rapturous, strange, death, and be entire,
>
>   Like syzygetic stars, supernly bright,
> Conjoined in the One and in the Infinite!

Most of the revisions to the poem in *Dream* are minor. They include marking the extended form of the participle "confusèd" and pluralizing "cypress" to improve the scansion – the insertion of the definite article in the first line of the manuscript's third quatrain is to the same purpose – and removing the archaic or Irish " 'Tis" in line 2. More significantly, it distances the poet from his beloved by the move from second to third person address in line 6 and pushes the poem further towards parody by the revision of the closing couplet. The holograph's "Like two merged stars, sublimely bright, / Conjoined in one + in the infinite", is improved in "Sedendo et Quiesciendo" by the revision of "sublimely bright" to the much stronger "intolerably bright," but the substitutions in revision of "syzygetic" for "two merged" and "supernly" for "intolerably" give the line a cloying, euphuistic timbre. The temptation to make this closing couplet do a little too much, which was already apparent in the capitalizations of the *transition* version, is made worse by the introduction of a rogue definite article before "One." The focus is definitively shifted from mystical union as a metaphor for tantric passion to tantric passion as a means of achieving mystical union: "the blue flower, Vega, [or, indeed] GOD." While these revisions, in Belacqua's appalling French–English pun, may "tighten the tender white worms" (*ver/vers*), they also justify his description of the relationship as "a sentimental coagulum, sir, that biggers descruption." It would be hard enough to take this at face value in a collection of poems, but it becomes impossible to do so when this "mystical adhesion" (70) is immediately parodied by the tale of Lilly Neary and "her pore Paddy" and their much less exalted passion, "a bitch-melba and a long long come and go before breakfast and."

As an exercise in the sonnet form, the poem is accomplished. The first quatrain discovers the poet, confused and incomplete. Its rhymes on "soul" and "whole" are complemented by the rhymes on "cypresses," the plant of Attic sanctuaries and

Mediterranean cemeteries, and the conjunction "unless" which leaves the first quatrain uncompleted and makes a bridge to the second. The word play on "confusèd" and "consummate" in the first quatrain is echoed in the second by "consumed" and "complete." The "dark flame" is partnered by "the white heat." Although new rhyme words are introduced, they maintain the semantic relationship that was established in the first quatrain. The notion of wholeness in the third line of the first quatrain is matched by completion in the third line of the second. The implicit numbering of "unless" is made explicit in the binary count of "none" and "one." The fusion of the poet and his beloved which is achieved in the octave is extended to the "birdless, cloudless, colourless skies" at the beginning of the sestet. His "dark flame" and her "white heat" are reimagined in "the bright purity of the fire / Of which we are" to give an Heraclitean cast to the poem. As Beckett will later (April 1933) record in his philosophy notes, "His radical substance [is] *ethereal fire,* by which he means something like the oxygen of modern chemistry. Air & water are cooling fire, earth is spent fire. The world is periodically dissolved & recreated in fire" (Beckett TCD MSS 10967/24). Heraclitus also "Identifies the real One with the apparent Many," an idea that is evident in this poem and which occurs also in *Whoroscope.* The "rapturous strange death" recalls the "little death" of Elizabethan and Jacobean love poetry but, as in the story "Assumption," also indicates a Freudian death wish.

From the opening quatrain to the closing couplet, the sonnet unfolds as a sinuous, long sentence, with subordinate clauses and phrases elegantly controlled, to lead, inexorably, from the poet, confused in his soul, to the stars and infinity. It achieves a sort of totalization of imaginative experience that Beckett will not attempt again until "The Vulture," but the conventionality of the sonnet form and the contrivance of the imagery do not sit well alongside Beckett's excursions into *vers libre* and the poem would be an anomaly in the projected collection of poems.

"Calvary by Night," according to the "homespun poet," is "a strong composition." This is a judgment from which we, like the author, or so the ironic tone insinuates, are free to dissent. These derogations are intensified in the circumstantial revisions from *Dream* to *MPTK*. In *Dream,* "he was making up his piece, almost an occasional one, whose main features he had established one recent gusty afternoon on the summit of the Hill of Allen" (213). The Bog of Allen figures prominently in the closing passage of "The Dead," so that mention here of the hill which overlooks it is a marker of the poem as Joycean *hommage.* The Hill of Allen has mythic connotations since it is the legendary site of a camp once occupied by Fionn MacCumhaill and the Fianna. However, for anyone who knows the site, these heroic pretensions may be undercut by the recollection of its most noticeable feature – the Victorian folly on the top of the hill. In *MPTK,* no such local knowledge is required, since "Calvary by Night" is now the work of a pot poet cycling back from the pub: "He was making up his piece, d'occasion perhaps in both senses, whose main features he had recently established riding home on his bike from the Yellow House" (65). The second-hand nature of the imagery is hinted at in the phrase "d'occasion perhaps in both senses," although there is an attempt to throw us off the source of the borrowing by altering the style of delivery from *Dream*'s "No, he would stand up at once and say" to the Yeatsian "No, he would arise and say" from "The Lake Isle of Innisfree," which was also written in the metropolis: "when walking through Fleet street very homesick I heard a little tinkle of water and saw a fountain in a shop-window which balanced a little ball upon its jet, and began to remember lake water. From the sudden remembrance came my poem *Innisfree*" (Yeats 1927: 153).

This change of inspirational location in *MPTK* necessitates a further change. The mode of presentation "best suited to his Hill of Allen manner" (*Dream*: 214) becomes "most worthy of his aquatic manner" (*MPTK*: 65). The introduction of the Latinate "aquatic" suggests that "Calvary by Night" belongs to a truly wet genre. "Most worthy" lays on the mockery using a tool you could lift turf with. Most of the changes made to the poem itself in *MPTK* also serve to undermine our efforts to take it seriously, but they cannot quite destroy the suspicion that there may have been a time when it took itself seriously.

Calvary by Night

the water
the waste of water

in the womb of water
an pansy leaps

rocket of bloom flare flower of night wilt for me
on the breasts of the water it has closed it has made
an act of floral presence on the water
the tranquil act of its cycle on the waste
    from the spouting forth
    to the re-enwombing
    untroubled bow of petaline sweet-smellingness
    kingfisher abated
    drowned for me
    Lamb of insustenance mine

    till the clamour of a blue bloom
    beat on the walls of the womb of
    the waste of
    the water

If "At last I find" is an Heraclitean fire poem, "Calvary by Night" is the Thalean poem of water. Taken together, they may signal a parodic relationship to Eliot's *The Waste Land* with its "Fire Sermon" and "Death by Water." Beckett later described the Thalean view of the universe in his Philosophy Notes:

Fundamental question of science: *What is the Weltstoff!* That this single cosmic matter lies at the basis of the entire process of nature was a self-evident presupposition of Ionic

School ... Experience suggests it as water to Thales. While the solid in itself seems dead, moved only from without, the liquid and volatile makes the impression of independent mobility and vitality ...

Whole history of cosmology at this period is the story of how the solid earth was gradually loosed from its moorings. Originally sky and earth were pictured as lid and floor of a box; but from an early date Greeks began to think of the earth as an island surrounded by river Okeanos. To regard it as resting in the water (as according to Aristotle Thales did) is an advance. To get the earth afloat was something. (Beckett TCD MSS10967/5–5.1)

Thales serves as the starting point for "Serena I" but also seems to underpin the imagery of "Calvary by Night." Calvary for Beckett, as early as *Proust* and as late as *Molloy*, signifies suffering without any end in sight: "But before this new brightness, this old brightness revived and intensified, can be finally extinguished, the Calvary of pity and remorse must be trod" (Beckett 1965: 44 cf. also 60); "A veritable calvary, with no limit to its stations and no hope of crucifixion" (Beckett 1959: 78). In *Dream*, Belacqua trundling "through the Tuileries on the platform of the A1 bis" experiences "calvary through the shock absorbers" (82). "By Night" darkens the mood still further. "The waste of water" in the second line, commences the overtly Joycean references with which the poem abounds. It recalls the association of water with music and sex in *A Portrait of the Artist as a Young Man* when Stephen awakes towards dawn: "O what sweet music! His soul was all dewy wet. Over his limbs in sleep pale cool waves of light had passed. He lay still, as if his soul lay amid cool waters, conscious of faint sweet music"(Joyce 1987: 221). When the "temptress of his villanelle" also awakes:

Her eyes, dark and with a look of languor, were opening to his eyes. Her nakedness yielded to him, radiant, warm, odorous and lavish-limbed, enfolded him like a shining cloud, enfolded him like water with a liquid life: and like a cloud of vapour or like waters circumfluent in space the liquid letters of speech, symbols of the element of mystery, flowed forth over his brain. (ibid.: 227)

More specific is the reference to "Flood" where "A waste of water ruthlessly / sways and uplifts its weedy mane." Joyce's "weedy mane" is alluded to in the phrase "an pansy leaps" where the older (not much in evidence since 1300!) and fuller form of the indefinite article parodies the precious tone in Joyce's "Flood." The archaic form of the indefinite article "pansies up" Beckett's poem. The slang term "to pansy up" was still current in the 1930s; its contemporary British equivalent is "to tart up." At the same time, "an pansy leaps" is a recollection of the etymology of pansy in the French "*une pensée*." It is a thought, therefore, that leaps in the womb of the water. A Thalean demiurge – "all things full of gods" (cf. "Sanies I") – merges with the Judeo-Christian creation myth – "And the spirit of God moved upon the waters (Gen.1:2). The upward movement of Joyce's poem ("lift and sway" in line 2, "sways and uplifts" in line 6, and "uplift and sway" again in line 9) is exaggerated in the phrase "rocket of bloom flare," which simultaneously shifts the frame of reference from "Flood" to the *Nausicaa* episode in *Ulysses*, where Leopold Bloom's voyeuristic encounter with Gertie MacDowell on the beach culminates in onanistic wetness as the fireworks explode:

> And then a rocket sprang and bang shot blind and O! then the Roman candle burst and it was like a sigh of O! and everyone cried O! O! in raptures and it gushed out of it a stream of rain gold hair threads and they shed and ah! They were all greeny dewy stars falling with golden, O so lively! O so soft sweet, soft! (Joyce 1960: 477)

"Flower of night wilt for me / on the breasts of the water" determines a briefer moment of orgasm in "Calvary" than Bloom's protracted pleasures in *Ulysses*. Here, it is even more a matter of "up like a rocket, down like a stick" (Joyce 1960: 483). The masturbatory nature of the climax is emphasized by its locus "on the breasts of the water" rather than "*in utero*." The pansy now seems an apt choice of flower with its vulgar names: "heartsease," "kiss me at the garden gate," and, best of all, "love in idleness." For Joyce, in *Finnegans Wake*, the pansy also has onanistic significance. His phrase "with a pansy for the pussy in the corner" (1964: 278) recalls Beckett's solitary, self-pitying, and deleted introduction to "Serena I":

> no my algos is puss in the corner I just feel fervent
> ardent in a vague general way
> and my little erectile brain God help her
> thuds like a butcher's sex

The act over, calm descends in perfect tenses that foreshadow the post-coital closure of "Dortmunder": "it has closed, it has made an act of floral presence on the water." The doublings that have characterized the poem from its beginning now become more like a nervous tic, and the repetitions that might, just, have seemed musical in the opening lines now take on the quality of doggerel. "The tranquil act of its cycle on the waste" reiterates the sense of the preceding line but weakens it by flabby paraphrase. "An act of floral presence" is a little stronger, because it is less abstract, than "the tranquil act of its cycle" and "water" is better than "waste" because it names what it describes. In the next lines, the desire to play variations on medial "o" / "ou" / "ow" sounds seem to determine the sense. "From the spouting forth / to the re-enwombing" just about works to describe this (surprisingly tranquil) act of ejaculation, but its recapitulation as "an untroubled bow of petal and fragrance" (*Dream*) or worse still "an untroubled bow of petaline sweet-smellingness" (*MPTK*) is *de trop*. "Kingfisher abated" is a vivid enough image of a flash of color disappearing, but its abrupt incorporation into the Christian redemption story in "drowned for me / lamb of insustenance mine" yokes together sex and salvation in a manner that seems designed to shock rather than to develop the argument of the poem. This Eucharistic imagery, which colors Stephen's vilanelle, may, in "Calvary," be traced back to the *Lotuseaters* episode in *Ulysses*, where Bloom's glimpse of the Turkish baths sets off masturbatory yearnings:

Enjoy a bath now: clean trough of water, cool enamel, the gentle, tepid stream. This is my body.

He foresaw his pale body reclined in it at full, naked, in a womb of warmth, oiled by scented smelling soap, softly laved. He saw his trunk and limbs ririppled over and sustained, buoyed lightly upward, lemonyellow: his navel, bud of flesh: and saw the dark tangled curls of his bush floating, floating hair of the stream around the limp father of thousands, a languid floating flower. (Joyce 1960: 107)

Bloom's "gentle tepid stream" realizes his previously expressed urge to piss in the bath: "Hamman, Turkish, Massage. Dirt gets rolled up in your navel. Nicer if a nice girl did it. Also I think I. Yes I. Do it in the bath. Curious longing I. Water to water" (ibid.: 105). This, in turn, informs Beckett's "from the spouting forth / to the re-enwombing," while the very idea of the "womb of water" derives from Bloom's term for the bath as a "womb of warmth," and perhaps also from Stephen's representation of poetic inspiration in terms of the Annunciation: "In the virgin womb of the imagination the word was made flesh" (Joyce 1987: 221).

"Lamb of insustenance mine" combines an act of communion with a Joycean neologism and so plays up Bloom's Eucharistic musings: "They don't seem to chew it; only swallow it down. Rum idea eating bits of a corpse why the cannibals cotton to it" (Joyce 1960: 99). There is a sort of arc of negation that traces the final word in Joyce's "Flood" ("incertitude") via its positive occurrence in "At last I find" ("the certitude that I cannot be whole") to "insustenance" here. The kingfisher/Lamb of God may be "drowned for me" but the sacrifice provides no sustenance and, as the last four lines make clear, the cycle begins anew. These concluding lines are drowned, in their turn, under a word music that overdoes alliteration and assonance, even as it brings the poem to a satisfying conclusion, finishing like an *alba*, where it started with "the waste / of the water."

Like the Yeatsian reference that introduces the poem in *MPTK*, the apparent allusion to the blue flower of Novalis, which refers us back to the short story "Assumption," is designed to throw us off the scent of Joyce. This poem is in part homage, in part pastiche. It may also be an oblique refutation of Joyce's *obiter dictu* on poetry: "poetry ought to be rimed and [addressed] 'à une petite femme'!" (Samuel Beckett to Thomas MacGreevy, March 1, 1931). "Calvary by Night" breaks both these rules.

"Text" / "Text 1" maintains this *hommage*.

TEXT 1

oh and I dreamed he would come and come come come and cull me bonny bony double-bed cony swiftly my springal and my thin wicklow twingle-twangler comfort my days of roses days of beauty week of redness with mad shame to my lips of shame to my shamehill for the newest of news the shemost of shenews is I'm lust-be-lepered and unwell oh I'd liefer be a sparrow for my puck-fisted coxcomb bird to bird and branch or a cave of coal with veins of gold for my wicked doty's potystick trimly to besom gone the hartshorn and the cowslip wine gone and the lettuce nibbled up nibbled up and gone nor the last day of beauty of the red time opened its rose struck with its thorn oh

I'm all of a gallimaufry and a salady salmagundi singly and single to bed she said I'll have no toadspit about this house and whose quab was I I'd like to know that from my cheerfully cornuted Dublin landloper and whose foal hackney mare toeing the line like a Viennese Taübchen take my tip and clap a lock on your Greek galligaskins ere I'm quick and living in hopes and glad to go snacks with my twingle-twangler and grow grow into the earth mother of your clapdish and foreshop. (Revised, previously unpublished version [Beckett TXR C00-A3])

At first sight, this is distinctively Joycean. Cohn says that, "as a young man, Beckett saw the comically repulsive aspects of sex, and they appear in this light in his prose poem entitled 'Text,' which reflects the influence of the multi-puns of Joyce's work" (1962: 17). Gross asserts that "Text" is a reduction of Molly Bloom's soliloquy at the end of *Ulysses*: "There is nothing in Beckett's 'Text' that is not in the original. And there is surprisingly little in the original that has not found its way, albeit in drastically reduced form, into its parody" (Gross 1970: 125). However, she does not offer a close reading to support this assertion. If there is a specific, textual point of departure in Joyce, it seems just as likely to be in the breathless conclusion to "Nausicaa":

O sweety all your little girlwhite up I saw dirty bracegirdle made me do love sticky we two naughty Grace darling she him half past the bed met him pike hoses frillies for Raoul to perfume your wife black hair heave under embon *señorita* I young eyes Mulvey plump years dreams return tail end agendath swooney lovey showed me her next year in drawers return next in her next her next. (Joyce 1960: 498)

The tone is similar and there are a number of superficial points of contact. An "Oh!" begins both passages, both allude to ejaculation ("love sticky," "toadspit"), are furnished with beds and exotic items of clothing ("pike hose frillies," "Greek galligaskins"), and make use of intimate endearments ("sweety", "swoony lovey" and "bonny bony double-bed cony … my springal and my thin Wicklow twingle-twangler"). However, as John Pilling has demonstrated, although the end result looks decidedly Joycean, the method of its construction is different and quite distinctively so:

Joyce treats borrowed material in both *Ulysses* and *Work in Progress* in an open manner; completely to have obscured a source would have run counter to his ambition to display the uses to which it could be put. In "Text", by contrast, Beckett offers not the slightest clue that his prose piece depends in large part on a pre-existent group of texts that Joyce either did not know, or in any event was not disposed to use. (1999: 212)

Pilling traces 10 percent of the words in "Text" to the works of John Ford and provides a useful glossary, but Beckett divorces these words from their meanings to substitute an insistent sexual innuendo. As Cohn says, "the female person is imaged as a coalcave, a cowslip, a lettuce leaf, a rose, a squab (*recte* quab), a mare, whereas her partner is relentlessly phallic" (2001: 34). This is highly gendered language which might seem to portray the sexual act, but which, contrarily, depicts an enforced abstinence. As the other commentators have noted "my days of roses days of beauty week of redness" suggests a heavy menstrual period during which intercourse is not possible despite the lady's being "lust be-lepered."

Like the other three poems included in *Dream*, "Text 1" is also delivered *in persona*; it is given to the Smeraldina. Things have not been going well between her and Belacqua since his return to Germany with the "collywobbles" (75). After a long passage of prescriptions for this ailment (80–2), the scene apparently shifts to "the platform of the A1 bis" bus in Paris; the Smeraldina is clasping a scroll, with which she strikes the hapless Belacqua. "Text" expresses her disappointed longing, although the source of this frustration is her indisposition rather than his. Belacqua's immediate response may be to the slap he has received from the scroll or to the prose poem "Text"/"Text 1" if, as Pilling suggests, this is what the scroll contains (2003: 172). "'Hure!'" is certainly returned in Kassel where Belacqua settles "his bottom on the sill" (83). In the *New Review* and Texas versions, it is equally clear that in this prose poem, a woman addresses a man, and it is this aspect of the piece that invites the comparison with Molly Bloom's soliloquy, for here we have a male poet imagining something he can never experience personally, the frustrations arising from menstruation. In this sense, as much as in its seeming appropriation of a Joycean idiom, "Text 1" is very clearly an exercise in style.

"Ce qu'on dit du style, et je veux dire, à coup sûr, ce que ce cochon de Marcel en dit, me plait, je crois," so commences the long passage in French (19–22), which includes towards its end what must be Beckett's first poem in French. The opening French phrase suggests that, like "Text 1," it is principally a matter of style, and, as Proust has it, style is "une question non de technique mais de vision" (1929: 47; Beckett 1965: 87–8). Like the other poems, "Ce n'est au Pélican" is given to one of Beckett's fictional creatures, and his distance from it is, seemingly, even greater than from the other poems. It is in French and has a decidedly homosexual edge; it is offered to Belacqua by Lucien who has it from Liebert. Yet, despite this distancing, the poem has a freshness that is not to be found in the other three pieces. Perhaps this is because the "Pélican" is a product of vision rather than technique, as Lucien's letter implies. His account of its composition certainly makes it seem considerably less labored than the homespun poet's efforts on "Calvary": "L. se lève d'un bond, se déshabille, fait son poème, fuit de tous les côtés. Devant moi, croisée tennysonienne, ta belle face carrée bouge, bat comme un coeur" ("L[iebert, the poet] gets up with a bound, undresses, composes his poem, runs all over the place. In front of me, grown tennysonian, his handsome square face stirs, beats like a heart"). Even the elaborately contrived pathetic fallacy, in which the rising sun serves as a metaphor for the dawning poetic inspiration, does not quite destroy the illusion of effortlessness. Dawn's rosy illumination seems first to cover Liebert with shame and then to bathe his poetic baby in blood: "L'intérêt de l'état de l'orient s'affirme. Il n'y a que lui, me dis-je, qui sache avoir honte, laisser percer une honte frivole, rougir. Les tiraillements du bas ciel cassent les carreaux. Du matin le tiroir s'entrouvre, crache le bébé, Polchinelle, sanguinolent à en mourir. En attendant que monté le thé simple que par consequent je viens de commander, au fond des yeux clos le poéme se fait" (The state interest of the East asserts itself. Only he, I tell myself, knows how to be ashamed, to let a frivolous shame prick him, to blush. The pangs of the low sky break the flagstones. The drawer of morning opens, the baby sputters out. Punch, covered in blood, as if bleeding to death. Waiting until the simple tea which, as it happens, I had just ordered, is served, in the depths of his closed eyes the poem is made). There is an implication that the poem which is made behind closed eyes is inspired. It has something in common with the "eye-suicide" Beckett detects in Rimbaud's "Les poètes de sept ans," which is "pour des visions" (Samuel Beckett to Thomas MacGreevy, November 3, 1931) and the "blank unsighted thing," "Serena I" (Samuel Beckett to Thomas Mac-Greevy, September 13, 1932).

TEXT 2

        Ce n'est au pélican
pas si pitoyable
ni à l'égyptienne
pas si pure
mais à ma douce Lucie
opticienne oui et peaussière aussi
qui ne m'a pas guéri
mais qui aurait pu
et à mon doux Jude
dont j'ai adororé un peu de la dépouille
que j'adresse la cause désespérée
qui a l'air d'être la mienne

(Revised, previously unpublished version,
Leventhal papers, Texas)

It is not to the pelican / not so piteous / nor to the Egyptian / not so pure / but to my sweet Lucy / optician and skin-dresser / who has not cured me / but who could have / and to sweet Jude / whose hide I have adored somewhat / to whom I offer the lost cause / which seems to be mine. (My translation)

The revised version in the Leventhal papers expands "C'n'est ," "n'm'a,' and qu'j'adresse"; does not capitalize "pélican" or "l'égyptienne," qualifies both Lucie and Jude as "douce"/"doux" and plays down the adoration of Jude by the insertion of "un peu" before "de la dépouille."

The poem begins with another frankly Christian reference. Beckett takes the legend of the pelican feeding his children with drops of blood from his breast, from de Musset's "Allégorie du Pélican," the same poem which had led him to characterize "At last I find" as a "Night of May hiccupsob." The next two lines recall Baudelaire's sonnet "La Beauté," a hint of which has already been given to the alert reader in the concluding phrase of the opening sentence of this French section: "si j'ose accepter, en ce moment, les hauts-de-petit-coeur-de-neige." The second quatrain of "La Beauté" reads,

Je trône dans l'azur comme un sphinx incompris
J'unis un coeur de neige à la blancheur des cygnes;
Je hais le mouvement qui déplace les lignes
Et jamais je ne pleure et jamais je ne ris.

(A sky-throned sphinx, unknown yet, I combine
The cygnet's whiteness with a heart of snow.
I loathe all movement that displaces line,
And neither tears or laughter do I know.

(trans. Roy Campbell)

In both of these poems, the poet is being addressed on his art, in de Musset by the Muse, in Baudelaire by Beauty herself. De Musset's Muse tells the poet that great poems are made from sorrow and disappointment with a few drops of blood to nourish the reader ("Quand ils parlent ainsi d'ésperances trompées, / De tristesse et d'oubli, d'amour et de malheur, /Ce n'est pas un concert à dilater le coeur / ... / Mais il y pend toujours quelques gouttes de sang"); Baudelaire's Beauty warns that the poet's days will be consumed in austere study ("Les poètes ... / ... / Consumeront leurs jours en d'austères etudes"). The phrase "pas si pitoyable" is ambiguous; it could mean "not so pitiful," but here, in apposition, it means "not so full of pity," and describes Lucie and Jude who are "pas si pitoyable" as the pelican. The purity of Baudelaire's mysterious sphinx, and therefore of Liebert's Egyptian, is expressed in the line "J'unis un coeur de neige à la blancheur des cygnes." Compared with her, Lucie and Jude are "pas si pure." Despite Lucien's opening endorsement of "les hauts-de-petit-coeur-de-neige," "pas si pure" distances Liebert from Baudelaire's austere conception of beauty just as "pas si pitoyable" does from de Musset's poetics of suffering. At the same time, these negations also abolish the Proustian distance from, in Belacqua's phrase, the "réel dermique," which Lucien had "proposed" to Liebert yesterday. Since both Lucie and Jude will be characterized in the poem precisely in terms of their skin-deep reality, it is clear that Liebert does not share Proust's disgust with it: "P. se paye de mots. Il ne sait jamais resister à l'extase du décollage. Il realize (et avec une morgue) des loopings verbaux. Si loin, oh dégoût !, du réel dermique qui le fait tant trembler et transpirer" (*Dream*: 20) ("P[roust] is taken in by words. He can never resist the ecstasy of coming unstuck. He profits from and takes pride in verbal loopings. So far — urrgh! — from the skin-deep real which makes him tremble and perspire" [my translation]).

Having rejected these idealized forms of poetic beauty, Liebert turns to the "real," but thinly disguised as Catholic saints. St Lucia, often represented with her eyes on a plate, is the patron saint of the blind, and an appropriate invocation for an "unsighted" poem. In the poem she is also *peaussière*, or skin-dresser, which may allude to her condemnation to work as a prostitute, a sentence that could not be carried out because she was, miraculously, so heavy that the soldiers could not move her. St Jude is the patron saint of lost causes, hence Liebert addresses to him "la cause déseperé / qui à l'air d'être la mienne." De Musset has taught us that "les plus désespéré sont les chants les plus beaux" and that the human feasts at which great poets sing most resemble those of the pelican when they speak of "espérances trompée."

In the Texas revision, Beckett introduces the adjectives *douce/doux* to qualify these secularized saints (their titles of canonization are not supplied in the poem). The word *douceur* has a particular significance for Belacqua in *Dream*, and for Beckett at the time. It denotes a Joycean epiphany with, inevitably, sexual undertones. Georges Belmont (*né* Pelorson, identified by James Knowlson as the real-life original of Liebert) tells the following anecdote in his memoir of Beckett's time at the *École Normale*:

> Then, one day, exasperated by running round in circles with the word douceur from Rimbaud's "Barbare," and by expatiating on the difficulty, nay, the impossibility of turning such typically French abstractions from the concrete into English, I suggested to him that a little stroll, to ventilate the brain and the imagination, would do us good. He refused. I set out alone. On my return, the light that always shone from his window suddenly sparked both my remorse for going off so abruptly and my curiosity about the progress of his struggle. I went up and found him in his favorite position, feet on mantelpiece; but he had slumped so deep into his armchair that the painful-looking angle of the back of his neck had folded his chin down on the front of his neck. His arm spilled over the armrest; his hand hung down, inert, fingers open, as if suspended in their fall. The almost empty whiskey bottle was in its place on the floor; the glass had rolled over without breaking, spilling the last drops. The tall oil lamp on the table behind the two armchairs which, customarily, shed light on our reading, seemed to scowl at the scene before me. Its flame was naked. Shattered shards of the enormous white porcelain shade which had covered the dazzling dome lay on the floor like snow. I froze at this littered debris. Sam's eyelids were closed; his glasses had fallen to the other side of the chair. I thought he was asleep and prepared to leave on tiptoe, when I saw his lips move. He turned his head painfully towards me, as much as his hunched up position allowed, and his eyelids opened. His eyes were lifeless but they knew I was there. His lips moved again with an indistinct word. I leant over and asked if he wanted anything. He applied himself to what could only be the laborious repetition of the word. "Mozart," he said. I said if he wanted to hear some Mozart, I only had the Requiem and I would have to go and get my record-player as well as the disk. "No," said he. "Douceur." As I remained dumb, he repeated it louder and with the German pronunciation: "Mo-tzarrt." Then his head fell forward and, as if collapsing into himself and into immobility, he closed his eyes.
>
>   It was only in crossing the courtyard of my quadrangle that, from the rudiments of my schoolboy German, churned up no doubt by the unconscious, I suddenly realized that *zart* means *doux* in German. (2001: 284–5, my translation)

In *Dream*, the Smeraldina is described as the "douce Vega" and "the darling blue flower" to whom Belacqua "inscribes" "At last I find" (*Dream*: 70). Early dawn, in phrases which recollect Lucien's account of Liebert in the throes of poetic composition, has its *douceurs* for the travel weary Belacqua: "a magic dust lapsed from the desolate hour, from the disastrous expulsion of the morning, livid strands in the east of placenta praevia, dust of his dove's heart, and covered him. Douceurs" (31). Lucien himself, or rather his capacity for silence, provokes the apostrophe: "Nor did he lay himself out to persuade, à la Liebert, nor titillate and arouse, à la Syra-Cusa, he did not talk at a person, he just balladed around at his own sweet aboulia, and – oh douceurs ! – he kept on the mute" (46). In a long passage that follows the prose poem, the word gives Belacqua "the chinks." He is still suffering, it seems, from his diarrhea, and it may be the sight of "a complete Racine drowning in the bidet" that has brought the word to mind. A few lines later, he takes a strange pleasure imagining the occasion of his death when "Florence shall be instructed shall she not or reminded to foist deep down oh douceurs the antiseptic tampons" (85). However, here it is probably most closely aligned with Chas's Ginette, who is "intelligente et douce, mais douce, mon cher" (143).

Jude's rather adored "dépouille" (skin or hide) aligns him with Lucie in her role as "peaussière," or skin-dresser, and sets them both at the opposite end of the artistic spectrum from Proust who is "si loin du réel dermique." Since Liebert remarks that Lucie has not, though she could have, cured him, it is evidently to the flesh rather than to the Muse or to Beauty incarnate that he turns for inspiration. For Lucien this seems to be a winning formula since he learns "dominando l'orgasmo," or holding back the orgasm that the poem provokes, inhaling the odorless placenta of dawn (21). Belacqua, on the contrary, seems less taken, though whether this is because of Liebert's homosexual badinage, which is directed at him ("'Il est si beau etc.'" [20]), or Liebert's poem is unclear: "He has no call, thought Belacqua, to throw his demented Liebert at me, and he need not crook his fingers at Smerry, whether fresh or frail or Jungfrau or none of the three." (22).

Lucien's letter began with an observation on style. Beckett continues this discussion many pages later but still in relation to Lucien, Liebert, and Lucie in her Syra-Cusa incarnation. Lucien has let fall a "little sparkle hid in ashes":

"'Black diamond of pessimism'" (47; in real life, Beaufret's phrase, Samuel Beckett to Thomas MacGreevy, March 11, 1931). Belacqua muses that this is precisely what "the conversationalist, with his contempt of the tag and the ready-made, can't give you; because the lift to the high spot is precisely from the tag and the ready-made. The same with the stylist." Into this phrase can be read Beckett's rejection of Proust, of de Musset, and through him of the contrivance of a poem like "At last I find," and perhaps even of Baudelaire. There is no comparable "high-spot" in "Pélican," but it does achieve what Beckett claims "only the French language can give you," the ability to "write without style" (*Dream*: 48). Some years later, the *Petit sot* poems will represent a similar exercise. "Ce n'est à pélican," short as it is, is more satisfying than the other poems in *Dream*. It plays the trick of the extended sentence less obtrusively than "At last I find," uses repetition more effectively than "Calvary by Night," and integrates its repertoire of allusions less flamboyantly than the prose poem "Text"/"Text 1." For all that it eschews style, it is an exercise in style. Surely Belacqua cannot be thinking of "pélican" when he remembers Liebert "declaim[ing] Valerian abominations of his own" (ibid.).

For any reader of James Knowlson's *Damned to Fame*, it is almost impossible not to read *Dream* as a *roman à clé*, and equally difficult to judge the extent to which the poems presented in it can be considered as Beckett's rather than pastiche pieces created for the various characters in role. Ezra Pound, in his adoption of the term "persona," took advantage of the interesting ambiguities created by assigning his poems to fictional characters with whom he was not fully identified. They might share his sentiments, but he was at liberty to make fun of their mode of expression. Something similar seems to happen to Beckett's poems in *Dream*. As they are subject to revision for incorporation in fiction, they become less able to stand up as his poems in their own right. This is particularly apparent with "At last I find" and "Calvary." It is less evidently so with "Text"/"Text 1" and "Pélican"/"Text 2." The four poems are very different in tone, in form, and in language. "At last I find" is an accomplished exercise in sonnet form; "Calvary" is mocked as the work of a pot-poet; "Text"/"Text 1" is an exercise in Joycean interior monologue while the "Pélican"/"Text 2" is offered as the tortured elucubration of the "inénarrable Liebert." Nonetheless, all four are closely linked, despite their obvious differences, in a system of references which includes de Musset ("At last I find" and the "Pélican"), Joyce ("Calvary" and "Text"/"Text 1"), and the blue flower of Novalis ("At last I find" and "Calvary"). Complementary fire and water imagery link "At last I find" and "Calvary," but the "Pélican" also qualifies as a watery poem both because of the long sea-journey of de Musset's pelican and because of Liebert himself "beau sans blague comme un rêve d'eaux" (20). All four poems share a concern with the male orgasm which is mystically achieved in "At last I find" and "Calvary" and denied in "Text"/"Text 1" and the "Pélican"/"Text 2." The successive revisions of "At last I find" and "Calvary" show Beckett gradually pushing these poems beyond the pale, so that there is no possibility of including them in a "serious" work of poetry. With the "Pélican," it is different. The poem is slight and simply expressed, but Beckett's revision continues to take it seriously and smartens it up for consumption by a wider public by removing the slangy elisions of the *Dream* original. "Text"/"Text 1" is neither fish nor fowl. It begins and ends its life as a prose poem (in the *New Review* and the Leventhal revision), and the changes that are made from first to last state do little to alter the impulse or the impact of the piece. It is rather lost in *Dream* as just another, not immediately comprehensible paragraph, delivered in a voice that puts it at odds with its neighbors, but it stands up as a tone poem and seems no odder than the other early poems that Beckett reworked for inclusion in *POEMS*. The irony is that Beckett's editors have chosen to republish from *Dream* the two poems that Beckett had abandoned while the poems that he continued to work on remain uncollected.

References

Beckett, Samuel. Leventhal papers, "POEMS" 1932–3, Harry Ransom Humanities Research Centre. Austin, Texas.

Beckett, Samuel. Leventhal papers, TXR C00-A3. Harry Ransom Humanities Research Centre. Austin, Texas.

Beckett, Samuel. HRHRC "Whoroscope" MS, Harry Ransom Humanities Research Center, University of Texas, Austin, Texas, n.d.

Beckett, Samuel. TCD MS 10402, "Letters to Thomas MacGreevy," Trinity College Library Dublin, Republic of Ireland. Dublin, 1929 seq.

Beckett, Samuel. TCD MSS 10967, "Philosophy Notes" 1930s, Trinity College Library Dublin, Republic of Ireland.

Beckett, Samuel (1927). "Assumption." *transition* 16–17: 268–71.

Beckett, Samuel (1932), "Sedendo and Quiescendo." *transition* 21: 13–20.

Beckett, Samuel (1959). *Molloy, Malone Dies, The Unnamable*. London: John Calder.

Beckett, Samuel (1965). *Proust and Three Dialogues with Georges Duthuit*. London: Calder.

Beckett, Samuel (1970). *More Pricks Than Kicks*. London: Calder and Boyars.

Beckett, Samuel (1992). *Dream of Fair to middling Women*. Dublin: Black Cat.

Beckett, Samuel (1995). *Complete Short Prose, 1929–1989*, ed. S. E. Gontarski. New York: Grove Press.

Beckett, Samuel (2002). *Poems: 1930–1989*. London: John Calder.

Belmont, Georges (2001). *Souvenirs d'outre-monde*. Paris: Calmann-Lévy.

Cohn, Ruby (1962). *The Comic Gamut*. New Brunswick, NJ: Rutgers University Press.

Cohn, Ruby (2001). *A Beckett Canon*. Ann Arbor: The University of Michigan Press.

Gross, Katherine Travers (1970). "In Other Words: Samuel Beckett's Art of Poetry." Columbia University PhD thesis.

Jeffares, A. Norman (1968). *A Commentary on the Collected Poems of W. B. Yeats*. Stanford, CA: Stanford University Press.

Joyce, James. (1960). *Ulysses*. London: The Bodley Head.

Joyce, James (1964). *Finnegans Wake*. London: Faber & Faber.

Joyce, James (1987). *A Portrait of the Artist as a Young Man*. London: Collins.

Knowlson, James (1996). *Damned to Fame: The Life of Samuel Beckett*. London: Bloomsbury.

Pilling, John (1999). "Beckett and 'The Itch to Make': The Early Poems in English." *Samuel Beckett Today/Aujourd'hui* 8: 15–25.

Pilling, John (2004). *A Companion to Dream of Fair to Middling Women*. Tallahassee, FL: Journal of Beckett Studies Books 2004.

Pilling, John (2006). *A Samuel Beckett Chronology*. Basingstoke: Palgrave Macmillan.

Proust, Marcel (1929). *Le Temps retrouvé, oeuvres complètes*, Vol. 7, Part 1. Paris: NRF.

Yeats, W. B. (1927). *Autobiographies*. London and Basingstoke: Macmillan.

17

Figures of Script: The Development of Beckett's Short Prose and the "Aesthetic of Inaudibilities"

Dirk Van Hulle

"I know nothing about short story or any other aesthetics," Beckett wrote in a letter to Kay Boyle in May 1957 (Beckett 1991: 265). Still, the first literary texts Beckett published – apart from the critical writings "Dante...Bruno.Vico..Joyce" and "Proust" – were short stories, together with fragments from the novel *Dream of Fair to middling Women*. Gradually the notion of "fragment" seemed to become more appropriate to describe the short prose. Beckett often provided his (collections of) short pieces with titles that consciously stress their fragmentary nature, such as *Odds and Ends, Disjecta, Residua, From an Abandoned Work, Texts for Nothing* ... The focus also tends to shift from the story to its telling – *How the Story Was Told*. As S. E. Gontarski notes in the *Collected Short Prose 1928–1989* (Beckett 1995, hereafter *CSP*), "Beckett's short prose pieces not only outline his development as an artist, but suggest as well Beckett's own view of his art, that it is all part of a continuous process" (Gontarski 1995: xxix–xxx). That process includes the writing process – which will be taken into account as an integral part of Beckett's poetics. This essay on the development of the short prose investigates how the "continuous process" of Beckett's writings is driven by an "aesthetic of inaudibilities."

Starting Assumption: The 1920s and Early 1930s

The way Beckett insisted on his ignorance about writing short stories is as telling as the way the narrator in Herman Melville's story "Bartleby" denies any knowledge of his former employee: "I know nothing about him" (1986: 38–9). The opening lines of the fifth of Beckett's *Texts for Nothing* suggest an attitude that resembles Bartleby's job: "I'm the clerk, I'm the scribe, at the hearings of what cause I know not" (*CSP*: 117). After reading Beckett's short prose, a reader loses his innocence, and, with the advantage and disadvantage of hindsight, Bartleby's passive resistance becomes strangely "beckettian" – *avant la lettre*. Beckett's work has had a retroactive impact on the way we read Melville's writings now, with appreciation, as opposed to the incomprehension they met with during Melville's lifetime. In that retrospective sense the setting of "Bartleby" also shows "beckettian" elements. Apart from being located in Wall Street, the narrator's offices are surrounded by walls: "At one end they looked upon the white wall of the interior of a spacious sky-light shaft"; at the other end "my windows commanded an unobstructed view of a lofty brick wall, black by age and everlasting shade." In between, "the view might have been considered … deficient in what landscape painters call 'life'" (Melville 1986: 4–5). That is the landscape Clov enjoys in *Endgame* when he has "things to do" in his kitchen: "I look at the wall." Bartleby's life between the white and the black wall and his death in the Tombs, "strangely huddled at the base of the wall" (ibid.: 45), not only echo the embryonic posture of the lutemaker Belacqua in Dante's *Divina Commedia*, but also prefigure many of Beckett's protagonists, notably Belacqua "with his palpitations and adhesions and effusions and agenesia and wombtomb and *aesthetic of inaudibilities*" (Beckett 1993: 141; my emphasis). When the narrator tells Bartleby he "must quit this place" he assumes his scrivener will be relieved, but instead Bartleby's reply remains unaltered: "I would prefer not to." When the narrator insists – "You *must*" – he "*assumed* the ground that depart he must; and upon that assumption built all I had to say" (Melville 1986: 30).

The *assumption* upon which Beckett built perhaps not "all" but certainly much of what he had to say was the notion of impotence as expressed in the first sentence of his first story, "Assumption" (published in June 1929 in *transition*): "He could have shouted and could not" (*transition* 16–17; see also *CSP*: 3). This sentence already prefigures much of the ambiguity that marks Beckett's later works, but the story also tends to "melodramatize" the content, as John Pilling notes (Pilling 1997: 32). The *Sturm und Drang* that characterizes the protagonist's emotions oscillates between sound and silence. The unnamed protagonist is blessed or cursed with the "remarkable faculty of whispering the turmoil down" (*CSP*: 3). The turmoil is described as a "wild rebellious surge that aspired violently towards realization in sound" (4). The protagonist's attitude towards this "prisoner" is again quite ambiguous: he dreads lest it should escape and simultaneously longs that it might escape, until "the Woman" enters his life. From a Joycean perspective the story can be read as a rewriting of Stephen Dedalus's visit to the prostitute in *A Portrait of The Artist as a Young Man*, as suggested by P. J. Murphy, who interprets the title "Assumption" in terms of Beckett's "assumed identity as a Dedalus Redux" (Murphy 2009:43).

The style of Beckett's early prose generally reflects the protagonist's mental convolution, but contrasts sharply with the stylistic simplicity with which the woman's conduct is described: "She turned on the light and advanced carelessly into the room" (5). Whenever she leaves again, he feels as if "something of the desire to live" (6) has left him. After being "released, achieved" – a condition that is described in romantic and religious terms ("the blue flower, Vega, GOD"), he feels "one with the birdless cloudless colourless skies, in infinite fulfilment" (6–7).

The climax of the story is the *Sturm* of the finally released *Drang*: the pent-up cry bursts forth as "a great storm of sound" (7) and leaves the lifeless body of the protagonist in the arms of the Woman. Ruby Cohn's analysis summarizes the central dilemma as the impossibility "to serve woman *and* art. Or even self and art. Expression becomes a form of suicide" (Cohn 2001: 6). In this sense "Assumption" already foreshadows an important theme of *Krapp's Last Tape*, in which the protagonist's inability to serve both woman and art results in his "farewell to love." This was to remain a dilemma throughout Beckett's life, as is evidenced by a letter to Pamela Mitchell (March 30, 1968), written 10 years after he created *Krapp's Last Tape*, in which he mentions having considered another version of the play, this time with a protagonist who has preferred serving his girl instead of art.[1]

No matter how immature Beckett's early story with its many references to romanticism may seem, the impasse expressed by the opening sentence makes it a worthy first sentence of his published works of fiction and an adequate expression of their default situation.

The Impact of the "Dante Revelation": The 1930s

Beckett's story "Sedendo et Quiescendo," also published in *transition* (in March 1932), harks back to phrases from "Assumption." The line "one with the birdless cloudless colourless skies" reappears in the sonnet, written for Peggy Sinclair and incorporated in "Sedendo et Quiescendo," which in its turn was an extract from *Dream of Fair to middling Women* (Beckett 1993: 64–73). The volta is marked by the word "One" and the line recycled from "Assumption":

> One with the birdless colourless skies,
> One with the bright purity of the fire
> Of which we are and for which we must die
> A strange exalted death and be entire. (*CSP*: 14)

By forcing the turbulent emotions of his first story into the confines of a sonnet and thus employing formal constraints to separate its content from the rest of the story, Beckett creates a distancing effect, ironically exposing the bathos of his first story. The sonnet is said to be one of "the finest Night of May hiccupsobs that ever left a fox's paw," "inscribed" by the protagonist "to his darling blue flower," who is also referred to as "his sweet Vega" (13). Here, Vega and the romantic image of the blue flower are not applied to the state of bliss as in "Assumption," but to the woman who can bring it about – "what name shall we call her. What name would you suggest?" (*CSP*: 10).

This interruption by the narrator already foreshadows a more sustained metafictional move in the later prose. In answer to his rhetorical question to the reader, he immediately suggests, "I'm rather inclined myself to think / SMERALDINA-RIMA / and anything that comes in handy for short" (10). The protagonist is traveling by train to go and see her. That is the only action determining the "plot" of this fragment, ending with the arrival and the retreat into the lavatory, to reflect upon this "Beschissenes Dasein" (*CSP* 16).

The final focus on "Dasein" indicates Beckett's tendency to constantly stress the futility of human actions and existence in general, especially in combination with the adjective *beschissenes* (shitty). Beckett thus inscribes his prose in a long tradition of presenting writing as a form of defecation. The closest exponent of this tradition for Beckett was Joyce with his portrait of Shem the Penman as an artist who produces ink from his own excrements in Chapter 7 of "Work in Progress" (*Finnegans Wake* [Joyce 1939: 185.14–26]). This image was to become more explicit in Beckett's prose when he presented the "logorrhoea" (Beckett 1993: 14) and other compulsions to express as *Foirades* and *Fizzles* – "just as in *How It Is* the word and the fart have come to be equated," as James Knowlson and John Pilling note in *Frescoes of the Skull* (1979: 200).

The impact of Joyce's verbal "diarrhio" (1939: 467.19)[2] is undeniable in "Sedendo et Quiescendo," and even more so in the short "Text," published in the *New Review* (in April 1932). As *The Grove Companion* suggests, "The 'Joyce method' is as much exorcism as imitation" (Ackerley and Gontarski 2004: 287). Nonetheless, Beckett did learn the craft of writing from Joyce, which is reflected in his early habit of jotting down short odd phrases in a notebook. The *Dream* Notebook, edited by John Pilling (1999), contains jottings from source texts ranging from Robert Burton's *Anatomy of Melancholy* to Max Nordau's *Degeneration*. A remarkable source text is Pierre Garnier's *Onanisme seul et à deux sous toutes ses formes et leurs conséquences*. The extent to which this form of note-taking resembles Joyce's is especially striking with reference to note 442 (in Pilling's edition; corresponding to Garnier 1895: 31), where Beckett has marked the notions "Incubus satyriasis" and "Succubus nymphomania" respectively with T and Δ, the sigla which Joyce used in his notebooks to refer respectively to Tristan and to ALP. Apart from uncommon words such as "glabrosity," "clitoridian (exuberance)" or "confrication," which seem to be noted down mainly for their linguistic exoticism, some notes have more conceptual importance. For instance the notion of "involuntary seminal exoneration" recurs as "involuntary exonerations" in a letter to Thomas MacGreevy to describe two poems (Pilling 1999: 65).

One of the "involuntary exonerations" that thematize this poetical onanism is "Calvary by Night," a poem included in the story "A Wet Night," originally part of the novel *Dream of Fair to middling Women* (1993: 199–241), then recycled to become the fourth story in *More Pricks Than Kicks*. Here, the blue flower that had its origins in Novalis's *Heinrich von Ofterdingen* and denoted a longing for the sake of longing appears again. First it was on a par with Vega and God (in "Assumption"); then it was applied to Smeraldina-Rima (in "Sedendo et Quiescendo"); now it alludes to Leopold Bloom's masturbatory adventure in the "Nausicaa" episode of Joyce's *Ulysses*: "rocket of bloom flare flower ... blue bloom" (Beckett 1970: 57).

As S. E. Gontarski's invaluable "Bibliography of Short Prose in English" indicates, "The distinction between a discrete short story and a fragment of a novel is not always clear in Beckett's work" (*CSP*: 287). This certainly applies to a few stories in *More*

Pricks Than Kicks, such as "The Smeraldina's Billet-Doux" and "A Wet Night," with its rainy parody of the snow in Joyce's story "The Dead." Joyce's double chiasmus ("falling softly ... softly falling"; "falling faintly ... faintly falling") is more than merely parodied in Beckett's story ("It fell upon the bay ... and notably upon the Central Bog it fell"; Beckett 1970: 75); the chiastic structure gradually became an important element in Beckett's developing poetics as a stylistic equivalent of the emblem of the cross, linked to St Augustine's formulation of the predicament of the two thieves at the crucifixion of Christ ("Do not despair, one of the thieves was saved. Do not presume, one of the thieves was damned") and to an attitude of uncertainty and ambiguity that is central in Beckett's works. Rather than just a figure of speech, the chiasmus thus becomes a "figure of script" (Van Hulle 2008: 148) underpinning Beckett's writing method.

It is probably not a coincidence that *More Pricks Than Kicks* opens with the word Dante. The story "Dante and the Lobster" indicates the important role the Italian poet played not only in Beckett's life but also in that of his main character. The surname of the protagonist in the early stories is Shuah, referring to Genesis 38:2–4 ("And Judah saw there a daughter of a certain Canaanite, whose name was Shuah; and he took her, and went in unto her. And she conceived, and bare a son; and he called his name Er. And she conceived again, and bare a son; and she called his name Onan" [*King James Bible*]). Beckett came across this name in Garnier and had jotted down that Onan was one of the sons of Shuah. The protagonist's first name – "BELACQUA we'll call him" – is introduced in much the same way as Smeraldina-Rima in "Sedendo et Quiescendo." Again the *Dream* Notebook contains a wealth of background information to situate this protagonist in his intertextual context, but even then the references to Dante in this notebook pale in comparison with Beckett's much more extensive, earlier notes on the *Divina Commedia* preserved at Trinity College Dublin.

Dante is important in Beckett's developing poetics for several reasons, one of them being the issue of translation that was to become so important, especially after World War II. In the story "Dante and the Lobster" Belacqua refers to the line "Qui vive la pietà quand'è ben morta" (Dante 2002: canto 20 1.28) as a "great phrase." In his Dante notes Beckett summarized canto 4 of the *Inferno*, recounting how Dante and Virgil arrive at an abyss: Virgil invites Dante to follow him, but the guide's face has suddenly gone pale. Because Dante is a bit alarmed, Virgil explains that he is not pale because of fear but out of pity ["pietà"] for the unbaptized patriarchs and illustrious pagans in Limbo. Sixteen cantos further on, the "pietà" that made Virgil's face turn pale in Limbo is now "dead," for it is no longer appropriate to feel the same pity with regard to the soothsayers in the fourth Bolgia of *Inferno* as it is to the patriarchs and illustrious pagans in Limbo. In his Dante notes (TCD MS 10966/7r), Beckett comments that compassion is legitimate in Limbo, but not among the damned proper. Here another "pietà" – in the sense of "piety" – lives only when its homophonous counterpart is dead, since it would be impious to think that God shows passion in his judgment. As opposed to the translation "Here *piety* lives when *pity* is quite dead" the original is much more ambiguous in that the dead and the living "pietà" coincide. Because of this ambiguity it is also a "great phrase" in view of Beckett's developing poetics, since it reflects what Rosemary Pountney calls Beckett's tendency towards increasing ambiguity. When Belacqua asks his teacher how one could translate the great phrase, she eventually replies with a counter question: "Do you think it is absolutely necessary to translate it?" (1970: 17). The issue thus remains undecided and already prefigures the idea of proceeding "by aporia pure and simple" – as the Unnamable puts it, with a question mark.

The "Dante revelation," which Beckett mentioned to James Knowlson, occurred to him when he was 20 years old, without the help of his professors at Trinity College Dublin. This "revelation" may have been just as significant as the one that is said to have taken place shortly after World War II. Beckett's personal Virgil during this revelatory experience was his Italian teacher Bianca Esposito (Knowlson 1996: 715n.35), the model of Signorina Adriana Ottolenghi in "Dante and the Lobster." The way in which Dante's guide is "revealed" is a central element in Beckett's "Dante revelation," and a key to the "aesthetic of inaudibilities". In the first canto of *Inferno*, before Virgil's name is mentioned, a "figure" appears: "Before my eyes a figure showed, / Faint, in the wide silence." (Dante 2002: canto 1, lines 62–63). In his Dante notes (TCD MS 10966/1r), referred to the line "chi per lungo silenzio parea fioco", noting the paradoxical nature of the figure's faintness since Virgil had not yet spoken. In rhetorical terms, this may seem a rather trivial case of synesthesia. But the aural impression as a metaphor of a visual perception is more than just a figure of speech. Not unlike the chiasmus, this trope gradually became more significant to Beckett, especially after his reading of Max Nordau's *Degeneration* (see 1993). In the *Dream* notebook he took a few notes on "coenaesthesis" and the way "the organic dimly-conscious 'I'" (Nordau 1993: 249) relates to, or fails to relate to, the altruistic realm of the "Not-I." This mental state of intermingled sensory experiences (or "self-aesthesia," not dissimilar to the embryonic situation) finds its formal expression in the Dantean synesthesia, the stylistic figure of speech mixing different sensations, which thus becomes another "figure of script."

The synesthesia involved in the passage from Dante's *Divina Commedia* does not simply involve a mix of sensory experiences, it is also important that the appearance of Virgil is not marked by loud exuberance or radiant luminosity, but rather by faintness. The dimly-conscious mental figure becomes a figure of speech, but initially it is rather a figure of speechlessness or inaudibility. "Don't be so beastly inaudible," Belacqua says to Doyle in the unpublished story "Echo's Bones" (Beckett HRC 24), and the same inaudibility also applies to the first character he meets in this story. Belacqua feels he has been dead for at least 40 days when a woman shoots out of the hedge and presents herself as Zaborovna. Belacqua does not hear what she says and asks her to speak up. The scene with Zaborovna accords with what Belacqua calls his "aesthetic of inaudibilities" in *Dream of Fair to middling Women*. Not unlike Virgil in the first canto of *Inferno* she appears as an inaudibility. Throughout Beckett's works the appearance of Virgil "per lungo silenzio (…) fioco" is a primal scene, representing the attempt to give shape to recollections. Every creation by Beckett somehow examines the problem of its own creation. In this respect "Echo's Bones," written in October 1933 and originally intended as an extra story in *More Pricks Than Kicks*, is

an important document. After being ravished by Zaborovna, Belacqua appears again
in the "familiar attitude" – that is, the embryonic posture – when he receives a crack
on the coccyx from a golf ball, hit by Lord Gall of Wormwood. The Lord is described
as an "aspermatic colossus" with a thousand golf balls to compensate for his impotence. The golf balls may be read as a reference to Benjy in the first chapter of William
Faulkner's *The Sound and the Fury* (1929), the castrated "idiot" who spends most of
his time looking for (golf) balls. Analogous with the ruin of *The Sound and the Fury*'s
Compson family, Lord Gall's Wormwood will be doomed unless a male heir is produced. That is why he enlists the help of Belacqua, "green as Circe's honey" (a reference
based on Beckett's notes on Victor Bérard's translation of the *Odyssey*): Lord Gall
invites him to go in unto his lady Moll, and Belacqua obliges. The adjective "clitoridian" to describe her "croon" shows that, in 1933, Beckett was still drawing on his
verbal booty, notably the excerpts from Garnier. The sexual performances that are
expected from Belacqua fail to yield the results that are hoped for. While Lord Gall
is counting his golf balls and hoping for a male descendant, the foreman comes to
tell him that the child is "essentially" a girl. The scene concludes with words to the
effect that this is how it goes in the world. These words are repeated at the very end
of the story, when Belacqua, like Echo in Ovid's *Metamorphoses*, first turns into voice
and bones, until the bones turn into stone and only voice remains. This voice is rhetorically quite skilled, so that twice Lord Gall has to urge him to cut out the style.
That is what Beckett – by his own account – tried to achieve by starting to write
in French.

"Cut Out the Style": The 1940s

Apart from the prewar French poetry, the first short prose in French is the story "La
Fin," published partially in *Les Temps Modernes* as "Suite." But although this is Beck-
ett's first publication after the war, he did not suddenly decide to write a story in
French. As Ruby Cohn points out, the manuscripts nuance the traditional view of
Beckett's decision to become a French writer. On February 7, 1946, he started writing
a story in English, opening with the line: "They dressed me and gave me money."[3]
He worked on it for more than a month, and on March 13, on page 28 of his notebook, he stopped, drew a line, and rewrote the passage about the protagonist's tutor,
who gave him his dark glasses and *The Ethics* by Arnold Geulincx. The seventeenth-
century Flemish philosopher's occasionalist philosophy had already inspired Beckett
while he was writing *Murphy* in 1936. Regarding the problem of the dualism between
mind and matter Geulincx had suggested that there is no causal interaction between
the two, but that a change in either one of them occasions God to intervene and bring
about a change in the other. Man may think he has a free will, but in that respect he
is, according to Geulincx, comparable to the baby, deluding itself that by crying it
can make the cradle rock, whereas it is simply on occasion of the crying that his
mother's hand rocks the cradle. Against this occasionalist background it is interesting

that Ruby Cohn presents the death of the tutor in "La Fin" as "the occasion of Beckett's birth as a major French writer." However the attributes he bequeaths to his pupil indicate a continuation ("Suite") of, rather than an end ("La Fin") to, the prewar English writing. The dark glasses – his interest in the notion of pessimism, his reading of Schopenhauer, Mauthner, Geulincx, Proust ... – keep coloring his writing, and the major consequence of the Geulincxian view on the dualism of mind and matter, is that the mind is limited to knowledge of itself.

A more sudden postwar change in Beckett's work is the shift from a third- to a first-person narrator. According to Max Nordau, the conscious "I" gradually develops from the dimly conscious state of coenaesthesis and usually withdraws behind the "Not-I" as it learns more about the external world. If this latter process is unsuccessful, however, the "I" tends to revert to itself. After the turbulent years of the war and a period of involvement in the big world (for example, in the Résistance), Beckett seems to have focused even more resolutely on the "little world" of the "I" and the "degeneration" this entailed, according to Nordau, implying that the adult "remains a child" (1993: 254). In "The End" the narrator–protagonist describes the dark glasses accordingly: "They were a man's glasses, I was a child" (*CSP*: 91). Only in drops does the big world seep into the narrator's little world when he is begging at his sunny corner and hears snatches of the "discourse" of a man perched on the roof of a car: "Union ... brothers ... Marx ... capital ... bread and butter ... love" (94). While the Marxist orator urges the passers-by not to give alms, since charity would be an endorsement of the system, the text's mild allusion to the Marx Brothers is a comment in itself.

The "cloudless sky" that was already mentioned in "Assumption" and "Sedendo et Quiescendo" is linked to an arch-scene, which recurs in Beckett's later works: a young boy's question relating to the sky and his mother's "cutting retort" (as it is later called in *Company*); in "The End" her words are quoted directly: "Fuck off" (*CSP*: 81). Ruby Cohn laconically summarizes the plot of the story: "expelled from his room, the protagonist seeks a substitute home and eventually finds it in a kind of suicide at sea," but she immediately adds that "the imposition of linearity would render most of the story digressive" (Cohn 2001: 131). Apart from the suicidal aspect, her summary can serve as a rather universal basic plot of human existence, expelled to start with and moribund by definition: "I knew it would soon be the end, so I played the part, you know, the part of – how shall I say, I don't know" (*CSP*: 96). It is remarkable how the interjection "comment dire" ("how shall I say"/"what is the word") in this first postwar story called "The End" already prefigures the end of Beckett's oeuvre – *what is the word* – concluding in incompleteness. The bareness of this rudimentary plot turns the digression into the *condition humaine* – life as a form of beating about the bush.

That is precisely how the working title of Beckett's next work (in an early stage of the writing process) describes the journey of its protagonists: *Voyage de Mercier et Camier autour du pot* (...). While he was writing *Mercier et Camier*, Beckett was concerned about the publication of "La Fin." When he finished it in May 1946, he had written to George Reavey that he hoped he could have the complete story published as a separate work. Jacoba van Velde managed to have the first part published in *Les Temps Modernes*, but when Simone de Beauvoir decided not to publish the second part, Beckett wrote the draft of a rather passionate letter in defense of his "creature," as he significantly calls it in the final version of the letter: "Je ne vous demande pas de revenir sur ce que vous avez décidé. Mais il m'est décidément impossible de me dérober au devoir que je me sens vis-à-vis d'*une créature* ... Vous immobilisez une existence au seuil de sa solution" (Beckett in Lake 1984: 82; emphasis added).

The way Beckett describes his work, as a creature with an existence, resembles the way Malone talks about his "little creature" as a Faustian "homunculus," that is, an artificial but living result of literary alchemy in a long tradition that links putrefaction to creation (Van Hulle 2008: 171). The conception, creation, and "birth" of such a creature is a major theme in Beckett's postwar prose, as well as in his radio plays. The story "L'Expulsé" opens with the protagonist's expulsion from a house, by the anonymous "them," after which the door is slammed shut. If this expulsion can be read as a form of birth (comparable to Mouth's opening word "out" in *Not I*, a substitution for the original opening word "birth"), the expelled's efforts to re-enact this traumatic expulsion toward the end of the story – this time of his own accord – seem to parody Otto Rank's *Trauma of Birth*, which Beckett had read before the war. Because he cannot open the door of the stable, he has to leave by the window, head first and afterwards he remembers the tufts of grass on which he pulled in his effort to extricate himself (*CSP*: 59). The link with literary creation is subtly suggested by means of the allusion to Wordsworth's description of literary composition in his Preface to the *Lyrical Ballads*, combined again with the idea of the circular journey "autour du pot": "Recollecting these emotions, with the celebrated advantage of tranquillity, it seems to me he did nothing else, all that day, but turn about his lodging" (*CSP*: 58).

The story ends with a metafictional twist: the first-person narrator claims he does not know why he told this story; he could just as well have told another (60). That is what Beckett did. From July 5 to October 3 he had been working on *Mercier et Camier* in his notebooks, and three days later he already started writing "L'Expulsé," which he finished in little more than a week's time, on October 14. Two weeks later he started telling yet another, *Premier Amour*. Here, the starting point is the graveyard, with which the narrator has "no bone to pick." From the death of his father he switches rapidly to the date of his own birth. Later on, the same rapid switch from the end to the beginning is repeated when his own child is born and he thinks of what it must have been going through: "What finished me was the birth" (44–5).

Again, the protagonist is subject to "eviction" when his father dies. His passive subjection to the anonymous "them" is stressed a few pages further on when, after his "eviction," he is "at the mercy of an erection" (31). Beckett erects this "rigid phallus" as a *"trait de désunion"*[4] between the self and the "execrable frippery known as the non-self" or "the world, for short" (31). Towards the end the protagonist re-enacts his eviction or expulsion by working his way out through the mass of junk that bars the door, pursued by the cries: *"They* pursued me down the stairs and out into the street"

(45; emphasis added). Here, the story suggests that "they" – whenever they are mentioned – are not necessarily anonymous characters but, rather, abstract, existential cries. "For years I thought they would cease", the story concludes: "Now I don't think so anymore" (45). Forty years later, in *Stirrings Still*, the cries can still be heard, and they do not cease. (Beckett 2009: 113).

The cries at the end of *First Love* gradually grow fainter, "but what does it matter, faint or loud, cry is cry" (45). Whenever the word "faint" occurs in Beckett's works it subtly echoes Dante's description of Virgil's appearance, "per lungo silenzio ... fioco." In Beckett's next story, "The Calmative," which he started writing two days before Christmas of that extremely creative year 1946, the protagonist finds himself facing a young boy and resolves to speak to him, but the strange rattle he utters is unintelligible, even to himself. It is described as "mere speechlessness due to long silence, as in the wood that darkens the mouth of hell" (*CSP*: 66) As a reverberation of the opening sentence of "Assumption" – "I could have shouted and could not" – this impasse also prefigures the first of the *Textes pour rien*: "Suddenly, no, at last, long last, I couldn't anymore, I couldn't go on" (*CSP*: 100).

"What Matter Who's Speaking": The 1950s

After the extremely productive period of writing in the second half of the 1940s, Beckett abandoned the technique of the quest structure, notably in his *Textes pour rien* and subsequent fragments, such as "Au bout de ces années perdues," "Hourah je me suis repris," "On le tortura bien," "Ici, personne ne vient jamais," "Coups de gong". These texts reflect what Porter Abbott has called Beckett's first deployment of an "aesthetic of recommencement" (Abbott 1996: 93). With its reverberation of the opening sentence of "Assumption," the first of the *Texts for Nothing* formally presents itself as a recommencement. What is new in these *Texts* is the way Beckett chooses to make language "perform" a decomposition, in both a musical and a theatrical sense. The silent measure, or *mesure pour rien*, to which the title refers, represents – unlike Joyce's hybrid chaosmos – a zone between the chaotic tuning preceding it and the organized composition it announces, the "decomposition" that is neither chaos nor cosmos. What the *Texts for Nothing* express, according to Beckett in a letter to Barney Rosset (February 11, 1954), is "the failure to implement the last words of *L'Innommable*" (in Gontarski 1995: xiv). At that moment these last words (in the first Minuit editions) were not yet the famous, paradoxical line "I can't go on, I'll go on," but a less problematic "il faut continuer, je vais continuer." When the French ending was changed into "il faut continuer, je ne peux pas continuer, je vais continuer" in the beginning of the 1970s, this crucial variant was only the confirmation of a turn Beckett's prose had already taken in the beginning of the 1950s. Instead of the journeys and quests of the earlier prose, the *Texts for Nothing* radically focus on the impasse: "I couldn't stay there and I couldn't go on ... I could have stayed ... I couldn't" (*CSP*: 100). On the first page of the "Texts" Beckett introduces the crucial word "neither," which – as he later told Morton Feldman – was to become the central theme of his work: "I need nothing, neither to go on nor to stay where I am" (100). Since there is no more need for a composition, the text can fully concentrate on the complex process of decomposition, for – as Molloy recognizes – "to decompose is to live too, I know, I know, don't torment me, but one sometimes forgets" (Beckett 1955–8: 25).

Here the so-called Dante revelation is fully realized: what appears to Dante is a set of words, barely audible. Only later do these words become "Virgil." The inaudibility before the full appearance (comparable to the opening murmurs in *Not I*) corresponds with the "lungo silenzio" just before the start of the composition: this is the enclosed space of time, the *mesure pour rien* in which Beckett tries to work from now on. He is not so much interested in "successful composition," as Wordsworth called it, but in the tranquility that precedes it, as "Text 6" suggests: "what tranquillity, and know there are no more emotions in store" (*CSP*: 125). What Beckett "stages" in his *Textes pour rien* is the moment Edgar Allan Poe – in his "Philosophy of Composition" – dismissed as irrelevant, that is, "the necessity – which, in the first place, gave rise to the intention of composing a poem" (Poe 1986: 482). Otto Rank would probably see this focus on the "not yet" before the composition as a sublimation of the trauma of birth, but the distance Beckett kept from his readings on psychology suggests more intricacy in coming to terms with decomposition: "Oh I know I too shall cease and be as when I was not yet, only all over instead of in store" (*CSP*: 160).

When Beckett suggested a staging of one of the "Texts" to Joseph Chaikin in 1980, "the idea was to caricature the labour of composition" (Beckett qtd. in Gontarski 1995: xvi). S. E. Gontarski argues that what this suggested staging caricatures is "the Romantic notion of creativity, the artist's agonized communion with his own pure, uncorrupted, inner being, consciousness, or imagination" (ibid.: xvii). At the same time this also indicates how deeply Beckett's work is affected by his efforts to come to terms with this romantic notion of creativity. The staging indicates the complexity of his efforts: the notion of the "author (A)" is problematized in that he can simultaneously be seen as Audience – as Stan Gontarski suggested. Moreover, A is also an Actor, reacting to what "voice (V)" prompts: "Prompt not always successful, i.e., not regular alternation VAVA. Sometimes: Silence, V, silence, V again, A. Or even three prompts before A can speak" (ibid.: xvi).

This complex view of creation suggests that the phrase of Beckett's from "Text 3" quoted by Michel Foucault in his lecture "What is an Author?" – "What matter who's speaking, someone said, what matter who's speaking" (*CSP*: 109) – expresses more than merely indifference.[5] The voices prompting the author in *Texts for Nothing* were not a matter of indifference to Beckett but one of continuous investigation and re-examination. If the self is the object of investigation, the question is who is examining it: "who says this, saying it's me? … It's the same old stranger as ever, for whom alone accusative I exist" (*CSP*: 114). The reference to the accusative case is also an accusation, since every human being is an accused if "to be is to be guilty" (*CSP*: 117). The voices of the dead, associated with the "murmuring" of the leaves in *Waiting for Godot* (Beckett 1990: 58) recur in the last *Text for Nothing*: "there is nothing but a voice murmuring a trace. A trace, it wants to leave a trace, yes, like air leaves among the leaves" (*CSP*: 152).

The homograph "leaves," signifying both the verb and the objects, is a nice example of the way these "Texts" "perform" their content. The trace ("like air leaves among the leaves") marks the nominalist irony of applying the same label to different things. While Beckett's prose increasingly focuses on the "neither" between going and staying, the problematized notion of the author crystallizes in homophones and homographs. Not unlike Beckett's definition of the individual as a succession of individuals in his early essay on Proust, the authorial or initiating agent never simply coincides with itself. Any attempt to fix it on paper is doomed to fail. Whereas homographs (such as the word "pietà" in "Dante and the Lobster" or the "leaves" and "leaves" in *Texts for Nothing*) stress the deceiving idea of identity, homophones (such as I/eye, seen/ scene, know/no, quite/quiet, horse/hoarse [*CSP*: 159]) emphasize the non-coincidence and the illusion of being able to capture a phenomenon by giving it a name: what looks like a still usually turns out to be still stirring. The need neither to go nor to stay (*CSP*: 100) is not simply stasis, but an uncomfortable situation, which Beckett referred to as the fidgets. *From an Abandoned Work*, for instance, mentions "those awful fidgets I have always had" (*CSP*: 162). In the 1930s, in a review of Rilke's *Poems*, Beckett wrote he did not understand why these fidgets are sometimes elevated to a divine status: "But why call the fidgets God, Ego, Orpheus and the rest? This is a childishness to which German writers seem specially prone" (Beckett 1984a: 67; Nixon 2005: 150). Beckett's skepticism also indicates his awareness of the affinity between the fidgets and the "obligation to express." The sheer restlessness without purpose of those literary fidgets is expressed in *From an Abandoned Work*: "I have never in my life been on my way anywhere, but simply on my way" (*CSP*: 156).

"Closed Space": The 1960s

Although the *Texts for Nothing* already indicate the break with the journeys that structured most of Beckett's prose up until the trilogy, the real departure from this departure-and-return structure had to be a "false start." "Faux départs," published in *Kursbuch* 1 (June 1965), prefigure what is usually referred to as the "Close space" pieces. They can be considered the direct "incipit" of "All Strange Away" (1964) and "Imagination morte imaginez"/"Imagination Dead Imagine." The closed space of "All Strange Away" is defined by bare walls, whose dimensions diminish as memory gradually deteriorates. The third of the "Faux départs" opens with the words "Le vieux je est revenu" (*CSP*: 272). The idea of a self imagining itself is further complicated by means of a mirror-in-the-mirror effect: "a self imagining itself imagining itself, often suspecting that it, too, is being imagined" (Ackerley and Gontarski 2004: 438–9). The "Faux départs" are some of the remains of an abandoned work that was to be called "Fancy Dying." In combination with the recurrent phrase "Fancy dead" (*CSP*: 171ff.), this tentative title crystallizes the ambiguity of "Imagination Dead Imagine," indicating the paradox of imagining the death of imagination. If the "closed space" is read as "the issueless predicament of existence" (Beckett 1984a: 97), death could be regarded as a way out of this state of being trapped in the body. The closed space is "tightened" round the figure it contains, which can be read as an echo of Joyce's reference in "The Dead" to the monks sleeping in their coffins. If it is at all possible to imagine that imagination is dead, fancy might be an alternative: "Fancy is his only hope" (*CSP*: 170). The combination of fancy and imagination confronts these closed spaces with the problematic issue of romantic poetics. Imagination was considered to be the superior, creative, and organic mental faculty according to Coleridge's *Biographia Literaria*, whereas fancy was a more mechanistic principle, an "aggregative and associative power" that can merely reproduce and recombine (1983: 1.293). "All Strange Away" seems to be conceived as a (de)composition that goes *diminuendo* from "Imagination dead" (the first words) to "fancy dead" (the last words). Similarly "All Strange Away" starts off by gradually eliminating all originally imagined elements ("no stool, no sitting, no kneeling, no lying, just room to stand and revolve" [*CSP*: 171]) and tightening the space. But no matter how hard the narrator tries to imagine imagination and fancy dead, they keep entering the room like the cat and the dog in *Film*: "*Imagine* him kissing, caressing, licking, sucking, fucking and buggering all this stuff" (171; my emphasis), and the same from a more passive perspective: "*Fancy* her being all kissed, licked, sucked, fucked and so on by all that" (172; my emphasis). Thus, the intent of undoing is counteracted and the intended effect is eventually even undone when the abstraction is suddenly broken by the introduction of a strikingly concrete "small grey punctured rubber ball" (178), described in all its particulars. If the aim was to imagine a situation in which imagination is dead, the attempt seems to be doomed to fail.

In combination with the images of Emma and Emmo projected onto the walls, recalling the Golo scene on the opening pages of Proust's *À la recherche du temps perdu*, the thematization of fancy and imagination in the closed space is a powerful metaphor of our limited mental capacities. The figure of Golo with his "robe rouge"[6] is only a projection by a "lanterne magique," a metaphor suggested by Schopenhauer to illustrate the inadequacy of our sensory perception. In a chapter "On the Essential Imperfections of the Intellect," Schopenhauer argues that "our thinking consciousness is like a magic lantern, in the focus of which only one picture can appear at a time; and every picture, even when it depicts the noblest thing, must nevertheless soon vanish to make way for the most different and even most vulgar thing" (1969: 2:138). In "All Strange Away" imagination works in a similar way: a red image is imagined and immediately replaced by a grey one: "No real image but say like red no grey say like something grey" (*CSP*: 178).

The idea of "failed attempts" that was explicit in the title "Faux départs" remains inherent in all the closed space texts, also in "Ping": here, the notion of trial and error becomes even more explicit in the 10 versions, published in *Cahier de l'Herne*. The series of drafts only seemingly comes to a close thanks to the fixating effect of the

English translation, which retroactively turns the tenth French version into a "texte définitif" (Beckett 1976: 24–43). While these "closed space" texts seem to frustrate "what was originally a plan to prove that imagination is dead and gone" (Davies 1994: 146), and thus may be regarded as the proof of its underlying power, they also indicate the limitations of our imagination as it proves to be impossible to think anything beyond the representation we make of it, according to the opening sentence of Schopenhauer's *magnum opus*: "The world is my representation." This situation simultaneously recalls Geulincx's view that the mind is limited to knowledge of itself.

The limitations of our mental capacities are powerfully captured in the word "issueless," which recurs frequently in the experimental text "Lessness" ("Sans"), consisting of 60 sentences, presented "first in one disorder, then in another," according to Beckett's blurb (qtd in Cohn 2001: 305). Rosemary Pountney has analyzed the structure of this text and shown how it suggests its own endless rearrangement. The $2 \times 60 = 120$ sentences are organized into 24 paragraphs according to a rigid system. First Beckett wrote six groups of 10 sentences. He subsequently mixed the separate sentences in a container and picked them out in random order twice. Yale University Library holds Beckett's own "key" to this text, explaining that *Lessness* is "composed of 6 statement groups each containing 10 sentences, i.e. 60 sentences in all. These 60 are first given in a certain order and paragraph structure, then repeated in a different order and different paragraph structure. The whole consists therefore of $2 \times 60 = 120$ sentences arranged and rearranged in $2 \times 12 = 24$ paragraphs."[7] The analogy with human conventions to systematize time, forcing it into a grid of seconds, minutes, and hours, is even more rigidly applied by means of the organization of the paragraphs: Beckett wrote the numbers 3, 5, 7 on two pieces of paper each, and the numbers 4 and 6 on three pieces of paper each, which were picked at random (twice). The arrangement of paragraphs of minimum 3 and maximum 7 sentences was thus determined by chance, and could be repeated endlessly, resulting in ever new arrangements. But the "endlessness" that occurs so frequently in the text and seems to have been the basis for the title of the English translation, is at the same time a terrible limitation, because the endless repetition of "the nothing new" is also "issueless." The suffix -ness that marks a difference between the English translation and the French original can be read as another instance of nominalist irony: on the one hand the idea of doing without ("Sans") is turned into an abstraction by means of the suffix "-ness"; on the other hand this all too human tendency (and all too easy linguistic trick) to turn particulars into universals by simply adding a suffix, is undermined by the first syllable "less-," so that the combination can be interpreted as a nominalist plea for fewer universals. Form and content are inseparable in this remarkable text; the endlessness is reflected in the text's lemniscate structure since the repetition of the same 60 sentences creates the textual equivalent of an infinity sign. The motif of the bicycle, which was so prominent in Beckett's earlier works, thus proves to be present in the later texts as well, albeit in a more abstract form.

"By Way of Neither": The 1970s and 1980s

The "closed space" idea continued to play an important role in Beckett's short prose of the 1970s, not only in *Le Dépeupleur / The Lost Ones*, but also in the *Foirades / Fizzles*. The most obvious instance is the *Foirade* "Se voir," opening with the words "Endroit clos," which Beckett first translated as "Closed space" and then replaced by "Closed place" (UoR MS 1550/19). Some of the *Fizzles* suggest a carnal closed space: "I'll be inside, he'll rot, I won't rot, there will be nothing of him left but bones, I'll be inside" (*CSP*: 234). Again, "Echo's Bones" reverberate here, recalling Echo's metamorphosis into voice and bones.

The *Fizzles* mark a shift of focus. While the first postwar texts were characterized by journeys and the paradoxical situation of going on in spite of the inability to do so, the late short prose tries to capture stillness, which turns out to be equally impossible, again because of the limitations of the human mind. *Fizzle 7* ("Still") fully exploits the power of homographs and homophony to express the paradox of expressing stillness with a brain that is never still, only "quite quiet" at best (*CSP*: 241). Even the ambiguous title "Still" is still much too vibrant to express stillness.

If the closed space is regarded as the enclosure between womb and tomb, the most suitable word to express the in-between situation is *neither*, the title of Beckett's only opera libretto (written for the minimalist composer Morton Feldman). From a narrative point of view *neither* also expresses the awareness that the volatility of existence cannot be captured, neither in English nor in French. In this sense Beckett's decision to write in two languages enabled him to create an intermediary zone, a no man's land in which the meanings of words can shift and the complexity of linguistic ambiguity can be fully appreciated.

Neither also expresses a situation of constantly being under way, being neither here nor there. In his short text "The Way," published in *College Literature*, Beckett links this idea to the old bicycle structure of the infinity sign: "The way wound up from foot to top and thence on down another way. On back down. The ways crossed midway more and less" (Beckett 2009: 125). The text further specifies that "the one way back was on and on was always back" (125). In one way the text can be read as a rather realistic description of two walks (not unlike the Swann and the Guermantes way in Proust's *À la recherche du temps perdu*); at the same time it can be regarded as a translation of a philosophical image, suggested by Heraclitus' aphorism that the 'way up' (earth – water – fire) and the way down (fire – water – earth) are one and the same, which Beckett noted down several decades earlier in his philosophy notes (TCD MS 10967/26v).

Not only the very early philosophy notes, but also the even earlier notes on Dante still played a role in the last decade of Beckett's career. In these notes (TCD MS 10963, f. 3r) the appearance of Virgil is explained in terms of Reason, which had been dormant and dumb in Dante for such a long time that it seemed faint from long silence. This transition from a mental image to a faint voice thus stands for a "coming

to," as it is called in "Ceiling" (1981 [Beckett 1985]). This short text is a confrontation with the whiteness of the ceiling, which is transposed to the blankness of the
page: "On coming to the first sight is of white" (Beckett 2009: 129). The starting
point is a "preverbal" state (Cohn 2001: 371) that resembles Max Nordau's dimly
conscious state of "coenaesthesis": "Dim consciousness first alone. Of mind alone.
Alone come to. Partly to" (130). The next effort to do anything beyond "partly"
opening the eyes is blocked: "Further one cannot." But this impasse is immediately
followed by the word: "On." The next section ends with "Further one – / On." And
the final words ("Further – / On") show how the decomposition of "Further one
cannot" eventually leads to a form of continuing nonetheless, and to the opening
and closing word of *Worstward Ho*.

Consciousness – however dim – is an important theme in the late texts. Not unlike
the setting of *Endgame* ("*Bare interior. Grey light. Left and right back, high up, two small
windows*" [Beckett 1990: 92]), the setting of *Stirrings Still* suggests the interior of a
skull, this time combined with the fear of mental *Umnachtung*: "This outer light then
when his own went out became his only light till it in its turn went out and left him
in the dark. Till it in its turn went out" (Beckett 2009: 107). In the opening lines of
the second section the protagonist begins to wonder if he is still "in his right mind,"
which in a way is a comforting thought in and of itself: "For could one not in his right
mind be reasonably said to wonder if he was in his right mind and bring what is more
his remains of reason to bear on this perplexity …?" (Beckett 2009: 111). Unlike the
bare interior of *Endgame*, however, the opening setting of *Stirrings Still* mentions only
one window, which suggests Proust's idea of a "chambre obscure," the setting of the
painter Elstir's studio with only one window. In this artistic "camera obscura" the
painter tries to capture outside reality. But if one tries to capture the *inside* reality of
the camera obscura itself, this turns out to be an impossibility because of consciousness's annoying property of always being conscious of itself. Not unlike O and E in
Film, consiousness is always being chased by self-consciousness. As a consequence the
interior of the skull is never quite still. The manuscripts give evidence of these stirrings. As Theodor Adorno noted, Beckett's work is not so much characterized by
abstraction but by subtraction (Adorno 1994: 73). Even towards the end the urge to
tell is expressed in a humorous way by presenting the textual production in terms of
relieving oneself: the protagonist may be improbable, but not so improbable as not to
must needs relieve himself once in a while. To this purpose one of the few items in
his bare room is a small heart-shaped plastic pot (UoR MS 2935/1/2). The writing
then proceeded by subtracting this material object and several others from the initial
drafts. In the third section of *Stirrings Still* the protagonist hears a sentence "from deep
within" but he cannot catch the crucial word that will give him a decisive answer as
to what it must be like to end: "oh how *and here a word he could not catch* it were to end
where never till then" (Beckett 2009: 114, emphasis added). The nature of the missing
adjective ("*sad*" or "*bad*," for example, or the reverse) will determine whether it is better
to stay alive, or rather "stir no more." But the "missing word" is too "faint" (114).
After tracing the impact of Beckett's Dante revelation in his short prose, it does no

longer come as a surprise that this late text contains a reference to the "fioco" phrase, as the manuscripts indicate (UoR MS 2934, 9v).

In his next and last work, Beckett went one final step further: he presented the published version as a kind of draft, with the interruption "comment dire" as its title: *Comment dire / what is the word*. He chose to end the way he started, in an impasse, in search of the missing word. As in *A la recherche du temps perdu*, the search (rather than its object) gradually became a subject in and of itself, and not unlike Proust, Beckett could have continued writing without end. But in order to do so he paradoxically needed an end to write towards. And to that end, the missing word's most crucial quality was its inaudibility.

NOTES

1 With many thanks to Mark Nixon for drawing my attention to this letter.
2 This is part of Joyce's response to Wyndham Lewis's criticism in *Time and Western Man*, describing *Ulysses* as a "stupendous outpouring of *matter*," "like a record diarrhoea" (108–9).
3 When Richard Seaver translated the story, the first sentence read the same as the first sentence of the original English: "They dressed me and gave me money." Beckett changed the verb into "clothed" as one of his additions on the typescript preserved in the Richard Seaver collection at the Harry Ransom Center.
4 This is the term Beckett employs in his manuscripts of *Comment dire* to describe the hyphens interrupting the text (UoR MS 3316, f. 2v).
5 "Beckett nicely formulates the theme with which I would like to begin: '"What does it matter who is speaking," someone said, "what

does it matter who is speaking.'" In this indifference appears one of the fundamental ethical principles of contemporary writing [*écriture*]" (Foucault 1979: 141–60).
6 "Le corps de Golo lui-même, d'une essence aussi surnaturelle que celui de sa monture, s'arrangeait de tout obstacle matériel, de tout objet gênant qu'il rencontrait en le prenant comme ossature et en se le rendant intérieur, fût-ce le bouton de la porte sur lequel s'adaptait aussitôt et surnageait invinciblement sa robe rouge ou sa figure pâle toujours aussi noble et aussi mélancolique, mais qui ne laissait paraître aucun trouble de cette transvertébration." (Proust 1987–9: 1.10).
7 For a detailed discussion of this text's structuring patterns, see Pountney (1988), which includes a montage of the six thematic "families" in appendix.

REFERENCES AND FURTHER READING

Abbott, H. Porter (1996). *Beckett Writing Beckett: The Author in the Autograph*. Ithaca and London: Cornell University Press.
Ackerley, C. J. and S. E. Gontarski (2004). *The Grove Companion to Samuel Beckett*. New York: Grove Press.
Adorno, Theodor (1994). "Skizze einer Interpretation des 'Namenlosen,'" In Rolf Tiedemann

(ed.), "'Gegen den Trug der Frage nach dem Sinn': Eine Dokumentation zu Adornos Beckett-Lektüre." *Frankfurter Adorno Blätter III*. Munich: edition text+kritik.
Beckett, Samuel HRC "Echo's Bones" typescript. A. J. Leventhal, Box 1, Folder 1. Harry Ransom Humanities Research Center, University of Texas at Austin.

Beckett, Samuel HRC Lake, Box 17, Folder 1. Harry Ransom Humanities Research Center, University of Texas at Austin.

Beckett, Samuel TCD MS 10963, 10966, Dante notes, Manuscripts Department, Trinity College Library Dublin, Republic of Ireland.

Beckett, Samuel TCD MS 10967, Philosophy notes, Manuscripts Department, Trinity College Library Dublin, Republic of Ireland.

Beckett, Samuel. UoR MS 2934–2935, *Stirrings Still* manuscripts, Beckett International Foundation Archives, University of Reading.

Beckett, Samuel UoR MS 3316, "Comment dire" manuscripts, Beckett International Foundation Archives, University of Reading.

Beckett, Samuel (1929). "Assumption." *transition* 16–17 (June): 268–71. Included in *The Collected Short Prose*, pp. 3–7.

Beckett, Samuel (1932a). "Sedendo et Quiescendo." *transition* 21 (March): 13–20. Included in *The Collected Short Prose*, pp. 8–16.

Beckett, Samuel (1955–8). *Molloy, Malone Dies, The Unnamable*. New York: Grove Press.

Beckett, Samuel (1970). *More Pricks Than Kicks*. London: Calder & Boyars.

Beckett, Samuel (1976). "Bing / Ping." In *Beckett: Cahier de l'Herne*. Paris: Editions de l'Herne. 24–43.

Beckett, Samuel (1981a). *Watt*. London: John Calder.

Beckett, Samuel (1981b). "Crisscross to Infinity." *College Literature* 8 (3): 311.

Beckett, Samuel (1984a). *Disjecta*, ed. Ruby Cohn. New York: Grove Press.

Beckett, Samuel (1984b). *The Way. No Symbols Where None Intended: A Catalogue of Books, Manuscripts and Other Material Relating to Samuel Beckett in the Collections of the Humanities Research Center*, ed. Carlton Lake. Austin, TX: Humanities Research Center / The University of Texas at Austin: 173. (Originally published in *College Literature* 8, nr. 3 [1981].)

Beckett, Samuel (1985). "Ceiling." In *Arikha*. London: Thames and Hudson.

Beckett, Samuel (1990). *The Complete Dramatic Works*. London: Faber and Faber.

Beckett, Samuel (1991). Letter to Kay Boyle. In "No Allegory Where None Intended: Beckett and Boyle on Joyce." *Joyce Studies Annual*.

Beckett, Samuel (1993). *Dream of Fair to middling Women*, ed. Eoin O'Brien and Edith Fournier. New York: Arcade Publishing.

Beckett, Samuel (1995). *The Collected Short Prose 1928–1989*, ed. S. E. Gontarski. New York: Grove Press.

Beckett, Samuel (2009). *Company, Ill Seen Ill Said, Worstward Ho, Stirrings Still*, ed. Dirk Van Hulle. London: Faber and Faber.

Cohn, Ruby (2001). *A Beckett Canon*. Ann Arbor: University of Michigan Press.

Coleridge, Samuel Taylor (1983). *Biographia Literaria; or Biographical Sketches of My Literary Life and Opinions*, ed. James Engell and W. Jackson Bate. Princeton: Princeton University Press.

Dante Alighieri (2002). *The Inferno*, trans. Robert and Jean Hollander. New York: Anchor Books/ Random House.

Davies, Paul (1994). *The Ideal Real: Beckett's Fiction and Imagination*. Rutherford: Fairleigh Dickinson University Press.

Foucault, Michel (1979). "What Is an Author?" In Josué V. Harari (ed.), *Textual Strategies: Perspectives in Post-Structuralist Criticism*. Ithaca, NY: Cornell University Press.

Garnier, Pierre (1895). *Onanisme seul et à deux sous toutes ses formes et leurs conséquences*. Paris: Garnier frères.

Gontarski, S. E. (ed.) (1995). Introduction. *The Collected Short Prose 1928–1989*. New York: Grove Press.

Joyce, James (1939). *Finnegans Wake*. New York: The Viking Press.

Knowlson, James (1996). *Damned to Fame: The Life of Samuel Beckett*. London: Bloomsbury.

Knowlson, James and John Pilling (1979). *Frescoes of the Skull: The Later Prose and Drama of Samuel Beckett*. London: John Calder.

Lake, Carlton (1984). *No Symbols Where None Intended: A Catalogue of Books, Manuscripts, and Other Material Relating to Samuel Beckett in the Collections of the Humanities Research Center*. Austin, TX: The University of Texas at Austin.

Lewis, Wyndham (1927). *Time and Western Man*, London: Chatto and Windus.

Melville, Herman (1986). *Billy Budd and Other Stories*. London: Penguin Classics.

Murphy, P. J. (2009). *Beckett's Dedalus: Dialogical Engagements with Joyce in Beckett's Fiction*. Toronto: University of Toronto Press.

Nixon, Mark (2005). "The German Diaries 1936/37: Beckett und die moderne deutsche Literatur." In Marion Dieckmann-Fries and Therese Seidel (eds.), *Der unbekannte Beckett: Samuel Beckett und die deutsche Kultur*. Frankfurt am Main: Suhrkamp.

Nordau, Max (1993). *Degeneration*, trans. George L. Mosse. Lincoln and London: University of Nebraska Press.

Pilling, John (1997). *Beckett Before Godot*. Cambridge: Cambridge University Press.

Pilling, John (ed.) (1999). *Samuel Beckett's "Dream" Notebook*. Reading: Beckett International Foundation.

Poe, Edgar Allan (1986). *The Fall of the House of Usher and Other Writings*. London: Penguin Classics.

Pountney, Rosemary (1987). "The Structuring of Lessness." *The Review of Contemporary Fiction* 7: Samuel Beckett Number (Summer 1987): 55–75.

Pountney, Rosemary (1988). *Theatre of Shadows: Samuel Beckett's Drama 1956–76*. Gerrards Cross/Totowa, New Jersey: Colin Smythe/ Barnes and Noble Books.

Proust, Marcel (1987–9). *À la recherche du temps perdu*. 4 vols. Paris: Gallimard Pléiade.

Schopenhauer, Arthur (1969). *The World as Will and Representation*. 2 vols. trans. E. F. J. Payne. New York: Dover Publications.

Van Hulle, Dirk (2008). *Manuscript Genetics, Joyce's Know-How, Beckett's Nohow*. Gainesville: University Press of Florida.

Weller, Shane (2000). "The Word Folly: Samuel Beckett's *Comment dire (what is the word)*." *Angelaki* 5:1 (April 2000), 165–80.

18

Molloy, or Life without
a Chambermaid

Patrick A. McCarthy

Written between May and November 1947 and published in French in 1951 (Beckett 1988, hereafter *M*), with the English version following in 1955 (Beckett 1991, hereafter *TN*), *Molloy* marked a turning point in Beckett's fiction. His earlier English fiction, including *More Pricks than Kicks* (1934) and *Murphy* (1938), was clever, erudite, and intellectually complex in ways that parodied and yet emulated Joyce and other high modernists, but in his French fiction, starting in the late 1940s, Beckett had different aims. To be sure, *Molloy* is not without its allusions and adaptations of literary structures, but there is a clear difference between the fiction written during the "siege in the room" and a story like "Dante and the Lobster" in *More Pricks*, which begins with a complex allusion to Dante's *Paradiso*. *Molloy* is not an intellectual exercise but a fundamental exploration of experience that began, Beckett said, "the day I became aware of my own folly. Only then did I begin to write the things I feel" (Knowlson 1996: 319). Moving from English to French and from third to first person narration, Beckett sought a form of expression closer to his own uncomfortable and bewildered experience of the world than to literature. The major fiction that he composed from 1946 through 1950 – "The End," "First Love," "The Expelled," "The Calmative," *Molloy*, *Malone Dies*, and *The Unnamable* – also exemplifies Beckett's increasing emphasis on weakness, uncertainty, and folly as subjects for exploration.

Molloy's Narrative

Molloy contains two narratives, Molloy's in Part 1 and Moran's in Part 2, each oddly constructed and incomplete, circular, or contradictory. At the outset of Part 1, Molloy says that he lives in his mother's room, where he writes about himself for a man who gives him money in exchange for pages of writing, later returning them with "signs" – presumably copy-editing marks – that Molloy neither understands nor bothers reading. Although Molloy learns that his narrative is wrong because he "began at the beginning, like an old ballocks" he gives us that narrative, which "must mean something, or they wouldn't keep it. Here it is" (*TN*: 8).

Thus ends the first paragraph of *Molloy*. The second paragraph, the remainder of Part 1, covers more than 80 pages and presumably contains all that Molloy wrote before the preamble. The order in which Molloy writes – the second paragraph, then the first – parallels the order in which Beckett wrote his manuscript, for Beckett added the first paragraph after completing the rest of the manuscript. Apart from that insertion, the major difference between the draft manuscript of *Molloy* and the novel published in French is the unification of many shorter paragraphs into the second paragraph of Part 1. Unlike the *Watt* notebooks, which provide evidence of Beckett's extensive planning for and revisions of the text, not to mention the frequency with which he found himself at an impasse, the notebooks for the trilogy indicate that those narratives were largely unplanned, almost at times consisting of what would now be called free writing. Beckett's decision to fuse all but the first paragraph of Part 1 into a single paragraph reinforces the impression that the narrative's main structural principles are digression and free association.

The basic structure of Part 1 may be seen in this outline:

1 First paragraph (*TN*: 7–8): Statement of themes. Time: present.
2 Second paragraph (*TN*: 8–91): Development of themes. Time: past.
   (a) Molloy sees A and C (*TN*: 8–15).
   (b) Molloy goes on quest for his mother (*TN*: 15–91).
        (i)   Discovery of bicycle (*TN*: 16).
        (ii)   Digression about mother (Mag) (*TN*: 16–19).
        (iii) Run-in with police (*TN*: 20–6).
        (iv)   Night on canal bank, meeting with shepherd and dog, digressions (includes digression on farting) (*TN*: 26–32).
        (v)   Stay at Lousse's house (*TN*: 32–59).
               • Molloy runs over Lousse's dog (*TN*: 32).
               • Lousse buries dog (*TN*: 36–7).
               • Molloy sleeps, wakes, demands clothes, verifies their contents, puts on clothes (*TN*: 38–46).
               • Molloy stays at Lousse's house – mainly in garden – and vegetates (*TN*: 47–56).
               • Molloy digresses on his "true love" (*TN*: 56–8).
               • Molloy departs from Lousse, leaving bicycle (*TN*: 59).
        (vi)   In town: Molloy finds various shelters (*TN*: 60–8).
        (vii) Resumption of quest, visit at seashore (*TN*: 68–75); includes problem of sucking-stones (*TN*: 69–74).
        (viii) Continuation of quest: Molloy goes through swamp, which becomes a forest (*TN*: 76–91).
               • Molloy's good leg gets worse (*TN*: 77).
               • Molloy meets charcoal-burner (*TN*: 83), kicks him (*TN*: 84).

- Method of going in a straight line (*TN*: 85).
- Molloy's digression on meaning (*TN*: 88).
- Molloy crawls (*TN*: 89–90).
- Molloy ends in ditch (*TN*: 91).

Part 1 has something like the episodic structure of a picaresque novel, but Molloy is one of the oddest and most hapless picaros on record. Moreover, he is often uncertain about his narrative: "Perhaps I'm inventing a little, perhaps embellishing, but on the whole that's the way it was" (*TN*: 8); "I crouched like Belacqua, or Sordello, I forget" (*TN*: 10); "A or C, I don't remember"; "a pomeranian I think, but I don't think so" (*TN*: 11); "the less I think of it the more certain I am" (*TN*:12). When he does think, he is uncertain about names: "a Mrs. Loy ... or Lousse, I forget, Christian name something like Sophie" (*TN*: 33); "She went by the peaceful name of Ruth I think, but I can't say for certain. Perhaps the name was Edith" (*TN*: 56). Later, he again has trouble with Ruth's (or Edith's) name: "nothing like the old woman, I've lost her name again, Rose, no, anyway you see who I mean" (*TN*: 83). He struggles to remember his own surname (we never learn his given name, if he has one), and can only assume that his mother's surname was Molloy as well (*TN*: 23).

Often the narrative seems to deteriorate or go astray. So do individual sentences, as when Molloy explains why, if he were to return to the site of his encounter with the police and find them changed beyond recognition, he knows they will be the same police: "For to contrive a being, a place, I nearly said an hour, but I would not hurt anyone's feelings, and then to use them no more, that would be, how shall I say, I don't know" (*TN*: 28). Like Molloy's narrative as a whole, this example of what Christopher Ricks calls a "Struldbruggian sentence" (1993: 25–6) peters out. Ricks cites another: "For [one leg] was shortening, don't forget, whereas the other, though stiffening, was not yet shortening, or so far behind its fellow that to all intents and purposes, intents and purposes, I'm lost, no matter" (*TN*: 77). The repetition of "intents and purposes" (lost in the Grove edition of *Three Novels* but present in other English editions; the French *Molloy* [*M*: 104] repeats "tout comme") delays the end of the sentence without helping in any way to get it back on track, as Molloy tries to remember where he is headed.

Part 1 is oddly asymmetrical: not only is the first paragraph far shorter than the second, but the first "episode" of the second paragraph, Molloy's reflections on his observation of A and C, is minuscule compared to the second, his search for his mother. He introduces that search casually: "But talking of the craving for a fellow let me observe that having waked between eleven o'clock and midday (I heard the angelus, recalling the incarnation, shortly after) I resolved to go and see my mother" (*TN*: 15). Despite unspecified "reasons of an urgent nature" for seeing his mother, no sooner does Molloy decide to visit her than he finds a bicycle that he didn't know he owned and takes pleasure in describing the bicycle and its rubber horn (*TN*: 16). Later, his statement that he "did not lose sight of [his] immediate goal, which was to get to [his] mother as quickly as possible" (*TN*: 29) is belied by the fact that almost immediately he reverts to his favorite subject, himself, commenting on his preference for gloomy weather and the frequency of his farts, which he inaccurately calculates as "Not even one fart every four minutes" before concluding "I hardly fart at all, I should never have mentioned it" (*TN*: 30). Here and elsewhere Molloy gives the impression that he has no real control over his narration – that his words slip out, much like his farts.

Kevin Dettmar says that Molloy "constructs his narrative from whatever is at hand" and in this way "is mastered *by* rather than the master *of* his material" (1990: 73). Observations, events, commentaries, random thoughts arise as they occur to Molloy, who makes little attempt to shape or select. Indeed, like his discovery of the bicycle, Molloy's narration often surprises him: thus, after describing the death of his "true love," the "idealist" Ruth (or Edith), he exclaims, "Well, well, I didn't think I knew this story so well" (*TN*: 58). From one sentence to the next the narrative takes turns that he does not foresee:

> Could a woman have stopped me as I swept towards mother? Probably. Better still, was such an encounter possible, I mean between me and a woman? Now men, I have rubbed up against a few men in my time, but women? Oh well, I may as well confess it now, yes, I once rubbed up against one. I don't mean my mother, I did more than rub up against her. And if you don't mind we'll leave my mother out of all this. (*TN*: 56)

Molloy's inability to control or even predict the direction of his narrative may be illustrated by his reference in the opening paragraph to the mother of a son he might have had: "It was a little chambermaid. It wasn't true love. The true love was in another" (*TN*: 7). Molloy mentions the chambermaid only once again, after the story of Ruth or Edith, with whom he might (or might not) have experienced true love: "Don't talk to me about the chambermaid, I should never have mentioned her, she was long before, I was sick, perhaps there was no chambermaid, ever, in my life. Molloy, or life without a chambermaid" (*TN*: 58–9). The first chambermaid reference, in the preamble, leads us to expect that she will play a part in the narrative, and the second, in the narrative, implies that he has just mentioned her, but in neither case is the implication true. Unless we endorse John Fletcher's theory that the chambermaid resurfaces in Part 2 as Martha – Moran's servant and, in Fletcher's reading, his mother (1970: 167) – references to the chambermaid serve mainly to demonstrate how little control Molloy has over his narrative.

"And to think I try my best not to talk about myself" (*TN*: 13) says Molloy, who in fact talks incessantly about himself and his narrative. He even questions his use of tense: "This should all be re-written in the pluperfect" (*TN*: 16); "I speak in the present tense, it is so easy to speak in the present tense, when speaking of the past" (*TN*: 26); "My life, my life, now I speak of it as of something over, now as of a joke which still goes on, and it is neither, for at the same time it is over and it goes on, and is there any tense for that?" (*TN*: 36). Narration, he says, is a matter of choosing "between the things not worth mentioning and those even less so" (*TN*: 41). Even as he apologizes for an excess of "details" and promises to move through his narration more quickly he warns that he might "relapse again into a wealth of filthy circumstance" (*TN*: 63). Such a relapse is typical of Molloy's inability to control the narration of a life that in some way has already ended. Curiously, Molloy says that "it is only since I have ceased to live that I think of these things and the other things" (*TN*: 25), which if taken literally would mean that his is a postmortem narrative, as in other works Beckett wrote around the same time – "First Love," "The Calmative," and *Texts for Nothing* 1 and 2. When Molloy says that "It is in the tranquillity of decomposition that I remember the long confused emotion of my life" and adds, "To decompose is to live too" (*TN*: 25), he not only parodies Wordsworth's description of the origins of poetry but sets forth a parallel between life, which for Beckett is a continual process of decomposition, and narrative.

Richard Ellmann notes that we can recognize *Murphy* as a work of Beckett's early period because it has a plot (1986: 8). *Molloy* retains a vestigial plot (or pair of plots), but the world of the novel has disintegrated to the point where Molloy even has trouble distinguishing between himself and others: "People pass too, hard to distinguish from yourself. That is discouraging" (*TN*: 8). Maurice Blanchot sees this "principle of disintegration" as one "not confined to the instability of the wanderer, but further requiring that Molloy be mirrored, doubled, that he become *another*, the detective Moran, who pursues Molloy without ever catching him" (1986: 142). Having become progressively lost in his own narrative, Molloy finally emerges from the forest only to find himself in a ditch. Although he says "I longed to go back in the forest" he adds that this was "not a real longing. Molloy could stay, where he happened to be" (*TN*: 91). Molloy's final reference to himself, in the third person, serves as a transition to Moran, who uses the third person when referring to Molloy and on occasion refers to himself the same way (*TN*: 111, 124, 147).

Molloy and Moran

As Molloy searches for his mother, Moran seeks Molloy. That is his assignment, sent by an authority figure named Youdi through his "messenger," Gaber; yet Moran is generally more preoccupied with himself than with Molloy, much as Molloy forgets about his mother for much of his narrative. There are other parallels between Molloy and Moran, whose bodies and memories generally deteriorate as their narratives proceed. Both confuse blue and green (*TN*: 83, 89, 103); Molloy pedals his bicycle with one leg, and Moran believes he could learn that trick (*TN*: 16, 161); Molloy cannot remember which was his sick leg, nor can Moran recall which bicycle tire was punctured (*TN*: 156). As Raymond Federman notes, both are writers who "negate" their narratives by making and then retracting statements (1970: 106–7). After describing what he said (to himself), Molloy admits that he "did not say it in such limpid language. And when I say I said, etc., all I mean is that I knew confusedly things were so, without knowing exactly what it was all about ... For what really happened was quite different" (*TN*: 87–8). Moran says, "When I said I had turkeys, and so on, I lied. All I had was a few hens" (*TN*: 128); his report begins "It is midnight. The rain is beating on the windows" and ends "Then I went back to the house and wrote, It is midnight. The rain is beating on the windows. It was not midnight. It was not raining" (*TN*: 92, 176). While in the conclusion of "Dante and the Lobster" an omniscient narrator contradicts Belacqua's comforting reflection that the lobster will have a "quick death," in *Molloy* the narrators deny their own statements, which are always subject to revision.

Whereas Molloy is uncertain about names, even his own, Moran initially seems assured, declaring that his name is Jacques Moran, that his son has the same name, and that "This cannot lead to confusion" (*TN*: 92). Yet when he asserts that he knew something about Molloy before his present assignment, Moran introduces an element of uncertainty: "Molloy, or Mollose, was no stranger to me" (*TN*: 111). The Molloy/Mollose alternatives, which parallel Molloy's hesitation between "Loy" and "Lousse" (*TN*: 33), undermine Moran's confidence that he already knew about Molloy, who might be the product of his own imagination: "Perhaps I had invented him, I mean found him ready made in my head" (*TN*: 112). He tries to think which is the right name and decides that "Mollose" is "perhaps the more correct" before opting for "Molloy" because "Gaber had said Molloy, not once but several times." (Since the occasions on which Gaber used the name "Molloy" do not appear in Moran's narration, the argument for "Molloy" over "Mollose" seems less than conclusive.) Before putting "Mollose" to rest for good, Moran introduces "a thought which did not so much as cross my mind" at the time: that Molloy and Mollose are distinct people rather than alternate versions of one man (*TN*: 113). Moran arrives at this possibility only while writing his report, one sign that the past is reshaped with each act of memory.

As their names imply, Molloy seems to be Irish and Jacques Moran is French; hence Moran notes that "the Molloy country ... was situated in the north, I mean in relation to mine" (*TN*: 133). There are many other differences between them, as when Molloy says he cannot bear watching things disappear from sight whereas Moran wishes to do precisely that (*TN*: 12, 147). A crucial difference may be seen in their references to principles. Molloy refers to principles that he never learned, like "the guiding principles of good manners" (*TN*: 25), or that he knows must exist but cannot express or define: "And then doing fills me with such a, I don't know, impossible to express, for me, now, after so long, yes, that I don't stop to inquire in virtue of what principle ... And if I speak of principles, when there are none, I can't help it, there must be some somewhere" (*TN*: 45–6). His simultaneous disavowal of principles and belief that "there must be some somewhere" resembles Beckett's own persistent interest in, and denial of, philosophical systems. To the extent that he understands principles, Molloy seems to deny their validity, as when he remarks, "If I go on long enough calling that my life I'll end up by believing it. It's the principle of advertising" (*TN*: 53). Later, unable to decide how to suck each of 16 stones before sucking any stone twice, he suddenly realizes that he could do so "by sacrificing the principle of trim," but he admits that "this illumination" is somewhat dimmed because he has never before encountered the word "trim" and does not know what it means (*TN*: 71). J. D. O'Hara says that "trim" connotes directness (1997: 170–1), but "le principe de l'arrimage" (*M*: 95) suggests order and balance, since *l'arrimage* refers to stowing things on a ship. Molloy's "principle of trim" soon becomes one of equal distribution of stones among his pockets, and when he abandons this principle he says "it was something more than a principle I abandoned ... it was a bodily need" (*TN*: 74).

Whereas for Molloy principles either are imposed from without or involve "bodily need," Moran's few references to principles tend to represent his arbitrary wishes. He calls his decision to begin his search for Molloy by autocycle, a mode of transportation that he prefers, an instance of "the fatal pleasure principle" (*TN*: 99), apparently meaning that deferring to his preferences mars the quest from the beginning. Yet Moran repeatedly follows his preferences. He has little interest in others: even his son is not an independent person but, as we might guess from their shared name, someone for Moran to shape in his own image. His real desire is to be in control, as he reveals when he says, "I liked punctuality, all those whom my roof sheltered had to like it too" (*TN*: 98). This may be why he prefers "things" to men, animals, and God: "I used to think that men would never get the better of me. Not I. I still think I am cleverer than things. There are men and there are things, to hell with animals. And with God. When a thing resists me, even if it is for my own good, it does not resist me long" (*TN*: 165). A desire for control underlies Moran's struggle over the stamps that his son wishes to bring on their trip. He gives himself credit for being an indulgent parent, allowing Jacques to bring duplicates of common stamps and noting, self-approvingly, "When I can give pleasure, without doing violence to my principles, I do so gladly" (*TN*: 104), but the only principle at stake is his domination of his son. When the boy tries to take rare stamps that he cannot bear to part with, Moran says he must teach his son self-denial: "*Sollst entbehren*, that was the lesson I desired to impress upon him, while he was still young and tender" (*TN*: 110). As Ackerley and Gontarski note, the principle that Moran embraces – *sollst entbehren*, "you must renounce" – is precisely what Goethe's Faust rejects (Ackerley and Gontarski 2004: 233, 534). Unlike Faust, Moran is a hypocrite who wants his son to learn self-denial but does not practice it himself.

Much later, after being approached by a man dressed as a fisherman, Moran says, "I shall have to describe him briefly, though such a thing is contrary to my principles" (*TN*: 150). He never explains, and seems not to know, why he must describe the man or why doing so would violate his principles. Moran dimly sees his visitor and fails to recognize him, but he realizes that the man resembles him. When the man presses Moran for information about another old man whom Moran saw earlier there is a lapse in the narration ("I do not know what happened then") before he discovers the man "stretched on the ground, his head in a pulp" (*TN*: 151). Given that "forgetting is Beckett's presentation of repression" (Baker 1997: 93), the scene appears to be the remnant of a terrible memory that Moran has repressed and still refuses to face directly: hence the reluctance to describe the man, which Moran does only under an inner compulsion that he cannot explain. The man's resemblance to Moran might suggest that this repressed scene represents the murder of Moran's father.

Some differences between Molloy and Moran are a matter of degree. Both have bad legs that get worse, but Molloy's are generally stiffer and more useless at comparable stages of Parts 1 and 2; Molloy has an insecure sense not only of his identity but of the relation of names to things – "Yes, even then, when already all was fading, waves and particles, there could be no things but nameless things, no names but thingless names" (*TN*: 31) – whereas Moran is initially buoyed by certainties that he later comes to question, as he begins to resemble the man he is sent to find. The problems Molloy discusses tend to be more about the body, and less about religious doctrine or transcendent reality, than Moran's. Molloy has a recurrent interest in problems related to his body: the frequency of his farts, whether or not anal intercourse is "true love" (*TN*: 57), the "incompatible bodily needs" he faces in distributing his sucking-stones (*TN*: 74), the process by which a man on crutches may kick another man in the ribs. Moran becomes increasingly Molloy-like during his narrative, but even when he faces "the problem of what I should do if my leg did not get better or got worse" he does not explain his thoughts on the subject, as Molloy would, but says instead, "I shall not expound my reasoning. I could do so easily, so easily" (*TN*: 140).

Similarities and differences between Molloy and Moran may be illustrated by two parallel scenes in which they refer to their dangling testicles, bad legs, bicycles, and loss of desire. In the first scene, following his lament that his "sick leg" has left him "virtually onelegged," Molloy says that his testicles hung very low, "dangling at mid-thigh." He adds, "there was nothing more to be squeezed [from them], not a drop. So that non che la speme il desiderio, and I longed to see them gone" (*TN*: 35). Molloy alludes to Giacomo Leopardi's "A se stesso" ("To Himself"): "Non che la speme, il desiderio è spento" (Not just hope but even the desire [for dear illusions] is extinguished); instead of losing hope and the desire for hope, as in the poem, Molloy loses sexual desire. In a related passage, while riding on the back of a bicycle pedaled by his son, Moran says "I trembled for my testicles which swing a little low." Soon they arrive in Ballyba, where he speaks of his unwillingness to augment his narrative with "the obstacles we had to surmount, the fiends we had to circumvent, the misdemeanours of the son, the disintegrations of the father." Moran had meant to tell all of this, but "Now the intention is dead, the moment is come and the desire is gone"; he adds, "My leg was no better. It was no worse either" (*TN*: 157). Similar in many respects, the passages demonstrate two crucial differences between the narrators. First, Molloy's reference to Leopardi illustrates Vivian Mercier's point that, apart from theology, Molloy seems better educated than Moran (1977: 49). Second, even if both passages begin with the body and end with loss of desire, there is an obvious difference between Molloy's loss of sexual desire and Moran's loss of the desire to narrate events. Here and elsewhere, Molloy's focus on the body is more consistent than Moran's.

In a perceptive article originally published in 1959 Edith Kern noted that "Moran lays hesitant claim to authorship of Molloy" when he says, "Perhaps I had invented him, I mean found him ready made in my head" (1970: 36; *TN*: 112). The relationship of the narrator-protagonists to one another is a crucial element in the novel, whose persistent doubleness is never resolved. In the fiction composed in the late 1940s Beckett experimented with monologue, which became his characteristic fictional and dramatic form. With two monologues that at times appear to be in dialogue with one another but never quite connect, however, *Molloy* is a singular work even within the Beckett canon.

Molloy et/and *Molloy*

Originally Beckett envisioned *Molloy* as the next to last in a series of novels from *Murphy* to *Malone Dies* (Pilling 2006:102). He alludes to that plan early in the French *Molloy*, where the narrator's words are basically those of the first draft: "Cette fois-ci, puis encore une je pense, puis c'en sera fini je pense, de ce monde-là aussi" (M: 8; This time, then again I think, then I think it will be finished, with that world too). Yet before he sent the final manuscript to Les Éditions de Minuit Beckett wrote *L'Innomable* (*The Unnamable*), a development recorded in the English *Molloy*: "This time, then once more I think, then perhaps a last time, then I think it'll be over, with that world too" (TN: 8). In French, Molloy believes he is in "l'avant-dernier" (penultimate) stage of his writing, but in English he is still only at "the last but one but one" (TN: 8); the tentative "then perhaps a last time" also indicates uncertainty that the series can ever end. As Leslie Hill notes, the different passages in French and English demonstrate "considerable hesitation on Beckett's part as to the underlying structure of the three novels" (1990: 54). Further evidence of hesitation may be seen in the fact that although there have long been American and British editions of the "trilogy" there has never been a one-volume edition of *Molloy*, *Malone Dies*, and *The Unnamable* in French.

Although Beckett translated parts of *Molloy* into English in 1950, the full English version was "translated by Patrick Bowles in collaboration with the author," as the title page attests. The final text demonstrates Beckett's careful revision of this translation, resulting in a parallel *Molloy*, or a different stage of the *Molloy* process, rather than just a translation. In working on the English version Beckett sometimes added material or otherwise altered the text significantly; at other times the English is quite similar to the French in its effects. Both patterns are evident in the passage, cited earlier, in which Molloy comments at length on his testicles (TN: 35–6; M: 46–7). Beckett added the allusion to Leopardi's "A se stesso" to the English version, yet the following lines in both versions involve similar puns about Molloy's testicles. In thinking that his testicles "bore false witness," Molloy puns on the derivation of "testicle" from Latin *testis*, "witness"; in French his testicles are "ces témoins" (these witnesses). He says his testicles "accused me of having made a balls of it" – "avoir couillonnés" – although he later adds, "these cullions, I must be attached to them after all" (TN: 36), much as in French: "Mais au fond je devais avoir de l'attachement pour ces couillons" (M: 47).

Marjorie Perloff notes that although one reason Beckett gave for turning to French was to escape the rhythms of English poetry – "to write without style" – those rhythms sometimes resurface in the English versions: thus *Ill Seen Ill Said* contains an "elaborate web of poetic references" in contrast to the spare style of *Mal vu mal dit* (1987: 39–44). Likewise, besides the Leopardi quotation, *Molloy* in English contains other allusions that are not in the French. When Gaber finds Moran near the end of his journey, he quotes Youdi as saying "la vie est une bien belle chose, Gaber, une chose inouïe" (life is a very beautiful thing, Gaber, an incredible thing), but the passage in English points clearly to Keats's "Endymion": "life is a thing of beauty, Gaber, and a joy for ever" (*M*: 224, *TN*: 164). Even Molloy's initial observations of two men whom he calls A and B in the French version, A and C in the English, become more "literary" in English (*M*: 9, *TN*: 8): readers of the English text often assume that A and C are Abel and Cain (as indeed they might be, although neither man murders the other), whereas "A et B" appears to be a simple alphabetical sequence. Some of the sentences Molloy uses in the A and C episode are typical Beckett reductions ("They looked alike, but no more than others do"), but others read like poetic clichés: "The road, hard and white, seared the tender pastures, rose and fell at the whim of hills and hollows" (*TN*: 9). Although the parodic tone may be found in each version, it is more obvious in the English, and the hackneyed phrase "serried ranges" (*TN*: 9) has no equivalent in the French. The sequence as a whole illustrates Ruby Cohn's observation that the French *Molloy* is more colloquial, less literary, than the English (1962: 274).

The two texts diverge significantly when Gaber delivers Youdi's message that Moran should return home. In English, Gaber opens his notebook, shines a light on it, and reads, "Moran, Jacques, home, instanter," a message that is even shorter the second time: "He opened his notebook again, shone the torch on his page, studied it at length and said, Moran, home, instanter" (*TN*: 163). Asja Szafraniec perceptively notes that Youdi's order "sounds like an entry in a census record (last and first name, address, profession)" (2007: 145), but the same cannot be said of the order in French, first given as "Moran, Jacques, rentrera chez lui, toutes affaires cessantes" and then as "Moran regagnera son domicile toutes affaires cessantes" (*M*: 222). By suppressing the predicate, the English text increases the curtness of the order. Moreover, in English, where the message is virtually identical when it is repeated, the omission of "Jacques" the second time might seem to be a hurried second reading of the same passage. Conversely, in the French, the difference between "rentrera chez lui" and "regagnera son domicile" makes it appear that there are two distinct orders, or two drafts of one order.

Sometimes, when the two versions are close, one may confirm the other. Moran complains, "Mais je devenais la proie d'autres affections, ce n'est pas le mot, intestinales pour la plupart" (*M*: 225), "But I was succumbing to other affections, that is not the word, intestinal for the most part" (*TN*: 166). Not only are the passages similar but in both languages he says "affections" when he means "afflictions." Much the same thing occurs when Moran tries to describe why he is so intent on taking communion: "It's this, I said, Sunday for me without the Body and Blood is like –. He raised his hand. Above all no profane comparisons, he said. Perhaps he was thinking of the kiss without a moustache or beef without mustard" (*TN*: 100). Elizabeth Barry notes that "above all" is a pun that calls attention to the problem of making comparisons between sacred and profane matters, since religious matters are above all others (Barry 2006: 131). The same effect may be seen in the French, "Pas de comparaisons profanes surtout, dit-il" (*M*: 136), since "surtout" means "above all." In both cases the pun calls attention not only to a hierarchy of subjects (the religious above the everyday) but to the confusion of literal and figurative meanings in terms like "above all"/"surtout." Other passages seem to call for a bilingual reading, as when Molloy imagines himself "all shame drunk, my prick in my rectum" (*TN*: 19). To understand the final phrase it is useful to consult the French *Molloy*, where we find "la queue dans le rectum" (*M*: 24), "with one's tail in one's rectum," apparently an adaptation of the expression *la queue entre les jambes*, "with one's tail between one's legs."

In Part 2 Beckett uses similar phrasing at the beginning of two scenes to connect the episodes. In French the first scene, Moran's encounter with the man whose face resembles his own, begins, "Je venais d'allumer mon feu et le regardais prendre lorsque je m'entendais interpeller" (*M*: 203), but the English version starts a sentence earlier: "It was evening. I had lit my fire and was watching it take when I heard myself hailed" (*TN*: 149). The second scene, in which Gaber finds Moran, begins, "C'était un soir. Je venais de me traîner hors de l'abri pour ma petite pouffade et pour mieux sentir ma faiblesse" (*M*: 221) – "It was evening. I had just crawled out of the shelter for my evening guffaw and the better to savour my exhaustion" (*TN*: 163). The parallelism between the openings of the two scenes, which the French text suggests with the shared phrase "je venais de" – I had just – is intensified in English through the addition of "It was evening" to the first scene; perhaps to avoid an overly mechanical repetition of phrases, however, Beckett changed the phrase "I had just lit" ("Je venais d'allumer") in the first scene to the less specific "I had lit." Other parallels between the scenes, such as the lapses in Moran's awareness just before the man dressed like a fisherman dies and Gaber disappears, are established, or signaled, by these parallel openings.

Perloff notes that some of Beckett's critics "seem to assume that the Beckett text is a stable and unitary entity"; encountering a work that he wrote in one language and translated into another, they often regard one version as "better" or more "real" than the other (1987: 44–7). Yet, like the Molloy and Moran narratives, the French and English language editions engage in an uneasy, imperfect dialogue. Each may be read on its own, but sometimes the most striking effects of Beckett's rich, yet spare, language may be discerned only through a bilingual reading.

REFERENCES AND FURTHER READING

Ackerley, C. J., and Gontarski, S. E. (2004). *The Grove Companion to Samuel Beckett*. New York: Grove Press.

Baker, Phil (1997). *Beckett and the Mythology of Psychoanalysis*. New York: St. Martin's Press.

Barry, Elizabeth (2006). *Beckett and Authority: The Uses of Cliché.* New York: Palgrave Macmillan.

Beckett, Samuel (1988). *Molloy {French, 1951}.* Paris: Les Éditions de Minuit; rpt. with afterword, "'Molloy': Une Événement littéraire, une oeuvre," by Jean-Jacques Mayoux.

Beckett, Samuel (1991). *Molloy,* "translated from the French by Patrick Bowles in collaboration with the author" [English, 1955]. Rpt. in *Three Novels: "Molloy," "Malone Dies," "The Unnamable."* New York: Grove Press, Evergreen Edition.

Blanchot, Maurice (1986). "Where Now? Who Now?" In S. E. Gontarski (ed.), *On Beckett: Essays and Criticism.* New York: Grove Press.

Cohn, Ruby (1962). *Samuel Beckett: The Comic Gamut.* New Brunswick: Rutgers University Press.

Cousineau, Thomas J. (1999). *After the Final No: Samuel Beckett's Trilogy.* Newark: University of Delaware Press.

Dettmar, Kevin J. H. (1990). "The Figure in Beckett's Carpet: *Molloy* and the Assault on Metaphor." In Lance St. John Butler and Robin J. Davis (eds.), *Rethinking Beckett: A Collection of Critical Essays.* New York: St. Martin's.

Ellmann, Richard (1986). *Samuel Beckett: Nayman of Noland.* Washington: Library of Congress.

Federman, Raymond (1970). "Beckettian Paradox: Who Is Telling the Truth?" In Melvin J. Friedman (ed.), *Samuel Beckett Now: Critical Approaches to His Novels, Poetry, and Plays.* Chicago and London: University of Chicago Press.

Fletcher, John (1970). "Interpreting *Molloy.*" In Melvin J. Friedman (ed.), *Samuel Beckett Now: Critical Approaches to His Novels, Poetry, and Plays.* Chicago and London: University of Chicago Press.

Hill, Leslie (1990). *Beckett's Fiction: In Different Words.* Cambridge: Cambridge University Press.

Kern, Edith (1970). "Moran-Molloy: The Hero as Author". In J. D. O'Hara (ed.), *Twentieth Century Interpretations of "Molloy," "Malone Dies," "The Unnamable."* Englewood Cliffs: Prentice-Hall.

Knowlson, James (1996). *Damned to Fame: The Life of Samuel Beckett.* New York: Simon & Schuster.

Mercier, Vivian (1977). *Beckett/Beckett.* New York: Oxford University Press.

O'Hara, J. D. (1997). *Samuel Beckett's Hidden Drives: Structural Uses of Depth Psychology.* Gainesville: University Press of Florida.

Perloff, Marjorie (1987). "Une Voix pas la mienne: French/English Beckett and the French/English Reader." In Alan Warren Friedman, Charles Rossman, and Dina Sherzer (eds.), *Beckett Translating/Translating Beckett.* University Park: Pennsylvania State University Press.

Pilling, John (2006). *A Samuel Beckett Chronology.* New York: Palgrave Macmillan.

Ricks, Christopher (1993). *Beckett's Dying Words.* Oxford: Clarendon Press.

Szafraniec, Asja (2007). *Beckett, Derrida, and the Event of Literature.* Stanford: Stanford University Press.

19

Malone Dies:
Postmodernist Masculinity

Susan Mooney

The *Bildungsroman* in its twentieth-century guise develops a narrative of self-analysis and autobiographical retrieval, with the masculine subject often displaying signs of unraveling, liminality, and disillusionment. The narrative becomes fixated on an undoing of the development of character, especially the premises of mastery of the masculine character. The twentieth-century *Bildungsroman* as story of character cannot aspire to the novel's equivalent of Fernand Braudel's dream of collecting *"l'histoire totale,"* but it can use narration to work the margins and framework of such a dream. Samuel Beckett's *Malone meurt* (1951) (first published in English in 1955 as *Malone Dies*) presents the "story" of the masculine character in forms of a postmodernist narrative of personal history. In the novel, the narrating subject oscillates between two imperatives – telling stories and telling his story or state of being – with a deadline of death. These two imperatives can be seen as creative extensions of the traditional *Bildungsroman*'s imperatives for the protagonist: realizing his inner desires and negotiating a coherence of these with the demands of the social world. In *Malone Dies*, narrating and the narrative of self-reflexivity have become prioritized, while displacing (but not abandoning) the *Bildungsroman*'s earlier sense as a novel of apprenticeship with its attendant aim towards completion and fulfillment, and masculine mastery (for example, Goethe's *Wilhelm Meisters Lehrjahre* [1795–6] *Wilhelm Meister's Apprenticeship* [1989]). Beckett's weary, at times jaded, character–narrator Malone carries out an apprenticeship of sorts: he adheres to certain social and physical conditions of the larger world beyond the self, as well as interrogating the masculine *Bildung* role via his little stories of Sapo and Macmann. In these two ways, through confrontation with Malone's state of being and with his narrative acts, the novel considers masculine mastery as both centrally constitutive and precariously ephemeral for the subject.

Malone Dies sets up oppositions of history and narrative through the narrator Malone, who is compelled to alternate between the telling of his stories and inserting his own story or history. With the foregrounding of telling and playing, combined with gender and the prospect of ending and dying, Beckett maintains a modernist project of self-reflexivity, while introducing the postmodernist tensions between history and story, and masculine subject's construction in these. As a postmodern *Bildungsroman* (that is, a novel that undoes the novel of becoming and its achieving heroic masculine protagonist), *Malone Dies* rewrites masculinity as both possibility and failure, as a subjectivity oscillating between dominance and submission.

The exploration of masculinity in *Malone Dies* depends partly on apparent contrasts with the feminine subject. Women characters participate within the Sapo and Macmann stories. In Sapo's story, his mother Mrs Saposcat, Lizzy Lambert, and Mrs Lambert perform maternal roles; in Macmann's story, the maternal role becomes overtly tyrannical and phallic as seen in his grotesquely romantic interlude with his keeper Moll and his episode with Lady Pedal. Feminine counterparts in Malone's diary entries are traced to the old woman who brings him his soup and pot and early, overlapping memories of his mother, such as discussions about an airplane and the limits of the sky. The old woman frames the end of his life, the old Malone reduced to being cared for like a grown infant, and the mother frames the beginning of his life at the point of inquiry into the limits of human perception and knowledge. Malone's mother simplifies his first educational steps by curtailing his questions: "It [the sky] is precisely as far away as it appears to be" is a treacherous statement, both truthful and false (Beckett 1958: 268–9). Women seem to hold the keys to an unknown area of information, and do not dispense it; their alignment with the symbolic and the Law-of-the-Father (for example, Lizzie and Mrs Lambert's submission to Louis Lambert; Moll's upholding of the rules) make them perfidious alternative allies for filial rebellion. Further, the female principle is linked to stability, the hearth, and the law, and in the novel the feminine accommodates the masculine subject in awkward or suffocating ways.

In her *Gender of Modernity*, Rita Felski describes the modern era's "ideology of bourgeois masculinity: the narrative of history as progress, the valorization of function over form, the sovereignty of the reality principle" (1995: 101). Malone clings to a shard of this ideology in his declared intention to craft his four themed stories, account for his possessions, and report his state of being, all before he dies. Although he proposes an aesthetics of neutrality (as opposed to "prettiness"), his narrative retains traces of a previous aesthetics of process. The narrative arc suggests a kind of masculine birth or resurrection, with his early narrative possibly coinciding with late June and July and the feast day of St John the Baptist and Bastille Day and his conclusion accompanying Easter. His fragmented stories rely on traces of master or grand narratives of the son's coming of age and his development pertaining to the *Bildungsroman*. Malone himself posits himself in the text as both paternal and filial: he is paternal in his Faustian or God-like creation of his characters, and filial in his *méconnaissances* of self in the others he creates. Further, despite his age and doubts, Malone still coheres to a logic of *Bildung* – of cultivation or education. He seeks to contemplate, write, reflect, and achieve, despite his flaws and setbacks. The function of his narrative is meant to be privileged over its uncrafted form, composed as his text is in an exercise book with a diminishing pencil. The text emphasizes its realism through its documentary quality

– a reflection of what a real writer might compose in such limited circumstances – and consequently some stretches of the imagination. All of these narrative features suggest a kind of urge to progress and achievement, but Beckett sets his protagonists (Malone, Sapo, Macmann) in anti-bourgeois positions, thus disrupting conventional motifs of modern masculinity.

Felski suggests that modernist male narrators and characters can play up traits associated with the feminine. In her explorations of texts like Wilde's *The Picture of Dorian Gray*, she explains,

> If the hero's preoccupation with style, quotation, and linguistic play is linked to his femininity, so in turn his mimicry of femininity confirms the authority of the parodistic world-view. The feminized male deconstructs conventional oppositions between the modern, bourgeois man and the natural, domestic woman: he is male, yet does not represent masculine values of rationality, utility, and progress; feminine, yet profoundly unnatural. His femininity thus signifies an unsettling of automatized perceptions of gender, whether hailed as subversive or condemned as pathological, whereas the same traits in a woman merely serve to confirm her incapacity to escape her natural condition. (1995: 101)

I suggest that Malone and his narrative counterparts Sapo and Macmann do not display this brand of modernist feminine masculinity. While the masculinity in *Malone Dies* is often subversive and posits men as wayward infants, helpless types, or wanderers, the narrative line of becoming nonetheless playfully echoes both modern bourgeois ideals and the *Bildungsroman*'s tensions of the protagonist's self-integration and integration into society. Beckett manages to work those tensions without providing achievement. For Malone, Sapo, and Macmann integration is a preoccupation, but they remain at the threshold. Beckett refuses a bourgeois integration as a conclusion for his characters, but rather shows the problems with such an integration, for example, in the lives of the Lamberts and Saposcats. Malone rejects a pleasing tale of masculine accomplishment and mastery. Within the *mise-en-abyme* texts, Sapo refuses the paths of his bourgeois father and surrogate peasant father, whose values differ only superficially. Macmann, who as a man in the world fails in work ("when given the job of weeding a plot of young carrots for example, at the rate of threepence or even sixpence an hour, it often happened that he tore them all up, through absent-mindedness" or tears them up through an "urge to make a clean sweep" [Beckett 1958: 243]), knows nothing, and prefers to wander, or better, remain motionless, sit or lie down (ibid.). As an inmate at the asylum, Macmann refuses to submit completely to its aggressive aid (his subversion can be noted, for example, in his affair with Moll).

Malone (and his narrative counterparts) – marked by his signature armor or envelope of great coat, hat, stick, and aging, sagging genitalia – resists typification within the modernist tradition. He does not correspond to a grand mythology or symbolism as do Joyce's key men. Nor does he fulfill the qualities of the dandy-aesthete of early modernism (Wilde; Huysmans), who would seem to lay claim to feminine mystery and allure. The Beckettian man does not approximate the hypermasculinist desires of a Wyndham Lewis or Ezra Pound for some kind of lean, muscular epic figure (such as the warring figures of Hanp and Arghol in Lewis's *Enemy of the Stars*). It would be hard to imagine such modernists admiring Molloy's sucking stones or Malone's punting in a bed. Beckett's masculine characters perhaps most approximate T. S. Eliot's fisher king figure – with its dual filial–paternal characterization – and D. H. Lawrence's exhausted men, displaced by overly desiring phallic women and at odds with the bourgeois and working-class status quo. In this comparative grouping, Beckett's masculinity places impotence and uncertainty in the path of possible achievement in class terms, and yet still traces emphatically a path of solitary achievement, especially of creative production.

Among the postmodernist and postwar writers, Beckett could be grouped with those representing a post-patriarchal masculinity, with his works of self-conscious gender specificity. Schoene-Harwood discusses how postwar writers like Angela Carter, Iain Banks, Alisdair Gray, and Ian McEwan develop an *écriture masculine*, that is a writing "employed to describe the anti-phallogocentric and non-patriarchal disposition that characterizes (pro-)feminist men's writing" (2000: 102). However, unlike writers of this group, I suggest that Beckett accepts many traditional notions and practices of gender and sexuality, while playfully subverting and resisting them at times. Moreover, in *Malone Dies* and most of his oeuvre men upstage women (in contrast to the progressive indebtedness to feminism of *écriture masculine*). If we were to call Beckett's novelistic discourse *écriture masculine* at all, it would entail his deconstruction of the masculine subject, with its non-integrated relation to the paternal and maternal.

Beckett's investigation of masculinity probes the foundations of masculine subjectivity as these are produced through the incest prohibition and Name of the Father, and also through kinship arrangements. For Freud and Lacan, masculine subjectivity is based on a failure to recognize lack, and a displacement of male castration (symbolic) onto the female subject and the primary object of desire in their secondary form (the breast, excrement, the gaze, the voice, and fetishes, such as high heels, earrings, etc.). The incest prohibition obliges the boy to identify with his father and to relinquish his mother as object of desire; through kinship relations, he can seek another woman. Masculinity is strongly preoccupied with mastery, with psychic mastery often accomplished through repetition. Kaja Silverman elaborates the dynamics of masculine subjectivity: "Masculinity is particularly vulnerable to the unbinding effects of the death drive because of its ideological alignment with mastery. The normative male ego is necessarily fortified against any knowledge of the void upon which it rests, and – as its insistence upon an unimpaired bodily 'envelope' would suggest – fiercely protective of its coherence" (Silverman 1992: 61).

While mastery and the death drive are distinct, they appear similar. In Beckett's novel, these psychic negotiations are subversively entertained by the masculine subjects. The novel represents the paternal order in the figures of Mr Saposcat, Mr Louis Lambert, Lemuel, and Malone's recollection of his father, partly memory, partly phantasy. Male lack is assigned to the women in the text: Lizzy, Mrs Lambert, Moll, Lady Pedal. At the asylum, Lemuel assumes a subversive paternal position as the keeper of Macmann; Lemuel's character also mimics the authorship of Malone, in his decisive yet seemingly senseless murderous actions on Dalkey Island during the excursion, his hatchet corresponding to Malone's pencil. Malone's paternity of his "sons" or little creatures made in his own image, Sapo and Macmann, is centrally attached to the masculine dream of mastery and embedded in the context of Malone's narrative invention. Malone dominates his text, and his sons can be ordered and reordered, even renamed and allotted a new age and position. The narrative mastery exceeds the bounds of everyday paternity, surpassing yet reflective of the bourgeois father's worrying and planning and of the peasant father's despotism and violence. In fact, underlying Malone's mastery and play – veiled by his repeatedly declared impotence ("my stories are all in vain" [Beckett 1958: 234]) – is an anxious preoccupation with violence and, at times sadistic, domination (as seen in such examples as his manipulative use of a hunchback in narration, whom he humiliates by asking him to undress [ibid.: 180]; the various killing of characters; his desire to keep a "little girl" [ibid.: 273]). Beckett develops a postmodernist masculinity that models itself self-consciously along notions of mastery and its oppositions of failure and impotence. In taking apart the grand narrative of the *Bildungsroman*, Malone reveals a *Bildung* impulse that combines with the self-conscious narration of the modernist and postmodernist male subject. He explains how he uses his narrative subject: "I slip into him with the hope of learning something" (ibid.: 226). This function and goal of self-development, at the heart of the *Bildung* project, are reconfigured by the writing subject Malone, who uses his little men, his little creations, as models of experimentation and play.

Postmodernist *Bildungsroman*

Malone's text juxtaposes narratives of the self (or self-reflection) and action. Abbot evaluates *Malone Dies* as an example of writing as action: the text shows Malone as actively writing his diary. Meanwhile, in *Reflection and Action: Essays on the Bildungsroman*, Hardin explains how reflection and action are the two primary modes of being of the *Bildung* protagonist. While I certainly agree with Abbott's vision of Malone as a diarist whose acts of writing are foregrounded in the novel, I also view the novel as reassessing the tensions between reflection and action that pertain to the *Bildungsroman*. Whereas it can be argued that the traditional *Bildungsroman* affirms societal values, Beckett's hybridized *Bildungsroman* questions the logic and values of ideals of progress, accomplishment, and with these, the mastery that seems to come with masculinity (even when the masculine subject is physically limited to a bed and a stubby pencil).

In *Postmodern Genres*, Perloff notes that while modernism seeks to reinvent genres, postmodernism moves away from genres; she follows Blanchot's line of vision in the 1950s. If we turn to Blanchot's *Le Livre à venir* (1959) (*The Book to Come* [2003]), we can note how he emphasizes the transcendence of the book, above generic concerns. He argues,

> Only the work matters, the affirmation that is in the work, the poem in its compressed singularity, the painting in its own space. Only the work matters, but finally the work is there only to lead to the quest for the work ...
>
> Only the book matters, such as it is, far from genres, outside of categories – prose, poetry, novel, testimony – under which it refuses to be classed. (Blanchot 2003: 200)

We should remember that, in *Le Livre à venir*, Blanchot does recognize genres, while also noticing how Mallarmé's poetry and Beckett's novels resist generic typology. The "quest for the work" refers to the reader's activity of discovery and reinvention. Perloff importantly asserts that "It is the paradox of postmodern genre that the more radical the dissolution of traditional generic boundaries, the more important the concept of genericity becomes" (1989: 4). My discussion posits the *Bildungsroman* as one of the key genres informing the hybrid text of *Malone Dies*. The *Bildungsroman's* preoccupation with achievement, formation, and development operates as a guiding tension that Malone and his masculine narrative counterparts resist, but cannot entirely avoid. Castle notes the elasticity of the *Bildungsroman*, with its few conventions, and he discerns in Beckett's novels "the rudiments of the form – a biographical narrative, problems of socialization, the influence of mentors and 'instrumental women,' the problem of vocation – even when such rudiments are pared down to their essence, then to their absence" (2006: 4). Like me, Castle notes the *Bildungsroman's* hybridizing potential in the modern (and postmodern) novel: "Often what we find are ensemble narratives in which *Bildung* plots are embedded and thereby re- or decontextualized by a larger narrative structure that contains them (ibid.: 192). For Castle, the experimental *Bildungsroman* of modernist writers "model[s] both the possibilities of nonidentity and the failure of the Bildungsroman form to represent these possibilities adequately" (ibid.: 251). In my view, Beckett's *Malone Dies* falls well into this company defined by Castle: nonidentity is the negative side of the dialectic of self-formation; the subject often resists, for various reasons, harmonious social integration, and identity then becomes a contested site.

Malone Dies is situated on the overlapping borders of modernism and postmodernism. It highlights and problematizes self-representation, using and abusing realist techniques (such as the confessional first-person voice and documentary-style presentation) and modernist self-reflexivity (such as the narrator's intensive introspection and assessment of the status of the text is composing). Calinescu surveys shared modernist and postmodernist devices (1987: 302–4). *Malone Dies* belongs to a genre of fictional diary writing and topos of the endangered manuscript, which both augment the documentary quality of the literature. Abbott particularly develops this view, suggesting how Malone's diary conflates action and time, exploits the blank entry, and both promises and reneges playfulness in composition. Postmodernist elements can be noted in the novel's emphasis on Malone's state of becoming, through his reflections and actions. Malone's narrative acts during the state of dying subvert the genre of the *Bildungsroman*. Additional parodic and mimetic layers are introduced in Malone's coincidence in the calendar with the day of St John the Baptist, the Assumption, and finally Easter ("Can it be Easter Week?" [Beckett 1958: 208]); these inferences of a Christ-like quality point to both a mock-self-aggrandizement as well as a somber reference to the pitiful state of man, his state of suffering in the world. We can observe such traces of Christ in the character–narrator and his primary narrative subjects or counterparts, the young Sapo and the aging Macmann, these two characterized as "sons." Sapo is first typified as the son of the suffocating parents Saposcat, and he goes through "stations" (ibid.: 206); Macmann's name signifies son of man, and his initial wandering and spread-eagled prone position on the grass point to Christ's wandering in the wilderness and crucifixion. The modernist and postmodernist elements of the novel relate to the male character's liminal and documentary position; Malone reflects the male author writing of reflexive male subjects on the edge of initiation.

Malone Dies emphasizes problems in masculine subjectivity by examining the potential power of gender. In his identity as writer, despite his physical weaknesses and extremely reductive confinement to a bed in a room with scarcely any variation to his day or night, Malone ("man alone") suggests conflicting gendered power (that is, his writing explores sons submitting to paternal law and breaking from it; man's potential submission to woman, who as maternal or phallic figure, possesses power). As several scholars have noted (for example, Kenner, Cousineau, Begam, Abbott, Connor, Davies), we readers are completely dependent on Malone's words, having access to virtually no other direct source of novelistic discourse outside of his. But Malone's extreme narrative dominance is countered by ample displays of lack of mastery (for example, his many retractions, contradictions, absences, repetitions, fumblings, and ramblings), along with many other lacks (his lack of delicacy, tact, balance, perspective, bodily strength, and dexterity). Thus Malone embodies and expresses a modern masculinity of renunciation and paradoxical retention of power. In his alienated state of reflection, he dramatizes himself as a man who contemplates the world and attempts creative action in the form of his stories. Malone's mastery of the double-pointed pencil, with its obvious phallic implications, is qualified by the pencil's diminishing state and its temporary loss in the bed. He views his stories in both phallic and uterine terms:

> clinging to the putrid mucus, and swelling, swelling, saying, Got it at last, my legend ... I shall never get born and therefore never get dead, and a good job too. And if I tell of me and of that other who is my little one, it is as always for want of love, well I'll be buggered, I wasn't expecting that, want of a homuncule, I can't stop. And yet it sometimes seems to me I did get born and had a long life. (225)

Malone's confessional reveals previously unconscious desires for love of the other, as well as desire for a little other ("a homuncule") or baby, much like women's wish for

a child in the Freudian schema. Further, Malone's uncertainty about his existence –
has he been born or not? – indicates a reflexivity with his narrative creations, for he
poses himself this extreme existential question only part way through the telling of
his stories.

In this transitional point of the novel, Malone insists on his desire for

> a little creature, I shall try and make a little creature, to hold in my arms, a little creature
> in my image, no matter what I say. And seeing what a poor thing I have made, or how
> like myself, I shall eat it. Then be alone a long time, unhappy, not knowing what my
> prayer should be nor to whom. (226)

Malone's plan for this little creature made in his own image echoes both God's creation of Adam and Christ in his own image, as well as Goethe's Faustian experiment
that resulted in the homunculus (Second Act). If we consider the composite Sapo-
Macmann as Malone's Faustian homunculus, we can recognize certain parallels in the
two works in terms of man's urge to create man (a reproduction fantasy). In the Second
Act of *Faust*, Faust's pupil Wagner, copying his master, produces an homunculus, a
little man in flask, whom we could compare to Macmann, a narrated little man in
Malone's little story. The little man in the flask is outside the domain of Nature,
having no body and being composed of fire; Macmann, as fictional creation of Malone,
exists nowhere in Nature, but only in Malone's imagination and exercise book. The
transformation of the homunculus is similar to Macmann's (and Malone's) final state
at sea. While Faust is unconscious, the homunculus takes him to Ancient Greece,
seeking to become a whole being. He determines to unite with water to attain birth,
to become real outside his flask. With the help of Proteus, the god of metamorphosis,
the homunculus makes a kind of mystic, sexual union with the sea and Galatea, the
sea-nymph. The little man's surrender to the sea can be seen as a harmonious entry
into the feminine element; later, in Act Four, Faust tries to dominate the ocean, in a
kind of violent rape, leading to his downfall. Macmann's and Malone's partially syn-
thesized endings reflect these dual Faustian resolutions with the sea. For Macmann,
with his murderous keeper Lemuel, is cast out to sea, oarless, while Malone lapses
into silence, his pen and Lemuel's violent hatchet coinciding, and water, air, and fire
mingling alchemical images of the feminine and masculine: "The night is strewn with
absurd ... absurd lights, the stars, the beacons, the buoys, the lights of earth and in
the hills the faint fires of the blazing gorse. Macmann, my last, my possessions, I
remember, he is there too, perhaps he sleeps. Lemuel" (287).

Malone's composite creature, Sapo/Macmann, demonstrates qualities of the mar-
ginalized modern man, reflective of the fictive author. Consistent with his hesitance
and ambivalence, Malone desires both a mimetic self (narcissistic desires) and a distinct and original one (the writer's impossible dream of the original creation and
mastery, exclusive of the feminine domain). As Malone admires his early achievement
in portraying Sapo, he asserts, "Nothing is less like me than this patient, reasonable
child, struggling all alone for years to shed a little light upon himself, avid of the

least gleam, a stranger to the joys of darkness" (192). Malone's pleasures are located in a sense of rebirth in Sapo, or at least a sense of escape from his state of darkness ("Here truly is the air I needed, a lively tenuous air, far from the nourishing murk that is killing me"). Malone's sense of masculine authorship coheres with a fantasy of the womb and of worldly things, or domain of Mephistopheles ("For I want as little as possible of darkness in [Sapo's] story. A little darkness, in itself, at the time, is nothing ... But I know what darkness is, it accumulates, thickens, then suddenly bursts and drowns everything" [190]). Sapo is depicted as the precocious, brooding, "eldest" yet oddly solitary son of the intrusive, judgmental, petty bourgeois, "poor and sickly parents" (187). They fuss over their bills, work, his education and future employment, his lack of action. They prepare a fountain-pen (a "Bird" [210]; in *Malone meurt*, a "Blackbird" [60]) to give him as a present after his exams, a pen symbolic of paternal authorization and entry (flight or wings) into the adult world. Sapo further lingers around the home of the Lamberts: Mr Louis Lambert (or Big Lambert), Mrs Lambert (his young cousin and third or fourth wife), son Edmund and daughter Lizzie. In these Lambert scenes, Sapo observes but does not integrate himself with the peasant family of four that presents the phantasy and prospect of incest (215–16). In contrast to the laboring Big Lambert and Edmund, who will follow in his father's footsteps ("the son, or heir" [201]), including their desire for sex with Lizzie, Sapo distinguishes himself by his inaction and perpetual meandering and contemplation. He wanders in and out of the Lamberts' horizon; when with them, he becomes entranced by the grey hen and moons over a bowl of goat's milk, both signs of his resistance to paternal coding and of a preference for a maternal space. For Lambert, marriage is a matter-of-fact, unromantic affair, involving aggression in sex when he needs his way:

> Lambert was feared and in a position to do as he pleased. And even his young wife had abandoned all hope of bringing him to heel, by means of her cunt, that trump card of young wives ... And at the least sign of rebellion on her part he would run to the wash-house and come back with the beetle and beat her. (200)

Big Lambert and Edmund are portrayed almost as lumbering farm animals, while Mrs Lambert and Lizzie are crystallized as introspective young women in a yawning domestic setting. Mrs Lambert's meditation and labor over the lentils situate her as an unrealized woman arrested in traditional activities. The text hints at possible liaisons between Sapo and the two young women, Mrs Lambert and Lizzie. Lizzie endures the banal aggression in her father's announcements ("To-morrow we'll kill Whitey" [216]) and the bedroom shared with the oafish Edmund. Her marked absence from the household at dinnertime at one juncture points to a rendezvous she has with Sapo, who lingers in the field, neither coming nor going, but soon to go forever. He has told her that "he was going away and would not come back. Then ... they summoned up such memories as he had left them, helping one another and trying to agree. But we all know that little flame and its flickerings in the wild shadows. And agreement only comes a little later, with the forgetting" (217). Both women are sleepless the night he leaves; Lizzie only discloses to Mrs Lambert Sapo's definitive departure a day or two after the fact, implying that his departure is significant for both women, that there has been a special relationship between him and them. Sapo does not so much integrate temporarily into the family as he infiltrates its web of relations.

In contrast to the non-reflective phallic peasant men, the Lambert women seem absorbed in reflection, brooding on each other, memories, thoughts, "formless questions," the moon, stars. While Malone draws for us a portrait of traditional women, he installs a modern sense of lack in them, a lack commensurate with that of Sapo's: these women desire something beyond their local experience, but are unable to articulate or achieve it, unable to come and go as Sapo does.

The women of Sapo's story contribute to the hybridized coming-of-age narrative of the *Bildungsroman* "hero." The kind of feminine fulfillment or plenitude they can offer (the milk, the hen, reproduction) is mediated by the Law of the Father. Sapo departs, implicitly rejecting the two paternal paths in his world, those of Saposcat and Lambert. Malone eventually renames his errant protagonist "Macmann" and posits him in his middle and late years. The Macmann story also involves women to qualify the protagonist's masculine subjectivity as infertile and paradoxically powerful.

The second conception of Malone's protagonist, the aging Macmann, finds new women to watch over him. Moll and Lady Pedal offer two versions of the nurturing woman. Beckett recognizes an aggressive quality in care-giving: it is not altruistic, but rather controlling and self-serving. In both women's cases, nurturing or caring is portrayed as problematic, if not negative; both women are physically repulsive yet comic. Moll's hideous crucifix earrings and carved tooth make a mockery of the erotic love relation. Moll and Macmann are so aged that they can hardly physically or mentally love each other. Moreover, Moll's care for Macmann is superceded by her love for the rules (267). Lady Pedal's ridiculous charity – one paltry outing in a whole year – is indicative of a feminine power that sides with conservatism and colonial rule (she is a "lady" in the British social order). She insists on joining the patients on their outing to witness their enjoyment of her charity. Lemuel seems to serve to punish her for her vanity and overarching power: he murders her helpers and leaves her broken and perhaps dying (286–8).

Beckett's text is saturated with images of unheroic but resilient masculinity and femininity. While these roles are also seen to be dreary, unappealing, unfulfilling, and linked to masculine power in terms of submission, subservience, and performing sexual functions, traditional conservative roles are retained for the women in *Malone Dies*. In both the Sapo and Macmann stories, the male protagonists are set up in relationships with women that eventually end without a resolution of *Bildungsroman* harmonious integration. Sapo makes a departure from the Saposcats and Lamberts, but neither he nor Malone offers a direct explanation or motivation. On a narratological level (since Malone allows us to see the scaffolding of his literary creation), Sapo later "departs" or merges into the character of Macmann, a metamorphosis based not on an apparent narrative plan of character development but on Malone's disgust with the name "Sapo" and disenchantment with his once prized creation. In the case of Macmann, Malone supplies him with unclear resolutions in the prospect of death and violence (for example, Malone decides to "kill" Moll [264]; Lady Pedal is left with a broken hip or worse) and with a final narrative merging – or coincidence – with his creator Malone and keeper Lemuel in the last indeterminate lines of the novel. In Sapo's and Macmann's cases the masculine subject recedes from his feminine others into a world of solitude and a merging with a masculine domain, indicative of an uncertain renunciation of the Law of the Father and a desire for the curiously empowering position of the indeterminate.

In the *Bildungsroman*, the protagonist's environment or surroundings have a strong impact on his character and development. In the fragmented *Bildung* pieces of *Malone Dies*, Sapo and Macmann seem dominated by their surroundings, while also being often lost in reflection. The women who care for these men do not receive much in the way of reciprocation. The tension or conflict in both of these little stories relates to the men's lack of priorities in the world, their lack of self-integration, and relatively meagre social integration. Macmann suffers by being in the world, finds it "galling" to have been conceived in his mother, and does not procreate to extend his lineage (240–1). One could call Sapo and Macmann failures of the *Bildung* credo. Indeed, Malone points out that Macmann is incapable of acting like "true men, true links, [who] can acknowledge the error of their ways" (241). Malone proposes an alternative filial masculinity, not a definitive or dominant one, nor necessarily one approved by him.

Wilhelm Dilthey, an early leading theorist of the *Bildungsroman*, identifies the hero's double task of self-integration and integration into society. Goethe's *Wilhelm Meister's Apprenticeship* is prototypical of the genre: the novel confirms and validates society, and is essentially conservative in its world view of relating the individual to having a productive place in society; Wilhelm Meister does reject the bourgeois man's prosaic life for a more mysterious calling, a dedication to an aristocratic Castle. *Malone Dies* subverts this genre, and essentially questions the productivity of society and the ethics underpinning it. Malone offers us fathers who would be difficult for the modern male subject to emulate. Mr Adrian Saposcat is a fussy salesman and Louis Lambert a bullying peasant who overworks animals and is preoccupied with slaughtering them and lording his power over others. Both fathers toil enormously to little effect, and their relationships with their women are anti-modern. Sapo has possibly sought out the Lamberts in a bourgeois illusion of the nobility of the peasant class. Ultimately, neither class model offers Sapo much to look forward to. He makes his departure, effectuating what I call the filial renunciation – giving up the Law of the Father. The renunciation is both a transgressive act of counter-mastery and an act reifying Sapo's pre-oedipal masculinity. Even Sapo's and Macmann's largely non-productive states of being – for their lives are characterized by very little action or education except for wandering and looking – indicate man's resilient ability to make some course in life yet resist self-development. The modernist and postmodernist novel may lack the

teleological and totalizing structure of the traditional novel of development or education, but Beckett retains the sense of teleology in having his characters, such as Sapo,
Macmann, and Malone, carry out failed or uncertain efforts in life. Their actions and
thoughts are characterized by indecision, ambivalence, redoing and undoing, suggesting and retracting, erasing and reappearing, and hesitating. These three men are
marked by time; teleology is further supplied in the foregrounding of man's body,
his life determined by his aging and ultimate death. Despite Malone's, Sapo's, and
Macmann's prolonged instances of hesitation, they are drawn to some sort of end,
indeterminate, but concluding. Within the temporal regime of *Malone Dies*, two forms
of time compete – the *chronos* and *kairos*, blank, unfolding time or mere successiveness,
and meaningful, shaped, end-directed time (see Kermode 1967). The result of the
novel's *chronos* and *kairos* is a confusion and blurring of time. For example, Malone's
bodily limitation to the bed prevents him from knowing clearly calendar or clock
time; his guesses suggest a narrative time related to signification, such as Easter (resurrection) or summer (youth), as opposed to mere mechanical time used in the modern
metropolis.

Beckett's examination of the masculine subject can be compared to Lacan's assessment of the human subject in the mirror stage. Lacan discusses the tendency to imitation in human and other animal life; further, in man's case, it is possible that
developmentally he may be born too early and is helpless too long after birth. In the
mirror stage, he notes, we can recognize a "specific prematurity of birth in man"
(1977: 4). Lacan's premature man is commensurate with Beckett's men, who do not
seem to be ready to apprehend a vision of their wholeness in the mirror of the symbolic
register. Within Beckett's fictional world, the creators, such as a character–narrator
like Malone, both seek and reject imitations of themselves in their creations (for
example, Sapo, Macmann). They are both drawn to self-expression and its obverse,
and this oscillation shows an indecisive posture towards masculine subjecthood;
Beckett's writing of the masculine subject calls into question what masculinity – or
more specifically its armor – consists of.

Lacan explains the process and result of the mirror stage for the human subject:

> This development is experienced as a temporal dialectic that decisively projects the
> formation of the individual into history. The mirror stage is a drama whose internal
> thrust is precipitated from insufficiency to anticipation – and which manufactures for
> the subject, caught up in the lure of the fragmented body-image to a form of its totality
> that I shall call orthopaedic – and, lastly, to the assumption of the armour of an alienat-
> ing identity, which will mark with its rigid structure the subject's entire mental devel-
> opment. (1977: 4)

In terms of the narrative of *Malone Dies*, a mirror stage of sorts is re-enacted for the
creating masculine subject (Malone) and his masculine creation (Sapo/Macmann).
Paternal Malone creates in his image a little creature or son. The text serves as a kind
of mirror to reflect the imitative parts of the illusory image. Malone is frequently

dissatisfied with the resulting images in the mirror of his little stories, and alternately turns to the accounts of his own state of being and his possessions, which also do not satisfy. Lacan describes the results of the subject's encounter with his image in the mirror as "this moment of the identification with the imago of the counterpart and the drama of primordial jealousy" (ibid: 5). By extension, Malone's dissatisfaction and frequent interruptions are those of the artist both drawn to and jealous of his creation. Malone's wavering between his creative process (his mirror work or action, his narrating of the little stories) and his reflective processes (memory, his examination of his state of being, surroundings, abilities) dramatizes the imperfect and process-based act of writing and its relation to identity. Writing is both a highly personal act and one that forces one into an exaggerated split subjectivity ("my fingers too write in other latitudes" [Beckett 1958: 234]). In writing, one imagines or anticipates the other's position and judges it; it is no accident that Malone writes with a drafting writing instrument, the pencil (and not, say, an indelible Blackbird pen), and writes in an exercise book, much like a pupil who is learning and preparing something in draft and possibly for later examination.

The writing that creates the text of *Malone Dies* carries out that *Bildungsroman* motif, the tensions between acting and reflecting, while draining them of sweeping or totalizing enunciative power and reducing (but not erasing) social relevance. The question of mastery of the masculine subject remains central through the narrative. Malone turns away from certain imperatives in masculinity in his text (the renunciations of Sapo and Macmann), yet he (and shadowing him, Beckett) continues to fulfill his articulation of the Name of the Father.

REFERENCES

Abbott, H. Porter (1983). "The Harpooned Note-book: *Malone Dies* and the Conventions of Intercalated Narrative." In Morris Beja, S. E. Gontarski, and Pierre Astier (eds.), *Samuel Beckett: Humanistic Perspectives*. Columbus: Ohio State University Press.

Abbott, H. Porter (1984). *Diary Fiction: Writing as Action*. Ithaca and London: Cornell University Press.

Beckett, Samuel (1951). *Malone meurt*. Paris: Minuit.

Beckett, Samuel (1958). "Malone Dies." In *Three Novels*. New York: Grove.

Begam, Richard (1996). *Samuel Beckett and the End of Modernity*. Stanford: Stanford University Press.

Blanchot, Maurice (2003). *The Book to Come*, trans. Charlotte Mandell. Stanford: Stanford University Press.

Braudel, Fernand (1980). *On History*, trans. Sarah Matthews. Chicago: University of Chicago Press.

Buckley, J. H. (1974). *Season of Youth: The Bildungsroman from Dickens to Golding*. Cambridge, MA: Harvard University Press.

Calinescu, Matei (1987). *Five Faces of Modernity: Modernism, Avant-Garde, Decadence, Kitsch, Postmodernism*. Durham: Duke University Press.

Castle, Gregory (2006). *Reading the Modernist Bildungsroman*. Gainesville, FL: University Press of Florida.

Connor, Steven (1988). *Samuel Beckett: Repetition, Theory and Text*. Oxford: Blackwell.

Cousineau, Thomas (1999). *After the Final No: Samuel Beckett's Trilogy*. Newark: University of Delaware Press; London: Associated University Presses.

Davies, Paul (1994). "Three Novels and Four 'Nouvelles: Giving up the Ghost Be Born at Last.'" In John Pilling (ed.), *The Cambridge Companion to Beckett*. Cambridge: Cambridge University Press.

Dilthey, Wilhelm (1985). *Poetry and Experience*. Princeton: Princeton University Press.

Eliot, T. S. (1961). "The Waste Land." In Maynard Mack, Leonard Dean, and William Frost (eds.), *Modern Poetry*. Englewood Cliffs, NJ: Prentice-Hall.

Felski, Rita (1995). *The Gender of Modernity*. Cambridge and London: Harvard University Press.

Goethe, Johann Wolfgang von (1989). *Wilhelm Meister's Apprenticeship*, ed. and trans. Eric A. Blackall in cooperation with Victor Lange. New York: Suhrkamp.

Goethe, Johann Wolfgang von (2006). *Faust: Parts One and Two*, trans. John Clifford. London: N. Hern Books.

Hardin, James (ed.) (1991). "Introduction." In *Reflection and Action: Essays on the Bildungsroman*. Columbia: University of South Carolina Press.

Kenner, Hugh. (1973). *A Reader's Guide to Samuel Beckett*. New York: Farrar, Straus and Giroux.

Kermode, Frank (1967). *The Sense of an Ending*. New York: Oxford University Press.

Kontje, Todd (1992). *Private Lives in the Public Sphere: The German Bildungsroman as Metafiction*. University Park: Pennsylvania State University Press.

Kontje, Todd (1993). *The German Bildungsroman: History of a National Genre*. Columbia: Camden House.

Lacan, Jacques (1977). "The Mirror Stage." *Écrits: A Selection*, trans. Alan Sheridan. New York: Norton.

Lewis, Wyndham (1979). "Enemy of the Stars." In *Wyndham Lewis: Collected Poems and Plays*. Manchester: Carcanet. Originally published 1914.

Perloff, Marjorie (1981). *The Poetics of Indeterminacy: Rimbaud to Cage*. Princeton: Princeton University Press.

Perloff, Marjorie (1989). "Introduction." In *Postmodern Genres*. Norman: University of Oklahoma Press.

Schoene-Harwood, Berthold (2000). *Writing Men: Literary Masculinities from Frankenstein to the New Man*. Edinburgh: Edinburgh University Press.

Silverman, Kaja (1992). *Male Subjectivity at the Margins*. New York and London: Routledge.

Wilde, Oscar (2006). *The Picture of Dorian Gray*. New York: Norton.

20
"The Knowing Non-Exister": Thirteen Ways of Reading *Texts for Nothing*

S. E. Gontarski and C. J. Ackerley

Samuel Beckett's ground-breaking set of short, apparently disjointed narratives, the 13 *Texts for Nothing*, represents an attempt to move beyond the creative impasse caused by the writing of *The Unnamable*. Through them Beckett hoped "to get out of the attitude of disintegration," as he said to interviewer Israel Shenker in 1956. They thus bridge the last of the three French novels, *L'Innommable* (*The Unnamable*), and Beckett's final lengthy novel of 1961, *Comment c'est* (*How It Is*). In fact, the stories themselves, in both French and English, form something like a continuous bilingual devolutionary narrative of some 26 stories, since the translations of *Texts for Nothing* followed hard upon the completion of *Textes pour rien* in December 1951 and continued over the next year. Beckett's title was derived from the musical term *mesure pour rien*, a silent prelude to performance, a soundless interval conveying nothing but tempo and so an essential part of the musical whole even in its silence. One can argue that the great dramas of the 1950s are derivative of earlier prose, and that Beckett's original works, the genre-altering innovations of thought and expression, were only possible as he came to terms with the complexities of disintegration that reside in such prose. Even so, these difficult *Texts* have received scant critical attention. The best accounts remain John Pilling's discussion in *Frescoes of the Skull* (Knowlson and Pilling 1979), which examines them according to an aesthetics of failure and Susan Brienza's *Samuel Beckett's New Worlds* (1987), which elaborates that theme. In *The Complete Short Prose of Samuel Beckett*, S. E. Gontarski sets them against the *Quatre nouvelles* (*Four Novellas* [*Stories*]), and sees them as performing "a leap from Modernism to Post-Modernism, from interior voices to exterior voices, from internality to externality" (1995: xxv) as they dismantle the stream of consciousness narrative technique, the interior monologue, and reduce it, or at least its essentialism, to nothing, or rather to performance. They appear to be shards and aperçus of continuously unfolding narratives that can never be complete or completed, as the coherent entity of "character" is disbursed amidst a plurality of disembodied voices and echoes, origins unknown. Others have noted, perhaps too glibly, the impulse towards minimalism, and the instability of "I" as the distinction between the self as subject and as object (the "not I" and the "not me") is dissolved. They can be seen in many respects as the narrative equivalent of the late plays in that each can stand alone as an exquisitely etched image, and they can be grouped so that each plays off its predecessors and anticipates subsequent images. Below the 13 are treated separately, even as we stress the interrelationship of the narrative fragments and images.

"Text 1" does not so much "begin" as emerge from a void, the empty pages preceding it, without any "signs" of character, plot, or resolution, but with seemingly meaningless statements of negation ("Suddenly, no") and impasse ("I could have stayed … I couldn't") which offer few concessions to the reader's orientation and so to his or her understanding. The effect is unnerving, yet a pattern of counterpoint emerges, a disintegrating narrative marked against yet held together by details with a biographical basis, words as stepping-stones through a quagmire of the unsaid. The tone is gentle, repetition creating cadence, sustained with a lilting rhythm that signals the slow entropic decline of one caught between telling and listening, the life sentence of one unable to make for himself a place in the grammatical sentence. John Pilling suggests (Knowlson and Pilling 1979: 45) that the narrator is concerned with preserving an integrated self, but emphasis may be more properly placed on his holding onto an integrated narrative, however fictitious it might be. "Text 1" initiates a difficult journey, across an abstract landscape, universal yet sharply particularized, the Beckett country of *Molloy* and *Waiting for Godot*, and, more precisely, that of Chapter 7 of *Mercier and Camier*. Yet the place, like the body, is "unimportant," and descriptions annihilate themselves: "Glorious prospect, but for the mist." An exact sense of place is paradoxically the nowhere of a story that moves away from external "description" towards a narrative about narrating. There are moments of rare beauty: the distant sea as hammered lead, the night sky open over the mountain, the final image of father and son; yet the tone is pessimistic. Metaphors and intertextual references delineate the process, and the text is built around a heap of broken images from Beckett's earlier work: the body as a "foundered" old hack, as at the end of the short story "Dante and the Lobster"; the haggard vulture face, as in poem "The Vulture"; the biblical (Proustian) city and plain, as in *Molloy* (1951: 91); the pun about being "attached" to his hat; the phrase (in the English text only) *stultior stultissimo* ("an unparalleled fool"), invoking Thomas à Kempis and his "fool for Christ," as in "Echo's Bones" (1961: 20); and retelling the story of Joe Breem or Breen, the lighthouse-keeper's son, as in "The Calmative" (1995: 64). This fable of Joe Breem or Breen, shapes Samuel Beckett's text intriguingly as it invokes the adventure story of childhood and reduces it to a cultural shard, a piece of memory that seems to fit with no other piece. At best, it is perhaps company; it fills the emptiness and offers the comfort of closure; our narrator is finally able to compose himself for sleep. This will prove a false solace, a deceptive victory, for the fight on the linguistic battlefield of the self is barely engaged, and the narrator has taken refuge in a story of another, a story for children, rather than narrate himself into the story as it is told.

"Text 2" begins with a descriptive passage of night and day, and the image of Mother Calvet. The plain telling is subverted by the double articulation of words like "endurable" (lasting, having to be endured) which create metaphysical uncertainty and unreliability, prompting the narrator to wonder if he is better off "here," now that he "knows"; knows, that is, the horror of the light. The meliorist sense that he is somehow better off is fleeting, and he is forced to admit that he is in a head, an "ivory dungeon" (in Beckett's French original, an "oubliette"), with a fear of coming to the last, like a crucified Jesus. Details are recalled (Mr Joly, the verger), or misremembered (Piers pricking over the plain, say); journeys, coming and going, an equilibrium sustained between negations and affirmations; then a final image of Schubert's *Winterreise* (and the Graves brothers) marking the futility of any hope. The narrator has tried to assert a sense of connection and familiarity by remembering "above," but (unlike "Text 1") there is no comforting closure, and memory "here" will not constitute a unified self.

"Text 3" treats these themes intently, the differing articulation of "I am alone" and "I alone am" revealing a profound metaphysical solitude. There will be a departure, and he starts (not suddenly) by stirring, "there must be a body ... I'll say it's me." This is "I" in the accusative, object rather than subject, which undercuts the effort to imagine himself into existence, as a man, an "old tot." "Text 3" thus introduces the body according to the criteria of Descartes and Schopenhauer, as immediate object to the self in a way that the rest of the world is not; but the narrator strains vainly towards corporeality, until he concludes that "There is no flesh anywhere, nor any way to die." Before reaching that conclusion, however, he surveys several aspects of his self: the Nanny fantasy (in English, Bibby, and St Stephen's Green), which reveals him in limbo between childhood and old age; the dark blue tie with yellow stars (which Samuel Beckett's mother had given him); the desire for a crony, a fellow, to whom he can listen and tell improbable tales of war and the Easter Rising, familiarized narratives of heroism. As "Text 2" exhausted memory, "Text 3" tires imagination. Having survived, there is old age to "look forward" to: sitting and spitting; getting into the Incurables (the Mater Hospital); the "sere and yellow" (*Macbeth*); unreliable memories (Hohenzollerns); going literally and figuratively to the dogs; or ending up like "Vincent" (van Gogh), brought home for burial in the rain. He wants to "cut a caper," to be "bedded in that flesh," to move through the *carnival* of life; but in accordance with the dictum of Thomas à Kempis, the joyous setting out and sorrowful coming home, the story ends in a sad stasis, the jaded admission that it is all in vain, that nothing has stirred and no one has spoken.

"Text 4" asks, where would he go, if he could go; who would he be, if he could be; what would he say, if he had a voice. Simple questions are complicated by the sense of himself as stranger, the earlier "it's me" generating "for whom alone accusative I exist" (which will in turn generate the metaphor of trial in "Text 5"). A kind of schizophrenia ensues, between the nominative ("he" and "I") and the accusative ("him" and "me"), as pronouns vie for supremacy, the struggle generating such forms as "me who am everything." Syntax breaks down as speechlessness is intuited, the voice which cannot be his – for it is there that he would go, if he could go; it is that who he'd be, if he could be. At the end of "Text 4" he finds himself "almost restored to the feasible": this, in the interviews with Georges Duthuit (103), signifies the realm of quotidian life, from which art must break. In the tension between the two realms, the narrator lives out the perennial difficulty of relating life to art.

"Text 5" anticipates *How It Is* directly with the imagery of the trial, the narrator defining himself as merely a clerk and scribe, playing the major roles in this tribunal of reason, and peopling the "court" with many voices, the narrative gliding in and out of these, prosecutor, witness, judge, and accused, much in the manner of James Joyce's *Finnegans Wake*. This is an "obscure assize where to be is to be guilty" (117). The crime, apparently, is that of having been born; the penalty a life sentence. No manner of representation can mitigate this, but equally on trial is the language through which identity is shaped and asserted, the sentence sentenced, so to speak. "Text 5" thus marks the disintegration of the fundamental ordering units of language, punctuation losing its power, "I" denoting the third person, and definite and indefinite articles interchangeable. The body too disintegrates, ears straining "for a voice not from without" (118), were it only to tell another lie. He is aware of the great gulf between himself and others present. He says: "I say it as I hear it." This theme will dominate *How It Is* and reflect an inability to determine (or to trust) that authoritative voice. The session ends, not entirely one of sweet silent thought, and phantoms of memory return; weariness sets in, the quill falls (Hamlet's "special providence in the fall of a sparrow" [5.2.233]), and though the "minutes" are incomplete "it's noted."

"Text 6" sustains the imagery of "Text 5" by noting the "keepers" of his prison, and wondering how the "intervals" (the "rests" implied in the title) might be filled. The answer is by memory, past "apparitions" conjured up in such a way (the narrative voice imagines fleetingly) that, in an implied chiasmus, if he cannot live again in the world, the world might exist in him again, "a little resolution" being all that is needed to come and go again under the changing sky. Such "high hopes" are condemned to futility, however, as he will fail to find the words to fill the intervals or to tell a story, not because he has failed to "hit on the right ones," but because the enterprise is doomed from the start. Yet out of that "farrago of silence" intimate images arise. He recalls standing in Picadilly Circus on Glasshouse Street, and the clatter of bones and castanets (see *Murphy*, 1957: 115–16). The famous ant is here to memory what it was there to vision; dead flies that appeared in "Serena I," "La Mouche," and *Watt* are obsessional images of futility and dream. The "eyes" (of cousin/lover Peggy Sinclair, perhaps) that he must have believed in for an instant will open poignantly in *Krapp's Last Tape*. These remind him of his father's shaving mirror which remained when his father went; and his mother doing her hair in it in her New Place. The butterfly refuses to be an emblem of the soul surviving death, and the dust remains slime despite all efforts of the Eternal and his son. The "apparitions," however fragmented, serve to counterpoint the pattern of textual disintegration (tears are a "crystalline humour," and like Mercutio he jests, "I'll be grave"), so as to offer, if not high hopes, the possibility of a little story told or heard, a way of filling the interval, he gives us his word.

"Text 7" dashes such hopes, with its despairing query, "Did I try everything?" The purgatory of waiting is imaged in the "Terminus" where he sits in memory, as so often in the past, in the third-class waiting room of Harcourt Street Station whence trains departed for the Dublin suburb of Foxrock. He recalls when he could move, but motion has slowed and the narrative loses momentum. He compares himself with X, "that paradigm of human kind, moving at will," a carcass in God's image with wife and brats, and tries (in vain?) to distance himself from such a likeness. The station turntable parodies the *Paradiso*, the universe rotating about God; the sense of waiting at the Terminus and the vision of Eternity are transposed into the remarkable image of the balance-wheel of the station clock, which effects the transition from timelessness to time passing. Although time has slowed, and this text has been a static interval, tentative conclusions are reached, but not in haste, "not so fast": that to search for himself elsewhere would be a "loss of time"; that there is no time to lose; that the time has come for him to begin. This seventh text, the mid-point of the 13, is the balance wheel of the sequence.

"Text 8" reverts to the silence, broken only by words and tears, assuming its place on the continuum of decline, and reflecting a deep pessimism directed at both the inevitability of aging and his "stupid old threne." Continuing the imagery of imprisonment, the narrator imagines himself thrown out by the past, or having burrowed his way out, for the moment free of memories. But what is an old lag to do? He does not understand whom he can have offended to have been punished this way, and he repeats the old cry: "It's not me, it can't be me." A bifurcation takes place, one self as a ventriloquist's dummy in the image of a head left behind, in Ireland, perhaps, "that other who is me," while to his "certain knowledge" (the irony is unstated) he is somewhere in Europe. While the sense of living by proxy is manifest, and the "right aggregate" unlikely, he cannot but see himself as in imagination he might be, with a white stick and ear-trumpet, at the *Place de la République* adjacent to the Père Lachaise cemetery, begging for alms without any concession to self-respect (a "previous song"), yet simultaneously aware that this was not he (or him), not his real self.

"Text 9" suggests a way out, an image more powerful in French in which "issue" generates a sense of the issueless predicament of existence, Molloy's "senseless, speechless, issueless misery." Yet Dante's image of the beauties of the skies and stars at the moment of emergence from the *Inferno* is powerful in both languages. This is how "Text 9" concludes, and so the narrative vibrates between these two polarities, the predicament less resolved than contemplated. As befits his textual history, the narrator has "convictions," but these pass, and he feels himself instead buried beneath an avalanche of "wordshit," unable to dig (himself) out. His alternative to the prison is the graveyard, emphatically *there* ("là"), as the "way out" is not. But *something* is struggling to emerge, which he can't quite grasp, and although everything is in the conditional ("if I could say") and there's a "minor" difficulty about the body, Dante's great image has revived (if only momentarily) the "high hopes" of "Text 6."

"Text 10" destroys such nonsense. Time to give up, the heart is not in it any more, the appetite not what it was. There is uttering, agreed, but the image of the mouth as anus of the head defines the worth of what is expelled. This is a pessimistic little text, sentences connected by "and" and "or" in a vain attempt at meaningful concatenation, and with a Malone-like lapse: "This is awful, awful, at least there's that to be thankful for." The prospect is unredeemed misery, with the barest gesture towards "a voice of silence" (143), the theme of what follows. "Text 10" closes with the narrator's attempts to sleep, but the closure possible at the end of "Text 1" is here reduced to a verbal wish, less than an act, as befitting one not really there.

"Text 11" struggles to begin when all sense of the self is "scattered by the everlasting words" (a pun on "winds"), where nothing is namable. One possibility is the musical turn, adding "him" to the repertory, executing him "as I execute me," one dead bar after the other, the puns giving a double articulation of movement and death. The outcome is vaguely successful, like a patch of sea under the passing lighthouse beam, a comforting reminder of the close of "Text 1." He knows that triumph is delusory, vile words to make him believe he's here, but he can affirm he's getting on, getting on, though the repetition makes the assertion less convincing. The theme he is trying to utter begins: "when come those who knew me," but its first articulation has failed, and the second is "premature" (the imagery of birthing sustained). Striking images of his condition are executed: the square root of minus one, an imaginary number rendered symbolically as *i* (something less than "I"); a student's face covered with ink and jam, the phrase *caput mortuum* implying "worthless residue" but meaning literally "dead head"; then as an old clot (French "con") alone in the two-stander urinal on the corner of the Rue d'Assas (in French, "dans la vespasienne à deux places rue Guynemer"), rending the air with painful ejaculations (physical and religious), Jesus, Jesus. These, and especially the last, are moving and compelling images of the humanities he insists he has terminated, and through these he is able to overcome, if only temporarily, the disjunction between the "I" and the "he" and move to the third utterance of the failed theme. This time it's going to work: "when comes the hour of those who knew me ... it's as though I were among them," in their "company." Thus, "he" *is*. For all its insistence on failure, this is a text carefully structured to build to this triumph, dubious as it may be.

"Text 12" returns to the *Winterreise*, a journey towards death. Picking up the theme of identity ("so long as the others are there"), he sets aside "believing in me," or the need for a voice and the power to move as *witness* of his existence, of his being "on earth." He sees his body as a "veteran" (Napoleon's retreat from Moscow may be implied), the "me" in "him" remembering, forgetting. Although (changing the metaphor) he is trapped in the dungeons of this moribund, this represents his "last chance to have been," to listen to the voices that are everywhere, and again to ask, Who's speaking? This composite sense of being, the "me" in "him" and the awareness that sees the disjunction (the "I"), is described as "a pretty three in one," a Trinity of sorts (in French, "un joli trio"), but the hypostasis is insubstantial, "one" being equally "no one." Finally, he is back to a point of departure, "the long silent guffaw of the knowing non-exister," Democritus, for whom Nothing is more real than nothing. The hard-won victory of "Text 11" must be set aside, for to accept it as reality would be like joining the accountants' chorus, "opining like a single man," that is, accepting unquestioningly the existence of the body ("riding a bicycle") and the need for a god as ultimate witness, whereas the reality is, as it was and ever shall be, "nothing ever but nothing and never, nothing ever but lifeless words." The *Winterreise*, if it has not moved beyond this point of departure, has negated any other option.

"Text 13" is an elegy to the dying voice, the "weak old voice that tried in vain to make me," which has foundered on the nothingness of being (like the old hack of "Text 1"). Still, it "embodies" the unnamable, indefinable, incomprehensible, impossible urge to express, to leave a "trace" of its passing, of the life that has passed. This text reaches equilibrium between the forces that have shaped the others, a kind of peace as the "I" of self is absorbed into the "it" of voice, a *diminuendo al niente* which is also an affirmation, the authoritative voice at last assuming its role as subject of the narrative. For the narrator, now almost absent, this is the end of the farce of making, of the silencing of silence, of the wish to know, an acceptance of death, and of the inevitable failure of his attempt to create himself, a startling reminder of which yet breaks out in the extraordinary metaphor of "no's knife in yes's wound," a scream which stains the silence to which the text aspires, a "trace" of its author's passing. In the final sentence the narrator takes his farewell of the light, the verbal tense moving from the subjunctive ("were there one day to be") and conditional ("all would be silent") to the mythological present: "it murmurs." Against the odds, despite all, "a coda worthy of the rest" has emerged, a poetical apotheosis of the impossible paradox of being and not-being.

References

Beckett, Samuel (1951). *Molloy*. New York: Grove Press. (Reprinted [1955] in *Three Novels*. New York: Grove Press, 7–176.]

Beckett, Samuel (1957). *Murphy*. New York: Grove Press. (London: Routledge, 1938).

Beckett, Samuel (1961). *Poems in English*. London: John Calder.

Beckett, Samuel (1974). *Mercier and Camier*. New York: Grove Press.

Knowlson, James and John Pilling (1979). *Frescoes of the Skull: The Later Prose and Drama of Samuel Beckett*. London: John Calder.

Beckett, Samuel (1995). *Samuel Beckett: The Complete Short Prose, 1929–1989*, ed. S. E. Gontarski. New York: Grove Press.

21

What We Are
Given to Mean: *Endgame*

Paul Shields

Whatever one thinks, Endgame *puts it to the test.*

Herbert Blau

In his essay "Ending the Waiting Game: A Reading of Beckett's *Endgame*," Stanley
Cavell argues that Beckett's characters endure the curse of meaning. Hamm, Clov,
Nagg, and Nell are "sealed away by a universal flood of meaning and hope" (1969:
149), though they yearn for "solitude, emptiness, nothingness, meaninglessness,
silence" (ibid.: 156). Cavell writes, "*Endgame* is a play whose mood is characteristically
one of madness and in which the characters are fixed by a prophecy, one which their
actions can be understood as attempting both to fulfill and to reverse" (ibid.: 123).
The most recent scholarship on *Endgame* reveals that the author shares in his characters'
struggles. S. E. Gontarski's 2006 study of Beckett as a director and commentator,
"Greying the Canon: Beckett in Performance," suggests a man of many minds, a
schizophrenic author who both retreats from and pursues meaning. Beckett inhabits
a shelter similar to that of the characters, suffering from a desire not to understand
his meaning but also from a need to be meaningful, or, to adapt one of Cavell's key
phrases, an inability *not* to be meaningful. Gontarski (among others) helps to show
that Beckett is also "fixed by a prophecy," even as he attempts to undo his meaning
and strives not to mean what he is given to mean.

As it reaches its fiftieth anniversary, *Endgame* remains among the most prodigious
dramas in Western culture, which is to reiterate what many critics and scholars have
been saying for five decades. In its early years, the play attracted the attention of
Martin Esslin, Ruby Cohn, Hugh Kenner, and Theodor W. Adorno among others.
Beckett's American director, Alan Schneider, quickly knew the play would stand the
test of time. For Schneider, *Endgame* "lifted me out of myself, exhilarated me, provided
a dramatic experience as strong as the one I had when I first discovered *Oedipus* or
Lear" (1969: 16). In the twenty-first century, the play continues to elicit praise from
critics and scholars, many of whom, like Schneider, measure *Endgame* against works

by Sophocles and Shakespeare. In 2003, from a podium in Sydney, Australia, Herbert Blau called *Endgame* the greatest play of the twentieth century, echoing his own words in a 1964 essay, "*Endgame* – in my opinion the most profound drama in the modern theater" (2004: 42). One of the play's most inspiring commentators, Blau describes its profundity:

> One feels inside those gray walls, as amid the odalisque splendors of Stevens' *Sunday Morning*, the dark encroachment of old catastrophe ... What is amazing about the play is its magnitude. Haunting the limits of endurance, it finds grandeur amid the trash, trivia, and excrement of living. More than any modern drama I know it creates explicitly that place where Yeats said Love has pitched its mansion. (ibid.: 43)

In a telephone interview with me (April 23, 2006), Harold Bloom concurred with Blau's judgments: "I suppose, aesthetically speaking, if I had to choose a single work by Beckett, in spite of the power of the trilogy, it would be *Endgame*, which is certainly, together with perhaps two plays by Pirandello, *Henry IV* in particular ... a candidate for the major drama of the twentieth century." According to Bloom, if trends continue, *Endgame* may reign in the present century: "There are good novelists alive, but there are no great dramatists alive in any western country that I'm aware of. Mr. [Tony] Kushner is still a figure of enormous promise, but not Samuel Beckett's." For Bloom, Beckett achieves his place in the Western canon because of his misreading of Shakespeare, the ghostly author of *Endgame*. "But whose play is it anyway," Bloom wonders, "Beckett's or Hamm's – or, to state the point more harshly, Beckett's or Shakespeare's? ... Is not *Endgame* part of Shakespeare's creation?" (1993: 474). Bloom shares Jan Kott's vision of Beckett's work. In his book *Shakespeare Our Contemporary*, Kott argues that *Endgame* is Beckett's paring down of *King Lear*: "Edgar is leading the blind Gloucester to the precipice at Dover. This is just the theme of *Endgame*; Beckett was the first to see it in *King Lear*, he eliminated all action, everything external, and repeated it in its skeletal form" (1964: 157). *Endgame* indeed reveals Beckett's reading of Shakespeare, but 50 years of criticism yield a vast range of other perspectives.

The location of the shelter is central to the debate. Some critics locate the play in the skull, some at the site of the crucifixion. Richard N. Coe suspects the play might be set in Hell (1968: 95), and Blau suggests the "suburbs of Hell" (2004: 47). Katharine Worth believes the setting evokes a more specific kind of hell: "Comparison with the other most celebrated 'room' play of the century, the *Huis Clos* of Sartre, brings out the expressive power of Beckett's set. The grey light, high windows, and so forth are a language, speaking directly to us, telling us something profound and real about the state we are entering" (2001: 36). H. Porter Abbott sees the setting as a dystopia, comparing the play to the work of writers such as H. G. Wells (1996: 133), and in a more recent study, Geoff Hamilton envisions the play as an anti-pastoral drama. "This is obviously no Arcadia," Hamilton writes, "but Arcadian (or near-Arcadian) subjects haunt each character's speech, while appeals to God to account for suffering – corresponding to invocations of pagan deities in pastoral poetry

– are a definitive obsession … Flora and fauna seem to be extinct in this (suggestively post-nuclear) landscape, but memories of more vital, more pastoral worlds remain" (2002: 612, 615).

Other critics argue that the play's setting is Ireland, or, as Nels C. Pearson surmises, a one-time Ireland. In his 2001 article, Pearson theorizes that Hamm and Clov are ghosts of a defunct colonial (or decolonization) struggle between Britain and Beckett's homeland. The system is dead, the world in ruins, but the characters cannot manage to stop saying their lines and living out their parts. They perform according to a master-script: "The important thing is that Hamm and Clov maintain their respective roles of ruler and ruled, as well as the assumption that there is no alternative to these roles, long after the external causes or specific historical circumstances of those roles have deteriorated" (Pearson 2001: 216–17). In *Inventing Ireland*, Declan Kiberd focuses on the notion of role-playing and the characters' reliance on "an approved text." Kiberd writes, "*Endgame* is, in fact, the most extreme example of a repeated revivalist theme: the study of the sufferings of characters who make themselves willing martyrs to an approved text" (1996: 545). Kiberd continues, "Clov is as in love with his subjection as Hamm is with his gloom … Beckett's is a world whose characters are constantly tempted to allow others to do their thinking for them, to resign their wills to a higher authority" (ibid.: 546, 548). Pearson's and Kiberd's readings are intriguing postcolonial reinventions of Cavell's essay on *Endgame* and the curse of meaning, though Cavell locates the characters neither in Ireland nor in its after-image. For Cavell, the play unfolds in a far more universal, or at least Western-universal, environment. His essay demands careful scrutiny.

Cavell argues that the setting of *Endgame* is rather ordinary, a place of ordinary beings. Inside, a family lives its days – talking, arguing, cursing. He writes, "Take a step back from the bizarrerie and they are just a family. Not just any family perhaps, but every unhappy family is unhappy in its own way, gets in its way in its own way" (Cavell 1969: 117). As he discusses this ordinary group, Cavell makes reference to the Bible, Shakespeare, Pascal, Nietzsche, and even Alfred Hitchcock. The force of the diagnosis makes one wonder whether Cavell has been to the shelter and met with the characters. Perhaps he has. "[There] is no distance at all," he writes, "or no recognizable distance between them and us" (ibid.:131). (Blau makes a similar assertion concerning the distance between audience and characters: "A friend of mine once objected to *Endgame* because 'You can't call the characters on the telephone.' True. But if you could, you'd only be talking to yourself" [Blau 2004: 47].) Out to undo early critics who suggest the play is a commentary on nothingness (for instance, Esslin), Cavell argues that the very opposite is the case:

Beckett, in *Endgame*, is not marketing subjectivity, popularizing *angst*, amusing and thereby excusing us with pictures of our psychopathology; he is outlining the facts – of mind, of community – which show why these have become our pastimes. The discovery of *Endgame*, both in topic and technique, is not the failure of meaning (if that means the lack of meaning) but its total, even totalitarian success – our inability *not* to mean what we are given to mean. (1969: 116–17)

The last few words are most important. Beckett's characters, an ordinary family living ordinary lives, are cursed with meaning, unable to stop meaning what they "are given to mean." Unlike Blau, who remarks that Hamm is "in defiance of Nothingness" (2004: 48), Cavell sees him as desperate to find it. As Pearson asserts in his postcolonial reading, Hamm, Clov, Nagg, and Nell perform their parts even in a ruined world.

The characters receive their meaning from art, pictures, and stories about God. The play's various allusions to the story of Noah (a focus for many critics) intimate that they endure the curse because of a story in which God chooses to destroy humanity, but then chooses not to, saving eight individuals. In *Endgame*, the family is cut in half, four survivors in a small shelter. They check the weather, say prayers, and discuss the notion of the earth's replenishment. (James Knowlson's biography on Beckett informs us that the author was reading about Noah while writing *Endgame* and that in early versions of the play one of the characters reads passages from the Genesis account [1996: 366].) In his reading of the play, Bloom is uncertain as to the significance of Noah to the drama:

> Palpably, as many critics have shown, the Biblical reference of *Endgame* is the story of Noah and his son Ham, who was cursed for witnessing the Primal Scene reenacted between his father and his mother, perhaps indeed for a more serious outrage against Noah. We do not know (because Beckett won't tell us) whether Hamm's blindness was caused by this Oedipal curse, nor can we say how relevant Noah and the Flood are to *Endgame*. (1993: 474)

Cavell is much more convinced of the pertinence of Beckett's allusions: "The entire action of the play is determined by the action of that tale" (1969: 138). The story of Noah provides the characters with meaning, hope for another day, the need to continue playing the waiting game. They recognize, however, that their wait is merely that. Their dilemma is that "they do not know how to end" (ibid.: 132). For "even where it is a happy change," Cavell remarks, "a world is always lost" (ibid.: 118). The characters are, to recall Kiberd's vision, "in love" with their world, with their subjection and their gloom. Hamm nevertheless attempts to accomplish the task God chooses not to finish: "Hamm's strategy is to undo all covenants and secure fruitlessness" (ibid.: 140).

One of Hamm's strategies concerns the infamous picture that hangs in the shelter, its face to the wall. Cavell surmises that the picture (perhaps a drawing of the creation or a family portrait) reveals an attempt to destroy the power of religion, stories, and art (1969: 152). In an insightful move, Cavell links the tyranny of God with that of the artist. In *Endgame*, "It is art itself which is disgraced, cursed because it makes the artist special, bullies his audience into suffering for him, contains his meaning, tells stories, loves floods" (ibid.: 152). As with all his other efforts, however, Hamm fails to undo the curse of meaning. The picture faces away from the characters, but its image, its meaning, remains. Hamm and his family linger in a nightmarish world, a world Cavell likens to King Lear's, "a world pervaded by madness and the fear of madness – a fear not of chaos but of naked meaning" (ibid.: 155). Essentially, Cavell's reading is an elaboration on one of Blau's remarks: "*Endgame* is a play with a tenacious memory … History dank and stagnant, ineliminable, the characters forget nothing" (2004: 42–3).

At first glance, Gontarski's more recent essay on *Endgame*, which continues his 1985 investigation into Beckett's intent to undo himself from his art, might seem to have little in common with Cavell's reading. In the earlier study, Gontarski writes, "Beckett has given us all that he knows in the play [*Endgame*] and that is, as he told Alan Schneider, 'all that I can manage, more than I could.' Such a response is not a simple perversity, but a statement that devalues authority, that shifts emphasis from author to text, that insists on the tropological nature of texts" (1985: 5). In his more recent investigation, Gontarski argues that Beckett knows much more than what is in the text. His thesis concerns Beckett's letters and comments as a director and the ways in which "directing … would allow Beckett to liberate a repressed voice" (Gontarski 2006: 144). Gontarski finds that Beckett is inconsistent in his remarks about *Endgame*, sometimes admitting to nothing, while at other times divulging specific information about the characters' past and their motivations: "While he often recoiled from the role of omniscient author, projecting for himself instead an image of authorial impoverishment, indigence, and impotence, a diminished author-ity, he finally extended such authority, insisting on the primacy of the playwright in the process of performance" (ibid.: 142–3). To some inquirers, Beckett (when "perform-ing" or playing dumb) offers only "Don't know" and "no one knows" (ibid.: 142, 155). Yet on other occasions, Beckett not only provides clarification but "demystifies the text and thus desacralizes it" (ibid.: 145). For example, "Beckett often treated [Alan] Schneider much like a pupil, outlining key themes and associations for his director" (ibid.).

According to Gontarski, Beckett's remarks and insights concerning *Endgame* and its secrets succeed in "greying the canon," frustrating the idea of any printed text (minus Beckett's thoughts) being a definitive edition of the play: "As more of the peripheral, secondary, or what we might call the ghost or grey canon comes to light and is made public (letters, notebooks, manuscripts, and the like), it inevitably inter-acts with and reshapes, redefines, even from the margins (or especially from the margins), the white canon (or the traditional canon)" (2006: 143). As Gontarski ulti-mately argues, the definitive *Endgame* is a Beckett-directed performance (or a Beckett-guided performance) in which Beckett manages to include all his revisions, remarks, reinventions, and afterthoughts. Gontarski writes,

> The texts on stage are fuller, more complete in Beckett's direction since much of the
> grey canon that he reluctantly communicated to friends and fellow directors is folded

into those productions. These are not the only way to stage Beckett's plays, but they are the fullest expressions of the texts themselves, the soundest argument I know for the performance being the text itself. (ibid.: 155)

Endgame on stage is finally more Beckettian than *Endgame* on page. Under Beckett's direction, the "fullest expression" – the fullest story, the fullest meaning – shines through.

Gontarski's study thus enters into a dialogue with Cavell's philosophical reading of the play. Through a "performance," Beckett attempts to conquer the same demon of meaning that haunts his characters, a demon Gontarski spends his career chronicling. As director and commentator, Beckett mirrors the major themes of the play itself. Both the family in the shelter and their creator struggle not to mean what they are given to mean, not to suffer the curse of meaning. Juxtaposing Cavell and Gontarski helps to show the ways in which *Endgame* is a blooding of the artist's abstract contention, to use Blau's infamous trope. Hamm, Clov, Nagg, and Nell want their farce to end and their wait to be over. They would prefer to trade the shelter, as Cavell argues, for a place free of received meaning. Yet they also play the waiting game and accept their meaning. Beckett's comments about his play and his characters show that he, too, looks for an end to meaning, but also that he struggles with the desire or the impulse for his meaning as an artist not to end. As Gontarski theorizes, Beckett seeks to abolish "the traditional presumption of authorial authority, what he called the supposed privilege of authorship, which he himself has been struggling to undo" (2006: 142). On one hand, Beckett is another Hamm who wants to end all covenants with his audiences, all insight and understanding into his works of art. As he writes in a 1949 letter to Georges Duthuit, "I have always thought that he [painter Bram van Velde] hadn't the faintest idea of what he was doing and neither do I" (Beckett 2006: 20). Beckett as ignorant "conduit" (Gontarski's word [2006: 155]) seeks to be silent and to suggest he has nothing to aid one in search of meaning. On the other hand, Beckett as God-like artist cannot give up power over his creation, speaking with authority and assuming the role of omnipotent creator. Where one Beckett is a void, the other Beckett is replete with meaningful insights. Two roles: a double blooding of his own contrary thought.

At one point in his essay, Cavell meditates on God's motives for choosing not to end his covenant with humanity, which helps to explain why Beckett cannot give up authority over *Endgame*. God may decide to save a few souls in the ark not because Noah and his family are indeed worthy of salvation, but for a more profound reason. Cavell writes:

God saves enough for a new beginning because he cannot part with mankind; in the end, he cannot really end it. Perhaps this means that he cannot bear not to be God. (Nietzsche said that this was true of himself, and suggested that it was true of all men …). Not ending it but with the end come before him, he cannot avoid cruelty, arbitrariness, guilt, repentance, disappointment, then back through to cruelty. (1969: 139)

Beckett's contradictory voices concerning his play reveal that he suffers from a yearning similar to that of God in Cavell's reading. Beckett strives to eliminate himself from the picture and to bring an end to his God-like authority as an author, yet he finds himself needing to have his say. Despite attempts to become free of meaning, free of intentions, free of all control over his creation, he lands in the realm of the divine, saving enough information, enough commentary for a new beginning. As evidence in Nietzsche's favor, Beckett cannot really end it, cannot fully part with his audience of critics and actors, cannot bear not to be God. He suggests in comments of ignorance that he wishes the dialogue would stop, but in comments of authorial control that the dialogue should continue. Beckett does not allow his involvement with *Endgame* to end, just as Hamm does not allow his world to end. The need to take his course is greater than the desire to switch off for good. To adapt Blau's earlier remark about the play, Beckett himself has a too-tenacious memory – the characters' dank and stagnant history ineliminable from his mind.

In *The Intent of Undoing*, Gontarski indirectly compares Beckett to God in the Old Testament to indicate Beckett's *helplessness* in destroying his connections to his works: "The creative struggle is to undo the realistic sources of the text, to undo the coherence of character and to undo the author's presence ... In composition those origins recede near the vanishing point as a repentant creator struggles to efface them, but they never wholly disappear" (1985: 4). Yet the evidence now suggests that Beckett seeks to play a much more prominent role in the discussion and direction of *Endgame*. If he is a repentant creator, he finally repents of his repentance and *chooses* to invite himself back into the work, revealing that he knows much more than what he offers in the text.

The portrait of the artist grows darker still. Indeed, as a director, Beckett may not only be unable to give up authority over his play but may also be fulfilling sadistic urges – if Abbott's theories are correct. In his intriguing study, *Beckett Writing Beckett: The Author in the Autograph*, Abbott considers Beckett's turn to the theater in 1948:

> What were the motives and effects of this sudden immersion in the theatrical on the author ...? ... Beckett's directorial reputation was for exactitude: the precise realization of his will on stage. One should keep in mind, moreover, what Beckett did to his actors. He tied ropes around their necks and crammed them in urns ... He tied them to rockers. He buried them in sand under hot blinding lights. He gave them impossible scripts to read at breakneck speed. If this is not torture, it bears a strong resemblance to it. (1996: 117–18)

Abbott helps to reveal that Beckett uses his plays to count himself king of theatrical space, to achieve, like a god, the "precise realization of his will." As Gontarski reveals, Beckett may suggest his ignorance at times, but he also knows what he wants – often, as Abbott observes, to the detriment of his cast.

Abbott's study offers further insights into Beckett's desire to mean exactly what he is given to mean. As Abbott explains, theater and tyranny have much in common:

"It requires a director, and directors can be tyrants" (1996: 111). Cavell, as aforementioned, argues that art is cursed in Hamm's shelter because it forces an audience (a culture) to suffer for the artist; the picture (art) thus faces the wall. Beckett's direction of the play, however, is another means of turning the picture back toward the characters. In the Schiller-Theater, for example, Beckett ensures that he is in control of his work, in control of his meaning, in control of others. Gontarski's phrasing is telling: "Taking full charge of his own work would at least allow for accurate productions ... Watching those [productions] of others or even reviewing production photographs often dismayed him" (Beckett 1992: xv).

Beckett fails, then, like Hamm, to put an end to his meaning. He fantasizes about an art without purpose, or at least about being an artist without purpose or without access to purpose, but his urge to be authoritative overcomes him. Beckett is an artist with too many qualities, too much to add, too much to offer, too much to mean. His "don't know" and "no one knows" responses are a means of keeping the tyrant at bay and ensuring that his art is free of his meaning. Yet, to invoke Cavell's term cited earlier, Beckett finally "bullies" his audience, his critics, his directors, and his actors by revealing his intentions and control over his creation. He refuses to abandon it to others, investing it with his own meaning after claiming he has nothing useful to offer. If, as Cavell argues, *Endgame* reveals an effort to escape from the meaning of stories, pictures, and art, then Beckett is one of the assailants, finally cursing his play with his intent, his "fullest expression," as Gontarski refers to it. *Beckett* wants to be special, to contain meaning, to tell stories, to love floods. He aims to keep his face to the wall, but ends up flipping over time and again, revealing what Cavell calls meaning's "totalitarian success." If Beckett's strategy is to find a way around the curse of meaning and bottle that part of him that seeks to be God, he is never able to keep up the act for long. As its creator, Beckett does not know how to end his covenant with *Endgame*, though he makes a conscious effort to "repress," as Gontarski proffers, the voice of knowledge and insight. The irony, of course, is that despite Beckett's attempt to control his meaning and infuse the play with his total vision, *Endgame* nevertheless takes on a life of its own. At some point, it outmaneuvers its creator, meaning things other than what Beckett intends. Yet the yearning for power remains. As an artist, he wants to play God, even though such a role has its limits. Like his characters, Beckett vacillates between meaning and nothingness, intent and ignorance. In Gontarski's words, Beckett wants to be "both a knower and non-knower, both master of his work and mere conduit through which it seeps to a public" (2006: 155). Beckett and his creatures all suffer the same fate, commiserating in their desire to mean and not to mean.

According to Abbott, Beckett's entire oeuvre represents the author's attempt not to mean, through "autographical" methods. His texts reveal an effort to unwrite narrative and, in effect, unwrite Beckett. "Only by laying waste to story itself," Abbott writes, "does one create the opportunity of finding oneself outside an ancient story that absorbs all identity into its relentless functioning" (1996: 16). For Abbott, a work such as the late novel *Company* exemplifies Beckett's attempt to unwrite himself, to become a man without a biography, to find himself outside the "oldest narrative of identity, older than the quest ... the narrative of parents begetting children" in the opening chapters of Genesis (ibid.: 12). Beckett's novel thus wears away at both the idea of fatherhood and the idea of narrative, which is "the formal equivalent of generative fatherhood" (ibid.: 19). Indeed, Abbott suggests that *Company* is Beckett's way of undoing what Deirdre Bair did to him in her biography, "a narrative present-ing itself as the story of Samuel Beckett's life" (ibid.). Abbott continues, her "work would have threatened roughly forty years of concentrated endeavor" (ibid.).

Eleutheria is another example of Beckett's concentrated endeavor, a play in which the main character wishes, as Abbott explains, "to step outside of time" (ibid.: 72): "Cor-respondingly, Victor's dramatically unsatisfying nonpattern of anarratological move-ment, his oozing, is of a piece with his non-relation to the paternal home. Both belong to the narratricidal matrix" (ibid.: 72). *Company* and *Eleutheria*, in their themes and his style of writing, illustrate Beckett's resentment at becoming part of the myths of Western culture and his attempt not to. The attempt to unwrite narrative (as well as fatherhood) demonstrates Beckett's desire not to mean what he is given to mean. "This undoing is not to the end of fictional creation," Abbott writes, "but to the end of being Beckett, Beckett as it were *avant la lettre*, Beckett before he is Beckett" (ibid.: 18).

Like Victor's isolation, Beckett's "performance" concerning his understanding of *Endgame* represents a similar attempt to find himself outside a myth of identity. In moments of ignorance, Beckett lets go of his play and its meaning, just as his writing of *Company*, as Abbott explains, helps him let go of his life story. Like Hamm, Clov, Nagg, and Nell, Beckett wants to exist outside the myths of culture. Yet the author returns time and again to his play, piecing it together, offering illumination, asserting himself back into the discussion, even admitting the play's connection to his own life and times with his wife Suzanne: "Several times, in rare unguarded moments, Beckett has said that Hamm and Clov are Vladimir and Estragon at the end of their lives. Once he qualified this remark, stating that Hamm and Clov were actually himself and Suzanne as they were in the 1950s – when they found it difficult to stay together but impossible to leave each other" (Bair 1978: 468).

A study of both *Endgame* and Beckett's "performance" is vitally important in the early years of the twenty-first century. Beckett's attempt to avoid meaning and knowl-edge as an artist has both philosophical and political implications. In the age of terror, meaning reigns supreme. Human beings continue to maim, kill, destroy, engage in holy wars. While one country searches for weapons of mass destruction, another test-launches them. Blau's observations from 1982 apply. In *Take up the Bodies*, he writes, "We are suicidal and genocidal. We are randomly destructive. We violate our space by the mere living of it ... The damage we've done to the world is appalling, immeas-urable. We are the ruins of time" (1982: 7). Like the characters of *Endgame*, cultures live according to the story, or to borrow Kiberd's phraseology, according to "an approved text." Rather than abandon the past, many call for its conservation, for the conservation of traditional values. Many place hope in the old questions, the old answers, unable to recognize that such questions and answers are responsible for the evils of the present. "Some day," Cavell writes,

> if there is someday, we will have to learn that evil thinks of itself as good, that it could not have made such progress in the world unless people planned and performed it in all conscience. Nietzsche was not crazy when he blamed morality for the worst evils, though he may have become too crazy about the idea. This is also why goodness, in trying to get born, will sometimes look like the destruction of morality. (1969: 136)

Beckett's proclamations of ignorance, his desire not to understand his own art, not to know more than others, are evidence of his fear of meaning, of saying too much, of living up to his authoritative potential, of sadistically binding others in accordance to his will. Beckett lived through some of the darkest moments in human history, witnessing where certainty and perfect meaning can lead. Abbott remarks, "Without question, Beckett wants us to feel the weight of political injustice, the outrage of tyranny, the stifling inhumanity of engineered lives, the bitter residue of a system of self-interest ... From beginning to end, Beckett's art is one long protest. It is written out of a horror of human wretchedness and a yearning that this wretchedness be lessened" (1996: 138, 147).

In his 1959 production of *Endgame* at The Actor's Workshop in San Francisco, California, Blau's costume choices for Clov reveal the servant's wish to be separated from the world in which he lives. In his retrospective of the production, Blau explains the effort "to seal him [Clov] off as much as possible from the air, the world, the presence of others, who are the source of pain" (2004: 75). Were Blau to direct the play in the twenty-first century, he might choose similar garments for Clov. Indeed, he might wear the cowl himself, as one so obsessed with solitude and silence, one who named his own theater group after the kraken, a sea monster who lives far beneath the surface. In the present age, sealing oneself off is not a bad idea, as answers to the human dilemma are few, which is why *Endgame* is as important to early twenty-first century audiences as to those in 1957. The play is a period piece, for the period that includes human grief. It chronicles humanity's problem of meaning, of needing to mean what it is given to mean at all costs. It demonstrates that terror begins at home, in small places where individuals learn what to mean, how to mean it, and the consequences of disobeying the given commands.

Fifty years of *Endgame*, 50 years of critical study, mandate disobedience. Pearson's insights are invaluable: "The endgame, that is to say, is only an inevitable result because, like Hamm and Clov, we have assented without scrutiny to the black and white rules and oppositional strategies of the game" (2001: 237). Pearson's commentary concerns a colonial dilemma, but his insights extend well beyond the struggle between Britain and Ireland. As Cavell helps to show, colonialism begins in the most ordinary places, the most common living rooms. The shelter may be reminiscent of Ireland, but it could, as Blau sees it, also be a living room in Moscow:

You might say Beckett begins where Chekhov leaves off. I remember a drawing by Robert Edmond Jones of the last moment of *The Cherry Orchard* as produced at the Moscow Art Theater: a brooding pointillist darkness; a sliver of light, like the vertical beam of the Cross (which you complete in your mind), the slumped figure of old Firs crawling toward the couch to die. Look again: it might be the opening of *Endgame*. Adjust your eyes to the darkness. Now you see the closed shutters, the covered furniture, the spaces on the walls where the pictures had been. (2004: 27)

Endgame demands that humanity find ways to escape the shelter and dive kraken-deep below meaning's surface, or like Blau's Clov, seal itself off, sew itself in. The play exemplifies the need to "flee" what Gilles Deleuze and Félix Guattari refer to as molar life: "Courage consists … in agreeing to flee rather than live tranquilly and hypocritically in false refuges. Values, morals, homelands, religions, and these private certitudes that our vanity and our complacency bestow generously on us, have as many deceptive sojourns as the world arranges for those who think they are standing straight and at ease, among stable things" (1983: 341). Beckett's "performance" as non-knower, his attempted stuttering of the voice of authority and power, is a move in the molecular direction, despite its failure. His "don't know" comments serve as a model for a world that has yet to stop meaning, has yet to stop playing the waiting game.

Late in his essay, Cavell alludes to a comment by Pascal, in which the French thinker considers the source of evil in the world: "How did Pascal put it? 'All the evil in the world comes from our inability to sit quietly in a room.' To keep still" (1969: 161). The characters in *Endgame* are unable to sit still, generating evil, cruelty, and hate in the world around them. Yet their plight need not be the plight of their audience. There may be, as Cavell asserts, no distance between the characters and us, but, if Beckett's audiences heed the warnings of *Endgame*, humanity might be able to understand why it behaves so horrifically, and how it may come to abandon the quest to mean what it is given. "To accomplish this," Cavell writes, "will seem – will be – the end of the world, of *our* world. The motive, however, is not death, but life, or anyway human existence at last" (ibid.: 148–9).

References

Abbott, H. Porter (1996). *Beckett Writing Beckett: The Author in the Autograph.* Ithaca: Cornell University Press.

Bair, Deirdre (1978). *Samuel Beckett: A Biography.* New York: Harcourt Brace Jovanovich.

Beckett, Samuel (1992). *The Theatrical Notebooks of Samuel Beckett Vol. II: Endgame*, ed. S.E. Gontarski. New York: Grove Press.

Beckett, Samuel (2006). "Letter to Georges Duthuit." In S. E. Gontarski and Anthony Uhlmann (eds.), *Beckett after Beckett.* Gainesville: University Press of Florida.

Blau, Herbert (1982). *Take up the Bodies: Theater at the Vanishing Point.* Urbana, IL: University of Illinois Press.

Blau, Herbert (2004). *Sails of the Herring Fleet: Essays on Beckett.* Ann Arbor: University of Michigan Press.

Bloom, Harold (1993). *The Western Canon: The Books and School of the Ages.* New York: Riverhead Books.

Cavell, Stanley (1969). "Ending the Waiting Game: A Reading of Beckett's *Endgame*." *Must We Mean What We Say?: A Book of Essays*. Cambridge: Cambridge University Press.

Coe, Richard N. (1968). *Samuel Beckett*. New York: Grove Press.

Deleuze, Gilles and Felix Guattari (1983). *Capitalism and Schizophrenia: Anti-Oedipus*. Minneapolis: University of Minnesota Press.

Gontarski, S. E. (1985). *The Intent of Undoing in Samuel Beckett's Dramatic Texts*. Bloomington: Indiana University Press.

Gontarski, S. E. (2006). "Greying the Canon: Beckett in Performance." In S. E. Gontarski and Anthony Uhlmann (eds.), *Beckett after Beckett*. Gainesville: University Press of Florida.

Hamilton, Geoff (2002). "Life Goes On: *Endgame* as Anti-Pastoral Elegy." *Modern Drama* 45(4): 611–27.

Kiberd, Declan (1996). *Inventing Ireland*. Cambridge, MA: Harvard University Press.

Knowlson, James (1996). *Damned to Fame: The Life of Samuel Beckett*. Charles Scribner and Sons.

Kott, Jan (1964). *Shakespeare Our Contemporary*. New York: W. W. Norton.

Pearson, Nels C. (2001). "'Outside of Here It's Death': Co-Dependency and the Ghosts of Decolonization in Beckett's *Endgame*." *ELH* 68: 215–39.

Schneider, Alan (1969). "Waiting for Beckett: A Personal Chronicle." In Bell Gale Chevigny (ed.), *Twentieth Century Interpretations of Endgame*. Englewood Cliffs, NJ: Prentice-Hall.

Worth, Katharine (2001). *Samuel Beckett's Theatre: Life Journeys*. Oxford: Oxford University Press.

22

"In the Old Style," Yet Anew:
Happy Days in the "AfterBeckett"

William Hutchings

With the extraordinary exactitude of its stage directions, which specify not only the cadence of delivery but also the performer's smallest gestures (even including the movements of the eyes), *Happy Days* was unprecedented not only within Beckett's stagecraft but within drama as a whole. With the possible exception of those plays that constrict movement even further (*Play*, *Not I*) or exclude it altogether and rely on a recorded soundtrack (*Breath*), *Happy Days* might seem to be the most visually replicable of Beckett's plays, even though the myriad indeterminacies of its plot and characterization have led it to be likened to *Hamlet* in its nearly infinite complexity. The stark simplicity of the set, a single mound, also affords scant variation – or so it would seem. Nevertheless, Winnie can be played as self-deluded or self-aware, complacent or courageous, oblivious or defiant, a combination of any of these or somewhere in-between – and the mound itself has been creatively reimagined by set designers in an astonishing variety of ways. Yet, with particular emphasis on the years since Beckett's death, the production history and stage design of the play reveal a surprising range of interpretations – and calls for a reassessment of the play that, among his full-length works, has been described as Beckett's "neglected masterpiece."

In many ways, the production of *Happy Days* by CSC Repertory in New York City in 1990 can serve as the baseline for post-Beckett productions of the play (though it had originally been produced with the same director and cast at the Mark Taper Forum in Los Angeles). Starring Charlotte Rae as Winnie and Bill Moor as Willie, it was directed by Carey Perloff, the CSC's Artistic Director, with faithful attention to Beckett's production details in the script. Rae's interpretation emphasized the differences in Winnie's character between the play's two acts: loud and exuberant in the first act, she became introspective and sober in the second until, as Tom Bishop observed in *The Beckett Circle: The Newsletter of the Samuel Beckett Society*, she "gained tragic stature by the end of the play, despite her reassuring smile"; he also commended Rae's facial expressiveness, though he considered her voice at times too shrill and "The Merry Widow," Winnie's final song, was "excessively charged" (1990). David

Richards of the *New York Times* concurred, remarking that it was delivered "shrilly [and] raucously … like a dirty barroom ballad" (1990: 15). The mound in which she is entrapped was "precisely as the author wanted it[:] high enough, scorched, lunar, [and] forbidding" (Bishop 1990), but the "very pompier trompe-l'oeil backcloth to represent unbroken plain and sky receding to meet in far distance" (Beckett 1961: 7) was not used; in production photographs, the set designed by Donald Eastman appears to be an interior space with large dark vertical cracks in its wall(s), and two massive black rectangular forms are visible behind her, one of them several inches taller than her head but otherwise unidentifiable. As always in Beckett's works, such changes in the play's visuals have thematic implications that are far more extensive than those made by similar adaptations in other writers' works: if, indeed, the set of *Happy Days* suggests an interior rather than an exterior locale, and if "the light was suitably blazing and the bell properly piercing" (Bishop 1990), it implies an extent of human agency if not direct control over Winnie's plight: the room is obviously a *built* construct, possibly under human control and monitoring in ways that Beckett's specified stark and seemingly infinite outdoor terrain is not.

Also in New York, The Whole Theater production of *Happy Days* was actually, early in 1990, the first major production of the play after Beckett's death. With Olympia Dukakis as Winnie, directed by William Foeller, and with set design by Nancy Thun, the play was also not only set in an interior but unmistakably a theater's interior at that. According to Alvin Klein's review in the *New York Times*, this version was "happening in a theater, not on a desert, or in limbo – to reinforce the here and now – as though we could have thought we were really elsewhere. The mound rises from the floorboards, the jagged edges of ripped wood surround it, and a stagehand comes peering out at the audience before each act" (1990: 15). Such production details (which Klein considered a "valueless embellishment") accentuate the play's already-apparent metatheatricality:

- Winnie's "strange feeling that someone is looking at me" acknowledges an in-theater audience that remains by her unseen (Beckett 1961: 40);
- the rhythm of Winnie's self-described routine reiterates that of daily theatrical performance: she is "clear, then dim, then gone, then dim again, then clear again, and so on, back and forth, in and out of someone's eye" in a *literal* theatrical "here" where, indeed, "all is strange" (ibid.);
- the Cookers or Showers, erstwhile passers-by who commented callously on her plight, parody bewildered "show-goers" who have been misled into buying tickets by the play's title perhaps and are utterly baffled by their encounter with the absurd: "[']What does it mean?['] he says – [']What's it meant to mean?[']" (ibid.: 43).

The addition of the peering stagehand at best gratuitously reduplicates the metatheatrical aspects of the play; however, his presence introduces, in effect, an additional character who could conceivably intrude or intervene in Winnie's plight, particularly in the direr second act. (Why, after all, doesn't *he* dig her out?). Dukakis's portrayal of Winnie was described as "irreverent ... bemused, sensual, possessed of sly wit and ... 'well-preserved'" but with "an extraordinary ability to comment wryly on the role she is playing while playing it" (Klein 1990) that is itself the quintessence of metatheater.

For the State Theatre production in Adelaide (and later Sydney) Australia in 1991, however, set designer Mary Moore sought exactly the opposite effect – and suggested that, particularly in Australia, with its many beaches and often relentlessly bright sunlight, *Happy Days* would even "be a wonderful play to perform on the beach" (Bramwell 1991). She explained her conception of the set as follows:

> I think it is important that the audience can relate to the essence of Winnie's predicament so they don't just feel they are looking at an actor poked into a pile of papier mache, that they can relate to the idea that this woman is embedded in earth. But the set also concedes that the theatre is not reality, it is an exercise in artifice. (ibid.)

To reviewer Samela Harris, however, Moore's set was "[an] anthill-like dung pile ... place[d] in an incongruously squared environment of cracked clay" (1991). Given the play's physical demands, however, Ruth Cracknell, who played Winnie, was probably well pleased that it was not being produced on a beach under actual blazing sun. As she explained to journalist Murray Bramwell,

> On the first day we made a mistake ... In Act One [the mound] is only up to [Winnie's] waist and when we are playing [it] we are only there for an hour. But in rehearsal we were concentrating for a long time without thinking to take a break and, when I finally got out, I nearly collapsed. We now take what we call our "mound breaks." (Bramwell 1991)

Regarding the role's demands on the actor, Cracknell was "heard to use the word torture" – and about the second act she was "diplomatically brief: 'All I can say is that it is only half an hour!'" Nevertheless, like countless other performers, directors, critics, and Beckett aficionados before her, she discovered that, notwithstanding its manifest physical and psychological challenges, *Happy Days*

> is like a piece of music which is limited by the bars, the crotchets and quavers. You can't, in certain kinds of music, muck about too much. You are not in free form and you are very much governed by how the composer has noted it down. It is very like that with Beckett. But as a performer you still have to discover how to make it breathe. (ibid.)

In accord with director, Simon Phillips, Cracknell – using specifically Australian idiom – contended that "while dense, there is nothing woolly about [Beckett's] text."

The most notable production of *Happy Days* in 1991, however, was staged in Dublin, Ireland, as part of the city's year-long Beckett Festival, during which all 19 of his plays were staged. Directed by Caroline Fitzgerald, with set design by Tim

Reed, this rendition of the play starred Fionnula Flanagan as a "confident, witty Winnie [whose] range of voice lent a rich variety to the play" (Ben-Zvi 1991: 3); like the other productions in the series, it emphasized both fidelity to Beckett's specifications and, given its location, reminded audiences of the distinctive Irishness of Beckett's idiom and worldview. For reviewer Katharine Worth, however, the most memorable impression made by the production was visual, "the extraordinary image of the second act[,] a face with streaming hair rising out of the mound like an epic being in some archaic sculpture" (ibid.: 5).

Certainly no "epic" similes were utilized regarding the production directed by Simone Benmussa at the French Institute in London in 1994, starring Angela Pleasence, who gave Winnie "an accent so precisely filled with lower-middle-class English nuance ... [that] *Happy Days* [becomes] simply the slow extinction of what used to be called the soul of a housemaid" (Macaulay 1994). Michael Billington (1994) of the *Guardian*, however, contended that the production offers "living proof you can re-think Beckett without distorting his essential values" or otherwise "tearing the fabric of the play apart." Much of the rethinking had to do with the set, apparently, which Billington described as "a sloping cardboard construct like a desolate relic of urban neglect"; furthermore, her parasol had been replaced by a "tatty umbrella and her capacious handbag [was] a black bin-liner," making her "a bird-like bag-lady engrossed in her survival-tactics, ironically mimicking upper-class tones when she speaks 'in the old style' and sounding almost apologetic when sorrow bursts in on her determined cheerfulness" (ibid.). The biggest surprise of the performance, however, came when "at the last, having gazed wistfully at the prostrate Willie, [Winnie] vanishe[d] into thin air as the cardboard mound collapse[d]" after her final glimpse at Willie (Peter Bayliss), duly characterized as "the saddest of smiles" (ibid.).

An even more radical reimagining of the set greeted theatergoers who attended the production of *Happy Days* directed by Per Zetterfalk at the Samuel Beckett Theatre in Dublin in April 1995. As described by Gerry Colgan in the *Irish Times*,

> [Whereas t]he play usually opens with ... Winnie ... buried to her waist in a sand-hill[, h]ere she seems to be in mid-air, behind a black-draped structure which leaves her visible to mid-thighs. Her bits and pieces – lipstick, parasol etc – are suspended by glistening filaments and float around distractingly. Where the author gives us, without explanation, a recognisable physical environment, here we are offered inchoate metaphor. (1995)

This semi-free-floating Winnie, played by Aisling Murphy, was "concealed to her neck" as usual in the second act, Colgan noted, though he contended that as "an appealing young woman with vigorous voice and movements" Murphy had been "miscast and misdirected" – as well as (mis)positioned in such a way that Willie (played by Bernard Berts Folens) and Winnie "clearly cannot see each other" even though the play's near-monologue was "laudably word-perfect" (ibid.).

For the production of *Happy Days* at the Pleasance Theatre in Glasgow, Scotland in August 1995, the play's mound of parched earth had become an urban rubbish-heap of collapsed cardboard boxes and scattered newspapers. Winnie, played by Angela Pleasence, rummaged through a trash bin by her side to garner her meager possessions. According to reviewer Peter Whitebrook in *The Scotsman* (1995), Pleasence's characterization was "gentle, meticulous, [and] peaky [as] she grins, chuckles, and mutters about 'the old style' of things, champing her jaws like a squirrel and staring [with] flickering pity and contempt at her husband, old Willie," played by Howard Goorney. Sara Villiers (1995), writing in the *Herald* found Pleasence's Winnie "a very bird-like creature, perched atop her pile of rubbish, virtually trilling out her repetitive 'in the old style' – always followed by a mawkish gnashing of the [presumably non-bird-like] gums." In this production, the two acts were played without intermission, "with only the lowering of the lights and the sound of a violent wind before Winnie is revealed buried up to her neck" (Whitebrook 1995).

Given such bold and unorthodox reimaginings of the play's *mise-en-scène*, theatergoers might well have expected an even more audacious staging when it was announced that the world-renowned theatrical innovator Peter Brook would be directing *Oh les beaux jours*, Beckett's French translation of *Happy Days*, in Lausanne, Switzerland in 1995, transferring it later to his Centre International de Recherches (later to become Créations) Théâtrales in Paris at the Bouffes du Nord. Natasha Parry, Brook's wife, was a native English-speaker who had learned French in order to perform the role of Winnie – after having demurred when her husband first suggested it in the previous decade (Donnelly 1996). Willie was played by Francis Berte. The production was indeed surprising – primarily because it was done so literally "by the book." Its most unusual innovation occurred when,

> At the start of both halves of Brook's production, we see stage hands slotting a very scrubby, parched-looking mound around Ms. Parry. The harsh whiteish light dies for a moment and then rears up on her in character. It's a directorial decision which may have been made for pragmatic reasons but it has the effect of sensitising you to the way, as in *Godot*, the experience of the protagonists is likened to that of actors having to put on a play night after night. The repetitiveness of Winnie's days, the mysteriously replenished "props" in her bag and the bell that reminds her to perform all minister to this feeling. (Taylor 1996)

Reviewers noted only minor modifications of Beckett's specifications: Matthijs Engelberts, writing for *The Beckett Circle*, noted that "the mound was maybe more rocky than usual[, t]here was no painted back-cloth … [, and a]t the start of both acts, there was a haze that gradually disappeared – a deliberately incongruous, realistic evocation of morning" (1996: 3). Another concession to realism was that "in the second [act] … as in the Royal Court production [in 1962] … make-up made [Winnie] look markedly older" than in the preceding one.[2] Reviewer Mark Fisher (1996) described Parry as "pensive and poetic … a glamorous Winnie[, an] elegant Parisian, not the buxom Dubliner" of other productions. In 1997, Brook's production was brought to the Riverside Studios in Hammersmith as part of its French Theatre Season, co-produced with the National Theatre; it was also subsequently shown at the Tramway

Theatre in Glasgow as well as other venues. Writing of the Riverside production, Beckett's biographer James Knowlson contended that "the play is, I am now sure, less comic, more poignant, and more poetic in French than it is in English," and he claimed that "the bravura passages in both acts of the Shower[s] or Cooker[s] ('Piper ou Cooker' in French) ... and the Millie and the mouse story ... have never been more sensitively (or in the case of the mouse story) more powerfully delivered" (1998: 2).

Whether buxom or not, Winnie was definitely "all breezy Dublin determination" when portrayed by Rosaleen Linehan in the production directed by Karel Reisz at the Gate Theatre in Dublin, which then transferred to the Almeida Theatre in London at the same time that Brook's production was running in Paris (Billington 1996). Reviews of the production are sharply divided over its tone, though not over its excellence. In the *Guardian*, Michael Billington contended that "Linehan emphasizes not just Winnie's stoicism and courage but the stark nature of her declension" in a performance that he found "much grimmer than ... previous productions" (ibid.). In the *Independent*, however, Paul Taylor argued that "the English text is much funnier than the French." He contended that, whatever its "existential extremes," the play

> is also a brilliantly naturalistic and tragi-comic portrait of a marriage ... Winnie rabbits away, with a would-be gentility and many a borrowed air, to cover over the boredom and fear caused by being steadily ignored in favour of a newspaper ... She tries to fool herself, simply by fussing around with the contents of her bag, that she's leading a busy, rewarding life. (Taylor 1996)

He also noted class implications in Linehan's performance, as she "adopt[ed] a different parodically prunes-and-prism posh voice ... when quoting wisps of the classics" (ibid.). Furthermore, "the landscape in which this Winnie finds herself has an altogether more surreal quality to it – a cliff of deep ochre and technicolour blue sky ... [of] incongruous richness"; without explanation, he also termed the play's action "an interminably repeated day at the seaside" (ibid.). The set, designed by Tim Hatley, was described by Robert Hanks of the *Independent* as "the Platonic form of Beckett, looking exactly the way you imagine it should," with "a rising slope of bare, red earth, with a sharp drop into nothingness" (1996a). Along with other plays from the Gate Festival, this production was subsequently transferred to Lincoln Center in New York; Linehan also reprised the role at the Barbican Theatre in London during its Beckett Festival in 1999.

In 1996, *Happy Days* was also produced with no set whatsoever when, with the approval of the Beckett estate, it was presented as a radio drama by London's Radio 3. Directed by Peter Woods, and starring Geraldine McEwan as a "strangely lovable Winnie," it was nevertheless greeted by reviewer Robert Hanks of the *Independent* (1996b) as "surely a far bigger betrayal of the author's intentions than anything short of a nude mud wrestling *Footfalls*." Stage directions – though surely not every pause and eye movement specified in the text – were spoken by Phil Daniels, whom Hanks praised as "one of very few actors who has really grasped the naturalistic flattening out of nuance and tone that sits best with the intimacy of radio." Nevertheless, Hanks continued,

> There is a huge difference between knowing that someone is supposed to be buried in their mound, and seeing them trapped there in front of you for the duration ... To keep the image of Winnie earthbound in your head for 80 minutes requires a level of concentration that's beyond most of us ... Not only could [the radio production] not reproduce the perfectly monotonous context, but neither could it bring out the occasional moments of drama (such as the spontaneous combustion of Winnie's parasol). (ibid.)

Though rare, such transpositions from one medium to another were not without precedent even in Beckett's lifetime; however, they had never involved *Happy Days* heretofore.

Another type of technological transposition accompanied the production of *Happy Days* at the Traverse Theatre in Edinburgh in June 1996. Director Stewart Laing sought, in the words of reviewer Neil Cooper, "to drag the play into that post-modern hybrid of 'live art,' a vague arena with an emphasis on technology" (1996). Although Myra McFadyen was said to have given "the performance of her life" as Winnie, letting "the power [of the play] come through the words," the mound was apparently surrounded by a "small array of [video] screens" on which "the odd cursory video image [was] sneakily tucked in, to little effect." The play's "visual marvel," however, came in the second act as "Laing shifts the action so far back as to give the audience a brand new perspective, a theatrical equivalent of a long shot or fade out." Exactly how this was accomplished is not clear.[3]

Although the most acclaimed productions of *Happy Days* in 1996 were those directed by Brook and Reisz, the most renowned actress to have undertaken the role of Winnie during that year was without doubt Academy Award winner Estelle Parsons, who starred in the Splinter Group's production in Chicago. Directed by Richard Block, it was part of the "Buckets O' Beckett" Festival, which presented 18 of Beckett's 19 plays – his entire dramatic canon except *Godot*. Parsons, who was then best known for her role on the television series *Roseanne*, was paired with Mike Nussbaum as Willie. According to Eileen O'Halloran, who reviewed the Festival for *The Beckett Circle*, "[the] mound was creatively designed: a cross section complete with roots, bones, rocks, and broken branches. However, the backdrop was overdone: red scorched clouds, freshly painted, gave off noxious fumes, making the backdrop seem too literally a site of a nuclear explosion" (1996: 7). Disconcertingly, however, the production's pre-show music was the bouncy pop oldie "Red, Red Robin" which, however cheery, creates an odd and ironic context for a play about a woman buried in a hole. Late in 1998, Parsons reprised the role (again under Block's direction but with Frank Raiter as Willie) at the Hartford Stage in Connecticut – where she stayed for discussion with the audience after almost every performance. In describing her interpretation of the role and its "wild, tear-filled laughter," Alvin Klein of the *New*

York Times wrote that "Ms. Parsons radiates a gripping power of mastery, of an artist dedicated to a higher calling, whatever it is … [Her] Winnie is the capstone of a remarkable life in the theater" (1998).

In the Chueca district of Madrid, the theater company "El Canto de la Cabra" presented an outdoor production of *Happy Days* from July 4 through September 1, 1996, utilizing a small courtyard in an outdoor annex to their playhouse. Directed by Juan Úbeda, the production starred Elisa Gálvez as Winnie and Carlos Iglesias as Willie; the translation, *Los días felices*, was by Antonia Rodríguez-Gago. As Antonio Ballesteros González reported in *The Beckett Circle*, however,

> Theatre in the open air in Madrid in summer presents many disadvantages. On the one hand, the audience had to face the interruptions of crying babies in the flats surrounding the courtyard … and those of their mothers preparing dinner. But on the other hand … the eager spectator is compelled to hear the music played by hostile neighbours, who, always so fond of culture, try to boycott the performance. And the big surprise is that, despite the strange amalgam of operatic sounds and Beckettian voices, they cannot. For Beckett's words and silences … attract the entire attention of the audience, turning the uneasy mixture of sounds into an unforgettable theatrical experience … The rustle of tree leaves produc[es] a ghostly effect as they accompany Winnie's words. (1997: 6)

Winnie's mound, designed by director Úbeda, was equally unorthodox and particularly urban, "formed by a huge pile of rubbish and demolition materials: old chairs, pieces of fences, bricks, miscellaneous boxes, paper, old streetlamps, exhaust pipes and a collection of other broken objects and débris, everything combined with plaster" (ibid.). Willie, who was "dressed as a bricklayer throughout the first act," seemed to have "slid down the wide tubes jutting out from the plaster" to his current position (ibid.). Winnie, who looked nearly two decades younger than the "about fifty" that is specified in the text (Beckett 1961: 7), wore "long silvery eyelashes," mascara, face powder, and a flat white hat and partial veil (González 1997: 6). Quotations from well-known Spanish authors were substituted for the English and Irish allusions that had been translated literally in Rodríguez-Gago's rendering of the play.

In two instances in the late 1990s, critics themselves became involved in productions of *Happy Days*. In Columbus, Ohio, in 1996, Katharine Burkman, Professor Emerita at Ohio State University and a widely recognized authority on Beckett and Pinter, played Winnie in a production of the theater company known as Women at Play. In London in 1998, Claire Armitstead, the Arts Editor of the *Guardian*, was invited to become a producer for Battersea Arts Centre; her production of *Happy Days* (for a production company called Leap of Faith) starred Amanda Bellamy and was directed by Caroline Smith. "As someone used to the short-concentration clatter of the newsroom," Armitstead explained in her autobiographical account of the experience, "I have found myself astonished by the calm determination and staying power required by a play which, in any other walk of life, would be ruled out as a breach of health and safety regulations" (1998: 12). She also recounts what happens when "the Beckett initiates began to scuttle out of their burrows … rang[ing] from academics

to actors, from stage managers to his old mates," all of whom proffer tips and suggestions of more or (often) less usefulness (ibid.). Armitstead's own perspective on the
playwright was more prosaic: having "read and re-read *Happy Days* ... suddenly it hit
me – Beckett's great virtue was that he could look up his own bum and see the universe, whereas other monologuists are prone to look up their's [sic] and see, well ..."
(ibid.). Bellamy, two decades younger than the 50-year-old that Beckett's notes
specify, proved to be a "very English Winnie [who] could have stepped out of the
papered-over suburban depression of an Alan Ayckbourn play," according to reviewer
Paul Taylor of the *Independent*, and she "tend[ed] to put the tight inverted commas of
conscious self-doubt round the word 'happy' in phrases such as 'Oh, this is going to
be another happy day!' which reduces rather than enhances a sense of the pathos that
stems from Winnie's prattling stoicism" (1998). He also noted that "in the second
half, the set fails to make her look properly stuck [since] ... she appears to be wearing
a neckbrace of sandstone that could detach from the mound like a jigsaw piece" (ibid.).
David Murray of the *Financial Times* remarked that Bellamy, "in kewpie-doll makeup,
squeaks her way girlishly through the first act ... [but] is much older and greyer in
Act 2" (1998). Producer Armitstead may have felt much the same way as a result of
her experience; she concludes her account of it by saying that "it has made me
think about life and storytelling and the miraculous fact that anyone has the energy
(and money) to go on making theatre at all in such an appallingly inhospitable
climate" (1998).

From April 20 to May 9, 1999, at the Théâtre de la Tempête in Paris, the production of *Oh les beaux jours* directed by Miloud Khetib surely startled theatergoers who
assumed they knew Beckett's play. The production opened in darkness rather than
the blazing light specified in the script, and an alarm rang loudly. Then, as described
by Helen Astbury for *The Beckett Circle*,

> [the audience] catch[es] a glimpse of a stagehand, who enters carrying a dummy, which
> he unceremoniously dumps at the foot of a rubber mound that is being inflated before
> our eyes. The originality of this is that the role of Willie will be shared throughout the
> play by the dummy and the stagehand [Pierre Clarard]. When the mound is fully
> inflated, the same stagehand turns off the alarm, a piercing white light reveals Winnie
> [Betty Raffaelli] in the center of the mound, and he activates the bell, which signals
> the beginning of Winnie's day, before returning to join his inanimate double. "Willie"
> will be constantly fluctuating between this role, outside of the play, as he busies himself
> with the lighting, the bell, setting fire to the parasol, etc., and the role more familiar
> to us ... The stagehand's presence on stage is deliberately accentuated and his presence
> and movements isolate Winnie even further, as he is obviously indifferent to her words,
> and she to his actions and his very presence. (1999: 3)

Often, indeed, Willie's "presence" was signified by a shadow projected onto the left-
hand wall of the stage – reading his newspaper, adjusting his hat, donning his handkerchief, and so on. In the second act, according to Astbury,

When we expect Willie to attempt to join Winnie, the stagehand drags the dummy to the front of the mound where he has him perform a series of grotesque jerking movements ... He will obviously never attempt to climb up towards Winnie as the slopes of her mound are clearly too steep and slippery to permit his reaching her. (ibid.)

At the end of the play, the stagehand, carrying the dummy, moved to the corner of the stage from where he activated the bell. Thus, as Astbury notes, "Willie's final 'Win,' uttered almost from the wings, is ... difficult to interpret, making the dénouement a little weak" – a fact that she considered "the only reproach which could be directed against this production" (ibid.). However, in a terse review in *Le Figaro* that mentioned few specifics about the production, Jean-Louis Pinte contended that "Meloud Khelib est comédien ... Sa familiarité avec Beckett n'est pas évident. Dans un mise en scéne maladroit et scolaire il banalise la parole de l'auteur, la réduit à des mots qui, mis bout a bout, n'ont pas aucun sens" ["Meloud Khelib is a comedian ... His familiarity with Beckett is not at all evident. In a maladroit and school-like production he banalizes the words of the author, reducing them to words that, juxtaposed, make no sense whatever"] (1999). More traditional-minded Beckettians (not to mention the representatives of the Beckett estate) might have managed to find a few more reproaches as well – perhaps even enough to have raised a *tempête de théâtre* all their own.

In 2001, the release of the "Beckett on Film" set of four DVDs containing his complete 19-play dramatic oeuvre directed by 19 different filmmakers aroused a surprising amount of controversy when it was discovered that a number of the plays had been "creatively re-imagined" with varying degrees of success (or lack thereof) in transposing them from stage to screen. *Happy Days*, directed by Patricia Rozema, proved to be among the less controversial films in the series, not only because she remained faithful to the script and to the basic visual imagery of the play but also because of the presence of Rosaleen Linehan as Winnie, which she had performed to much acclaim at the Gate Theatre's Beckett Festival, described above. The sole significant change was that an actual, appropriately desolate outdoor setting was used – though even this difference provoked dissent, including the following from Fintan O'Toole in *The Irish Times*:

Rozema makes one huge change, placing the action in a real and beautifully filmed landscape of sky, mountain and stone. This may seem like a rather obvious thing to do when turning a play into a film, but it interferes quite radically with the nature of the piece. For one thing, what Beckett wanted was a visual monotony which makes Winnie's determined cheerfulness all the more poignant. For another, he was also making a deliberate joke of the audience's utter incredulity at a set that features a woman stuck in a hole in the ground. As he wrote to [the American director Alan] Schneider, "what should characterise [the] whole scene, sky and earth, is a pathetic unsuccessful realism, that kind of tawdriness you get in third rate musical or pantomime ... laughably earnest bad imitation." When you get, not a laughably bad imitation, but a real and lovingly shot landscape, the tone of the play changes and the joke is lost. (2001)

It is, of course, axiomatic among ardent Beckettians that no change, however slight, is too insignificant to escape scrutiny, risk denunciation, or provoke debate. Rozema's change was quite modest in comparison to others in the series, however – including Anthony Minghella's placement of the three urns in *Play* on a vast terrain containing countless similar ones, Damien O'Donnell's relocation of *What Where* into a vast library, and Damien Hirst's reconfiguration of the setting for *Breath* as a floating island of discarded hospital equipment careening through outer space like the Starship Enterprise. Linehan explained to Andrew O'Hagan of the *Daily Telegraph* that "For me, the text is God. A profound frivolity is what Beckett hoped for, and that is totally essential to the piece. It is his greatest note in the play. And with Winnie, Beckett really got right inside a woman" (2001). Since Linehan has been widely acclaimed as among the finest interpreters of the role, it is fortunate that her performance has been preserved on film and made widely available.

One noteworthy production of *Oh les beaux jours* was given for one performance only at the Beckett Festival sponsored by the Association pour la Maison Samuel-Beckett in August 2001. Staged at the Théâtre des Terrases in Gordes, France, it featured Tsilla Chelton, the favorite actress of Eugène Ionesco, as Winnie – her first performance in any Beckett play. Dominique Ehlinger, who played Willie, had performed that role many years earlier opposite Madeleine Renaud in one of the most respected French productions of the play. Details of the current production were reported by Annie Joly for *The Beckett Circle*, as follows:

> The innovative directing of Arlette Reinerg somewhat surprised veteran Beckettians, who are used to a more respectful attitude towards the author's intentions. Reinerg, with Chelton's approval, departed from Beckett's own stage directions rather than allowing them to interfere with her directorial creativity. She decided, for example, to create a much more substantial stage presence for Willie than is usual in traditional productions. She also opted for an unconventional setting, one that took advantage of the striking natural rock-formation that serves as a backdrop to the amphitheater at Gordes. Instead of burying Winnie in an earthen mound, she placed her at the mouth of a raised well, to which Willie would climb from time to time on a ladder. (2001: 7)

The Beckett Festival also included an exhibition of photographs entitled *Beckett et son théâtre*, in addition to scholarly presentations; these attracted many Beckett specialists, who reportedly gave Reinerg's revisionist production a standing ovation.

Working with what he termed "purely abstract creativity" (and with the approval of the Beckett estate), the choreographer Maurice Béjart adapted *Oh les beaux jours* into a ballet titled *L'heure exquise*, which starred Carla Fracci and Micha von Hoecke in the lead roles. It was first performed in Turin, Italy, in 1998 at the Teatro Carignano as part of the eleventh biennial Torino Danza International Ballet Festival. It was revived in Lausanne, Switzerland at the Théâtre de Vidy, starring Maïna Gielgud (the niece of Sir John) and Martyn Fleming in 2002. Béjart seems to have been more influenced by Madeleine Renaud's performance of the role in the early 1960s than by Beckett's text itself. Details of the production were provided by Diane Luscher-Moreta in *The Beckett Circle*:

When the curtains open, we behold a sleeping woman trapped in the middle of a mound that is entirely covered with faded pink ballet slippers of a fleshy hue. A man – seated on the front to the left of the mound and wearing a pair of black trousers, large shoes, and a hat – reads a newspaper. Like Winnie, the female character begins her day with a prayer …

Béjart [then] creates bursts of movement that return his aging dancers to their past. The mound opens, liberating its prisoner. The dancers' movements – awkward at the beginning, as though they were awakening from a state of petrification – quickly become fluid, thus conveying a sense of energy and grace.

The moment when the earth opens is breathtaking and intense in its daring simplicity. The visual image of the circular mound splitting and opening up evokes demented "rondes des heures" (the two hands on a clockface that have split asunder). (2002: 6)

At the beginning of the second act, Winnie is once again entrapped in the mound – though this fact is concealed behind the stage curtain, which Willie tries futilely to penetrate. Luscher-Moreta continues:

He moves alongside the curtain, as if it were an impassable wall, puts on a tailcoat and dons a top hat, which replaces his bowler. Parading in front of the audience, with his belly protruding, he offers them, like Pozzo in *Waiting for Godot*, an image of bourgeois self-satisfaction.

The rituals of dance wind down variously, as … when her companion falls to the ground, exhausted by the series of repetitive exercises that he imposes on himself. The more the motions are repeated, the emptier they seem. The endless series of efforts result in nothingness, even if, through the repetition of forms and movements, the performance becomes more and more perfect. (ibid.: 7)

A mirror becomes a key prop in the dance, evoking both time present and time past. At times, the happy days of the title seem to be relived, but during the second act "the female dancer, now deathly pale, looks increasingly like a statue [as] she comes slowly to a standstill and her gestures stiffen" (ibid.). The mound, which had opened in the first act, recloses around her during the second. At the end, Willie crawls away, "leav[ing] Winnie without looking back, in a series of numb and mechanical motions" (ibid.). Music by Webern, Mahler, and Mozart was used, though the production also utilized spoken words from a "considerably curtailed and amended [French] text, but there is still quite a lot of speaking, which Gielgud does most clearly and eloquently," as John Percival (2002) noted in his review in the *Independent*. Gielgud, at age 57, had returned to the ballet for this performance 15 years after her stage farewell as a dancer, he reported – adding that she "include[d] fast turns across the stage, some jolly, almost jazzy jigging, bold balances, and a deal of small, precise footwork, besides eloquently expressive arm movements."

Just over 40 years after its American premiere there, the Cherry Lane Theater in New York City was the site of a production of *Happy Days* in October 2002, directed by Joseph Chaikin, with Joyce Aaron as Winnie and Ron Faber as Willie. As a director, Chaikin was (as always) scrupulously faithful to Beckett's text – although as a result of physical limitations of the stage (an inability to lower Aaron into the mound for the second act), the mound was noticeably higher in the second act than it was in the first, implying that it was rising rather than that she was sinking. Reviewing the production for the *New York Times*, Ben Brantley remarked that Aaron "wears a battered kewpie-doll face that appropriately shifts between chipper animation and forlorn stillness" (2002). In my interview with her in *The Journal of Beckett Studies* Joyce Aaron gives her perspective on the play. Although Chaikin was then suffering from partial aphasia, which made communication quite difficult for him, Aaron notes that he nevertheless insisted that her portrayal of Winnie should be neither "sentimental ... [nor] heavy and dark ... [He] was after the humor that was in the play ... [but] he was also clear that we had to go in a different direction in the second act, emphasizing the tension between the humor and the untenable circumstances in which Winnie finds herself" (Hutchings 2002: 92).

In 2003, Peter Brook directed his second production of *Happy Days* – this time in German, titled *Glückliche Tage*, starring Miriam Goldschmidt as Winnie and Wolfgang Kroke as Willie. The play had its premiere in Basel, Switzerland and subsequently toured Europe. Having had a long-term professional relationship with Goldschmidt, whose native language was German, Brook felt that she "could make her own unique contribution to the play [since she] had, in particular, developed a fine sense for linguistic nuances that she could bring to a play that imposes severe restrictions on bodily forms of communication" (Tönnies 2003: 1). Although the production included revisions that Beckett had himself made for the 1979 Royal Court production of *Happy Days* (published by James Knowlson in 1985), Brook insisted on a "musical" faithfulness to the text, that is, treating the script as a musician treats a classical composer's score. The set, which was designed by Abdou Ouologuem, placed the mound at center stage for purposes of symmetry, but it "reduced the sky to a turquoise ribbon on Winnie's hat (and a decoration on her dress in Act II)" – reportedly because "Brook considered the trompe-l'oeil backcloth as belonging too much to the 'theatre of the absurd' of the previous century" (Tönnies 2003: 2). Instead, "uniformly dark brown fabric emphasized the walls at the back and at the two sides of the set" (ibid.). The mound itself was covered in goat and sheep hides that had been imported from Mali; only a few "dried-up plants" were present to suggest the effects of the heat, but the stage floor remained visible beyond the edges of the mound. Another alteration involved the props:

> Instead of a bag ... [Winnie] is equipped with an open, box-like construction that allows her to survey her possessions at any given moment. According to [Brook's assistant director Hendrik] Mannes, Brook did not see this change as problematic, because for him the bag was a "secondary" prop, less central to the orchestration of the play than the "primary" ones of revolver, toothbrush, and parasol. (ibid.)

Brook's German production also emphasized the play's physicality, energy, and earthiness (in both senses of the word): Winnie delighted in viewing Willie's raunchy postcard despite professing some indignation, and her primping accentuated her body as well. Even Willie was visibly bare-shouldered behind the mound. Tönnies reports that "according to Mannes, Brook paid special attention to creating a tension between these two extremes [her philosophical thoughts and her down-to-earth attitude to life]; Winnie is part of earth *and* of heaven, always pulled down again when she feels she is about to float upwards into the light" (2003: 2). The result was that laughter from the audience was much more common, particularly in the first act, than in Brook's previous French version. Accordingly, "instead of expressing despair, her voice was harsh, almost sarcastic when she twice qualified her 'happy day' with *'trotz allem'* ('after all') in the final scene ... stay[ing] mentally in control until the very end" (ibid.). After the play ended, Goldschmidt extricated herself from the mound (with Kroke's assistance) to take a full-bodied bow.

Although Brook's touring German production has not been mounted in England (it was in Berlin in 2006), a contemporaneous revival in London was directed by Sir Peter Hall in 2003 at the Arts Theatre, starring Felicity Kendal as Winnie with Col Farrell as Willie. For Hall, who had directed Peggy Ashcroft in the much-heralded production that inaugurated the National Theatre's then-new building on the South Bank in 1976, this was, as for Brook, his second major staging of Beckett's play. The set, designed by Lucy Hall (the director's daughter), quite literally gave audiences a new perspective on Winnie's plight: instead of the usual eye-level (horizontal) gaze at the vertical mound, the audience seemed to have a more aerial view, with Winnie "at the centre of a tilting, scrub-coloured spiral ... seem[ing] to be trapped in a serpentine coil rather than earthily incarcerated" (Billington 2003). Terming the perspective thus created "more intrusive ... than normal," Paul Taylor of the *Independent* described it as "a tilted-up spiral of earth that looks like the electric ring of a Baby Belling as magnified and reimagined by the Surrealist movement" (2003). The effect, according to Charles Spencer of the *Daily Telegraph*, "is of a character simultaneously trapped, and floating free, in a terrible unearthly void"; he notes that the "spiral of parched grass [is] surrounded by streaks of cerulean blue" (2003). Best known for her starring role in the long-running television series *The Good Life*, Kendal brought to the role what Spencer described as her "familiar air of game, gamine jauntiness," though she also proved capable of delivering her lines "almost through clenched teeth, as if Winnie is defiantly willing herself to be happy, and throughout there are sudden glimpses of the mask slipping to reveal the terror that compels her to talk, talk, talk" (ibid.). That terror soon became a recurrent motif in a production that Billington described as "revelatory" in that "instead of a reverent revival about a heroine greeting living entombment with stoical cheer, it becomes a study of a woman on the verge of a nervous breakdown ... [as] Kendal emphasizes Winnie's panic and fear more than her cheerful fortitude" (2003). Such a reimagining of her character was not without cost, however; David Bradby, reviewing the production for *The Beckett Circle*, complained that Kendal's vocal delivery "seem[s] intended to give relief to the text more than to serve the Beckettian rhythms, and she ignores almost every one of the pauses in Beckett's text" (2004: 10). Ian Shuttleworth of the *Financial Times* was even more forthright, not only disparaging the "Expressionist spiral of scorched grass almost perpendicular to the stage, slightly concave towards its centre, with ribbons of blue sky above and below" but also Kendal's "putting a recognisable, warm individual at the centre of this whirling artscape, mak[ing] us likelier to question the play's strategy." His unabashed and unambiguous conclusion: simply "This is wrong" (2003).

When *Happy Days* was produced as *Los días felices* at the Teatro San Martín in Buenos Aires in 2003, the production's most startling innovation came from an even more unexpected (indeed, virtually unprecedented) source: the characterization of Willie. According to Laura Cerrato, the reviewer for *The Beckett Circle*, Marilú Marini, who played Winnie, "looked like an average well-to-do Argentinian housewife, with a conventional coiffure and make-up, who was musing ineffectually about life in her beautiful garden" (2004: 1) – an interpretation of the role that, like many of those described above, emphasized her interest in the domestic mundane. Willie, however, as played by Marc Toupence, "provided a contrast to Winnie's upper middle class style with his almost surrealistic apparitions, *half naked and with a wounded head*, reminiscent of a World War I refugee from the trenches" (ibid.; my emphasis). The director was Arthur Nauzyciel, using a translation by Antonia Rodríguez Gago. Marini, who had previously performed the role of Winnie in French in Paris at the Théâtre de l'Odéon and subsequently in Morocco, commented on her choices for the production as follows: "I chose an 'Argentinian version' to achieve a greater intimacy between Winnie and that other to whom she speaks, whether it be her husband, or death, or whatever life-supports she chooses to imagine. It was a risky decision. At times I was afraid the text would seem too much like something from a soap opera" (ibid.: 2). Of all the worries of all the stars in all the productions in all the world, never before had a concern with an audience possibly confusing *Happy Days* with "something from a soap opera" been so brought to the fore. Nor had Willie ever so seemed a refugee from *All Quiet on the Western Front* on the (battle-scarred?) scorched-earth slope of the mound. The production was also mounted in Barcelona at the Teatre Municipal Mercat de les Flors for a three-day run in late June of 2003.

In the January 2006 production of *Oh les beaux jours* directed by Frederick Wiseman at the Théâtre du Vieux-Colombier (the home of the Comédie Française in Paris's Latin Quarter, the venue for its staging of a range of contemporary classics), the mound was a surprisingly tall four-tiered equilateral triangle of beige canvas that, in production photographs, looks like an extremely wide, flounced hoop-skirt. According to Alexandra Poulain in *The Beckett Circle*,

> set-designer Paul Andreu ... recall[ed] finding a new angle to the play's scenography in Winnie's enigmatic musing, "Is gravity what it was, Willie, I fancy not. Yes, the feeling more and more that if I were not held – in this way, I would simply float up into the blue." In Andreu's set, it is not so much Winnie who sinks down into the mound between acts one and two, as the mound that rises up to her neck and seems to carry her skyward. (2006: 1)

As Winnie, Catherine Samie "look[ed] as if she were going to 'float up into the blue' at any moment – if she only could," and she gave a performance that was "entirely free of pathos" as she "deliver[ed] her lines like a hypnotic song, improvising an astonishing vocal tour de force as she ramble[d] on, yet always preserving the halting rhythm with which Beckett gives a voice to silence" (ibid.). Willie was played by Samie's long-term friend and frequent artistic partner Yves Gasc; their rapport obviously enhanced the relationship between their characters. Following *En attendant Godot* in 1978 and *Fin de partie* in 1988, *Oh les beaux jours* had at last entered the repertoire of the Comédie Française – even if, coincidentally, Winnie herself seemed for the first time to be nearing her own almost-Ascension.

Within days of Beckett's death, the Beckett scholar Tom Bishop (who was also a close friend of the playwright) speculated that "the plays will now be more available for interpretation. I think they're strong enough to support all that" (in Gussow 1989: 13). Now, nearly two decades later, his prediction that productions of the plays would proliferate has certainly come true – though neither he nor anyone else could have foretold the startling variety of interpretations of *Happy Days* that would include an aerial view of Winnie's confinement, a war-wounded half-naked Willie sprawled almost all quiet on the western not-front of the mound, or a ballet in which Winnie suddenly danced free of her pink-slippered pile, to name but a few. That controversy ensued (and will certainly continue) is predictable, even desirable: in the theater, as anywhere else, still waters stagnate. Endlessly replicable productions, even if theoretically possible, might as well be embalmed. In surveying the startling variety of productions of *Happy Days* since Beckett's death, the visual ingeniousness and irrepressible artistic creativity of performers, directors, and designers is unmistakable. Less apparent, but no less important, is their respect for – even veneration of – Beckett's inimitable words, a recognition of genius and stage poetry that exists quite apart from contractual demands of the author's estate. Perhaps even more than the two tramps idling beside a desolate tree, the image of Winnie entrapped in the mound has become iconic in modern theater. With each new production, her plight is necessarily reimagined, re-explored, and reconceived, as only the greatest literary characters demand of their performers. And so, even as she speaks, yet again, in and of "the old style" – played sometimes suburban and sometimes not, sometimes vulgar and sometimes elegant, sometimes comical and sometimes distraught to the verge of a nervous breakdown – she is perennially (re)created.

NOTES

1   Harris's review also contains what is possibly the single most incongruous simile ever used to describe an actress in performance: "In the second act, Winnie [Cracknell] is embedded up to the neck, her head looking like the nipple on a vast and rugged reclining breast."

2   Although the production credited George Devine as the director, Beckett's biographer

James Knowlson writes that Beckett was
"allowed by Devine more or less to take over
as director" (1996: 446); the designer was
Jocelyn Herbert. For a detailed account of the
rehearsal period and the production, see
Knowlson (1996: 445–8); he does not confirm
the detail about makeup in the second act,
however.

3   Cooper's review (1996) also includes one of the
most peculiar descriptions of an actor's performance ever written: "Willy [sic], Winnie's
almost silent foil in this arrangement, drips
from every orifice as she desperately fills the
void with her chatter." Mercifully, the actor is
unnamed in the review, perhaps to prevent
embarrassment over this unusual medical predicament, an affliction surely surpassing even
any of Lucky's in *Waiting for Godot*.

REFERENCES

Armitstead, Claire (1998). "Up to my neck in it,"
Guardian, p. 12 (February 4).

Astbury, Helen (1999). "*Oh les beaux jours* in Paris."
*The Beckett Circle: Newsletter of the Samuel Beckett
Society* 21(2): 3.

Beckett, Samuel (1961). *Happy Days*. New York:
Grove Press.

Ben-Zvi, Linda (1991). "Dublin Salutes Beckett."
*The Beckett Circle: Newsletter of the Samuel Beckett
Society* 13(1): 2–3.

Billington, Michael (1994). "*Happy Days*: French
Institute." *Guardian*, T6 (June 6).

Billington, Michael (1996). "Savage Twist in
Happy Days." *Guardian*, p. 2 (October 31).

Billington, Michael (2003). "*Happy Days*: Last
Night's Show." *Guardian*, p. 30 (November 19).

Bishop, Tom (1990). "*Happy Days* in New York."
*The Beckett Circle: Newsletter of the Samuel Beckett
Society* 12(1): 1.

Bradby, David (2004). "Peter Hall's *Happy Days*."
*The Beckett Circle: Newsletter of the Samuel Beckett
Society* 27(1): 10–11.

Bramwell, Murray (1991). "*Happy Days* Is Here
Again." *Advertiser* (May 18).

Brantley, Ben (2002). "Becket's Earthy Idea of
Optimism." *New York Times*, p. 4 (October 2).

Cerrato, Laura (2004). "*Los días felices* in Buenos
Aires." *The Beckett Circle: Newsletter of the Samuel
Beckett Society* 27(2): 1–2.

Colgan, Gerry (1995). "*Happy Days* – Samuel
Beckett Theatre." *Irish Times*, p. 15 (April 17).

Cooper, Neil (1996). "*Happy Days*: Traverse
Theatre, Edinburgh." *Independent*, p. 9 (June
26).

Donnelly, Pat (1996). "Oh *Happy Days*: Renowned
Theatre Director Peter Brook Finally Tackles
Samuel Beckett." *Gazette* E1 (May 18).

Engelberts, Matthijs (1996). "*Oh Les Beaux Jours*
Directs Peter Brook." *The Beckett Circle:
Newsletter of the Samuel Beckett Society* 18(1):
2–3.

Fisher, Mark (1996). "*Oh Les Beaux Jours*, Bouffes
Du Nord, Paris." *Herald*, p. 24 (October 1).

González, Antonio Ballesteros (1997). "Open-Air
Happy Days in Madrid." *The Beckett Circle: Newsletter of the Samuel Beckett Society* 19(1): 6–7.

Gussow, Mel (1989). "Beckett's Plays: Can His
Fiat Last?" *New York Times* (December 30).

Hanks, Robert (1996a). "How Not to Succeed
at Being a Failure." *Independent*, p. 13 (November 3).

Hanks, Robert (1996b). "Radio Review." *Independent*, p. 9 (April 2).

Harris, Samela (1991). "Day by Day, Cracknell
Tackles the Dungheap." *Advertiser*, n.p. (May
27).

Hutchings, William (2002). "Interview with
Joyce Aaron." *The Journal of Beckett Studies* 11(2):
90–7.

Joly, Annie (2001). "Roussillon 2001," trans.
Thomas Cousineau. *The Beckett Circle: Newsletter
of the Samuel Beckett Society* 24(2): 6–7.

Klein, Alvin (1990). "Hope Wins in Beckett's
Happy Days." *New York Times*, sec. 12, p. 15
(January 28).

Klein, Alvin (1998). "Beckett's Many Mercies,
Abounding Mercies." *New York Times*, sec.
14CN, p. 15 (November 15).

Knowlson, James (1996). *Damned to Fame: The Life
of Samuel Beckett*. New York: Simon and
Schuster.

Knowlson, James (1998). "*Oh Les Beaux Jours* in
London." *The Beckett Circle: Newsletter of the
Samuel Beckett Society* 20(1): 1–2.

Luscher-Moreta, Diane (2002). "Béjart's Beckett." *The Beckett Circle: Newsletter of the Samuel Beckett Society* 25(2): 6–7.

Macaulay, Alistair (1994). "Happy Days." *Financial Times*, p. 17 (June 7).

Murray, David (1998). "Life at the End of the Road." *Financial Times*, p. 15 (February 19).

O'Hagan, Andrew (2001). "Filming the Poetry of Pain in an Inspired New Project ..." *The Daily Telegraph*, p. 25 (February 6).

O'Halloran, Eileen (1996). "Buckets O' Beckett in Chicago." *The Beckett Circle: Newsletter of the Samuel Beckett Society* 18(2): 6–7.

O'Toole, Fintan (2001). "The Reel Beckett." *Irish Times*, p. 60 (January 27).

Percival, John (2002). "Happy Memories are Made of This; Dance L'Heure Exquise Lidy Theatre Lausanne." *Independent*, p. 19. (June 20).

Pinte, Jean-Louis (1999). "Théâtre de la Tempête: Sale temps." *Le Figaro* (April 28).

Poulain, Alexandra (2006). "*Oh Les Beaux Jours* at the Théâtre du Vieux-Colombier." *The Beckett Circle: Newsletter of the Samuel Beckett Society* 29(1): 1–3.

Richards, David (1990). "One Good Laugh That Deserves Another." *New York Times*, sec. 2, p. 15 (October 21).

Shuttleworth, Ian (2003). "*Happy Days*: Arts Theatre, London." *Financial Times*, p. 17 (November 20).

Spencer, Charles (2003). "Bleak, Terrifying, yet Delightful." *Daily Telegraph*, p. 18 (November 19).

Taylor, Paul (1996). "*Happy Days*: Almeida Theatre, London / Bouffes du Nord, Paris." *Independent*, p. 19 (November 1).

Taylor, Paul (1998). "Up to their necks in happiness." *Independent*, p. 6 (February 17).

Taylor, Paul (2003). "First Night: Kendal Up to her Neck in Stunning Revival of *Happy Days*." *Independent*, p. 11 (November 19).

Tönnies, Merle (2003). "Peter Brook's *Glückliche Tage*." *The Beckett Circle: Newsletter of the Samuel Beckett Society* 26(2): 1–3.

Villiers, Sara (1995). "*Happy Days*, Pleasance." *Herald*, p. 10 (August 12).

Whitebrook, Peter (1995). "*Happy Days*: Angela Pleasence, Pleasance Theatre." *Scotsman*, p. 7 (August 15).

Worth, Katharine (1991). "Beckett Festival, Dublin 1991." *The Beckett Circle: Newsletter of the Samuel Beckett Society* 13(1): 5.

Part IV
Acts of Performance

Beckett's Production of *Waiting for Godot* (*Warten auf Godot*)

David Bradby

Beckett's own production of *Waiting for Godot* at the Schiller-Theater, Berlin in 1975 provides the key point in what Stanley Gontarski has called his "reinvention of himself as an artist" through having to direct his own work (Gontarski 1998: 131). He dreaded the experience because he considered the play to be undisciplined, but it gave him the opportunity to revise the text and to clarify aspects that he felt were still confused. To his assistant director, Walter Asmus, he described the play as "a mess" and explained that, because of his lack of theater experience when he was writing it in the late 1940s, the play was not visualized to his satisfaction (Knowlson 1993: xi–xii). For the Schiller-Theater production, which was in German, he completely revised both text and stage directions and these revisions were then incorporated into an English text for subsequent productions by Walter Asmus closely modeled on Beckett's work in Berlin. This is now the authoritative English text (McMillan and Knowlson 1993: 7–85), although the standard Faber edition still reproduces a partially revised version dating from 1965. In this chapter, *TN* denotes page references to Beckett's revised text, published in *The Theatrical Notebooks of Samuel Beckett Vol. 1*, and "Faber" those to the standard Faber edition.

In his work on the play Beckett demonstrated a remarkable understanding of how theater performance communicates differently from written text. The shaping of the non-verbal elements of theater performance – action, gesture, voice, light, sound, pace, rhythm – occupied the center of his attention for the months he spent working on the production, evidence of the development that had taken place in his approach to theater over 25 years. This development began as early as the late 1950s: from *Krapp's Last Tape* onwards, Beckett's dramatic compositions demonstrated a new awareness of the visual dimension and of the poetic force of a dramatic situation in which vocal and visual elements depend on one another. It is possible to imagine productions of both *Waiting for Godot* and *Endgame* in a variety of settings. But in all his subsequent plays, Beckett made the setting part of the stage action in such a way that the two are inseparable. The force of *Krapp's Last Tape* (1959) lies in the image of an old man trying to recover memories of his earlier life by listening to his own voice on a tape recorder. It would make no sense to perform the play without a tape recorder. *Happy Days* (1962) makes similarly effective use of the image of a woman being buried alive. After *Happy Days*, every new play he wrote incorporated some striking new visual image in such a way that the stage picture itself summed up and embodied the experience the play had to offer: the urns in which the characters are confined in *Play* (1964), the single spot-lit mouth in *Not I* (1974), the obsessively pacing feet of *Footfalls* (1976) or the rocking chair in *Rockaby* (1982).

In *Waiting for Godot* the scenic situation does not have the same sharp originality – the play's originality lies rather in its whole dramatic structure. So part of Beckett's work as director was to supply this. He began by expanding the initial stage direction which, in its original form, was: "A country road. A tree. Evening" (Route à la campagne, avec arbre. Soir.) This was changed to read "A country road. A tree. A stone. Evening" and the description of Estragon "sitting on a low mound" was changed to "seated on a stone." In addition, where the original had begun with Estragon alone on stage, Beckett decided to have Vladimir already there too, from the start. By such means, Beckett was looking for opportunities to visualize more intensely the interplay of thematically linked pairs or complementary opposites, such as the tree and the stone, with their distant echo of cross and grave. These were used to set up a series of mirror images, cross references and echoes, giving the final production its poetic complexity. The rather Synge-like country road has given way to a more general evocation of evening – it is not just the evening of the day but the evening of life, as the countless references to death in the play confirm.

Although it was his first attempt at directing the play, Beckett was by no means a novice in the practicalities of directing. By the time he agreed to direct *Waiting for Godot* he had acquired considerable experience of theater production. Not only had he attended rehearsals for many of his plays, from Roger Blin's first *Godot* onwards, he had also undertaken three productions of his own at the Berlin Schiller-Theater's small studio theater named the Werkstatt: *Endgame* (1967), *Krapp's Last Tape* (1969), and *Happy Days* (1971). So, when he accepted the offer to direct *Godot* on the main stage of the same theater, he knew what to expect and evidently enjoyed the challenge of working in German with German actors. Despite this, he found it a great strain going back over *Godot*, and, instead of approaching the work with the authority of its creator, he assumed his characteristic stance as the artist of failure. As has been noted, he described the play as "a mess" and wrote in his preliminary notebook that his purpose in taking on the production was "Der Konfusion Gestalt geben" (i.e. to give shape to the confusion) (Knowlson 1993: xi). The key word here is "Gestalt." Beckett's production demonstrated his central preoccupation with the way art can shape experience, drawing out patterns, both visual and musical. The shapes, rhythms, echoes, and recurrent patterns on which Beckett laid such emphasis are exactly those elements which are only perceptible in performance, and almost impossible to recover after a given production has run its course. But a unique record of Beckett's shaping work as director of his own play survives in the form of his production notebook. This shows how he planned the production and also, through its erasures and additions, how his direction evolved.

Beckett's Production Notebook

Beckett's notebook is highly original. It does not resemble Brecht's *Modellbücher*, which aimed to give a clear record of a production, since it was written before rehearsals started, as an aid to the director. Nor is it similar to Stanislavsky's production notebooks for Chekhov's plays, in which he pasted the text onto one page and then set out, on the facing page, detailed descriptions of what the actors should be doing while speaking the playwright's text. It is more analytical than either of these models and also less exhaustive, since not every line of the play is dealt with. But it does set out the manner in which Beckett visualized his play running its course on stage, both in general outline and in precise details. It shows how Beckett broke the play down into sections for rehearsal purposes and which aspects he picked out for special emphasis in seeking to "give shape to the confusion." There are two notebooks, a preliminary version, known at the Reading University archive, where both are housed, as the "green" notebook, and a final version, known as the "red" notebook. Beckett had the red notebook with him throughout rehearsals and made additions or deletions to it as he worked with the actors. It is this notebook which is reproduced in *The Theatrical Notebooks of Samuel Beckett Vol. 1*. It begins by breaking the play up into 11 sections, six in Act 1 and five in Act 2. These are listed as A 1–6 and B 1–5. Each of these sections has a few pages devoted to it, giving detailed indications for movements, gestures, manipulation of props, together with occasional comments on tone of voice or desired effect on the audience. The textual location of a given move is indicated by a short quotation from the German text, followed by a telegraphic evocation of what movement is to take place. Only the right-hand pages of the notebook are used for these indications, except that, occasionally, Beckett has filled out his description by drawing a small diagram on the left-hand page, tracing out the pattern of a character's moves using lines and arrows. Apart from these diagrams, the left-hand pages were left blank for alterations or new ideas to emerge in rehearsals, and these were noted by Beckett in red to distinguish them from the black ink used for his preparatory notes. This takes up the first 53 pages of the notebook.

Beckett's sections are not all the same length and are best seen in musical terms as "statements" or "developments" of thematic patterns. His section A1 runs from the opening to just after Estragon's line "People are bloody ignorant apes" (Faber: 13). Beckett's note at the end of the section reads:

Thus establish at outset 2 caged dynamics, E sluggish, V restless.
+ perpetual separation and reunion of V/E. (*TN*: 185)

The function of the opening section was thus to bring out the predicament of the two characters, stressing both their opposition and their complementarity. In the following section he concentrated on developing the theme of perpetual separation and reunion, "like a rubber band, they come together time after time," commented Stefan Wigger in rehearsals. The central part of Act 1, with Pozzo and Lucky, were divided into sections A3, A4, and A5. Finally, A6 ran from their exit to the end of the act. Beckett's notes for A6 provide a good example of his concern for very precise lighting effects combined with equally precise moves to be made by the boy. With regard to lighting effect, what he wanted was for the boy to emerge from deep shadow, and this was achieved in the Schiller-Theater. As for the moves, these were to be a variation of a pattern he named "approach by stages," which he had already specified on more than one occasion for moves by Vladimir and Estragon: as the boy moved hesitantly towards Vladimir he was to reciprocate with moves towards the boy. The boy's moves as he exited were to mirror his entry. In the production, Vladimir's last words to the boy – "You did see us, didn't you?" – emerged "as an important motif in Beckett's Schiller production where this despairing cry from Vladimir became something of a climactic moment" (*TN*: 143). This was an occasion for another successful lighting effect: "The Boy's exit was co-ordinated here with the moon which, in Schiller, rose in a perfect arc from the point where Vladimir was standing and stopped above the spot where the Boy had just been" (*TN*: 143).

The second act was divided into five sections. The staging notes for this act show Beckett developing variations on the patterns of movement he had established in the first act, contrasting straight lines with arcs and circles, and echoing the theme of the "approach by stages."

The second half of the notebook, from page 54 to page 109, is devoted to a series of 20 analytical headings bringing together recurring themes or actions in the play. Most of these consist simply of lists, devoid of commentary. The first of these headings, "L's moves A3," catalogues in meticulous detail each step taken by Lucky so as to avoid any confusion about how he carries his burdens and how he responds to Pozzo's stream of commands. These pages of the notebook generally restrict themselves to outlining moves, although on rare occasions general principles underlying the moves are alluded to. The lists in this part of the notebook are invaluable pointers to what Beckett himself saw as the key themes. For example, one page, headed "Help," lists 21 cries for help in the play; among that number 14 go unanswered, and only four are answered. Other headings include "Sky," "Sleep," "Remembering" and three pages listing "Doubts confusions."

Beckett's Handling of Actors in Rehearsal

When Beckett arrived to begin rehearsing in Berlin on December 26, 1974, he had already completed the production notebook described above and had completely revised the German translation, making many hundreds of changes, cuts, and revisions in order to bring the text "closer to the French and English versions and establish more precise verbal repetitions and echoes" (Knowlson 1993: xi). To facilitate the rehearsal process, he had also committed the German text to memory, leaving him free to concentrate on the actors' work without constant scrabbling in the pages of his copy. The production opened on March 8, 1975, so the rehearsal period lasted more than two months, a great luxury by the standards of most English-speaking theater. Rehearsals took place in the mornings only (11:00 a.m. to 3:00 p.m.) and were mostly on the main stage. This extended time period allowed him ample opportunity to try out and, where necessary, revise his initial staging ideas.

Beckett's relationships with the cast were friendly; he had worked with them before and had been given a free hand to cast any actor he chose from among the members of the company. He deliberately picked actors of contrasting body shape for Vladimir and Estragon. Stefan Wigger, tall and thin, played Vladimir, while Estragon was taken by Horst Bollmann, who was short and fat. Martin Held, who had played Krapp in Beckett's 1969 production, was to play Pozzo, but after two weeks withdrew from the production on grounds of ill-health and was replaced by Karl Raddatz. Klaus Herm, as Lucky, showed enthusiasm from start to finish and was judged by Beckett to be "a remarkable Lucky. Most moving" (Knowlson 1996: 608). The rehearsal diary kept by Walter Asmus provides invaluable insights into the process; it was published in two English-language versions, whose wording differs slightly; in quoting from it, therefore, I will give references either to one or both editions depending on whether the relevant extract is available in each source. Asmus's diary stresses the friendly atmosphere in which rehearsals were conducted and the absence of any authoritarian note in Beckett's dealings with the actors:

> Beckett subjects his own script constantly to critical control in the most amazing and sympathetic way. He is also open to suggestions at any time, and he even asks for them. He is not at all interested in carrying out a rigid concept, but aims for the best possible interpretation of his script. Should uncertainty occur, he is ready with a new suggestion the next day, always precise and thought-through, even if it does not always work immediately. (Asmus 1975: 20; McMillan and Fehsenfeld 1988: 136)

This account shows that although he always began with the moves and stage business which he had worked out in advance in his notebook, Beckett was ready to adjust them in the light of what appeared most effective in rehearsal. He adopted several of the actors' suggestions, especially those which increased comic impact through the use of repetition. In Act 1, for example, when Pozzo is trying to introduce himself to Vladimir and Estragon, they built up a comic repetition of the names "Bozzo ... Bozzo," "Pozzo ... Pozzo," each actor intercutting his line with that of the other. Again, when Pozzo and Lucky depart, Vladimir and Estragon continued to repeat their "adieux" and to raise their hats in a gesture of farewell long after the other two had left the stage. Knowlson points out that Beckett's creative work with the actors in rehearsal cannot be deduced from the notebook, especially the way he encouraged them to build up the physical routines, transforming "vaudeville movements into something almost balletic" (Knowlson 1996: 609). An example of this was the "three hats for two heads" routine in Act 2, when Vladimir and Estragon discover the hat left behind by Lucky, based on a sequence which appears in the Marx Brothers' film *Duck Soup*.

Despite Beckett's intense concern for precision in everything that was done on stage, Asmus records "an atmosphere of 'relaxed tension', which could also be described as an occupation of pleasure" (Asmus 1975: 26; McMillan and Fehsenfeld 1988: 147). Beckett was unwilling to discuss the play's meaning or content in discursive terms but was always ready to help the actors with explanations concerning the characters' motivation at any particular moment. He rejected explanations of the kind commonly associated with the Stanislavskian school of naturalism, such as those relating to background, earlier events that have taken place before the action begins, or subtextual details only hinted at in the text of the play. On the other hand, he was quite forthcoming on the subject of the complex way in which the characters on stage relate to one another. While he was rehearsing Lucky's "Think," Asmus reports in translation the following exchange between Beckett and Klaus Herm (playing Lucky):

> HERM: He [Lucky] gives Estragon once, a long look. What do you mean to say
> with this long look?
> BECKETT: It's a kind of look you can't explain in a few words. There is a lot in that
> look. Lucky wants the piece of bone, of course. Estragon, too. That is a
> confrontation, a meeting of two very poor people.
> HERM: Something like solidarity, is that in it, too?
> BECKETT: Yes, there are so many things in his head. Recognising the other one's
> situation, that is very important – but also some pride, that he is free to dispose
> of the bones, as opposed to Estragon. But Lucky does not forget either. The kick in
> the shin should be interpreted as Lucky's revenge for the fact that Estragon took
> the bone. (Asmus 1975: 22–3; McMillan and Fehsenfeld 1988: 139)

While Beckett may not have wanted his characters to be considered in naturalistic terms, he nonetheless envisaged their reactions to one another being built up from a complex interplay of different motives, and expected his actors to convey a range of very subtle nuance through something as simple as a look.

Sometimes the actors yearned for the naturalistic acting style to which they were accustomed. When Beckett was describing the non-realistic way he wanted Lucky to fall, Stefan Wigger asked, "But how can one prevent the loss of all human consideration, how can one prevent it from becoming sterile, to which Beckett replied that 'it is a game, everything is a game'" (Asmus 1975: 23; McMillan and Fehsenfeld 1988: 140). He frequently returned to this assertion that the play was a game, albeit a game played in earnest: "It should become clear and transparent, not dry. It is a game in order to survive"(Asmus 1975: 24; McMillan and Fehsenfeld 1988: 140). He was determined to avoid imitation of reality, but he respected the real tensions, desires and frustrations present in the ways people interrelate. An example of this realistic yet playful approach to character emerges from the following description:

Starting with "Sweet mother earth", the scene is being played in context until the exit of Pozzo and Lucky [in Act 2]. When Estragon and Vladimir – all lying on the ground – shout "Pozzo", Beckett slips in a small alteration. Instead of speaking all the time towards the back, towards Pozzo, Estragon should say his "We might try him with other names" directly to Vladimir. There is thus a small intimate moment of conspiracy created at this point, which is reminiscent of similar moments throughout the play. (Asmus 1975: 26; McMillan and Fehsenfeld 1988: 148)

The conspiratorial, game-like approach was evident in a number of key sequences of action devised by Beckett for his actors; it helped them to come to terms with the precise, sometimes deliberately artificial patterns of movement which he described as "balletic."

As can be seen from the examples given, a move was never permissible, as it is in so many productions, simply on the grounds that it made the actor feel comfortable or looked natural. On the contrary, every move had a purpose within the overall structure of the production; no move was either gratuitous or superfluous. The same was true of the delivery of the lines. This had to respect the reality of the characters' emotions, provoked by their relationships and the situations in which they were placed, but also the overall thematic patterning. The effect of the moments of stillness and silence was further enhanced by the speed of much of the dialogue. Beckett's production was timed by Ruby Cohn at 70 minutes for Act 1, 55 minutes for Act 2, which is considerably faster than most. For purposes of comparison, Luc Bondy's production – which had a considerable success at the Théâtre Vidy of Lausanne in 1999 – ran for more than half an hour longer than this. In Beckett's production, the overall experience for audiences was one of lightness and speed, interspersed with haunting moments of anguish.

Lucky's "Think"

The first thing Beckett chose to tackle when the rehearsals got under way was Lucky's single long speech in Act 1, known as his "Think." This is striking, since it is the last thing a professional director might think of doing, and we know for a fact that the play's earliest directors, Blin, Hall, and Schneider all left it till very late in the rehearsal process. The priority which Beckett gave it perhaps resulted from his own preoccupations at the time: his dramatic writing over the previous years had tended more and more towards dramatic monologue. His most recent play was *Not I*, in which a single voice babbles semi-incoherently about her life, conveying an impression of fragmentation which has many similarities to that of Lucky's "Think." He had directed a memorable first production of *Not I* with Billie Whitelaw two years before, and so he was familiar with the performance problems posed by long sections of monologue. Moreover, he began to write *Footfalls* in Berlin while rehearsing *Godot*, so dramatic monologue continued to preoccupy him at this time.

His approach to the "Think" demonstrates in microcosm his approach to the whole play. He first broke it down into sections. This had two functions: first to help Klaus Herm to shape the speech, and, second, to help the other three actors to shape their reactions to it. His division of the speech into sections helped to change the way it was understood. Early interpreters had seen it all of a piece, with very little meaning or coherence. Beckett changed all that by showing that, despite the fragmentation of its form, it nevertheless has a clear structure. He divided it into five sections, set out on page 57 of the production notebook. They are as follows:

1   from the start to the first "but not so fast";
2   to "waste and pine";
3   to the first "the facts are there";
4   to "the facts are there but time will tell";
5   "I resume alas alas on on" to the end.

Beside section 1 Beckett wrote "Indifferent heaven." Sections 2 and 3 were bracketed together with the comment "Dwindling man." Sections 4 and 5 carried the comment "Earth abode of stones & cadenza." This clear progression from an indifferent heaven through dwindling man to the conclusion of an earth that is the abode of stones give a clear thematic shape to the speech. Two notes added beside section 5 during rehearsals read, "New elements Skull" and "Last straw – Tears."

In addition to these thematic pointers, Beckett's notes indicate the responses of the other three characters. In (1) Vladimir and Estragon are to be "concentrated in spite of early shock of quaquaquaqua and quaquaquaqua," while Pozzo watches attentively for their reactions; in (2) Pozzo grows increasingly unhappy as the other two become more restive; in (3) Vladimir and Estragon show "some interest" in physical culture but lose patience again and make "audible protestations," while Pozzo has "fingers in ears bowed forward"; in (4) it all becomes too much for Estragon and Vladimir, both of whom exit, re-enter and then exit again and only come back again in (5) on "the skull"; finally, Beckett notes, "Cunard Cunard all close in to down L." In rehearsals this was changed to exclude Pozzo: just Vladimir and Estragon closed in on Lucky and brought him down with a sequence of slow-motion stylised kicks and punches, while Pozzo looked on.

Beckett's advice to Klaus Herm, playing Lucky, showed a keen understanding of how an actor must relate to the part he is playing. He said for example: "'To shrink and dwindle…' will cause bewilderment for the public: but at this point everything will be absolutely clear for Lucky." He went on to explain that Lucky is anxious to please Pozzo:

> Lucky's thinking isn't as good as it used to be: "He even used to think prettily once …" says Pozzo. Herm could play it that way, watching Pozzo from time to time. And the two others, too. He is not talking simply to himself, he is not completely on his own, says Beckett.

HERM: But he kind of refuses first, he doesn't like the idea of thinking ...

BECKETT: He would like to amuse Pozzo. Pozzo would like to get rid of him, but if he finds Lucky touching, he might keep him. Lucky would like to be successful. (Asmus 1975: 22; McMillan and Fehsenfeld 1988: 139)

This is an invaluable note for any actor performing Lucky. It shows that for *him* the speech must make some sort of sense, and not be delivered in one great outburst as it is so often done. The audience should feel the despair of a man whose pride once lay in the "pretty" way he could voice his thoughts, but who now finds the control of his words slipping away.

Beckett's notes on Lucky's "Think" conclude with the words the actor should stress, followed by a list of "Main shocks." The words to be stressed show Lucky's desperate attempts to give academic credibility and a meaningful shape to his "Think." They begin with "all research tandems," by which Beckett meant "Poinçon and Wattman," "Testu and Conard," "Fartov and Belcher," "Steinweg and Petermann," after which he listed the following: "Hell to Heaven"; "but not so fast"; "established" (recurring three times, although each time used a slightly different phrase in the German text); "waste and pine"; "shrinks and dwindles"; "the facts are there"; "abode of stones." Under "Main shocks" (that is, the phrases eliciting shocked reactions from Valdimir and Estragon) were: "quaquaquaqua; quaquaquaqua"; "Acacacacademy"; "Anthropopopometry"; "established ter" (that is, third time); "As a result ter" (third time); "Testew and Cunard"; "Hockey in the air" (an addition to the German text not present in English editions); "I resume 3" (crossed out during rehearsals); "more grave 2 (exit Estragon)"; "more grave 4 (exit Vladimir)"; "I resume 4 (re-exit Estragon)"; "I resume 5 (re-exit Vladimir)"; "I resume 8 (Last straw)."

In the different expressive elements available to the director that Beckett mentions here, we can see an example of three key methods that he applied to the play as a whole. The first is his subdivision into manageable sections, not only for ease of rehearsing but also to bring out underlying thematic concerns. The second is his emphasis on stress and shock: the expressive dynamics of the speech have been carefully thought out so as to give shape to Lucky's torrent of words. The third is his attention to the positions and moves of the other characters; although he is dealing with a monologue, his concern is for the overall stage picture and for the patterns of movement traced by all four actors.

Design, Shape, Themes

Knowlson has shown convincingly how much of Beckett's writing was influenced by his knowledge and love of painting. When he began to direct, this influence emerged all the more powerfully. Knowlson comments that "Lucky is a grotesque who could have existed relatively unremarkably in the world of Bosch, Bruegel or, one of Beckett's favourite painters, Brouwer" (Knowslon 1996: 609). He goes on to cite a specific example where the pattern of stage movement calls to mind a painting by Bruegel, *The Land of Cockaigne*. It is in Act 2, where all four figures fall across one another. Beckett paid careful attention to the exact positions in which the actors were to fall. For Pozzo and Lucky, who fall first, he specified: "Stylize fall as throughout first knees, then forward on face" (*TN*: 43). He also added to his stage direction "They lie helpless among the scattered baggage," the words: "perpendicular across each other midstage off-centre right." When, a couple of pages later, Vladimir and Estragon fall onto the same heap they were to fall backwards, so as to add angled branches to the perpendicular shape of the cross formed by Pozzo and Lucky. This carefully constructed shape closely resembles the heap of men lying in the left foreground of Bruegel's painting identified by Knowlson. This was not to be done too realistically, nor too seriously, Beckett said: "It is a game, everything is a game. When all four of them are lying on the ground, that cannot be handled naturalistically. That has got to be done artificially, balletically" (Asmus 1975: 23; McMillan and Fehsenfeld 1988: 140). He exploited the extreme contrast in body shape between Bollmann (Estragon) and Wigger (Vladimir) to add to this "balletic" element, giving them gestures which at times made them seem almost to be puppets rather than live actors.

In all of these ways, Beckett wanted to evoke for his spectators images and shapes which would carry poetic resonances, and which he called "themes of the body." He explained that his aim was:

> To give confusion shape … a shape through repetition, repetition of themes. Not only themes in the script, but also themes of the body. When at the beginning Estragon is asleep leaning on the stone, that is a theme that repeats itself a few times. There are fixed points of waiting, where everything stands completely still, where silence threatens to swallow everything up. Then the action starts again. (Asmus 1975: 23; McMillan and Fehsenfeld 1988: 140)

When he spoke of these "themes of the body," Beckett was thinking not only of the actors' positions on stage, but also of the "fixed points of waiting." These are not indicated in the text, but were introduced by Beckett as he planned the production. He named them *Wartestelle* and used them to punctuate the action in the way that a composer introduces moments of silence between different movements of a musical score. These moments, in which everything stopped and the stage presented a tableau frozen in time, were introduced at the beginning and end of each act and at four further points within each of the acts. On page 75 of the production notebook, headed simply **W**, Beckett had noted, "Opening / close both acts," followed by a list of 16 points at which a *Wartestelle* might be interpolated. In the course of the rehearsals, he settled on eight of these, four in each act.

His underlying concern was to achieve a clearly defined contrast between the "themes of the body" as conveyed by Estragon and Vladimir. In rehearsals, he explained that "relaxation is a word of Estragon's. It is his dream, to be able to keep calm. Vladimir is more animated" (Asmus 1975: 24; McMillan and Fehsenfeld 1988: 140).

He also commented that Estragon was close to the ground and belonged to the stone, whereas Vladimir was light, oriented towards the sky, and belonged to the tree (Asmus 1975: 21; McMillan and Fehsenfeld 1988: 137). Such indications combined to create a "theme of the body" in which Estragon's dominant position was slumped on the stone. In order the better to state this theme, Beckett altered the play's opening, as we have seen. Instead of starting on Estragon's feverish attempts to get his boot off, followed by Vladimir's entrance, Beckett placed both actors on stage from the beginning, Estragon sitting on the stone, and Vladimir standing near the tree. Vladimir was looking up, listening; Estragon appeared to be half asleep, his head bowed. There was a long moment of silence and stillness, the first of the *Wartestelle* or Waiting points. Only after this prolonged pause did Estragon set the action of the play in motion by beginning to pull at his boot. The revised opening enabled Beckett to clarify from the outset the contrasted physicalities of Estragon and Vladimir while also stating the fundamental theme shared by both characters: that of waiting. A similar frozen moment of contrast was achieved at the beginning of Act 2, which was also changed so that it began with both characters on stage. The openings found an echo in the *Wartestelle* at the end of each of the acts: at the end of Act 1, both were sitting on the stone, "V looking up. E down"; at the end of Act 2, they were standing either side of the tree, "E looking down, V up."

Given his attention to physical and pictorial detail, the relationship he established with his designer was clearly important. With Beckett's approval, the Schiller-Theater appointed the French designer Matias Henrioud, known simply as Matias, who had worked on many previous Beckett productions in Paris, as well as designing the three studio theater productions Beckett had already done at the Schiller-Theater. As might be expected in a production so carefully prepared in advance, set and costumes both made a significant contribution to the images and concepts governing the whole performance. The set was simplicity itself: the stage was completely bare apart from the tree upstage left and the stone downstage right. The stone which replaced the "low mound" of the original marked an important step in Beckett's attempt to "give shape to confusion," since it echoes the references to stones in Lucky's "Think" and, more clearly than the mound, suggests a tomb. Beckett's symbols for sketching the tree and the stone in his notebook were a cross for the tree and a horizontal line for the stone, bearing unmistakable overtones of cross and tomb. These poetic or symbolic resonances required physical embodiment, as Beckett made plain, not just to the actors, but to the designer as well, repeating his comment that Estragon belonged to the stone, Vladimir to the tree. In this way, through concrete embodiment of contrasted characteristics, Beckett uses all the expressive means of the stage to develop one of his chief recurring themes: the mystery about why one person is favored while another suffers (explicitly discussed in the first big debate of the play, concerning the two thieves crucified with the Savior).

Equally important in clarifying the ideas behind the production was the costume design, which made a strong visual statement about the interdependence of the two pairs of characters. This was especially clear in the case of Vladimir and Estragon.

Beckett wanted to exploit the difference in height between the short Horst Bollman as Estragon, and the tall Stefan Wigger, playing Vladimir. His aim was to build up a paradoxical picture of two people who were very unlike each other and yet depended on each other completely; who were always longing to get away from one another, and yet entirely lost without one another; opposites who complemented one another and who were somehow incomplete as individuals if separated. "Vladimir is going to wear striped trousers which fit him, with a black jacket, which is too small for him; the jacket belonged originally to Estragon. Estragon, on the other hand, wears black trousers which fit him, with a striped jacket which is too big for him; it originally belonged to Vladimir" (Asmus 1975: 21; McMillan and Fehsenfeld 1988: 137). In the second act, this arrangement was reversed: Vladimir wore Estragon's black trousers, which were uncomfortably short on him, with the striped jacket that fitted, whereas Estragon had outsize striped trousers beneath a well-fitting black jacket. An incidental benefit of this arrangement was that the final moment of the play, when Estragon's trousers have dropped round his ankles, had a self-evident quality: it was a disaster that had been threatening to happen throughout the act.

Beckett also developed the leitmotif of complementarity in the costuming of the Pozzo–Lucky couple. Pozzo's trousers and Lucky's waistcoat were made from the same checked material, Pozzo's jacket was dark grey, matching Lucky's trousers. In this way, Beckett stressed the interdependence of Pozzo and Lucky rather than laying the emphasis on Pozzo's superior social status as landowner. In Walter Asmus's rehearsal diary, Beckett is reported as saying that Pozzo was "not to be played as a superior figure (as he usually is). Instead, all four characters should be equal. He plays the lord – magnanimous, frightening – but only because he is unsure of himself" (McMillan and Fehsenfeld 1988: 141). The clothes of both were shabby and broken down.

The lighting design echoed the play's overall theme of repetition with variations. Page 107 of the production notebook lists three lighting states:

A = ½ evening light
B = full " "
C = Moonlight (*TN*: 389)

Both acts opened and closed with a curtain. After the curtain had risen, in each act the lighting faded up from nothing to "A." In Act 1 Vladimir's move first towards Estragon (after "Nothing to be done") brought the light up to "B," while in Act 2 it was Estragon's move downstage after Vladimir's "dog song" which brought it up to "B." In both acts it faded down to "A" again on the departure of Pozzo and Lucky, and then changed to "C" on the first step back taken by the boy after his conversation with Vladimir. Here again, Beckett was evidently drawing on pictorial inspiration, since page 30 of the notebook bears the name "K. D. Friedrich" at the point when the moon rises. This refers to Friedrich's painting *Two Men Observing the Moon*, which Beckett had seen at the art gallery in Dresden. Both acts closed on a five-second *Wartestelle* before the lights were allowed to fade and the curtain came down. After the final curtain the actors took no curtain call because Beckett wanted to avoid break-ing the final silence and darkness before the house lights come up.

This careful patterning in the design elements of the production served to empha-size the shaping of the play of repetition and contrast on which Beckett's whole production was structured. A similar shaping could be seen at work in Beckett's indications for actions on stage. Page 73 of the notebook, headed "INSPECTION PLACE," contains four sketch maps of characters' moves. The first of these shows Estragon moving all round the stage during his speech "Charming spot. Inspiring prospects. Let's go" (Faber: 13–14). When, shortly afterwards, Estragon falls asleep, Beckett has Vladimir follow an almost exactly identical pattern of moves before waking him up with his three repeated exclamations of "Gogo!" (Faber: 15). In per-formance, such repetitions come across extremely clearly and encourage the audience to look for repeated themes or shapes in the movements as much as in the words. The third sketch shows Vladimir making an almost identical round of inspection at the start of the second act, thus establishing the pattern of the second act repeating (with variations) the action of the first act. The fourth sketch shows a movement made by Vladimir after the departure of Pozzo and Lucky in Act 2, but it does not completely reproduce the pattern of the three earlier moves, and Beckett has written beside it "Not properly inspection [sic]." This is consistent with other moves and shaping devices employed, which all tend to decline or fragment or fall apart as the play runs its course.

Similar to the "inspections" is his treatment of what he called "Approach by Stages," which is the heading for pages 101–3 of the notebook. These are another example of what Beckett termed "themes of the body." Sixteen of them are listed in the notebook, the last of which was deleted in the course of rehearsals. The first two occur early in the first act, on Estragon's speech "But what Saturday? And is it Sat-urday? Is it not rather Sunday? Or Monday? Or Friday?" (Faber: 15). During this exchange, Estragon moved across the stage towards Vladimir in short bursts, stopping between Sunday and Monday and between Monday and Friday. The same pattern of a three-stage approach was then repeated a few lines later for Vladimir's three excla-mations of "Gogo!" mentioned above. Similar moves were given to Pozzo when, soon after his entrance, he says: "I am Pozzo! (Silence.) Pozzo! (Silence.) Does that name mean nothing to you?" (Faber: 22) and to Vladimir and Estragon as they approach and inspect Lucky (Faber: 25). Finally, at the end of the act, the boy's approach and Estragon's angry questioning of him (Faber: 49) were accompanied by the same short bursts of movement. In the second act, the motif of the "approach by stages" was limited to moves by Vladimir and Estragon, being used to particularly good effect in the swearing match (Faber: 75).

Beckett himself, in one of his rare comments on directing and how it should be done, complained that:

Producers don't seem to have any sense of form in movement. The kind of form one finds in music, for instance, where themes keep recurring. When in a text, actions are repeated, they ought to be made unusual the first time, so that when they happen again – in exactly the same way – an audience will recognize them from before. (Cohn 1980: 231)

His use of the motif of "approach by stages" outlined above shows how he considered that such principles ought to be applied. The kind of musical form to which he refers is to be found in the work of most of the great composers in the Western tradition, and is a particular feature of many of the works of Schubert, a composer for whom Beckett felt special affection. At its simplest, it can be seen in the sonata form, which works with two fundamental elements: repetition and variation. Beckett is not the only playwright to have used musical form in this way. It is a major strand in modernist theater running from Strindberg (who entitled a play *Ghost Sonata*) to Michel Vinaver, who has described all of his plays as similar to musical compositions in their use of theme and variations (Vinaver 1982: 289). The principles of repetition and variation emerged especially clearly in the Schiller-Theater production from his design of the actors' movements. These form, in Knowlson's words, "a whole pattern of moves in semi-circles, arcs and chords, horizontals and verticals which create what may be termed a subliminal stage imagery" (*TN*: 401). There are no separate headings in the notebook for straight lines and semicircular curves, but the sketches which he included from time to time show how he rang the changes.

Tracing this in detail throughout the production is a monumental task, magnificently achieved in the 465 pages of McMillan and Knowlson's (1993) *Theatrical Notebooks of Samuel Beckett Vol. 1,* and the reader is referred to that volume's notes for a complete analysis. But one simple example can be extracted to show how different types of movement acquired thematic overtones, especially in respect to the relationships between the characters. Pozzo and Lucky were linked in linear fashion. This was apparent from their first entrance, in which the straight line of the rope going, like a dog-lead, from Lucky's neck to Pozzo's hand was emphasized in Beckett's note. This specified that the rope must be "just over ½ width of stage for P to stop just short of midstage – L to fall just off" (*TN*: 197). In other words, the audience witnessed Lucky cross more than half of the stage, dragging the rope behind him, before Pozzo appeared holding the other end, and Lucky had already disappeared offstage on the opposite side from his entrance before Pozzo pulled him up short and the audience heard the clattering of his fall. Following this, almost all the moves given to Pozzo or Lucky are in straight lines, either from one side of the stage to the other or diagonally across it.

Many of Vladimir and Estragon's moves were also made along straight lines: there was marked use of diagonal movement, for example, when they rushed to and fro in fright and horror at the entrance of Pozzo and Lucky. However Beckett varied their patterns of movement by sometimes giving them a curved, semicircular trajectory. This kind of move was often associated with the more contemplative moments of the play. An example is the end of Act 1 following the lines "Are you mad? We must take cover. Come on," where Beckett's revised stage direction reads "They begin to circle up towards the tree" (Faber: 53; *TN*: 49), and his notebook entry includes a semicircular sketch (*TN*: 236). On the page facing the sketch, Beckett has written, "V takes E's left hand or arm as for walks A2." By this he means that the move should be an echo of earlier "walks," which also conveyed similar moments of relative quiet or reflection. For example, on page 8 of the notebook, he wrote that Vladimir should take Estragon's arm and draw him in a semicircular movement around the stage (also illustrated by a sketch) in the course of the lines following "Let's wait and see what he says" (Faber: 18; *TN*: 17). In this way, through the use of repetition and contrast, particular patterns of movement echo one another, becoming associated in the audience's minds with motifs or moods in the play.

Conclusion: "Three-Dimensional Writing"

Beckett's production toured widely and was admired on both sides of the Atlantic. Peter Hall, who saw it in London, wrote in his diary, "This is a masterpiece ... It revived my shaken faith in the theatre" (Goodwin 1983: 230). It had the effect of finally persuading critics, directors, and actors that *Waiting for Godot* is a masterpiece at *both* the theatrical level (that is, taking all the expressive elements of the stage into account) *and* at the literary level. The play is now recognized as having its own peculiar shape and rhythm (encoded to a large extent in Beckett's stage directions for the revised text), and these are understood to be as central to the artistic work we know as *Waiting for Godot* as the words of Vladimir and Estragon, Pozzo, Lucky, and the boy. As James Knowlson has pointed out, this is not just a technical matter of interest to critics and theater people. The idioms of stage performance are as important to Beckett in articulating his themes as the words his characters speak (Knowlson 1987). The success of any given production must be judged on its ability to manipulate and counterpoint all the idioms of the stage in expressing such key themes as waiting, loneliness, symbiosis, the painful human awareness of being "irremediably present" yet subject to slow deterioration, building up a layered, poetic effect.

Beckett's production was satisfying because it achieved a clear counterpoint between the moments of absolute stillness, when both audience and characters shared the experience of waiting, and the contrasting bursts of activity, when the characters play their "games to survive." His actors did not become too involved with giving a realistic portrayal of down-and-outs, but concentrated more on giving musical shape and form to their performances. The performance was rapid, as has been noted, and parts of it were extremely funny, but it also managed to convey that mood of profound emotion which occurs when a whole audience feels that it has been touched, through art, by reality. Commentators have rightly picked out the theme of Vladimir's long speech over the prone bodies of Pozzo and Lucky in the second act: "To all mankind they were addressed, those cries for help still ringing in our ears! But at this place, at this moment of time, all mankind is us, whether we like it or not" (Faber: 79).

The extent to which any production is able to strike a balance between the universal truths of this play and the particular application to us, the audience, is a criterion of its success. So much of the play's action has to do with the intransigence of the real, physical world we all have to deal with: difficulties with standing up and sitting down, with boots, hats, food, and other necessities of life such as the need to piss at regular intervals. And this, in turn, is linked to Beckett's choice of archetypal figures: the two down-and-outs who long to separate at the same time as they depend totally upon one another; the master–slave relationship in which the master is as dependent on his slave as vice versa. The temptation, since the objects *are* so basic and since the relationships *do* possess the simplicity of binary opposites, is to perform everything at a one-dimensional level. But the play only comes to life through its contradictions, and it is the performance which can show both Pozzo's cruelty and his tenderness, both Estragon's truculent cynicism and his hopeful innocence, that ultimately creates an experience of emotional profundity for its audience.

The success of Beckett's production might lead one to the conclusion that the problem of how to perform *Waiting for Godot* has been settled, once and for all, and that the director needs only to copy Beckett's production, following his revised stage directions with care. But it is in the nature of dramatic texts that they only live through being embodied anew, and the fact that the stage directions are as important to *Godot* as the words spoken in no way changes this fundamental truth. The unusually integrated quality of word and action in *Godot* does not mean that its actions must always achieve realization by means of the same embodied shapes, movements, and images, any more than it means that its words must always be spoken with the same intonations. Rather, it points towards the originality of Beckett's dramatic creation and the need for each new production team to understand the nature of the work they propose to embody. It is neither a play in the tradition of naturalism, nor a Brechtian allegory; it is a new type of structure which comes closer to the theater dreamed of by Artaud than to any other twentieth-century model one might cite. This is also the insight of Pierre Chabert, an actor and director who worked with Beckett on a number of his plays, including the only work Beckett ever directed which was not written by him: Pinget's *Hypothèse* (1975). Chabert expressed in forceful terms the sense that Beckett writes through the body of the actor and the three-dimensional medium of space:

> Once the theory that action and psychology are all-important has been demolished, the emergence of the "stage" and its specific language (the language that, in Artaud's view, has been repressed since the very origins of "Western Theatre") becomes possible. This physical language, linked to space and to the materiality of stage (bodies, objects, movements, sounds, lights …) becomes the primary, fundamental, material out of which theatre is made. It participates on equal terms with words and action, in a new kind of three-dimensional writing. Space and words are woven into an integral whole, a single theatre work. Space and all the other expressive elements of the stage acquire a role in the dynamics of the play: they speak and act. (Chabert 1994: 9, my translation)

Interpreters who have grasped this fundamental quality of Beckett's work do not need to feel themselves limited by the contingencies of, for example, bowler hats. Once the "three-dimensional writing" out of which the play is constructed has been understood, all kinds of new possibilities will arise for weaving space, objects, bodies, and words into an integral whole.

First it was necessary that the play's multidimensional nature be recognized. The regular recreations of Beckett's own production by Walter Asmus, and Sir Peter Hall's 1997 revival, which followed almost all of Beckett's own stage directions, have confirmed that recognition, at least within the ambit of the British and American theater community. What had, for a long time, been thought of as an anti-play, one that denies the whole basis of Western dramatic tradition, has come to be seen as one which might be better described as commenting on it in self-aware modernist style, while at the same time exploiting all of its expressive devices, from movement to stillness, sound to silence, light to dark, and from laughter to tears. As the thousands of productions since 1975 have shown, the simple fact of performing with different actors, in a different theater, for a different audience and in a different context, introduces so large a quantity of variables that no one production can ever claim to exhaust every performance possibility, any more than this can be true of a piece of music. Performers can only hope to "Fail again. Fail better" (Knowlson 1996: 674).

REFERENCES AND FURTHER READING

Asmus, Walter (1975). "Beckett directs *Godot*." *Theatre Quarterly* 5(19): 19–26.

Beckett, Samuel (1965). *Waiting for Godot*. London: Faber and Faber.

Chabert, Pierre (1994). "Singularité de Samuel Beckett." In Jean-Claude Lallias and Jean-Jacques Arnault (eds.), *Théâtre Aujourd'hui 3: L'Univers Scénique de Samuel Beckett*. Paris: Centre National de la Documentation Pédagogique.

Cohn, Ruby (1980). *Just Play: Beckett's Theatre*. Princeton: Princeton University Press.

Gontarski, S. E. (1998). "Revising Himself: Performance as Text in Samuel Beckett's Theatre." *Journal of Modern Literature* 22(1): 131–55.

Goodwin, John (ed.) (1983). *Peter Hall's Diaries: The Story of a Dramatic Battle*. London: Hamish Hamilton.

Knowlson, James (1987). "Beckett as Director: The Manuscript Production Notebooks and Critical Interpretation." *Modern Drama* 30(4): 451–65.

Knowlson, James (1993). "Introduction." In Dougald McMillan and James Knowlson (eds.), *The Theatrical Notebooks of Samuel Beckett Vol 1: Waiting for Godot*. London: Faber and Faber.

Knowlson, James (1996). *Damned to Fame: The Life of Samuel Beckett*. London: Bloomsbury.

McMillan, Dougald and Martha Fehsenfeld (eds.) (1988). *Beckett in the Theatre*. London: John Calder.

McMillan, Dougald and James Knowlson (eds.) (1993). *The Theatrical Notebooks of Samuel Beckett Vol 1: Waiting for Godot*. London: Faber and Faber.

Vinaver, Michel (1982). *Ecrits sur le Théâtre*. Lausanne: L'Aire.

24

The Seated Figure on Beckett's Stage

Enoch Brater

I

Within the vast and varied repertory of late twentieth-century European drama, Beckett's work would surely be noticed for placing actors in odd, eccentric, and otherwise uncompromising stage positions. And that is, as *Footfalls* states things, "indeed to put it mildly" (Beckett 1984: 243). Planted in urns or standing stock still on a cold plinth, dumped summarily into trash bins or buried up to the waist, then the neck, in a mound of unforgiving earth, that "old extinguisher" (Beckett 1961: 37), the figures in this dramaturgy are more often than not subjected to a highly abbreviated form of physicality, one that demands the *doing* of more and more with less and less – even and especially so in those places where less did not seem possible before. In *That Time*, for example, the actor "plays" only a disembodied head; and in *Not I*, a *reductio ad hominem*, if not *absurdum*, the lead part is a mouth (as the author said, "just a moving mouth"), "*rest of face in shadow*" (Brater 2003: 107; Beckett 1984: 216). Little wonder that Jessica Tandy, who starred in the world premiere of *Not I* under Alan Schneider's disciplined direction at Lincoln Center in New York in 1972, demurred, "I'd like to do a musical next" (Jessica Tandy in Brater 1987: 4).

Beckett is, of course, much more than a mere provocateur, though his role as such should not be discounted in the making of such a heady theatrical mix. Yet here the pinpoint precision of his stagecraft has been designed to precede, if not entirely overwhelm, the seductive allure of metaphor and meaning. This playwright can surprise us by revealing his formalist credentials, and most particularly his grounding in theatrical convention, precisely at those moments when the work seems most suspect and most alarmingly avant-garde. What results is a far cry from the sturdy machinery of an Ibsen or a Chekhov, but make no mistake: it is not quite Robert Wilson or Pina Bausch either. Beckett's scenography looks both backward and forward at the same time, celebrating his theatrical inheritance in the very process of transforming it, a method that involves stripping his seemingly minimalist sets of every extraneous detail *plus one* (Menard 2007: 92–4). Nowhere is this technique more evident than in the uncanny use Beckett makes of the seated figure on stage. The performance history here is huge. Strindberg's *Ghost Sonata* is only one of many plays that revel in the dramatic potential of restricted and limited mobility, though in Beckett's case this particular cross-reference can be illuminating. The image of the old man confined to a wheelchair had a profound effect on him when, on Suzanne Dumesnil's urging, he saw Roger Blin's 1949 production at the Gaîté Montparnasse on the left bank in Paris, an interpretation the playwright later said was true to both "the letter and the spirit" of the drama (Knowlson 1996: 348; Brater 2003: 59–60) – *Endgame* (1957), was only eight years away. Tennessee Williams exploits the same theatrical trope in the highly atmospheric *Suddenly Last Summer*; though his female incarnation of the device, the gothic horror that is Mrs Venable, appears on stage to inhabit the full force of a sexually charged *drame bourgeois*. Beckett, like O'Neill before him, eschews any such holding of "the old family Kodak up to ill-nature" (O'Neill 1965: 1–2), and will pursue the seated figure for very different purposes and effects. The Western theatrical canon gave him a great deal to choose from.

Shakespeare's seated figures, those that are scripted, are most often discovered in public surroundings: banquet scenes, throne rooms, and senate chambers abound. The emphasis would appear to be on spectacle rather than intimacy. As early as *Titus Andronicus*, two noble families who have not previously consumed what remains of one another are prepared to go at it again, seated as they are, fatally, at this last of all suppers. And in a much later drama the irony cuts deep: Macbeth reminds Banquo not to "fail" his feast. A famous ghost obliges. The large interior spaces where characters are likely to sit in *King Lear*, *Hamlet*, or *King Richard III* are similarly ceremonial, just as they are when they turn legalistic in *Othello* or jury-rigged in *The Merchant of Venice*. Yet Shakespeare's hyperactive heroes rarely sit for long, reluctant as they are to forfeit their empowering vertical positions. No director would allow his stunned Macbeth to remain calmly seated when a ghost materializes on stage so sensationally; nor could the actress playing Lady Macbeth – no "little chuck" she – resist the opportunity to assert her control over the scene by the simple act of *rising*, as though the text itself were telling her what to do. "Sit, worthy friends," she urges Ross and Lennox and the other nobles gathered at her table, "my lord is often thus." Later in the same scene a newly confident Macbeth attempts to reclaim his authority over his wife in much the same way: "I am a man again. Pray you *sit* still" (my emphasis).[1] All of this may be nothing, of course, compared to *King Lear*, where the Duke of Cornwall demands that a chair be brought on stage for the blinding of Gloucester. The captive Earl, his hands bound, is in most modern productions thrown backwards as Cornwall plugs his heels into the "vile jelly." And then he does it again – because, according to Regan, "one eye will mock the other" – before this seated figure, as sightless as Milton's Samson Agonistes at Gaza, will be returned to his upright position. Only then is Gloucester set free to "smell his way" to Dover.

Kings, too, may willingly and literally abandon their thrones when the dramatic occasion encourages them to do so: think of Claudius delivering his highly polished

speech before the assembled courtiers as the second scene begins in *Hamlet*, or Lear
pointing to the redrawn map of the peaceful kingdom he plans to divide among three
troubled sisters. And just what is Horatio supposed to do with Hamlet's body at the
end of the play when, for this protagonist at least, "the rest is silence"? Chairs, especially ornamental ones, come in handy.

Writing in the second half of the nineteenth century for the quite different dimensions of a box set, Ibsen had the opportunity to explore the potential of the seated
figure in an entirely new perspective, one that allowed for a far more focused display
of psychological texturing. Shaw was quite right in his observation that modern drama
began when Nora sat her husband down in the final act of *A Doll's House* to discuss
the nature of their marriage (see Shaw 1957). Ibsen is terrific at this sort of thing,
efficiently arranging the scenic space to accommodate his characters' need to com-
municate their innermost thoughts and emotions (it's his substitute for the no–no of
soliloquy, realism's *bête noir*). Nora sits on a love-seat with Mrs Linde, her could-be
confidante, first communicating too little, then in a subsequent scene perhaps revealing too much. The same tableau works for her encounter with the love-sick Dr Rank;
she flirts, then recoils from the clumsy declaration that follows. Movement constitutes
meaning here, and how the furniture is used speaks volumes. Nora re-establishes the
boundaries of their relationship when she turns away, abandons the love-seat, and
stands, rigid, elsewhere. The same blocking on the same sort of settee accumulates
additional resonances when Ibsen further explores its dynamics in *Hedda Gabler*. Eilert
Lovborg joins Hedda on the drawing-room sofa as she invites him to, on the pretense
of sharing her honeymoon photographs. The tension is palpable; intimate glance and
innermost gaze make the most of it. Much of what happens next lies in everything
that is *not* said, except for Lovborg's trenchant murmur, "Hedda Gabler," married
name very conspicuously omitted. The predatory Judge Brack, a Hedda Gabler in
drag, insinuates his presence at her side, too, and on the same divan, at first appearing
to have greater success in penetrating the shell she has so elaborately constructed
around herself. "I never jump," she confides, though she may be forced to do so, and
soon, under the threat, albeit unstated, of blackmail. "Life is not tragic," Ibsen wrote
in the notebook he kept about this play and its lead character's motivation, "Life is
absurd – And that is what I cannot bear" (Goodman 1971: 43). Defeated, but also a
little triumphant, this female figure removes herself from the set and the set-up, sits
down at the piano, and shoots herself. Brack, startled, thrown off guard, even shocked
into recognition, falls into an armchair, prostrated, and delivers the play's refrain,
which also serves as its bitter curtain line: "But good God! People don't *do* such
things!"[2] He's right: people don't, but dramatic characters do.

Ibsen's contemporary Chekhov seems to have been equally astute in recognizing
the enormous range of possibility for the seated figure on stage. One could even argue
that sitting is what Chekhov's characters do best. *Uncle Vanya* opens on a quiet scene
like so many others in this canon: Astrov sitting and chatting with the old nurse, but
really talking to himself. Vanya awakes from his nap and soon joins him in the garden,
as do other members of the cast. They drink tea, and in one case perhaps a drop of

vodka. Yelena passes by with the Professor, she "too indolent to move."[3] Scenes from a country life – in four acts no less – indeed. Yet not every Chekhov set-to is quite so laid back. The provincial tranquility has been deceptive. Bedlam will erupt following a busy afternoon of revelatory tête-à-têtes. Serebryakov, the family members gathered all around him, announces a bizarre plan to sell the estate, invest in securities, and purchase a small villa in Finland. Vanya, his chronic lassitude for once upstaged, runs into the house to look for a gun. It misfires. "I missed!" he cries out in dismay and despair (this is, among other things, hilarious), "I missed twice!" The curtain falls on act 3 before he has a chance to sit back down.

There's so much going on in the first act of *Three Sisters* – preparations are in order for the big event marking Irina's name day while Olga is transfixed in monologue, remembering and inventing – that we sometimes forget that the third sister, Masha, is sitting there in full view, reading, detached, and bored. She whistles, then gets up to leave, but not before Vershinin, recently arrived from Moscow, makes a gallant entry into the Prozorov sitting room. "I'll stay ... for lunch," she says, tellingly, joining "the lovesick major" at the table and foreshadowing everything that will take place between them as time in this drama runs its steady course. Another play, *The Seagull*, even borrows a famous theatrical device from *Hamlet*. Arkadina and Trigorin, not exactly "guilty creatures sitting at a play" (*Hamlet* 2.2), take their assigned places as part of the makeshift audience for Konstantin's literally dumb show, in which poor Nina is forced to play the underwritten lead. "There are no real people in your work," she tells the crestfallen young author, who yearns so much to be the writer he will never be. As in Shakespeare, the scene, both the play and the play-within-the-play, devolves into chaos, with everyone soon on their feet. Chekhov's drama ends, by contrast, on a far more somber note, and with a far greater density of dramatic overtones. With characters concentrated around a card table, a fateful game of lotto is in full progress. But so is something else. "Get Irina out of here somehow," Dorn tells Trigorin, leading him downstage and away from his seat at the table. "Konstantin just shot himself." *Curtain.*

Beckett is by no means the only beneficiary of such a rich and all-inclusive theatrical vocabulary. Playwrights of his generation, as well as those before and after, have embraced the same legacy, retooling and refining it in a series of strategies for "making it new" and discovering their own voices. Caryl Churchill updates the banquet scene in her feminist drama, *Top Girls*; Sam Shepard finds a surprising locus for a benched father-figure in *Fool for Love*; and Harold Pinter, in a cycle of remarkable plays that runs the gamut from *The Hothouse* and *The Birthday Party* to *Old Times* and the "icy and cold" *No Man's Land*, invests his sedentary characters with blood-curdling, almost demonic, power. "If you take the glass," the seated Ruth taunts Lenny in *The Homecoming*, "I'll take you" (Pinter 1967: 34). Through a glass darkly indeed; passive aggression like this may never have been quite so dramatically potent before. Less successful, perhaps, is Arthur Miller's attempt to use the image to explore the multidimensionality of paralysis, physical, psychological, and political, in an ambitious work like *Broken Glass*. What distinguishes Beckett from his peers, however, is that his solution to the problem is not only practical from a theatrical point of view, but simultaneously analytical. It involves nothing less that a reconsideration of how this device might be used within the entire dramatic enterprise itself.

II

One of the things that makes Beckett an exceptional figure in the development of modern drama is his ability to think outside the box – and especially outside the box set, the theater space he was familiar with, and the one he was generally writing for. Beckett said he turned to the stage as an escape from the "awful prose" he was writing at the time. "I needed a habital space," he reflected, "and I found it on the stage" (in Brater 2003: 55).

But this was also a license to look elsewhere for the foundation and formulation of his image-making. His longtime interest in landscape painting and the representation of interior spaces on a canvas, light emanating from a source outside the frame (as in Caravaggio and Vermeer), would have enormous repercussions as he quickly adapted such values to the demands of the stage.[4] Yet it is perhaps in the portrait of the seated figure in its many variations, from Raphael to Rembrandt to Van Gogh, and to contemporary painters like Francis Bacon and Louis LeBroquy (or Picasso for that matter), that Beckett finds a grammar and an idiom that he can truly call his own. This is less a question of the one-to-one correspondences of the sort we might be able to locate between a provincial Chekhov scene and the evocative landscapes of his good friend the Russian painter Isaac Levitan (or between Munch, say, and the late Ibsen) than it is an appraisal of the specific ways in which form gives latitude to meaning.

As early as those gold-leafed Madonnas in Giotto, Cimabue, and Duccio, seated as they are so serenely on their earthly or celestial thrones, we already sense the profound mystery of inwardness and the dislocation caused by private thought – not yet "a voice dripping in [the head]" of the sort Beckett will pursue in *Endgame*, but certainly pointing us in that direction. And such magnificent Marias, flat and elongated though they may be (their chairs come off a whole lot better), are already equipped with distinct personalities. In the embrace of perspective that follows, the characterological basis of such figures will be defined even further in a steady preoccupation with three-dimensionality, sometimes in the fullness of looking out, sometimes through the pensive mediation of searching even deeper within. The seated figure, painted, repainted, and represented yet again, was well on its way toward becoming the sine qua non of that endless and elusive drama known as human consciousness.

Such implications were not lost by the cautious playwright who became, in the 1950s, Samuel Beckett. "*In a dressing gown, a stiff toque on his head, a large blood-stained handkerchief over his face, a whistle hanging from his neck, a rug over his knees, thick socks on his feet,*" the blinded Hamm, "*in an armchair on castors*" – a gender-bending Madonna on wheels – would seem to epitomize the playwright's fascination with the seated figure on stage. Never neglecting "the little things in life," *Endgame* allows us to study the image in a highly circumscribed form: a brief tableau punctuates the mime Clov performs in the drama's opening moments, while it is still *"covered with an old sheet"* (Beckett 1958). But it is really in the famous earlier play, *Waiting for Godot*, where this stylization can be seen to be most firmly rooted. Pozzo even goes so far as to make a fetish of this recurring motif: "But how am I to sit down now, without affectation, now that I have risen? Without appearing to – how shall I say – without appearing to falter" (Beckett 1954). Pozzo, like his author, recognizes a good thing when he has it going, and a few minutes later, eyeing the stool, he seizes the opportunity to advance its richly performative momentum:

POZZO: I'd very much like to sit down, but I don't know how to go about it.
ESTRAGON: Could I be of any help?
POZZO: If you asked me perhaps.
ESTRAGON: What?
POZZO: If you asked me to sit down.
ESTRAGON: Would that help?
POZZO: I fancy so.
ESTRAGON: Here we go. Be seated, Sir, I beg you.
POZZO: No, no, I wouldn't think of it! (*Pause. Aside.*) Ask me again.
ESTRAGON: Come, come, take a seat I beseech you, you'll get pneumonia.
POZZO: You really think so?
ESTRAGON: Why it's absolutely certain.
POZZO: No doubt you are right. (*He sits down.*) Done it again! (*Pause.*) Thank
   you, dear fellow.

(ibid.)

In *Godot*, however, the seated figure is assigned a much more primary role than this, and a far more vital one: nothing less than the opening image of the play itself. As the curtain rises (the playwright was certainly thinking of one), we first meet Estragon *"sitting on a low mound"* trying to take off his boot and failing to do so, followed by the quintessential Beckett line, "Nothing to be done."

Without calling undue attention to itself, the insistent figure of a man sitting by himself on a stone, Gogo's initial situation in *Waiting for Godot*, has a long provenance in the Beckett repertory. As a semblance of isolation, cosmic and otherwise, it appears not only in "The Calmative," but also in the second movement of *Stirrings Still*. Beckett seems to have derived this image from the Middle High German poet he much admired, Walther von der Vogelweide, though this is the first time he uses it, albeit ironized, in a play:

> I sat upon a stone,
> Leg over leg was thrown,
> Upon my knee an elbow rested
> And in my open hand was nested
> My chin and half my cheek.

> My thoughts were dark and bleak:
> I wondered how a man should live,
> To this no answer could I give.
> (von der Vogelweide 1938: 49;
> see also Knowlson 1996: 147, 613)

"Ich saz ûf eime steine," Walther's self-description in the first line of the medieval lyric, inspired the well-known painting of him in the Manesse manuscript. The poet is said to be buried in the cathedral at Würzburg, where Malone recalls having seen "Tiepolo's ceiling" – "what a tourist I must have been, I even remember the diaeresis, if it is one" (Beckett 1956: 62).

Sitting – and waiting – is Hamm's celebrated "speciality" in *Endgame*, though Beckett's bums already exploit most of the latter's potential in *Godot*. Thinking on his feet to pass the time that would have passed anyway, but "not so fast," Vladimir in fact rarely sits down, but he will do so, and poignantly, on those few occasions when he tenderly comforts his partner. Poor Lucky, of course, is never permitted the same luxury, even though "he carries like a pig" and falls down in an ever-maddening sequence of verticals and horizontals, culminating in a dance variously called "The Hard Stool" and, more significantly, "the Net." Much comes together for Beckett, however, in the work that explores the dark underside of *Godot*; and it will be *Endgame*, as "dark as ink" (Beckett in Brater 2003: 78), that finally allows him to write his own signature on the seated figure stranded on a lonely set: "Outside of here it's death" (Beckett 1958).

III

Even as a student at Trinity, Beckett saw Belacqua, the Florentine lute maker who appears early in his fiction by way of Dante (and who re-emerges in various guises throughout the prose writings), as the seated figure *par excellence*. In *Purgatory* his role is both tantalizing and suggestive. Chided for his negligence, he responds with the words Aristotle assigns to him, and which provide Beckett with the title of a short story published in 1932: *Sedendo et quiescendo anima efficitur sapiens*. The Poet's riposte in *The Divine Comedy* could not be more stinging: "Certainly, if to be seated is wise, then no one can be wiser than you."[5] In his fiction Beckett transforms such habitual laziness and such exquisite verbal sparring – for that is what it is – into his own version of some dematerialized "Belacqua bliss" (Beckett 1957: 111). But in theater indolence has to be animated; there's sitting, and then there's sitting, squared.

For the actor playing Hamm, planted so magisterially on his own throne, *Endgame* can be daunting in just how much it asks him to act, to do, and to perform (see Raynor 1994 and Garner 1994). Sloth does not enter into the equation. Clov, who has "work to do" and cannot sit down, is a whole lot more than stage manager, caretaker or mere retainer here; he is also the engineer for rapid transportation as he wheels his master from place to place around the circumscribed "world" of this interior set, placing him, one more time, smack "in the center" – or thereabouts. Hamm, too, is called upon to play any number of roles: he is (or has been) at various times a story-teller, a master jokester, a consumer of sugarplums, a dispenser of biscuits and pap, a vengeful son, a drug user, a sentimentalist, a tyrant, a dog lover, and an enviable appreciator of stage terminology. He may also be a father. *Endgame* requires a remarkable series of gestures from this seated figure in order to develop a complete character and take full charge of the stage.

Oddly enough, *Krapp's Last Tape* (in Beckett 1984), a work for only one player, presents a view of the seated figure that offers the audience both more and less. Krapp seems at first reluctant to play this part. Jangling keys, uncorking a bottle, or retrieving a dusty old dictionary, he shuffles back and forth into the darkness of the set before settling down into the dimness that reluctantly illuminates his small table. Preparatory rituals completed, the "play," so to speak, is now ready to begin for this "wearish" figure, face mostly forward as he confronts that perilous point where time remembered becomes the consciousness of time remaining. The past, transformed on tape, alternately startles and plagues him with its steadfastness, and it is his misbegotten "vision" that even at this late date still tampers with it. "Play" as it will be defined on this platform therefore involves mostly playback, this one from the resources of memory stored in "box three ... spool five." Reaction constitutes the action here – so much so that the actor must carefully calibrate his every move to accommodate the dictates of Beckett's multifaceted and highly literary script. Face and upper body are of crucial importance in *Krapp's Last Tape*, for, as light fades downward, it obscures all that might otherwise be revealed. On tape the recorded voice of Krapp-at-39 says he will "feel" a black ball in his grip until his "dying day," a cue for the most nuanced of hand gestures. And when, after a pregnant pause, the voice from the same past comments on the "new light" above the desk as "a great improvement," weary eyes grudgingly veer upward. As previously noted in the case of *Macbeth*, this text, too, goes a long way in stimulating the seated figure's animation. But not every suggestion of movement in this drama will evoke a similarly kinetic response, however discreet it may be meant to be. Some can only be taken at *face value*: the image of the lovers together on a punt before ardor compels a much younger Krapp to lie "down across her," his "face in her breasts," and his "hand on her," or the more recent and quite different memory Krapp records in the present, that time he went to Vespers "once," fell asleep, and rolled off a pew.

In a fourth major play, *Happy Days*, Beckett emerges once again as "a great leg-puller and an enemy of obviousness" (Dylan Thomas writing about Beckett in the *New English Weekly*, March 17, 1938; see Graver and Federman [1979: 46]). Winnie's physical situation, planted as she is in the earth, the playwright's update of some Mesolithic burial site from the Boyne Valley due north of Dublin (the scale more reminiscent of Loughcrew than Newgrange or Knowth), will be difficult to determine. It is hard to tell – "imagine," really, as Mouth says in *Not I* – "what position she is in," "whether standing or seating or kneeling" (in production, the solution is best left to the techies). Seated behind the mound, and barely within our sightline, is the ever-patient Willie – "ever," that is, until the play's ambiguous conclusion. And it is the blocking for this enigmatic figure that will be of most interest to us here. In the first act Winnie "sits," to speak strictly metaphorically, "in the old style," in the privileged position; for it is she – and she alone – who can twist her neck back in order to receive a better view of this less than demure seated male figure. As she shifts her observational position for greater visibility, we must take her word for it when she reports that he picks his nose, looks at pornographic postcards, or spreads sun-screen over the various parts of his body best left unmentioned. By contrast, we can just about see a snippet from the local newspaper when Willie turns a page to read from the obituaries: "His Grace and Most Reverend Father in God Dr Carolus Hunter dead in a tub." Winnie reacts to this alarming news with an exclamatory "Charlie Hunter!" in what the script calls a *"tone of fervent reminiscence."*

Two short works first produced in 1981, *Rockaby* and *Ohio Impromptu*, as well as the earlier *Come and Go* (written in 1965), offer us compelling variations of the same motif. These are highly compressed dramas that start with a specific image, ignite a complex emotion, and open up a universe of feelings and ideas (see Cotter 1977: B25, 30). "When did we three last meet?" Vi recites at the opening of *Come and Go* (in Beckett 1984), inverting a line of inquiry we may well recall as having been previously assigned to one of the three "weird sisters" in Shakespeare's *Macbeth*. Vi sits in the center side by side with Flo and Ru as Beckett's three female figures are stationed stage right, motionless, and very erect, facing front, hands clasped in laps. Each gets up, turn and turn about, then returns to the place of origin, re-inscribing the initial static tableau, isolated and illuminated as it is by a single ingot of unforgiving light. "Does she not know?"/"Does she not realize?" is this text's ominous take on the old game of who's-on-first; but in this case the consequences, unstated though everywhere implied, are likely to turn lethal. Closure is achieved when the seated figures are arranged somewhat differently, but only just so: resuming the same positions in which they were first discovered, they now have their hands clasped, resting on three laps to signal end of play. Flo delivers the curtain line, "I can feel the rings," followed by the palpable silence that finally engulfs them all.

Rockaby (in Beckett 1984) will be similarly attuned to the mysterious, even mysti-cal quality of inwardness portraitists have often found so seductive in the features assigned to their own seated figures. Beckett recycles the rocking chair from his novel *Murphy*, but in the play he elevates its status to that of a character in its own right. A "prematurely old" female figure sits "subdued" in *Rockaby* on a chair that is "con-trolled mechanically," without her assistance. The playwright was clear about one thing: the Voice of memory, recorded, initiates the rock, not the other way around, and certainly not the woman dressed in black who yearns to hear so much "More."[6] Beckett preserves the enigma as well as the integrity of this dramatic moment by insisting on "the absolute absence of the Absolute" (Beckett 1972: 22), relying instead on the image and the modesty of its scale to insinuate presence through a fusion of light, sound, and movement rather than narration. His dialogue is poetic, not surpris-ingly so in this case, as it is there to complement and elevate the stage's searing visual lyricism. Rarely has a seated figure on stage, "mother rocker" notwithstanding, been asked to carry the weight of so many competing discourses, one in which theater technology wears such a disarming human face. For the French translation of this play Beckett chose the title *Berceuse*, as Van Gogh had done for his well-known portrait of the seated Mme Augustin Roulin, but Beckett was doing much more than making a cross reference to "La Berceuse" or finding a convenient painterly analogue. While for Van Gogh, the word denoted the seated figure herself – it means "rocking chair," "cradle," and "lullaby" too – and Beckett's drama in performance will be, experientially, all of these things at once. The affective nature of such formal restraint achieves additional resonance in *Ohio Impromptu* (in Beckett 1984), where the figures seated at a plain deal table are both singular and doubled, "*As alike in appearance as possible.*" Reader and Listener are each other's Other; and each is each other's " – Hypocrite lecteur, – mon semblable, – mon frère!" (see Baudelaire 1964: 92). Perilously, as in Dante (1932: canto 9, 1.130), "Simile qui con simile è sepolto," like with like is buried here.[7] But are we really seeing double, or merely some liminal fantasy of a replication hysteria, an uptake of the riveting stage dynamics called for by Goldoni in *I due gemmeli veneziani*? Or are Beckett's spellbinding seated figures only two aspects of one man, for, inevitably, as you read you also in some sense profoundly listen? Stage left one figure intones the cherished lines from an old volume, monopolizing the soundscape and complicating its strangeness with the suggestion of narrative. Stage right the other "other" carefully weighs every word; his "knock" is opened wide when it signals an unexpectedly sudden interruption to the couple's tacit interaction, only to magnify it further when L compels R to retrace his steps. Only the rereading counts, as Nabokov said (Ondaatje 2007: 136). Then, when we least expect it, stage imagery is quietly redrawn as the seated figures achieve unprecedented momentum. The "story," such as it is, being done, Reader very slowly and very deliberately closes the book on us:

Knock.
Silence. Five seconds.
Simultaneously they lower their right hands to the table,
raise their heads and look at each other. Unblinking.
Expressionless.
Ten seconds.
Fade out.

IV

While Beckett's work for the mechanical media might be best discussed in another forum, it could be argued that his depiction of the seated figure is offered much greater amplitude and precision in the plays written for television. Subject to sharp definition by the camera lens, the images we see delineated in complex pieces like *Eh Joe*, *Ghost*

Trio, and *Nacht und Träume*, as in Beckett's "comic and unreal" *Film*, come to us both scrupulously edited and pre-recorded, like fleshly eruptions in an otherwise spectral world. But that is their limitation as well as their considerable strength, the fact that they are frozen, so to speak, in time and on digitalized tape. The illusion of spontaneity and of spontaneous gesture, so crucial to the impact of Beckett's seated bodies in live performance, as when Reader and Listener synchronize their movement at the conclusion of *Ohio Impromptu*, or when the actress suddenly utters "Fuck life" seemingly out of nowhere just before she bows her head in *Rockaby*, empowers such figures to command the space they inhabit with emphasis and authority. What may be lost in exactitude is made up for in fineness; and as the light slowly fades on the set for each play, it provides the theater audience with another kind of permanence: a fixed after-image that lasts for ever.

Beckett's stage, as this discussion of his innovative use of the seated figure attempts to show, is always full of "high-class nuts to crack" (Beckett 1958: 33). But that is not to say that the solutions he finds so appealing are without precedent. Beckett draws upon a rich vocabulary of theatrical convention, analyzes his inheritance, then takes it several steps forward. The hardest nut to crack for Beckett, as for Shakespeare, Ibsen, Chekhov, and so many other playwrights before him, will always be found, after all, in that delirious and probably delusional seeing-place he knows and we know as "theater." *See better. Fail better.* Followed in his case by that agonizing – but also inspirational – one word, "On."

NOTES

1 All citations from Shakespeare are from the second (1997) edition of The Riverside Shakespeare.
2 Citations from *Hedda Gabler* are taken from Ibsen (1992).
3 All citations from *Uncle Vanya*, *Three Sisters* and *The Seagull* are from Chekhov (1999).
4 For Beckett's interest in the visual arts, especially painting, see Knowlson (1996) and Oppenheim (2000).
5 On the figure of Belacqua as he appears in Beckett's work, see Ackerley and Gontarski (2004: 46–8).
6 For the playwright's comments on this piece, see Brater (1987: 173–4).
7 For a detailed study of the Dante–Beckett connection, see Caselli (2005).

REFERENCES

Ackerley, C. J. and S. E. Gontarski (eds.) (2004). *The Grove Companion to Samuel Beckett.* New York: Grove Press.

Alighieri, Dante (1932). *The Inferno of Dante Alighieri*, trans. J.A. Carlyle, rev. H. Oelsner. London: J. M. Dent.

Baudelaire, Charles (1964). "Au Lecture." In Maurice Z. Shroder (ed.), *Poètes français du dix-neuvième siècle.* Cambridge, MA.: Harvard University Press.

Beckett, Samuel (1954). *Waiting for Godot.* New York: Grove Press.

Beckett, Samuel (1956). *Malone Dies*. New York: Grove Press.

Beckett, Samuel (1957). *Murphy*. New York: Grove Press.

Beckett, Samuel (1958). *Endgame*. New York: Grove Press.

Beckett, Samuel (1961). *Happy Days*. New York: Grove Press.

Beckett, Samuel (1972). "Dante ... Bruno. Vico.. Joyce." In *Our Exagmination Round His Factification for Incamination of Work in Progress*. New York: New Directions.

Beckett, Samuel (1984). *The Collected Shorter Plays of Samuel Beckett*. New York: Grove Press.

Beckett, Samuel (1985). *The Unnamable*. New York: Grove Press.

Brater, Enoch (1987). *Beyond Minimalism: Beckett's Late Style in the Theater*. New York: Oxford University Press.

Brater, Enoch (2003). *The Essential Samuel Beckett*. London: Thames & Hudson.

Caselli, Daniela (2005). *Beckett's Dantes: Intertextuality in the Fiction and Criticism*. Manchester: Manchester University Press.

Chekhov, Anton (1999). *The Plays of Anton Chekhov*, trans. Paul Schmidt. New York: HarperCollins.

Cotter, Holland (1977). "Sonnets in Marble." *New York Times* (August 10).

Garner, Stanton B., Jr (1994). *Phenomenology and Performance in Contemporary Drama*. Ithaca: Cornell University Press.

Goodman, Randolph (ed.) (1971). "From Ibsen's Notes." In *From Script to Stage: Eight Modern Plays*. San Francisco: Rinehart Press.

Graver, Lawrence and Raymond Federman (eds.) (1979). *Samuel Beckett: The Critical Heritage*. London: Routlege & Kegan Paul.

Ibsen, Henrik (1992). *Hedda Gabler*. In *Four Major Plays*, Vol. 1, trans. Rolf Fjelde. New York: Signet.

Knowlson, James (1996). *Damned to Fame: The Life of Samuel Beckett*. New York: Simon & Schuster.

Menard, Louis (2007). "The Aesthete," *The New Yorker* (June 4).

Ondaatje, Michael (2007). *Divisadero*. New York: Knopf.

O'Neill, Eugene (1965). "Strindberg and Our Theatre." In Horst Frenz (ed.), *American Playwrights on Drama*. New York: Hill and Wang.

Oppenheim, Lois (2000). *The Painted Word: Samuel Beckett's Dialogue with Art*. Ann Arbor: University of Michigan Press.

Pinter, Harold (1967). *The Homecoming*. New York: Grove Press.

Raynor, Alice (1994). *To Act, to Do, to Perform: Drama and the Phenomenology of Action*. Ann Arbor: University of Michigan Press.

Shakespeare, William (1997). *The Riverside Shakespeare*. Boston and New York: Houghton Mifflin.

Shaw, Bernard (1957). *The Quintessence of Ibsenism*. New York: Hill and Wang.

von der Vogelweide, Walther (1938). *"I Saw the World": Sixty Poems from Walther von der Vogelweide, 1170–1228*, trans. Ian G. Colvin. London: Edward Arnold.

25
Clowning with Beckett

Mary Bryden

Groucho Marx once remarked, "Clowns work as well as aspirin, but twice as fast" (Steele 2004: 129). Beckett, on the other hand, voiced the opinion, in his well-known letter to Alan Schneider, that if people experienced headaches during his work they should supply their own aspirin (Harmon 1998: 24). Beckett's clowns, as this chapter aims to demonstrate, are not aspirin-dispensers or stand-in painkillers. I refer to Groucho Marx (1890–1977) at both the beginning and the end of the chapter, but not so much to establish affinities as to suggest a dissonance. Despite his comic genius, and despite Beckett's admiration of the Marx Brothers, Groucho's project is much more *in*compatible than compatible with that of Beckett.

It is not, of course, difficult to establish connections between Beckett's writing and an array of clowning traditions. His early enthusiasm for the silent movies of Buster Keaton and Charlie Chaplin is well known, as is his familiarity with theatrical entertainments which incorporated visual humor and repartee deriving from music hall and circus routines. As many critics have pointed out, these duly find their echo in Beckett's own writing, whether it be the quick-fire exchanges of words or hats in *Waiting for Godot* or the transactions of Beckett's only film, *Film*, with its cast of perturbed humans and mutely subversive animals.

There is, nevertheless, a difficulty in making these connections in any straightforwardly transferable way. Among the adjectives we might choose to apply to Beckett's *Film*, for instance – interesting; significant; profound; "great," in the case of Gilles Deleuze – we would not, I think, include "comic."[1] If Beckett was disappointed that the cat and dog ejection sequence in that film raised little more than a wry smile, he did not reveal it. No doubt he would have maintained that comedy was not his prime aim. His preparatory notes for the piece would confirm this. Yet surely he must have hoped that comedy would have been *one* of the outcomes, even if transient. Otherwise, why cast Buster Keaton, having failed to secure Charlie Chaplin for the role? Did he *really* intend them to suppress all of their comic instincts? There is in my view something too deliberate, too studied, about Beckett's *Film* to enable it to embrace humor, and this takes us to the heart of what comedy is and is not in Beckett's work. Comedic and clowning traditions already tread this tightrope. On the one hand, they have recourse to a repertoire of stock-in-trade gestures and situations; on the other hand, they rely on improvisation, on imparting a sense of mercurial creativity. There is, therefore, a potential problem in aligning Beckett's precisely conceived and often austerely choreographed scenarios with the performative traditions of clowning.

Clowning traditions are so rich, diverse, and ancient in their origins and cultural realizations that this essay does not attempt to navigate through them but, rather, to pick out some key elements of a range of clownish personae, and the nuanced use of them to be found in Beckett's work. The principal elements I shall focus on are the problematics of the clown body; the movement of clowns (including silly walks); the music of clowns; and the violence of clowning (both within the clowning act and within the spectatorly act). Throughout the discussion, I shall refer to individual clown practitioners in relationship to Beckett's work.

The Clown Body

Clowns often have an exuberant physicality. Their bodies subvert and undermine the clothes which drape them, which often hang loose and have to be suspended with braces or belts. In the tradition standardized by the Grimaldi clowns, but having its origins in the harlequin tradition, the extremities or features are often exaggerated, with long shoes, enlarged and reddened noses and whitened faces. As we know, early versions of Krapp had clownish purple noses before Beckett toned them down, as early as the first London production of *Krapp's Last Tape* in 1958 (see, for instance, Knowlson 1992: 13). This toning-down is one indication of the kind of clownishness which Beckett was working towards, which was not so much external as behavioral and attitudinal. He seemed not especially drawn to the acrobat clown, or to the kind of knockabout clowning which was cranked up to the point of vivid delirium. In 1937, having seen a performance by the great German comic Karl Valentin (then past his best), he wrote that the performance had been "reduced here and there to knockabout" (Knowlson 1996: 259). "Knockabout" clearly operates here as a pejorative term for Beckett.

What, however, would be the alternative to a knockabout clown? Can we conceive of a restrained clown? Certainly some of the most famous clowns of the past century have intrigued audiences because of their sense of containment. Beckett was a great admirer of the famous Swiss clown Grock, a truly international artiste and skilled linguist, who could perform in several languages. Grock features in *Dream of Fair to middling Women*, where he is associated with some of his well-known catchphrases, including "warum?" and "sans blague," with its equivalents "nicht möglich," or "you're kidding."[2] Yet, despite accomplishments and fame, Grock regarded his act as modest, uneffusive. Writing in his autobiography, *Life's a Lark*, he attributed his lack of success in America to precisely these characteristics: "I appeared in New York,

Chicago and Philadelphia. But I did not make a great hit. I was too simple for the Yankees, too restrained, not enough "pep" in me … They like a man to be a sort of human teetotum" (Grock 1931: 197).

The British comic Max Wall (1908–90) (who, in the last two decades of his life, was deeply immersed in Beckett's work), was strongly influenced by Grock, and even worked with the star for a time in Paris. In his own autobiography, called *The Fool on the Hill*, he draws attention to this sense of restraint, or holding back, within the comedic act. Wall refers to Grock as a "genius," and as "the greatest clown of the international halls," a description which was being applied to Wall himself by the 1970s. He writes, "The thing I remembered most about him was his shy, quiet and ambling way of performing: he did not depend on a lot of noise, breakages or explosions, but on projecting something that was more like an *alter ego* … The great element of humility in his performance made him a most lovable figure" (Wall 1975: 68; 70). Wall aligns Grock with the kind of clown referred to as "Auguste" – the one who is always struggling (and failing) to fulfill the prescriptions laid down by his more authoritative companion, the so-called "Whiteface" clown. This kind of clown hierarchy may be linked to some degree with the relationship between Vladimir and Estragon, and that between Pozzo and Lucky. It is Lucky's struggle to fulfill Pozzo's command to "think" which brings about the crescendo of incomprehension and chaos that is so often the environment of the "Auguste" clown.

This environment is also, to a greater or lesser degree, a conflictual one. Arguably, a successfully meek or victimized "Auguste" clown would also be as familiar with anger as a sadist might be with masochism. However contained Grock's demeanor might have been, he was given to being combative and choleric in his personal life. His brushes with authority have something in common with brushes with policemen in Beckett's early work. In his autobiography, he describes encountering in the street a magistrate who had recently unjustly fined him on the grounds of his being the accomplice of a thief. Seething with anger, and with a voice inside him telling him "*Do him in*; no one's looking" (Grock 1931: 105), he decides to follow the magistrate and push him over a bridge. He is only prevented from doing this by bumping unexpectedly into a friend, a tightrope walker. Without that, the magistrate might have met the sticky end which ensued for the constable who tried to arrest Mercier and Camier.

Of course, the subversive current, the potential disorder, which underlies every clownish act, is not achieved by chance, but by years of discipline bearing some relationship with the balletic. The clown's body must be trained such that it can be presented in astonishing contortions, with shifting centers of gravity. In his *Stages of the Clown: Perspectives on Modern Fiction from Dostoevsky to Beckett*, Richard Pearce points out, with particular reference to mime, that clowns have to turn their bodies into instruments. During his or her training, Pearce states, "the mime learns to analyze his body into all its component parts; then he learns to displace his center of balance from the inner ear, and finally to displace his center of orientation from the brain. The result is that each part of the body can receive a physical or emotional impact according to its own laws" (Pearce 1970: 153). He goes on to cite the example of Marcel Marceau who, when lifting an invisible heavy weight, is able to demonstrate the separate effects of the weight on each individual part of the body – head, neck, shoulders, arms, back, legs, feet, and so on. The whole body is affected by the strain, but the same body, at the micro-anatomical level, exhibits diverse and even conflictual pressures. Some of these demands can be seen in a work such as Beckett's *Act Without Words I*, the weight in this case being that of all-consuming thirst.

This ostensive capacity of the mime or clown is acquired only after sustained training and experimentation. In a Beckettian context, one might cite the case of Bill Irwin, who in the last few years has given mesmeric performances of a selection of Beckett's *Texts for Nothing*. Bill Irwin is a graduate of Ringling Brothers and Barnum and Bailey Clown College in Florida, and was an original cast member of San Francisco's Pickle Family Circus. Later, he went on to develop a more naturalistic clown persona relying less on make-up and more on what we might call *interior* bewilderment in the face of postmodern complexity. He became what some theorists characterize as "Auguste lite" (though I think this a poor title in Irwin's case, implying as it does a less profound alignment with the Auguste tradition). Irwin performed the *Texts* with his whole body, sectioning it and bending it like indiarubber to the orientations of the text in seemingly impossible ways.

To make body and voice speak together, sometimes contradicting or ironizing one another, is a demanding and grueling task. One reviewer of Irwin's Seattle performances, Roger Downey, drew attention to the emotional and aesthetic repertoire that Irwin had developed from the starting-point of a clown:

> When just one clown of many with the Pickle Family Circus, [Irwin] was already something rare: a funnyman who could turn every pratfall into a thing of beauty. For more than twenty years, through native talent, intelligence, and relentless work, he has turned himself into an actor of incalculable capacities. Now *two* talents struggle to possess that one amazing body. (Downey 2002: 2)

It was Downey's contention that Beckett's *Texts for Nothing* were not the right vehicle to allow both these talents – that of a clown and that of an actor – to shine without nullifying or at least interfering with one another. Yet it seemed to me that the *Texts* were in fact remarkably suited to the positing of an uneasy cohabitation between physical and psychic affectivities, since this mismatch is already there within Beckett's narrativity. Multiple passages from the *Texts* could illustrate this, but an example from "Text 3" will suffice:

> Is it possible I'll sprout a head at last, all my very own, in which to brew poisons worthy of me, and legs to kick my heels with, I'd be there at last, I could go at last, it's all I ask, no, I can't ask anything. Just the head and the two legs, or one, in the middle, I'd go hopping. Or just the head, nice and round, nice and smooth, no need of lineaments, I'd go rolling, downhill, almost a pure spirit, no, that wouldn't work, all is uphill from

here, the leg is unavoidable, or the equivalent, perhaps a few annular joints, contractile, great ground to be covered with them. (Beckett 1984b: 81)

Clowns Moving

This experimental or provisional attitude to enfleshment, and its relationship to the act of moving oneself about, is a deep vein running through Beckett's work. It is also one, I am suggesting, that runs through the identity and performance of a clown. A clown must face the arduous task of moving with controlled agility while at the same time conveying a *lack* of assurance, a *lack* of security in the graceful coordination, or even the legitimacy to exist, of his or her own body. This complementarity was precisely what in my view qualified and recommended Bill Irwin for the performance of *Texts for Nothing*. Moreover, his selection of texts, and his bodily vocabulary in projecting them, brought to the fore the difficult negotiations between stasis, projected movement, accomplished movement, hiatus, interruption, the stirrings still or still stirrings which pulse through Beckett's writing.

Those dilemmas in locomotion find expression, in both Beckett and in clown performances, in distinctive walks. The inspirational theater teacher Jacques Lecoq writes in his collection *Le Corps poétique* (translated by David Bradby as *The Moving Body*) of the process of developing such a walk, a process which begins at a level of psychic searching before it assumes any external locomotive manifestation.[3] Lecoq maintains that it

> involves looking for ways of walking that are buried deep within us. Watching the way each person walks, we can pick out the characteristic features ... and then exaggerate them progressively until we reach a personal transposition. I help the students to research their own clown walk, just as Groucho Marx, Charlie Chaplin or Jacques Tati all had their characteristic walks. It is never a question of the clown building something external, always a gradual development of their own, personal walk. (2002: 157)

Max Wall developed a walk for his celebrated Professor Wallofski character in which he appeared to divide his body into four incongruous zones – a prominent brow with professorial locks resting upon a heavy, erect upper body which sat oddly on a bulging pelvic region with protruding buttocks, all carried around in a chicken strut on impossibly spindly legs.

The walk, then, is linked to one's own personality and gait, and yet differs from it. It has a personal origin, and yet it must also have an outreach: audiences must not only recognize it, but also find it funny, incongruous, or somehow ill-adapted for the purposes of efficient transit. Such is the case with Beckett's Watt. Watt sums up all directional possibilities in his own body, covering all points of the compass as he turns his step to the east while pointing his torso to the north, launching his right leg to the south, then his torso to the south and his left leg to the north, and so on. Lady

McCann, coming up behind him, deems his articulations to be "extraordinary" (Beckett 1976: 29), and yet he usually seems to attain a destination in due course.

An illustration of this kind of combination of anarchic and yet all-encompassing movement may be seen in Bruce Nauman's video piece entitled "Slow Angle Walk" (1968), and subtitled "Beckett Walk." In this piece, Nauman films himself executing an agonizingly slow promenade around his studio. He lifts one leg up at right angles, holding it there while swiveling his torso round, then jackknifing at the waist to follow his descending leg as it plants its foot back on the ground. The whole process is repeated with the other leg, as Nauman makes irregular progress around the room, sometimes going out of sight of the viewer, and then heaving back into view, never renouncing his commitment to the impulsion to move. For Nauman, the intensity of these movements must have produced a bodily debilitation akin to that experienced by Billie Whitelaw in *Footfalls*. For the observer, the act of watching the piece, rather like that of watching the televised version of Beckett's *Quad*, produces initial hilarity but, at length, an obsessive uneasiness. This is the effect hoped for by Nauman, who described a dynamic which is applicable to much of Beckett's writing: "I wanted the tension of waiting for something to happen, and then you should get drawn into the rhythm of the thing" (Shaffner 2002: 167).

What amusement may be derived from Nauman's "Beckett Walk" emanates from the co-presence of an exquisitely deliberate pace-making with what appears to be a random trajectory. Similarly, a clown's walk, even if it becomes characteristic of him or her, does not have to remain constant. Much of its humor may arise from a veering between apparently aimless strolling on the one hand, and deliberately studied placing of the feet on the other. Both varieties may be found in Beckett. Gilles Deleuze, who finds Beckett one of the most humorous of writers, writes of the schizophrenic strolls of Beckett's creatures, always setting off on a mission but ending up tracing arcs or spirals. He frequently cites the description of journeying given in *Mercier et Camier*, in which Camier enjoins (I quote from the English text) that their watchword should be "lente, lente, and circumspection, with deviations to right and left and sudden reversals of course. Nor let us hesitate to halt, for days and even weeks on end. We have all life before us, all the fag end that is" (Beckett 1988: 67). Deleuze and Guattari align these human counter-currents of random, unattached walking (deterritorialization) and targeted journeying or patrolling (territorialization) with the movements of dogs, who need both the reassurance of habitual circuitry within known territory, and the exhilaration of freedom from the leash.

The two interlapping modes of journeying and wandering, sauntering and pressing on, the whole subject to obstacles and dilemmas, are applicable both to a large number of Beckett's wayfarers, and to the clown, especially of the "Auguste" variety. The kind of clowning undertaken by Grock, for example, often depended on infinite postponement in the accomplishment of a specific mission. He would embark on a task, only to be impeded, time and again, by obstacles or distractions, to the frustration of his taskmaster.

The Music of Clowns

The clownish act is often built around an act of music, or of attempted music. For Grock, music was not a supplement to his act: it inhabited it. Indeed, it is, in my view, likely that the musical thread running through all his performances created a further layer of involvement for the musically sensitive Beckett. Grock was in fact a trained piano tuner, and his autobiography relates tall tales of tuning exploits in remote castles involving piano strings in flitters to rival those of Beckett's Galls father and son (see Beckett 1976: 69). After examining the inside of Mr Knott's piano, Mr Gall Junior reports to Watt that "the mice have returned" (Beckett 1976: 68). Grock has a similar experience at an aged countess's castle, where, lifting the piano lid, he finds that "a multitude of tails darted hither and thither seeking refuge" (Grock 1931: 161). Having got rid of the mice, he has a great deal more trouble in evading the countess's erotic assault on him.

Grock's skills included not just piano tuning – an activity which does not in fact require its practitioners to be able to play the piano or read music – but also the ability to play a wide range of musical instruments. In the few bars of music that he ever did play before another element of his routine interrupted the performance his proficiency was briefly though tantalizingly demonstrated. The act of music-making was indispensable for Grock insofar as it enabled him to create that syncopated dynamic to which I referred earlier, in which the rhythm of one activity is sliced through or interrupted by a counter-rhythm. Grock on stage would sit down at the grand piano and prepare to play or to accompany another instrumentalist. However, a whole succession of obstacles or accidents would ensue. One by one, he would succumb to these, overcome them, and then fall victim to another, such that his whole act became a theme and variations, the theme being the intended music, and the variations being the diversions away from and back to the music. The few bars of music which the audience has heard plays on in their mind; its continuance, however, becomes a virtual music that plays alongside its own withdrawals and playbacks. Meanwhile, another rhythm, of pausing, preparing, beginning again, and ceasing again, is set up. Grock's act demonstrated within its apparent carelessness an extraordinary intricacy of rhythm and timing. The painstaking rehearsing and shaping of these intersecting timings for Grock's comedy-making is akin, I think, to the painstaking text-making processes undertaken by Beckett, who once stated that he *heard* all of his texts in advance of writing them (see Bernold 1992: 107).

Alive as clowns necessarily are to the performative exigencies of timing, it cannot be taken for granted that they can adapt easily to the musicality of another. Just as a clown may evolve a distinctive walk, he or she may evolve a distinctive rhythm which they feel reluctant to contravene. Not all clowns who have encountered Beckett's work have been prepared to let go of their routines and to listen to Beckett's music. For Bert Lahr (1895–1967), for instance, in the first American production of *Waiting for Godot*, this was a difficult challenge. He read the exchange between Estragon and

Vladimir: "E: All the dead voices. V: They make a noise like wings. E: Like leaves. V: Like sand. E: Like leaves," and advocated that the lines should be dropped (see Lahr 1970: 266–7). The music was subservient to its comic impact, which he considered minimal. The notion of containment was a suspicious one to Lahr. Like Buster Keaton, later on, in *Film*, he wanted to include his old tried-and-tested gags and mannerisms. Both he and Keaton eventually managed largely to suspend these, under persuasion, and to good effect, though it seems likely that Keaton remained mystified about what his contribution had been.

Max Wall, on the other hand, whose burlesque, music-hall apprenticeship had been similar to that of Lahr, responded immediately to Beckett. The British artist, Maggi Hambling, went to see Max playing Krapp in *Krapp's Last Tape* at the Greenwich Theatre in 1975. Later, she wrote,

> [Max] has the true face of the sad clown, and possesses that power I can only call magical to make one laugh and cry at the same moment. My first painting in oils at the age of fourteen was of a clown, and at various times over the years I have attempted this subject. The contradictory aspects of the clown's nature fascinate me. (Hambling 1983: 10)

Max Wall went on to play Vladimir in *Waiting for Godot*, and Hambling went about six times to the Round House in 1981 to watch it. She was fascinated by the elements of music-hall and clowning which Wall brought to the role. Her oil sketch of him as Vladimir is entitled *Voilà c'est tout* – "There you are, that's all" – an acknowledgement of Wall's hero Grock, who, like many French-speaking clowns, commonly used the phrase to conclude his act. Yet Beckett's music seemed to keep playing on in Max Wall's auditory memory, long after the performances were over. He was fascinated by the shapes, rhythms, and strangenesses of Beckett's language, and his correspondence with Maggi Hambling contains frequent echoes of Beckett's words.

The Violence of Clowning

Whether musical or not, many of the clown's comedic devices rely, of course, on repetition, verbal or physical. Repetition, though, is risky. It builds up weight; it builds up tension. The clown attempts an exploit, and messes up. He tries again, and takes a pratfall. Will he succeed next time? Will he *ever* succeed? As Jacques Lecoq states: "Ask a clown to do a somersault: he fails. Give him a kick in the backside and he does it without realising. In both cases we laugh. If he *never* succeeds, we are tipping over into the tragic" (Lecoq 2002: 156). As Nell observes in *Endgame*, unhappiness can be "the most comical thing in the world," but not when "it's always the same thing" (Beckett 1964a: 20). If an audience laughs at a clown who flops, their reaction includes a feeling that they are fulfilling expectation. If they laugh because he *never* succeeds, are they merely observers and he the observed, the performer, or is he the victim and are they somehow complicit in his victimization?

These are the issues which arise when confronted, for example, with Bruce Nauman's 1987 installation, *Clown Torture*. Nauman's clowns are embodiments not of reassurance and laughter but of tensions and insecurities. *Clown Torture* consists of four narrative sequences of clowns projected on giant screens as well as on small monitor screens in a darkened, enclosed room. Approaching the installation through a padded tunnel suggests the passageway to a torture chamber, or to Dante's Inferno. Entering it is terrifying, with shrieks, shouts, and even ambient noise turned up to ear-splitting volume. In one sequence, a clown repeatedly screams the word "No!" from a variety of postures, often lying kicking out on the floor. In another, a clown opens a door, causing a bucket of water to fall on his unprotected head. He staggers, dripping, to his feet, only to have to repeat the sketch, over and over again. In one of the most disquieting sequences, called "Clown Taking a Shit," a clown is viewed sitting in a public toilet, flicking through a magazine, weeping, fidgeting, incarcerated in an endlessly prolonged succession of mundane rituals and gestures. Surrounded and assaulted by this grammar of traumas played out to what seems like infinity, the viewer becomes drawn in, becomes herself the object of interrogation, in questionable association with the unseen powers of surveillance and control to which the clowns are subjected.

Is this the kind of clown that Lucky represents? Even the name is like that of a clown or a performing animal. When Lucky dances, the movement is not ludic or improvisatory: his spasms are always the same. His dance, according to Pozzo, is called "The Net," since he thinks himself trapped in a net. He performs it, as with Nauman's clowns caught in an infernal cycle of repetition, under duress. He has refused only once to perform it, Pozzo divulges: perhaps the punishment he experienced for not performing it was worse than the torture implicit in its performance. His "think," similarly, initially diverting because of its sheer impetus, its hurtling, baffling tennisball repetitions, arrives at last at the point of torture for everyone, its performer, its instigator, and its witnesses.

Meanwhile, what of the spectators, for Nauman's clowns as much as for Beckett's dispossessed? Perhaps they comfort themselves with the thought that clowns inhabit a separate sphere, a sphere in which sensation is more immediate and therefore perhaps more transient and bearable, a sphere which does not afford the luxury of remembering offences or nursing grudges. This is the sphere to which Pozzo consigns Lucky, observing dispassionately the cycle of his tears and his cessation of tears, and concluding that "Old dogs have more dignity" (Beckett 1965: 32). Even if they are accorded dignity and due recognition of acrobatic triumph, clowns are often assigned a status which is only partially human. In *The Confessions of Felix Krull*, Thomas Mann (an author well known to Beckett) has his narrator ruminate, after a visit to the circus in Paris,

> Take the clowns, for example, those basically alien beings ... are they, I repeat, human beings, men that could conceivably find a place in every-day daily life? ... I honour them and defend them against ordinary bad taste when I say no, they are not, they are

exceptions, side-splitting monsters of preposterousness, glittering, world-renouncing monks of unreason, cavorting hybrid, part human and part insane art. (Mann 1955: 203–4)

There is a sense in which clowns may cultivate and find desirable this perception of apartheid. In that marginal position – the Chaplinesque outlaw – they are, clearly, more at liberty to provoke, to challenge social, legal, and cultural norms. This process is fraught with the risk of a *volte-face*. Paradoxically, in becoming casualties of encompassing regimes, clowns may come to seem not subhuman but superhuman, by virtue of their very resilience, their constantly renewed ability to bounce back. In this understanding, their exclusions render them stronger, more impervious, more fantastical, more resourceful, than ordinary human beings. As Ingrid Shaffner theorizes it, "Possessed of superhuman strength, [clowns] endure what no right-minded person would tolerate" (Shaffner 2002: 170). But is this a manifestation of the superhuman, or is it that clowns are trapped in a process which *forces* them to endure what no right-minded person would tolerate? Like the three figures in Beckett's *Play*, they endlessly rehearse and revisit their routines under the caking plaster of their faces. From time to time a laugh may be incited by well-established methods, such as the onset of flatulence: "Give up that whore, she said, or I'll cut my throat – (*Hiccup.*) pardon – so help me God" (Beckett 1984a: 148). This *is*, however, just a hiccup, an escape of air; it is not an escape from the cycle of repetition.

This perpetuation of routine and frustration – the kind proposed, as I suggested earlier, by the Bruce Nauman clowns – is one that exposes the deep insecurities and alienation which may underlie the clownish event. In one of her paintings of Wall in the role of Vladimir, Maggi Hambling shows the tiny figure dwarfed by the giant, egg-shaped stage and its black anonymous audience. The title of this piece is "The Search is always Alone," and indeed the figure does seem to be threshing about within a cavernous space with few clues and few comforts. By this stage of his life, having lived through three divorces, bankruptcy, and numerous career setbacks, Wall could appear an isolated figure, traversed with regrets and resentments. He told friends that he spent long periods gazing out of his window, and in an interview with the *Times* in 1984, he said: "I think there's some little thing in [Beckett] that I've got. A wistfulness, a sort of reflection." He added, "I feel sorry for the human race and I have no way of expressing what I feel. I can't cry. I haven't cried for years. I feel numb about life, about the unfortunate people, the dreadful killings, the whole thing" (Appleyard 1984: 9). During the last years of his life, when he was preoccupied with Beckett, Wall's mind was as active as ever, but he felt a sense of dwindling. In one letter, he compared himself to an elephant where the huge body was behind him, leaving him resident in the trunk alone. In 1984, he struck his interviewer, Bryan Appleyard, as "a man to whom everything has been done, who has achieved a sort of irreducible minimum, a condition into which further tragedy can only be admitted as comedy."

Despite deep and recurrent melancholy, Wall continued to clown. The notion of a sad clown is all too familiar. A clown is popularly seen as a figure who hides his sadness, who puts on an act, in pursuit of amusing the world. Many great clowns have indeed been prone to deep depressive states. Beckett reported in a letter to Peter Gidal how moved he had been by the melancholy projected by Karl Valentin when he saw his act in Germany (see Knowlson 1996: 260). But we need to go further, I think, than simply to remark a discrepancy between internal state and outward demeanor, as if individual unhappiness is transcended in the attainment of collective joy. To do this is to impose a chronology on the clownish event. Sad face in the wings gives way to smiley face on stage, then returns to sad face in the dressing room, and so on. This is a kind of recuperative instinct, an antidote to the illusion we may have entertained that clowns are superhuman, or only partially human. As Richard Pearce observes, "In the theater the spectator responds immediately to almost every nuance of Beckett's expression; in the lobby he asks, 'What was it supposed to mean?'" (Pearce 1970: 142).

Freeing the clownish phenomenon from these reactive and chronological plateaux allows us to see it as something much more immediate, more naked, more confrontational. In this context, affects or ideas do not necessarily succeed one another; they may be coincident or optional elements of the same moment. The question "what was it supposed to mean?" is not consigned to the lobby; it is built into the act of theater, but in the present tense. A clown is always intensely alert; he is susceptible and full of incredulity precisely because he is always grappling with the unfolding of the present moment, always surprised at the turn of events. Nearly four decades after his first appearance on stage, Grock wrote, "No sooner do I get upon the stage than all my self-protective armour peels away from me and I am a recording instrument as sensitive as a mimosa plant. There is nothing I cannot feel and nothing I do not react to" (1931: 40).

With increased sensitization comes increased vulnerability. Many of Beckett's characters resemble clowns insofar as they struggle to create meaning, or simply to proceed to the next moment in a bewildering landscape. Vladimir and Estragon ask "why?" as frequently as Grock asks "warum?" and rarely receive answers that satisfy. As every child knows, "why?" may be a more interesting question – and produce more interesting answers – than "when?" But "why?" may also be a question which is more gut-wrenching in its implications. Not to receive an answer to "why?" may be much more costly than not to receive an answer to "when?" especially when human suffering or injustice is involved.

A clown is hit on the head by a bucket of water. He gets up, and asks "why?" The answer is that he is hit again and laughed at again. Christ when crucified is reported by two of the evangelists as having shouted out to God, "Why have you deserted me?" No answer is recorded. In Georges Rouault's paintings (much admired by Beckett), Christ takes on the features of a clown, and vice versa. In one painting from 1932, called *The Injured Clown*, a hurt, slumping clown is held up on each side by two other clowns, in a manner reminiscent of the crucifixion tableaus to be found in *Godot* when Vladimir and Estragon are joined on stage by Pozzo and Lucky. The composer Luciano Berio – influenced by both Grock and Beckett – lived as a child next door to Grock's residence in Oneglia. Profoundly indifferent to the old clown, he used to climb over Grock's garden gates to steal oranges and tangerines. When he was about 11, he was taken to see Grock's act. During the performance, Grock suddenly faced the audience pointblank and asked "Warum?" Berio was spellbound, on the point of tears. He said that, from then on, he never stole from Grock's garden again.

In the space created by that unanswered "why?" many emotions can flood in. In a context of resourcelessness, dispossession, these may turn more readily towards hatred, cruelty, and anger than towards love, kindness, and equanimity. The artist Cindy Sherman has exploited this interface between the comedic and the sinister in the persona of the clown fascinatingly. She herself finds clowns uncongenial and irritating, and in her Clown series, she photographs herself in a variety of gaudy but disturbing clown guises. Is the clown's mask simply providing a surface by means of which spectators may obtain a kind of splenetic catharsis? Or is it, as Maik Schlüter suggests of Sherman's work, "a sexualized and violent mask that veils or replaces identity for the moment of so-called perversion and enables the person behind it to fuck, beat, torture or deploy more subtle forms of mastery and repression in the name of someone else?" (Schlüter 2004: 14).

Within the kaleidoscope of clownish transactions, only a small shift is necessary to tip the balance. Gilles Deleuze draws attention to these crucial micro-shifts in the work of Charlie Chaplin. He gives the example of Chaplin, viewed from behind after having been abandoned by his wife. His shoulders appear to be shaking with sobs. Then he turns around, and reveals that he is in fact shaking a cocktail for himself. Deleuze comments on "la petite différence qui fait basculer la situation ... l'instant comme moment critique des situations opposables" ("the little difference which tips the situation over ... the instant as a critical moment in opposable situations") (Deleuze 1983: 232). The micro-shift might turn the possibility of horror towards comedy, or vice versa, potential laughter being diverted to horror or chaos. In the same volume on cinema, Deleuze also comments on the moment in Beckett's *Film* when O, played by Buster Keaton, is tipped towards terror by the sudden recognition of his own surveillance.

Alternatively, as I have suggested earlier, it might be the repetition or persistence of an action which achieves its transformation. A tin opener jabbed momentarily by one clown into the buttocks of another might set up a cacophony of bellow, counter-attack, and laughter; the sustained jabbing, carving, and crying of Beckett's *How It Is* shifts the relationship further along the continuum running from mischief to torture. Objects, or we might call them props, have a life of their own, or at the very least a spectrum of potential applications, both for Beckett's narrators, and for clowns. The material world may participate in the comic assault, taking its revenge on those who unthinkingly manipulate it. Part of the clown's improvisatory skill, according to Grock, derives from an ability to look afresh at each moment at both the animate and the inanimate world. In his autobiography, he attributes to the material world sentiments which might well be imagined emanating from Didi and Gogo: "Ever since I can remember, all kinds of inanimate objects have had a way of looking at me reproachfully and whispering to me in unguarded moments: 'We've been waiting for you ... at last you've come ... take us now, and turn us into something different ... we've been so *bored*, waiting'" (Grock 1931: 29).

Coda

In this chapter, I have tried to suggest productive areas in which Beckett's work can be drawn into affiliation with clownish phenomena. This affiliation, however, needs to be rather carefully established, and is not intended to be comprehensive. I have not, for example, approached the genre of the so-called hobo or tramp clown, which of course has underlain some persuasive performances of *Waiting for Godot*. Even though it is important to take account of Beckett's enthusiasm with twentieth-century clown figures, especially via the medium of film, it seems to me that some contemporary, twenty-first century explorations of the ambiguities and contradictions around clowning (Nauman, Sherman, and others) are particularly illuminating in a Beckettian context.

Finally, most clowns have at some point been imprinted with antecedent exemplars, although these may be unpredictable ones. Max Wall wrote that his greatest comic influence had come from Grock (Wall 1975: 70). After him, he placed Groucho Marx, on the grounds of his verbal delivery. Given some of these comic throughlines, might we expect, then, that Groucho Marx would also have responded positively to Beckett? In 1956, Goddard Lieberson, President of Columbia Records, sent to Marx the double LP recording of *Waiting for Godot*, a recording he had produced that year, with Beckett's agreement. This was the original cast performance of the New York production which included Bert Lahr. In his letter of response, Marx told Lieberson that he had just escaped from the clutches of his doctor, who, despite being an excellent physician, was, he said, "even daffier than Godot – if that's possible."[4] As for the experience of sitting through the double LP recording of *Godot*, Marx reports: "I listened, and I must say I'm still waiting for him. If he ever shows up, I'll break every bone in his body!" There could hardly be a better illustration of the violent undertow to be found both within clowning and within Beckett's enervating installations.

NOTES

1 See Gilles Deleuze, "Le plus grand film irlandais (*Film* de Beckett)" (1993: 36–9).
2 See "Voice of Grock: *Nicht mööööögliccchhh ...!*"; also, the Alba: "'Sans blahague!' she mocked grockly" (Beckett 1992: 115, 173).

3 I am grateful to Steven Barfield for directing my attention to this source of insight into clown pedagogy.
4 October 25, 1956. MSS 69, The Goddard Lieberson Papers in the Irving S. Gilmore Music Library, Yale University.

References and Further Reading

Appleyard, Bryan (1984). "Wistfully Watching the Sorrows of Humanity." *The Times*, Arts Section (May 23).

Beckett, Samuel (1964a). *Endgame*. London: Faber.

Beckett, Samuel (1964b). *How It Is*. London: John Calder.

Beckett, Samuel (1965). *Waiting for Godot*. London: Faber.

Beckett, Samuel (1976). *Watt*. London: John Calder.

Beckett, Samuel (1984a). Play. In *Collected Shorter Plays*. London: Faber.

Beckett, Samuel (1984b). Texts for Nothing. In *Collected Shorter Prose 1945–1980*. London: John Calder.

Beckett, Samuel. (1988). *Mercier and Camier*. London: Picador.

Beckett, Samuel (1992). *Dream of Fair to middling Women*. Dublin: Black Cat Press.

Bernold, André (1992). *L'Amitié de Beckett*. Paris: Hermann.

Deleuze, Gilles (1983). *Cinéma I: L'Image-Mouvement*. Paris: Editions de Minuit.

Deleuze, Gilles (1993). *Critique et clinique*. Paris: Editions de Minuit.

Downey, Roger (2002). "Tears of a clown: *Nothing* ventured, nothing gained." *Seattle Weekly*, Arts Section (May 1), available online at http://www.seattleweekly.com/arts/0218/arts-downey.php

Grock (alias Adrien Wettach) (1931). *Life's a Lark*, trans. Madge Pemberton. London: Heinemann.

Hambling, Maggi (1983). *Max Wall: Pictures by Maggi Hambling*, exhibition catalogue. London: National Portrait Gallery.

Harmon, M. (ed.) (1998). *No Author Better Served: The Correspondence of Samuel Beckett and Alan Schneider*. Cambridge, MA: Harvard University Press.

Knowlson, James (ed.) (1992). *The Theatrical Notebooks of Samuel Beckett: Krapp's Last Tape*. London: Faber.

Knowlson, James (1996). *Damned to Fame: The Life of Samuel Beckett*. London: Bloomsbury.

Lahr, John (1970). *Notes on a Cowardly Lion*. London: Allen Lane The Penguin Press.

Lecoq, Jacques (2002). *The Moving Body*, trans. David Bradby. London: Methuen.

Mann, Thomas (1955). *The Confessions of Felix Krull, Confidence Man*, trans. Denver Lindley. London: Secker and Warburg.

Pearce, Richard (1970). *Stages of the Clown: Perspectives on Modern Fiction from Dostoevsky to Beckett*. Carbondale: Southern Illinois University Press.

Schlüter, Maik (2004). "Fun That is No Fun." In *Cindy Sherman: Clowns*. Hanover: Schirmer/Mosel.

Shaffner, Ingrid (2002). "Circling Oblivions: Bruce Nauman through Samuel Beckett." In Robert C. Morgan (ed.), *Bruce Nauman*. Baltimore: Johns Hopkins University Press.

Steele, H. Thomas (2004). *1000 Clowns: More or Less*. Cologne: Taschen.

Wall, Max (1975). *The Fool on the Hill*. London: Quartet Books.

26

"Down, all going down ...": The Spiral Structure of Beckett's Theater

Xerxes Mehta

Waiting for Godot has famously been described as "a play in which nothing happens, *twice*."[1] This remark, prompted by the pressures of journalism, was perhaps not intended entirely seriously, although, taken literally and not idiomatically, it is, ironically, accurate. What it does do, however, in its common meaning, is point to a geometric figure, the circle, which is often considered *Godot*'s central organizing principle. My contention here is that this is not true, and that the spiral, and not the circle, is the figure that controls the design – not only of *Godot*, but of all of Beckett's theater.

A circle is by its nature a static and didactic form. Whether wielded technically – to structure events, words, images, or an entire work – or thematically – to proffer a vision of life – it is incompatible with the medium of theater, being neither actable nor stageable. It is not actable because, by robbing a character of the possibility of change, it leaves the actor with no way to enter existence, with, in effect, nothing to do. And it is not stageable because, by robbing the spectator of the possibility of change, it severs the compact between audience and action, leaving a mere "point of view" hanging in its stead. *Waiting for Godot*, on the other hand, is neither static nor didactic. It engages life and its audience with furious vitality. It is the seminal work in which Beckett discovered the full force of the spiral as a theatrical template, which he then forged into the varied and complex uses that sustained his subsequent work in the theater.

A spiral, of course, issues from the marriage between a circle and a straight line. The impalpable line – vertical – penetrates the center of the palpable circle – horizontal – and, depending on the direction of felt movement, either drags the circle down in ever-tightening constriction or lifts it upward in ever-more-spacious expansion. In either case, the circle is the passive principle, the line – no less for being invisible – the active one.

In briefest outline, here are *Godot*'s spirals, as I understand them. In a play in which everything appears to repeat, I suggest that in fact nothing does. Even in the rare instance when a perfectly closed system seems to present itself – for example, nightfall and moonrise at the ends of the two acts – the circle is an illusion. The design elements must repeat exactly if they are to do right by their relentless counterparts in what passes for real life. But the contexts in which they are received, by the characters and by the spectators, are as different as, to follow the figure, day and night. The first time, softened as we are by the play's initial charm, humor, and fascination, and by the no-nonsense abruptness of the pseudo-poetic effect, a slight smile might play on the lips. The second time, by when, in the writer's phrase, "the hooks have gone in," our reaction encompasses thoughts and feelings of far greater gravity and turbulence. In short, how a moment in the play's text functions in performance depends less on its ontological *donnée,* which is invariably unyielding, than on how the characters respond to those givens, and, especially, on how we in the audience respond to their responses (see Brater 1987: 130).

So far, I have spoken only of one of the rare incidents of apparent stasis in *Godot.* The greater part of the play, however, declares its spiral structures openly. Thus the second Pozzo – Lucky scene is half the length of the first, less satiric and more interior in intent, and far grimmer in tone. Silences fall twice as thickly in the second act as in the first. The second scene with the boy – or rather with *a* boy – wears its parody of the Annunciation less lightly than the first, being, again, half the length of its predecessor, its metaphysical hunger more naked, its tone more violent and desperate. As time stops and eternity presses in, the phenomenal world continues to recede. Sight fails and speech founders, ropes break, carrots turn into radishes – black ones, at that – and Pozzo's copious pacifiers are ground down into a bag full of sand. The earth reclaims its own in other ways too, as the vertical bipeds of the first act, who were once "respectable," and who even used to "think very prettily," are reduced to a rubble of horizontal flesh, silent and still in "sweet mother earth" 's indifferent embrace. Invention flags, rhythms slow, and the tramps listen ever more closely to suicide's siren call, the obscene jocularity with which they first greeted her overtures having collapsed by play's end into monosyllabic reminders to themselves to "bring a good bit of rope".

If one were now to step back from *Waiting for Godot* and look at the stage works that emerged over three decades, certain patterns suggest themselves. The descending spiral that is *Godot*'s central structural discovery and principle remains so for all the plays which follow. The overall movement of each work is always a spiral, and the direction of the spiral is always downward.

However, quite soon, Beckett devised a variation on the design of the downward movement, in particular on its rhythmic quality and on the way it is experienced in the theater. In *Act Without Words II,* character B displays a stunning energy and purpose as he races through his daunting daily routine, in starkest possible contrast to his sad-sack companion, A, who, drawing apparently equal doses of encouragement from pills and prayer, barely manages to dress himself before it is time to reverse his dismal procedure. Whatever one may think of these two approaches to life's journey, whether one sympathizes with A or B, or both, or finds them equally risible, equally inauthentic, equally victims of received ideas, what is of interest in the formal context is that the play's power derives from the contrast between the two. Two spiraling ironies flow in parallel, each generating humor and horror, one from the spectacle of human-as-machine grinding to a stop, while never quite stopping, and the other from the vision of human-as-machine winding up to the point of flying apart, while never quite flying apart. The first pattern, that of A, is the dominant one in Beckett's dramaturgy; we have encountered it before and will again. The second pattern, while glimpsed in embryo in Lucky's manic aria in *Godot*, is here, for the first time, accorded a structural importance equal to that of its partner in declension. The double-spiral design of this vicious little cartoon is, like the day/night example from *Godot* offered earlier, implicit rather than explicit. The play's surface presents the soothing exactitude of a perfect circle, whose downward tug is not fully felt until A's second ejection into Winnie's "holy light." As the repeat springs its trap into the infinite, the spiral's vertiginous drop bites into the prevailing jollity. Also of interest here are the dualities – two kinds of horror, two types of laughter – that the opposing rhythms produce. The result is a harsh brilliance that not only reinforces the onslaught of the play's blinding black and white frieze, but also sharpens the savagery and clarity that make cartoons indelible.

Act Without Words II is the first of Beckett's multi-spiral works that also resist closure, retaining the sense of infinite regression that admits the void and empties the spirit. The others, in my view, are *Play*, *Not I*, and *Quad*.[2]

Quad is patterned on the same two opposing spirals as the earlier mime – the leading design (*Quad I*) colorful, percussion-driven, "feverish,"[3] its shrunken follower (*Quad II*) monochromatic, near-silent, exhausted. Once again, the spirals are implicit, pulled by the spectator from the work's surface circularity under the pressure of repetition, end without end. There is, however, a difference from the earlier template. Whereas, decades ago, the spirals were intertwined and interdependent – sharing a single set of clothes, literally carrying each other through the stations of their common calvary – here they are offered in sequence as distinct and discrete visions, although the sense that one will decline into the other ("one hundred thousand years later" [Beckett in Fletcher and Fletcher 1985: 262]) is strong.

Play (see Beckett 1986), on the other hand, is, structurally, perhaps the most complex, original, and intricately shaped work in the Beckett canon. As I understand them, based on the two productions that I have directed (Baltimore/Washington, DC, 1978–9; Baltimore/Berlin, 2000), five spirals, controlling all aspects of sight and sound, determine the play's design. Four of these – volume of voices, intensity of light on faces, duration of choruses, and the play's repeats – are characteristically recessive; one – the speed of verbal delivery – is assaultive. Because Beckett made adjustments to all but one of these elements in productions with which he was associated – particularly those in Germany (1963), London (1964), Paris (1964), Paris (film of *Play*, 1966), and London (1976) – the work's production history is a necessary guide not only to production choices but also to an understanding of implicit forces at play within the text.

The most central of these choices and forces, and the one which instantly rivets an audience's attention, is the speed at which the characters speak. Hovering at the edge of intelligibility, *Play*'s sounds – all words, except for the man's nine hiccups and his mistress's five laughs – assault the audience at a tempo that forces acute listening and, initially at least, lunges at comprehension. When such an aural attack is combined with the lightning movement of the spot that jabs at faces and demands speech, the whole enterprise – thrusting light, desperate verbal response, and appearing and disappearing heads – takes on a quality somewhere between a hallucination and a high-wire act; one senses that the smallest miscue, on the part of actor or light operator, will snuff it out altogether. This tension, and the bond between performer and spectator that it enforces, are purely theatrical epiphanies. They reach full strength in less than a minute, well before character, narrative, theme, or in fact any aspect of content can work its spell. *Play*, thereby, immediately declares the first of its titular purposes – to investigate the nature and limits of theater itself – and simultaneously lays out the means through which such a self-probe will be administered – structure, shape, design, form.

Extreme assaultive patterns of any kind, however, cannot be sustained unchanged in the theater for extended periods. When they are, when spectators sense no development, the welcome onslaught of originality quickly sours into the oppressive hectoring of didacticism, and the audience withdraws. That Beckett was aware of this is shown in his remarks to Martin Esslin explaining his dislike of a radio adaptation of *Play* that he had heard. Here is the relevant excerpt from Esslin's recollection of what Beckett said:

> there must be a clear progression by which each subsection is both faster and softer than the preceding one. If the speed of the first Chorus is 1 and its volume 1, then the speed of the first Narration must be 1 plus 5 per cent and its volume 1 minus 5 per cent. The speed of the following segment, the first Meditation, must then be (1 plus 5 per cent) plus 5 per cent, and its volume (1 minus 5 per cent) minus 5 per cent. The implication is quite clearly that ... however soft, however fast, the same text will go on *ad infinitum*, even faster and even softer without quite ceasing altogether.[4]

If one considers for the moment only that part of Beckett's response which concerns *Play*'s tempo, one sees that the pattern of acceleration he describes is an exact summary of the work's dominant verbal spiral, the only one not explicitly called for in the work's text, stage directions, or note on permissible variations later attached to its English edition. What Beckett was presumably objecting to in the radio version was either that the pace was lax or, more probably, that it was static, circular, thus robbing the play of movement and subtracting one half of its dynamic structure – the *increasingly* aggressive verbal spiral that balances the combined weight of the recessive spirals arrayed against it.

Of the latter not much need be said. The fading voices and light, receding in the linked series of stutter-steps described in Beckett's note mentioned earlier, reinforce the play's mirage-like aspect; all grows fainter, dimmer, further away, as if love, pain, hatred, jealousy ("this stew of angry contempt and fetid sexuality" [Alvarez 1973: 106]) were no more than so many motes in the universe's indifferent eye. Of formal interest here is the contrast between these carefully calibrated step-downs and the relentless rise in pressure from the clean acceleration of the verbal impulse. The two other receding spirals are the shrinking chorus – "abridged chorus, cut short on laugh of W2, to open fragment of second repeat" (Beckett 1986: 320) – and the repeats-of-play themselves which, underlining the regression, promise to keep spinning "Down, all going down, into the dark" (ibid.: 312) long after the spectators have gone home, grown old, and passed on to their own purgatorial accountings.

So far I have suggested two designs for the downward spiral in Beckett's theater: the entropic single spiral originated by *Waiting for Godot* and the dual or multi-spiral variations discernible in *Act Without Words II*, *Play*, and *Quad*. To these Beckett added still another sub-variation in one play: *Not I*.

The spiral structure of *Not I* (see Beckett 1974) is nominally based on the same duality as that of the two mimes in this group, a duality that also underlies *Play*'s elaboration of it. In *Not I*, the recessive spiral is explicit in the auditor's gradually diminishing gestures "of helpless compassion," until, on the fifth and final occasion of Mouth's "vehement refusal to relinquish third person," there is no gesture at all (Beckett 1974: 14). Once again, the accumulating exhaustion and despair of this fading movement is opposed to the "scalding intensity" (Knowlson and Pilling 1979: 195) and hurtling momentum of Mouth's verbal assault. Such a balance of contrasting spirals, however, is more apparent than real.

Based on my three productions of *Not I* (Baltimore/Washington, DC, 1978–9; Baltimore, 1990; Baltimore/Strasbourg, 1996), and confirmed by others that I have seen, there is no longer much doubt in my mind that the auditor is a feeble presence in performance. The fascination and power of Mouth – both as blazing visual image and as amplified aural onslaught – render her giant companion theatrically insignificant. That Beckett was aware of this can be seen in his own omission of the auditor (*Pas moi*, Paris, 1975; Cohn 1980: 266–7), in his attempt to reinstate and reinforce the figure by adding an ultimate gesture "of increased helplessness and despair, as if unable to bear any longer the torrent of sound" (*Pas moi*, Paris, 1978; Beckett, cited in Brater [1987: 34]), in his acquiescence to the auditor's absence from the BBC Television version (1977), and in his resigned suggestion to Alan Schneider – which, to his credit, the director did not heed – to "try it without him" (*Not I*, New York, 1972; letter to Alan Schneider in Harmon [1998: 287]). "For me the play needs him but I can do without him. I have never seen him function effectively" (letter to David Hunsberger and Linda Kendall, dated November 16, 1986, in Gontarski 1999: xxiv).

Auditor's failure in *Not I* is not, finally, a technical one. Despite the notorious difficulties in lighting this apparition successfully, it can be done. A skilled designer can render the huge wraith dimly yet fully visible without losing the sense of float so essential to the hauntings of the late plays, and without compromising the inky ground of negative space in which and through which *Not I* defines itself. The source of the failure, I suggest, is that the auditor is dramatically inert, a conceptual construct – "a physical representation of an internal force that is developed clearly in dialogue" (Gontarski 1985: 148) – and, as such, lies outside the flow of visceral energy that ties audience to Mouth. At the same time, the losses are real and keenly felt. A necessary visual balance is obscured, especially in the theater, where Mouth's image cannot be expanded, as it can in film, to fill the frame.[5] A philosophical presumption close to Beckett's heart throughout his writing life – Bishop Berkeley's *esse est percipi* (to be is to be perceived) – is compromised (Cohn 1973: 205; Knowlson and Pilling 1979: 99). A clarifying and moving conduit for audience reaction to Mouth's self-destructiveness is enfeebled. And, perhaps most significantly in the present formal context, a cleanly equipoised double-spiral design progressively deteriorates into a de facto single spiral of overwhelming force.

Not I's weakness, in other words, is also its greatest strength and the source of its uniqueness; for nowhere else in Beckett's theater is there a play in which our sense of falling into a night without end is solely generated by a single upward surge of sound, voice, words, and tempo. What had first been tried out in Lucky's "think," then given central structural roles in *Act Without Words II* and *Play*, now floods a work in its entirety. Because there has been much fine writing on *Not I*, and in the interest of hewing to my argument, I will confine myself here to remarking only on those aspects of this upward surge that are of particular concern in performance and that are not explicit either in Beckett's stage directions or, as far as I know, in the play's production history.

Performer and production team work backward from an acknowledgment of *Not I*'s obvious authority to a search for those patterns in the text that generate that authority. Of special concern are sources of development, change, and movement, elements that lift the narrative out of a lifeless recital of woe to the headlong and *increasingly* desperate quest for identity that is the play's engine. Such patterns and sources are scattered throughout the text and not difficult to find, and all of them point to a gradual intensification of Mouth's already racing verbal tempo, which, in turn, is linked to the growing chaos in Mouth's life and her diminishing ability to cope with it.

There is, for example, the "ray of light" (Beckett 1974: 15), which Mouth tells us that "she" sees, presumably in her mind's eye ("found herself in the dark"), and which appears to be a ghost image of the ray of light that we in the audience see focused on Mouth herself. "She" is initially unthreatened by this occasional guest, which "came and went … such as the moon might cast … drifting … in and out of cloud." Barely a page later, however, "she" radically re-evaluates this phantom, now a constant presence ("all the time this ray or beam"), no longer drifting ("always the same spot") or benign ("just all part of the same wish to … torment"). Then, after a gap, during which "she" frantically tries to deal with other unwelcome surprises, such as the fact that, following a lifetime of near-muteness, a torrent of words is issuing from her mouth, a torrent that she can neither understand nor control, "she" again brings up her blazing tormentor ("all part of the same"), which is now "starting to move around." Vowing to "keep an eye on that, too ... corner of the eye," "she" hurries on, only to backtrack in a panic almost immediately as she realizes that the light is "ferreting around" and, soon after, even more invasively "poking around." Of Mouth's five references to "she"'s light across the play's eight-plus pages, the last three press in on her in the final two pages and a half.

A similar compression can be seen in Mouth's determined denials of selfhood ("what? ... who? ... no! ... she!"). Of the five occasions on which these occur, the last three erupt within two pages in *Not I*'s closing moments, the final denial repeating and pounding the word "SHE!"

Other such reductions are evident in the play's linguistic style – in the progressive foreshortenings of certain repeated narrative patterns and in the breakdown of syntax under the pressure of Mouth's cracking mind. For example, her four-line description of "she" "wandering in a field" at the start of the play gets pressed into "back in the field" on the penultimate line, just as "all that early April morning light" is cut down to "April morning." "She"'s confusion about "what position she was in" following the unspecified but catastrophic event in the field at the play's onset, a confusion explored at length over five lines, is telegraphed by "sink face down in the grass" later on, which shrinks to "face in the grass" at the very end. Similarly, "she"'s early amazement at the paralysis of her body, again explored over five lines, is crushed into "whole body like gone" in the closing moments.

Such foreshortenings are paralleled and reinforced by an equivalent syntactical collapse. However driven ("I hear it breathless, urgent, feverish, rhythmic, panting ..." [Harmon 1998: 283 quoting Beckett in a letter to Alan Schneider]), and however broken up into concentrated impulses (usually of three to five words each), Mouth's delivery nevertheless sustains several coherent narratives in the early going – "she"'s premature birth, her abandonment by her parents, her lack of love from any source, the event in the field, speculation about her physical position and condition, speculation about whether or not she is being punished for her sins (this theological mix-up lasts a good three-quarters of a page), and so on. Each of these narratives is several lines long and charmingly formal and decorous in grammar and syntax, the contrast between the near-pedantry of Mouth's style and the horror of "she"'s life providing one of *Not I*'s several sly provocations to humor. By play's end, however, all this has more or less collapsed. Bits of narrative – now shredded, but still semi-intelligible – alternate with a collage of panicked impulses and desperate lunges at salvation ("quick grab and on ... nothing there ... on to the next ..."). The bursts between breaths are now one to four words in length, the words are shorter, frequently monosyllabic, and no thought is sustained for more than a few seconds.

And finally, the downward spirals in Mouth's struggle with the light, denials of selfhood, and progressive constrictions of narrative and syntax are explicitly mirrored in the mounting chaos of her words themselves. Here are examples from *Not I*'s final minutes: "it can't go on ... all this ... all that ... mouth on fire ... stream of words ... can't stop ... no stopping it ... and the whole brain begging ... begging the mouth to stop ... if only for a moment ... couldn't pause a second ... like maddened

... now this ... this ... *quicker and quicker* ... the words ... the brain ... flickering away like mad ..." (my emphasis).[6] The overall impression is that of a soul perishing before our eyes.

From even so cursory a glance at *Not I*, it is clear that the play carries embedded in its structure the same principle of movement, the descending spiral, as do its predecessors. The variants are that while designed to be a member of the double-spiral group, it is in fact a single-spiral work, and that, unique to the canon, the single spiral is centrifugal rather than centripetal.

Before concluding with a few thoughts on the broader implications of the spiral-as-theatrical-template, I would like to consider a significant category of plays in which the spiral might appear in some way truncated, even cancelled, plays which have, or at least seem to have, clear-cut and definite endings. This group might include *Act Without Words I, Come and Go, That Time, Footfalls, A Piece of Monologue, Rockaby, Ohio Impromptu, Catastrophe,* and *What Where*.

Just as Beckett used *Act Without Words II* to try out, in miniature, his first double-spiral design, he used *Act Without Words I* to introduce a fresh pattern that he would deepen and complicate in the plays from the final decade of his writing life. The falling spiral in this caustic little cartoon is as clear, harsh, and unforgiving as the "dazzling light" which illuminates it (*Act Without Words I* in Beckett 1986: 203). It is also familiar. The stab at life's finer points (trimming one's nails), which is mocked, the attempts to secure life's necessities (water and shelter), which are dismissed, the repeated circlings of suicide, which abort, have all been seen before, mainly in *Godot*. What is new is the outcome: silence, stillness, resignation, the renunciation of desire, the absolute withdrawal from existence. "Whistle from above. He does not move. The tree is pulled up and disappears in flies. He looks at his hands. CURTAIN" (ibid.: 206). Both mimes, *I* and *II*, carry the elegance of a Picasso line drawing and the vitriol of a Daumier sketch; both dig new ground structurally; but whereas A and B, in *II*, struggle on in formally contrasting dynamic patterns, setting up opposing spirals of energy, rhythm, and engagement with life, their wordless cousin, in *I*, declines to go "on," gives up, stops. What such an ending does to the idea and theatrical reality of the spiral-as-world-view-and-organizing-principle I will attempt to address in a moment. For now, it is important only to recognize the advent of the changed pattern, which Beckett will worry as a dog does a bone in the years to come.

For present purposes, I exclude *Catastrophe* and *What Where* from this discussion, on the grounds that the latter is a slight and self-derivative work, and that the former, while powerful in performance and penetrating in its equation of theatrical and totalitarian impulses, is a political play whose relatively conventional agonistic structure lies outside the mainstream of Beckett's lifelong concerns.

The remaining six plays in this group join *Act Without Words I* in representing those works in the *oeuvre* that appear to achieve true and final closures, but do not do so, or so it seems to me. Rather, they are plays with false endings, transparent closures, which simply recast the plummeting spirals of consciousness in these works into slightly altered theatrical terms.

The conclusion of *A Piece of Monologue* provides perhaps the clearest example of this pattern. The 30-second fade out of the lamp – "skull-sized" and skull height – that acts as the speaker's "silent, totemic double" (Mel Gussow, quoted in Zeifman 1996: 248), accompanied by the death-infused cadences of his last words (delivered by the original Speaker, David Warrilow, in "an old hoarse voice [with] long, painful, gasping hesitations" [Fletcher and Fletcher 1985: 243]), all followed by a 10-second silence and final curtain, certainly would seem to qualify as an instance of definitive closure. And yet, Speaker's words throughout the work appear to negate the possibility of the end so longed for and feared, silence and darkness – as so often in Beckett – being the ever approaching and receding release ("they being one") from life's pain and loneliness. Darkness is denied: "Faint light in room. Whence unknown. None from window. No. Next to none. No such thing as none" (*A Piece of Monologue* in Beckett 1986: 425). Silence is denied: "Room once full of sounds. Faint sounds. Whence unknown. Fewer and fainter as time wore on. Nights wore on. None now. No. No such thing as none." Nothing is done or said at any point in the play, including its conclusion, to refute the absence of the absolute. On the contrary, the speaker makes plain the grim sequence of nights, 30,000 so far (82 years), in which he – or rather the doppelgänger in his necessary fiction – has performed almost the same sequence of bodily actions, relived almost the same memories, spoken almost the same words, and experienced almost the same emotions as those we see before us on "this night." "And now. This night. Up at nightfall. Every nightfall." "Gropes back in the end to where the lamp is standing. Was standing. When last went out." The lamp, in other words, goes out every night, only to be relit the next. The only difference – and it is a critical one – between this night, any night, and the one before it is that things are a little worse, the waking hours harder to bear, the dead ("he all but said the loved ones") both more absent and present, the isolation more insupportable. "Dying on. No more no less. No. Less. Less to die. Ever less." Here we hear, sharply and explicitly, the true note of the tightening spiral from which the play draws its deep structure, its emotional charge, and its dramatic movement – in short, its theatrical tension and viability. To posit against so irresistible a force, so coherent and deeply held a vision of existence, a self-contradictory, definitive closure, simply because the speaker's nights, including the one we attend, flicker out in devastation, is to permit a kind of wish-fulfillment, a need for release from grief over our own mortality, to intrude upon a shape that in its conviction and astringency will not admit it.

I have focused on *A Piece of Monologue* because, of the plays with what I have called false endings, its design is the simplest and clearest. However, the others, while more complex, highly particular, and at some level entirely mysterious creations, nevertheless seem to draw their energy from a common source. The spine of each of these plays continues to grow from the obsessive pursuit by its central consciousness (in the case of *Come and Go* a composite consciousness) of release from the suffering and isolation of his or her life. The falling spirals that the works embody use a variety of theatrical means, most of which we have encountered already, and to which I will return. At the heart of each of these spirals, however, is the effort to cope with a condition that can only incrementally worsen, and that therefore calls for incrementally greater degrees of endurance and will from the sufferer "trying to make sense of it ... or make it stop" (Beckett 1974: 20). Because this movement toward disaster is so ineluctable and basic, because it does not depend on the particulars of individual lives, which perhaps for that reason are largely withheld from us, and because it corresponds exactly to the audience's own intuition of our common fate, the endings of these plays are foregone conclusions, carrying neither surprise nor alteration. That they are also imagistically brilliant – a tribute to the writer's unflagging inventiveness – and emotionally insupportable – a proof of their penetration to our profoundest fears – does not change their provisionality or their transparency. For behind each lies the struggling consciousness that is "dying on," that reinvents its past to get through "this night," that has no choice but to endure the chaos at night's end, through the dawn that "shed[s] no light" (*Ohio Impromptu* in Beckett 1986: 447) and on, until "up at nightfall," "this night to be," when the fiction will be slightly different (see Gontarski 1985: 173–82), slightly more desperate, the life recast from its recastings, in the hope of fending off "his old terror of night" (*Ohio Impromptu*, in Beckett 1986: 446), in the hope that "she" will "hit on it in the end" (Beckett 1974: 22).

From such a perspective, the very notion of closure in Beckett's theater – early or late – becomes faintly absurd, at best a mocking nod to theatrical convention, at worst a sentimentalism. What is asserted in its stead is human consciousness, consciousness of self, as a kind of absolute compulsion, perhaps the only absolute to be found in the plays. It is offered as a force that is involuntary, undeterrable, and sharpened by life's darkest passages (all the plays); undimmed by physical catastrophe (*Godot*, *Endgame*, *Happy Days*, *Not I*); and immune even to death (*Play*) or failed birth (*Footfalls*).

VLADIMIR:	What do they say?
ESTRAGON:	They talk about their lives.
VLADIMIR:	To have lived is not enough for them.
ESTRAGON:	They have to talk about it.
VLADIMIR:	To be dead is not enough for them.
ESTRAGON:	It is not sufficient. (Beckett 1954: 40)

What the old men in *Godot* intuit, their successors embody, as they turn into the "they" in this exchange. Considered so, the ending of *Rockaby*, the most apparently "final" of the late group, can perhaps evoke two kinds of response, not mutually exclusive. Under the spell of the play's falling spirals – fainter voices, fainter echoes, fainter light, closing eyes – we grieve for the life, "prematurely old" (*Rockaby*, in Beckett 1986: 433), being extinguished before us. As I have suggested earlier, because this life is hardly individualized – all we are told through the fiction W summons is that "she" has spent her waking hours in an unrequited search for "another living soul," "another like herself" – our grief flows to her, through her, and back upon ourselves. It is possible, too, that our response to death in fiction, no matter how particular or complex the life at issue, always contains this component, and that our fearful knowledge that we are born alone, die alone, and, imprisoned by self-awareness, live alone through our moment in the light ("the same day, the same second" [Beckett 1954: 57]), is the fuel that energizes all engagement with others, real or imagined. Whether or not, then, the two women in the common rocker (like *Ohio Impromptu*'s two men with the common hat, or *Footfalls*' multiple women measuring out their common patch of ground) literally perish at play's end – and there are different views on this (Fletcher and Fletcher 1985: 250–1) – seems essentially beside the point. What matters, surely, in all these ghostly comings and goings, is that consciousness does not. As these wraiths seek meaning, order, or minimal solace from their obsessive relivings of life's chaos, the gallantry and endurance of the effort itself, along with the tightening vise of its inevitable failure, generate the audience's core reaction. An amalgam of tenderness, anger, and exaltation, our response reaches far beyond natural sympathy for a suffering – possibly even a dying – individual, to touch, for a moment, those white-hot currents of knowledge and refusal that animate and distinguish our kind.

The preceding perspective might suggest that the formal geometry of Beckett's theater is coherent and consistent – all of a piece from first produced play to last. Each work enters an ongoing and unending struggle midstream and leaves it a blink of an eye later. As, over time, the plays become shorter, their protagonists more generic, and their physical settings more abstract, this struggle, which is between the human consciousness of disorder and the need to still that consciousness through fiction, acquires an overwhelming centrality. In every case the fiction is shown in the process of failing, even as, in a kind of perverse inversion, the fictionalizing consciousness redoubles its effort to overcome the failure in exact proportion to the ever-growing burden of the failure itself. I have suggested that this war between the self and itself takes the form of a spiral because that shape embodies both the circularity of habit, the "great deadener" (Beckett 1954: 58), "Night after night the same" (*A Piece of Monologue*, in Beckett 1986: 427), and the linear, downward pressure stemming from the inability of life experience, reason, language, narrative, art, or thought itself to break free of circularity into some version of authentic existence – "hit on it in the end ... think everything keep on long enough ..." (Beckett 1974: 22). The theatrical tools through which Beckett releases his spirals are various. Among them, as we have seen, are: shrinkage in the lengths of acts, scenes, "canters," and – the smallest verbal unit – the three-or-four-word impulses between breaths; progressive darkening of tone; compression and shredding of syntax; deceleration or acceleration of verbal rhythm and energy; deceleration or acceleration of physical rhythm and energy; fading voices; closing eyes; the stripping of the physical world; the dismemberment and virtual elimination of the human body; diminishing or swelling sound; dimming or increasingly aggressive light; and disappearing or proliferating narratives. A note Beckett wrote to himself while rehearsing *Footfalls* in London (1976) pinpoints the method, if not the full range of its devices.

<u>Diminuendo</u>
4 chimes (fainter)
"   fade-ups (dimmer)
3 pacings (slower, fainter)
"   voices ("   ")
M's semblance (more tattered)? (Gontarski 1999: 305).

It is an irony of the form that, in any given work, Beckett's spirals simultaneously express both the central consciousness's rage against its ontological confine and the nature of the confine itself. For example, as dictated by the rehearsal note from *Footfalls*, the combined sinking spirals of sight and sound in that play record both life's withdrawal from M and the failure of M's anguished self-assertion in the face of that withdrawal – "the motion alone is not enough, I must hear the feet, however faint they fall" (*Footfalls*, in Beckett 1986: 401). (Doubly ironic, in this particular ghost tale, is that the same spirals, in the very act of distancing us, as they wave us away from the vanishing woman in the vanishing play, imprint both woman and play indelibly upon our hearts.)

One suspects that Beckett arrived at the spiral as his art's controlling shape because it exactly reflected his intuition of what once was called "the human condition," and of art's possibilities within that condition in the mid-twentieth century. That said, the spiral's central *structural* function is to inject drive, change, movement, and vitality into Beckett's theater. In every work, its characters' pursuit of meaning, solace, or relief from the torment of consciousness is presented not as a tilting at windmills, a quest mocked for its foreordained failure, but as a dynamic and evolving struggle of great consequence. The spiral both dictates to and accommodates this struggle, which, after all, is between forces that are simply in the nature of things. If it is in the nature of "all this" (Beckett 1986: 313) to get worse with time – less because "Night is drawing nigh-igh" (*Krapp's Last Tape* in Beckett 1986: 219) than because nourishment's lack is the more keenly felt the longer withheld ("Hope deferred maketh the something sick" [Beckett 1954: 8]) – then the spiral will enforce that declension – here and now, on stage, in front of us. If, under the millstone, it is in the nature of consciousness to keep "revolving it all" (Beckett 1986: 403) at ever more unbearable human cost ("Like dragging a great roller, on a scorching day. The strain ..." [Beckett 1986: 315]), then the spiral will expose those hideous increments – again in the living moment, the time and space shared by audience, actors, characters, situation, and play. (For there are no fourth walls here, neither illusion nor illusions.) In every case, the outcome is no secret; spectators grasp it immediately, for it is in plain sight, both before them and within them. To say so much is simply to try to finger the true suspense that these plays secrete, a suspense that has nothing to do with outcomes and everything to do with the struggle itself. At stake is nature – tangentially the nature of individuals, centrally the nature of the species.

VLADIMIR: Let us represent worthily for once the foul brood to which a cruel fate
consigned us! (Beckett 1954: 51).

VLADIMIR: We have kept our appointment and that's an end to that. We are not
saints, but we have kept our appointment. How many people can boast as much?
ESTRAGON: Billions. (ibid.)

For me, it is not sufficient to see the plays primarily as "an analysis of the evasions
that inhibit authentic vision" (Webb 1972: 141).[7] While on one level this view is
persuasive, particularly of the comic dimensions of the early plays, I suggest that the
crucible of loss in which Beckett grinds his characters has purposes that outstrip those
of farce or satiric comedy. The terrifying linear movement into the dark that is at his
work's core, and that his spirals enforce, draws its overwhelming conviction less from
his people's mulish limitations and incapacities – mulish, limited, and incapable as
they surely are – than from the tender toughness and rage-ridden endurance that they
eventually, sacrificially, embody, and that we devour. And thus the cannibalism that
marks all great theater reasserts itself, as we nourish ourselves on the sufferings of
our kind.

From which one might draw an inference that, structurally, the spiral in Beckett
suggests a classical reincarnation, owing less perhaps to the Irish playwrights of his
youth, or even to his beloved Racine (Mercier 1977: 20–45, 73–87) than to the
monster-imaginers who birthed the medium, Aeschylus and Sophocles. For despite
his affinities to the interwar modernist ferment that so influenced him, and despite
his work's obvious distance from several defining characteristics of tragedy as a
genre, Beckett never relinquished the ruthless massing of pressure and the terrifying
downward slide that together constitute the core of tragic form. This form is
linear, as is Beckett's, as is that of all great theater. The first of two major differences
between the modernist and his classical progenitors is that whereas in the latter
pressure intensifies from the burden of accumulating knowledge – knowledge of
the past, of the self, of the divine and fated world – in the former, the weight that
crushes feeds on compounding ignorance. The other, related, divergence is that, in
the Greeks, full disclosure generates finality – endings that are necessary, hortatory,
and summational – whereas, in Beckett, proliferations of the unknowable generate
incessant provisionality, endings that do not mean and therefore cannot end. It is
this last that lends Beckett's linearity – no less catastrophic than the Greeks' –
its curvature.

As the preceding link to classical form might imply, Beckett's spirals, by drawing
their magnetism from the singularity of their downward movement, turn each work
into an emblem. The source of the emblem is the same as the source of the spiral: the
conviction that the essential never arrives (Brater 1987: 22), that all we are left with
is "the collapsed ideal of the essentialist enterprise" (Webb 1972: 140), and, therefore,
that the artist's sole remaining path is to make us see and feel the absence of presence,
and the presence of absence, as exactly and as indelibly as possible. Not all ages,
however, have celebrated their emblem-makers equally. A style that might have

seemed, in the agora, a natural outgrowth of a people's myth-haunted imagination and ritual-ridden art can, in a more decentered time, appear artificial, obsessive, and inhuman. Put another way, I suggest that to contemporary actors, designers, directors, and audiences, the ruthless, emblematic singularity of Beckett's theater presents both a great hurdle and an offer of great renewal. (It is perhaps hardly necessary to say that all of the notorious difficulties over Beckett's stage-directions – pace, "color," settings, etc. – are at root a quarrel over the plays' emblematic core. For when this force is yielded to, it threatens an obliteration of self. When it is resisted, the works crumble in one's hands; one is left with nothing.)

As Dugald McMillan has pointed out, Beckett was himself ambivalent about the emblematic principle in his work (McMillan 1975: 128–35). In a poem from 1932, "A Casket of Pralinen for the Daughter of a Dissipated Mandarin," Beckett mocks his own "clumsy artistry," and is "ashamed / ... of everything but the ingenuous fibres / that suffer honestly" (in McMillan 1975: 128). McMillan finds other examples, primarily through the voices or portrayals of characters in the novels, of mockery of allegory, of "ironic treatment of the emblematic use of posture," of "the conflict between direct experience and artificial expression," and again, "between allegory and direct representation." This struggle to find "the means to present experience directly" and yet to "retain the emblematic mode," was one that would occupy Beckett throughout his working life. The struggle remained unresolved, for, of course, he did both, one through the other, though his techniques and balances changed over time. The late plays, for example, emerge, in a near paradox, as both less allegorical and more emblematic than the early ones, with Beckett hewing ever more closely to "the ingenuous fibres / that suffer honestly."

Beckett's ambivalence about the style is understandable. Emblematic performance in the contemporary world carries risks. Common responses to such an art focus on its didacticism, its predictability, its abstraction, its literariness, its coldness, its smugness, its oppressiveness, and its lack of fidelity to the flux of individual behavior and spontaneous event that characterize life as we know it. Beckett's controlling spiral, therefore, is very much a double-edged instrument. On the one hand, by introducing alteration within his works, it is those works' primary source of tension and feeling. On the other, its tyrannical nature courts dismissal.

Beckett's success, on the whole, in avoiding the pitfalls of an emblematic art is accomplished through a trio of related achievements: the peopling of his stage with figures who, while clearly emblems rather than "characters," somehow become distillates of humanity; the pinning of those emblems, like butterflies, to visual forms which are themselves emblems – emblem redoubled – but which, in turn, seem to become organic outcomes, concentrates, of the profoundly basic, existential realities that a web of language is weaving around them; and, finally, the capacity of those words to separate out irreducible human residue in formulations of unforgettable simplicity, beauty, and power.

Anchoring this tripartite design is the element in the center, for it is the interplay between the physical icon and the flow of consciousness that unlocks these grand and mysterious works. Beckett's frequent insistence on the primacy of the image, with the words a distant second in importance, should therefore be regarded with some skepticism, prompted as it almost certainly was by an understandable need to counter the subjectivism of Western acting and the decorative tendency in Western theater design and, by doing so, to get the image realized exactly. For, in any given play, its ceaselessly spinning central consciousness, made available to us in words of unerring simplicity and humanity, is the originating force which in effect creates its physical emblem. Thus, because May can't stop "revolving it all," May is physicalized as a wraith forever condemned to revolve her tiny patch of ground; because Mouth can't stop her "stream of words," Mouth is incarnated as a mouth that can't stop her stream of words, and so on.[8] What such a scheme mandates is a relationship between words and emblem that is analogous to that between a viewer and a movie screen. While the emblem's design exactly reflects the play's verbal content, it is itself emotionally neutral – hence Beckett's demand for impassive faces, which removes the actors' subjectivity from the equation. Thus is the audience freed to project upon the emblem – and receive reflected back from it – the full range of thought and feeling that the play's narrative web is spinning around both, emblem and spectator.

The centrality of consciousness, in short, makes it fairly clear that each work's dominant spiral grows out of the play's narrative and not out of its physical emblem. As a result, a significant thematic balance tilts away from the idea that such notorious physical dissolutions as Winnie's devouring mound, May's vanishing body, or the adulterous trio's fading imprint are the work of a malign external divinity. Rather, in every case, the plays' internal coherence and structural consistency, eschewing handy scapegoats, dictate that the diminishing spirals in the visible realm are intended to universalize, to summarize, to underline, and to lend a certain shocking overtness to the declensions of the controlling spiral, which always stem from the life at issue and which find their most devastating expression in the central consciousness's mind and words. For it is those words that, in the end, break our hearts and lift our spirits.

> Moments. Her moments, my moments. [*Pause.*] The dog's moments. [*Pause.*] In the end I held it out to him and he took it in his mouth, gently, gently. A small, old, black, hard, solid rubber ball. [*Pause.*] I shall feel it, in my hand, until my dying day. [*Pause.*] I might have kept it. [*Pause.*] But I gave it to the dog. [*Pause.*] Ah well ... (Beckett 1986: 220)[9]

Such passages – not rare in Beckett – render the individual mystery and trace the fine movements of a single soul as simply, spontaneously, complexly and profoundly as anything in realism's repertoire, even as the unyielding emblem – an old head bent over a memory machine – gathers into itself and offers back to us all those other souls, present and gone, who have obsessively sifted their lives' bitterest moments in search of succor. We watch with riven hearts – led by an incomparable language to union with the sufferer, pushed back into our own lives by the emblem's neutrality, and released to join our kind through the emblem's transparency. This gift from Beckett, which at root is a transformative modernization of the classical mask, is, to me, the single most important innovation in twentieth century theater for it re-legitimizes an emblematic art in a skeptical age.

NOTES

1 Mercier (1977: xii), "Nothing else I have written on Beckett has attracted so much notice as this ... one phrase in an *Irish Times* review of the Faber first printing of *Waiting for Godot*."

2 I include *Quad* despite its genesis as a work for television; it has been and continues to be staged. Beckett: "This original scenario (*Quad I*) was followed in the Stuttgart production by a variation (*Quad II*). ... No colour, all four in identical white gowns, no percussion, footsteps only sound, slow tempo, series 1 only." (Beckett 1986: 453–4).

3 Beckett, quoted by Martha Fehsenfeld, cited in Fletcher and Fletcher (1985: 260).

4 *Encounter*, September 1975, 44, cited in Fletcher and Fletcher (1985: 185–6).

5 See Brater (1987: 31) for an analysis of the shifts in visual focus that the Mouth/Auditor pairing is intended to enforce, and Knowlson and Pilling (1979: 195) for a perspective in which "this duality of focus has proved to be something of a dramatic weakness."

6 In this context it might be of interest to note that an analysis of Billie Whitelaw's performance in *Not I*, based on her filmed version, shows that her running time between the play's first printed word ("out") and last ("up") was 11 minutes and 30 seconds. However, she performed the first half of the text in six minutes, and the second in five and a half – an

8 percent acceleration. In my two most recent productions of the play, in which Wendy Salkind played Mouth, the overall running time was 11 minutes and 45 seconds, with the surge in tempo also registering at 8 percent. I did not ask Salkind to speak progressively faster, nor, as far as we know from the production information we have, did Beckett ask Whitelaw to do so. The intensification of the struggle is built into the journey.

7 See also Metman (1965: 120–32) for a similar judgment, though from a psychoanalytical perspective. It would be fair to keep in mind that these views were formed before the advent of the short plays from the last decade of Beckett's theater.

8 This would appear true of all the plays, early and late, the essential difference being that in the older works the physical icon includes relatively intact figures moving around in relatively recognizable ways, whereas in the newer works the icon is narrowed to the indispensable human bits isolated in the indispensable bits of light. In both cases, the emblem is stage-wide, the surrounding darkness in the later works forming the ground that defines the image – theatrically and ontologically.

9 For an extended analysis of this passage, and the play, *Krapp's Last Tape*, that contains it, see Knowlson and Pilling (1979: 81–92) and Knowlson (1972).

REFERENCES

Alvarez, A. (1973). *Samuel Beckett*. New York: Viking Press.

Beckett, Samuel (1954). *Waiting for Godot*. New York: Grove Press.

Beckett, Samuel (1974). *Not I*. In *Ends and Odds*. New York: Grove Press.

Beckett, Samuel (1986). *Play. Act Without Words I. A Piece of Monologue. Ohio Impromptu. Rockaby. Footfalls. Krapp's Last Tape*. In *Samuel Beckett: The Complete Dramatic Works*. London: Faber and Faber.

Brater, Enoch (1987). *Beyond Minimalism*. New York: Oxford University Press.

Cohn, Ruby (1973). *Back to Beckett*. Princeton: Princeton University Press.

Cohn, Ruby (1980). *Just Play: Beckett's Theatre*. Princeton: Princeton University Press.

Fletcher, Beryl and John Fletcher (1985) *A Student's Guide to the Plays of Samuel Beckett*. London: Faber and Faber.

Gontarski, S. E. (1985). *The Intent of Undoing in Samuel Beckett's Dramatic Texts*. Bloomington: Indiana University Press.

Gontarski, S. E. (ed.) (1999). *The Theatrical Notebooks of Samuel Beckett: The Shorter Plays*. London: Faber and Faber.

Harmon, Maurice ed. (1998). *No Author Better Served: The Correspondence of Samuel Beckett and Alan Schneider*. Cambridge, MA: Harvard University Press.

Kennedy, Andrew (1975). *Six Dramatists in Search of a Language*. Cambridge: Cambridge University Press.

Knowlson, James (1972). *Light and Darkness in the Theatre of Samuel Beckett*. London: Turret Books.

Knowlson, James, and John Pilling (1979). *Frescoes of the Skull*. London: John Calder.

McMillan, Dugald (1975). "Samuel Beckett and the Visual Arts: The Embarrassment of Allegory." In Ruby Cohn (ed.), *Samuel Beckett: A Collection of Criticism*. New York: McGraw-Hill.

Mercier, Vivian (1977) *Beckett/Beckett*. New York: Oxford University Press.

Metman, Eva (1965). "Reflections on Samuel Beckett's Plays." In Martin Esslin (ed.), *Samuel Beckett: A Collection of Critical Essays*. Englewood Cliffs, NJ: Prentice-Hall.

Webb, Eugene (1972). *The Plays of Samuel Beckett*. Seattle: University of Washington Press.

Worton, Michael (1994). "*Waiting for Godot* and *Endgame*." In John Pilling (ed.), *The Cambridge Companion to Beckett*. Cambridge: Cambridge University Press.

Zeifman, Hersh (1996). "The Syntax of Closure: Beckett's Late Drama." In Lois Oppenheim and Marius Buning (eds.), *Beckett On and On ...* London: Associated University Presses.

27
Beckett on Television

Graley Herren

No poet, no artist of any art, has his complete meaning alone. His significance, his appreciation is the appreciation of his relation to the dead poets and artists. You cannot value him alone; you must set him, for contrast and comparison, among the dead.

(T. S. Eliot, "Tradition and the Individual Talent")

Samuel Beckett situates his teleplays among the dead. The important effort to re-historicize his work in this area requires a kind of critical archeology, excavating layers of artifacts to reconstruct the uses Beckett makes of history, memory, and tradition. These compact plays for television are remarkably allusive, embedded with references to significant works of intellectual history, poetry, painting, and music – in other words, what once passed for Western civilization. But Beckett comes to bury tradition, not to praise it. He resuscitates the old masters only to kill them anew, working through his traditional sources toward decidedly countertraditional ends, erecting his teleplays upon the bones of the dead.

Beckett's own previous works must be numbered among the various expirations from which he draws inspiration in the teleplays. His proclivity for trilogies (or, more accurately, the proclivity of his critics to "trilogize" his works) makes it tempting to think of his six teleplays as a pair of trilogies. The thematic consistencies and intricate network of cross-references among the teleplays tend to reinforce the impulse. Nevertheless, this temptation should be resisted; Samuel Beckett was no George Lucas, and there is no evidence that he entered television with any kind of master plan. On the contrary, his ritual of preparation for a new production routinely concluded with a vow that this one would finally be his last. Yet he was periodically lured back to television as the most appropriate "memory machine" for working out a recurring obsession: namely, how to live with the dead. The teleplays are haunted by absent-yet-present specters whose traces and echoes animate the mourner's lonely room, much like the flickering, murmuring transmissions that emanate from the viewer's television set.[1] With each new teleplay he devised, Beckett revisited and revised his previous plays for the medium. Therefore, a cumulative sense of interconnectedness and trajectory does emerge, if only in retrospect. The result is that, as brief and quiet as these teleplays tend to be, each resonates with conversation, the latest installment in Beckett's long intertextual and intratextual dialogue with the dead.

Eh Joe

Beckett's first play for television, conceived in 1965 and produced in 1966, establishes the "telegiac" themes that dominate most of his subsequent work for the medium. As in most of the teleplays, a man sits alone in his room dwelling upon a lost love. In this case the man is Joe, a lapsed Catholic in his late fifties, and the lost lover assumes the form of Voice, a low, monotonous feminine voice-over. As the camera steadily closes in on the speechless Joe, Voice taunts him with reminders of his lecherous past. From a purely technical perspective, the conflict is straightforward. Just as Beckett routinely pitted words against music in the radio plays, he pits words against image in the television plays. Image struggles to strangle words into silence, while words strain to outlast the fading figure on screen. Judged solely on these technical grounds, Joe's image clearly prevails over Voice's words. We witness him "throttling the dead in his head" (Beckett 1986: 365), reducing Voice to a whisper before finally silencing her completely. In both the English premiere for BBC2 and the German premiere for SDR, Beckett punctuated Joe's technical knockout with an unscripted smile of victory. "I asked in London and Stuttgart for a smile at the end (oh not a real smile)," Beckett wrote Alan Schneider in April 1966. "He 'wins' again" (Harmon 1998: 202).

From a psychological perspective, however, Joe's conflict is far more complicated and his victory far less assured; his smile is not a real smile, and his win is only a "win." The original complication lies in the slippery ontological status of Voice. Though she is based upon a woman Joe once knew, her current manifestation is clearly something quite different: an imaginative recreation of Joe's own device, a ventriloquized voice inside his head. In effect, then, his conflict is internal – he is fighting himself. Furthermore, it is difficult to reconcile any claims of victory for Joe against the appalling – and potentially lethal – amount of psychic punishment he absorbs during the verbal barrage, particularly in the final rounds. After assuring Joe that she recovered completely from his jilting, Voice reminds him, "But there was one didn't ... You know the one I mean, Joe ... The green one ... The narrow one ..." The last time Joe saw the green one he was hustling her off to catch a flight, only to read shortly thereafter in the *Irish Independent* that she had died: "She went young ... No more old lip from her" (Beckett 1986: 365). She supposedly overdosed because she could not go on without Joe. I say "supposedly" because Joe simply cannot know for sure. She died alone, taking the mystery of exactly how and why she killed herself with her to the grave. In the absence of direct knowledge, Joe recreates a hypothetical account via his mental mouthpiece Voice. The extreme close-up on screen reveals a listener in rapt attention, as disturbed as he is fascinated, just like the engaged TV viewer staring and listening from his own lonely room. Joe ultimately squeezes his mind down hard enough to stifle out the voice, but not before the account of the green one's suicide is complete and the psychic damage is done.

Why would Joe, as the ventriloquist behind Voice, put himself through such a punishing ordeal? His morbid monologue assumes new resonance if one listens for echoes of Freud. Beckett's deep familiarity with Freud is by now well established. The most important Freudian intertext for the teleplays is "Mourning and Melancholia," his landmark study of what happens when grieving goes wrong and the mourner refuses to relinquish his dialogue with the dead. Unlike the "good" mourner, who works through his grief and eventually reconciles himself to the death of the loved one, the melancholic can neither accept the loss nor withdraw his libidinal attachment from the lost love-object. Instead, the melancholic keeps the undead love-object alive by internalizing her. The "self-reproaches and self-revilings" that Freud observes as symptomatic of melancholia are really hostilities designed for the lost lover but redirected inward, where the internalized object now resides. The melancholic's "delusional expectation of punishment" thus becomes a self-fulfilling prophecy, as the subject abuses the internalized object through reproaching and reviling himself. As Freud puts it, such self-abuse enacts "a satisfaction of trends of sadism and hate which relate to an object, and which have been turned round upon the subject's own self" (Freud 1975: 251). He even warns that, in extreme cases, the melancholic ego can become suicidal if "it can treat itself as an object – if it is able to direct against itself the hostility which relates to an object" (ibid.: 252). This is precisely Joe's condition by the end of *Eh Joe*.

For one attuned to the Freudian intertext, the teleplay reads like Joe's virtual suicide note. He sits on the edge of his bed, just as the green one is described before her suicide, and reviews her lethal trip to the water's edge as preparation for following in her footsteps. Voice speaks of and for a silenced woman driven to despair by abandonment. This is what her words tell us, but Joe's image tells a different story. We see a silenced man – no more old lip from him – who cannot reconcile himself to losing his lover. Like Freud's prototypical melancholic, Joe adopts various strategies for deferring and deflecting this loss, from sadistic resentment, to masochistic self-abuse, to psychic detachment complete enough to permit self-annihilation. *Eh Joe* depicts a virtual suicide, not an actual one. Like most of Beckett's characters, Joe is stalled in the penultimate stage, somewhere short of actually finishing himself off. But the deferral of his suicidal desire makes the impulse no less acute. Freud's "Mourning and Melancholia" provides the key to *Eh Joe*'s psychopathology, unlocking an otherwise banal play about hand-wringing Catholic guilt and revealing instead a complex rehearsal for self-martyrdom, "The passion of our Joe" (Beckett 1986: 364).

Ghost Trio and ... *but the Clouds* ...

In 1975 the BBC began planning a multimedia commemoration in honor of Beckett's seventieth birthday the following year. None of the available material on video added up to a satisfactory program, however, so Beckett set about devising a new work for the television portion of the celebration. His renewed efforts for the medium soon yielded two teleplays, *Ghost Trio* and ... *but the clouds.* ... Packaged alongside a filmed close-up of Billie Whitelaw's performance in *Not I*, the plays were broadcast together in 1977 under the "tele-trilogy" title *Shades* (in German *Schatten*).

  Ghost Trio and ... *but the clouds* ... must be considered in conjunction with one another, and not only because these two death-obsessed teleplays share the same birth date. Both pieces overtly announce their debts to previous artworks; *Ghost Trio* incorporates musical excerpts from Beethoven's Fifth Piano Trio in D Major (nicknamed "The Ghost"), and ... *but the clouds* ... takes its title and closing lines from Yeats's poem "The Tower." In addition to these intertextual dialogues, both works also maintain intratextual conversations with Beckett's previous filmed work. Gilles Deleuze describes *Ghost Trio* as "a kind of vocal and spatial purification" of *Eh Joe* (1997: 166). Just as *Eh Joe* presents a distillation of O's cluttered room in *Film*, *Ghost Trio* revisits the scenario of a man not-quite-alone in his room and pares it down further – only to be followed immediately by ... *but the clouds* ... with an even more austere treatment of the same theme. Moreover, *Ghost Trio* and ... *but the clouds* ... maintain an intratextual dialogue with one another, albeit muted and covert. Beckett admitted as much in a revealing letter to Dr Müller-Freienfels. He wrote to SDR's executive director on December 13, 1976 to stress the importance of casting the same actor as male lead in both teleplays (as Ronald Pickup had been in the BBC2 productions). He explained, "Though not expressly stated, the man in '... but the clouds ...' is the same as in *Ghost Trio*, in another (later) situation, and it would be a great pity if we could not have the same actor for the two parts" (BBC Written Archives, T51/350/1). This privileged communiqué confirms that *Ghost Trio* and ... *but the clouds* ... are more than mere stylistic companions or thematic cousins; the latter is in fact the direct descendent of the former. Accordingly, ... *but the clouds* ... should be credited as Beckett's first intentional sequel.

  Ghost Trio returns the viewer to the "familiar chamber." In the first section of the teleplay (labeled "Pre-action"), the viewer is directed through a visual tour of the room by a subdued female voice (V). She calls the shots for the camera, pointing out the room's few furnishings, culminating in the indispensable male figure (F). F spends most of his time slumped on a stool, listening to a cassette recording of Beethoven's "Ghost" trio and waiting for an unnamed "her" to arrive. The first interruption of this routine comes in the second section ("Action"), when V informs us (and him?), "He will now think he hears her" (Beckett 1986: 410). F checks at the door, finds no one, and then takes his own "tour" around the room. He follows the same pattern of examination established in the first section, with one notable exception. He stops and looks at the heretofore unacknowledged mirror, prompting a surprised exclamation from V. F's undirected and unanticipated deviation from V's established routine marks the beginning of a subtle power shift in the teleplay. V begins the play as the silent F's puppet-master (Beckett even advised his male actors to adopt the movement of an *Übermarionette*). Gradually, however, F cuts his puppet strings, usurping control over the governing patterns of this highly formalist play. The third and final section ("Re-action") is characterized less by its repetition of the established patterns than by its recomposition of them, introducing new close-ups, subjective shots, and even a silent boy who arrives at the door and shakes his head in the negative before retreating back down the corridor. *Ghost Trio* is itself a kind of recomposition of inherited forms. For instance, the excerpts from the Fifth Piano Trio are incorporated erratically and non-sequentially, a signature Beckettian gesture. The teleplay is at once mindful enough of Beethoven to quote him but irreverent enough to misquote him, counter-traditionally undermining the order and symmetry that characterized his traditional source. But Beckett even treats Beckett irreverently, returning to the "familiar chamber" established by his earlier work only to defamiliarize it. *Ghost Trio* decomposes the heated psychodrama of *Eh Joe* and recomposes it through the colder eye and ear of formalism.

Beckett uses his sequel to *Ghost Trio* to "Cast a cold eye / On life, on death," on memory and imagination, and on W. B. Yeats ("Under Ben Bulben," 1997: ll. 92–3). *... but the clouds ...* depicts the male figure (now labeled M instead of F) in a later situation, still waiting for the return of his woman lost (here abbreviated W). His situation has deteriorated in one sense: he crouches over his table throughout the teleplay, having lost his former mobility. However, his immobility is more than compensated for by his improved powers of speech and memory. With his newfound voice M recalls his ritualized vigil for W, when he would walk the roads all day, return home every night, retire to his "inner sanctum" and "beg, of her, to appear, to me" (Beckett 1986: 420). His narrative is accompanied by illustrative memory-images projected on screen. Whenever he describes his departures and returns, the camera dissolves to his former self (M1) walking marionette-style in hat and greatcoat; and whenever he narrates a trip to the "inner sanctum," the camera dissolves to M1 receding in robe and skullcap. Most remarkable of all, M calls to the mind's eye images of a Woman's face. He distinguishes three categories of W's appearance: 1) her face silently appeared and then immediately disappeared; 2) her face silently appeared, lingered briefly, and then disappeared; and 3) her face appeared, lingered briefly, mouthed out a few words from Yeats's "The Tower," and then disappeared. He also adds a fourth case, "by far the commonest, in the proportion say of nine hundred ninety-nine to one, or nine hundred and ninety-eight to two, when I begged in vain, deep down in the dead of night, until I wearied" (Beckett 1986: 421).

M testifies that his efforts to lure W back were largely unsuccessful, but the visual evidence on screen contradicts this testimony. In fact, M is able to conjure up W's image on screen eight separate times in a span of less than 20 minutes. Apparently M has become much more proficient at summoning his woman lost than F ever was.

Nevertheless, his efforts remain far from satisfactory; her features remain indistinct and she cannot, or will not, speak. M has acquired the *habit* of memory – the rote repetition of certain sequences and images – but only at the expense of involuntary memory's spontaneous revelation. As Beckett observes in *Proust*, "The man with a good memory does not remember anything because he does not forget anything. His memory is uniform, a creature of routine, at once a condition and function of his impeccable habit, an instrument of reference instead of an instrument of discovery" (1957: 17). Just so, M's habitual memory is merely an instrument of reference, a dependable machine devoid of any animating vitality. Henri Bergson explains this rote form of recollection in *Matter and Memory*:

> When we really wish to know a thing, we are obliged to learn it by heart, that is to say, to substitute for the spontaneous image a motor mechanism which can serve in its stead ... thanks to this faculty, we have no need to await at the hands of chance the accidental repetition of the same situations, in order to organize into a habit concomitant movements; we make use of the fugitive image to construct a stable mechanism which takes its place. (1912: 98)

M has learned how to produce a stable facsimile of W. Unfortunately, this deaf, dumb, and blind simulacrum lacks all the qualities that led him to long for her return in the first place.

The other problematic figure conjured on the memory screens of ... *but the clouds* ... is W. B. Yeats. In "The Tower," his masterful anthem to the imagination, Yeats asks the central question, "Does the imagination dwell the most / Upon a woman won or woman lost?" (1997: 113–14). Obviously, for Yeats as well as for M, the answer is the woman lost. But for Yeats she is never truly lost because of the recuperative powers of the imagination. He asserts that human consciousness is constitutive of all life, death, and after-life. Therefore, he draws comfort at the end of "The Tower" from his faith that the mind can overcome all the indignity, pain, and loss of this world and the next, making them

> Seem but the clouds of the sky
> When the horizon fades;
> Or a bird's sleepy cry
> Among the deepening shades. (ibid.: 192–5)

It should come as no surprise that Beckett rates the redemptive powers of the imagination considerably lower than Yeats. What is most interesting in ... *but the clouds* ... is how Beckett calls an earlier Yeats to the mind's eye to testify against the grandiose claims of "the Nobel Yeats."

Though the teleplay overtly acknowledges its debts to "The Tower," it actually draws more of its imagery from Yeats's earlier play *At the Hawk's Well*. That play opens with an invocation of the imagination by a chorus of musicians: "I call to the eye of the mind" (Yeats 2001: 1). The stage is thus established as an internal space, a mindscape much like the memory screens of ... *but the clouds* .... This mindscape features three characters: an Old Man besotted by memories and regrets; a Young Man (the Irish hero Cuchulain) seeking the elusive waters of immortality; and the mysterious Guardian of the Well, a speechless woman like W with "Pallor of an ivory face" (ibid.: 5), who guards the waters of immortality in the guise of a hawk. The Old Man has spent 50 years waiting in vain to drink from the well, and he rails against the pallid woman for refusing to speak to him (like M he ventriloquizes on her behalf) and for refusing to reward his vigilance. With the arrival of Cuchulain, the latest pilgrim to the well, the Old Man is reminded of his own youthful folly. As if he could turn back the clock to warn himself against wasting his life, the Old Man pleads with the Young Man to abandon the vain pursuit of immortality. The waters of immortality do eventually well up for a moment, but the weary Old Man and the distracted Young Man both miss their opportunities to drink. The play ends in bitter disappointment, unmistakably warning that the life dedicated to pursuing immortality is doomed to failure. Such a dark conclusion is far more consistent with ... *but the clouds* ... than with "The Tower." The pre-Nobel Yeats exhibited none of the post-Nobel Yeats's confidence in the omnipotence and death-defying immortality of the imagination – and neither does the post-Nobel Beckett. In ... *but the clouds* ... he essentially turns Yeats against himself, allusively enlisting *At the Hawk's Well* to help him destabilize the grand edifice of "The Tower." Once again, Beckett uses the "memory machine" of television to conjure up the dead, decompose his traditional sources, and recompose them for countertraditional purposes.

Quadrat I + II and *Nacht und Träume*

Even without recourse to Beckett's "sequel" letter to Müller-Freienfels, it is obvious that *Ghost Trio* and ... *but the clouds* ... work in tandem as companion pieces. They premiered side by side, they share common obsessions and performers, and they are constructed according to the same countertraditional blueprint. On the other hand, his next two television broadcasts, *Quadrat I + II* (1981) and *Nacht und Träume* (1983), are far more notable for their stark differences than for any similarities.[2] Nevertheless, they might be productively juxtaposed against one another since they represent opposite extremes in Beckett's approach to the medium.

"Quad," as it was called in manuscript form, was conceived upon the corpse of an abandoned mime for the actor Jack MacGowran. "J. M. Mime" (1963) posited a son and father (or mother) pacing through all the permutations of a bisected square playing area. When Beckett reconceived the mime some two decades later he erased all residue of naturalism, including character and conflict. *Quadrat I + II* features four players draped in colorful hooded gowns. They plod rapidly in rhythm with percussion instruments, following the bisected paths of a brightly lit square. They never acknowledge the camera or one another. The tele-mime's only complication is not a matter of dramatic conflict but of traffic control; whenever a player approaches the square's center, he or she (genders are indeterminable) deftly sidesteps the potential "danger zone" (Beckett 1986: 453). During production, Beckett happened to see a playback on an achromatic monitor and decided to append a brief "sequel" – with color removed, pace slowed, duration shortened, and percussion sounds replaced by the shuffle of feet – all said to take place "ten thousand years later" (Knowlson 1996: 593).

The resulting teleplay, transmitted by SDR as *Quadrat I + II*, is an aberration to every pattern Beckett had established in his previous work for the medium. There is no animating conflict between the characters and no countertraditional tension with artistic predecessors. For all its color and activity, this mime strikes me as Beckett's blandest and most static effort for television. Yet in some respects *Quadrat I + II* is a perfectly logical extension of certain nihilistic tendencies long latent in Beckett's work. He was always pulled between the poles of silence and speech, torn between the inability and the obligation to express. As an artist, Beckett was periodically driven to remount the Sisyphean slopes of memory and imagination in a foredoomed effort to "eff the ineffable." In a recently reprinted letter of March 9–10, 1949, to Georges Duthuit, Beckett perfectly captures these conflicting artistic impulses. Scrambling to account for the painter's irrepressible instinct, against all reason and desire, to continue expressing, he concedes, "If you ask me why the canvas doesn't remain blank, I can only invoke this clear need, forever innocent, to fuck it with color, if need be through vomiting one's being" (in Gontarski and Uhlmann 2006: 20). *Quadrat I + II* represents Beckett's most extreme televisual gesture toward realizing the nihilistic ideal of a blank canvas. Nonetheless, even in this most inscrutable telemime he cannot completely resist the urge to eff the ineffable, "to fuck it with color."

If *Quadrat I + II* represents Beckett's most radical attempt to empty a teleplay of expression, then *Nacht und Träume* represents his counterimpulse to apply layer upon layer of expression to the miniature televisual canvas. The action on screen is deceptively simple. The Dreamer (A) sits in the lower left quadrant of the screen. He hums the last seven bars of Schubert's lied *Nacht und Träume*, and then sings the final lines, "Holde Träume, kehret wieder!" (Sweet dreams, come again!). He then slumps over on his desk, apparently asleep. The upper right quadrant of the screen is slowly illuminated to reveal a mirror-image of the Dreamer, his dreamt self (B). A dumb show ensues, at once sacramental and maternal in its significance, between B and a pair of helping hands (the possessor of these hands remains invisible just off screen). The hands touch B upon the head, give him sup from a cup and wipe his brow with a cloth, and finally embrace him as he slumps back down upon his desk. Light fades down on B, and then the routines with A, B, and the helping hands are repeated exactly, with one important variation. The second time through the camera moves in for a close-up on the dream sequence, losing A from the screen. After B's embrace, the camera moves back, regaining A and losing B, before fading the entire screen to black. Once again, Beckett recycled a previously abandoned mime, "Mime du rêveur, A" ("Dreamer's Mime, A"), as his starting point for the teleplay. But he clearly consulted a number of other artistic sources in multiple media to complete the work.

The most blatant source is "Nacht und Träume," a romantic lied from his favorite composer, Schubert. In the lyric the singer pines for enchanting dreams that float down through the holy night. When daylight breaks and the dreams vanish, the woken dreamer pleads for the sweet dreams to return. On one level the teleplay seems simply to dramatize the action described in the lyric. Ultimately, however, Beckett manipulates his intertextual material in such a way as to break faith with Schubert just as he had with Beethoven and Yeats. He incorporates the closing line but removes its musical accompaniment, thus forcing the desperate lyric to stand without the crutch of Schubert's uplifting score. Furthermore, he arranges the teleplay so that it ends not on the dream's comforting embrace but upon the woken dreamer's lonely isolation. In other words, Beckett takes the closing prayer of "Nacht und Träume" – "Sweet dreams, come again!" – and remorselessly depicts it as an unanswered prayer.

Schubert is by no means the only source illuminating the holy night of *Nacht und Träume*. The teleplay is also strongly informed by Dante. Beckett's canon is replete with Dantean influence, most often from *Inferno* and *Purgatorio*. For his most meditative teleplay, however, he naturally turns to *Paradiso*. The imagery of B's dream sequence – chalice, cloth, and the "laying on of hands" – certainly suggests eucharistic connotations, but the dream is equally pregnant with maternal significance. Through the wish fulfillment of dream, the Dreamer returns to a maternal ideal where his basic needs – for someone to watch over him, feed him, clothe him, hold him – are all ministered by helping hands. These two lines of signification converge perfectly in the Holy Mother Mary. As Dante is led nearer to Mary in *Paradiso*, first by her surrogate Beatrice and then by her devotee St Bernard, his reactions anticipate those of B in the dream sequence. He can only look up briefly, so dazzling is Mary's brilliance, and he is reduced to the state of an infant. So, too, is Dante's heavenly supplicant "like the babe that stretches forth its arm / For very eagerness towards the breast / After the milk is taken" (2003: canto 23, ll.118–20).

More specifically, Beckett alludes to the pivotal scene in book 31 of *Paradiso* when Bernard replaces Beatrice as Dante's guide. The poet compares his adoration of Bernard to a pilgrim's awe while gazing at Veronica's famous cloth (ibid.: canto 31, ll. 93–101). SDR cameraman Jim Lewis confirms that Beckett had Veronica's cloth specifically in mind for B's dream sequence: "At the moment when [the hands] wipe the drops of perspiration from the brow of the character, Beckett simply said that the cloth made an allusion to the veil that Veronica used to wipe the brow of Jesus on the Way of the Cross. The imprint of Christ's face remains on the cloth" (Lewis 1990: 379). Veronica's cloth, the "vera icon" or "true image" of Christ, was one of the most venerated relics of the Church in Dante's time. This perfect replica was used to authenticate the physical existence of Christ. Beckett appropriates the concept from Dante but puts it to distinctly contemporary, unorthodox, meta-televisual use. The cloth within the dream is a rather straightforward allusion. But then B is himself a sort of "true image" of A as well, though not an exact replica. To add a final frame of complication, the television broadcast – *any* television broadcast – is itself essentially a "true image," a relic of seeming presence denoting performers who are in fact absent from the viewer, an artifact of a performance that is in fact already past. In its traditional use, Veronica's cloth sustained the continuing presence of Christ. In Beckett's countertraditional use, however, the "vera icon" instead becomes a reminder of ephemera and absence.

Ultimately the source with the most buried traces in this allusive teleplay is Christ's prayer in the Garden of Gethsemane. After scraping away a layer of Schubert and a layer of Dante, one finds that *Nacht und Träume* is at bottom an Agony in the Garden painting applied to the televisual canvas. During the evening of Christ's arrest, three of the four gospels record that he went with some disciples to the Garden of Gethsemane, where he prayed for deliverance from his looming sacrifice. The most detailed account is offered by Luke, who describes Christ, flanked by sleeping disciples, praying, "Father, if thou be willing, remove this cup from me" (Luke 22: 42, King James Version). Of course, God requires his son to drink from the cup of suffering, but in Luke's account he does send down a ministering angel to help strengthen Christ. Luke makes no mention of a cloth per se, but he does say "his sweat was as it were great drops of blood falling to the ground" (Luke 22: 44) – prefiguring that station of the cross where Veronica and her cloth will play their fateful parts. When Christ uses his own sweat and blood to reproduce a "self-portrait" on Veronica's cloth, he effectively initiates the tradition of Christian iconography that would dominate Western art for the next two millennia. As a lifelong student of that tradition, Beckett was well aware of painterly paradigms for depicting the Agony in the Garden, as the iconography of *Nacht und Träume* clearly demonstrates. Painters typically depict one or more sleeping disciples in a lower corner of the canvas. The viewer's gaze is directed toward the agonized Christ, who always dominates the center of the painting. But Christ redirects the viewer's gaze toward an upper corner of the canvas, occupied by one or more angels bearing one or more instruments of the Passion (for example, chalice, cloth).[3] Beckett faithfully reproduces all of these paradigmatic elements in his "Agony on the Screen." However, he exploits the dimension of time – an element at his disposal as a televisual artist but unavailable to the "Old Masters" – to undermine the traditional function of Agony in the Garden paintings. The Old Masters used their paintings didactically to elicit empathy for Christ's suffering and gratitude for his sacrifice, making our own redemption through Christ possible. Beckett, on the other hand, spurns any impulse for "televangelism." He indulges the beauty and solemnity of this fantasy, only to dissolve the image on screen. Having glimpsed this divine vision, the supplicant A is ultimately left alone, the dream fled, the prayers for comfort, deliverance, and redemption unanswered.

Was Wo

Nacht und Träume was the last play Beckett conceived originally for television. However, he did return to the SDR studios one more time in 1985 for a significantly reconceived TV-adaptation of his final stage play, *What Where*. This final teleplay aired under the German title *Was Wo* on April 13, 1986, Beckett's eightieth birthday.

Once again, the written text fixes its gaze firmly toward the past, alluding to numerous previous artworks including several from Beckett's own oeuvre. However, *Was Wo*'s greatest importance lies in Beckett's forward-looking methodology. He fundamentally revised the play in the transfer from stage to screen, proving that he was far more amenable to creative adaptation and collaborative input than his reputation as an intransigent despot would suggest. He readily and radically reinvented *What Where* as *Was Wo* to take advantage of the new opportunities afforded by a different medium. Beckett's disinclination to treat his final play as precious or sacrosanct should serve as a corrective to his overzealous protectors – and as an instructive model for future artists interested in adapting his work.

In its original stage conception, *What Where* is presided over by the disembodied Voice of Bam (V), funneled into the auditorium through a suspended megaphone. The stage itself serves as a mindscape on which V rehearses performances of memory. These memories take the form of interrogations. As the seasons and years pass, Bam summons one interrogator after another (Bom in the spring, Bim in the summer, Bem in the autumn, Bam himself in the winter). He assigns each interrogator to take a suspect off stage and "give him the works" until he confesses "what" and "where." When each successive interrogator returns having failed to coerce the required information, Bam turns on him and treats him as a suspect, sending him off with the next interrogator to be given the works. In the end Bam is alone with no one left to question and with no desire left to seek answers: "Make sense who may. / I switch off" (Beckett 1986: 476).

Making sense of this highly retrospective play leads one back to several intertexts. In his annotations to the revised script of *What Where*, S. E. Gontarski cites allusions to Franz Schubert's song-cycle *Der Wintereisse*, Thomas Moore's Scottish air "Oft, in the Stilly Night," and Arthur Rimbaud's sonnet "Voyelles" (Gontarski 1999: 449–52). The odd character names find their antecedents in Beckett's fiction: "Bim" and "Bom" Clinch are asylum nurses in *Murphy*, and Bem and Bom (and Pim) appear in *How It Is*. Still deeper intratextual roots connect *What Where* to Beckett's radio plays. The play's opening lines directly echo the beginning of *Cascando*, and V's function as detached "opener" and "closer" of the action seems modeled directly after Opener's job description in that play. *What Where* bears an even closer family resemblance to *Rough for Radio II*. This radio play likewise features interrogation and torture for purposes that seem as vague to the victimizers as to the victims. Animator admits to his prisoner Fox, "Of course we do not know, any more than you, what exactly it is we are after, what sign or set of words. But since you have failed so far to let it escape you, it is not by harking on the same old themes that you are likely to succeed, that much would astonish me" (Beckett 1986: 282). Though *What Where* differs stylistically a great deal from the more naturalistic *Rough for Radio II*, both works affirm Schopenhauer's observation about torture in *The World as Will and Representation*: "The inflicter of suffering and the sufferer are one. The former errs in believing he does not share the suffering; the latter, in believing he does not share the guilt" (1966: bk 4, l.219).

When Beckett agreed to "switch on" again and direct a German TV-version of *What Where*, he embarked upon a wholesale reconsideration of the play's iconography. In so doing he followed the exemplary precedent set by *Comédie*, the 1966 French film adaptation of *Play* on which Beckett collaborated significantly. Marin Karmitz, the primary director of the film, reports that his pre-production discussions with Beckett focused "first, on the abandon[ment] of filmed theatre. On what cinema, image and editing could bring" (Karmitz 2001: 73). Likewise, Beckett clearly had no interest in merely replicating his stage version of *What Where* for the screen. Instead he abandoned any notion of "filmed theatre" in favor of creative adaptation appropriate to the new medium. For instance, he recognized that the stage play's megaphone effect, whereby the Voice of Bam is funneled into the auditorium from some mysterious elsewhere, simply could not translate to television, where the sound source is necessarily the TV set. Rather than keep faith with an irrelevant stage concept, he dismissed the megaphone in favor of putting a face upon the Voice of Bam. Cameraman Jim Lewis called upon all his technical ingenuity to create a distorted "death mask" for V (Fehsenfeld 1986: 236). The Face of V occupies the entire upper-left quadrant of the screen, presiding over the action and dwarfing the other players. The B-ms are reduced in *Was Wo* to small illuminated faces against a black field, fading into and out of the darkness via the editing process rather than entering and exiting through their own volition. As innovative as these technical effects may seem, they are in fact borrowed almost exactly from the *Comédie* film, where illuminated faces of varying sizes stare back at the spectator from a dark screen. That intratextual debt notwithstanding, the salient point is that Beckett and his crew exploited all of the technical tools at their disposal to transform the stage play *What Where* into the teleplay *Was Wo*. Though the latter work is not completely consistent with the former, it is consistent with Beckett's countertraditional methodology as exhibited throughout the teleplays. He tenaciously decomposes and recomposes his source texts, even those that initiate from his own pen. *Was Wo* stands finally as Beckett's testament that transgeneric adaptations of his works are indeed possible, but only if the creative team renounces complete fidelity to the original in favor of creative medium-specific adaptation.

This same adaptive principle informs the best offerings in *Beckett on Film*, the ambitious film festival and subsequent DVD box-set that includes 19 new film versions of the stage plays. For all the legitimate faults one might find with individual productions, the project is on the whole a superb example of creative adaptation in the "after Beckett." For instance, Anthony Minghella's *Play* departs radically from the stage play in terms of mise-en-scène and lighting, much to the dismay of Beckett's purist defenders. Yet I would counter that Minghella devised a perfectly legitimate cinematic correlative to the original, a film imbued with Beckett's spirit of innovation rather than calcified in sycophantic restatement. The brightest prospect for the future of the teleplays would be for bold directors to breathe fresh life into them. A *Beckett on Television* project analogous to *Beckett on Film* could give creative artists the opportunity to reinvent Beckett's teleplays much as he reinvented his own artistic mentors. Beckett's productions for the BBC and SDR best evince this countertraditional approach, so one might hope that the groundwork for a *Beckett on Television* project might be laid by first distributing those earlier productions which now languish in archival obscurity. The "after Beckett" era also promises transgeneric adaptations in the opposite direction from *Was Wo*; witness the recent successful run of Atom Egoyan's stage adaptation of *Eh Joe*. This is precisely the sort of creative rethinking of the teleplays that is needed. Surely the best way to keep these works alive is for critics and practitioners to continue the countertraditional dialogues with the dead begun in the teleplays, even when the tradition being countered is Beckett's own.

NOTES

1 For a fuller discussion of Beckett's use of television as a "memory machine," see Herren (2007).

2 This teleplay is referred to variously as *Quad*, *Quad I & II*, and *Quadrat 1 + 2*; however, the videotape I have viewed of the SDR broadcast lists the title verbatim as *Quadrat I + II*. Since

most of my comments refer specifically to that production, as distinct from any published text of the play, I defer to that title.

3 For reproductions of several representative paintings from this tradition, see Herren (2001).

REFERENCES

Beckett, Samuel (1964). *Film.* Dir. Alan Schneider. Perf. Buster Keaton, James Karen, Susan Reed, and Nell Harrison. Evergreen Theater, New York.

Beckett, Samuel (1957). *Proust.* New York: Grove Press.

Beckett, Samuel (1966a). *Eh Joe.* Dir. Alan Gibson. Perf. Jack MacGowran and Siân Phillips. British Broadcasting Corporation, London.

Beckett, Samuel (1966b). *Comédie.* Dir. Marin Karmitz. Perf. Delphine Seyrig, Michaël Lonsdale, and Eléonore Hirt. MK Productions, Paris.

Beckett, Samuel (1966c). *He Joe.* Dir. Samuel Beckett. Perf. Deryk Mendel and Nancy Illig. Süddeutscher Rundfunk, Stuttgart.

Beckett, Samuel (1977a). *... but the clouds ....* Dir. Donald McWhinnie and Samuel Beckett. Perf. Ronald Pickup and Billie Whitelaw. *Shades.* British Broadcasting Corporation, London.

Beckett, Samuel (1977b). *Geistertrio.* Dir. Samuel Beckett. Perf. Klaus Herm and Irmgard Först. *Schatten.* Süddeutscher Rundfunk, Stuttgart.

Beckett, Samuel (1977c). *Ghost Trio.* Dir. Donald McWhinnie and Samuel Beckett. Perf. Ronald

Pickup, Billie Whitelaw, and Rupert Horder. *Shades.* British Broadcasting Corporation, London.

Beckett, Samuel (1977d). *... nur noch Gewölk ...* Dir. Samuel Beckett. Perf. Klaus Herm and Kornelia Boje. *Schatten.* Süddeutscher Rundfunk, Stuttgart.

Beckett, Samuel (1981). *Quadrat I + II.* Dir. Samuel Beckett. Perf. Helfrid Foron, Jürg Hummel, Claudia Knupfer, and Susanne Rehe. Süddeutscher Rundfunk, Stuttgart.

Beckett, Samuel (1983). *Nacht und Träume.* Dir. Samuel Beckett. Perf. Helfrid Foron, Dirk Morgner, and Stephan Pritz. Süddeutscher Rundfunk, Stuttgart.

Beckett, Samuel (1985). *Was Wo.* Dir. Samuel Beckett. Perf. Friedhelm Becker, Edwin Dorner, Walter Langwitz, and Alfred Querbach. Süddeutscher Rundfunk, Stuttgart.

Beckett, Samuel (1986). *... but the clouds.* Cascando. Eh Joe. Ghost Trio. Nacht und Träume. Quad. Rough for Radio II. What Where. In *The Complete Dramatic Works,* ed. S. E. Gontarski. London: Faber and Faber.

Beckett, Samuel (2001). *Play*. Dir. Anthony Minghella. Perf. Juliet Stevenson, Alan Rickman, and Kirstin Scott Thomas. Blue Angel, Dublin, 2001.

Beethoven, Ludwig von. *"Der Geist."* Piano Trio in D Major. Opus 70, Number 1.

Bergson, Henri (1912). *Matter and Memory*, trans. Nancy Margaret Paul and W. Scott Palmer. New York: Macmillan.

Dante, Alighieri (2003). *The Divine Comedy*, trans. John Ciardi. New York: New American Library.

Deleuze, Gilles (1997). "The Exhausted." In Daniel W. Smith and Michael A. Greco (trans.) *Essays Critical and Clinical*. Minneapolis: University of Minnesota Press.

Eliot, T. S. (1997). "Tradition and the Individual Talent." *The Sacred Wood: Essays on Poetry and Criticism*. London: Faber and Faber.

Fehsenfeld, Martha (1986). "'Everything Out but the Faces': Beckett's Reshaping of *What Where* for Television." *Modern Drama* 29(2): 229–40.

Freud, Sigmund (1975). "Mourning and Melancholia." *The Standard Edition of the Complete Psychological Works of Sigmund Freud*, Vol.14, trans. and ed. James Strachey. London: Hogarth Press.

Gontarski, S. E. (ed.) (1999). *The Theatrical Notebooks of Samuel Beckett, Volume IV: The Shorter Plays*. London, New York: Faber and Faber, Grove Press.

Gontarski, S. E. and Anthony Uhlmann (eds.) (2006). *Beckett After Beckett*. Gainesville: University of Florida Press.

Harmon, Maurice (ed.) (1998). *No Author Better Served: The Correspondence of Samuel Beckett and Alan Schneider*. Cambridge, MA: Harvard University Press.

Herren, Graley (2001). *"Nacht und Träume as Beckett's Agony in the Garden." Journal of Beckett Studies* 11(1): 54–70.

Herren, Graley (2007). *Samuel Beckett's Plays on Film and Television*. New York: Palgrave Macmillan.

Karmitz, Marin (2001). Interview with Elisabeth Lebovici. *Comédie / Marin Karmitz / Samuel Beckett*, trans. Catherine Facerias, ed. Caroline Bourgeois. Paris: Editions du Regard.

Knowlson, James (1996). *Damned to Fame: The Life of Samuel Beckett*. New York: Simon & Schuster.

Lewis, Jim (1990). "Beckett et la camera." Interview with Sandra Solov. *Revue d'esthétique*, special edition: 371–9.

Schopenhauer, Arthur (1966). *The World as Will and Representation*. 2 vols, 2nd edn., trans. E. F. J. Payne. New York: Dover.

Schubert, Franz. *"Nacht und Träume."* Opus 43, Number 2.

Yeats, W. B. (1997). *The Collected Works of W.B. Yeats, Volume I: The Poems, Second Edition*, ed. Richard J. Finneran. New York: Scribner.

Yeats, W. B. (2001). *At the Hawk's Well. The Collected Works of W. B. Yeats, Volume II: The Plays*, ed. David R. Clark and Rosalind E. Clark. New York: Scribner.

28
Staging Beckett in Spain: Theater and Politics

Antonia Rodríguez-Gago

Despite his unprecedented international popularity, Beckett remains a "marginal" playwright in Spain, where he is still seen as a difficult and obscure artist, his plays always produced outside the "official" theaters. The first of his plays to be produced in Spain was, of course, *Esperando a Godot* (*Waiting for Godot*), in 1955; the frequency and quality of subsequent productions of his works has, however, been inconsistent. In Spain, Beckett is usually considered a hard realist and a dramatic poet. As a result, his plays have often been, overtly related to the political and cultural climate of the moment when they were produced. They were least prevalent during the 1960s and early 1970s, the dark years of political repression and cultural censorship in Spain; however, they experienced a rebirth during the 1980s, and theatrical artists, audiences, and critics rediscovered Beckett's theater. This change was in good part the result of an improved climate of democratic "normalization" in the Spanish cultural and socio-political life in the decade after General Franco's death. Nowadays, Beckett's plays are often produced in "Salas alternativas" (fringe theaters) and seldom in large theaters.

Staging Beckett's Plays: 1955 to 1980

Beckett's theater arrived in Spain during very difficult times of political dictatorship. Trino Martínez Trives, a key figure in the introduction of French avant-garde theater to Spain, brought his plays over from France in the late 1950s. The premiere of *Esperando a Godot* attracted all of the forces opposed to the fascist regime and was both a political and artistic event.

> the play was not even granted a one day license by the censors and so no theatre wanted to produce it. In the 1950s and 1960s the fascist censorship exerted a stifling influence on the performing arts, and almost everything coming from abroad was

banned, especially if it came from France or Britain, nations which had helped the "wrong" party in the Spanish Civil War. (Rodríguez-Gago 1987: 45–6)

After being refused a license by the censors, Martínez Trives went to the Rector of the Universidad Complutense de Madrid, Pedro Laín Entralgo, and asked for permission to perform the play in the Assembly Hall of the Faculty of Arts. Its clandestine production there on May 28, 1955 by the group Pequeño Teatro, under the direction of Martínez Trives himself, transformed the staging into a symbolic act in support of the freedom of artistic expression. Martínez Trives told me that the tension on the first night was great, and the fairly large university theater was packed. He thought that the right-wing people who attended the performance were going to stop it at any moment, but the great support of the majority of the audience prevented the right-wingers from jeering. Next year, a different group, Dido Pequeño Teatro, directed by Josefina Sánchez-Pedreño, produced the play in the theater of the Círculo de Bellas Artes in Madrid on March 28. Audiences and critics alike were deeply divided in their response to the play. For some critics, Beckett was "a fraud admired by the Spanish cultural snobs" (Alfredo Marquerie, quoted in Alvaro 1960: 174); for others, he was "a theatrical genius, true heir of Calderón, Unamuno, and Valle-Inclán" (Domenech 1959: 4). This division was observable in the audience's immediate reaction to the work, as some gave a standing ovation while others jeered and walked out. This divided response to Beckett's plays was typical in the 1950s and 1960s and the response to *Endgame* was even more pronounced.

Two groups competed for the right to produce the premiere of *Final de partida* (*Endgame*). Dido Pequeño Teatro, possibly the best experimental group of the time, won the battle and presented the play on June 1, 1958, in the theater of the Circulo de Bellas Artes of Madrid. The Spanish version was translated by Luce Moreau and directed by González Vergel. A few days later, the acting group Los Independientes, under the direction of Javier Laffleur, staged the same play in the Teatro Recoletos using Trino Martínez Trives's version. Because of the different styles of the directors, the two productions were very dissimilar. González Vergel said that he wanted to transmit that beneath the anguish and desperation of the play lay a "certain serenity and harmony"; Javier Laffleur, on the other hand, thought that *Final de partida* should have "an irritating quality" and its pace should be rapid (González-Vergel and Laffleur 1959: 23). The critical response to *Final de partida* was similar to the one that greeted *Esperando a Godot*, except that the attacks from establishment critics, who considered Beckett an atheist and a nihilistic playwright and his dramatic language vulgar and obscene, were even more pronounced.

The premiere of *La última cinta* (*Krapp's Last Tape*) took place on November 5, 1962 and was directed by José Guevara. *La última cinta* once again raised the ire of conservative critics, but it also received some very positive reviews from a very significant minority. The passionate arguments the play caused for and against the importance of Beckett's theater reached their high point just after the first production. Gómez Picazo's review, which appeared in the newspaper *Madrid*, is perhaps the best example of this kind of anti-Beckett criticism: "[*La última cinta*] is an atheistic and amoral play ... with no value whatsoever in our world, which still believes in higher values. The actor was Italo Ricardi, God forgive him!"(Alvaro 1978: 162). On the other hand, García Pavón, a writer and drama teacher, wrote, "It is impossible to stage more economically and with such dramatic intensity, the tragedy of a man who suddenly sees frustration pouring upon him" (ibid.: 163). Such controversy died down some when Beckett was awarded the Nobel Prize in 1969.

Before this conservative backlash died out, *Días felices* (*Happy Days*) was staged by Trino Martínez Trives and premièred during a Theater Festival at the Teatro María Guerrero of Madrid in 1963. The play "officially" debuted the following year, May 14, 1964, at the Teatro Valle-Inclán in Madrid. This production was repeated in 1965 and, with slight changes, was taken on tour to various Spanish cities in 1974. *Los días felices* was the last Beckett production by Martínez Trives, who, unfortunately, abandoned the Spanish theatrical scene too soon.

The Madrid-based experimental group Los Goliardos, directed by Angel Facio, staged *Beckett 66* on December 10, 1966. This production included *Eh Joe*, *Vaivén* (*Come and Go*), and *Palabras y música* (*Words and Music*). The best comments on this production, which was well received by audiences, came from the group itself in its program note: "We were attracted by the interest of the texts and the unique personality of their Irish author ... our own failings due to our professional immaturity are compensated for by our findings in this risky field of theatrical experimentation. Spectators, you will be our only judges!" In 1967 *Beckett 66* was invited to the Festival de Teatro Independiente of Valladolid, where Los Goliardos introduced Julio Castronuovo, an Argentinean mime and theater director, to the Spanish public in an interesting two-part show titled *Pantomimas en blanco y negro*, by Julio Castronuovo, and Beckett's *Acto sin palabras I*. Castronuovo's performance in both mimes was very much praised by critics.

The political situation of Spain in the 1950s, 1960s, and early 1970s was not, in fact, very different from that of many Latin American countries of this period, and Spanish stage directors, like their Latin American colleagues, favored a theater of protest and political commitment, neglecting the more daring experimental plays. With few exceptions, radical theater directors turned to Brecht, not to Beckett, for their productions, a trend that helps explains why Beckett's plays have almost always been staged in small theaters.

With the arrival of political democracy in the late 1970s and early 1980s, some professional actors, stage directors, and established independent theater companies turned to Beckett, and their approach to staging his plays changed as well. The earlier stigma attached to him fell away, and he came to be regarded as a master of theatrical language with a corrosive sense of humor. By the end of the 1970s, Beckett had become relatively established in the official theater circles because of the initiative of a group of very well-known Spanish actresses who staged *Waiting for Godot*. Paz Ballesteros, who produced the play, told me in an interview (October 7, 1985, Madrid), that she fell in love with Beckett's 1975 Schiller Theater production when she saw it at Belgrade's International Theater Festival. She gave the text to her stage-director husband, Vicente Sáinz de la Peña, with a note: "write a Spanish stage version of this, because we are going to produce it." They looked for a male cast, but good actors refused or were unavailable, so they decided to produce the play with an all-female cast; on September 13, 1978, the independent theater company Teatro Estable Castellano staged *Esperando a Godot* in the Teatro Martín of Madrid. Paz Ballesteros was Didi, Rosa María Sardá, the popular Catalan actress, played Gogo, Maite Brik played Lucky, and Maruchi Fresno (the first Spanish Winnie) was Pozzo. Although a female *Waiting for Godot* has always been very problematic because the language of the play is clearly male, many found this production to be extremely impressive. Although the predominant tone of this production was comic, the underlying anguish latent in the play was brought to the fore by the acting and precise staging.

In the 1980s, Spain modernized and freedoms were expanded. These changes were especially important for the artists, and this period boasts many – and perhaps some of the best – productions of Beckett's plays in Spain. A series of events that ran parallel to this ideological liberation also revealed that there were more Beckettians in the country than many assumed. The 1980s opened with two outstanding productions of *Final de partida*, one in Logroño in 1980 and another in Madrid in 1984. In the same year, José Sanchis Sinisterra directed the first Catalan production of *Happy Days – Oh els bons dies* – in Barcelona February 28, 1984 at the Teatro Regina, with the great Rosa Novell as Winnie. In 1985, the Circulo de Bellas Artes of Madrid held an important homage to Beckett: "Muestra sobre la vida y la obra de Samuel Beckett." This event consisted of 10 Beckett plays, five of which were Spanish premieres, as we shall see below.

Nuclear Terror and the Death of a Dictator: Two Spanish "Endgame(s)"

In 1980 Julio Castronuovo directed *Final de partida* for the well-known theater group Teatro Estable Adefesio of Logroño. Ricardo Romanos played Hamm, Agustin Oteiza was Clov, and Damian Rodríguez and Pilar Santamaría were Nagg and Nell respectively. Since its Argentinean premiere in 1961, Castronuovo had directed *Final de partida* on four occasions and changed his staging very little. His different productions were centered on the theme of loneliness; for him the emotional isolation of the characters is prevalent in *Endgame*: "three generations are isolated and their relationships deteriorate, little by little, creating a situation of growing tension and violence … one *feels* the oppression of human beings over human beings" (interview with the author on his various productions of *Endgame*, May 4, 1986, Madrid). The play's set, created by Cesar Ocho, was a metal structure that looked like the interior of a submarine, and contained two small rectangular windows, which were placed very high up, and a door to the right, which led to Clov's kitchen. The props were limited to two huge tin dustbins and a big unfamiliar looking armchair on castors with two unusual long poles on its back.

The acting was non-realistic. Being a mime himself, Castronuovo devotes a great deal of attention to finding the specific movements and gestures best suited to the actors' roles. Thus, when directing *Final de partida*, he created "robot-like movements, with strong changes of rhythm" for Clov (ibid.). In the initial mime, there is a pattern to how Clov goes up and down the stairs, and it is balanced through opposition; Clov would often go up the stairs very slowly and come down very quickly or vice versa. Hamm's gestures were at times very stylized. Castronuovo says that sometimes, "he moved his arms very slowly and others with exaggerated symbolic gestures, especially when he is (or pretends to be) furious with Nagg or Clov. This created a certain parallelism between Clov's and Hamm's gestures" (ibid.), which helped to create a visual pattern in this production that echoed the verbal. Nagg's miming of the story of the tailor is characteristic of Castronuovo's emphasis on gesture. Castronuovo explains that the gestures made the story much funnier: "Nagg's gestures underlined the verbal comedy." Audiences liked Nagg's "little act" very much, but, judging from production photos, one could certainly argue that his body was too visible, and he seemed too alive for his role. The concepts of mutual dependence and enforced imprisonment were underlined in this production. The characters were portrayed as the only humans remaining after a nuclear explosion. In a program note, this idea of nuclear terror is emphasized together with other similar impending terrors, which brought the production into the historical present: "Under the empire of nuclear, multinational, microelectronic terror ... of hunger, of lack of energy, of Jomeinisms and apocalyptic redeemers around the corner ... etc, to stage Beckett seemed to us the necessary step to start this hopeful 1980" (program note). The performance was very well received and the most repeated adjectives in reviews of this *Final de partida* were "brilliant," "intelligent," and "imaginative."

On January 4, 1984, the company Teatro del Arte, under the direction of Miguel Narros, one of the best and most popular Spanish theater directors, staged *Final de partida* in the Sala Cadarso of Madrid. Narros's staging evolved around what he saw as the central idea of the play: the end of a dictator. His direction stressed the *nec tecum nec sine te* situation (neither with you nor without you), the mutual dependence between the two main characters, and the latent hatred and violence that such a situation engenders. Narros had two excellent actors in the main roles, Francisco Vidal as Clov and Manuel de Blas as Hamm, who were very well suited to their roles, Vidal small and thin and de Blas tall and corpulent. The set, a wonderful bare gray room, was created by Juan Gutiérrez and Andrea D'Odorico. They incorporated some extra elements to those suggested by Beckett, the most visible being a large closed door upstage center. They also suspended a conical lamp center stage and used it to project a circular luminosity on the central playing area, which included Hamm's chair and Nagg and Nell's large metal dustbins. A huge ladder stood stage right, close to Clov's kitchen door and established a sort of visual parallelism with the dustbins. The ladder was initially covered by a white cloth, which added a certain mystery to the set.

While these were the most significant additions to Beckett's set, they were by no means the only ones. Clov's possessions at the end of the play were enlarged to include a backpack and an oar, which was tied to his suitcase. The lighting created an atmosphere of grayness with a luminous touch of pale gray at center stage. An extra lighting effect was added at the end of the play, creating suspense. When Clov was ready to leave, he opened the large upstage door, which was closed during the whole performance. The door was now strongly illuminated only to reveal another closed door. This addition suggested an endless series of closed doors, and the audience was made to feel that there was no way out for Clov. However, at the same time, the fact that another door was there suggests the possibility that an opening to the outside world may lie behind it, and viewers might assume that if Clov were ever to gather the necessary strength to depart, he may finally open this door and abandon Hamm. This final image thus remains ambiguous because the final blackout occurs before the spectators know if Clov will find the strength necessary to open the door and go. One might argue that these added elements are totally unnecessary and that "less is always more" when staging a Beckett play. However, in this case, these extra elements worked and did not mar the visual economy that is essential in any staging of *Endgame*.

Narros slowed down *Final de partida* to make the action move at a relentlessly slow pace, which caused this performance to last about two hours. By prolonging Clov's painful and funny business of going up and down the stepladder, Narros irritated spectators who were waiting for some kind of action to take place but were instead faced with constant repetitions of the same inanities. In *Final de partida,* Narros says, "time turns around itself with endless monotony and it is measured only by Clov's trailing footsteps ... which reach us with a discontinuous rhythm, the only living beat in this dead space" (Narros 1984: 10). The director compared this oppressive relationship between the two protagonists and the violence it generates to the dynamic at work in countries under fascist regimes. The people who live in such countries are waiting for the death of the dictator in order to be released from an unbearable situation of torture and violence, but that death seems to be endlessly delayed and, like Clov, they endure all kinds of cruelties and humiliations while they wait. Narros sees Hamm not only as a dictator, but also as a symbol for a kind of cruel divinity on which people depend. He wanted Manuel de Blas to adopt a very majestic and hieratic attitude, like "a kind of Pantocrator," and de Blas's powerful physical presence was well suited to suggesting such an image.

During his production, Narros demonstrated his ability to get the most out of his actors. De Blas's excessive movements and gestures as Hamm were often difficult to control, and in order to address this problem, the director decided to have the actor tied to the chair during rehearsals to prevent him from falling off it during the show. After this forceful checking of his extra movements, de Blas's acting became superb. His imposing physical presence and extraordinary range of voice were especially impressive. He mastered Hamm's frequent changes of tone and rhythm, although he spoke too loudly at times. Francisco Vidal's Clov conveyed the right note of contained desperation through his rigid, painful walk, the monotonous tone of voice, and the constant doubts and hesitations he exhibits before obeying Hamm. Enrique Menéndez and Paca Ojea, their white, old but childish-looking faces covered with white plaster and so reminiscent of the characters in *Play*, were marvelous in the roles of Nagg and Nell. They produced a comic yet pathetic effect; the actors depicted talking corpses, but they deluded themselves and the audience into thinking they were still very much alive by evoking sentimental memories.

Theater critics saluted this production of *Final de partida* as excellent. The play proved to be far more accessible in 1984 than it was in 1958 when it premiered. Nearly every critic lauded the power of Beckett's characteristic humor: "now audiences laugh and laugh at that which is unhappy" (Haro-Tecglen 1984). Critics also appreciated the author's courage in presenting situations of human impotence through powerful stage images. As is common among Spanish theater critics, Beckett was again considered a hard realist and connections were made between *Final de partida* and Spain's recent political past. More personally, the poet and critic Juan Mollá confessed to having been "deeply moved and disturbed by this extraordinary play" in which "one is made to feel, dramatically, the last moments of a game, or of a life, reaching thus a kind of mystical experience" (Mollá 1984). Almost all reviews repeated the idea that Spanish audiences understood Beckett's theater much better now than they did in the 1950s and 1960s. Since the new generation had grown up with the menace of a possible nuclear war and hecatomb, they could easily imagine such empty and devastated landscapes and the limited and painful personal situations present in the play.

From Politics to Dramatic Poetry: Beckett in the Círculo de Bellas Artes

The most important and successful attempt in Spain to date to put Beckett's theater into perspective also took place in the 1980s. The 1980s opened with two outstanding productions of *Final de partida* discussed above, one in Logroño in 1980 and another in Madrid in 1984. José Sanchis Sinisterra directed the first Catalan production of *Oh els bons dies* (*Happy Days*) that same year in Barcelona, and in 1985, the Círculo de Bellas Artes of Madrid held an important homage to Beckett: "Muestra sobre la vida y la obra de Samuel Beckett." This event consisted of 10 of Beckett's plays, and five of them were Spanish premieres, as we shall see below.

In order to show Beckett as a bilingual playwright, the festival opened with a 1975 Théâtre d'Orsay production of *La Dernière Band*, which was directed by Beckett and featured Pierre Chabert in the role of Krapp. The acting was technically perfect but Chabert placed too much an emphasis on the pathetic and tragic aspects of the play. The closing event was the "Los Angeles Actors Theater" production of *Company*, which Stan Gontarski, who also directed this production, had adapted from the novel in

1985 with Beckett's assistance. One of the most interesting features of this production, very well received by the audience, was the way in which the protagonist, played by Alan Mandell, was placed in the middle of the audience. This decision made the spectators the close, personal listeners to the character's memories and of his present doubts and confusion.

The Spanish contributions to the festival included *Qué hermosos días*, Sanchis Sinisterra's Spanish version of the above-mentioned Catalan production of *Happy Days*, featuring the great actress Rosa Novell as Winnie. Novell was a memorable Winnie, her precise and stylized movements, sense of rhythm, and meticulous attention to the creation of Winnie's many voices were extraordinary. The play was directed by José Sánchis Sinisterra – a well-known Spanish dramatist and theater director – who was very meticulous and sensitive in his approach to the play. However, the production was somehow inhibited by the set. The lighting was not "hellish" enough, and the sound of the bell lacked the required terror. A number of extra effects were also added to the play. Winnie's mound was too small and non-scripted movements of the actor playing Willie were at times visible to the audience from behind it. Fragments of old broken objects, a violin, a clock, and several other items were buried with Winnie in the mound. They might have been her old possessions and were as deteriorated as her memories. These objects, although redundant, did not interfere too much with this production. "The Merry Widow Waltz" was repeatedly played as the spectators entered the theater; as a result, the sense of surprise at hearing the waltz when Winnie opens her musical box was nullified. Overall, however, these were minor controversial points in what was, certainly, a great production of the play.

The Madrid festival also included *Actos sin palabras I y II* (*Act Without Words I and II*), in a production by Julio Castronuovo, who played the protagonist of the first mime and directed *Acto sin palabras II*. Angel Facio staged *Vaiven* (*Come and Go*) using the same kind of experimental approach as in his 1966 production. He extended the three-minute playing time of this "dramaticule" to almost 10 minutes by repeating the play three times and he also added background music during the intervals that followed each repetition. In Facio's production the three protagonists meet inside a church, and they are seen kneeling on a pew as if whispering their prayers. When I asked Facio why he changed the setting from a playground to a church, he replied "In Spain three old spinsters like these surely meet in a church." Perhaps he was right, but the music and the three repetitions seemed redundant.

The five Spanish premieres included three short plays: *Nana* (*Rockaby*), *Impromptu de Ohio*, and *Catástrofe* (in my Spanish version authorized by Beckett), directed by Pierre Chabert. Sánchis Sinisterra also presented his dramatic adaptation of the story *Primer amor* (*First Love*), directed by Fernando Grifell; the above-mentioned production of *Company*, directed by Stan Gontarski, completed the five. The staging of *Primer amor* was well received by audiences and critics alike. For both Sinisterra and Grifell it was a challenge to recreate Beckett's dramatic situation without the author's precise stage directions. Grifell told me (interview with the author on directing *Primer amor* [*First Love*], Madrid, April 12, 1985) that he was worried about "the coherence of the character with the universe of everyday physical actions." He explained that he "did not want to create a logical but a coherent character." The created protagonist was finally a Beckett tramp, dressed in a long dark coat with a bowler hat. The setting was a kind of rubbish dump, with a large petrol can downstage right. This can was used at times as a chair for the protagonist. Downstage left was a pile of miscellaneous rubbish. Several realistic details were scattered about: sticks, papers, a bowler, plastic tea cups ... etc. The protagonist moved slowly and usually horizontally: sometimes he walked and other times he crawled on all fours as if searching for some lost object. However, the surprising feature of this production was a long string that fastened to a belt stage left and went down to the auditorium, crossing it half a meter above the heads of the spectators. A poster onstage bore the following inscription: "To make him act pull the string." This was not meant as a joke, and the play did not start until someone in the audience stood up and pulled the string. This trick was repeated several times during the performance, always when the main character took his hat off and looked intently inside it. He would remain silent in this position until a spectator got up and pulled the string. While this gimmick was certainly funny, it destroyed the rhythm of what was otherwise a fine production. The typical goads in a Beckett play, those that cause his characters to talk or keep silent, are usually internal. In this Spanish production of *First Love*, the whims of the spectators controlled, and ultimately destroyed, somehow, the rhythm of the play.

Produced by the theater department of the Círculo de Bellas Artes, Madrid, the Spanish premieres of *Nana*, *Impromptu de Ohio*, and *Catástrofe* took place in the Sala de Columnas of the Círculo de Bellas Artes on April 2, 1985. The plays were directed by Chabert and were acted by three excellent Spanish actors: Maite Brik, Francisco Vidal, and José Lifante. These three plays were staged on a black stage, a kind of black box created especially for this production. The light – created and controlled extraordinarily by Geneviève Soubirou – functioned as a "life-giver," bringing the characters to a fleeting existence and restoring them to their original darkness and silence at the end. The force of this production also made audiences feel the suspension of time. In *Nana* and in *Impromptu de Ohio* especially, time seemed to be abolished, and audiences were invited to descend deeper and deeper into what seemed to be the simultaneity of an instant. Chabert had previously directed the French premieres of these three plays and used this experience to enhance the Spanish production. Chabert's meticulous attention to detail was especially evident in the protagonists' stylized gestures and the different tones and rhythms of their voices.

Although all three performances were notable, Chabert's staging of *Nana* (*Rockaby*) was especially memorable, owing to Maite Brik's excellent performance as the protagonist. After the festival was over, Brik talked to me about the difficulties of acting in this play:

> First of all, it was very difficult to learn the text by heart with all its repetitions and its subtle variations ... it was also difficult to achieve a general rhythm for the play while, at the same time, adjusting your internal rhythms to the meaning of the words thus

avoiding falling into monotony. I wanted to *say* the play every night. It was a torture
to listen to my recorded voice, for I always thought I could have improved my recording
here and there ... I really fell in love with *Nana*, which is a beautiful calm song. (interview with the author, April 14, 1985, Madrid).

Brik had trouble, however, playing the assistant in *Catástrofe*: "I never quite got into
my role ... and I cannot explain why" (ibid.). José Lifante, who acted the part of the
director in this play, talked about the problems he and Maite had finding an adequate
"tonality" for their voices: "The way you say these short cutting phrases is crucial to
establish the right power/submission relationship implicit in *Catástrofe*" (interview
with the author, April 20, 1985, Madrid). Francisco Vidal, the reader in *Impromptu
de Ohio*, confesses that this was the most difficult role of his career: "It was very complicated," he says, "to search for an adequate neutral voice for the Reader which could
give to the words that kind of dream-like reality which is latent in the play." Vidal
apparently found the right tone one day when he approached the reading "in a sort
of contained rage," which, at the same time, was full of tenderness and sensibility
towards the listener. The resultant tone, he said, was a very Spanish mixture of tenderness and fury (interview with the author, April 22, 1985, Madrid).

These memorable productions of *Nana*, *Impromptu de Ohio*, and *Catástrofe* amazed
audiences who were not acquainted with Beckett's late style. Critics were respectful
but baffled by these plays, and the passionate arguments for and against Beckett
revived. Some critics claimed that, given the severe restriction of the actors' movements, the plays represented the end of theater. Others stressed the poetry and the
rhythm of the voices and the mastery of the staging. Theater people talked about
these productions long after they closed and they inspired future productions of Beckett's plays in the 1990s. This Madrid "Beckett Festival" was the seed of many other
Beckettian projects, the most interesting being the creation of the "Sala Beckett" in
Barcelona in October 1989.

Three Memorable *Los días felices* (*Happy Days*) in the 1990s

By the end of the 1980s, admiration for and interest in Beckett's theater was well
established in Spain among a significant, growing minority. However, official theaters
seemed still to be "afraid" of Beckett. Perhaps the most important attempt to make
Beckett's theater "official" was Lluís Pasqual's production of *Waiting for Godot* in
Catalan (*Tot esperant Godot*) at the "Teatre Lliure" in Barcelona in 1999 and, with the
same cast, in Spanish in Madrid and other Spanish cities in 2000. The well-known
stage director's production stressed the comic and grotesque elements to unburden
the play of the atmosphere of heaviness and solemnity characteristic of some previous
Spanish productions. His aim was to provoke as much laughter as possible from the
spectators and he certainly achieved this. Audiences laughed at Didi and Gogo's efforts
and routines to kill time, perhaps aware that their own daily efforts and routines were
not so different from those exhibited by the two protagonists.

Unfortunately, the play also suffered from a number of shortcomings particularly with rhythm and balance. The excessive emphasis on clowning destroyed the poetry and tragic aspects of the play. Pasqual, for example, substituted a popular Spanish pop song "No cambies, no cambies" (Do not change, do not change) for Didi's rendition of "A dog came in the kitchen," which opens the second act. This switch made audiences laugh, but it destroyed the tragic undertones of the moment by creating a climate of triviality. The most problematic aspect of the production was its setting. The stage was reduced to a narrow strip from which the characters seem to be expelled. As a result, the players acted downstage and so far too close to the audience. The location of the tree, downstage right, was also a problem. It did not allow the characters to run up, down, and around it when they felt lost. Consequently, most of the textual allusions to the tree and the characters' relation to it were lost. Yet despite such technical flaws, the prestige of its director ensured the production was well received by audiences and critics.

If *Final de partida* (*Endgame*) was the most produced play in Spain in the 1980s, *Los días felices* (*Happy Days*) dominated the 1990s. Three of these productions were especially notable. In 1993, it was produced by the group "Tabanque" from Zaragoza. The play was directed by John Strasberg and featured Dionisia Ridruejo as a very familiar Winnie. In 1996, Pablo Corral also directed this play for the Sala Círculo of Valencia. Corral slowed the action, emphasizing the tragedy and loneliness of the protagonist. Also in 1996 it was staged by El Canto de la Cabra, the well-known experimental group based in Madrid. Elisa Gálvez played Winnie and the play was directed by Juán Úbeda, who also played Willie. This production was staged in an open-air square close to the theater and featured a complicated setting made of plastic tubes. Willie would appear and disappear into the tubes. The company finally simplified the set so that they could take the play on tour. In place of the tubes they created a more conventional mound and also moved the play indoors. These changes yielded much better results. The new setting facilitated the necessary closeness between the audience and the main character. The ability to immobilize Willie behind the mound also improved the production. Elisa Gálvez was a memorable Winnie; her impressive range of voice moved easily between tragedy and comedy, and her ability to fix her big threatening eyes on the audience made them accomplices to her misfortunes and let her share her jokes with them. This popular production of *Los días felices* has been repeated in Madrid almost every year since its inception and has been taken on tour to other Spanish cities.

Throughout the 1990s, in the wake of Beckett's death, various homages were created in his honor. In Barcelona, the Sala Beckett organized a "Memorial Beckett," which included lectures, theater productions in French, Spanish, and Catalan, dramatic readings, and video sessions. In February of 1999, the Sala Pradillo of Madrid celebrated a similar homage, entitled "Beckett ... ¿quién?" ("Beckett ... Who?"), which also included different productions, lectures, round table discussions, and video sessions. In the 1990s, the Centro Dramático Nacional staged four of Beckett's short plays, *Rockaby, A Piece of Monologue, Ohio Impromptu* and *Not I*, under the title "Beckettiana," in a production best forgotten. The director, Alvaro del Amo, a newcomer to staging Beckett, completely and arbitrarily changed the settings of these plays. For example, the female protagonist of *Not I* walked up and down the stage in a blue nightdress, her body reflected in mirrors, and she carried a tape recorder that reproduced her own voice. The visibility of her body and her movements rendered the text meaningless. Such misdirection was regrettable because the actors were very good and included the famous film actress Marisa Paredes as well as Joaquin Hinojosa. This production underscored the lack of experience that some Spanish theater directors had with producing Beckett's work, especially his later plays.

Beckett's Theater in Spain at the Turn of the Twenty-First Century

In 2001, the experimental theater group "Ultramarinos de Lucas," based in Guadalajara, produced a very poetic *Esperando a Godot* under the direction of Juan Berzal. The play's setting was almost bare and contained only a very stylized metal tree in the background. Movements and gestures were beautifully choreographed, at times echoing circus games. And the Teatro Lagrada of Madrid also organized a season of Beckett's plays in 2001; this series included *Los días felices*, and *La última cinta* (*Krapp's Last Tape*), both directed by Pablo Corral, as well as *Final de partida*, directed by Rodolfo Cortizo. These productions seem to confirm that Beckett's theater is now well established in Spain

Perhaps the most extraordinary event of 2001 related to Beckett's work was the première of a film on Beckett's work *Company* (I am not aware of any other long film of a Beckett's novel having been made elsewhere). The film, entitled *Voz*, was based on my Spanish adaptation and translation of *Company*. Javier Aguirre, one of the best experimental and most daring film directors in Spain, produced this film, which featured one of the greatest Spanish actors, the late Fernando Fernán Gómez, as the silent protagonist listening to a recording of his own voice coming from the dark. The film's lighting was superb and its almost total stillness has pictorial qualities reminiscent of a Zurbarán or a Rembrandt painting (Rodríguez-Gago 2001). In another of his famous *tours de force*, Aguirre maintained a single shot during the entire 75 minutes of the film's duration. The only mobile elements on screen are the silent figure of the protagonist, moving from the table to a pallet at the beginning of the film and from the pallet to the table at its conclusion, and a burning candle whose light is totally extinguished at the end of the film.

Rodolfo Cortizo and his company, La pajarita de papel, deserve especial recognition for their continuous dedication to Beckett's theater. In their 2004–5 theater season, Cortizo's company devoted his small theater, Teatro de la Puerta Estrecha, in Madrid, entirely to Beckett's plays. Cortizo directed all their productions and was also the protagonist of *Krapp's Last Tape*. Among his productions was an *Esperando a Godot* with an all-female cast (in male costumes). It was followed by two different collections of short plays. One production entitled "Voces femeninas" (Female Voices) included

Nana (Rockaby), *Pasos (Footfalls)*, *Ir y venir (Come and Go)*, and *Yo no (Not I)*. A second show entitled "Voces masculinas" (Male Voices) included *Fragmentos de teatro I y II* and *Solo (A Piece of Monologue)*. Productions were very simple, a necessity given the small stage space, and the acting was good in general. However, the compelling performances of Rodolfo Cortizo as Krapp and Eva Varela as Mouth in *Not I* deserve special note.

Even in so brief a history of staging Beckett in Spain, one can discover both the range of responses to his theater by critics and audiences and how these responses have changed over the years. In the 1950s and 1960s, except among a devoted minority of critics and spectators, productions of Beckett's plays were greeted with overt hostility and his texts were altered and mutilated by the fascist censorship of the time. Beckett was depicted then as a nihilist and pessimistic author, and his dramatic language was seen as obscene and vulgar. In the 1970s and 1980s, with few exceptions, Beckett was seen as a "hard realist" with a bitter sense of humor, and almost all productions of his plays were staged to echo the political climate of the time. From the 1990s to the present, Beckett has usually been admired as a great dramatic poet with a dark sense of humor who drastically transformed the language of drama, even as his most radical search for the essence of the theatrical seems still too risky and daring to be produced in "official" Spanish theaters.

REFERENCES

Alvaro, Francisco (ed.) (1960). *El Espectador y la crítica. El teatro en España en 1958*. Editorial propia. Valladolid.

Alvaro, Francisco (ed.) (1978). *El espectador y la crítica: El teatro en España en 1962*. Valladolid.

Domenech, Ricardo (1959). "Un teatro crepuscular." *Acento Cultural*. February (4): 4.

González-Vergel, Alberto, and Javier Lafleur (1959). "Nuestros montajes de *Final de partida*" (Our Productions of *Endgame*). *Primer Acto*, December (11): 53.

Haro-Tecglen, Eduardo (1984). "Risas para Beckett" (Laughter for Beckett). *El País* (January 6), p. 28.

Mollá, Juan (1984). "Viaje al fondo del problema" (Journey to the Heart of the Problem). *El Ciervo*. January: 41–2.

Narros, Miguel (1984). "Notas sobre *Final de partida*." *Diario 16*. February 5.

Rodríguez-Gago, Antonia (1987). "Beckett in Spain: Madrid (1955) and Barcelona (1956)." In Ruby Cohn (ed.), *Beckett: Waiting for Godot*. London: Macmillan.

Rodríguez-Gago, Antonia (2001). "Translating and Adapting *Company* for the Screen." In Angela Moorjani and Carola Veit (eds.), *Samuel Beckett: Endlessness in the Year 2000/Fin sans fin en l'an 2000. Samuel Beckett Today/Aujourd'hui*. Amsterdam: Rodopi.

Index